p7k

WITHDRAWN

The Wild Ass of the Ozarks

*Jeff Davis and the Social Bases of
Southern Politics*

Jeff Davis

The WILD ASS of the OZARKS

Jeff Davis and the Social Bases of Southern Politics

Raymond Arsenault

Temple University Press

Philadelphia

Temple University Press, Philadelphia 19122
© 1984 by Temple University. All rights reserved
Published 1984
Printed in the United States of America

Library of Congress Cataloging in Publication Data
Arsenault, Raymond
The Wild Ass of the Ozarks
Includes bibliographical references and index.
1. Davis, Jeff, 1862–1913.
2. Arkansas—Politics and Government—To 1950.
3. Legislators—United States—Bibliography.
4. United States. Senate—Bibliography.
5. Arkansas—Governors—Bibliography.
I. Title.
E664.D28A85   976.7′051′0924 [B]   83-5103
ISBN 0-87722-326-2

For Kathy

Contents

Tables   ix

Figures   xi

Acknowledgments   xiii

1   Introduction   3

2   Arkansas Traveller   21

3   Democracy and Disfranchisement   35

4   Bryanism and Reform   47

5   The Stormy Petrel   61

6   Redneck Messiah   78

7   The Boys up the Forks of the Creek   97

8   The Democratic Warrior   110

9   The Tribune of Haybinders   119

10   Hillbillies and Swamp Democrats   137

11   Just a Pint Baptist   158

12   High Crimes and Misdemeanors   173

13   The Old Guard   185

14   "Multiply the White Man and Subtract the Nigger"   204

15   King Jeff I   223

Appendix A   247

Appendix B   260

Notes   271

Index   323

Tables

1. Voter Turnout in the Arkansas Black Belt, 1888–1900, Gubernatorial Elections   41
2. Comparative Voting Strength of Political Parties in Arkansas, 1880–1910   45
3. The 1900 Davis Vote: Precinct Returns, Five County Sample   98
4. The Distribution of Wealth and the 1900 Davis Vote in Washington County: Rank-Order Correlation   103
5. Illiteracy, Farm Tenancy, and the 1900 Davis Vote in St. Francis County: Rank-Order Correlations   104
6. Illiteracy, Farm Tenancy, and the 1900 Davis Vote in Howard County: Rank-Order Correlations   105
7. Rank-Order Correlations Between the 1900 Davis Vote and Selected Electoral Variables, Five County Sample   107
8. Populist Precincts: Support for Jeff Davis in the 1900 Gubernatorial Primary, Five County Sample   108
9. Prohibitionist Precincts: Support for Jeff Davis in the 1900 Gubernatorial Primary, Three County Sample   109
10. Turnover and Persistence in the Arkansas Legislatures of 1891, 1893, 1899, and 1901   123
11. Age, Occupational, and Religious Composition of the Arkansas Legislature, 1897–1901   124
12. Factionalism in the 1901 Arkansas Senate: Support for the Davis Position on Eight Important Roll Call Votes   127
13. Age, Occupational, Religious, and Tenure Composition of the 1901 Arkansas Senate: Pro-Davis, Anti-Davis, and Neutral Factions   129
14. The Growth of the Anti-License Movement in Arkansas, 1882–1910   150
15. The 1902 Davis Vote: Precinct Returns, Eleven County Sample   153
16. Illiteracy, Farm Tenancy, and the 1902 Davis Vote in Four Sample Counties: Rank-Order Correlations   154

17. The Distribution of Wealth and the 1902 Davis Vote in
    Washington County: Rank-Order Correlations   155
18. The Distribution of Wealth and the 1902 Davis Vote in Sharp
    County: Rank-Order Correlations   156
19. Age, Occupational, Religious, and Tenure Composition of the
    1903 Arkansas House of Representatives: Pro-Davis, Anti-Davis,
    and Neutral Factions   181
20. The 1904 Davis Vote: Precinct Returns, Eleven County Sample   201
21. Illiteracy, Farm Tenancy, the Distribution of Wealth, and the 1904
    Davis Vote in Six Sample Counties: Rank-Order Correlations   201
22. Baptist Counties: Democratic Primary Vote for Jeff Davis,
    1898–1912   202
23. Racial Bills: Comparative Voting Behavior of Pro-Davis, Anti-Davis,
    and Neutral Factions in the 1903 Arkansas House of
    Representatives   216
24. The 1906 Davis Vote: Precinct Returns, Nine County Sample   221

Figures

1. Arkansas in 1900   19
2. Arkansas Counties   20
3. Voter Turnout in Arkansas General Elections, 1880–1910   42
4. Racial Composition and Voter Turnout in Arkansas General Elections, 1888–1910   44
5. 1898 Democratic Primary for Attorney General: % for Jeff Davis   52
6. 1900 Gubernatorial Election   116
7. Factionalism in the 1901 Arkansas Senate   130
8. 1902 Democratic Gubernatorial Primary: % for Jeff Davis   151
9. 1902 Democratic Senatorial Primary: % for James P. Clarke   152
10. The 1903 Impeachment Controversy   182
11. 1904 Democratic Gubernatorial Primary: % for Jeff Davis   199
12. 1906 Democratic Senatorial Primary: % for Jeff Davis   220
13. 1912 Democratic Senatorial Primary: % for Jeff Davis   242

Acknowledgments

An admiring literary critic once commented that the genius of Robert Penn Warren, the author of *All the King's Men,* lay in his ability to impose "the order of art on the chaos of actuality." The historian has less room to maneuver than the novelist, but the goal is the same: to bring order out of chaos without distorting the truth. In this study, I have tried to develop a general hypothesis about the nature of Southern demagoguery without losing sight of the chaotic complexity of historical reality. Whatever success I have had can be traced to the kindness and intelligence of the many people who have helped and guided me along the way. I owe an incalculable debt to Sheldon Hackney, a cherished friend and mentor. My experiences as his research assistant at Princeton laid the groundwork for this study, as well as for my continuing interest in Southern history and culture. His uncompromising commitments to humanitarian values and the highest ideals of scholarship remain a source of inspiration. I am also heavily indebted to the members of my dissertation committee, Professors Morton Keller and Marvin Meyers of Brandeis University, and Professor Ronald Formisano of Clark University. Morton Keller was an exemplary dissertation director; his intellectual toughness and attention to detail saved me from disaster on more than one occasion. I would also like to thank David Hackett Fischer and John Demos for awakening my interest in social history.

During an extended visit to Arkansas, several people provided me with invaluable assistance: Dr. Samuel Sizer, the director of Special Collections at the University of Arkansas Library, Russell Baker of the Arkansas History Commission, Tom Dillard, and Professors Walter Brown, James Chase, and Willard Gatewood of the Department of History at the University of Arkansas at Fayetteville. I am also indebted to Alvin Jacobson and Rabbi Ira Sanders, both of Little Rock, for their cooperation and assistance. I am also deeply grateful to the staffs of the University of Arkansas Library, the Arkansas History Commission, the American Antiquarian Society, the Massachusetts Statehouse Library, the Boston Public Library, the Library of Congress, the National Archives, the Washington County (Arkansas) Courthouse, Firestone Library at Princeton University, Widener Library at Harvard University, Goldfarb Library at Brandeis University, Wilson Library at the University of Minnesota, and the Nelson Poynter Library at the University of South Florida. This study was also aided by generous financial assistance from the Irving and Rose Crown Foundation and the Faculty Summer Research Fund of the University of Minnesota Graduate School.

I would like to acknowledge the support and encouragement of my former colleagues at the University of Minnesota, especially Sara Evans, Stuart Schwartz, Edward Griffin, John Modell, Rus Menard, Allen Isaacman, Lansine Kaba, Bob McCaa, Clarke Chambers, David Noble, Elaine May, John Howe, and George Green. I also owe a debt of gratitude to several of my present colleagues at the University of South Florida: Gary Mormino, David Carr, James Swanson, Darryl Paulson, Danny Jorgensen, and Steve Turner. During the course of this project, several other friends have offered thoughtful suggestions or criticisms. I would like to thank Harry Boyte, Jim Green, Vernon Burton, Clark Miller, H. L. Mitchell, Bob Randolph, Ed Kopf, Richard King, David Starr, Mills Thornton, Jim Horton, Jim Stewart, Fred Hoxie, Chuck Cheape, Ted Hammett, Mike Grossberg, Steve Whitfield, and the irrepressible Tim Bird. I owe a special debt to Steve Whitfield, who was always willing to listen to my ideas and who gave me moral support when I needed it most. Bill Barnard, Tom Terrill, and Paul Gaston took time out of a busy schedule to read a large portion of the manuscript; their insightful and constructive criticisms are greatly appreciated. David Gould, Robert Cohen, Richard Tedlow, Mitchell Snay, and Sam Fustukjian also deserve thanks for their help, both on the tennis court and off. I would also like to thank Luis Tiant and the 1975 Boston Red Sox for the season that gave me the strength to go on.

During the past four years, the participants in the Fulbright Commission Summer Institute on American Regionalism have taught me a great deal about regionalism, political culture, and friendship. I will never be able to repay their many kindnesses. I would also like to express my appreciation to Sheldon Hackney, Alan Brinkley, and the late T. Harry Williams for participating in a memorable session on Southern demagoguery at the 1978 Southern Historical Association Convention in St. Louis. During that session, Morgan Kousser offered several valuable suggestions and criticisms that forced me to rethink and recast some of my arguments.

I am deeply grateful to Lorie Miros for her skillful typing and understanding heart, to Jim McHugh for his help with the maps, and to Helen Berliner for copyediting. I would also like to thank Ken Arnold, who supervised the early stages of publication, and the staff of Temple University

Press—especially Michael Ames, Jennifer French, and Candy Hawley—for their patience and professionalism.

My greatest debt is to my family: to my daughters, Amelia and Anne, whose bright smiles and innocent questions put everything in proper perspective; and to my wife Kathy, who shouldered more than her share of the burden and who patiently and lovingly helped me find my way out of the Ozarks.

The Wild Ass of the Ozarks

Jeff Davis and the Social Bases of
Southern Politics

1

Introduction

This is a book about the other Jeff Davis. Long after the president of the Confederacy passed from the scene, an extraordinary politician with the same name roamed the hills and valleys of Arkansas. One of the post–Reconstruction South's most colorful figures, Davis earned such sobriquets as the Wild Ass of the Ozarks, the Tribune of Haybinders, and a Karl Marx for Hillbillies.[2] Vilified as a demagogue by his enemies, he became famous for his picturesque crusades against Yankee trusts, city dudes, and "high-collared aristocrats." One scornful Arkansas editor described him as "a carrot-headed, red-faced, loud-mouthed, strong-limbed, ox-driving mountaineer lawyer that has come to Little Rock to get a reputation—a friend to the fellow who brews forty-rod bug juice back in the mountains."[3] Davis gloried in such descriptions and played the role of hillbilly folk hero to the hilt. Elected state attorney general in 1898, he went on to serve three stormy terms as governor before moving up to the United States Senate in 1907. He was re-elected to the Senate in 1912, but his career was cut short by a fatal heart attack in January 1913.

In his day, Jeff Davis was a national celebrity and a major figure in Southern politics. Yet he has received relatively little attention from historians. While most general studies of Southern political history devote a paragraph or two to his escapades, the published literature on Davis is very thin.[4] The major reason for this neglect—aside from the inability of many historians to take him seriously—is the absence of personal papers. Davis himself left no private papers, and the sparse manuscript collections left by his Arkansas contemporaries reveal very little about his activities.[5] Although a lengthy personal memoir written by his private secretary, Charles Jacobson, fills some of the void, the materials required for a full-fledged, intimate

3

biography are lacking. Even though we have access to the public man through newspapers and government documents, the private Davis will always remain a shadowy figure.

Fortunately, some of the most intriguing historical questions raised by Davis's career lie outside the realm of personal biography. Who voted for Jeff Davis? What were the sources of his extraordinary popularity? Why did he evoke such fierce loyalties and hatreds? What was the relationship between "Jeff Davisism" and other mass movements, such as Populism, progressivism, and Prohibitionism? What impact did the Davis movement have on the political, economic, and social institutions of early twentieth-century Arkansas? We may never know why Davis did what he did, but we can recapture the broader historical significance of his career.

The present study is conceived as a merger of public biography and social history. Although Davis is the focal point of the book, this study is also an analysis of a mass social and political movement that encompassed thousands of voters and hundreds of politicians. Using data from a wide variety of sources—federal census returns, local tax records, business directories and gazetteers, state reports, and newspapers—I have attempted to reconstruct the social fabric and political tendencies of a large sample of Arkansas counties, cities, towns, villages, and rural townships. Despite its imperfections, this patchwork quilt of electoral and ecological data should help us to understand not only Jeff Davis but also the society that produced him.

A careful examination of Davis's career promises to shed some light on the political and social history of a much-neglected state. But there is a more important reason for undertaking such a study. The saga of Jeff Davis is part of a much larger story—the story of a political tradition that dominated Southern politics for nearly three-quarters of a century. Along with Pitchfork Ben Tillman of South Carolina, Fiddlin' Bob Taylor of Tennessee, Tom Watson of Georgia, and James K. Vardaman of Mississippi, Davis served as a prototype for the twentieth-century "Southern demagogue."[6] His remarkable career influenced countless politicians, including Huey Long, who was mesmerized by a Davis stump speech in 1911.[7] Although Davis was the product of a particular time and place, his style of politics was rooted in a regional folk culture that has persisted into the late twentieth century.

The phenomenon of Southern demagoguery has been a source of fascination for several generations of Americans. Unfortunately, it has also been the source of a great deal of confusion, much of which has stemmed from the inherent ambiguities of the word "demagogue." The term originated in classical Greece, where Euripides defined a *demos agogos* as "a man of loose tongue, intemperate, trusting to tumult, leading the populace to mischief with empty words."[8] To the Greeks, any rousing street-corner orator who did not speak for the political establishment was a demagogue, plain and simple.

When later cultures adopted the term, they reshaped the concept of demagoguery to fit their own political traditions. During nearly twenty-five hundred years of usage, the word "demagogue" has meant many different things to many different people. In the United States alone, politicians have been accused of demagoguery for engaging in democratic reformism, collusion with professed enemies, emotional and rhetorical manipulation, racial and religious scapegoating, xenophobic parochialism, political bossism, and so on.[9] Like "democracy" or "republicanism" or any of the basic words of our political vocabulary, "demagogue" is an imprecise term that defies authoritative definition. The fact that it is not only a political term but also an epithet further complicates the problem of definition. As Cal Logue and Howard Dorgan recently observed, "colorful, popular, and plebeian politicians we do not like we call 'demagogues,' whereas those we like we are apt to identify as 'leaders of the common man' or 'champions of the people.'"[10]

True enough, but where Southern politics is concerned this distinction is frequently forgotten. For some reason, if we are to believe conventional wisdom, the South has been long on demagogues and short on champions of the people. As Wilma Dykeman once noted, "the term 'Southern demagogue' seems as natural a combination as cornbread and turnip greens."[11] Yet the region's reputation as a breeding ground for unscrupulous demagogues may not be totally deserved. If the incitement of emotion-laden mass politics constitutes demagoguery, the South has produced more than its share of demagogues. But if demagoguery implies treachery and deceit, the pantheon of Southern demagogues becomes much smaller. Jeff Davis, for example, could be characterized as a demagogue under the first definition, but probably not under the second.

To some degree, the stereotype of the Southern demagogue has been based on elitist and cosmopolitan biases. The folksy politicians of the rural South have been routinely classified as demagogues, whether or not they were unprincipled charlatans. In many cases, their sincerity, not their duplicity, has earned them the demagogue label. To H. L. Mencken, who probably did more to popularize the phrase "Southern demagogue" than anyone else, these "yokel" politicians were fitting representatives of the South's "poor white trash" society. "Every now and then," he wrote in 1920, "they produce a political leader who puts their secret notions of the true, the good and the beautiful into plain words, to the amazement and scandal of the rest of the country."[12] Defining demagoguery as "the trick of inflaming half-wits against their betters," Mencken claimed that "to get rid of its demagogues the South would have to wait until the white trash were themselves civilized. This would be a matter demanding almost as much patience as the long vigil of the Seventh Day Adventists."[13]

In a less grandiloquent fashion, many professional scholars have followed Mencken's lead. Reinhard Luthin, the author of the highly influential

American Demagogues: Twentieth Century, offered the following description of a typical Southern demagogue in 1951:

> Promising seemingly everything to everybody, proclaiming love for the "common man," preaching from Bibles, praising Founding Fathers and Confederate heroes, protesting against "nigger-lovin" Yankees and Republicans, and purveying jokes, anecdotes, histrionics and hillbilly music, as they performed on the stump, in legislative halls, and before news reporters, these "demagogues" won hearts and votes. Talented actors, showmen and exhibitionists, they pandered to the pride and prejudices of poverty-pinched "wool hat and one gallus" white rural voters as they barked against county courthouse "rings" and town "machines" and merchants. Hardy perennials of Dixie politics, they took to the hustings in each Democratic campaign season. They attracted publicity by their picturesque personalities, distinctive dress, unorthodox electioneering, pointless programs, and "hot air" harangues.[14]

Such condescension has led a number of Southern historians and intellectuals to question the legitimacy and utility of the concept of Southern demagoguery. As long ago as 1938, C. Vann Woodward, in the preface to *Tom Watson: Agrarian Rebel,* insisted that "the term 'Southern demagogue' should be recognized for what it is, a political epithet. It does not contribute anything to our understanding of the men to whom it is applied."[15] Reflecting on the saga of Huey Long, the Louisiana journalist Hamilton Basso reached the same conclusion. "Merely to say that he was a demagogue," Basso wrote in 1946, "is to say nothing more incisive than that he made use of certain methods and tactics that are as old as recorded political history. . . . The statement that Huey Long was a demagogue . . . tells us nothing."[16] In 1967, Thomas D. Clark and Albert D. Kirwan, the authors of *The South since Appomattox,* concluded that "Southern political history, confusing at best, is hopelessly confounded by too free usage of the term demagogue. It would be better to forget the word altogether and to classify politicians, if indeed they must be classified, as reformers or non-reformers, as progressives or conservatives."[17] T. Harry Williams, who probably has commented on the concept of Southern demagoguery more than any other scholar, expressed similar reservations in a 1960 essay on Huey Long:

> Let us dispense with the word demagogue in dealing with men like Long and employ instead a term suggested by Eric Hoffer, mass leader. . . . It is possible that we have been too apologetic about and too patronizing toward all the Southern demagogues. Some of them were hopelessly confused and some were merely clowns. Some did nothing to control the interests they attacked and some sold out to those interests. But the best of them tried to do something for their people. Throw out the crudities they had to employ to arouse a submerged electorate and the race baiting, and these men are the Norrises, the La Follettes, and the Borahs of another section. . . . Indeed, many of the Southern demagogues, in their genuine concern for the welfare of the masses, in their essential respect for the democratic system, conform in their own peculiar fashion to Eric Hoffer's picture

of the good mass leader—the leader who does not hesitate to "harness men's hungers and fears" to weld a following in the service of a cause but who, because of his faith in humanity, does not attempt to use the frustrations of men to build a brave new world.[18]

Although there is a large measure of truth in Williams's statement, the fact remains that the agrarian insurgents of the early twentieth-century South were something more than rustic progressives. Whether we call them "demagogues" or "mass leaders," they were genuinely paradoxical figures. They were legitimate folk heroes, yet (with the exception of Huey Long) their heroics were largely illusory. They were agrarian radicals, yet for the most part they practiced a politics of catharsis and symbolic action that probably inhibited radical change.[19] They were innovative politicians who knew how to acquire and hold power, yet their careers had surprisingly little impact on the overall distribution of power in Southern society. Despite a lot of tough talk about the need for radical reform, they produced more politics than government, more ritual than legislation. In their romantic, myth-laden approach to political conflict, the demagogues resembled the Bourbon Democrats of the late nineteenth century; yet with the Bourbons there was no pretense of radicalism, no messianic posturing.[20] As Williams himself has written, "The great wonder of it all was that out of the sound and fury nothing happened."[21] In a similiar vein, a friend of mine once remarked that Southern demagoguery reminded him of professional wrestling: there is always a lot of grunting and groaning and gouging, and bodies flying across the ring, yet no one ever seems to get hurt. Perhaps this is what the journalist Clarence Cason was thinking of in 1935 when he insisted that most Southern political news belonged on the sports page.[22]

The paradox of Southern demagoguery presents historians with two challenging sets of questions. The first concerns the origins of mass arousal and mass appeal. Why were the demagogues so popular? Why was factional conflict between agrarian demagogues and other Southern Democrats so persistent and so intense? Why did political battles which had little functional impact on the distribution of governmental services attract so much attention and produce so much heat and emotion? In essence, what was all the shouting about? The second set of questions approaches the paradox from the opposite end. Why was most of the intensity described above channeled into symbolic rather than functional protest? Why were the demagogues such ineffectual reformers? Why didn't early twentieth-century Southern society produce a more authentic brand of agrarian radicalism, a true neo-Populism? Why did it take so long for a Huey Long to emerge?

In attempting to identify the sources of mass arousal and mass appeal, Southern historians collectively have come up with a long list of contributing factors: racial scapegoating; xenophobic sectionalism; "Lost Cause" romanticism; resentment of a colonial economy and the desire for local self-determination; rural chauvinism; class conflict; the emotionalism of evangelical religion; personal charisma and fiery oratory; buffoonery and exhibitionist campaign stunts; personal contact between politician and constituent; the promise and, in some cases, the reality of economic and social reform; the desire for a democratization of party politics; intrastate sectionalism; nativism; and anti-Semitism.

Similarly, the attempts to explain the prevalence of symbolic politics in the early twentieth-century South have produced a long list of possible explanations: personal insincerity; collusion with professed enemies; preoccupation with the race issue; religious and nativist diversions; the gullibility and ignorance of the Southern electorate; a regional proclivity for romanticism; a one-party system, which placed restrictions on political conflict and a premium on personal magnetism; a lack of faith in government as a problem-solving institution and an ambivalent attitude towards governmental power; an organizational rather than an ideological approach to political conflict; administrative inexperience and ineptitude; and the ability of conservatives to obstruct legislative reform programs.

Most serious students of Southern demagoguery have recognized the complexity of the subject and thus have avoided mono-causal interpretations. Nearly everyone seems to agree that there are many pieces to the puzzle. Unfortunately, however, no one has had much success in fitting the pieces of the puzzle together. Despite a half century of diligent scholarship, the Southern demagogue remains an enigma. The fundamental question of why the post–Populist South produced a strain of agrarian radicalism that was as ineffectual as it was strident has never been answered satisfactorily. As Sheldon Hackney observed in 1972, "One of the unsolved, even unposed, riddles of twentieth-century southern politics is why a two-party system did not develop after disfranchisement. The absence of an opposition party, of course, did not mean the absence of conflict, because fierce conflict did occur between personal followings or through intrastate sectionalism. The question really is why was there not enough strength or persistence in the factional alignments for one or more opposition parties to emerge."[23] To pose the riddle in more specific terms, if factional strife between agrarian rabble-rousers and their more respectable opponents was so rampant and so bitter, why didn't the "Solid South" come apart at the seams?

The inability of Southern historians to solve this riddle can be attributed, at least in part, to a serious and recurrent methodological problem: the history of Southern demagoguery has been written almost exclusively from the top down. Focusing almost all of their attention on the demagogues themselves, Southern historians have consistently neglected the grassroots dimension of mass politics. While the personal and institutional history of Southern demagoguery has been studied with great care and sophistication, the broader social history of Southern demagoguery has been handled in a haphazard and cursory manner. To cite just one example, although we know a great deal about the personal and political life of Pitchfork Ben Tillman, we know next to nothing about the mass of voters who participated in the Tillman movement.[24]

The historiography of Southern demagoguery suffers from the limitations of a biographical synthesis. This criticism is based on the simple proposition that you cannot study mass politics properly without looking closely at the masses themselves. The literature on Southern demagogues includes a number of excellent biographies—of Tom Watson, Ben Tillman, James K. Vardaman, Sidney Catts, Eugene Talmadge, and Huey Long, just to name a few.[25] By treating their subjects in a serious and unpatronizing manner and by painstakingly separating fact from folklore, the authors of these studies have fostered a greater awareness of the richness and complexity of Southern political history. Nonetheless, the collective impact of these volumes on our understanding of mass politics has been somewhat disappointing. This lack of progress, I would argue, stems from a lack of research on the social bases of Southern politics. Until we learn a great deal more about the social and cultural landscape of the early twentieth-century South, and until we gain a fairly precise sense of who voted for and against the demagogues, the phenomenon of Southern demagoguery will continue to be shrouded in mystery.

Most historians, of course, have been well aware of the social dimension of the Southern demagogue—the political symbol of the social pathology of Southern life. Since a demagogue is by definition a mass leader, many historians have recognized the dual, sociopolitical nature of Southern demagoguery. These same historians, however, have failed to come to grips with the methodological implications of this dualism. With very few exceptions, analyses of the social composition and social psychology of the Southern electorate have been based almost exclusively on an examination of political rhetoric.[26] In many instances, historians have simply echoed a politician's description of his own following or even more commonly a description offered by the opposition. Impressionistic evidence of this kind is extremely valuable, but it is no substitute for hard ecological and electoral data. The use of such evidence should not obscure the fact that, as an area of serious inquiry, the social history of Southern demagoguery remains an unexplored frontier.

In recent years, quantitative analysis, or more accurately what Samuel Hays has termed "the social analysis of politics," has reshaped and refined our understanding of Reconstruction, Populism, disfranchisement, and numerous other aspects of Southern history.[27] Perhaps social analysis will effect a similar transformation in our understanding of Southern demagoguery. At the very least, it should shed a little light on a murky subject. Of course, here, as elsewhere, it would be a serious mistake to embrace quantitative social analysis as a methodological panacea. As Richard L. McCormick once pointed out in a critique of the ethnocultural school of political historiography, voting behavior represents only one facet of political life.[28] Or, as the novelist Samuel G. Blythe once put it, "Politics is politics, and that explains many things."[29] Still, we should not forget that politics as politics does not explain everything, even in the South. Despite its many flaws and peculiarities, early twentieth-century Southern politics was more democratic than authoritarian.[30] Although they were often characterized as "cotton-patch fascists" during the 1930s and 1940s, the demagogues of the South were actually democratic leaders who had limited power over their followers.[31] In the South, as in the rest of the United States, the character of political protest movements was shaped by voters as well as politicians.

Historians of Southern demagoguery need to develop a creative synthesis of political and social history—a synthesis which recognizes that politician-constituent interaction flows both ways. Looking at the grass roots dimension of Southern demagoguery should help historians to move away from a preoccupation with the moral and personal aspects of mass politics—a preoccupation that has led a number of observers to overemphasize the theme of mass manipulation. When dealing with larger-than-life characters who did everything they could to surround themselves with an aura of power and personal magnetism, it is easy to forget that politicians are seldom as powerful or pansophical as they claim to be. The failure of Southern historians to examine the social determinants of mass politics is a serious oversight, not only because it leaves part of the story untold, but also because it distorts our view of mass leadership.

A thoroughgoing social analysis of Southern demagoguery will require the efforts of dozens of scholars and will take many years to complete. But we have to begin somewhere. Despite the obvious limitations of a case study, the contours of Arkansas politics should tell us something about the broader contours of Southern politics. Although the extent to which the South's demagogues were variations on the same theme remains an open question, social analysis of the Davis movement lends strong support to a "cultural" interpretation of Southern demagoguery.[32] As practiced by Davis, "demagoguery" was a sincere attempt to defend the principles of individualism and local autonomy and to reassert the primacy of traditional rural values in the face of an expanding metropolitan society. Rooted in the folkways of an embattled agrarian subculture, "Jeff Davisism" was essentially a politics of cultural resistance. The bitter rivalry between pro-Davis and anti-Davis factions represented a form of cultural conflict that was similar, in many respects, to the ethnocultural conflict that characterized Northeastern and Midwestern politics during the nineteenth century.[33]

To date, Southern historians have contributed very little to the ongoing debate over the validity of the ethnocultural model of American voting behavior.[34] Most historians have assumed that the ethnocultural model is totally inapplicable to the South, where ethnic and religious homogeneity have almost always been the norm. Yet, as both George Brown Tindall and Robert Kelley have pointed out, this assumption is based on a rather narrow definition of ethnicity and culture. According to Kelley, "if the term 'cultural' is understood to refer to home-grown ethnic groups like Yankees and white Southerners, and their attitudes, as well as to those whose ethnicity is of foreign origin," and "if we can realize that economic rivalries often have a cultural dimension," the usefulness of the ethnocultural model is greatly expanded.[35] Kelley's point is well taken, but his focus on "Southern" ethnicity obscures the fact that the most important cultural identities in the white South (at least as far as early twentieth-century Southern politics was concerned) were subcultural identities. Although Southern sectionalism was the primary source of cultural identity for some Southerners, most had a deeper identification with either an agrarian or an urban subculture. A number of Southern historians have suggested that the factional battles between agrarian demagogues and more respectable Democratic politicians hinged on cultural conflict between town and country.[36] But no one has been able to marshal enough evidence, quantitative or otherwise, to sustain a fully developed cultural interpretation of Democratic factionalism.

The cultural split between town and country was the primary basis for Democratic bifactionalism in early twentieth-century Arkansas. This is not surprising, since the urban-rural cleavage was the deepest division in white Arkansas society. There were several dimensions to this cleavage, but the most obvious was a fundamental difference in lifestyle. To some degree, Arkansas's farmers and town dwellers, despite their economic interdependence, had always lived in separate worlds.[37] But the cultural distance between town and country increased dramatically during the half century following Reconstruction. The animating force behind this cultural divergence was the coming of the railroad. As sleepy villages became bustling railroad towns, a distinctively urban "county seat town culture" began to emerge. By the end of the nineteenth century, most Arkansas town dwellers who lived in communities with populations of a thousand or more were surrounded by many of the trappings of modern urban life: electric lights, telephone and telegraph service, daily mail deliveries, local banking and brokerage facilities, indoor plumbing, hotels and restaurants, an expanded network of voluntary associations and public institutions, and relatively easy access to the outside world. Many larger towns also boasted electric streetcar lines, paved roads, municipal sewage systems, and daily newspapers.[38] Viewed from the perspective of New York or Chicago or even

Memphis, these communities were little more than overgrown villages masquerading as towns. Nonetheless, from the perspective of the rural Arkansawyer the county seat town was distinctly and unmistakably urban.

In most areas of Arkansas, the urban conveniences and institutions described above did not make their way into the countryside until the 1920s or 1930s. (Some of these things, of course, never made it into the countryside.) By the beginning of the twentieth century, most Arkansas farmers and villagers were part of a metropolitan economy; but, in most cases, they did not become members of a metropolitan society until much later. Despite their involvement in an increasingly integrated national economy, in cultural terms most Arkansas agrarians continued to live in what Robert H. Wiebe has termed "island communities."[39] The "urbanization" or "metropolitanization" of rural life did not become the dominant trend until after the spread of rural electrification, rural telephone exchanges, country highways, automobiles, and radios. In other words, agrarian culture in Jeff Davis's Arkansas retained much of its integrity and distinctiveness long after it lost most of its economic independence and social status.

This divergence between urban and rural lifestyles was not unique to the South. During the late nineteenth and early twentieth centuries, urban-rural differences were an important source of political and social conflict throughout the United States. But in the South, more than in any other area of the country (with the possible exception of New England), the cultural gap between town and country was reinforced and deepened by a roughly parallel division of socioeconomic class and status. Although the degree of parallelism varied from county to county, this alignment of urban-rural and class cleavages tended to divide the white South into two distinct subcultures, one rural and poor, the other urban and relatively prosperous. Significantly, the wide socioeconomic gap between "agrarian" and "New South" subcultures represented a reversal of the pattern that had prevailed in the antebellum South, where wealth and status had been concentrated in the countryside. In many Southern counties, this reversal process was not completed until after the turn of the century. But the basic pattern was already in evidence in some areas by the end of Reconstruction.

In Arkansas, this fundamental change in the relationship between class and geography was largely the result of one extremely significant development: between 1880 and 1920 a large number of Arkansas planters moved to town. By the beginning of the Davis era, approximately half of the state's planters lived not on plantations but in towns or cities.[40] The town-dwelling planter was hardly a new phenomenon. During the antebellum period, it was not uncommon for planters—especially wealthy planters—to spend part or even most of the year in town. Nonetheless, the impact of absentee landlordism on patterns of class and culture was far more significant in the New South than in the Old. Not only did the proportion of planters residing in town increase substantially during the post-Reconstruction period, but also, as noted above, the social and cultural implications of town dwelling became increasingly profound. As the nineteenth century drew to a close, the relatively straightforward class division between Old South planters and small farmers became a broader and more complex cultural division.[41]

Although the town-dwelling planters of the New South continued to make most of their money in the countryside, in many respects they were no longer members of an agrarian society. As Davis once put it, they were businessmen who liked to "farm with their mouths on the edge of town."[42] Supervising their tenants from a distance, usually with the help of a country merchant or a resident farm manager, and often reinvesting part of their wealth in the nonagricultural sector of the economy, many planter-merchants became almost indistinguishable from their urban neighbors. As members of a New South commercial elite, they generally exhibited a style of life that was more in tune with the values and institutions of the metropolitan North than with the traditional agrarian culture of the rural South.[43] Of course, even when they managed to retain their rural values, their relationships with other farmers tended to become strained. After their exodus from the countryside, there was far less opportunity for a paternal bond to develop between planters and small farmers. From the perspective of the Arkansas dirt farmer, the urban planter-merchant was, at best, an outsider and, at worst, a colonial agent of a Northern-based culture and a Northern-controlled economy. When Davis referred to Arkansas-born planters as "Yankees," his followers did not have to be told why.[44]

By the end of the nineteenth century, the lower- and middle-class white farmers of Arkansas found themselves at odds with the town-dwelling planter-merchants, culturally and politically. The "metropolitanization" of much of the planter class was an important development because it accentuated the declining status of agrarian life. As money and influence flowed out of the countryside, an agrarian political revolt began to take shape. Frightened by the aggressiveness of an encroaching metropolitan society and goaded by urban wealth and power, many farmers were willing recruits for a political protest movement that combined the themes of rural chauvinism, sectionalism, and relative deprivation.[45] Following the lead of the Agricultural Wheel, the Farmers' Alliance, and the People's Party, the Davis movement tapped the farmers' desire for local self-determination, dignity, and economic reform.[46] Unlike the agrarian radicals of the 1880s and 1890s, Davis completely ignored the plight of black farmers.[47] But, within the confines of white-supremacist one-party politics, he tried to harness many of the same forces that had fostered earlier agrarian movements.

Jeff Davis was an extraordinarily successful mass leader, not because he was adept at trickery, but rather because he understood the cultural forces that divided white Arkansas better than any other politician of his generation. His popularity was based on much more than racial scapegoating and an issueless politics of personality. Although Davis was a devout white supremacist and a racial demagogue of considerable skill, his coalition was not held together primarily by racial prejudice. Racial concerns were clearly predominant in determining the structure of Arkansas's political system— one-party politics, black disfranchisement, the white primary, etc.—but racism was not the primary force *within* that system. Although race-baiting became an obligatory ritual on the Arkansas stump during the Davis era, Democratic primaries were seldom won or lost on the basis of the race issue alone. Moreover, the political salience of racism often depended upon sectionalist antipathy towards "outside agitators." When Davis lashed out at blacks, it was usually part of a broader assault on "meddling Yankees."

Similarly, Davis's flamboyant personality was an important element of his appeal largely because it was culturally keyed to the myths and realities of the agrarian South. Combining two hallowed Southern traditions—a sense of place and a sense of honor—he became the embodiment of community pride and country virtues. Whether he was dispensing homely witticisms or vitriolic diatribes, he was a master of the rural idiom.[48] Full of swagger and geniality, he was the epitome of the down-home good old boy. His personal escapades and folksy speeches provided rural Arkansawyers with a means of expressing their feelings about the impersonal forces that affected their lives, as well as their feelings about themselves. Davis articulated their fears and anxieties and prejudices, especially their xenophobic distrust of Yankees and city folks; he also gave voice to their hopes and dreams and aspirations. His emotional stump campaigns were celebrations of agrarian folk culture—celebrations that provided a ritualistic affirmation of the vitality of rural life. As the poet-historian John Gould Fletcher once observed, Davis's mission was "to reveal to his own people . . . the still-unused and long-wasted human ability of the Ozarks."[49] He was not an effective reformer in the classical "progressive" sense, but he did bring about a temporary redistribution of psychological power by enhancing and legitimizing an agrarian world-view. When it came to trumpeting the cultural superiority of the agrarian South, Davis was in a class by himself. As he told a crowd of cheering farmers in 1912, "If some of them high-collared, flyweight dudes of the East had sense enough to sit down to a big dish of turnip greens, poke salad and hog jowl, they might sweat enough of that talcum powder off to look and smell like a man."[50]

It was no accident that Davis's electoral support was concentrated in rural townships, especially in the more remote precincts, or that his farm support cut across class lines. Although he often resorted to class rhetoric, he did not speak for an underclass of poor whites.[51] Instead, he appealed to all farmers who resented the fact that the locus of power was shifting away from rural communities. His supporters were angered by the quasi-colonial relationship between town-dwelling merchants and farmers, and by the similar relationship between Northern capitalism and the Southern economy. But economic malaise, per se, was not the driving force behind the Davis movement. Davis's followers wanted economic reform; but, more than anything else, they wanted respect.[52] Their loyalty to Davis and their enthusiasm for his romantic style of politics suggest that their most deeply felt grievances were cultural. They wanted someone to stand up for them, someone to defend their collective sense of honor. And this Davis did in full measure. This is why they stuck by him, why he went to his grave "unbeaten and unbeatable."[53]

A progressive critic might argue that if Davis had truly respected his followers he would have spent more time drafting reform legislation and less time out on the stump. But Davis and the "Old Guard," as he called his followers, did not see it that way. To them, the battle for economic reform was but one part of a larger battle—a life-and-death struggle for self-respect and cultural self-determination. In the long run, the preservation of cultural autonomy depended upon a thorough redistribution of economic power—a redistribution that could only come about through reform legislation or revolutionary violence. But in the short run, merely standing up to the "high-collared crowd" was a victory of sorts. Jeff Davisism was little more than a politics of catharsis, but no one, with the possible exception of the agrarian socialists, offered the Old Guard anything better.[54] With all its flaws and false hopes, Davis's flesh-and-blood politics was more attractive than progressive reform, which smacked of accommodationism and which was invariably grounded in the insulting concept of "uplift." In Arkansas, as in most Southern states, the progressive movement was dominated by urban "business progressives"—instrumentalist, efficiency-minded reformers who were not centrally concerned with the economic and cultural grievances of small farmers.[55] As T. Harry Williams once observed:

> Southern progressivism was too conservative, too withdrawn, really, to appeal to the masses. . . . The Progressive representation of leadership did not provide the psychological outlets that rural and poor people craved and needed: a sense of identification with their spokesmen; a feeling that however drab their life or despised their estate they were somehow expressing themselves through these spokesmen, were through them flinging defiance at their enemies; an assurance that because their chiefs were swaggering characters who told the mighty where to head in, they were pretty hell-for-leather fellows themselves.[56]

This kind of mentality has often been ascribed to mass ignorance and gullibility. The Southern masses, spell-bound by charismatic oratory and preoccupied with conspiratorial specters, allegedly followed their demagogic leaders in mindless, lock-step fashion. Perhaps in some cases they did, but I suspect that such explanations generally tell us more about the assumptions of the observer than about the social psychology of the Southern electorate. Without denying that the Davis movement had its share of irrationality, I would like to offer an alternative explanation for the movement's romantic character.

Part of the explanation can be found in the legacy of Jacksonian democracy. To a great degree, Davis and his followers were throwbacks to the anti-institutionalism of the nineteenth-century frontier. Like the Jacksonians, they distrusted all concentrations of power and were ambivalent about governmental activism.[57] Although Davis advocated a populistic reform program, he and his followers had limited faith in government as a problem-solving institution and remained wedded to the ideals of low taxes and small government. Most of the Old Guard put more stock in politics than government. They knew that good politics would make them feel better, but they were not sure what good government would do for them. One of the secrets of Davis's success was his intuitive sense that most of his followers did not want to be governed—even by him.

A second factor which encouraged the Old Guard to settle for a romantic illusion of power was the social and cultural structure of white Arkansas society. Davis's penchant for symbolic politics was grounded in an ambiguous cultural order. His agrarian jeremiads were based on a mythic conception of rural life—a reductionist oversimplification of the division between town and country. The cultural split between "agrarian" and "New South" subcultures was only a semblance of a dichotomy. The alignment between class, cultural, and urban-rural cleavages was blurred by several groups: planters who continued to live in the countryside, prosperous yeoman farmers, working-class rural-to-urban migrants, villagers who both envied and resented the culture and power of larger communities, and town-dwelling lawyer-politicians who represented the interests of farmers. In short, not everyone in the Arkansas countryside was a poor dirt farmer. And not everyone in urban Arkansas was a prosperous cosmopolitan. In many communities, a significant number of voters were either ambivalent or confused about their cultural loyalties.

This confusion was one of the reasons why Davis did not push harder for radical economic reform. Class divisions within the countryside prevented the development of an agrarian consensus in the Davis movement. Some Jeff Davis men did not want radical economic reform. In a slightly modified form, Lawrence Goodwyn's "shadow movement" thesis, originally developed to explain the demise of Populism, could be applied to Jeff Davis-ism.[58] Davis was the leader of both a movement and a shadow movement. The movement attracted the support of struggling yeomen and tenants who harbored deeply-felt cultural and economic grievances. The shadow movement, in contrast, was made up of rural planters, prosperous yeomen, and middle-class villagers—men who found Davis's defense of agrarian culture attractive but who were less enthusiastic about his periodic attacks on the local economic elite.[59]

To maintain control of state politics, Davis had to have the support of both the movement and the shadow movement. Although the planters, yeomen, and villagers of the shadow movement accounted for a relatively small proportion of Davis's mass following, they dominated Davis's political organization. These middle-class politicians did not always have their way with Davis. Nor did they exercise paternalistic hegemony over the small farmers who made up the bulk of the Davis movement. But they did have enough influence to soften Davis's commitment to radical reform. Their presence encouraged him to direct most of his hostility towards external enemies. It was politically advantageous for him to play to the lowest common denominator, which was either a non-class-based defense of agrarian culture or a defense of Southern rights. Davis's willingness to accommodate the shadow movement demonstrates that he was something less than "a Karl Marx for Hill Billies." But it would be a mistake to dismiss him as a mere tool of the agrarian elite. Politically and ideologically, he straddled the line between the movement and the shadow movement. He was a pragmatic politician, not a duplicitous charlatan. There is every indication that he sincerely believed that Yankee trusts, not Arkansas planters, posed the greatest threat to the state's struggling dirt farmers.

Most small farmers seem to have agreed with him on this point. For the most part, they did not interpret their problems in class terms. This was true, in part, because Davis and other political leaders discouraged them from doing so. But their attitudes also reflected a genuine conservatism rooted in a cultural environment that was beyond Davis's control. In a sense, they were victims of cultural confusion. Simultaneously Southerners, agrarian Southerners, and poor agrarian Southerners, many members of the Old Guard had difficulty maintaining a consistent frame of cultural reference. This multiple "ethnicity" placed severe limits on their agrarian radicalism. The mystique of regional unity tempered their criticism of urban Southerners, and the mystique of agrarian unity tempered their criticism of the rural elite. They were angry about their declining status. But like the dispossessed tenant farmer Muley Graves in *The Grapes of Wrath*, they did not know whom to shoot.

Here the comparison with the ethnocultural politics of the non-South is revealing. As a number of historians have pointed out, the non-South's ethnic and religious makeup provides part of the explanation for the persistence of a coherent and vigorous two-party system. Members of both parties had strong frames of reference, both positive and negative. They knew who they were, culturally and politically. And they knew who their enemies were. In contrast, the South has lacked both a strong two-party system and an ethnoreligious basis for political division. Because of its ethnic and religious homogeneity, the white South has developed its own distinctive style of political conflict—a style based on geography and social class rather than on ethnicity and religion. Significantly, as sources of cultural identity, geography and class seem to hold a greater potential for ambiguity and change than do ethnicity and religion. The cultural identity of the average Southern voter has been less fixed and more susceptible to political manipulation than that of the average non-Southern voter. Thus, the fact that political conflict in the South has been geocultural rather than ethnocultural may help to explain why the region has produced more than its share of demagogues. To explain Southern demagoguery primarily in terms of one-party politics and Negrophobia may be correct as far as it goes. But a more fundamental cause of demagoguery may have been a distinctive social structure that insured the persistence of one-party politics, encouraged the use of reductionist rhetoric, and promoted the political salience of racism.

In Arkansas, and perhaps in other Southern states as well, the two primary characteristics of Southern demagoguery—an extraordinary intensity of feeling and an unproductive, symbolic form of protest—were partially determined by the cultural makeup of white society. A cultural polarity between agrarian and New South subcultures fueled the fires of agrarian insurgency and encouraged bifactionalism; yet at the same time the almost inherent ambiguity of a cultural cleavage based primarily on geography insured that this conflict would stop short of disrupting the one-party system or of effectively challenging the status quo. Jeff Davis and the demagogues of the early twentieth-century South were prisoners, not only of their own personal failings, but also of an ambigous cultural landscape.

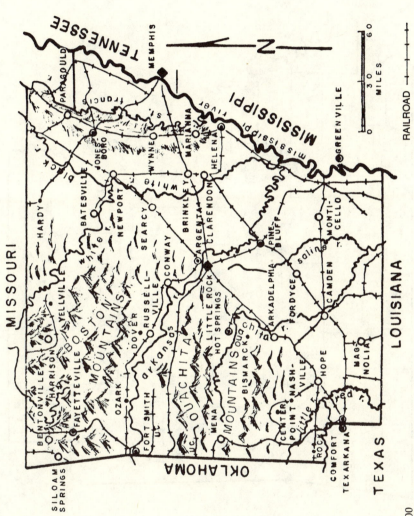

FIGURE 1.
Arkansas in 1900

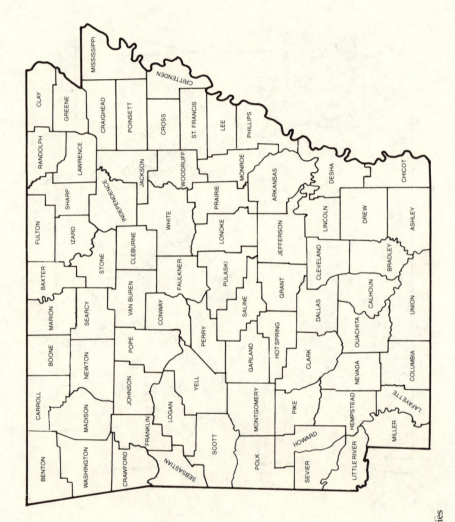

FIGURE 2.
Arkansas Counties

2

Arkansaw Traveller

I was born over here in the swamps of Red River Valley, where the
ladies had to wear boots when it was muddy. All that I am, all that
I have, all that I expect to be is centered in Arkansas. It is the land
of my nativity ... all up and down the hills and valleys of
Arkansas there lives as noble, as brave, as generous, as gentle a
race of people as ever sunned themselves in the smile of Omnipo-
tent God.

—*Jeff Davis (1900)*[1]

Jeff Davis began his life as he later lived it, with a large measure of
grit and a touch of grace. He was born near the backcountry village
of Rocky Comfort, Arkansas, on May 6, 1862, the first anniversary
of Arkansas's secession from the Union. Named for the most famous of
Rebel partisans, he was both a child of the Confederacy and a son of the
Southwestern frontier.[2] For a man who would one day become a master at
blending "log cabin" politics with the romantic symbolism of the Lost
Cause, it was a fitting, almost prophetic beginning. Although he was born
too late to become an authentic buckskin hero or a gallant brigadier, his
name and the circumstances of his birth gave Davis a personal identification
with the Old South which few politicians of his generation could muster.

As is often the case in American politics, the legend of Davis's origins was
part hyperbole. Although many of his followers believed otherwise, he was
not a descendant of the president of the Confederacy. Never one to waste a
political advantage, Davis actively encouraged this misconception
throughout his career—a practice that his enraged opponents condemned
as blasphemous. Out on the campaign trail, he was invariably clad in a
Prince Albert suit of Confederate gray, an outfit that bore a striking resemblance to a Rebel uniform. On occasion, he went so far as to ride from
village to village on a mule sporting the brand "C.S.A." (Confederate States
of America) on its rump.[3] In fact, some voters who were a little hazy about
the past actually believed that he was the old man himself. One old ex-
Confederate from Van Buren County told a reporter in 1900, "You must be a

d———d fool to think that after I had fought for Jeff Davis thirty-eight years ago I wouldn't vote for him now."[4] "I fought for him in the sixties," another veteran once exclaimed, "and I'm going to go on voting for him if he lives forever. He is the greatest and longest lived man that ever was."[5]

The frontier image also contained elements of exaggeration. Rugged as it was, heavily timbered and floodridden, Davis's birthplace was not the howling wilderness that he described on the stump. Rocky Comfort, located only a few miles northwest of the Davis family farm, was one of the most important farming and trading villages in southwest Arkansas. Settled in the 1830s, on the eve of Arkansas's admission to statehood, the village boasted a population of nearly 200 in 1860, which made it the largest community in Sevier (appropriately pronounced "severe") County. Situated on the highest point of land between the Little and Red Rivers, Rocky Comfort was a popular haven for lowland planters trying to escape the blistering heat and violent floods of the valley. Located along a major wagon road, the village also served as a final way station for weary homesteaders heading south towards the East Texas Prairie. Thus, even though it was tucked away in the extreme southwestern corner of the state, by Arkansas standards Davis's boyhood home was not particularly remote.[6]

Like most areas of the Red River Valley, Sevier County had passed out of its raw frontier stage long before Jeff Davis arrived on the scene. By the end of the antebellum period, the frontier line had been pushed well into Indian Territory, hundreds of miles west of Rocky Comfort. Blessed with a rich alluvial soil, most of Sevier County was well-settled plantation country by the 1850s. Though large plantations were relatively rare, nearly half of the county's eight hundred white farmers were slaveholders in 1860. Of a total population of 10,516 inhabitants, 3,366, or 32 percent, were slaves. In the southern half of the county, where the Davises lived, slaves were actually in the majority. Except for a handful of sawmills and a few cattle ranches, cotton plantations dominated the local economy, giving the area the unmistakable aura of the Black Belt South.[7]

Still, there was an ample measure of truth in Davis's characterization of himself as a son of the frontier. Plantation country or not, Sevier County was part of rural Arkansas, which was a land apart during the mid-nineteenth century. Throughout its history, Arkansas has been a cultural backwater and a land of incurable isolation. The butt of countless jokes, "Arkansaw," according to local legend, "was made on Saturday night after all the rest of the universe had been finished."[8] From the early travel accounts of Thomas Nuttal and Henry Rowe Schoolcraft (the geologist who started it all in 1819 with his caricature sketch of "the lazy mountaineer squatter, with hookworm, bare feet, fiddle and jug, sitting before his log shack among his greasy dirty children and his moronic looking wife, his hound dogs and his filth"), to the tall tales of Pete Whetstone and Opie

Read, to the ballad of "The Arkansaw Traveller," to the radio humor of Lum and Abner, to the comic strip antics of modern Dogpatch, the state's image has been dominated by isolated hollows, God-forsaken mudflats, and inbred mountain clans.[9] Few elements of the American folk tradition have enjoyed longer currency than the backward and isolated Arkansawyer—especially the Ozark variety. In 1845 the Jesuit historian Abraham Reynolds described the Ozarks as the "most lost" area of the "near West," and more than a century later journalists were still writing about "the amazing and all but timeless Ozarkian talent for sustaining remoteness."[10]

The major causes of this physical and cultural isolation were an unusually rugged terrain and a hopelessly inadequate system of roads. Arkansas's topography stymied the traveller at almost every turn, especially in the Ozark upcountry. In the northwest, the rugged Boston Mountains blanketed the area between the Missouri border and the Arkansas River Valley. Dotted with limestone peaks and winding hollows, and heavily forested with hardwoods, the region was a traveller's nightmare. South of the Arkansas River lay the Ouachita Mountains. Covered with long narrow ridges, jagged rock formations, and a dense growth of shortleaf pine, the Ouachitas were almost as inpenetrable as the Boston Mountains.[11]

In the South Arkansas lowlands the landscape was somewhat less forbidding. Except for several low ridges running north to south, the land was flat or gently rolling. Yet even here travel could be a harrowing experience. Known as the "great timber belt," South Arkansas was essentially a trackless pine forest. In a state where dense forestation was the norm—as late as 1902 Arkansas was the most heavily wooded state in the nation—the piney woods of South Arkansas were legendary.[12] The only treeless area of any size in antebellum Arkansas was the region known as the Grand Prairie. Seventy miles long and twenty miles wide, the Grand Prairie would later become the heart of the Arkansas rice belt.[13]

Northeast of the Grand Prairie was a second topographical anomaly, Crowley's Ridge, a 150-mile-long spine of rocks and yellow topsoil. Jutting into the delta lowlands almost to the banks of the Mississippi, Crowley's Ridge was a nuisance to travellers but a godsend to generations of farmers fleeing the Mississippi's floodwaters. Nicknamed "God's Levee," the ridge gave the northeastern corner of the state a distinctive character. Elsewhere in the East Arkansas Delta the land was monotonously flat. Here all the traveller had to face were cypress swamps, gargantuan mudflats, and endless stretches of thick underbrush. Floods frequently made a bad situation worse, and even the best roads were sometimes under water.[14]

Throughout the nineteenth century, Arkansas roads were among the worst in the nation.[15] Comments on their quality ranged from the unprintable to the hilarious, a tradition parodied in the folk tale of "The Arkansaw Traveller":

TRAVELLER: My friend, can't you tell me about the road I'm to travel tomorrow?

SQUATTER: Tomorrow! Stranger, yew won't git out'n these diggins for six weeks. But when hit gits so yew kin start, ye see that big sloo over thar. Wal, yew haf to git crost that fust, then yew take the big road up the bank, and in about a mile, yew'll come to a two-acre-and-a-half cawn-patch, the cawn's mightily in weeds, but yew needn't mind that, just ride on. In about a mile and a half, or mebbe two miles, yew'll come to the damndest swamp yew ever seen. Hit's boggy enuf to mire a saddle blanket. Thur's a fust rate road about six feet under thart.

TRAVELLER: How am I to get at it?

SQUATTER: Yew cain't get at hit noways, till the weather stiffens down some. Wal, about a mile from thar, yew'll come to whar thur's two roads. Yew kin take the righthand one, if yew want to; yew'll foller hit a mile or so, and yew'll find hit's just plum run out; then come back and try the left one; when yew git about two miles along on that, you may know ye air wrong; for thur ain't no road thar. Then yew'll think yerself mighty lucky if yew kin get back here. . . .[16]

Despite its poor roads and backward image, antebellum Arkansas was a land of promise and opportunity for many Americans. During the 1840s and 1850s, the state boasted many of the advantages of the Western frontier without subjecting its citizens to the perils of Indian attack. Notwithstanding its status as a slave state, the Land of the Razorbacks was renowned for its rugged equalitarianism and openness of spirit. Not only was land plentiful and cheap, but also a man could make his way in the world relatively free from the fetters of government and tradition.[17] Here almost any white man, regardless of background, could make a fresh start. In the words of a popular song of the period:

> The folks are plain down there,
>   Brave, modest and true,
> Wear homespun dresses and cotton pants
>   And coats of indigo blue.
>
> Hurrah! for Arkansas,
> Hurrah! for Arkansas,
> A four-horse team will soon be seen
> On the road to Arkansas.[18]

The waning years of the antebellum era were "flush times" in Arkansas. The coming of the river steamer, the extension of railroads into west Tennessee and the Mississippi Valley, the migration of restless slaveholders from the Upper South and the Southeast, the Mexican War and the subsequent opening of the "Great Southwest"—all of these factors helped to provide the "Nazareth of states" with its first legitimate boom. Between 1850 and 1860, corn production in the state doubled, the total value of livestock more than tripled, and cotton production increased by nearly six-fold. Most important, the local population more than doubled—from 209,857 in 1850 to 435,450 in 1860—as the state welcomed a steady stream of hopeful settlers.[19] One such settler was Jeff Davis's father, Lewis W. Davis.

Born in Todd County, Kentucky, in 1832, Lewis Davis was the son of Rebecca and Joshua Davis, a struggling blacksmith and dirt farmer who eked out barely enough to keep his family alive. Although they lived in the heart of south-central Kentucky's rich plantation belt, the Davises were poor whites who knew little of the romantic Old South that their grandson later revered. As an apparent consequence of this poverty, Lewis Davis left home at the age of twelve to become a blacksmith's apprentice in the nearby town of Russellville. Soon thereafter, in a turn of events worthy of Horatio Alger, he became the ward of Professor J. W. Ross. A local educator and philanthropist, Ross financed his education, first at a private academy in Bowling Green and later at Bethel College, where he prepared for the Baptist ministry. Ordained at the age of eighteen, the young preacher set out for the wild but promising land of southwest Arkansas. Arriving in Rocky Comfort sometime in 1850, he soon settled down to a life of farming and preaching the gospel.[20]

Information on Lewis Davis's life during the 1850s is sketchy, but according to family tradition he fared relatively well during these years. There is no evidence, however, that he rose to slaveholding status, the normal badge of prosperity in Sevier County, until July 1861 when, against a backdrop of war and secession, he married a well-to-do young widow, Elizabeth Phillips Scott. Born near Tuscaloosa, Alabama, in 1832, Elizabeth Davis was the daughter of Bolen C. Phillips, a wealthy planter (he owned thirty-six slaves and $10,000 worth of real estate in 1850) who had migrated to Sevier County from Alabama in 1835. Her first husband, William Scott, with whom she had three children, was a prosperous farmer who owned nine slaves at the time of his death in 1860. [21]

During the early years of the war, Lewis Davis remained at home with his new family and what was left of his congregation. While he was enough of a Rebel partisan to name his only natural son after the president of the Confederacy, he did not see action in the Confederate Army until he was drafted in 1864—a fact which later caused his son a good deal of political embarrassment. After serving a short stint as a private, he accepted a chaplain's commission in the 19th Arkansas Infantry, a position he held for the remainder of the war.[22]

However unpatriotic it may have seemed a half-century later, Lewis Davis's belated response to the Confederate call to arms probably raised few eyebrows at the time. Except for Quantrill's Raiders, who operated out of the Red River Valley as early as 1862, and a few Confederate steamboats cruising downriver with cargoes of Texas beef, the war did not come to Sevier County in any real sense until after the Confederate evacuation of Little Rock in September 1863. With the fall of Little Rock, the Rebel line of defense fell back to the Ouachita River; and the village of Washington, located less than forty miles northeast of Rocky Comfort, became the new Confederate state capital. For the rest of the war, southwest Arkansas was an area of major strategic importance. During the spring of 1864, a massive Union army commanded by General Nathaniel Banks attempted to capture the entire Red River Valley. But decisive Confederate victories at Poison Springs, Arkansas, and Mansfield, Louisiana, permanently stalled the Federals' drive.[23] Sevier County was thus spared the trauma of having a battle fought within its borders, and at the close of the war was one of the few counties in the state that remained in Rebel hands.

At the war's end Sevier County was little more than a Confederate garrison. From December 1864 on, Laynesport, a river village located southwest of the Davis homestead, served as the headquarters for General Sterling Price and his army of six thousand war-weary veterans. Thus, even though the war as a clash of armies never quite made it to Sevier County, there is some truth to the claim that Davis's early childhood was spent amidst "the acrid odor of burnt powder" and "the dull, dead boom of cannon." As one old friend pointed out at his funeral, Davis saw enough of the war to have the violent, combative "spirit of the times impressed . . . upon his nature."[24] The final Confederate surrender—that of Cherokee General Stand Watie, in late June 1865—took place at Doaksville, Indian Territory, less than fifty miles west of Rocky Comfort. Such stubbornness of spirit was characteristic of southwestern Confederates, a number of whom preferred exile to reunion.[25] In the hearts and minds of the unreconstructed veterans who populated Davis's youth, the romance of the Confederacy remained alive. It is little wonder that young Jeff became enraptured with the mythology of the "cause." Forty years after Gettysburg, he was still verbally storming the heights at Cemetery Ridge:

> How many old Confederate soldiers are there here? Hold your hands up. (A great many hold up their hands.) God bless you; you are the sentinels upon the watch towers of Liberty. I love the old Confederate soldier. Most of them have already crossed the dark river and pitched their tents upon Fame's eternal camping ground. God bless you. No man will bow with greater reverence to the old Confederate soldier than I. . . . Judge Bryant [one of Davis's opponents in the 1900 gubernatorial primary campaign] said he was a patriot; he is glad the Union is preserved. . . . He said that he didn't regret that our old flag trailed in the dust; he did not regret that we lost. I do. . . . You will never get me to say that I don't regret it. God bless you, I am not built that way.[26]

Davis was particularly solicitous of disabled Confederate veterans, those "with an empty sleeve" or "an empty boot leg." His own father was one of the lucky ones who returned from the war in one piece. For Lewis Davis, the period immediately following the war was not so much a time of tragedy or suffering as it was a time for new directions and fresh starts. Soon after his return he abandoned the ministry and took up the practice of law. Though he had little or no legal training, his rise in the profession was nothing short of meteoric. In the fall of 1866, less than a year after being admitted to the bar, he was elected county and probate judge of Sevier County. After July 1867, when the southern half of Sevier became Little River County, his jurisdiction was limited to the new county. During this period the local judiciary was completely politicized, and Judge Davis was essentially a care-taker for the interests of Democrats who hoped to forestall Radical Recon-struction. Unfortunately for the judge, the politicization of the judiciary proved to be a double-edged sword: in 1868 he and other local Democratic officeholders were swept out of office.[27]

The Republican victories in the state and local elections of 1868 marked the beginning of Radical Reconstruction in Arkansas—a development which most Democrats refused to accept gracefully. During the next four years, the Ku Klux Klan, the Knights of the White Camellia, and other ex-Confederate vigilante organizations terrorized black and white Republicans across the state. Nearly every Arkansas county had its share of Democratic avengers, but nowhere was the level of violence and terrorism higher than in the border country of Little River County, where gangs of ex-Confederate desperadoes took advantage of law enforcement officers who were seriously hampered by jurisdictional boundaries. (Later in the nineteenth century, the Red River borderlands would become a favorite haunt of outlaws such as the James brothers and Belle Starr.)[28]

Cullen Montgomery Baker, the most infamous of the Red River desper-adoes, reportedly murdered more than a hundred freedmen between 1866 and 1869. In October 1868, a few miles outside of Rocky Comfort, members of Baker's gang ambushed and killed a United States revenue assessor and a local Freedmen's Bureau agent, and wounded the county sheriff. This out-rage prompted Republican Governor Powell Clayton to place Little River County and nine other South Arkansas counties under martial law. Clayton also dispatched a company of state militiamen (most of whom were black) to the county to drive Baker's gang out of the state. Baker accepted Clayton's challenge and recruited several hundred men from Little River and Sevier Counties to do battle with the militia. But in the end he scurried across the Texas border, leaving the locals to fend for themselves. After several skir-mishes, one of which pitted more than 400 local "Klansmen" against a smaller force of militiamen, the militia gained control of the county, and by January 1869 order was restored. According to local Democratic mythology, the months that followed were a time of infamy in Little River County; allegedly, homes and businesses were pillaged, prisoners were tortured and murdered, and white women were ravaged by black militiamen. Many years later, Davis blasted Clayton as the "despoiler of our homes" and recalled the period of martial law as the most bitter episode of his youth. Though

Clayton vigorously denied the charge, Davis claimed that one of his aunts had been murdered by the Reconstruction Governor's "nigger gang."[29]

By the fall of 1869 Lewis and Elizabeth Davis had had enough of the rough-and-tumble Red River country. Journeying more than a hundred miles to the north, across the Ouachita Mountains and into the Arkansas River Valley, they resettled in the foothills of Pope County. Straddling the southern edge of the Ozarks, Pope County was a sparsely settled area enjoying its final years of rustic isolation. (Only a decade earlier the county was the primitive setting for Edward Payson Washburn's classic painting, *The Arkansas Traveler*.) The Little Rock and Fort Smith Railroad, which promised to rouse the Arkansas River Valley from its economic and demographic lethargy, was still under construction. The great flood of settlement, which would more than double the county's population between 1870 and 1885, was yet to come.[30]

Rich in potential and restless in spirit, Pope County was a good place for a young country lawyer to make a fresh start. From 1869 to 1873—as Jeff passed from childhood into early adolescence—the Davises lived and prospered in the county seat town of Dover, a small inland trading center fifteen miles north of the Arkansas River. As a former judge, Lewis Davis had little difficulty making his mark on the local legal community, which consisted of a handful of lawyers. By the early seventies, he was the acknowledged leader of the Dover bar. In 1870 the family's wealth, including real property, was assessed at $2,800, a relatively large sum for hard times.[31] Though hardly wealthy, by the end of Reconstruction the Davises were far better off than most local families, many of whom were caught in a spiral of ever-increasing debt. When Jeff Davis later thundered against the injustice of the crop lien system, he spoke for his less fortunate neighbors—the struggling dirt farmers were in danger of forfeiting their land to supply merchants.[32]

Moving to Pope County brought success and prosperity to the Davis household, but it did not provide an escape from the violence of Reconstruction politics. The postwar struggle between Democrats and Republicans proved to be even more rancorous there than in the Red River country. Here, as in most areas of the Ozarks, the primary challenge to Democratic rule came not from Yankee carpetbaggers or freedmen but from white scalawags. Home-grown and largely intraracial, local Reconstruction politics was rooted deep in the county's past. Throughout its early history, Pope County was plagued by a cultural and political rift between lowland slaveholders and upland yeomen—a rift that widened with the coming of the Civil War. In 1861 a substantial minority of the citizenry opposed secession, despite the fact that nearly a thousand slaves lived within the county's borders. During the early years of the war, many local Unionists defied the Confederacy and were subsequently harassed or imprisoned. But when Federal troops gained control of the Arkansas River Valley in the fall of 1863, the situation was rudely reversed. Once strident Rebel partisans suddenly found themselves under the control of the Unionist minority, many of whom promptly enlisted in the Federal army. For the remainder of the war, the county was ravaged by political violence, guerrilla warfare, and bushwhackers of every persuasion.[33]

After the war both sides harbored deeply felt grievances. Throughout most of Reconstruction, with the Republicans in control of local politics and the Democrats in control of the local economy, Pope County hovered on the brink of renewed civil war. Finally, in July 1872, after seven years of simmering hatred and intermittent violence, the county erupted into what was later known as the Pope County Militia War. This violent drama, much of which took place in Dover, began with the attempted murder of a Republican deputy sheriff and ended with the military occupation of the county by the Republican-controlled state militia. During more than six months of disorder, the county was rocked by a series of politically motivated murders and by the alleged "plundering" of the local Democratic yeomanry by black Republican militiamen. According to one pro-Democratic historian, under the guise of martial law "stores were robbed, barns pillaged, private homes forcibly entered," and "respectable" citizens murdered. (Embellished tales of marauding black militiamen dominated local Democratic mythology for decades.) Although their ability to muster armed resistance was limited, the embattled Democrats of Pope County became heroic figures to frustrated ex-Confederates all across the state.[34] By engaging in open conflict with the militia, they helped to set the stage for the Brooks-Baxter War of 1873–74, the epic struggle which put an end to Radical Republican rule in Arkansas.[35]

Although it is unclear whether Lewis Davis acted as a peacemaker or a firebrand during the Militia War, there can be little doubt that the conflict had a profound effect on his ten-year-old son. Coming on the heels of a similar experience in Little River County, the Militia War must have convinced young Jeff that the entire world was a battleground where Democrats and Republicans routinely gunned each other down. Cast in the forge of childhood experience, his memories of Reconstruction violence would shape Davis's personality and politics for the remainder of his life.[36]

Soon after the close of the Militia War, in early 1873, the Davises abandoned the war-torn village of Dover and moved ten miles south to the town of Russellville. This move, prompted in part by the war, was mainly due to the completion of the Little Rock and Fort Smith Railroad. With the coming of the railroad to the southern part of the county, Dover's days of local preeminence were over. Although Dover would remain the county seat until 1887, the locus of trade and settlement quickly shifted southward to the railroad towns of Russellville and Atkins. By the mid-1870s Russellville was a full-fledged boom town, complete with brick storefronts, fancy carriages, and businessmen sporting three-piece suits and silk hats. By 1876 Russellville's population had swelled to 800, more than twice that of Dover.[37]

No one benefited from this boom more than the Davises. The opening of the Little Rock and Fort Smith Railroad inaugurated an era of boosterism and development in Pope County that was ideally suited to the talents and ambitions of an enterprising man like Lewis Davis. As an attorney specializing in homestead cases, as a real estate agent and, for a short time, as the editor of a local weekly, the Russellville *National Tribune,* "Judge" Davis played a leading role in the economic and social modernization of the county.[38] In the process he became one of Russellville's most prosperous citizens.

But Judge Davis was more than just a successful lawyer and businessman. During the decade and a half following the end of Reconstruction, he was probably the most visible member of the local elite. He was a leader in almost every facet of local community life, from religion to railroad promotion, from politics to public education. In March 1875 he was instrumental in organizing "the friends of the Dardanelle, Dover and Harrison railroad." Three months later, he was accorded the honor of sending Russellville's first telegraph message. The following week he became the first president of the Pope County Immigration Society. In 1876 he was elected to the state legislature. In 1878 he chaired the first meeting of the Pope County Agricultural and Mechanical Association, a booster organization interested in sponsoring annual county fairs. In 1880 he served as chairman of the Russellville School District. In 1882 he was chairman of both the Pope County Sunday School Association and the Russellville Auxiliary of the American Bible Society. In 1886 he served as a delegate to the Arkansas State Temperance Convention.[39] Judge Davis was a go-getter of the first order, a classic New South gentleman.

As the son of such a man, Jeff Davis enjoyed a privileged adolescence. Though hardly bookish—his favorite pastimes were hunting and target shooting—he made his way through the Russellville public school system with relative ease. Graduating at the age of sixteen, he applied for an appointment to West Point, but was rejected—allegedly because of his poor spelling. Lowering his sights a bit, he enrolled at the Arkansas Industrial University (later the University of Arkansas) in the fall of 1878. He remained in Fayetteville for two years, preparing for a law career and mingling with the sons of the Arkansas gentry. In 1880 he transferred to the law department of Vanderbilt University in Nashville, Tennessee. While there he proved to be an able student, completing the standard two-year law program in a single year. But, because he had failed to meet the university's residency requirement, Vanderbilt refused to grant him a diploma; and he returned home in a huff.[40]

Within a few weeks of his less-than-triumphant return to Pope County, Davis applied for admission to the bar, even though he was technically underage. Through his father's influence the minimum age limit of twenty-one was waived, and he was admitted to the bar of Arkansas's Fifth Judicial Circuit in the summer of 1881. But his college odyssey was not quite over. In the fall he returned to Tennessee, this time to attend Cumberland University in Lebanon. The following spring, with his law degree finally in hand, twenty-year-old Jeff Davis became a junior partner in L. W. Davis and Son, Attorneys at Law.[41]

In late October 1882, only a few months after beginning his law practice, Jeff married Ina MacKenzie, the stepdaughter of the late Judge Frank Thach. A close personal and political friend of Lewis Davis's, Thach had served two terms (1874–1878) as county judge before his death in 1878.[42] Jeff had entered into a politically advantageous marriage, solidifying the Davis family's position within the local county courthouse elite. Described as a woman with "a masterful mind" and a "powerful personality," Ina Davis was an asset to her husband throughout his political career. Although she played no direct role in his political campaigns, her moderating influence on his fiery temperament saved him from disaster on more than one occasion. As Senator James P. Clarke once commented, "She was the only person I ever knew who could influence Senator Davis against what appeared to be his settled conviction, whim, or purpose."[43] Before her death in 1910, she bore twelve children, eight of whom survived past infancy.[44]

Fortunately for Davis, his law practice kept pace with his growing family. As his long-time friend Judge Jeptha Evans once remarked, "He was from the beginning a man of marked ability and adaption [*sic*] to the law." According to Evans, Davis "forgot nothing, overlooked nothing, neglected nothing, and saw through everything."[45] In the best tradition of the leather-lunged razorback lawyer, he could make a mixture of humor and country horse sense sound like irrefutable legal logic. Perhaps most important, his combative personality was ideally suited to the rough-and-tumble give and take of the country courtroom. Quick-witted and fearless, he liked nothing better than to engage in verbal brawls with his older and more respectable opponents. A powerful speaker with a natural flair for courtroom drama, he was virtually unbeatable before a jury. Despite his youth, Davis was the most sought after defense attorney in the district by the mid-1880s.[46]

For all his later claims on the stump, not all of Davis's time as a young lawyer was spent in trial work defending the "horny-handed sons of toil." Like most small town Southern lawyers, he also acted as a middleman in the local agricultural economy—a role that did not always endear him to local farmers. Beginning in 1883 Davis and his father served as loan agents for Shattuck and Hoffman, a large cotton factor firm operating out of New Orleans. Offering loans at 10 percent per annum, the Davises were profiting from an exploitative credit system that was driving many small farmers into hopeless debt. As one irate local editor described the situation:

... no farmer in this country, with the present low price of cotton, can afford to pay ten percent on the money he makes the cotton with, and that farmer who borrows money on this plan, had as well at once adjust himself to the consequent misery of never owning anything. ... We would advise a farmer to strain every point, live on bread and water, and finally go and hire himself out, rather than borrow money on such a plan.[47]

During the mid and late eighties, Davis also began to dabble in real estate speculation. In July 1887, "Davis and Son, Real Estate Agents" advertised several large tracts of land, including valuable coal lands located in the southern part of the county. By August of the same year, Davis and his family were wealthy enough to spend "the remainder of the heated term" at cool and fashionable Mount Nebo, the summer vacation spot of the local gentry.[48] Like his father, Jeff Davis was a man on the make.

In up-and-coming towns like Russellville, activities such as cotton factoring and real estate speculation were generally interpreted as signs of a healthy commercial spirit. This was not the case in the countryside, where real estate lawyers and loan agents often were viewed as parasitic opportunists. From the struggling farmer's perspective, lawyers, like merchants, were non-producers—men who made a living out of fleecing farmers.[49] Davis's image as an exploiter was softened somewhat by his "good old boy" personality, by his country wit and hell-raising reputation, and by his willingness to defend poor farmers in court. Nevertheless, he bore little resemblance to the simple haybinder, the one-gallus hillbilly, whom he later canonized on the campaign trail. Set apart by his education, his manner of dress, his occupation, not to mention the size of his wallet, Davis during these years was unmistakably a townsman, a member of the new "urban" middle class.

Tension between local farmers and villagers was as old as the county itself. But with the coming of the railroad, the cultural gap between town and country in Pope County took on new dimensions. Railway and stage lines, electric lights, telephone and telegraph service, daily mail deliveries, store-bought clothes, a local bank or two—from the 1880s onward, all of these sharply differentiated urban and rural life.[50] Significantly, the cultural impact of urban development was greatly accentuated by rural decline. While lazy villages such as Russellville and Atkins were turning into bustling towns, most of the surrounding countryside was drifting deeper and deeper into economic and psychological depression. As the journalist Charles Morrow Wilson once noted, in the "rural Ozarks the eighties were almost unbelievably depressed, so much so that a dollar looked at least as big as the moon and was only slightly easier to lay hands on."[51]

What angered the farmers of Pope County most was not economic depression per se—they and their parents and grandparents before them had lived with hard times off and on for decades—but rather what sociologists now call "relative deprivation."[52] Everyone in the county was well-aware that wealth and power were flowing out of the countryside and into the towns; the independence and social status of the yeoman farmer were slipping away. For the first time, town dwellers were determining the future of the county; and a large number of local planters, probably a majority by 1890, were living not on plantations but in town. Supervising their plantations from afar and often reinvesting part of their wealth in commercial ventures (such as the Melrose Cotton Mill which opened in 1882), these upper-class "agrarians" became almost indistinguishable from their non-planter neighbors.[53] This development—an alignment between class and urban-rural cleavages—divided the local white population into two distinct societies, one rural and poor, the other urban and relatively prosperous. In Pope County, as in most areas of the South, this polarization process did not gain a full head of steam until after the turn of the century, but the basic pattern was in evidence by the early 1880s.

The economic and cultural split between town and country sometimes led to open conflict, as in March 1891, when gangs of young "rubes" and "city slickers" brawled on the streets of Russellville. On occasion, signs of conflict also appeared in angry letters written to local newspapers by frustrated farmers. In October 1883 a farmer from Illinois township informed the editor of the *Russellville Democrat* that "the merchants of this county have got the working class with their hands crossed and are ready to tie them, but we don't aim for them to do it. And now they are mad and say they are going to starve us out. . . ."[54]

The most important manifestation of cultural and economic conflict in Pope County was the emergence of the Brothers of Freedom, a semisecret agrarian order similar to the Agricultural Wheel (with which it merged in 1885) and the Farmers' Alliance. Dedicated to agricultural self-sufficiency and non-intercourse with merchants and capitalists, and laced with rural chauvinism, the Brothers of Freedom began as a strictly apolitical order, but it quickly developed into a militant political organization that disrupted the solidarity of both major parties. As the leading historian of the movement put it, "When cotton prices robbed the farmers of their independence, when they had to swallow their pride and beg merchants for credit, when the government became an instrument of oppression, they realized that their freedom could be secured only by joining together 'as a band of brothers' in order to protect the interests of agriculture."[55] Originating in 1882 in Johnson County, the Brothers of Freedom swept across northwest Arkansas like wildfire during the hard times of 1883 and 1884.

The order first appeared in Pope County during the fall of 1883, and by the following spring the local membership numbered nearly two thousand, two-thirds of whom were Democrats. Lewis Davis and other local Democratic leaders claimed to be sympathetic to the Brothers' platform, but roundly condemned the organization's drift towards political involvement and party independence. When the Brothers refused to withdraw their independent ticket, enraged and frightened Democrats accused them of preaching "communism and socialism" and claimed that their lack of loyalty to the Democratic party endangered white supremacy. Despite such tactics, most of the Brothers kept faith during the local election of 1884. Supported by the local Republican party, which included several hundred black voters, the Brothers fought the regular Democrats to a draw, winning four of eight county offices.[56]

Such was the condition of the Pope County Democracy when Jeff Davis began his political apprenticeship. Badly splintered and stunned by the Brothers' militancy, the Democratic party was in serious danger of losing its local hegemony. With the yeomanry on the rampage, the tide of local politics seemed to be running against men like the Davises, who were closely associated with the ruling county courthouse elite. As a lawyer, man about town, and son of Lewis Davis, Jeff had no choice but to align himself with the Democratic stalwarts. Even if he had supported the Brothers' insurgency, he would not have been welcome in the councils of agrarian radicalism. For the man who would later gain fame as the Tribune of Haybinders, it was an ironic beginning.

3

Democracy and Disfranchisement

It is true that all power ultimately rests with the party. The party can make and unmake.

—*James G. Wallace (1890)*[1]

Although Jeff Davis occasionally joined his father in speaking out against agrarian insurgents in 1884, he did not become heavily involved in politics until the summer of 1886, when he served as a delegate to the Democratic county convention. In the weeks following the convention, he actively campaigned for Jeremiah V. Bourland, an old friend of Lewis Davis's from Franklin County who was running for district prosecuting attorney. Bourland, who later became one of Jeff's closest political advisors, ultimately lost his bid for the Democratic nomination for prosecuting attorney. But in the process, his young friend from Pope County made quite a sensation as a stump speaker.[2] Brandishing the same oratorical fire and bombast that had dazzled juries for four years, Jeff smoked his way across the district, giving the voters a brief glimpse of things to come.

By the time the 1888 campaign came around, Davis was in great demand as a stump speaker. In Pope County, the agrarian radical threat had subsided considerably since 1884, thanks to a steady barrage of racial demagoguery.[3] On the state level, however, the Democrats found themselves locked in a desperate struggle with the newly formed Union-Labor party, a biracial coalition of Republicans, Wheelers (the Agricultural Wheel absorbed the Brothers of Freedom in 1885), Greenbackers, and Alliancemen. The Democrats remained in power only by resorting to massive electoral fraud, intimidation, and a vicious campaign of race-baiting reminiscent of Reconstruction days. Even by the official count, the Union-Labor candidate for governor in 1888, Charles M. Norwood, came within 15,000 votes of victory.[4]

Davis did his part in the state election campaign, giving speeches in several counties; but his major contribution came during the national campaign, when the incumbent President Cleveland was challenged by the Republican Benjamin Harrison, and the Union-Laborite A. J. Streeter. Selected as a Democratic presidential elector, Davis stumped the state for "reform," white supremacy, and Grover Cleveland. It was an experience which marked his arrival as a serious politician, one which he recalled again and again in later years, sometimes with a humorous twist:

> In 1888 I was chosen by the Democracy of this State, a freckle-faced, red-headed boy, as one of their presidential electors, and nothing gave me more pleasure than to fight the Pops of our State. . . . I came very nearly getting mixed up with "Cyclone" Davis one time, the Populist leader of Texas. I had been invited to make a speech in Batesville. . . . They telegraphed for "Cyclone," who was in St. Louis. When I discovered this, I was almost scared to death, knowing what a mighty man he was, but the old Pops received a wire from him saying that he could not come. Someone had slipped into his room the night before and stolen his pants and his money, and the train left so early that he could not get out and get more, and I have thanked God ever since that "Cyclone" lost his breeches.[5]

Jeff may have been overmatched by the "Cyclone" from Texas, but the locals regarded him as a hell-for-leather politician who could hold his own against anyone. Twenty-six years old and full of grit, he seemed ready to tackle the world. The glories of the 1888 campaign, as one observer recalled many years later, merely "whetted his appetite for politics. . . . Like a young giant that had been sleeping for ages . . . he began to stretch himself and flex his muscles and look about for something upon which to test his strength."[6]

The test came in 1890 when he ran for district prosecuting attorney, a potentially lucrative position and traditional takeoff point for ambitious young politicians. Supported by his father's ex-law partner James G. Wallace, who was running for circuit judge, Davis was part of an unofficial Pope County ticket. His opponent for the Democratic nomination was Charles C. Reid of Conway County, a young Vanderbilt law graduate who later served five terms in Congress.[7]

The campaign between Davis and Reid was a good-natured affair, but it was not without controversy. Reminding the voters that Reid's home county was the only county in the district that had not outlawed saloons, Davis tried to skewer his opponent with the temperance issue. (At the time, Lewis Davis was probably the best-known temperance advocate in the district.)[8] Promising to rid the district of "blind tigers" and other liquor law violators, he declared war on the liquor interests, whom he claimed were behind Reid's candidacy. He also interjected the race issue into the campaign, vowing to "fill the penitentiary so full of negroes that their feet would be sticking out the windows."[9] This was an obvious attempt to take advantage of the fact that Conway County was the only "Black Belt" county in the district: 39.4 percent black in 1890, Conway had more black inhabitants than the other three counties combined.[10]

At only one point during the campaign did Davis find himself on the defensive, but that one episode nearly cost him the election. In late April, at the height of the contest, he got into a heated argument in a local store over the political future of the Farmers' Alliance, a powerful national farmers' organization then sweeping the county. Several Alliancemen who were present claimed that Davis had spoken out against the Alliance, an act tantamount to political suicide.[11] Davis denied the charge but was ultimately forced to defend himself in a public letter addressed "To the Farmers of Pope County":

> On my return home from Johnson County I find that a few men are trying to make political capital out of a statement that I made in Mr. Tucker's store in Russellville a short time since, and have so perverted that statement and given such publicity to it that I deem it my duty to set myself right with my farmer friends at least. . . . I stated then, and state now, that the Alliance or any other organization that was for the good of the farmer met my hearty approval and endorsement, but that the men who had organized the farmers formerly for political purposes only had better be attending to their own business and letting every body else's alone.[12]

In the end, Davis survived his scrape with the agrarian radicals, winning a narrow victory over Reid. Though he carried only two of the district's four counties, his victories came in the relatively populous counties of Pope and Yell. Unopposed in the general election, he became the prosecuting attorney of Arkansas's Fifth Judicial District on October 30, 1890.[13] A new political star was on the rise.

Already a local legend as a defense attorney, Davis had no trouble adapting his skills to the art of prosecution. By the end of his term, he had kept his promise to fill the local jails to overflowing. According to Judge Jeptha Evans, who witnessed many of Davis's triumphs during this period, he "was one of the ablest and most successful prosecuting attorneys the State of Arkansas ever had in its commission."[14] Charles Jacobson, who served as one of Davis's deputy prosecuting attorneys, offered a similar appraisal:

> I doubt if ever in this state there was a Prosecuting Attorney more active, more vigorous and more to be feared than he, throughout the district. The fee system being in vogue and the revenues of the office depending upon conviction, few guilty men had a chance to escape the meshes of the law. He was fearless and pugnacious in his prosecutions. . . . His cross-examinations were skillful and vigorous and he was a terror to any witness who undertook to misrepresent the truth. He was not only familiar with the psychology of his jury, but impressed upon them his own personality, and it was difficult to get an acquittal when Jeff Davis made the last appeal to the jurors. . . . It was during the four years that he served as Prosecuting Attorney that he began to realize his power over the people and his ability to sway them.[15]

Davis's success as a prosecutor improved his financial situation considerably, but politically it proved to be a mixed blessing. In a state where the county court was regarded with contempt by a large portion of the farming population and where the expression "actin' like a judge" generally meant "behaving like a pompous jackass," the local prosecuting attorney was not apt to be the most popular of men.[16] Because of his vigorous style of prosecution and his unusually large number of convictions, Davis "made a great many enemies throughout the district," particularly in Conway County where the local machine did not appreciate his stern prosecution of liquor law violators. Although he was unopposed for re-election in 1892, these enemies would come back to haunt him four years later when he ran for Congress.[17]

The early 1890s in Arkansas was a time of severe economic depression, interracial violence, and political instability.[18] Yet the era was not as turbulent as it might have been. In 1890 the Union-Laborite Napoleon B. Fizer came almost as close (44 percent of the vote) to capturing the governorship as Charles Norwood had two years earlier, but the agrarian radicals would never come that close again.[19] Before it had even made an appearance in some Southern states, "populism" had reached its peak in Arkansas. In fact, the unexpected weakness of the People's party in Arkansas, where agrarian radicalism had once been so vital, was one of the great disappointments of the Populist movement. Although the Arkansas People's party attracted a solid core of dedicated followers, the ruling Democrats were never seriously challenged during the nineties. In 1892 the Populist candidate for governor, James P. Carnahan, won only 19.9 percent of the vote. James B. Weaver, the Populists' presidential standard-bearer, fared even worse, polling 8 percent. By 1896 even in the state races Populists accounted for less than 10 percent of the electorate.[20] By then the dreams of Populist conquest, which had seemed so reasonable at the beginning of the decade, were shattered forever. "Populism is so dead," one Democratic editor wrote in 1901, "that not enough remains are left for an inquest."[21]

Several factors contributed to the early decline of third-party agrarianism in Arkansas, but the farm economy was not one of them. In economic terms, the case for agrarian revolt was stronger than ever. Arkansas farmers, like most Southern farmers, were significantly worse off in the mid-1890s than they had been a decade earlier when the Agricultural Wheel and the Brothers of Freedom had first erupted. And there was no relief in sight. Cotton prices continued to plummet, the farm tenancy rate continued to swell, and the economic and cultural gap between town and country widened with every passing year.[22]

Why then did Arkansas Democrats have so little trouble in beating back the Populist challenge? Perhaps the most obvious reason was the race issue. Fusion with the Republicans in 1888 and 1890 was a courageous strategy that almost brought the agrarian radicals to power; but it also made them an easy mark for race-baiting Democrats. Tar-brushed with the charge of "Black Republicanism" from the outset, the Arkansas People's party never had a chance. "All roads in Arkansas that lead from Democracy," the *Arkansas Gazette* declared in July 1892, "lead to the Republican party, controlled by Powell Clayton. . . . A vote for Whipple [the Republican candidate for governor] or Carnahan [the Populist candidate] is a vote for negro supremacy and bayonet rule."[23] According to the Democratic press, the Arkansas People's party was nothing more than the old Union-Labor party with a new name. Ironically, one of the People's party's greatest problems was its inability to reconstruct the Union-Labor coalition. Populist and Republican leaders flirted with fusion throughout the early 1890s, but both sides were too ambivalent and too cautious to enter into a solid alliance.[24] Although fusion was common on the local level, the two parties offered competing candidates for most state and national offices. As a result, the Populists ended up with the worst of both worlds: tainted with Republicanism, they received few Republican votes.

Another factor that hurt the Populist cause was the liberalization of the Democratic opposition. During the 1870s and 1880s, the Arkansas Democratic party was dominated by a Bourbon oligarchy of planter-merchants and lawyers—men of property whose primary concerns were economic development and class rule. Wedded to the gold standard and bound by traditional theories of small government, they had little to offer the common farmer other than white supremacy and the rhetoric of self-help. By the early nineties, however, the Bourbons were in full retreat. The near defeats of 1888 and 1890, combined with a major financial scandal in 1891 (the State Treasurer William E. Woodruff, Jr., son of the founder of the Little Rock *Arkansas Gazette*, embezzled more than $100,000) discredited the conservatives, bringing a younger and more flexible class of leaders to the fore. By the time the Populists appeared on the scene in 1892, Alliance and free-silver Democrats were in control of the party. A liberal party platform endorsed free silver and the abolition of the convict-lease system; and William M. Fishback, the debt repudiationist, was nominated for governor. An ardent free-silverite, Fishback had won the hearts of many economic liberals in 1880 by sponsoring a constitutional amendment which prohibited the state from repaying millions of dollars of railroad and levee bonds.[25] Fishback was a pragmatic politician, who was willing to go to great lengths to keep the unruly Alliance Democrats in the party. Like many moderate Democrats, including young Jeff Davis, he fervently believed that reform would forestall revolution.

A third factor in the Populists' demise was disfranchisement. The disfranchisement movement of the 1890s fundamentally altered the structure of Arkansas politics. During the 1880s the contours of Arkansas politics were not those of the "Solid South." Party politics was competitive, voter turnout was high, and blacks voted almost as often and as freely as whites. Though the Democrats controlled the state, they did so without the aid of formal disfranchisement mechanisms. Intimidated by the lingering specter of Federal intervention, they were forced to rely on violence and electoral fraud whenever they needed an extra advantage over their opposition. For Arkansas Democrats, then, the 1880s was an era of caution and limited power. For their opponents, it was an era of hope and opportunity.[26]

Under the open electoral system of the 1880s, Democratic leaders found themselves acknowledging, even encouraging, the right of black suffrage. In some counties, Democratic and Republican candidates openly competed for the black vote as they had done during Reconstruction. But in most Black Belt counties, particularly in the East Arkansas Delta, a more complicated set of arrangements prevailed. Here black Republicans and white Democrats customarily entered into "fusion" agreements, which allowed each party an uncontested share of local offices. Under the terms of such agreements, local Republicans were allowed to poll a full vote for Republican presidential candidates and for some state candidates as well. As long as the Democrats' opposition remained divided into competing parties, such arrangements posed no threat to the statewide Democratic hegemony. The fusion system represented a workable compromise, which assuaged Northern public opinion, precluded federal intervention in local elections, and provided Black Belt Democrats with many more local offices than they would have had under an unrestricted electoral system.[27]

By the standards of the twentieth-century South, the level of black suffrage in Arkansas during the 1880s was remarkably high. Using ecological regression analysis, Morgan Kousser has estimated that 72 percent of the potential black electorate participated in the Arkansas gubernatorial election of 1888. The comparable estimate for whites was 78 percent.[28] These estimates are consistent with the data in Table 1, which cross-classifies voter turnout and black population. In 1888 the average voter turnout level (74 percent) in Arkansas's twenty-one Black Belt (40 percent black or more) counties was only slightly lower than the statewide average of 76 percent. In the 6 counties where blacks made up 70 percent or more of the local population, the average turnout was 76 percent. Moreover, the absence of a significant relationship between race and political participation in the election of 1888 is confirmed by simple correlation and multiple regression analysis (see Appendix A, Tables B–C).

The openness of electoral politics in Arkansas during the 1880s can also be seen in the voting behavior of lower-class whites. Like race, poverty and illiteracy were seldom barriers to political participation. Judging by the correlation and regression analysis in Appendix A, voter turnout was almost as high among poor white farmers as it was among middle-class and upper-class whites. With few exceptions, the simple and partial coefficients that

TABLE 1
Voter Turnout in the Arkansas Black Belt, 1888–1900, Gubernatorial Elections*

County	% Black 1900	% Voting						
		1888	1890	1892	1894	1896	1898	1900
Chicot	87.1	71.9	76.2	36.0	20.4	23.5	19.1	21.6
Crittenden	84.6	81.5	61.3	21.4	13.9	18.7	12.8	19.3
Desha	81.7	83.4	75.4	33.0	23.0	23.5	9.4	14.7
Phillips	78.6	70.5	55.4	37.4	20.0	18.6	14.3	26.8
Lee	77.8	84.6	80.6	43.6	22.7	28.3	44.9	45.5
Jefferson	72.8	64.2	74.3	30.9	23.8	21.8	25.4	23.4
Monroe	65.4	77.5	73.3	38.5	24.0	35.8	18.8	30.6
St. Francis	64.1	82.7	76.9	60.0	48.8	49.6	16.2	26.3
Lincoln	63.1	58.1	82.3	69.3	44.6	41.8	40.1	33.3
Lafayette	61.2	69.2	66.8	53.5	39.3	41.4	39.3	33.8
Woodruff	61.0	74.5	72.9	77.2	44.8	61.6	35.2	45.9
Ouachita	55.7	73.8	73.4	52.9	51.3	55.1	39.2	41.8
Ashley	53.7	70.9	67.6	42.6	27.6	44.5	18.2	30.4
Drew	52.9	72.5	75.9	52.6	55.7	57.0	33.7	31.5
Mississippi	50.8	66.9	69.8	45.6	16.7	19.5	26.9	30.8
Hempstead	49.7	92.1	93.5	63.4	53.1	58.7	50.0	60.3
Pulaski	46.1	47.2	54.9	40.8	22.9	32.1	16.2	23.1
Cross	44.0	87.4	91.0	64.6	46.9	51.2	20.1	39.9
Miller	43.4	80.3	76.8	54.5	36.9	45.3	25.4	38.1
Union	43.2	75.1	65.9	48.9	44.6	40.5	24.9	31.3
Columbia	42.9	67.3	67.3	52.0	47.4	41.7	23.4	37.3
Little River	41.9	76.5	83.7	57.9	48.3	42.4	35.1	32.8
Lonoke	41.2	74.8	67.5	64.0	47.7	54.2	46.2	37.1
Black Belt Mean		74.0	73.2	49.6	35.8	39.4	27.6	32.9
Statewide Mean		76.1	75.9	60.4	47.8	51.1	38.6	44.3

*Based on inter-census estimates of males of voting age.
SOURCES: Calculated from *Compendium of the 10th Census, 1880,* Part 1, 562–563; *11th Census of the United States, 1890, Population,* Part 1, 755; *12th Census of the United States, 1900, Population,* 2: 175; *Biennial Report of the Secretary of State of Arkansas, 1889–1890 . . . 1899–1900.* The racial figures are from the *12th Census of the United States, 1900, Supplementary Analysis,* 264.

describe the relationship between class and political participation are very low. In Arkansas during the 1890s politics was everybody's business.

Unfortunately, this openness came to an abrupt end in the early 1890s. Frightened by the sudden ascendance of the Union-Labor coalition and faced with the very real possibility of becoming a minority party, the ruling Democrats instituted a series of measures that "legally" disfranchised a sizable portion of their opposition. In 1891, with Black Belt legislators leading the way, the Democratic-controlled state legislature passed a "secret ballot" election law which set up complicated new voting procedures. Under the new law, it was no longer permissible for private citizens to help illiterate voters to mark their ballots. Only election judges (the vast majority of whom were Democrats) could administer such aid, which effectively disfranchised thousands of illiterate Populists and Republicans. A year later, Democratic leaders sponsored a constitutional amendment that called for a compulsory

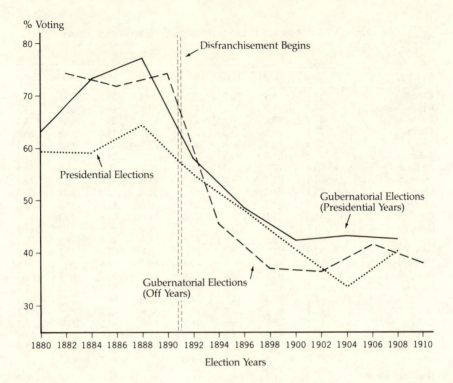

% Voting

Disfranchisement Begins

Presidential Elections

Gubernatorial Elections
(Presidential Years)

Gubernatorial Elections
(Off Years)

1880 1882 1884 1886 1888 1890 1892 1894 1896 1898 1900 1902 1904 1906 1908 1910

Election Years

FIGURE 3.
Voter Turnout in Arkansas General Elections, 1880–1910

SOURCE: See Figure 4.

poll tax. Though there is some evidence that many voters were uncertain as to what they were voting for, the poll tax amendment was ratified by the electorate in a September 1892 referendum, 75,847 to 56,589. Finally, in 1895 the Democrats pushed through a revision of the 1892 poll tax law. Under the revised statute, the poll tax had to be paid between January and June (when most poor farmers were strapped for money), and each poll tax receipt indicated the race of the taxpayer, making it easy for Democratic leaders to estimate and control the size of the black vote.[29]

The electoral "reforms" of the early 1890s had a devastating impact on voter turnout. Beginning in 1892 the upward trend (see Figure 3) in turnout, which had characterized the 1880s, was dramatically reversed. In the 1892 gubernatorial election, the first election held under the new secret ballot law, the level of participation (58 percent) was nearly 20 percent lower than it had been in 1888 (77.2 percent). A comparison of the off-year gubernatorial elections of 1890 and 1894 (the first election held under the poll tax law) reveals an even more striking decline, from 74.2 to 45.3 percent. In just four years, the number of non-voters had more than doubled! Although the rate of decline decreased after 1894, the downward trend continued through the rest of the decade. By 1898 the gubernatorial turnout level (37 percent) had fallen to less than half that of 1890. In less than a decade, a political system that had approached universal manhood suffrage had been replaced by a highly restrictive system in which only a minority of the potential electorate took part.[30]

The main thrust of the disfranchisement movement, as the leaders of the Arkansas Democratic party were quick to point out, was directed at black voters. However, the new laws also disfranchised a larger number of whites—many more than the Democrats cared to admit.[31] In the twenty-five counties (see Figure 4) where whites made up 94 percent or more of the local population, the average turnout fell more than 30 percent between 1890 and 1898. While part of this decline can be attributed to a decrease in party competition, the primary factor at work was clearly disfranchisement. As the correlation and regression coefficients in Appendix A (Tables D and E) indicate, in the postdisfranchisement era non-voting whites tended to be lower-class whites—men who could not afford to pay a poll tax. Although the analysis registers no significant relationship between disfranchisement and illiteracy, this undoubtedly reflects the fact that the Democratic party made sure that most illiterate Democrats continued to vote. Among illiterate Populists and Republicans it was a different story.

The effect of disfranchisement on Republican and Populist voting strength was just what the Democrats had hoped for. Prior to disfranchisement, the Democrats controlled approximately 55 percent of the electorate in state elections. After disfranchisement, they controlled between 65 and 70 percent. The Arkansas Republican party continued to do fairly well in

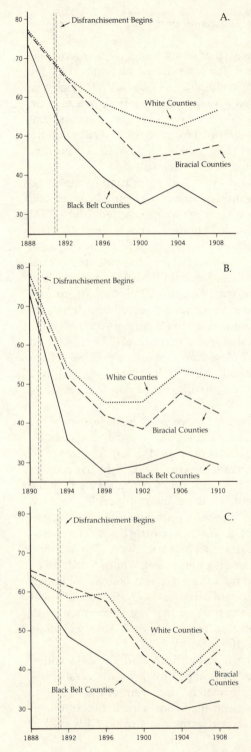

FIGURE 4.
Racial Composition and Voter Turnout in
Arkansas General Elections, 1888–1910

COUNTY RACIAL COMPOSITION
Black Belt: 40% or more black
Biracial: 6-39.9% black
White: 0-5.9% black

SOURCES: See Table 1; *13th Census of the United
States, 1910, Population*, 2: 119–131; *Biennial
Report of the Secretary of State of Arkansas,
1879–1880 . . . 1909–1910*.

A. Gubernatorial Elections, Presidential
    Years
    Mean percent Voting
B. Gubernatorial Elections, Off-Year
    Mean Percent Voting
C. Presidential Elections
    Mean Percent Voting

TABLE 2
Comparative Voting Strength of Political Parties in Arkansas, 1880–1910

Election	% Voting			
	Democratic	Republican	Populist	Greenback/Union-Labor
Gubernatorial				
1880	72.8	—	—	27.2*
1882	59.6	33.5	—	6.9*
1884	64.0	36.0	—	—
1886	55.3	33.0	—	11.7†
1888	54.1	—	—	45.9
1890	55.5	—	—	44.5
1892	57.7	21.5	19.9	—
1894	58.9	20.5	19.3	—
1896	64.3	25.3	9.9	—
1898	67.3	24.5	7.6	—
1900	66.7	30.6	2.7	—
1902	64.6	31.4	—	—
1904	61.4	36.0	—	—
1906	69.5	26.9	—	—
1908	68.2	27.9	—	—
1910	67.5	26.4	—	—
Presidential				
1880	55.8	39.0	—	3.8*
1884	57.9	40.7	—	1.5*
1888	54.8	38.0	—	6.8
1892	59.3	31.7	8.0	—
1896	72.0	26.7	—	—
1900	63.5	35.0	1.2	—
1904	55.0	40.6	2.0	—
1908	57.4	37.2	0.7	—

*Greenback-Labor Party.
†Wheeler Party.
SOURCE: *Biennial Report ot the Secretary of State of Arkansas, 1879–1880 . . . 1909–1910.*

presidential elections—in 1904 Theodore Roosevelt came within 18,000 votes of carrying the state—but its days as a competitive party in state politics were over.[32] Although disfranchisement had less impact on the predominantly white Populist coalition, a surprisingly large number of Arkansas Populists became non-voters in the late 1890s and early 1900s (see Appendix A, Tables D and E). While many Populists dropped out of the political system voluntarily out of disgust or frustration, there can be little doubt that legal disfranchisement also took its toll.[33] Certainly, most Populist leaders believed that it did. In the spring of 1900, as Jeff Davis stormed across Arkansas shadowboxing with the trusts at every crossroads hamlet, the state's leading Populist editor, W. Scott Morgan, gazed at the ruins of his party and offered the solemn comment that in Arkansas "the most dangerous trust is the one in politics."[34]

Democratic leaders viewed the situation in an entirely different light.

When questions arose about the morality of disfranchisement, they pointed out that the vast majority of disfranchised whites were non-Democrats— latter-day "scalawags" who, in effect, had forfeited their rights of citizenship. Since voter turnout among the poorer elements of the Democratic party remained relatively high, there was no cause for alarm and no reason to apologize. In the spirit of "herrenvolk democracy," which tended to define non-Democrats and non-whites as non-people, party leaders insisted that Arkansas politics was becoming more democratic, not less so. To men like Jeff Davis, disfranchisement was the ultimate electoral reform, a prerequisite for honest elections, responsible government, and the preservation of white supremacy. While the more populistic Democratic leaders may have had some misgivings about white disfranchisement, no one thought the matter was important enough to warrant a disruption of the party. For liberals and conservatives alike, disfranchisement had foiled the tyrannical designs of Republican and Populist bosses, setting the stage for a golden age of democracy in Arkansas. Ambitious young Democrats, many of whom had come perilously close to being swept aside by the agrarian radical tide, could now look to the future with confidence.[35]

4

Bryanism and Reform

In 1896, when we nominated the grandest and truest man the world ever knew—William Jennings Bryan—for President, we stole all the Populists had; we stole their platform, we stole their candidate, we stole them out lock, stock and barrel. . . . Populists—why, I used to hate them; but I did not know as much then as I do now.

—*Jeff Davis (1905)*[1]

As the Populist revolt subsided and the new one-party order took shape, Davis's career entered a period of transition. In October 1894 he retired from the prosecuting attorney's office and returned to private practice at the age of thirty-two. However, his law practice, though more lucrative than ever, could not satisfy his desire for political fame or his hunger for political combat. In less than a year, he was back on the hustings, this time in a race for Congress. Calling himself a free-silver Democrat and claiming to be the farmer's friend, Davis announced his candidacy for the Democratic nomination for Congress in the Fourth Congressional District, which consisted of four counties in the Fifth Judicial District, plus Franklin, Logan, Perry, and Pulaski. His opponent was W. L. Terry, a popular three-term congressman from Little Rock. One of the most respected lawyers in the state, Terry had handily defeated Judge James G. Wallace for the Democratic nomination in 1894. Although Davis was clearly a much better campaigner than his friend Judge Wallace, few observers thought he had much chance of winning.[2]

One of Davis's biggest disadvantages was that the nominating process was controlled by delegates to county conventions, not by votes cast in a party primary (the primary system would not become mandatory until 1898). Under the convention system, political friends and political favors counted far more than rousing stump speeches. Aided by six years of federal patronage, Terry had many more political friends than Davis, who found himself reaping a bitter harvest sown during four years of successful prosecutions.[3]

Davis's campaign for Congress ended almost before it began. On February 1, at the Pope County Democratic Convention, he expected to receive a unanimous endorsement; instead, more than a third of the convention's delegates threw their support to Terry. Stunned, Davis rose from his seat and delivered a tearful, emotional speech. Without the wholehearted support of his home county, he could not continue as a serious candidate. Pledging his loyalty to the eventual Democratic nominee, he withdrew from the race.[4] After nearly a decade in politics, he had suffered his first political defeat.

Davis's loss to Terry was a chastening experience, which led to a rethinking of his political values. Disillusioned with the convention system, he became increasingly receptive to the politics and ideology of agrarian radicalism. Although a formal break with the Democratic establishment would not come until 1899, his move toward insurgency began during the summer of 1896, when he threw himself headlong into the Bryan crusade. Selected as a presidential elector for the second time, he set out on the campaign trail like a political evangelist, preaching the Bryanist gospel of free silver and free trade to anyone who would listen.[5] Slashing away at "goldbugs" and Republican bankers, and pleading for a fair deal for the farmer, he shed most of what was left of his New South, Bourbon background. Exhilarated and inspired by the Great Commoner, he had reached a major turning point in his career. Jeff Davis the respectable small town lawyer was fast becoming Jeff Davis the agrarian avenger.

Because of a fusion agreement with the People's party, Davis ultimately was replaced by a Populist elector, but he continued to campaign for Bryan until the bitter end. Acknowledging his enormous contribution to the campaign, Arkansas's presidential electors gave him the honor of delivering the official vote to the electoral college in Washington.[6] For Davis, an Ozarker who had never seen a city larger than Memphis, the trip to Washington was an eye-opening adventure. This first glimpse of the capital city, with its men of power and gleaming white buildings, stirred his soul and fueled his ambition. A decade later he would return to Washington as a United States Senator.

The emergence of Bryanism was a pivotal experience in Davis's career. In terms of style and temperament, he had always been something of a rabble-rouser, but it was not until 1896 that he began to take the ideological substance of agrarian radicalism to heart. Bryan gave him a pattern to follow—a political style and philosophy that bridged the gap between middle-class democracy and agrarian insurgency. As Charles Jacobson recalled, Davis "sincerely believed William Jennings Bryan was the most wonderful man of the age and he never failed in any of his speeches to pay him tribute accordingly. . . . He carefully read everything that he could get his hands on that Bryan ever wrote, including the 'Commoner,' never failed to attend a

Bryan lecture or speech whenever opportunity presented itself, and really believed everything he said about the great Nebraskan. . . . his admiration for Bryan was genuine and unbounded, and he believed that everything Bryan said or did was right."[7]

Fortunately for Davis, most Arkansas Democrats shared his enthusiasm for the Great Commoner from Nebraska. In Arkansas, as in many areas of the South and Midwest, it took a long time for the excitement of the first Bryan campaign to die down. In 1897 and 1898 the free-silver and railroad regulation issues continued to dominate state politics; and the progressive elements of the Democratic party, with an infusion of ex-Populists, continued their ascendance. Moreover, the new governor, Dan Jones, was one of the most reform-minded chief executives in the state's history. A Confederate war hero who had served two terms as state attorney general in the 1880s, Jones was widely acknowledged as the patriarch of the party's progressive wing. Thus, despite a powerful railroad lobby and a persistent strain of conservatism in the legislature and the state supreme court, the political winds seemed to be blowing favorably for reformist Democrats like Jeff Davis.[8]

It was in this context of rising expectations that Davis decided to take the biggest political gamble of his career. In January 1898, after considering and ultimately rejecting the idea of a second race for Congress, he announced his candidacy for the Democratic nomination for state attorney general.[9] Since he had the solid backing of the Democratic leadership of the Fifth Judicial District, he immediately was pegged as a serious candidate by the Democratic press. The Little Rock *Arkansas Gazette*, the most powerful newspaper in the state, described him as "a ripe lawyer and a young man of great promise." The local press was even more enthusiastic. The *Russellville Democrat* touted him as "the brilliant young statesman of Pope County," while the *Atkins Chronicle* hailed him as "a lawyer who stands the peer of any within the limits of the state. Everywhere throughout the State," the *Chronicle* claimed, "he is recognized as a power in the courts of law, and his eloquence upon the hustings in behalf of democratic truths have time and again thrilled the hearts of the people."[10]

Although no politician from the Fifth Judicial District had ever been elected attorney general, Davis had good reason to feel confident about his candidacy. His success as a prosecuting attorney was well known, his reputation as a stump speaker was unmatched, and his opposition was surprisingly weak. None of his three opponents was well known or particularly distinguished: J. B. "Buck" Baker, the most formidable of the lot, was a former prosecuting attorney from Izard County; John T. Hicks was a young prosecuting attorney from White County; and E. P. Watson was a small town lawyer from Bentonville. Moreover, with the new mandatory primary rule in effect, Davis would have the opportunity to make the most of his spellbinding oratory.[11] Out on the stump, where there were no county convention delegates to worry about, he expected to make short work of his respectable, well-mannered opponents.

But Davis's hopes were soon shattered. Less than a month after announcing his candidacy, he suffered a minor stroke while arguing a case at Ozark. The stroke sapped his strength and temporarily paralyzed his left arm and part of his left side. Fearful of a total collapse, his friends and family urged him to drop out of the race. But he stubbornly refused to do so. After several weeks of recuperation in Little River County, he was back on the campaign trail. Unfortunately, he was only a shadow of his former self. At the opening of the official county canvass in Eureka Springs on April 4, he was a pitiable figure. Too weak to stand up for more than a few moments at a time, he remained seated throughout his speech, which was read almost inaudibly from a prepared text. Though he managed to poke a few jabs at the railroad interests, most of the speech was a rambling discussion of his medical problems and the difficulties he had had in arranging his campaign schedule. The response of the crowd was respectful but cold. Having trudged through the rain to be entertained by a rough-and-tumble spellbinder, they were understandably disappointed. All in all, it was a pathetic send-off for a candidate who had once held so much promise but who now appeared to be going nowhere.[12]

Davis's weakened physical condition was not his biggest problem. In February, his candidacy was dealt a second severe blow when Judge Frank Goar entered the attorney general's race. Dean of the University of Arkansas Law School and deputy commissioner of mines, manufactures and agriculture, Goar was widely regarded as the most distinguished lawyer in the state. Arkansas's political landscape was heavily populated with his former law students. Extremely popular and "entirely acceptable to the conservative old guard," he was a formidable opponent. Some observers predicted that he could win the nomination without even bothering to campaign.[13]

By the end of the first week of county primaries, these predictions seemed to be confirmed. With a total of 700 votes in the first four county primaries, Davis was well ahead of Baker (603), Watson (62), and Hicks (22), but he was far behind Goar, who had polled 1,165. Although the great majority of county primaries were yet to come, the pattern was set and Davis knew it. The best he could hope for was second place. For the second time in two years, he was losing out to an older, more conservative opponent. Angry and frustrated, he began to make plans to move his family to Oklahoma Territory, which was then in the midst of its first oil boom. He could only hope that the road to the top would be smoother in the land of the Sooners, where there was virtually no political establishment to contend with.[14]

Fortunately for Davis, fate intervened in the campaign once more. On April 6, at Hindsville, just hours before the first major speaking engagement of the campaign, Judge Goar dropped dead of cerebral apoplexy. With this sudden twist of fortune, Davis once again became the frontrunner. Pushing all thought of migrating to Oklahoma out of his mind, he "threw himself into the campaign with as much vigor and earnestness as his physical condition would permit."[15]

Compared to his later efforts, the campaign that Davis waged in 1898 was a mild affair, full of temperate rhetoric and polite debate. The fire-breathing Jeff Davis who liked to scorch the earth when he went out on the stump was nowhere in sight. But even in subdued form he had little trouble outdistancing his rivals. Although he received relatively few votes in the East Arkansas Delta and the northern Ozarks, he ran extremely well in the Arkansas River Valley (which included Pope County) and South Arkansas (which included Little River County), where he was well known.[16] Unable to build a coalition based on social class and ideology (see Appendix A, Table F) as he did in later campaigns, he depended heavily on localism and intrastate sectionalism. Fortunately, his "friends and neighbors" were numerous enough to pull him through.

By the time the last county primary was over, Davis (with 30,029 votes) enjoyed a large plurality over each of his three opponents: Baker (17,513), Hicks (14,672), and Watson (8,093). Though he lacked an actual majority, when his vote was converted to delegate strength Davis controlled over half (229) of the Democratic State Convention's 455 delegates.[17] When the convention met in late June, he was nominated on the first ballot, thanks in part to a rousing speech by George W. Murphy, a well-known Little Rock lawyer, who would later become one of Davis's most bitter enemies. With unintended irony, Murphy paid tribute to Davis in Lincolnesque terms:

> It has been said of him that in his boyish days he followed the plow and rigged up a place on the plow where he could place a law book and read as he plowed. (Laughter and cheers.) Mr. Davis stood a rigid examination for admission to the bar and quickly advanced to the position of prosecuting attorney. He had been born to poverty, but of parentage just. He bore the name of the grandest embodiment of heroism and patriotism the sun of God ever shone upon—Jefferson Davis. (Loud and prolonged applause.) When Jeff Davis entered the legal forum he would have not escaped oblivion [even] if he possessed no merit, because the people of Arkansas would not have tolerated a failure bearing his name.[18]

The general election campaign that followed was anticlimactic. Neither the Populist party nor the Prohibitionist party offered a candidate for attorney general, and the Republican candidate, J. J. Henley, conducted only a token campaign. By this time Davis had fully recovered from his stroke, but he too made only a handful of speeches. Even these were unnecessary: demoralized by disfranchisement and racial demagoguery, the Arkansas Republican party was at its lowest ebb in decades. In the September elec-

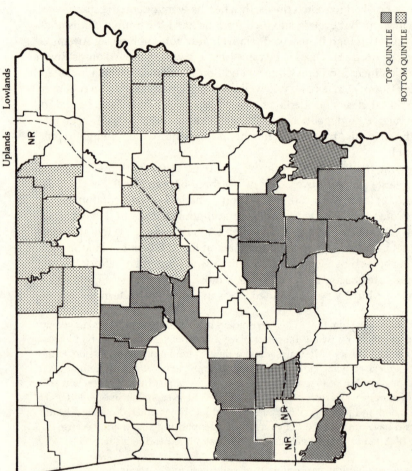

FIGURE 5
1898 Democratic Primary for Attorney General:
% for Jeff Davis

SOURCE: Little Rock *Arkansas Gazette*, June 17, 1898.

tion, Davis defeated Henley by a margin of nearly three to one and carried all but two of the state's seventy-five counties.[19]

Davis's election to the attorney generalship came at the end of a distinct era in the history of the Democratic party. During the preceding five years, the character of the party had been shaped largely by two ongoing crises: the Populist revolt and the economic depression which followed the panic of 1893. Together, these two problems pushed the Democratic party onto a leftward course, which ultimately led to the crypto-Populism of William Jennings Bryan. Faced with hard times and pressured by the Populist challenge, many Democrats said and did things which they would not have said and done under normal circumstances. In Arkansas, as in the rest of the nation, this shift to the left stemmed partly from a genuine ideological transformation and partly from political expedience.[20]

One obvious manifestation of the Arkansas Democratic party's leftward shift was the ascendance of free-silver Democrats. The first clear sign of this ascendance appeared in 1893 when the normally cautious Senator James K. Jones defied President Grover Cleveland and voted against the repeal of the Sherman Silver Purchase Act. As the depression deepened, the free-silver forces continued to gain strength. At the Democratic State Convention in the summer of 1894 they were strong enough to place an endorsement of free silver in the party platform. During the next two years, "goldbug" Democrats made a spirited effort to regain control of the party, but there was nothing they could do to stem the free-silver tide. When William Jennings Bryan and William Hope ("Coin") Harvey visited the state in late 1895, they were welcomed as conquering heroes by most Arkansas Democrats.[21]

By the summer of 1896 many of the state's "sound money" Democrats had either retreated into silence or gone over to the Republicans. Many others had swallowed their pride and reluctantly joined the free-silver chorus. "The man who is not with us on this question is not a Democrat," Dan Jones, the free-silver candidate for governor, announced in February 1896. "I don't care what he calls himself."[22] When a number of counties placed the free-silver question on the ballot during the spring primaries, the results seemed to confirm Jones's judgment. In county after county, an overwhelming majority of Democrats endorsed free silver. Even in Pulaski County, which included the city of Little Rock and which was considered to be the bastion of "goldbug" Democracy in Arkansas, free-silver Democrats outnumbered gold-standard Democrats by nearly seven to one. A poll conducted by the *Helena Weekly World* in March 1896 revealed that more than 80 percent of the state's editors supported free silver. In May, the "goldbug" faction even lost control of the powerful Little Rock *Arkansas Gazette*. W. B. Worthen, a conservative Cleveland Democrat, sold the paper to James N. Smithee, an eccentric reformer who had recently returned to Arkansas from Colorado, where he had flirted with free-silver Populism. With this, the "goldbug" Democrats of Arkansas threw in the towel.[23] The free-silverites were now in complete control of the party, and the stage was set for the Bryan love feast that was to follow.

The party's leftward drift could also be seen in a rising tide of anti-monopolist sentiment. During the mid-nineties, an increasing number of Arkansas Democrats advocated stringent corporate regulation and expressed resentment towards the economic and political power wielded by railroads and other Northern corporations. Most important, such attitudes were no longer confined to disgruntled farmers. The mounting number of bankruptcies, the absorption of floundering local businesses by large Northern corporations, the apparent ease with which these same Northern corporations weathered the economic storms of the day, and the need to find someone to blame for their economic problems led many Arkansas businessmen to view certain segments of Northern capitalism with jaundiced eyes. Although the business community continued to be the most conservative element of the Arkansas Democratic party, the ideological gap between local businessman and farmers was at its narrowest point in years. For a time, the antitrust issue tended to unite rather than to divide the party.[24]

Arkansas businessmen, like Arkansas farmers, vented most of their anger at the railroads, particularly the powerful Iron Mountain Railroad owned by Jay Gould. In December 1896, many of the state's leading businessmen attended a conference in Fort Smith where they discussed ways of developing the Arkansas River into a waterway which could "deliver the state from the hands of the railroad monopolists." Infuriated by freight rates—which discriminated against local wholesalers and discouraged the development of local manufacturing—a solid majority of the merchants in Little Rock, Fort Smith, and most other Arkansas cities and towns enthusiastically supported the movement for a state railroad commission.[25] Many of these same businessmen also supported the Bush Bill, a Populist-inspired plan to build a number of state-owned railroads. When the Bush Bill was approved by the 1897 legislature, the Little Rock business community was given much of the credit for its passage.[26]

In Arkansas, as elsewhere, the Democratic party's move to the left remained somewhat formless until the Bryanist crusade took the party by storm in 1896. The emergence of Bryanism established a new Democratic orthodoxy: what had been tendencies and inclinations now became official policy. By serving as a rallying point, Bryan accelerated the trend towards ideological consensus within the party, or so it seemed to many contemporaries. No other political figure in the state's history had ever evoked such enthusiasm or attracted such a broad base of suppport. Men who had been at odds for years agreed that Bryan was the greatest Democrat since Old

Hickory himself. Farmers and planters, workers and businessman, young and old, rich and poor—all were united behind Bryan and reform.[27]

Or were they? In retrospect, it seems clear that this unity was more apparent than real. The Bryanist Democrats of Arkansas shared common political slogans and a common standard-bearer, but they did not all share a common political philosophy or a common vision of what Southern society should be. The leftward shift of many moderate and conservative Democrats blurred the ideological divisions that had splintered the party during the late 1880s and early 1890s, but it did not eliminate them. The deep cleavage between agrarian and New South cultures continued to divide the party, even though all Bryanist Democrats publicly subscribed to a common creed of free silver, free trade, and local control. In effect, there were two types of Bryanists: radicals and moderates (in some cases "conservative" would be a more appropriate label). Generally speaking, this dichotomy paralleled the split between town and country. Small farmers, timber workers, and village merchants—along with a few renegade politicians like Jeff Davis—tended to be radical Bryanists. Planters (many of whom lived in town), urban businessmen, Democratic politicians, and most other town dwellers tended to be moderate Bryanists.[28]

The radical Bryanists were those Democrats who were imbued with certain elements of the Populist spirit. Along with the right wing of the People's party, they were part of what Lawrence Goodwyn has called the "shadow movement of Populism." Like the third-party agrarians, the radical Bryanists of Arkansas believed that the new economic order was fundamentally unjust, that an increasing inequality of wealth and power threatened to destroy the fabric of American democracy, and that farmers and other workingmen were rapidly losing control over their own lives. Even though, as Goodwyn has recently reminded us, most of these crypto-Populists did not have a clear vision of the "cooperative commonwealth," they had absorbed enough of the agrarian radical ethos to insure that never again would they tolerate the complacent conservatism of the old Bourbon Democracy.[29] Of course, during the late 1890s a more pressing question was: how long would they continue to accept the leadership and authority of the moderate Bryanists who dominated the local Democratic establishment?

The moderate Bryanists were reformers of a different stripe. Some were hardly reformers at all; they simply did what they had to do to defuse the Populist challenge. However, it would be a mistake to attribute the reformism of moderate Bryanists solely to political expedience. Southerners of all classes and backgrounds were susceptible to anti-Northern and anticolonial feelings. Like any colonial elite, the planters, businessmen, and political leaders of Arkansas and other Southern states resented the power and privileges of the colonizing society—even though they themselves acted as agents of that society. If the conditions were right—as they often were during the mid-1890s—normally conservative men expressed this resentment in surprisingly radical terms. As the Southern progressive movement would later confirm, a commitment to New South commercialism was not incompatible with a strong desire to bring the locus of power closer to home.[30]

However genuine, the brand of reform practiced by moderate Bryanists was qualitatively different from that practiced by radical Bryanists and Populists. Although moderate Bryanists sometimes mouthed the rhetoric of agrarian radicalism, for the most part they were neither agrarian nor radical; they were what might be called metropolitan liberals. In terms of spirit and motivation, they were closer to the progressives of a later era than to the agrarian radicals of the 1890s. The moderate Bryanists of Arkansas were practical, adaptable men, willing to go along with the times. Guided by essentially moderate instincts, they sought to protect middle-class society against threats from above and below. Their dissatisfaction with the new urban, metropolitan order tended to be superficial and intermittent—hardly surprising, since in most cases they were part of that new order. Bonds of class and culture cemented them to the Northern elite, which they sometimes attacked. They did not share the Southern agrarian's intense anger and frustration—or his profound sense of relative deprivation—because with few exceptions they did not share his desperate economic plight. In most respects they were no longer part of agrarian society. As men who generally lived and worked in towns or cities, moderate Bryanists exhibited a style of life and a vision of the future that was more in tune with the institutions and values of the urban North than with the culture of the rural South.[31]

Because the division between moderate and radical Bryanists was not always apparent to contemporaries, it is an extremely difficult subject for a historian to deal with. Moreover, like most political dichotomies, this division contains elements of artificiality and oversimplification. Some Arkansas Bryanists were undoubtedly more ambivalent than anything else. Nonetheless, the significance of the division becomes clear when we examine the origins of the Davis movement. Jeff Davis's rise to power was made possible by a simple paradox: while most of Arkansas's Democratic voters were radical Bryanists, all of the party's leading figures were moderate Bryanists. As Davis ultimately demonstrated, the leaders of the Democratic establishment were wide open to an attack from the left. A survey of the four most powerful politicans in the state during the late 1890s illustrates this point.

James P. Clarke, an East Arkansas lawyer who served as governor from 1895 to 1897, was an avid free-silverite and trust-baiter. Known for his fiery temperament and unrestrained rhetoric, Clarke often sounded like a Populist firebrand on the stump. Yet he also sat on the board of directors of the Springfield, Little Rock and Gulf Railroad, which was owned principally by a Chicago financier. During the 1897 session of the legislature, Clarke alienated many agrarian radicals by lobbying long and hard for the Smith Bill, which offered the Springfield, Little Rock and Gulf up to a thousand acres of delinquent tax land for every mile of track laid.[32]

Daniel Webster Jones, who succeeded Clarke as governor in 1897, had the best agrarian radical credentials of any of the party's leading figures. He played a leading role in the local free-silver crusade, frequently complained that the corporations were not paying their fair share of state taxes, called for full valuation of all railroad property, vigorously supported an 1897 railroad commission bill that required the railroads to pay for the commission's expenses, and once declared that a state of war existed between "the toiling masses of mankind" and "insidious . . . money changers."[33] Yet, like Clarke, Jones had enjoyed a long and successful career as a railroad attorney. During his governorship, he did his best to throw off his corporate past, but few radicals were willing to forget that he had been a moderate attorney general during the late 1880s, or that as recently as 1895 he had directed the Iron Mountain Railway's lobbying effort against a railroad commission bill. An ex-Confederate officer with an aristocratic bearing, Jones was more of a genteel paternalist than an authentic agrarian radical.[34]

The most powerful politician in the state during the 1890s was Senator James K. Jones, "the Plumed Knight of Arkansas." Elected to the Senate in 1885, Jones served as chairman of the Democratic National Committee during the election of 1896. One of the major architects of the national Democratic party's capitulation to free silver, he was also a staunch advocate of organized labor, the sponsor of an 1898 income tax bill, and a close friend of William Jennings Bryan. It was Jones who asked Bryan to give the keynote free-silver speech at the 1896 National Democratic Convention. Nevertheless, few people ever accused James Jones of being a radical reformer. A corporate lawyer (he was Dan Jones's long-time law partner) with basically conservative instincts, he was more adept at compromise than agitation. As chairman of the Democratic National Committee he did everything in his power to keep the party on a moderate course and to make sure that the party absorbed Populist votes without absorbing radical Populist doctrines. Haughtily respectable, Jones showed his true colors when he was openly contemptuous of the bedraggled farmers who attended the 1896 Populist Convention in St. Louis.[35]

James H. Berry, the state's lesser-known Senator, was an ex-governor (1883–1885) and a one-time leader of Arkansas's repudiation movement. A self-made man who spent most of his life in the mountains of Carroll County, Berry, like Jones, had served in the Senate since 1885. He was an ardent supporter of free silver and, according to one observer, "more of a free trader than any man in the Senate." Yet, like the other half of the "Jones-Berry" coalition, he was a cautious reformer who preferred moderation to insurgency. A one-legged Confederate veteran, Berry was a living symbol of the Lost Cause who spent much of his time in the Senate reminiscing about the Civil War.[36]

The leaders of the Bryanist Democracy were transitional figures in the history of Arkansas politics. Though flexible enough to abandon the Bourbon conservatism of the 1880s, they were woefully unprepared for the mass politics of the early twentieth century. Moving far enough to the left to keep themselves and the Arkansas Democratic party in power, they did not move far enough or fast enough to preempt the Davis movement. As the decade drew to a close, the political storm which came to be known as Jeff Davisism loomed menacingly on the horizon.

During the latter half of 1898, the peculiar conditions that had pushed so many Arkansas politicians and businessmen to the left began to disappear. By the time Davis had entered the attorney general's office in January 1899, one of the two crises which had dominated the mid-1890s had all but vanished, and the other had begun to fade noticeably. The Populist revolt was the first to go. On the verge of collapse since the ill-fated fusion of 1896, the Arkansas People's party was virtually annihilated in the election of 1898. W. Scott Morgan, the Populist candidate for governor, polled only 8,332 votes, less than 8 percent of the total; and the Populist contingent in the legislature, which had numbered eleven in 1897, was completely wiped out. Not a single Populist was elected to county office in the entire state, and even in White County, "the Gibraltar of Populism," the party's candidates received less than a third of the vote. Although Arkansas Populists would continue to hold conventions and offer a truncated slate of candidates for another five years, the party had essentially passed from the scene by the end of 1898.[37] "Populism has gone into the hands of a receiver," a Democratic editor from South Arkansas gleefully reported, "it is defunct and with no available assets."[38]

The demise of Arkansas Populism coincided with the passing of hard times. Full economic recovery would not come until after the turn of the century, but signs of a partial recovery appeared as early as 1898. For the first time in years the *Arkansas Gazette*'s annual crop report was cautiously optimistic. Although heavy rains and bitter cold ultimately destroyed a sizable portion of the 1898 cotton and fruit crops, most observers sensed that the depression was finally beginning to lift. In 1899 promise became reality: cotton prices edged upward, land values began to rise, and the credit squeeze became somewhat less severe.[39] News of an upturn in the agricultural economy was on everybody's lips. "Once more the South is getting upon its feet," the *Gazette* declared in October 1899. "We may expect in a short time that ten cents will be the ruling price in the market for the staple. The planter is out of the woods now. . . . The wait has been a long one, but the hour of prosperity has come, and come to stay. Once more cotton is king."[40]

The quickening of the economic pulse was even more dramatic in the nonagricultural sector. In January 1899 the Little Rock Board of Trade launched a campaign to raise $500,000 to help finance the construction of a huge cotton mill in Little Rock, and later in the year several large zinc mines were opened in Marion County near the Missouri border. But most important, Arkansas led the nation in miles of railway construction in 1899. "People who think this country is living from hand to mouth," the *Gazette* exclaimed in November, "should visit Arkansas and see the railroad building that is going on."[41] Spurred on by a heavy demand for railroad ties, the local lumber industry was also booming. In fact, the only local industry that continued to flounder was the coal industry, which was hit with a crippling strike in February 1899.[42]

The general upturn in the local economy did little to improve the economic condition of workers and poor farmers. Indeed, inflated land prices made the average tenant farmer's situation even more desperate, since his access to landowning status depended largely on a continued decline in land values. But for merchants, planters, and many middle-class farmers a bright new day was dawning.[43]

Combined with the passing of the Populist challenge, economic improvement had a dramatic effect on the ideological orientation of the Arkansas business community. Although a measure of ambivalence remained, in cities and towns across the state, attitudes toward Northern capitalists changed significantly as the practicality of class overruled the emotionalism of sectional loyalty. Slowly but surely, the angry rhetoric of Bryanism was replaced by the upbeat rhetoric of development and progress. In June 1899, instead of clamoring about the trusts, the state's business leaders were busy organizing the Arkansas Agricultural and Development Association to advertise Arkansas's resources on Northern railroad cars. In addition, many New South boosters who had supported the movement for an effective railroad commission earlier in the decade now began to worry that such a commission might inhibit Northern investment.[44]

Newspaper editors and publicists were in the forefront of the resurgent New South crusade. As the century drew to a close, editorials calling for regulation and reform gave way to editorials calling for more economics and less politics. One editor assured his readers that "People are too busy to talk politics these days"; while another claimed that "If Arkansas could only escape the baneful influence and expense of so many elections, she would be one of the most prosperous states in the Union."[45] Perhaps the best barometer of change was the editorial page of the *Arkansas Gazette*. A bulwark of Bryanist liberalism in the mid-1890s, the paper had become obsessed with New South commercialism by the end of the decade. "Development of Arkansas' resources," a *Gazette* editorial declared in October 1899, "is now the all-absorbing question of the hour."[46]

Among politicians, adjustment to the new conditions was somewhat slower and less complete than among businessmen and editors. But there were definite signs of a conservative trend. In larger cities and towns, conservative "goldbug" Democrats who had been swept aside by the Bryanist tide began to make a comeback. And many moderate Democrats, most of whom had never firmly embraced the agrarian radical tradition, began to have second thoughts about the Bryanist creed. Regardless of their ideological persuasion, few politicians with urban constituencies could afford to ignore the growing pressure from conservatives, particularly after Charles Collins, one of Arkansas's leading free-silverites, failed to win election as one of Little Rock's delegates to the 1898 State Democratic Convention.[47]

The resurgence of the New South crusade and the shift in political attitudes among merchants and other town dwellers had a polarizing effect on Arkansas's Democratic party. As local editors and businessmen renewed their love affair with Yankee commercialism, ripples of anger surged across the Arkansas backcounty. Convinced that Main Street was in cahoots with the Yankee trusts after all, many poor Arkansas farmers began to look closer to home for their enemies.[48] The traditional agrarian conviction that merchants, lawyers, and most other townsmen were not to be trusted was given new life. No longer obscured by the local business community's flirtation with Bryanism, the cultural cleavage between town and country re-emerged starker than ever. Galled by the new-found prosperity of merchants and planters, many poor farmers harbored anticolonial, antiurban feelings, deepened by an awareness of relative deprivation and a sense of betrayal. Having survived the economic and political crises of the Populist era, the Democratic party was now faced with a potentially explosive cultural crisis.

At the time of Davis's election to the attorney generalship, it remained to be seen whether the widening gap between agrarian and New South cultures would find effective political expression. The rednecks of Arkansas awaited a politician who was bold enough and tough enough to lead them—a politician who could articulate their grievances, strike back at their enemies, and restore their self-respect. With a firebrand like Jeff Davis around, they did not have long to wait. As John Gould Fletcher later put it, "The hour and the man had met."[49]

5

The Stormy Petrel

Trusts are what we are after. Monopolies are what we are after. If
you are a member of any of these things, you can't do business in
this state. . . . It is the entering wedge; it is the first stroke in the
great battle of the masses against the classes. . . . The tocsin of war
has been sounded, and these gentlemen may as well prepare for
the fray.

—*Jeff Davis (1899)*[1]

Davis's first order of business after the 1898 election was to choose
an assistant attorney general. His choice was Charles Jacobson, a
talented young Jewish lawyer from Conway County, who had acted
as his campaign manager during the latter stages of the attorney general's
race. The two men had been friends since 1893, when Jacobson had served
as Davis's deputy prosecuting attorney for Conway County. Born in 1874 in
Missouri, Jacobson was the son of a Prussian-born supply merchant who
had emigrated to the United States in the 1850s. An 1897 graduate of
Vanderbilt University Law School, he was an up-and-coming attorney in
Morrilton, the county seat of Conway County, when Davis approached him
for help at the beginning of the 1898 campaign.[2]

During his years as district prosecuting attorney, Davis had made a great
many enemies in Jacobson's home county: his relentless prosecution of
"blind tigers" and other liquor law violators had infuriated the county courthouse ring, which was controlled by local liquor interests. The Conway
County ring had already gained a measure of revenge by helping to foil
Davis's bid for a Democratic congressional nomination in 1896. It was under
these circumstances that Davis offered Jacobson the unenviable task of
managing his Conway County campaign. "I am not even going in that
county to speak," he promised, "but if you can carry it for me I will appoint
you as my assistant [attorney general]."[3] Despite the long odds, Jacobson set
out to convince the locals that Davis was their man. And to nearly everyone's surprise, his efforts proved successful. The obvious advantages of
having a Conway County man as assistant attorney general persuaded the

local Democratic machine to bury the hatchet. As a result, Davis carried Conway County in the Democratic primary by more than a thousand votes. No one was more surprised than Davis himself, who immediately named Jacobson campaign manager.[4]

When Davis selected Jacobson as his assistant, he made one of the wisest decisions of his career. For nearly a decade, first as assistant attorney general and later as private secretary to the governor, Jacobson was Davis's most trusted and valued political advisor. The two men formed a close personal and professional relationship, despite striking differences in temperament, background, and political philosophy. To a great degree, these differences held them together: each man had what the other lacked. Davis, the flamboyant and unpredictable rabble-rouser, was a master politician who had little interest in public administration. Jacobson, the calm and efficient bureaucrat, was an administrative wizard who had neither the background nor the skills to become a powerful politician on his own. Jacobson's administrative labors gave Davis the freedom to remain out on the stump week after week, grinding his opponents into the dust and communing with the voters as no Arkansas politician had ever done before.[5]

Throughout Davis's attorney generalship, Jacobson was the workhorse of the attorney general's office. While Davis was out beating the bushes for votes, his assistant was back at the courthouse preparing or arguing cases. Of the 150 cases handled by the attorney general's office during Davis's tenure, more than 100 were briefed and argued by Jacobson. Even on those occasions when Davis appeared in court, Jacobson did most of the legal groundwork. In his biography of Davis, he describes his orchestration of one of Davis's most celebrated appearances before the state supreme court:

> I had a large array of books brought down, none of which had ever been examined by Senator Davis. When we got up to argue the case, I would simply hand him the book open at the case and he would read the syllabi—for the first time and then proceed to argue the same. Very few would or could realize that he had not given the matter deep attention.[6]

When Jacobson stood next to Davis and took the oath of office in mid-January 1899, he clearly had no idea of what he was getting himself into. No one would have predicted that the new attorney general would spend most of his term out on the stump running for governor. When the *Arkansas Gazette* compiled a long list of possible contenders for the governorship in the summer of 1898, Davis's name was nowhere in sight. Davis himself gave no hint that he was on the verge of launching a political protest movement. During the 1898 campaign, he repeatedly declared that he had no interest in a long career in state politics. Other politicians could spend the rest of their days in Little Rock if they liked, he told the voters, but he preferred to spend his life in the quiet hills of Pope County, surrounded by his wife, his six children, and his nine pointer hunting dogs.[7] Some may have questioned the sincerity of such remarks, but few doubted that Davis would get his wish.

Attorney General Davis's first weeks in office were quiet. Except for the inevitable stream of job-seekers, there was little activity at the executive end of the state house. Most of the action was at the other end of the building where the new general assembly was in session. When the previous legislature adjourned in June 1897, it left behind much unfinished business. How the new legislature would deal with such unresolved issues as the structure and scope of the state railroad commission, the need for more effective antitrust legislation, a proposal for a new state house, and the advisability of giving tax exemptions to new industries were matters of great concern for conservatives and reformers alike.[8]

Some political observers predicted that the new legislature would be more conservative than its immediate predecessor. Not one of the eleven Populists who had served in the 1897 legislature had survived the Democratic landslide of 1898; the new senate was completely Democratic; and, in the new house of representatives, the Democrats controlled all but two of the one hundred seats. Still, beyond Democratic hegemony, most Arkansawyers did not know quite what to expect from the new legislature. Less than half of the 1899 senate had served during the previous session. And in the house, where rapid turnover was traditionally more common, the holdover rate was barely 20 percent. The only thing certain about the new legislature was an element of unpredictability. When the editor of the *Arkansas Gazette* nervously assured his readers that the majority of the new legislators "are practical men who have been sent here to legislate for the material interests of the state," he was probably expressing more hope than conviction.[9] And despite the *Gazette's* hopeful prediction, it was not long before Arkansas conservatives realized that they had an unruly legislature on their hands.

In the house, the reformist tone was set by the first bill introduced, which required all corporations "to settle with their employees on a stated day of each month." In the weeks that followed, legislators in both houses filed a rash of bills calling for various types of corporate regulation. One bill, infuriating insurance agents and businessmen alike, proposed "to make insurance policies taxable for their cash surrender value." A second bill stipulated that the railroads would pay for the operation of the new railroad commission. A third required all railroads to fence their tracks. A fourth called for a stringent fellow-servant law. Still another required all legislative lobbyists to wear badges.[10] Whether or not any of these reform bills would actually become law, many New South–oriented conservatives viewed the situation with considerable alarm.

By late February, the conservatives' fears centered around House Bill 87, an antitrust measure calling for the "punishment of trusts, pools and conspiracies to control prices." Antitrust bills were nothing new in Arkansas; in fact, an innocuous and largely symbolic antitrust measure had been enacted into law by the 1897 legislature. Thus, when the new antitrust bill passed the house by a unanimous vote on February 2, few observers were surprised. But as the bill made its way through various senate committees, some conservatives began to worry out loud that this time they were dealing with more than a paper tiger. Closely patterned after a recent Missouri antitrust law, House Bill 87 was full of imprecise language and open-ended assertions of regulatory power. If interpreted literally, the proposed statute, carrying penalties of up to $5,000 a day, threatened any corporation, large or small, involved in pricing agreements. Conservatives argued that even if it were unenforceable, such a law would tarnish the state's image in the eyes of Northern capitalists. By the end of February, many Arkansas businessmen had begun to take the new antitrust bill seriously; but few were prepared for the drama that was about to unfold.[11] Aided and abetted by Jeff Davis, House Bill 87 was to change the course of Arkansas's political history.

The troublesome antitrust bill had originated from an unlikely source. The sponsor of the bill, Elias W. Rector, was anything but a wild-eyed agrarian rebel. A forty-eight-year-old corporation lawyer from Hot Springs, Rector was a graduate of the University of Virginia and an ex-speaker of the house. The son of Henry Massey Rector, Arkansas's Civil War governor, and son-in-law of former Mississippi Governor and Senator James Lusk Alcorn, he belonged to one of the most distinguished political families in the state. He was a man of wealth and bearing, a legitimate "broadcloth" aristocrat. Nonetheless, during his four terms in the house, he had earned a reputation as a moderate mugwump-style reformer. An early advocate of a railroad commission, he had been instrumental in the passage of a law prohibiting state and county officials from accepting free railroad passes.[12] A man of strong convictions and unimpeachable integrity, Rector would see his commitment to reform sorely tested during the spring of 1899.

When he first introduced his antitrust bill, Rector had no intention of locking horns with the corporate establishment. Though he had some hope of restricting the local operations of corporate giants such as Standard Oil, the primary purpose of the bill was to break up a powerful state association of fire insurance underwriters. For sixteen years, the state fire insurance association had maintained uniform fire insurance rates which Rector and many other Arkansawyers regarded as outrageously high. Along with a number of other bills pending before the legislature, the Rector Bill was part of a growing movement to regulate an increasingly aggressive and powerful insurance industry.[13]

The leaders of the fire insurance association appeared before the senate judiciary committee on February 16 to plead for exemption from the antitrust bill. When Rector refused the request, the insurance lobby turned to the press and the business community for help. Though few Arkansas businessmen had much sympathy for the insurance industry, many were bothered by the broader implications of the Rector Bill. Consequently, pressure was brought to bear on the legislature, and for a time it appeared that the Rector Bill was in deep trouble—particularly when the Collins Bill, which proposed to tax insurance policies for their cash surrender value, was unexpectedly defeated in the house.[14] Three days before the Rector Bill was scheduled to reach the senate floor, the campaign against the bill was tacitly endorsed by the *Arkansas Gazette*. Although reluctant to declare itself firmly against an antitrust bill, the paper warned that the legislature was playing with fire:

> Capital will not come to the state nor will it remain in a state where the laws are hostile to it. Some of the bills pending before the present legislature if enacted into law would clog the wheels of progress and put Arkansas fifty years behind the times. The people did not elect the legislature to give death blows to the progress of Arkansas. They sent the members here to frame laws that would invite capital and immigration to the state, and not drive them away.[15]

Despite such pressure, or perhaps because of it, on March 6 the senate steeled its nerve and passed the Rector Bill by a comfortable margin. Later in the week, with Attorney General Davis looking on, Governor Jones signed the controversial act into law.

Jones hailed the Rector Act as a mighty blow against the malefactors of wealth. He had railed against the trusts for years, and in his opening message to the legislature in January, he had reminded the trusts that "the state is more powerful than any corporation created by it." Nonetheless, Jones was a cautious reformer who had no intention of picking a quarrel with the local business community. He had his political future to consider, and alienating the merchant class was no way to get elected to the United States Senate. Thus, he was quick to assure anxious conservatives that there were no Populists in the woodpile. Notwithstanding the new act's militant language, he confidently predicted that the courts and the attorney general would protect the legitimate interests of the local business community.[16] After all, who but a demagogue or an anarchist would endanger the livelihoods of honest and respectable businessmen? He would soon find out.

As the debate over the Rector Bill raged on, Attorney General Davis watched and waited. No one doubted that he supported the bill, but many people wondered how literally he would interpret the new law. Did the Rector Act apply to all trusts doing business in the state, even if the price fixing in question were national or worldwide in scope? If so, nearly every insurance and express company in the state, and scores of other corporations, would be in direct violation of the new statute. The consequences of such an interpretation would be immense. Thus, even though the attorney general's distaste for big business was well known, nearly everyone, including most of the legislature, expected him to deny the extraterritoriality of the new law.[17] They were wrong.

On the morning of March 25, Davis issued a public statement that sent shock waves across the state. The Rector Act, according to Davis, meant just what it said: "Any corporation organized under the laws of this or any other state" which entered into an agreement with other corporations to fix prices "shall be deemed and adjudged guilty of a conspiracy to commit fraud." As far as the attorney general's office was concerned, the new law prohibited *any* trust from doing business in Arkansas—regardless of where the trust had been organized. More specifically, dismantling the state fire insurance association would no longer get the insurance companies off the hook. They would also have to withdraw from industry-wide pricing agreements, which were administered by rate-setting boards in New York and London.[18] Conservatives shook their heads in disbelief. Incredibly, at a time when the Arkansas economy was in desperate need of capital, a redneck lawyer from Russellville had taken on the entire capitalist establishment. Some Arkansas businessmen refused to take the upstart attorney general seriously. But many others knew that their worst fears had been confirmed: the "Populist virus" had spread to the Democratic party.

By the afternoon of the 25th, much of the business community was in an uproar. The Little Rock Board of Trade, the most powerful businessmen's organization in the state, immediately convened an emergency meeting which was attended by most of the city's leading merchants and bankers, several conservative politicians, and representatives from more than a dozen large insurance companies. The mood of the meeting was indignant, and several of the insurance men angrily threatened to call the attorney general's bluff: if the Rector Act were not repealed or amended, their companies would be forced to withdraw from the state. The local businessmen must have winced. More than insurance protection was at stake; many retail merchants routinely used fire insurance policies as collateral when purchasing from wholesalers. Without such policies, many of them would be unable to stock their stores. Some businessmen believed that the entire credit structure in Arkansas might collapse. Thus, it came as no surprise when the meeting unanimously decided to petition the legislature for relief.[19]

During the following week, the legislature was barraged with similar petitions from business organizations all across the state; lobbying efforts in the corridors of the state house were equally intense. Much of the pressure being applied was anything but subtle. By March 29, even Governor Jones had gotten into the act. After meeting with the delegation from the Little Rock Board of Trade, he announced that he would urge the legislature to pass the desired amendment. Some members of the legislature did not need to be persuaded to restrict the antitrust law; they were moderates who had never intended to provoke a full-scale financial crisis. But many others bitterly resented the insurance companies' threats of withdrawal, which they considered to be tantamount to blackmail. In most cases their original conception of the Rector Act had been relatively modest, but they now began to see the wisdom of the attorney general's interpretation. In a display of questionable hindsight which galled conservatives, they began to claim they had never doubted the extraterritorial scope of the antitrust law.[20]

To add fuel to the fire, William Jennings Bryan arrived in Little Rock on March 27. A special guest of the legislature, Bryan treated an overflow crowd in Glenwood Park to an hour-long oration, urging Arkansas Democrats to stand firm against the trusts. The Democrats in the legislature did not disappoint him. When the businessmen's amendment, sponsored by Representative George W. Williams of Little Rock, reached the house floor on March 30, it became clear that their high-handed tactics had backfired. By a vote of 48 to 31, the house immediately tabled the amendment. A similar amendment introduced in the senate a week later was also defeated.[21] Though many conservatives could scarcely believe it, a majority of the legislature had sided with the attorney general.

On March 31, a jubilant Davis filed antitrust suits against sixty-three out-of-state fire insurance companies. And he warned, this was only the beginning:

> It is not only the fire insurance companies that I am after, under the law, but many others. I waited to see whether the legislature would change the law, and it was not until I saw the temper of the house that the proceedings were begun in the courts. These suits are to test the law and the legislature ought to play hands off. They were brought in dead, down-right earnest. If any of them think it is a bluff, we'll take a tilt at them for each day they have been doing business since the act became effective. They are in violation of the law for every day they have transacted business since then. I don't want to be captious, but if the insurance companies can't do business here without belonging to combinations, the sooner they quit the better. I don't think a single syllable of the law should be changed. It is a good law and I think it ought to stand. . . . I am here to execute the law, not to make it. If my construction of this law is not right, the courts can settle it.[22]

Predictably, many of the fire insurance companies responded to Davis's challenge by immediately cancelling thousands of policies. Within a week, virtually all out-of-state insurance companies had withdrawn from the state. Conditions were so unsettled that most independent insurance brokers simply closed their doors. Others remained open but refused to issue new insurance policies of any kind. The result was utter chaos. Faced with a tottering credit structure and a mountain of worthless policies, the Arkansas business community began to panic. In towns and cities from Helena to Fort Smith, outraged businessmen held protest meetings demanding that the Rector Act be repealed or amended. Except for a few small town weeklies, the press was equally upset. Surveying editorial opinion across the state, the editor of the *Arkansas Gazette* could "not recall any measure ever passed by an Arkansas legislature that had met with so much disapproval as the Rector antitrust law."[23] One editor characterized the law as "the infamy of '99," while another insisted that the legislature had obviously "gone daft," sarcastically predicting that it would soon "pass a law regulating the number of stalks of corn to be planted to the hill."[24]

Most of the anger was directed at the legislature and not at Davis. Sensing that the attorney general was all too eager for martyrdom, the *Arkansas Gazette* continually downplayed Davis's role in precipitating the crisis. The attorney general, the paper assured the public, was "merely obeying orders." Most Arkansas newspapers followed the *Gazette's* lead, but not all. The *Helena Weekly World,* a conservative paper published in the heart of the East Arkansas Delta, contemptuously proclaimed that Jeff Davis was nothing more than "a carrot-headed, red-faced, loud-mouthed, strong-limbed, ox-driving mountaineer lawyer that has come to Little Rock to get a reputation—a friend to the fellow who brews forty-rod bug juice back in the mountains." This characterization would follow Davis for the remainder of his career. Davis himself relished the description and repeated it at every opportunity, especially when stumping the Ozark backcountry.[25]

During the second week of April, the battle over the antitrust law reached new levels of intensity. On April 10, Davis filed antitrust suits against a number of express, tobacco, and cotton oil companies—including the American Tobacco Company and Wells Fargo. Later the same day, conservatives suffered a second disappointment when both houses of the legislature beat back attempts to amend the Rector Act. Two days later a desperate business community counterattacked. Aided by the railroads, which offered half-price fares to all businessmen travelling to and from Little Rock, the State Board of Trade transformed its annual convention into a massive protest meeting. Businessmen from all over the state jammed into Glenwood Park to vent their anger at the Rector Act. Not since ex-President Grant's visit in 1880 had the city seen so many silk hats and three-piece suits. In Davis's words, it was a gathering of the "high-collared crowd."[26]

Despite the high collars, the tone of the meeting was more raucous than respectable. For more than five hours, speaker after speaker alternated between flourishes of New South rhetoric and angry denunciations of the antitrust law. At one point, George Latta of Hot Springs read a news story describing the plight of an Arkansas widow who, after being denied a fire insurance policy, had lost her home to fire. "Who is responsible for this?" Latta asked the crowd. Many shouted back, "Rector! Rector!" Others screamed, "Jeff Davis! Jeff Davis!" Though merchants and bankers did most of the talking, some of the convention's more memorable moments were provided by conservative politicians. Representative James Wood of Lee County, later one of Davis's most bitter enemies, told the businessmen that they had no one but themselves to blame for the crisis. The business community had "stood aloof" from politics and was now paying the price. "You have got to send intelligent, progressive people to represent you here in the legislature," Wood exclaimed, "not that class of men who simply vote yes or no when their names are called. If you do not take more interest the state will go to the devil."[27]

The most dramatic moment came when Davis addressed the convention. Spotted at the back of the audience, he was asked to present an impromptu defense of his actions. Despite the obvious hostility of the crowd, he did not have to be prodded too hard. Defiant and implacable, he gave the businessmen more than they bargained for, telling them bluntly that it was time to throw down the gauntlet. As far as he was concerned, the question of the hour was whether or not Arkansas would "surrender and grovel in the dust before this mighty combine of wealth." He demanded to know why the Arkansas business community complained about the Rector Act but not about trusts like the Pacific Express Company and the American Tobacco Company. At this point his voice was drowned out by angry cries from the crowd. When he resumed, he warned the hecklers that if they shouted him down they would have to answer to the true businessmen of Arkansas—the men who tilled "in the fields and hollows." He closed with the prediction that "the courts would sustain every syllable of the antitrust law." As he left the podium there was a ripple of polite applause, but most of the audience booed and hissed. This scene later became one of his stock campaign stories. Time and again he would remind the voters how he had been "hissed, hooted, and howled down" by the "high-collared crowd."[28]

Davis's impromptu speech was a masterful piece of political maneuvering. Unequivocally and unmistakably, he had thrown himself into the breech. In the process he had proved his mettle and established himself as the unquestioned leader of the Arkansas antitrust movement. Jeff Davis, even his critics now had to admit, was a man to be reckoned with.

The aftershocks of the businessmen's convention were considerable. The next day, the house formally censured Representative Wood for his intemperate remarks (his colleagues did not take kindly to being called "anarchists" and "idiots"), and the legislature presented Davis with a gold-headed cane in appreciation of his speech at Glenwood Park.[29] As he thanked the legislators for the cane, which was inscribed with the words "Stand by your guns," an emotional Davis assured them that they "would take a place in history for the masses against the classes, for the people against the combines."[30] Arkansas businessmen did not know whether to laugh or cry. Although no one had known what the effects of the meeting in Glenwood Park would be, the "caning" of Jeff Davis was obviously not what they had had in mind.

To make matters worse, the controversy was beginning to receive national attention. When the news got out that a young politician by the name of Jeff Davis was jousting with the corporate establishment down in Arkansas, correspondents from many of the nation's major dailies descended upon the state. Predictably, most of what the correspondents sent back to their editors was anything but complimentary about the state of Arkansas. "Nearly every newspaper in the United States," the *Arkansas Gazette* complained, "has had something to say about our anti-trust law, and with very few exceptions, all condemn the act. They are creating the impression that Arkansas is un-friendly to capital and that it wants no further immigration. This is not true. . . . The business men of Arkansas will not tolerate any interference with the progress of their state."[31]

Fortunately for the business community, the battleground shifted to the courts in late April. Despite their troubles, most businessmen were confident that it was only a matter of time before the courts overruled the attorney general's interpretation of the Rector Act. On April 22, Davis went before Circuit Court Judge Joseph Martin and attempted to block a general demur-rer against the antitrust suits. The attorneys for the fire insurance companies contended that the demurrer was justified because the extraterritorial inter-pretation of the antitrust law was invalid. Davis responded in the way he knew best. As an incredulous audience of corporate lawyers and executives looked on, he put on a show which would have shaken up the roughest of country courthouses. Comparing himself to Old Hickory Jackson during the fight against the Monster Bank and challenging the opposition's head coun-sel to a debate on the hustings, he let loose with everything he had:

> . . . thank God, that [the] house and senate stood like a stone wall, deaf as an oyster to the pleas of one of the most gigantic, far-reaching, blood-sucking, dia-bolical trusts on the face of the earth—fire insurance. . . . I say that fire insurance business is an outlaw, and as conducted in these United States, it ought to be an outlaw. . . . Jesus Christ whipped just such a gang of fellows out of the temple, when they were selling doves. . . . I say, sir, the question is, shall the creature control the creator, or shall the creator be supreme? Shall the strong arm of the law be paralyzed? Shall the law bow down in humble obeisance to this monster combination, fire insurance? Ah, the pitiful howl that is being raised all over this state! Whenever you touch capital, whenever you touch money, whenever you touch aggregated wealth, you hear them howl out, the people are ruined. You know that is not your sentiment. Your sentiment rather is, "The people be damned. God bless the rich; the poor can beg." . . . [The Rector Act] is the entering wedge; it is the first stroke in the great battle of the masses against the classes. . . . The tocsin of war has been sounded, and these gentlemen may as well prepare for the fray.[32]

Judge Martin was not impressed. On April 27, he ruled in favor of the insurance companies, stating that the Rector Act applied only to trusts organized in Arkansas. Davis immediately appealed the decision to the state supreme court, vowing to continue to assess the insurance companies fines of $5,000 a day. Governor Jones pointed out that state law protected companies from fines during litigation, but Davis assessed the fines anyway.[33] He was not about to give up; neither was most of the legislature. In early May, as Davis and Jacobson prepared their supreme court brief, the general assembly appropriated $5,000 to help finance the attorney general's prosecution of the trusts. Davis promptly hired two additional assistants, Jesse Cleveland Hart and Hal Norwood. Both men would later become part of the Davis organization's inner circle, and Hart went on to become chief justice of the Arkansas Supreme Court.[34]

In mid-May, Davis presented his oral argument to the state supreme court. For nearly a week he sparred with a battery of distinguished corporate lawyers, and once again he put on quite a performance. Though he was better prepared than he had been in circuit court, he spent most of his time pacing back and forth in front of the justices, flailing his arms and growling at the trusts. At one point, he got so lathered up that he began to remove his coat, whereupon the chief justice reminded him that no gentleman would appear in shirt sleeves before such a high court. This unnecessary bit of stodginess would later rebound in Davis's favor out on the stump: asking voters if he could take off his coat, after reminding them that the highfalutin court would not put up with such common behavior, was always a sure-fire way to send the wool hats flying in the air.[35]

The business community's ordeal finally came to an end on May 27, when the state supreme court unanimously rejected Davis's appeal. However, the court did leave the attorney general some basis for further prosecutions under the Rector Act, ruling that the extraterritorial interpretation *was* valid if the combination in question attempted to fix prices in Arkansas specifically. Davis had won a partial victory, though he did not see it that way. Immediately after the decision was rendered, Davis held a press conference and announced that he was dropping all pending antitrust suits. As far as he was concerned, the Rector Act was dead: "Will I prosecute any further trust cases? No, indeed. If I cannot get the support which, in my humble judgment, I am entitled to from the judiciary, I wouldn't prosecute a trust if it should organize in front of the state house with a brass band. . . ." After calling for a special legislative session that would enact additional antitrust laws, he hinted that he would ultimately take his case to the people. For the time being, however, he had had enough. If the press wanted to find him, they would have to travel to "the wild wastes of Red River bottom" where he would be hunting and fishing with old friends.[36]

In the aftermath of the antitrust fight there was much speculation about Davis's motives and about how and why the situation had gotten out of hand. How could the Arkansas Democracy have elected such a troublemaker to the attorney generalship? Where had this wild man come from?

Was he a demagogue? Was he an anarchist? Was he crazy? Though the puzzlement would continue for years, most political observers concluded that Davis was more demagogic than radical. By dropping all of the antitrust suits in late May, he allegedly showed his true colors.

Some historians have accepted this interpretation as self-evident, but its validity is questionable.[37] Davis's decision to drop the suits could be interpreted as a legitimate tactical maneuver. Most likely, his political and ideological instincts dictated that he, not the supreme court or the *Arkansas Gazette,* should decide when and how the counterattack against the trusts would take place. If his critics failed to understand the relationship between power politics and reform, that was their problem. The major difference between Davis and most other Democratic politicians was ideology, not morality. Davis had internalized the anticolonial, anticommercial ideology of the agrarian revolt; his critics, moderate and conservative alike, had not. When he stated that he hated the trusts and had no intention of kowtowing to Northern capitalists, he meant it—even though he clearly did not understand all the implications of what he said.

On the other hand, there can be little doubt that he shaped the antitrust controversy to fit his own political purposes. Seeing the Rector Act as a vehicle that could transport him to the governorship, Davis jumped aboard and never looked back. Elias Rector, Dan Jones, and just about everybody else were left in the dust. Davis himself probably did not know where his ideological motives ended and his political motives began, and at this point in his career he certainly had no intention of choosing between the two. According to Jacobson, the man closest to Davis during this period, he was simply following the lead of his idol, William Jennings Bryan. As Jacobson put it, "Bryan's rise to national fame on the silver question opened his eyes to the possibilities of prominently getting into the public spotlight on some issue, even if that issue had to be forced."[38]

Davis took Bryan's lesson so much to heart that he found not one but two such issues during the tumultuous spring of 1899. Just as the furor over his antitrust speech at Glenwood Park was spreading, Davis stoked the fires of a second major controversy. This second controversy, which would disrupt Arkansas politics for more than a decade, was Davis's one-man crusade against the construction of a new state capitol. The battle over a new state house required Davis to rise to new heights of recklessness, since this time he had the spotlight all to himself. Many of the same legislators who supported his interpretation of the Rector Act fought him tooth and nail over the state house issue.[39]

The existing state house had been built in the late 1830s, during Arkansas's early years of statehood. An impressive building in its day—one observer described it as "one of the most beautiful old buildings in the nation"—the two-story wooden structure had suffered more than its share of neglect and rough treatment. In one incident, which epitomized Arkansas's rough-and-tumble heritage, a group of prominent citizens rode their horses up and down the main spiral staircase. Despite a major renovation in 1885, by the late 1890s the old building had deteriorated almost beyond repair. Described as an "ancient rookery" by one legislator and as a "chicken coop" by another, it was full of peeling paint, chipped plaster, threadbare carpets, and bowed walls. By 1899, state officials were afraid to allow large crowds to meet in the capitol for "fear it would fall down."[40] Though a measure of decayed elegance remained, the old capitol was simply too small and too rickety to meet the needs of a modern state government.

Of course, many advocates of a new state house were motivated less by an awareness of the existing building's shortcomings than by visions of a glorious new building. From the mid-1890s on, New South boosters saw the construction of a grand new capitol as essential to the state's well-being. Editorials called for a gleaming, marble-columned edifice to serve as a symbol of the new Arkansas.[41] "Building a million-dollar state house," the *Arkansas Gazette* argued in 1900, "is one of the best evidences of a state's progress." George Sengel, a former president of the State Board of Trade, predicted that the laying of the new capitol's cornerstone would be "the greatest event in our history."[42]

Talk of a new state capitol had been rife since the 1880s, but its proponents had been frustrated by the lack of a suitable site, as the grounds of the existing capitol were far too small to accommodate a modern state house. When Governor James P. Eagle proposed a relocation of the state penitentiary in 1893, New South enthusiasts hailed the penitentiary site as the perfect location for a new state capitol. But the idea of building a state house on the penitentiary grounds proved to be controversial. When a bill calling for a new state house was introduced in the 1895 legislature, it was soundly defeated by legislators who were unwilling to endorse such an expensive project in the midst of a severe depression.[43]

Later in the decade, as the depression began to fade, the supporters of a state capitol bill tried again, this time with more success. In January 1899 Senator John D. Kimbell of Hot Springs introduced a comprehensive bill that provided the relocation of the state penitentiary and the construction of a new state capitol. The Kimbell Bill called for an appropriation of $1,000,000 for the construction of the new state house, established a Board of Capitol Commissioners consisting of the governor and six appointees, authorized the Board to purchase a brick factory and a granite quarry (both of which were to be manned by convict labor), stipulated that the new state house would be built on the present grounds of the penitentiary, and directed the Penitentiary Board to find a site for a new penitentiary. By Arkansas standards, it was an extremely complicated and expensive bill. And few bills in the state's history had invested so much power in the hands of a few state officials. The bill met with stiff opposition: some opponents were afraid of a taxpayers' revolt; others considered the bill to be an outrageous boondoggle. Nonetheless, surrounded by the squalor of the old state house, most legislators could not resist the lure of a new building. On March 20, the senate approved the Kimbell Bill by a vote of 19–8, and on April 14, by a vote of 48–35, the house followed suit.[44]

Backers of the proposed capitol project were jubilant. All they needed now was Governor Jones's signature—or so they thought. On April 15, Davis stunned the local political community by declaring that the capitol bill had not passed after all. According to Davis, since the Kimbell Bill entailed a new tax levy, it was essentially an appropriations bill; as such it required the approval of two-thirds, not one-half, of the legislature. By his calculation, the bill had been handily defeated in the house. Proponents of the new capitol were stunned, but fortunately for them they had Governor Jones on their side. Assuring the legislature that Davis did not know what he was talking about, Jones signed the bill into law. Within a week, the newly appointed Board of Capitol Commissioners was hard at work examining proposals for the new state house.[45]

With the vast majority of politicians that would have been the end of it, but not with Davis. Like a barroom brawler, Davis did not consider a fight a fight until after the first knockdown. As far as he was concerned, Dan Jones had merely landed the first blow. During late April and early May, Davis was too busy jousting with the trusts to pay any attention to the state house issue. But as soon as he finished arguing the antitrust case before the supreme court he renewed his fight against the Kimbell Act with a vengeance.

On May 17, after a month of silence on the issue, he suddenly ordered the state auditor to withhold the capitol commissioners' per diem expenses. According to Davis, since the Kimbell Act had never passed the house, it was an unconstitutional law; therefore the capitol commissioners were not entitled to a nickel of state funds. When the state auditor refused to cooperate, Davis filed quo warranto proceedings in circuit court to enjoin the Capitol Commission from any further activity. The quo warranto procedure, which had not been used in Arkansas since the Brooks-Baxter War of 1874, provided Davis with a means of testing the constitutionality of the Kimbell Act. But it did so at considerable risk. As the conservative press was quick to point out, Davis had turned to a legal procedure associated with Radical Republicanism in the public mind. That proved he was a desperate man.[46] Davis agreed. Resorting to an extreme measure, he explained, was his way of alerting the public to the seriousness of the situation. The so-called Capitol Commission was on the verge of stealing the people blind, and someone had to blow the whistle. "I have no objection per se to building a new state house," he insisted, but it must "be built without increasing taxation."[47] With this statement, Davis admitted that his opposition to the Kimbell Act was substantive as well as procedural. Supporters of the act now had an inkling of what the attorney general was after: he wanted to convince the public that he was the taxpayer's best friend. And he was willing to sacrifice the new capitol to do so. As one historian has written, Davis was shrewd enough to realize that "a capitol site bestrewn with moss covered building blocks and infested with willows and weeds might lead to power more quickly than the splendor of a stately granite structure."[48]

During the month of June, Davis stalked the Capitol Commission. On June 5, he petitioned the chancery court to enjoin the Penitentiary Board from carrying out the Capitol Commission's orders to tear down the state penitentiary; three days later his petition was denied. On June 7, Circuit Court Judge Joseph Martin had rejected Davis's quo warranto claim and affirmed the constitutionality of the Kimbell Act. As most observers had predicted, Judge Martin ruled that, since the new capitol had been endorsed by a joint legislative resolution prior to the passage of the Kimbell Act, the appropriation in question was a necessary expense of state government; thus the Kimbell Act required only a majority vote. Undaunted, Davis went back to chancery court and asked for a temporary injunction against the Capitol Commission. When the chancery court turned him down on June 29, he immediately appealed the decision to the state supreme court, with virtually no chance of success.[49]

At the end of June, Davis had little to show for all his efforts. Twice he had taken a controversial stand on an important issue, forcing the issue through the courts, and twice he had been rebuffed. In the process, he had become a social and political pariah. The governor refused to speak to him, prominent citizens looked the other way when he walked down the street, the hotel where he was lodged tried to drive him out by doubling his rent, and one Little Rock bank even refused to cash his checks.[50] An ordinary politician would have regarded all this as a chastening experience and retreated to the security of moderation. But Jeff was no ordinary politician.

In late June, to the amusement of conservatives certain that he was well on his way to political oblivion, Davis announced his intention to run for the governorship. The announcement was made in a form letter which he sent to a number of state legislators:[51]

Little Rock, Ark., June, 1899

My Dear Sir—,

I have concluded to enter the race for governor in the coming campaign, and do not think it ill-advised at this time to let my friends know in a quiet way my intentions in this matter, as I am informed other probable candidates are doing the same thing.

I had not intended to enter this contest until the scurrilous attacks upon me by the subsidized press of this city forced me to take the defensive, not only myself, but as they term it, "the late lamented legislature." I have noticed that they say they intend to make "our name odious" in this state, and it is my intention, while they are giving us Hail Columbia, to take a little hand in this game myself. I intend to defend the action of the legislature and myself in connection with our recent antitrust law in no uncertain way. If my health will permit, whether I carry a single county or get one vote, from every stump in this state to take the hide off of some of the fellows in high places, because I believe they need a general shaking up. I have not yet made my candidacy public in the papers, and don't think it will be proper to do so at this time, although I am told that some are actively in the field; still, in a quiet way, if you are not pledged to others, you can render me any assistance in your county. I shall esteem it a great honor. I shall attend the meeting of the governors and attorneys general to be held at St. Louis in September to assist in devising some means to get rid of the trusts, although I think we had the best law upon this subject we could have had, but the trusts seemed to get their assistance from the supreme court which they vainly sought at your hands. Hoping that I may have the pleasure of seeing you, and visiting your people and speaking to them along the lines above suggested, I beg to remain very truly yours,

Jeff Davis

Few politicians took Davis's candidacy very seriously.[52] In the eyes of most Democratic leaders, an attorney general who had disrupted the business community and badgered the courts with misguided legal interpretations hardly deserved to be elevated to the governorship. At this point no one could have predicted that Davis possessed a "peculiar genius for turning defeat into victory." Of course, most of Davis's "genius" lay in the simple fact that he was the first Arkansas politician to realize that the new primary system had fundamentally altered the rules of state politics.[53] Unlike his critics, Davis understood the extent to which the Democratic establishment's power had depended on the convention system. Under the primary system, a renegade Democrat with a flair for mass politics had the capacity to turn the party upside down. No one knew exactly how the boys up the forks of the creek would react to the antitrust and state house controversies. Davis had a hunch that they would react much differently than the "high-collared crowd" in Little Rock and Fort Smith, particularly if he went out among them and told his side of the story.

Davis's turn to mass politics was probably dictated as much by circumstance as by design. According to Jacobson, from the beginning of his attorney generalship, "Davis had his eye fixed upon the Governor's office, but he never permitted himself to give expression to that thought nor how he expected to attain it. I am sure he himself had no idea nor even any tentative plan nor method of procedure. He was rather like a ship at sea without a rudder, dependent wholly upon the caprice of the winds. . . ."[54] Whatever his original intentions, by late June Davis had no one else to turn to but the masses. On the state house issue, virtually the entire political establishment was arrayed against him. Although he was still awaiting a decision on his final appeal to the state supreme court, the capitol commissioners were so confident that the court would rule in their favor that they organized a groundbreaking ceremony for the Fourth of July, to which every political and business leader in the state, including the attorney general, was invited.[55]

Davis, of course, would have no part of it. While most of Arkansas's political and economic elite celebrated the nation's birthday in Little Rock, Davis was standing on a makeshift grandstand in the small Ozark hill town of Hardy.[56] Surrounded by a crowd of leathery-skinned, one-gallused dirt farmers, he delivered the first speech of the most memorable political campaign in the state's history. Though it would be some time before the revelers in the capital city realized what was happening, the revolt of the rednecks had begun. Arkansas politics would never be the same again.

6

Redneck Messiah

. . . the war is on. It is knife to knife, hilt to hilt, foot to foot, knee to knee, between the corporations of Arkansas and the people.
—Jeff Davis (1900)[1]

The Independence Day celebrations in July 1899 dramatized the growing rift between urban and rural Arkansas. At the ground-breaking ceremonies in Little Rock, the mood was that of a New South festival—respectable, progressive, and incurably optimistic. Aside from Senator John Kimbell, who could not resist calling Davis "a bag of hot air," the speakers of the day talked of nothing but the promise of the new century.[2] In the dusty streets of Hardy, a hundred miles to the north, the mood was quite different, despite the best efforts of the local merchants and politicians who had organized the festivities.[3] The farmers who poured into Hardy to catch a glimpse of their notorious attorney general had little to celebrate but a day away from the fields. Nonetheless, they were always ready for a good show—particularly an old-fashioned, hammer-and-tongs stump speech. Some farmers had come because they considered Davis to be their champion, but most were there because they were either bored or curious. Neither group would go away disappointed. Spurred on by the gallus-snapping, foot-stomping enthusiasm of the crowd, Davis used the occasion to declare war on the "high-collared" aristocrats of the New South.

Davis began by disassociating himself from the corrupt environment of Little Rock, reminding the crowd that he was a simple country boy: "In his introduction the chairman stated that I live in Little Rock. Oh, no, I live in Russellville and while looking in the faces of these Sharp County Democrats I feel that I am in my father's house." Next, he indulged in a bit of self-serving Southern patriotism:

> The speaker who preceded me spoke of Washington, Jefferson and Lincoln as the three greatest Americans. While I am as proud as he of these three great Americans, there is another equally great whose name has not been mentioned. He lies buried at Beauvoir, Mississippi, with the constitution of the United States pillow-

78

ing his head—Jefferson Davis. An Arkansas paper has lately said that we would be made infamous in the state of Arkansas. I apprehend that newspaper did not refer to the name of the man buried at Beauvoir, Miss., but to my name. . . .[4]

Having assured the crowd that he was one of them, Davis was ready to talk about the issues. Reaffirming his opposition to a state-financed railroad construction scheme, he turned to the state house question, and for the first time publicly declared that the proponents of the Kimbell Act were nothing more than extravagant boodlers:

They say we want a new state house. I, too, would like to see a new state house. But I am going to tell you the truth. We have a depleted treasury. Did you know it? Our treasury is empty and taxes have already been increased. Can we afford to pay more taxes? They are breaking dirt for what they claim is to be a million-dollar state house, but it will cost three million dollars and prove to be the most infamous steal ever perpetrated against the people of Arkansas. My legal opinion is that our property, the beautiful park where the state house now stands, will, when they move it to the present penitentiary grounds, revert to the Beebe heirs. They are going to buy for the new penitentiary site 3,500 acres of land that is belly deep in poison water and pay $120,000 of your money for it. Because I am opposing such profligacy the newspapers say I am drunk or crazy.[5]

Turning to the antitrust controversy, he blasted the press and the courts—convenient symbols for Little Rock's trust-ridden establishment:

Look me in the face. Do I look like a maniac? Do I look like I'm drunk? The newspapers of the state accuse me of being . . . a lunatic because I honestly tried to enforce a good law placed on the statute books by your legislature. . . . We have an anti-trust law that would have knocked every trust cold had the Arkansas supreme court not killed it. The judges have lived too long at Little Rock, which is why they ruled against the people. The railroads and express companies combine on rates and rob the people and our law, if the courts would let us enforce it, would put a stop to their tyranny.[6]

At the close of his speech, Davis warned his enemies that they were in for a long struggle. "I am in this fight for the people," he roared, "and I shall not desert them. The men who have started out to make my name infamous in this state shall hear some truths. I intend to tell the people the truth in each of the 75 counties of the state and before the canvass for the governorship is over you will not be able to see me for the dust."[7]

Davis had fired the first shot of the redneck revolt—but he hardly had the conservatives quaking in their boots. After all, the Populists had filled the air with similar invective for years with little effect. Although Davis was a powerful public official who had already proven that he could be a nuisance, conservatives were confident that anything Davis did could be undone by the courts. As if to confirm this point, on July 5 the state supreme court unanimously upheld the constitutionality of the Kimbell Act.[8] Once again the attorney general seemingly had made a fool of himself.

In the state press, reaction to the Hardy speech ranged from amusement to outrage. Most editors regarded Davis as a loud-mouthed politician and a sore loser. Two powerful Little Rock papers, the *Arkansas Gazette* and the *Arkansas Democrat*, did take him seriously. The *Gazette* offered a point-by-point rebuttal of Davis's analysis of the antitrust and state house issues, complained that he had unjustly impugned the honor of several distinguished politicians, and claimed there was no evidence to support the charge that the Kimbell Act was a swindle. S. R. Cockrill, a former chief justice of the Arkansas Supreme Court and one of the principal heirs mentioned in Davis's speech, told a *Gazette* reporter that none of the heirs in question "have any more claim to the state house grounds . . . than they have to the moon."[9] The paper also pointed out that the original Jefferson Davis was buried not in Beauvoir, Mississippi, but in Richmond, Virginia. The *Democrat*, owned and edited by the ultraconservative James Mitchell, was even rougher on Davis. "The attorney general has attempted to besmirch the names of men whom Arkansas has often honored, and would gladly honor again," Mitchell declared. "He has done a deed that is inexcusable. While accusing his betters of foul deeds he has committed a crime that will now, and for all time to come, stench in the nostrils of honest men. He has shown himself to be a buffoon."[10]

If Davis's critics thought this kind of ridicule would force him to back off, they were in for a rude awakening. As far as he was concerned, the "squirrel-headed" editors of Little Rock could laugh at him all they liked.

But Davis had seen fire in the eyes of the farmers at Hardy, and he knew he was on to something. Trusting his instincts, he delivered a blistering stump speech at Conway on July 13. Printed in full in the *Arkansas Gazette*, Davis's blunt remarks left conservatives shaking their heads in disbelief:

> The *Helena World* says I am a red-faced, loud-lunged, deep-voiced, ox-driving mountaineer. He says I am a friend of the fellow that brews the forty-rod bug juice, and all that sort of stuff. If he attempts to classify people like them, and call in the people who live on the outskirts of Little Rock, and in the hills and valleys of this beautiful state, men of that character, I thank God that I am their friend and that I live among them. . . .
>
> The hardest task that I ever tried to perform in my life, fellow citizens, was leaving one of the prettiest, blue-eyed, black-haired little women up yonder at Russellville, with those babies, and going down to Little Rock, and being separated from them; that is the hardest task that I ever had to undergo in my life. I wasn't able to move to Little Rock. I wasn't able to support my family upon the salary of that office, and I had no idea of being a candidate before the people at this time. But, while attending to the duties of the attorney general's office, it came in my way so that I crossed the interests of somebody else, and then they began to lambast me; they began to shoot at me from the brush, and from behind and in front, and they began by their artilleries and their batteries. But I have never yet faltered in the discharge of a duty; I have never yet shown the white feather,

although down there in Little Rock the banks refused to cash my check; that may be good policy. The hotel where I boarded raised my board from $25 to $50 a month to price me out of the hotel. I paid my board and quit. The long distance telephone refused me long distance connection in my office, and made me go to the pay station and drop my money in the slot before I could send a telephone. I want to put a bed in my office, and I will put a cooking stove there and do my own cooking before they shall bulldoze me out of that town. . . .

I have not lost my faith in man. There are lots of good, pure noble men in the world. I wouldn't go through under the flare of the gas light; I wouldn't go to midnight revelries; I wouldn't go to men who never knew a real sorrow; I wouldn't go to men who keep late hours under bright, beautiful gas lights to find all the noble men in the world. Rather would I go to the man that awakes with the morning sun, the man that brushes the first dewdrops from the grass, sees the sun that rises in its beauty, and has felt real true sorrow, and that grasps the plow handle, where the day before he left it, and earns his bread as God has commanded him, "by the sweat of his face." These are the men that I would go to to hunt for true, pure manhood. There are lots of them. God bless them. . . .

You have got two classes. The wealth producing and the wealth consuming class, and the men who make the laws of the land, and the men who execute the laws, even the supreme judges, come from the wealth consuming class. Now, for years laws have been made in the interest of the wealth consuming class against the wealth producing class. I want to tell you that it is woe to the robbers who have gathered in fields that they have not sown, who have stolen the jewels from labor and built upon them a throne. . . .

They say I am a demagogue. Every time a man comes out and stands for the interests of the people, he is denounced, either as a crank or a demagogue. I thank God that if that is demagoguery that I am a demagogue. . . .

If I win this race I have got to win it against the telegraph, the telephone, the express companies, the Standard Oil, the tobacco company, every trust and combination of the face of the earth. I have got to win it against all the banks, against all the railroads, against all the corporations; not all the banks; some of the bankers are my personal friends, but the majority of them. Don't you see what an uphill pull I have got? . . .

Let them call it demagoguery if they please, but [the] farmer is the bravest man on earth. I have seen them up in my country on a little hill place, raising a family of noble sons and daughters, and every year they are scratching right on that same little old piece of ground, and the wealth-consuming class are tightening the strings every year; the product of your labor is growing less in value. You are working from early dawn until dewy eve; your wife is busy with your household cares, and the daughters and the sons are in the fields, and if you would sit down at night and let your son figure up what you would likely make you would quit the next morning. You know you can't make a cent—not a cent—and yet you work and toil and labor—the bravest man on earth. God bless them. These are my sentiments. You may call it demagogy or call it what you will. That is what they are. This wealth-consuming class has got the money; they have cornered everything. . . .[11]

The Conway speech and the stir that it created made many conservatives extremely uncomfortable. Davis's candidacy, originally considered something of a joke, was becoming less amusing. The political atmosphere was heating up much too fast. The first county primary was still eight months away, and already the gubernatorial campaign was in full swing. In a state where politicking rivaled drinking and hunting as the most popular pastime, long and arduous campaigns were hardly unknown; but never before had a contest for statewide office begun quite so early. By mid-summer, no less than five candidates had entered the race for the Democratic gubernatorial nomination: Jeff Davis; Elias Rector; James Wood, the conservative legislator from Lee County who had been censured by his colleagues in April; A. F. Vandeventer, a lumber merchant from Morrilton, who had served as speaker of the house during the 1899 legislative session; and Edgar Bryant, a sentimental New South enthusiast from Fort Smith who had earned the sobriquet "the Silver-tongued Orator of Arkansas." Although an early withdrawal by Rector cut the field to four, the *Arkansas Gazette* predicted that as many as a dozen candidates would enter the fray before the campaign was over. To conservatives, who preferred the sound of ringing cash registers to the din of political bombast, this was hardly encouraging news.[12]

Some conservative editors and politicians, sensing that Davis thrived on criticism and controversy, tried to calm things down by paying as little attention to the campaign as possible. Others tried to fight fire with fire and began to search for a spellbinder of their own—a hatchet man who could cut Davis down to size.

It appeared that James Wood might fill the bill. As editor of the *Lee County Courier*, Wood was well known for his stinging editorials. Described as a "roaster" by one observer, he needed no prodding to go after Davis, who had been skewering him ever since the businessmen's convention in Glenwood Park. At one point, Davis had called him "a traitor" and a "dirty filthy little squib." A week after the Conway speech, Wood—who had not yet formally announced for the governorship—invited Davis to meet him on the stump for a joint speaking engagement. "I am ready to expose him at any time he will give me the opportunity to do so," he declared. When Davis turned down the invitation, arguing that he had no time to waste on a noncandidate, Wood threw his hat into the ring.[13]

On August 25, before a huge crowd at Morrilton, the two men had their first head-to-head encounter of the campaign. Reporters and politicians from across the state were on hand to witness the bloodletting. Wood spoke first. Long-winded and pompous, he spent most of his speech reading lengthy newspaper clippings endorsing his actions during the antitrust fight. After two hours of this, the crowd became impatient and began screaming for Davis—so much so that Wood was forced to sit down without finishing his speech. As the crowd roared its approval, Davis made Wood wish he had never left the mudflats of Lee County. Ridiculing Wood's speech and chiding him for "foaming about the mouth," he vowed never again to waste his time debating a political lightweight. "Hasn't old man Wood fell flat?" he asked the crowd. "Say, boys, would you go down to Little Rock and meet him if you was me?" As Wood sat fuming on the grandstand, the crowd responded with a resounding "no."[14]

The following morning even the *Arkansas Gazette* had to admit that Wood had been no match for the fiery-tongued attorney general. Wood promptly called a news conference, during which he desperately tried to regain the offensive. "Jeff Davis of Arkansas compared to Jeff Davis of the Southern Confederacy," he thundered, "[is] as a dunghill to a diamond, mud to marble, a savage cat to a Royal bengal tiger, a whining cur to the big mastiff." When "the shyster attorney-general of Arkansas . . . strutted around in his suit of gray," he reminded him "of the jackass parading in the lion's skin."[15] But no amount of bluster could undo the damage that had been done: the Morrilton debate all but finished Wood as a serious candiadate.[16]

The next candidate to try his hand at besting Davis on the stump was A. F. Vandeventer. On September 7, the two men met at Bentonville, a prosperous county seat in the northwestern corner of the state. Even though much of the crowd was made up of unsympathetic townsmen, Davis dominated the proceedings, lashing out at the trusts and the courts one minute and dispensing gems of country humor the next. One unsympathetic commentator characterized Davis's speech as "agin everything that is and fer everything that ain't," while another complained that he "sawed the atmosphere with his coarse talk and clown-like antics . . . he bellowed like an angry male bovine, showing both ignorance of the proprieties and lack of common sense and decency. His actions thoroughly disgusted the ladies present, to say nothing of his male auditors."[17]

Despite a spirited effort, Vandeventer had no chance to gain center stage. A forceful speaker on the floor of the legislature, he was neither a spellbinder nor an entertainer.[18] And, unlike Davis, he had no burning issue to bring before the voters. A respectable businessman and self-proclaimed moderate, he was unable to champion the disgruntled Arkansas redneck. He counseled patience and moderation when most rural voters wanted action or, at the very least, tough talk.

In mid-September, while Wood and Vandeventer licked their wounds, Davis took time out from the campaign to attend antitrust conferences in Chicago and St. Louis. At the Chicago conference, he stole the show with an antitrust speech that was as comic as its was radical. Putting on his best hillbilly manner, he alternated between jabbing at the trusts and poking fun at himself. "Trust! It is the sweetest word that ever fell from mortal lips, perhaps," Davis informed the Yankee crowd, which was obviously unaccustomed to his folksy style of oratory, "but is wrongly named. They ought to have called it octopus, or anaconda, or something that squeezes the very life blood from its victims. They have stolen the livery of heaven in which to serve the devil." According to the Chicago *Times-Herald*, "the audience was in an uproar from the beginning to the end of the address."[19]

At the St. Louis conference, which was attended by governors and attorneys general from a dozen states, Davis—with the help of Governor Dan Jones—caused an uproar of a different sort. Caught in the glare of the metropolitan press, the long-simmering feud between the two Arkansas officials boiled over. Although they stayed in different hotels and avoided each other as much as possible, neither man could resist trying to upstage the other. Jones told a reporter from the St. Louis *Post-Dispatch* that Davis's interpretation of the Rector Act was ridiculous; Davis countered by asking the conference to endorse the extraterritorial principle. When the conference approved the resolution, Davis gloated and Jones burned with anger.[20] This triumph deepened his feud with Jones and provided new ammunition for his ongoing assault on Arkansas's political establishment.

With his interpretation of the Rector Act endorsed by high officials from nearly a dozen states, Davis could discuss the antitrust controversy without being put on the defensive. Most important, his claim that the Arkansas Democratic party was riddled with trust-heelers had been given added credibility. When he returned to the campaign trail in late September, he was more aggressive than ever. He challenged Jones to a debate, promising to "skin him alive" if he refused. When Jones ignored the challenge, Davis called him "a dirty, miserable, contemptible, political coward."[21] Jones made a serious mistake when he refused to meet Davis on the stump. The image of the governor cowering in the state house while his attorney general taunted him to come out and fight cost him dearly in his campaign against Senator James Berry the following winter.[22]

Through the fall and into the winter, Davis kept up a steady barrage of invective against a host of enemies: his opponents, Governor Jones, the trusts, the press, the Capitol Commission, and the members of the state supreme court, whom he labeled "the five jackasses." As one observer put it, he went "up and down the state like a political roaring lion seeking whom he might devour."[23] He saved his sharpest barbs for the Little Rock papers, which he claimed were involved in a grand conspiracy to defeat him. Richard Brugman, the editor of the *Arkansas Gazette*, was "one of the meanest, dirtiest little Republicans who is owned and controlled by the money power"; James Mitchell, the editor of the *Arkansas Democrat*, was nothing more than "a broken down gold-bug crank."[24] Both Little Rock papers, Davis insisted, were controlled by Northern capitalists who were trying to squelch his crusade against the trusts. He told a crowd in early February:

Never in the history of public offices in Arkansas has such an unjust, merciless, cruel, unnecessary war been waged against any official in Arkansas as has been made against me by the metropolitan press of the city of Little Rock. . . . I stood their vituperation and abuse until it was unbearable. I had no idea of entering into this race, but finally this proposition was made: "We will make his name infamous in Arkansas." "Infamous" in the State where I was born, where my children were born, where I was married and received my education, and hope to be buried when I die. I took that paper home and showed it to my wife, as good and brave a little Southern woman as God ever gave to any man, and asked her what I should do. She said: "Notwithstanding the fact that we are poor, notwithstanding the fact that we had little when were married, notwithstanding the fact that we have little now, yet if it takes everything that we have, even the little home over our heads, and we have to walk out into the street, and begin life over again, go before the people of the State and give the reason for the faith that is in you." And that is the reason why I am here today. . . . I have a little boy, God bless him, a little pale-faced, white-haired fellow. I love him better than anybody on earth except his mother. If I find that boy is a smart boy . . . I will go and make a preacher out of him; if I find he is not so smart a boy, I am going to make a lawyer out of him, and if I find that he has not a bit of sense upon earth I am going to make an editor out of him and send him to Little Rock to edit the *Arkansas Democrat.*[25]

Davis made it clear that the Little Rock papers were simply the worst of a bad lot. He constantly complained that the county seat papers were out to get him. Whenever he went into a town to speak, he invariably attacked the local editor, who more often than not had already come out against him. Even in the early stages of the 1900 campaign, all but a handful of the state's newspapers openly opposed his candidacy, which led him to charge that he was up against a "subsidized press." At one point, he claimed that a candidate could buy the support of any newspaper in the state for $2.50. The editors who opposed him were a bunch of "squirrel heads who could not buy on credit five cents' worth of beef steak in the town in which they lived."[26]

Some editors were angered by Davis's charges. Others were amused. But sooner or later, most of the "squirrel heads" responded in kind, filling their editorial pages with anti-Davis diatribes. They matched Davis epithet for epithet, calling him everything from an anarchist to a buffoon. The following excerpt from the *Camden Beacon* is typical:

Jeff is certainly a character. It required only a short time for him to work himself into a rage. He foamed and frothed and shouted like a dervish. He said he was loaded for grizzly, and he fired his old pot-metal blunderbuss loaded with buzzard intestines, wildly but harmlessly into the air. He sawed the atmosphere like a sand lot orator. Jeff was all action and while he made his quixotic charges against windmills of his own creation, he perspired like the proverbial African at an election. He roared and ranted all over the stage and in his mad dashes at Fletcher and Bryant, he looked like he was pawing dirt with one hand and sawing wood with the other. He led every charge against his foes dashingly but disastrously. Jeff evidently thought he was thinking, but the audience was convinced that if one good original idea should ever find its way into his cranium, it would burst it wide open. His burden was trusts, and throughout his harangue there was an incoherent flow of dirty billingsgate and vulgar allusions. . . . His speech was an effusion of egotism, effrontery and buffoonery never equaled in our experience. . . . Davis is a spoiled boy. His candidacy would have fared better had he not visited Camden. He lost most of his friends and the audience voted him crazy.[27]

By indulging in this kind of name calling, the press played right into Davis's hands. Seizing upon the themes of martyrdom and persecution, he benefited from every heated exchange. His style of campaigning—which one historian has called "the politics of combat"—depended upon extended conflict and a continuing sense of drama.[28] Libelous attacks by "trust-heeling" editors solidified his image as a beleaguered defender of the common man's interests and helped him to keep the emotional level of the campaign at a fever pitch. Charles Jacobson once noted, "These attacks had the same effect on him as pouring water on a duck's back. He welcomed them. He courted them. Did they not serve to center the public eye upon him? To draw the concentrated attention of all toward him and give him a weapon which he was in turn to use upon them? Instead of these attacks dismaying him, they served only to strengthen his arm and steel his soul to combat and to conquer."[29]

One anti-Davis editor warned that "if the *Arkansas Democrat* and several other papers don't let up abusing Jeff Davis, they will elect him Governor."[30] Fortunately for Davis, such warnings went unheeded. As the campaign progressed, it became increasingly clear that many voters were drawn to Davis because they felt he was being persecuted. "I know he is with the farmers and hard-working people," one Davis supporter declared, "and that is why the papers are so against him, for the trusts and money corporations have got them bought over now against the voters of Arkansas." According to a man from Greene County, Davis had "been abused, maligned, insulted more than any man who ever held office in the state . . . simply and only because he stood shoulder to shoulder with the honest lawmakers of the state in their efforts to check the hellish greed of the corporations. These corporations and trusts have had at their back a lot of snarling, snapping jackals, ready to do their dirty work in besmirching the characters of honorable men for the sake of gnawing the picked bones left at their master's tables." A pro-Davis editor from Yell County urged his readers to vote for "the worst berated and abused man in the State."[31]

During December and January the campaign quieted down considerably, although Davis did everything he could to keep the fires of conflict burning. While his opponents were content to let matters simmer for awhile, he refused to let up. Day after day, week after week, he maintained an incredible pace of speechmaking and politicking. Jacobson, the man who arranged and coordinated the 1900 campaign schedule, once observed that Davis practiced a brand of mass politics unlike anything his opponents or anyone else in Arkansas had ever encountered:

> If Senator Davis became a popular idol with the masses of the people of Arkansas, he paid a price for his popularity that none other, either before or since, has been willing to pay. . . .
>
> He seemed to care little for the condition of the weather or the impassability of the roads, or the difficulty in reaching his appointments, most of them being in the remote parts of the state, and off the railroad lines. In arranging his appointments, he persistently enjoined upon me to fix them in the country and away from the larger towns. We therefore find him in the mountains of northwest Arkansas, far off the railroad, driving day and night, with icy winds chilling him to the bone, and the sleet and snow beating upon his face. At times he was compelled to speak at 10 o'clock in the morning at one point, then drive in an iron-rimmed buggy all day in order to reach the next speaking engagement in the evening, leaving again at the break of the following day for his next appointment, driving all that day, and so on, day after day, in rain or snow with but very poor hotel accommodations and at points where he could not possibly speak to more than forty or fifty people at a time. At other times we find him in the swamps fighting along the same way.
>
> To any man except Jeff Davis, a little of this kind of campaigning would have gone a long way, but the icy blasts could not cool the warmth and enthusiasm. To him it was a labor of love. . . . He constantly impressed upon me in fixing his itinerary to cover just as much territory as was possible within a given period of time, even to the extent of speaking as many as four or five times a day. Then is it any wonder that, enduring the hardships he did, in order to reach the people, he should become their idol? He used to tell them the trouble and difficulty he had in order to reach them, that his opponents, they of the silk-stocking brigade, the high-brows, would not come to the people, would not try to reach them in person, because they did not love the masses as he did; that he was one of them, that he had rather be sitting around with them and talking to them, than be seated at banquets with the highbrows or in the palaces of the great.[32]

Throughout the winter of 1899–1900, anti-Davis editors and politicians tried to convince the voters that Davis's stump-speaking odyssey was a shameless, irresponsible exhibition. How, they asked, could the attorney general fulfill his responsibilities when he spent most of his time out on the backwoods stump? Though neither side was willing to admit it, the answer was obvious: while Davis was out on the campaign trail, his assistant Charles Jacobson was back in Little Rock serving as a surrogate attorney general. Since Davis was reluctant to admit that he relied so heavily on his "Jew clerk," the charge of irresponsibility continued to plague him.[33] In most respects, however, the campaign continued to go his way. On December 16, James Wood withdrew from the race, stating that he had never intended to remain in the contest until the bitter end, but had entered the campaign only to debate with Davis on the stump.[34] The field was now reduced to three candidates, though not for long.

On February 7, less than a week before the official county canvass was scheduled to begin, John G. Fletcher, a sixty-nine year old Little Rock banker, announced that he was entering the governor's race. A Confederate veteran, Fletcher had already served three terms (1875–1881) as mayor of Little Rock, one term (1882–1884) as sheriff of Pulaski County, and had narrowly missed winning the Democratic gubernatorial nomination in 1884 and 1888. Originally a Whig, he had been a Democrat since the early years of Reconstruction, except for a brief flirtation with the Wheeler party in 1886. One of the wealthiest and most influential men in the state, Fletcher was the president of the German National Bank, which allegedly had refused to cash Jeff Davis's checks. During the battle over the Rector Act, he had been one of the primary spokesmen for the Little Rock business community, sharply criticizing Davis for his demagogic attack on the insurance industry. A forward-looking conservative—Davis called him the "solid stage-horse of the business interests of Arkansas"—Fletcher was the state's leading exponent of New South boosterism. In announcing his candidacy, he promised to give "the people a conservative administration of state affairs, viewed from the standpoint of a practical business man."[35]

This provided conservative Democrats with a much-needed rallying point. It also provided Davis with a conservative foil—the counterpoint that had been missing from the campaign since the withdrawal of James Wood. Unlike Bryant and Vandeventer, who portrayed themselves as moderate alternatives to Davis, Fletcher was unmistakably and unapologetically a conservative. The contrast between Davis and Fletcher could hardly have been more extreme. Young and full of bluster, Davis was pure insurgent. As the self-proclaimed champion of the dispossessed and the downtrodden, he was, in the language of the day, a "calamity howler." White-haired and distinguished—more businessman than politician—Fletcher was the epitome of the New South commercial elite. Having Old Man Fletcher out on the stump where the wool hat boys could see him was just what Davis needed to dramatize his attacks on the "high-collared crowd."

On February 12, the four candidates for governor gathered at Center Point for the opening of the county canvass.[36] An old tradition in general election campaigns, the county canvass was becoming an integral part of the new primary system. For more than a month, a political carnival would wind its way across the state, leaving a trail of hoarse voices, littered picnic grounds, and well-watered voters. Day after day, the candidates would speak from a common platform, testing and retesting each other's civility and stamina. The county canvass could be a grueling experience for older candidates or those unaccustomed to the rigors of stump speaking. But for gritty young politicians like Davis it was an ideal system.

Center Point was a friendly setting for a Davis stump speech. One of the oldest settlements in the state, it was located in Howard County, on the southern edge of the Ouachita foothills. Davis's birthplace in Little River County lay forty miles to the south. Long a center of agrarian unrest, Howard County had more than its share of struggling dirt farmers. Center Point, a small village with a declining population, had been bypassed by the railroads and lacked electric lights, banking facilities, and telephone and telegraph services. It had the look and feel of an antebellum farming community, whose culture was almost indistinguishable from that of the surrounding countryside.[37]

Davis's oration at Center Point was probably the most important stump speech of his career. Transcribed by a stenographer whom Davis had hired, the text of the speech was later reprinted in pamphlet form and distributed throughout the state. A masterful exhibition of spellbinding oratory and political theatrics, the performance at Center Point signaled Davis's coming of age as a mass leader. According to John Gould Fletcher, the Center Point speech was "Davis's greatest effort," and "stands as a landmark in Arkansas's cultural and social history."[38] Here, for the first time, Davis tried out many of the homely anecdotes and ringing phrases for which he would soon become famous. Drawing upon a clever blend of class rhetoric, rural chauvinism, sectionalism, and pure sentimentality, he alternately touched the heart and stirred the anger of the Arkansas backcountry:

Ah, gentlemen, the war is one. Not a battle between my opponents and me—they are gentlemen—but the war is one. It is knife to knife, hilt to hilt, foot to foot, knee to knee, between the corporations of Arkansas and the people. . . . I sued the Standard Oil Company, I sued the American Tobacco Company, I sued the Cotton Seed Oil Trust, I sued the express companies, I sued everything that looked like a trust. I sued them all.

I said everywhere and I say it here now, that the farmers are the bravest class of men upon the face of the earth. Why do I say that? The men who marched up the bloody heights of El Caney, or who stormed the forts of Manila were not braver than the farmers and laborers. Why?

The farmers toil day in and out trying to support themselves and families as God Almighty commanded them, in the sweat of their face, but if they were to sit down at night and figure up what they are going to make they would quit the next morning, and you know it. The fellow at the other end of the line is controlling prices. Are you going to dally with it; are you in earnest about this matter? Then, shut them out; don't let them come here. . . .

If I had wanted to take what apparently seemed to be the popular side at that time, wouldn't I have gone with the business men, where my distinguished friend, Col. John G. Fletcher, was? If I had wanted money out of it, as the newspapers seem to think I want out of the Governor's office, couldn't I have just held my hand behind me and got all I wanted? Then, ladies and gentlemen, at least give me credit for being honest. I have stood by the guns. I have gone through the fiery furnace, my opponents have not. There is no chance for trusts with me in this office. There might be with my opponents. . . .

Mr. Vandeventer will also tell you that I have not attended the Penitentiary Board meetings. They have been held in the private office of Governor Jones. Governor Jones does not speak to me. I told Mr. Sloan, the president, that as long as they met in Governor Jones's private office I would not be with them. When I fight a man upon principles, I want to fight him beside the clear waters, under the blue sky, in open, noble combat. I don't want to get shot in the back. If I die I want to die with my face to the rising sun, with my windows open towards Jerusalem. . . .

I say to you that the building of this Statehouse under the present plan is the biggest steal that was ever attempted to be perpetrated upon the people of Arkansas. . . . I did not start this row, but I am going to keep it up. They went out the other day on the Nineteenth Street Pike and bought fifteen acres of land upon which to build a new penitentiary. What did they give for it? Five thousand dollars. Fifteen acres of land! That land is so poor that two drunken men could not raise a difficulty upon it. It is so poor you could not raise an umbrella upon it. It is so poor you have to manure it to make brick out of it. . . .

I am not trying to array the country against Little Rock. There are many noble men and women living there: lots of them. God bless them. But there is a gang down there that needs cleaning out, and needs it awful bad. I would give ten years of my life in jail, if it were possible, to be Governor of the State of Arkansas two years to clean out some of the things down there; I will clean that gang so clean, if I am elected, that it will look like the Red River had run through it, and that's why they are after me. . . .

Gentlemen, I may never see you again. I hope that I will hold out physically in this race, if God will only give me strength. That is all I ask. . . . The fight is on. It is between the trusts and the corporations and the people. If I win this race I have got to win it from 525 insurance agents scattered all over the state. I have to win it from every railroad, every bank, and two-thirds of the lawyers and most of the big politicians. But If I can get the plain people of the country to help me, God bless you, we will clean the thing out.[39]

Each of Davis's opponents was accused of committing treason of one kind or another. Edgar Bryant had informed a Yankee audience at Chicago in 1893 that he was glad that the Confederacy had lost the Civil War. Vandeventer, who claimed to be a free-silver Democrat, had proven that he was still a goldbug at heart by refusing to contribute a dollar to help defray the travel expenses of William Jennings Bryan, a guest of the legislature in March 1899. Fletcher could not be trusted because he had bolted the Democratic party in 1886: "We needed your help then, Colonel Fletcher. Ah, you deserted us then. You said, 'Thank God, I was not born a Democrat.' You may say in answer to this that you was born a Whig. I thank God that I was born a Democrat and I am a Democrat yet. I have never camped in the camp of the enemy for one night." And if this were not enough to discredit Old Man Fletcher, there was the matter of his bank. "He is the president of a National Bank, in the biggest trust on earth," Davis reminded the crowd. "Gentlemen, didn't the National Banks, as a rule, help to defeat Mr. Bryan? Didn't Jefferson refuse to recharter them? Doesn't McKinley propose to turn the issuance of all money over to the National Banks? The money trust is the biggest trust on earth."[40]

In the weeks that followed, the state was flooded with copies of Davis's Center Point speech. In country stores and on country porches, farmers who had never seen a gubernatorial candidate, much less read one of his speeches, learned about the bravery and martyrdom of their attorney general. Since Davis was the first politician in Arkansas history to resort to pamphleting on a large scale (he had little choice, considering his relationship with the press), it is not surprising that the boys in the backwoods put on their reading glasses, or at least perked up their ears.[41] Whatever their politics, readers of the Center Point speech had to admit that Jeff was a fighter. "Our Jeff," as he came to be called, might be a bit crazy taking on the "high-collared roosters" all by himself, but he was clearly someone special.

As the county canvass proceeded across the state, Davis's three opponents tried unsuccessfully to push him from center stage. Every time one of them delivered a speech which focused on good roads or good morals and not on Jeff, he would say something outrageous which forced his opponent into a personal confrontation. Using a mixture of humor and pathos, he had little trouble keeping the opposition off stride. He criticized lumber merchant Vandeventer for "just lumbering around town." And he ridiculed Fletcher by repeatedly asking him how much buttermilk he had consumed while running as a Wheeler candidate in 1886. At Benton, Davis brought down the house when he ordered Fletcher to quit fidgeting in his seat: "Sit right still, colonel, for I am going to take the hide off and stick the mustard to you." Later in the same speech, he claimed that his campaign was "but a repetition of the Goebel race in Kentucky, where a good, true Democrat was assassinated." As the crowd stirred, he shook an angry finger at Fletcher and thundered: "I am not dead yet, colonel." These theatrics prompted Edgar Bryant to suggest mockingly that "the political savior of Arkansas" should be renamed "Saint Davis."[42]

Davis's extraordinary campaign had cast him into the spotlight, creating much heat and emotion. But as the county canvass drew to a close in early March it remained to be seen whether Arkansas Democrats would actually vote for such a man. Anti-Davis Democrats were hopeful that, once the county primaries began on March 10, the traditional conservatism of the average voter would reassert itself. Such hopes were soon dispelled.

The results of the first week of primaries sent Arkansas conservatives into a panic: running stronger than anyone had predicted, Davis won sweeping victories in five counties. In Howard County, the scene of the Center Point debate, he polled 62.5 percent of the vote, outdistancing his nearest rival by more than 600 votes; and in Lincoln County he polled a staggering 83.4 percent. Davis's showing was most impressive in that none of his victories could be attributed to a "friends and neighbors" vote. All five counties were located either in southwestern or southeastern Arkansas, and only one, Hot Spring County, was located within seventy-five miles of Russellville. If Davis was this popular in the South Arkansas lowlands, conservatives shuddered to think what the returns from the Ozark mountain counties were going to be like.[43]

The size of Davis's majorities in the early primaries stunned and demoralized his opponents. Convinced that he had no chance of winning the nomination, Bryant withdrew from the race on March 17. Five days later, after a disappointing showing in Miller County, John Fletcher followed suit. Always a somewhat reluctant candidate, Fletcher was too old and proud to subject himself to one humiliating defeat after another. Though he refused to discuss the matter publicly, his decision to withdraw was undoubtedly made easier by Davis's mudslinging tactics—particularly Davis's cruel insinuation that Fletcher had hounded his Populist brother into the grave.[44] Never at ease on the stump, Fletcher returned to his life as a gentleman banker with a sigh of relief.

By March 22, only A. F. Vandeventer stood between Jeff Davis and the Democratic gubernatorial nomination. With more than 90 percent of the county primaries left to go, the anti-Davis Democrats were hardly ready to throw in the towel. But even the optimists among them must have realized that Vandeventer faced a steep uphill climb. On March 31, Vandeventer eked out a narrow victory in Sebastian County, thanks to a large anti-Davis vote in Fort Smith, the state's second largest city. But from then on it was all Davis. During April and May, he piled up victory after victory, winning by increasingly large majorities. In several of the upcountry counties, he garnered more than 90 percent of the vote. On April 17, he even carried Pulaski County, which included the city of Little Rock.[45]

To the horror of the Democratic establishment, Davis was not only winning the nomination, he was becoming a living legend. As the unparalleled nature of his popularity became apparent, he began to take on the aura of a folk hero. According to the sociologist Rupert Vance, in Arkansas "fact becomes folklore if it is allowed to simmer overnight," and Davis's strength at the polls was no exception.[46] In late April, the newspapers carried an apocryphal story claiming that the invincible Jeff Davis had even carried a township in Louisiana. An enthusiastic campaign worker who reportedly had "lost all connection with geographic locations" had wandered into a Louisiana polling place and was shocked that Davis's name was not on the ballot. Informing the locals that they were "victims of a villainous political trick," he convinced them to vote for Jeff, who "carried the township solidly." A second story told of a ten-dollar bill, accompanied by a sign reading "The man who votes for Vandeventer may reach up and get me," placed above the door at a polling place in Wilson Township, in Ouachita County. When the polls closed that night, the bill was still there. Davis had won all of the township's 134 votes.[47]

As the inevitability of Davis's nomination became apparent, many editors retreated into silence. Tired of publicizing Davis's triumphs, they turned their attention to less painful subjects—national politics, the Boer War, anything to take their minds off of his impending victory. Anti-Davis editors who continued to cover the campaign began to tone down their criticisms of Davis; a few even feigned neutrality.

One prominent anti-Davis Democrat refused to give up. Colonel James Mitchell, the crusty old editor of the Little Rock *Arkansas Democrat*, published a series of editorials presenting a plan to derail the Davis express. It was based on the proposition that the county primaries in which Davis was doing so well were illegal. Mitchell reminded his readers that the Democratic State Central Committee had ordered all counties to hold their primaries on the same day, June 9, 1900. The fact that a majority of Democratic county organizations had ignored this order did not obviate party rules. Party leaders had the right—indeed, it was their duty—to invalidate the results of the early primaries and to order the county organizations in question to hold new primaries on June 9. Such a ruling would give anti-Davis leaders time to regroup and the voters time to come to their senses.

Davis supporters saw darker purposes in Mitchell's legalistic interpretation of party rules. According to John Page, the editor of the Dardanelle *Post-Dispatch* and a close friend of Davis's, Mitchell's plan was a front for a conspiratorial attempt to circumvent the primary system. As Mitchell and the other members of the "Little Rock gang" well knew, it was unlikely that the offending county organizations would agree to hold second primaries on June 9. The real Mitchell plan, Page contended, would unfold at the Democratic State Convention in June when the Central Committee recognized the credentials of anti-Davis delegations—delegations chosen not by the electorate but by ad hoc county conventions under the control of local oligarchies.[48] In this way Davis's seemingly insurmountable lead could be wiped out, or at least whittled down to the point where the state convention would be forced to turn to a dark horse candidate.

Although it soon became clear that very few Democratic leaders were willing to follow Mitchell's lead, the Davis camp continued to worry out loud about the likelihood of anti-Davis conspiracies. Through the final weeks of the campaign, there were rumblings that many anti-Davis Democrats planned to vote for the Republican candidate for governor, no matter whom the Republicans nominated. In early May, Page reported that "some of the Democratic politicians" were plotting "to work conjointly with the Republicans to obtain the appointment of election commissioners in the negro counties with a view to giving Jeff Davis the worst of it in the general election."[49] Anti-Davis editors filled their pages with pleas for Democratic solidarity, suggesting that these were more than empty rumors. "We have had enough of republican rule in Arkansas and don't want any more of it," the editor of the Arkadelphia *Southern-Standard* wrote in late April. "We voted for Jeff Davis for president of the Confederate States, and 'I reckon' we can stand it to vote for his illustrious namesake, Jeff Davis for Governor, that's the kind of democrat we are. It's true it will be a bitter pill for some to swallow, but we think when the proper time arrives they will walk up and take their medicine before they will vote for a republican."[50] The editor of the *Benton Democrat* predicted that the fact that a Republican governor might appoint "a buck nigger ought to be sufficient to bring the kickers into line. The *Democrat* is not fond of Jeff, and as long as there was reason in so doing, it opposed him, but right or wrong the democrats of the state have nominated him. Now let us all give him a fair trial."[51]

Many anti-Davis leaders may have considered the option of helping the Republicans to defeat Davis, but in the end very few were willing to take such a risk. Their decision to stick with the Democratic party can be attributed to a number of factors: the deeply held belief that white supremacy depended upon Democratic solidarity; the suspicion that Davis was more demagogic than radical; the fear of sharing the fate of the anti-Tillman Democrats, who had bolted the party in South Carolina in 1890; the realization that bolting would be a futile gesture, since the voters would almost certainly put Davis in the governor's office anyway; and, in the latter stages of the campaign, the recognition that the Davis movement was no longer exclusively a mass movement. The significance of this final factor cannot be overemphasized. As the probability of Davis's nomination became high, many Democratic politicians began to grab onto his coattails. By the end of April, the few politicians who had supported Davis all along had been joined by hundreds of recently converted "Jeff Davis men."[52] Some of these new recruits were drawn to Davis because of his political style or ideology; others were opportunists who simply wanted to go with a winner. Whatever their motivation, they permanently altered the relationship between Jeff Davis and the political elite.

Most of the politicians who rushed to identify with Davis were minor figures, such as delegates to county conventions and other local politicos. But as the magnitude of Davis's following became apparent, bifactionalism began to emerge in the upper echelons of the party. Several candidates for other state offices let it be known that they considered themselves to be friends of Jeff Davis. No one went so far as to identify himself as part of a

Davis ticket, because at that time it was considered unethical for a group of Democratic candidates to form an official slate. But press charges that there was such a ticket were not altogether groundless, since in several cases Davis issued reciprocal endorsements.[53] Davis's endorsements of other statewide candidates were communicated behind the scenes either through the political grapevine or leaks to the press. Despite this discretion, by the beginning of May there was little doubt as to whom Davis was supporting in each of the four contested statewide races.

Davis's choice for attorney general was George W. Murphy, a fifty-nine year old Alabama-born Confederate veteran. He had served under Nathan Bedford Forrest and had been crippled by a Yankee bullet at Murfreesboro. One of Arkansas's best-known criminal lawyers, Murphy had practiced law in Little Rock since 1891. He was the former law partner of Judge Thomas B. Martin, the chancery judge who had foiled Davis's attempt to prevent the destruction of the state penitentiary in 1899. For secretary of state, Davis supported John W. Crockett of Arkansas County, the son of a Confederate colonel and the great-grandson of the folk hero Davy Crockett. For state auditor, he supported Thomas C. Monroe, a rather colorless Confederate veteran from Columbia County. Finally, in the United States Senate race, Davis backed the incumbent, Senator James Berry, who was being challenged by Governor Dan Jones. Here, Davis openly campaigned for his favorite, though his remarks were invariably more anti-Jones than pro-Berry.[54]

Jones, who withdrew from the race on March 23 after losing seven of the first eight county primaries, never forgave Davis for interfering in the senatorial campaign. With his political career in ruins, he came to hate Davis and verbally attacked him at every opportunity. In a May 25 speech at Little Rock, Jones told the following story:

> A distinguished gentleman in Washington city said to me last week, "What's the matter with your people down in Arkansas? I thought you had one of the greatest states in the union, but why are your people now electing an anarchist to the governorship?" I told him to watch the future and see how the people of Arkansas can surmount and survive the severest catastrophe which may overtake it.[55]

Davis, as always, had the last laugh. Before the day was over, he had retaliated with a series of low blows which left Jones reeling:

> When I go to a funeral I never kick the corpse, but we have a political funeral on now and I propose to give the corpse one parting kick, although it is hardly safe to kick so defunct a corpse as we have on our hands. Gov. Jones says I am an anarchist. If anarchy means to stand for the rights of the laboring man, then I'm an anarchist. Thank the Lord, I never deserted from the Southern army. I make a serious charge, but it is the absolute truth when I say that Dan W. Jones, the Democratic governor of Arkansas, is now conjuring a scheme to secure election

officers so that I can be counted out and Mr. Remmel [the probable Republican nominee for governor] counted in. He was hobnobbing and champaigning all over Hot Springs yesterday with Mr. Remmel, but I say let them name the best man the Republicans can put forward and if they dare rob the Democrats of Arkansas they will rue the day.[56]

Davis's sweetest revenge came the following day, when he clinched the gubernatorial nomination by winning primary elections in White and Johnson Counties. More than thirty of the state's seventy-five counties had not yet held primaries, but Davis's showing to date insured that he would have the support of a majority of the delegates to the Democratic State Convention. When the final thirty-two county primaries were held on June 9, Vandeventer's name was still on the ballot, but in most cases he received only a token vote.[57] Jeff Davis, the wild man from Pope County, had swept all before him. Carrying seventy-four of seventy-five counties, he had won the most resounding political victory in the state's history.

Reactions ranged from stunned silence to outright awe. John Page, the fiery pro-Davis editor from Yell County, could hardly contain himself: "The Jeff Davis groundswell has thrown some of the little jack-snapper politicians who belong to the 'more intelligent' and 'better element class,' so high in the air that they are coming down with benighted minds as well as bespraddled limbs." Anti-Davis editors, however, were surprisingly good-natured in defeat. Even the *Arkansas Gazette*, which had pilloried Davis throughout the campaign, poked fun at the anti-Davis coalition: "Gov. Jones and the capitol commissioners deny that Attorney General Jeff Davis is the state of Arkansas, and they are right about it. Gen. Davis carried only seventy-four of the seventy-five counties of the state. He is only seventy-four seventy-fifths of the state of Arkansas, and thus he lacks a little, at least, of being the whole thing." Adam Clark, an anti-Davis editor from Clarke County, warned his readers that they had to face facts: the upstart attorney general had eclipsed "any record made by any candidate for any office in Arkansas."[58] In the same spirit, an anti-Davis man in Montgomery County sent Davis a half-dead rooster along with a note that read:

I am the fellow that voted against Jeff Davis in Montgomery County. I am on my way to the state convention. I am originally from Sebastian County. I have not been in Little Rock since the business men's convention in 1899.

   Boys, I've done the best that I could, but I met the Davis boom, and you see the condition in which I am left. If I am dead when I arrive have the hearse meet me at the depot and give me a decent burial for I represent the only opposition that is left to Jefferson Davis.[59]

7

The Boys up the Forks
of the Creek

The papers say that nobody will vote for me except the fellow
who wears patched breeches and one gallus and lives up the forks
of the creek, and don't pay anything but his poll tax. I don't know
how true that is, but I want to tell you that there is no great
reformation that originated on the earth that did not come from
the ranks of the humble and lowly of the land.

—*Jeff Davis (1900)*[1]

Who voted for Jeff Davis in 1900? Who voted against him? Any
attempt to answer these questions is complicated by the peculiar
nature of the 1900 primary. Since nearly half of the state's counties
held their primaries after Davis had clinched the nomination, a statewide
analysis of county-level returns would be meaningless. In any event, such
an analysis is impossible because the primary returns for a number of
countries were never published. Our only alternative is to rely on scattered
precinct-level data.

Fortunately, precinct returns from five "sample" counties have survived.
These counties are: Howard, an isolated county located on the southern
edge of the Ouachita Mountains in southwest Arkansas; Pulaski, a predominantly lowland plantation county which includes the city of Little Rock;
Sebastian, a semimountainous Arkansas River Valley county which includes
the city of Fort Smith; St. Francis, an East Arkansas plantation county which
straddles Crowley's Ridge; and Washington, an Ozark mountain county
which includes the city of Fayetteville. Though they do not represent a
systematic or random sample, these precinct returns should give us a rough
idea of the size and shape of the 1900 Davis coalition.

Any analysis of Davis's following must take into account the sheer magnitude of his victory. When a candidate carries seventy-four of seventy-five
counties, his support is broad-based. This was certainly the case in the five-
county sample, where Davis won a majority of the vote in 80 of 101 pre-

TABLE 3
The 1900 Davis Vote: Precinct Returns,
Five County Sample

Type of Precinct*	N	Group Mean % for Davis 1900
City	3	46.2
Large Town–Farm	5	58.2
Small Town–Farm	7	62.2
Village-Farm	11	72.3
Hamlet-Farm	19	75.2
Farm (Suburban)	3	60.1
Farm (Central)	23	65.2
Farm (Isolated)	23	74.7
Farm (Very Isolated)	7	62.1

*The criteria used to construct this categorization scheme are described in Appendix B.
SOURCE: See Appendix B.

cincts. Nevertheless, as the data in Table 3 and Appendix B demonstrate, Davis ran much better in some precincts than in others.

The precincts in Table 3 have been grouped according to community type. Ranging from city precincts to "very isolated" farm precincts, the nine categories in the table represent a continuum of urbanization/metropolitanization. Most of Davis's opposition was concentrated at the urban end of the scale, which is not surprising given his running feud with the business community and a campaign rhetoric that featured a hardy strain of rural chauvinism. Predictably, he was least popular in the city precincts. In Little Rock, he polled only 40.5 percent of the vote, despite the fact that he was extremely popular (79.7 percent) in the rural precincts of Pulaski County. He did even worse in Fort Smith, polling barely a third of the vote. Only in Argenta, a city dominated by railway employees and other working class voters, did Davis poll a respectable vote (62.2 percent) among city dwellers.[2]

Davis did somewhat better in the "county seat town" precincts, but here too he ran well behind his showing in rural Arkansas. Since these precincts included a substantial number of farm voters, it does not appear that Davis's following in the county seat towns was any larger than his following in the cities. With few exceptions, the same was true in the smaller incorporated towns.

When we drop to the next level of urbanization, however, we find a markedly different situation. Davis was extremely popular in precincts that included small villages and hamlets—more popular, in fact, than in exclusively rural areas. His strong showing was related to the fact that most of these small communities had few of the trappings of modern urban life. Electric lights, telephone and telegraph service, daily mail, paved streets, streetcars, hotels and restaurants, banks and brokerage houses were generally limited to the larger towns and cities.[3] Although most villages and some hamlets were located along railway lines, their residents had more in common with the farmers of the surrounding countryside than with the businessmen and planter-merchants of Arkansas's burgeoning "electric light" towns. Like the small farmers with whom they did business, they lived on the fringe of the new metropolitan society. Many villagers obviously were caught between two worlds, but the vast majority apparently were more comfortable with Jeff Davis's nostalgic agrarianism than with the New South commercialism of his opponents. Arkansas villagers lived on one side of a political and cultural fault line, it seems, while most town and city dwellers lived on the other.

Table 3 and Appendix B demonstrate that Davis's claim that he was "the Tribune of Haybinders" was not an idle boast. Not all Arkansas farmers were Jeff Davis men. Indeed, in some farm precincts Davis was extremely unpopular. But by and large he made a strong showing in exclusively rural precincts. He won at least 65 percent of the vote in 36 of the 56 rural precincts listed in Appendix B. In 24 of these precincts, he won more than 80 percent of the vote.

Why did Davis do so well in some farm precincts and so poorly in others? An authoritative answer to this question is beyond our reach. Since the published version of the 1900 federal census contains very little precinct-level data and since the manuscript returns of the agricultural and manufacturing censuses have been destroyed, we must rely on the limited data found in business directories, local tax records, and the manuscript returns of the 1900 population census schedules. Using these three sources, we can at least estimate the impact of physical isolation and socioeconomic class on the distribution of the Davis vote.

The anti-Davis press often claimed that most of Davis's support came from the ignorant hillbillies who lived in the backwoods. Davis himself did little to dispel this notion. He expressed his affection for "the boys who live up the forks of the creek" at every opportunity, and he loved to repeat the *Helena Weekly World*'s charge that he was "a friend to the fellow who brews forty-rod bug-juice back in the mountains."[4] Was his support concentrated in remote backcountry townships? Table 3, which uses proximity to the nearest railroad stop as a crude measure of isolation, yields mixed results.[5] Davis did not win a large majority of the vote among farmers who lived within five miles of the nearest railroad stop. Yet he made an equally poor showing at the other end of the spectrum—in remote farm precincts located more than fifteen miles from the nearest shipping point. His popularity was greatest among farmers who lived in townships that were isolated but not remote—townships between six and fifteen miles from the nearest railroad stop. Although this data is obviously too rough to support fine lines of interpretation, it is clearly an oversimplification to say that Jeff Davisism and isolation went hand-in-hand.

In the absence of additional ecological data, we can only speculate as to why Davis ran so well in moderately isolated precincts. This pattern may have had as much to do with economic vulnerability and cultural autonomy as it did with physical isolation per se. Farmers in these precincts were less commercial and less prosperous than farmers who lived in more centrally located townships. Yet, unlike their backcountry cousins, they did have some direct interaction with town-dwelling businessmen and the metropolitan economy. In other words, their position on the fringe of the new order made them especially receptive to Davis's message, which focused on the dangers of an encroaching New South colonialism. At the same time, Davis's relatively poor showing in remote precincts was probably partly a function of a lack of political information. Although Davis made a Herculean effort to spread his message to the backcountry, there were hollows and mountain coves that even he could not reach.

The class dimension of the Davis movement is even more difficult to assess (though you would never know it by looking at previous studies of Davis's career). No one has ever systematically examined the class composition of the Davis coalition, but historians have generally agreed that class conflict was at the heart of Jeff Davisism.[6] Rupert Vance, in a classic essay entitled "A Karl Marx for Hill Billies," claimed that "in a state that possessed no aristocracy against whom they might rebel Davis led a revolt of the dispossessed poor whites." Using the concepts of class protest and anticolonialism almost interchangeably, Vance concluded:

> It was farmer against planter, common man against enfeebled aristocrat, Populist against Democrat, rustics against city dudes. But if Arkansas had no aristocrats to overturn, its towns had grown up and were developing a professional class of lawyers, doctors, merchants, and absentee landlords rising mildly above the dead level of reconstruction poverty. The capital had already grown into the wonder and envy of the haybinder. As Davis was to tell them, the horny-handed sunburned sons of toil yearly pulled the bell ropes over old Jerry only to have the price of their fleecy product set by the gamblers of the New York Cotton Exchange. . . . In no abstruse terms of economics he led the red neck and the patched britches brigade on a holy crusade against the malefactors of great wealth. Instead of seven against Thebes it was Arkansas against the trusts. Before he reached the Senate this Jeff the Giant Killer who had never heard of Karl Marx was to carry his truly grotesque version of the class struggle to the coves of all the mountains, forks of all the creeks, and banks of all the bayous in Arkansas. In the South one must understand that politics like agrarian religion is likely to be the outgrowth of poverty experience. A clear conscience and the witness of the spirit to the soul's salvation, things denied the wealthy, compensate the rustic for his ungained competence. Likewise the poor but honest yeoman of the plough arises on election day, and with the untainted ballot thrust in his hands by Democracy, strikes down the minions of pelf, pride, and plutocracy.[7]

Following Vance's lead, C. Vann Woodward concluded that Davis was a spokesman for the "'one gallus' proletariat." "In the dialectics of this 'Karl

Marx for Hill Billies,'" Woodward writes, "the class struggle was waged between the 'red necks' and their mortal enemies, the 'high-collared roosters' of the city." Similarly, John Ezell has argued that Davis "campaigned for governor by pitting class against class." David Y. Thomas, who observed early twentieth-century Arkansas politics at close range, described Davis as the "one gallus statesman." More recently, Richard Niswonger argued that "Davis' agrarianism . . . became a conscious appeal to class interest."[8]

Most contemporary political commentators expressed similar judgments. "There is never any issue in a Jeff Davis campaign but class against class, and Jeff Davis the martyr of the common kind," one New York journalist declared.[9] James E. Wood, Davis's bitter rival during the early stages of the 1900 campaign, claimed "that three-fourths of the Davis supporters" were so low-down that they "did not even pay poll tax."[10] In a more dispassionate vein, J. N. Heiskell, the editor of the *Arkansas Gazette*, concluded that Davis's greatest political asset was "his infinite democracy."

> He makes honest people out in the State think that at Little Rock there is an aristocracy of purse-proud plutocrats who menace the interests of the plebeians, and that all may be lost unless their tribune of the people is kept in power, so that he can effectually oppose the sinister machinations of the patricians. To an audience of workingmen he ridicules that harmless institution called "society"—that is, the folks who wear formal dress and play bridge whist. Then he tells the workingmen that he is one of them, and that if he ever "gives a party" they are the people he wants for his guests. It is an easy game. Envy inheres in the human breast.[11]

The only political commentators who seemed reluctant to characterize Davis as a predominantly lower-class spokesman were his political allies. Speaking at the 1902 Democratic State Convention, Davis's close friend Judge Emon Mahoney denied that the governor was essentially a rabble-rouser. "He is at once a patrician and a plebian," Mahoney insisted. "He is neither demi-god nor demagogue: neither sockless nor 'silk stocking,' but a comely, manly man."[12] L. S. Dunaway, a Little Rock journalist who was close to Davis throughout his career, wrote in 1913:

> It has been said that Senator Davis tried to array class against class. I do not think this is true. I do know that his heart was always beating in tune with the great throbbing heart of the people, and his sympathies were with those who toil in the various walks of life. . . . While it is true that the so-called "red-necks" and "hill-billies" (terms coined by him) were lined up with Senator Davis, it is also true that the leading business and professional men in the largest towns and cities of the State were often his staunchest supporters. He classed among his closest friends some of the leading citizens and wealthiest men of the State; men who stood high in social, business and intellectual circles.[13]

Mahoney and Dunaway, like most middle-class politicians who become involved in a mass movement, obviously wanted to have it both ways. To a limited extent, this was true of Davis himself. On the one hand, he relied heavily on class rhetoric. No Davis stump speech was complete without an affectionate reference to "the humble and lowly of the land," "the horny-handed, sunburned sons of toil," "the farmer with a patch on the seat of his pants as big as the map of South America," and "the fellow who wears patched breeches and one gallus and lives up the forks of the creek, and don't pay anything except his poll tax." Such references were usually accompanied by an equally class-oriented caricature of the opposition: "the wealth consuming class," "the robbers who have gathered in fields that they have not sown," "the silk-stocking crowd," "the high-collared crowd that wear collars so high they can't see the sun except at high noon. . . . the crowd that when they shake hands with you they only give you the tip of their finger."[14] It is little wonder that Rupert Vance dubbed old Jeff "A Karl Marx for Hill Billies."

Still, it is not clear how the voters interpreted all this. Throughout the 1900 campaign, Davis's class rhetoric was as vague as it was abundant. Like most American politicians, he was purposely ambiguous on the class issue. Although he talked about economic oppression in class terms, his working definition of class was based more on the cultural and social gap between town and country, or the gap between North and South, than on the distribution of wealth per se. While he had harsh words for the urban business community, he did not attack the equally wealthy planter class, at least in 1900. Nor did he make a specific appeal for the votes of tenant farmers, as Farmer Jim Ferguson would later do in Texas.[15]

Where did the "toiling masses" end and the "priviliged classes" begin? After stacking the deck a bit, Davis let each voter decide for himself. In a state where class lines were relatively fluid and where divisions of social and economic class were seldom perfectly aligned, it would have been foolish to do otherwise. As J. N. Heiskell observed in 1906, Davis's political strategy was simple: "He labors to divide the people against themselves in order that he may become the champion of the bigger class, those whom he invidiously calls 'the common people.'"[16] The end result, in terms of rhetoric, was a distinctly lower-middle-class orientation. For the most part, Davis directed his campaign efforts not at the low-down poor whites, but at the "honest yeomen" who had fallen on hard times, a category that even some planters could identify with. This strategy conformed to Arkansas's economic and social class structure and made good political sense. At least 55 percent of the state's Democratic electorate was made up of landowning yeomen, some relatively prosperous, but most struggling to keep their farms. The remaining 45 percent was divided among tenant farmers and farm laborers (approximately 30 percent), town dwellers and villagers (10 percent), and agrarian planters and country merchants (5 percent). There was also a small leaven of miners, timber workers, railroad workers, and draymen.[17] If Davis had restricted his appeal to landless tenants and other poor whites, it would have been political suicide. Despite a large measure of eschatological oratory, Davis was a shrewd politician who sought to maximize his friends and minimize his enemies. Making no attempt to disentangle the class issue from anticolonialism and antiurban sentiment, he left the door open for the entire agricultural community to support him. Of course, whether or not he actually attracted the support of a significant number of planters and prosperous yeomen is another question.

A limited class analysis of Davis's following is possible using three measures of socioeconomic class: assessed value of personal property (for Wash-

TABLE 4
The Distribution of Wealth and the 1900 Davis Vote in
Washington County: Rank-Order Correlation

Township	Personal Property Per Taxpayer, 1903	Rank	% for Jeff Davis, 1900	Rank
	$			
Vineyard	450	1	83.3	9.5
Springdale	357	2	64.6	26
Prairie	354	3	68.3	22
Prairie Grove	338	4	87.7	4
Marrs Hill	305	5	87.0	5
Illinois	284	6	88.5	2
Goshen	264	7	85.8	8
Wheeler	260	8	65.7	24
Rheas Mill	259	9	70.7	19
Cane Hill	258	10	79.4	14
Center	258	11	86.9	6
Price	256	12	83.3	9.5
Richland	242	13	75.3	15
Elm Springs	238	14	68.4	21
Wyman	234	15	73.9	16
Wedington	230	16	83.0	11
Brush Creek	228	17	87.8	3
Dutch Mills	220	18	65.2	25
Star Hill	186	19	81.8	12
Durham	183	20	67.6	23
White River	183	21	55.7	27
Boston	180	22	35.0	29
Valley	178	23	80.2	13
Cove Creek	164	24	73.5	17
Winslow	155	25	46.3	28
Reed	149	26	86.7	7
West Fork	147	27	73.3	18
Lees Creek	146	28	100.0	1
Crawford	145	29	68.8	20

$R_s = +.187$

SOURCES: Washington County Tax Book for 1903, located at the Washington County Courthouse, Fayetteville, Arkansas; *Springdale News*, April 20, 1900.

ington County), illiteracy (for Howard and St. Francis Counties), and farm tenancy (for Howard and St. Francis Counties). While none of these indices is an ideal measure of socioeconomic class or status, collectively they should provide us with a rough estimate of the class composition of the Davis vote.

An analysis of personal property tax data in Washington County lends little support to the notion that Davis's following was concentrated among the poorest elements of the white population (see Table 4). Instead of uncovering a strong negative correlation between wealth and the Davis vote, the analysis reveals a mildly positive rank-order coefficient, +.187. Davis was just as popular in Washington County's more affluent precincts as he was in the poor precincts. Although his amazing showing in Lees Creek, the second poorest township in the county, is suggestive, most of the evidence points the other way. In Vineyard, the county's wealthiest township, Davis received 83.3 percent of the vote; while in Crawford, the county's poorest township, he received only 68.8 percent. Most strikingly, Davis won less than 60 percent of the vote in three of the poorest precincts in the county.

The illiteracy and farm tenancy statistics in Tables 5 and 6 are more difficult to interpret, but they present a similar picture. The high positive correlations between the Davis vote and illiteracy (+.800) and farm tenancy (+.764) in St. Francis County suggest that Davis's popularity was greatest

TABLE 5

Illiteracy, Farm Tenancy, and the 1900 Davis Vote in St. Francis County: Rank-Order Correlations

Township	White Illiteracy Rate 1900*	Rank	White Farm Tenancy† Rate 1900*	Rank	% for Jeff Davis, 1900	Rank
Blackfish	29.3	1	54.3	3	94.7	3
L'Anguille	19.4	2	40.9	9	89.3	7
Griggs	18.0	3	64.5	1	100.0	1
Johnson	14.5	4	50.3	5	95.3	2
Franks	11.2	5	56.4	2	92.2	5
Goodwin	10.3	6	45.7	8	93.1	4
Telico	8.8	7	51.2	4	91.3	6
Wheatley	7.4	8	46.3	7	82.3	9
Prairie	5.1	9	47.6	6	88.5	8
Madison	0.0	10.5	33.3	11	73.3	10
Forrest City	0.0	10.5	38.4	10	53.1	11

Illiteracy and Farm Tenancy: R_s=+.589
Illiteracy and the Davis Vote: R_s=+.800
Farm Tenancy and the Davis Vote: R_s=+.764

*Among white heads of households.
†"Farm laborers" have been grouped with tenant farmers.
SOURCES: *12th Census of the United States, 1900, Population Schedules,* Manuscript Returns for St. Francis County, Arkansas, located at the National Archives, Washington, D.C.; Forrest City *Times,* April 13, 1900.

TABLE 6
Illiteracy, Farm Tenancy, and the 1900 Davis Vote in Howard County:
Rank-Order Correlations

Township	White Illiteracy Rate 1900*	Rank	White Farm Tenancy† Rate 1900*	Rank	% for Jeff Davis, 1900	Rank
Muddy Fork	25.2	1	38.4	7	76.5	8
Madison	21.7	2	25.0	12	93.1	1
Holly Creek	21.4	3	14.3	16	79.2	6
Mountain	20.7	4	16.5	15	87.8	3
Clay	18.9	5	22.6	13	17.6	18
Sulphur Springs	18.6	6	14.1	17	85.7	4
Dillard	14.5	7	40.7	6	45.6	14
Blue Ridge	14.1	8	9.8	18	51.9	12
Baker	13.3	9.5	18.7	14	79.2	7
Franklin	13.3	9.5	55.2	4	31.6	17
Center Point	13.3	11	45.0	5	63.9	10
Saratoga	12.2	12	60.0	2	65.7	9
Saline	11.5	13	31.6	10	47.1	13
Blackland	9.0	14	61.5	1	62.3	11
Brewer	8.4	15	27.8	11	92.3	2
County Line	8.2	16	35.6	8	81.0	5
Mineral Springs	8.1	17	56.9	3	44.8	15
Nashville	2.3	18	33.5	9	44.4	16

Illiteracy and Farm Tenancy: $R_s=-.481$
Illiteracy and the Davis Vote: $R_s=+.301$
Farm Tenancy and the Davis Vote: $R_s=-.387$

*Among white heads of households.
†"Farm laborers" have been grouped with tenant farmers.
SOURCES: *12th Census of the United States, 1900, Population Schedules,* Manuscript Returns for Howard County, Arkansas, located at the National Archives, Washington, D.C.; *Nashville News,* March 21, 1900.

among lower-class voters. Nevertheless, Davis's support in St. Francis County was consistently strong. With the exception of Forrest City, the county seat, every township in the county, regardless of its class profile, rallied behind Davis's candidacy. Even in Madison Township, where the majority of Democratic voters belonged to the planter class, Davis received 73.3 percent of the vote.[18]

In upland Howard County, where white illiteracy and white farm tenancy did not always go hand-in-hand (the illiteracy rate was 12.7 percent among white farm owners and 18.4 percent among white tenants and farm laborers), a rather curious pattern emerges. Here Davis's popularity was greatest in precincts with *high* illiteracy rates and *low* farm tenancy rates. Why this was so is unclear, though we might speculate that anti-Davis planter-merchants were influencing the votes of their tenants. It is clear that, for the most part, these figures do not support a lower-class interpretation of the early Davis movement. Once again most of the evidence suggests that in 1900 Davis was as popular among the landowning yeomanry as he was among poor whites. Although the most downtrodden elements of the white population may have been Davis's most enthusiastic supporters, they did not dominate the Davis coalition numerically.

Precinct returns can also provide us with a glimpse of the relationships between Jeff Davisism and other political movements, such as the Populist and Prohibitionist movements. The nexus between the Davis movement and Populism is particularly interesting. Noting that the two movements were similar in style and ideology, historians have routinely described Davis as a "neo-Populist."[19] It has generally been assumed that Davis's militant agrarianism and trust-busting exploits evoked memories of a lost cause among Populists, even though Jeff himself was never a member of the People's party. As Clifton Paisley has written, Davis was one loyal Democrat who "learned to speak their language." Correspondingly, most students of Arkansas politics have assumed that Davis attracted the support of a large number of ex-Populists. Richard Dixon has argued that Davis's "resiliency in incorporating agrarian demands into his program caused many Populists to support Davis with loyalty." Similarly, Richard Niswonger concluded that "much of Davis' strength came from those within the Democratic party who had assimilated Populist doctrine and attitudes or who formerly voted with a third party." Niswonger tried to prove his case by conducting a rudimentary county-level voting analysis of the 1900 general election returns, but most students of the continuity question have based their conclusions solely on rhetorical analysis.[20]

Although it is certainly plausible that the Davis coalition included a number of ex-Populists, there is reason to believe that historians have overestimated the amount of electoral continuity between the two movements, at least as far as the 1900 campaign is concerned. For one thing, prior to the 1906 primary campaign Davis did not make an explicit appeal for the votes of former Populists. Like most Democratic leaders, during general election campaigns he urged the old Populists to return to the party of Jefferson and Jackson. But he did not make an overt attempt to pad the Davis faction with ex-Populists. Secondly, not one of the leading figures of the Arkansas People's party endorsed Davis's candidacy during the 1900 primary campaign. On the contrary, several Populist leaders were openly contemptuous of Davis's brand of agrarian radicalism. W. Scott Morgan, the state's leading Populist editor, thought that Davis was an unprincipled charlatan. "The Hon. Jeff Davis, the so-called Attorney General of Arkansas," Morgan wrote in October 1899, "is a conspicuous example of a little man in a big place. . . . a conspicuous example of the fact that people can go crazy enough about politics to elect a crazy man to a responsible position." The 1900 primary campaign did not lessen Morgan's contempt for Davis. "Jeff Davis may not be a fair representative of Arkansas Democrats," he wrote in July 1900, "but he is a legitimate result of their methods. Rotten methods will put rotten men and blatherskites in office."[21]

Did former Populists constitute an important element of the 1900 Davis coalition? While it is impossible to offer an authoritative answer to this question in the absence of individual-level voting data, the aggregate data in Tables 7 and 8 suggest that this was not the case. If a large number of former Populists supported Davis in the 1900 Democratic primary, the correlation between the Davis vote and the old Populist vote should be strongly positive. Significantly, with the exception of the Pulaski County coefficient, the rank-order correlations between Populism and the Davis vote are all either extremely low or, in the case of Washington County, moderately negative.[22] Although Davis polled a relatively large vote in most of the old Populist strongholds (see Table 8), he did equally well in non-Populist precincts. Though somewhat inconclusive, these figures demonstrate that the amount of electoral continuity between Populism and Jeff Davisism varied widely from county to county and from precinct to precinct, and that in some areas Davis had limited success in attracting the votes of former Populists. In later campaigns, he would fare somewhat better among ex-Populists. But it would never be an easy task to convince the old radicals that he was an authentic neo-Populist.

TABLE 7
Rank-Order Correlations Between the 1900 Davis Vote and Selected Electoral Variables,
Five County Sample

	Counties				
Variable	Howard	Pulaski	St. Francis	Sebastian	Washington
Populist Vote For Governor, 1892* or 1894	.038*	.353	−.009*	.135	−.383
Prohibitionist Vote (Anti-License), 1900	NA	−.198	−.155	−.052	.206
George Murphy (Att. General), 1900 Primary	.402	.426	.464	.335	−.263
John Crockett (Sec. of State), 1900 Primary	.206	.197	.182	.163	.003
Sheriff or Prose. Attorney (**)	.587	.047	.300 .127**	NA	NA
County Judge or Assessor (**)	.331	.187	.100**	.016	NA

SOURCES: *Nashville News,* September 24, 1892, March 21, 1900; *Arkansas Gazette,* September 7, 1894, April 22, September 7, 1900; *Forrest City Times,* September 9, 1892, April 13, September 14, 1900; *Fort Smith Elevator,* September 14, 1894, April 6, September 14, 1900; *Springdale News,* September 21, 1894, April 20, September 14, 1900.

TABLE 8
Populist Precincts: Support for Jeff Davis in the 1900 Gubernatorial Primary,
Five County Sample*

			Populist Vote		
Precinct	County	% for Jeff Davis, 1900	% for J.P. Carnahan, 1892	% for D.E. Barker, 1894	% for A.W. Files, 1900
Union	Pulaski	96.9	NA	41.1	3.4
Johnson	St. Francis	95.3	36.2	40.9	3.0
Goodwin	St. Francis	93.1	27.0	40.2	0.0
Madison	Howard	93.1	64.0	NA	NA
Telico	St. Francis	91.3	56.1	41.0	0.0
L'Anguille	St. Francis	89.3	69.3	54.4	0.0
Prairie	St. Francis	88.5	60.8	69.9	3.0
Owen	Pulaski	87.3	NA	52.8	1.2
Ellis	Pulaski	86.6	NA	48.8	0.0
Vineyard	Washington	83.3	NA	54.1	11.2
Wheatley	St. Francis	82.3	44.4	9.6	0.0
Maumelle	Pulaski	81.4	NA	72.0	0.0
County Line	Howard	81.0	46.5	NA	NA
Mineral	Pulaski	77.3	NA	42.2	2.5
Muddy Fork	Howard	76.5	52.6	NA	NA
Cove Creek	Washington	73.5	NA	45.1	21.0
Crawford	Washington	68.8	NA	60.4	10.1
Mississippi	Sebastian	63.3	NA	44.7	0.0
Blue Ridge	Howard	51.9	53.3	NA	NA
Dillard	Howard	45.6	65.5	NA	NA
Boston	Washington	35.0	NA	75.5	13.8
Franklin	Howard	31.6	53.8	NA	NA
Clay	Howard	17.6	44.9	NA	NA

*Populist precincts are defined here as precincts in which the Populist gubernatorial candidate received 40
  percent or more of the vote in 1892 or 1894.
SOURCES: See Table 7.

The Prohibitionist movement had even less impact on the distribution of
Davis's support in 1900. Using the anti-saloon license vote in the September
1900 local-option referendum as a measure of Prohibitionist sentiment,
Table 7 demonstrates that the level of association between Jeff Davisism and
the temperance crusade was extremely low. As Table 9 illustrates, Davis ran
well in some Prohibitionist strongholds and poorly in others. This is hardly
surprising, since the liquor issue was never raised during the campaign.
Although conflict between "wets" and "drys" ultimately would play an important role in Davis's career, it did not affect his rise to power in 1900.

Our five-county sample also allows us to measure the degree of Democratic factionalism in the 1900 campaign. Did the voters perceive a "Davis
ticket" in 1900 and vote accordingly? The figures in Table 7 indicate that, in
most cases, they did not. Factional voting was most obvious in the attorney
general's race, where there was clearly a significant overlap between the

Davis and Murphy coalitions. Yet even in the attorney general's race, split-ticket voting was relatively common. The low magnitude of the positive correlations between the Murphy vote and the Davis vote suggests that many voters were either unaware of or unmoved by the two candidates' factional ties. In the case of John W. Crockett, Davis's choice for secretary of state, there is even less evidence of factional alignment. Moreover, as the coefficients in Table 7 indicate, there was no consistent pattern of bifactionalism where local offices were concerned. The vast majority of Arkansas Democrats either did not know or did not care whether a given candidate for local office was pro- or anti-Davis. Of course, these figures do not tell the whole story. Although gubernatorial politics had relatively little impact on most local races prior to the county primaries, many counties witnessed a good deal of post-election coattail grabbing.[23] Once Davis had clinched the nomination, many local politicians who had been reluctant to commit themselves during the campaign jumped on the Davis bandwagon.

TABLE 9
Prohibitionist Precincts: Support for Jeff Davis in the 1900
Gubernatorial Primary, Three County Sample*

Precinct	County	% Anti-license, 1900	% for Jeff Davis, 1900
Prairie	St. Francis	84.3	88.5
Bates	Sebastian	80.6	51.7
Prairie Grove	Washington	76.6	87.7
Mississippi	Sebastian	76.3	63.3
Centre	Sebastian	73.6	69.7
Dayton	Sebastian	73.2	94.9
Wheatley	St. Francis	69.8	82.3
Sugar Loaf	Sebastian	69.4	23.0
Boston	Washington	66.2	35.0
Prairie	Sebastian	66.2	33.8
Wedington	Washington	66.0	83.0
Brush Creek	Washington	65.8	87.8
Reed	Washington	65.6	86.7

*Prohibitionist precincts are defined here as precincts in which the anti-saloon license vote (i.e. the vote for a dry county) exceeded 65 percent in the September 1900 biennial referendum. These figures include non-Democratic voters.
SOURCES: *Forrest City Times*, April 13, September 14, 1900; *Fort Smith Elevator*, April 6, September 14, 1900; *Springdale News*, April 20, September 14, 1900.

8

The Democratic Warrior

This is the eve of the greatest of all national contests. . . . It is not a time for fraternal bickerings. Imperial armies at this moment are marshalling from ocean to ocean; ruthless beneficiaries of popular subjugation are capitalizing by untold millions their Christless, hell-born plans for binding in irrevocable chains, not you only, but posterity also, until God shall paralize the womb of motherhood and resolve into the original elements the universe by a holocaust of fire.

—*Jeremiah V. Bourland (1900)*[1]

When the Democratic State Convention met in Little Rock in late June 1900, "Jeff Davis men" were everywhere. Though loosely aggregated, they were in firm control of the convention from beginning to end. Judge Jeptha Evans, Davis's old friend from Logan County, was chairman of the convention, and Congressman Thomas C. McRae, another Davis supporter, headed the platform committee. Even the entertainment was provided by the Russellville Cornet Band, which honored its favorite son with countless renditions of "Dixie."[2]

Considering the bitterness that had characterized the recent primary campaign, the convention was a surprisingly harmonious affair. According to the *Arkansas Gazette*, the state had never witnessed "a more orderly or intelligent convention." The anti-Davis delegates, who were heavily outnumbered and had little to gain from prolonging Davis's alienation from the Democratic establishment, were in a conciliatory mood. The selection of Evans and McRae as the convention's leaders went uncontested; and there was little opposition to Davis's selection as one of the state's four at-large delegates to the 1900 Democratic National Convention. Even Vandeventer, who was serving as a delegate from Conway County, voted for Davis; and Edgar Bryant, who had battled Davis in the early primaries, graciously seconded Davis's nomination and moved that the nomination be made unanimous.[3]

On the second and final day of the convention, the peace was disturbed by W. H. Martin, an anti-Davis delegate from Garland County, who introduced a resolution endorsing the Kimbell plan for a new state house. But the resolution provoked so much protest, including an admonishment from Senator James Berry, that Martin withdrew his motion. The one serious challenge to Davis's authority came when Carroll Armstrong of Conway County was re-elected chairman of the Democratic State Central Committee, narrowly defeating Jeremiah V. Bourland, Davis's old friend and advisor from Franklin County. Bourland's defeat was a clear indication that the Davis faction had not yet crystallized and that many seemingly pro-Davis politicians were wary of giving their new leader too much power. At this point in Davis's career, his hold over other politicians was weak and conditional. Politicians like Bourland, who were unreservedly committed to him, were relatively rare.[4]

Earlier in the convention Bourland had been accorded the honor of placing his friend's name in nomination. His flowery, rather long-winded nominating speech portrayed Davis as a throwback to the pure Democracy of Old Hickory:

> Jacksonian, not less in faith than in personality, he grasps in a massive brain the basic principles of government. A student of our colonial history, he realizes that the old enemy of liberty still threatens the body politic; apprehending present direful conditions, economic, sociological, he sees with eagle eye in modern commercial conspiracy at home, no less than in imperial war upon liberty in the Orient, the old spirit of the dead kings of England, who attempted by the sword to wrest from the fathers, government by the people.[5]

Bourland's speech was both conciliatory and tough-minded. Reiterating the major themes of Davis's primary campaign—especially the antitrust issue and the charges of persecution by the press—he also made it clear that the future governor had no intention of disrupting legitimate business activities:

> Sirs, it has been unwisely and untruly asservated that the election of Davis will discourage investment, and drive capital from the state. . . . The election of Davis is inimical only to questionable methods, to unjust, dishonest commerce. . . . Commerce, so overrun by trusts, honeycombed with trade conspiracies, its standard of morality the bunco game, its only law the code of highwaymen, subsidizing, so far as is in its power, the metropolitan press, arrogantly denounces as a demagogue him who yet dares boldly to appeal to the masses.[6]

Davis's acceptance speech, which was uncharacteristically brief (he explained that he was saving his strength for the upcoming general election campaign), was similar in tone to Bourland's. Offering no apologies, he reaffirmed his commitment to reform and economic democracy; at the same time, he did his best to calm the fears of conservative Democrats. Denying that he was a dangerous radical, he insisted that his brand of democratic reform represented a return to the progressive conservatism of the early Republic:

> Ah, gentlemen, if we would be a happy, prosperous, united people, we must adhere to the old landmarks of Democracy hewn out for us by the consecrated hands of the patriot fathers, and not be led to catch at the sunshine and bubbles of seeming prosperity, which in the end will leave us desolate and without hope.... Prosperity should not descend from an upper circle, but rather should ascend from that true source of all wealth, LABOR, until it blesses all alike. Prosperity is not a long, lean, stealthy creature that would by law or otherwise take from one to bestow upon another, but rather is that jolly, round-faced, fat, good-natured fellow that scatters sunshine and gladness in the hovel of the poor as well as in the mansions of the rich.... I would not be unjustful to capital nor unmindful of its beneficent influence, nor will I be unjust to labor. In the great achievements of life, these two great forces should go hand-in-hand, inseparable, united, harmonious and together.[7]

The moderate rhetoric and diplomatic behavior that Davis exhibited at the state convention did not go unnoticed. Democratic editors and politicians who had been unable to reconcile themselves to Davis's nomination prior to the convention did so soon afterwards. Most Democratic leaders now believed that Davis could be tamed, or at least controlled. For many, supporting Davis was a bitter pill to swallow, yet the situation no longer seemed to warrant a disruption of Democratic solidarity. One notable exception was ex-Governor William M. Fishback who, in July, denounced Davis as an irresponsible demagogue. Asked to stump the state for Davis and the Democratic ticket, Fishback angrily refused in a public letter addressed to the secretary of the Democratic State Central Committee:

> Dear Sir:
>   Your letter requesting me to make some speeches in behalf of the State ticket is just to hand.
>   You must pardon me for declining to do so. I should do violence to my sense of duty, alike to my State and myself, if I were even to vote for Jeff Davis.
>   Mr. Davis, as also his father before him, has been a political, and I believe a personal friend of mine for many years, and it would have given me great pleasure to support him upon merely personal grounds. But his course within the last year and a half, since he has been in the office he now holds, as I view it, proves him an exceedingly dangerous man in any office of trust.
>   I am a Democrat because I love my State and country, and for precisely this reason I shall not vote for Jeff Davis.[8]

Fishback found few supporters among Democratic leaders and received a barrage of criticism from the Democratic press. Some papers even reported an old rumor that Fishback, once a staunch Unionist and close friend of Abraham Lincoln, had spied for the Union while serving in the Confederate Army.[9] Although such charges damaged Fishback's credibility, party leaders worried about the electoral impact of his defection. Conservative Democratic politicians had refused to abandon their party; but conservative Democratic businessmen, whose partisan ties were weaker than those of professional politicians and publicists, might not follow suit.

The threat of a mass defection by conservative Democratic voters insured that the general election campaign would be a spirited affair. Convinced that the ruling Democratic party was more vulnerable than it had been in years, Arkansas Republicans mounted a vigorous campaign. In early July, the Republican State Convention nominated Harmon L. Remmel for the governorship. A former state legislator and a former secretary of the State Bureau of Immigration, Remmel was a veteran campaigner who had been the Republican gubernatorial nominee twice before (in 1894 and 1896). Born in upstate New York in 1852, he had lived in Arkansas since 1876. A respected businessmen, he had enjoyed a long and successful career as a lumber manufacturer, bank director, and insurance executive. At the time of his nomination, he was manager of the Arkansas branch of the Mutual Life Insurance Company of New York. Distinguished, respectable, and eminently practical, Remmel was everything that Davis was not. He was the kind of candidate who might lure a large number of disgruntled Democratic businessmen into the Republican camp. Many prominent Republicans, including Marcus Hanna, predicted that most respectable Arkansawyers would choose Remmel over Davis who, as one party leader put it, was nothing but "a cheap pretender of mock heroics."[10]

Davis's other opponent was the Populist A. W. Files, an ex-Democrat and a former state auditor who had run for governor on the People's party ticket in 1896.[11] Demoralized by mounting defections to the two major parties, Files and the Populists played an inconsequential role in the 1900 election.

The contest between Davis and Remmel proved to be, in the words of one historian, "the greatest gubernatorial campaign in the history of the State up to that time." Public interest in the race was keen, and the county canvass was the most ambitious ever, calling for thirty-eight joint speaking engagements in little more than a month.[12] The canvass began on July 30 at Conway, where Davis set the tone of the campaign by dropping a political bombshell in Remmel's lap. Somehow Davis had obtained a copy of a telegram to Remmel from Richard A. McCurdy, the president of the New York Mutual Life Insurance Company. The telegram, which Davis repeated over and over again to the crowd, read: "I cheerfully consent and urge you to accept the Republican nomination for governor." There it was—according to Davis—undeniable proof that Remmel was the hand-picked candidate of the trusts! No honest candidate, no candidate of the people, wanted or needed a Yankee capitalist's consent to run for governor. As the Democrats in the audience moved to the edge of their seats, Davis turned to Remmel and demanded to know how much blood money McCurdy was pouring

into the campaign. Without waiting for an answer, he declared that
McCurdy was trying to tell the people of Arkansas how to run their state.
McCurdy, Davis assured the crowd, "did not draw $50,000 a year for doing
nothing." He had hired Remmel to sabotage the Democratic party's crusade
against the trusts. In his rejoinder, Remmel explained that the McCurdy
telegram was simply a response to his request for a thirty-day vacation in
order to make the county canvass.[13] But the damage had been done.
Throughout the campaign, Davis bludgeoned Remmel and the Republicans
with the infamous McCurdy telegram.

The *Arkansas Gazette* felt obliged to assure its readers that "it is not
Remmel the businessman, but Remmel the politician, whom Jeff Davis is
after." But the paper continued to echo Davis's charge that Remmel was a
minion of McCurdy and the trusts. "Dick McCurdy will find it an up-hill
task dictating the politics of Arkansas," the *Gazette* declared, ". . . Mr. Remmel is not quite as gay as he was before the McCurdy telegram fell into the
hands of the common people. . . . He is representing no one but the president of one of the largest corporations in the country."[14] To the Republicans'
dismay, most of the Democratic newspapers that had criticized Davis's anti-
business radicalism earlier in the year voiced similar sentiments. According
to one conservative editor, who had expressed nothing but contempt for
Davis during the primary campaign, the voters of Arkansas were faced
with a clear choice between "a servant of the people" and "a servant of
McCurdy."[15] In the best Gilded Age tradition, partisanship had gained the
upper hand over ideology.

In addition to branding Remmel as a trust-heeler, Davis and the Democrats continually reminded the voters that he belonged to the party of
imperialism, the gold standard, and Black Reconstruction. Discovering that
Remmel had once appointed a black tax collector, Davis turned the appointment into a major political issue. "Why did you appoint a kinky-headed
nigger to collect your revenues in the eastern part of the state?" he demanded of Remmel in a speech at Little Rock. "Why didn't you appoint a
white man?" After all, he reminded Remmel, "this is a white man's government." Earlier in the same speech, Davis had attacked Remmel for being an
imperialist. "I would not give the life of one American boy or Confederate
soldier," he told the crowd, "for the whole Philippines. God never intended
that civilization should be put into a people with a pump gun."[16] On other
occasions the free-silver issue was Davis's primary weapon. At Huntsville,
dramatizing the hallowed "sixteen to one" ratio between silver and gold, he
was escorted to the speaker's platform by "sixteen men mounted on white
horses, each man wearing one-gallus of bed-ticking, broad-brimmed straw
hats, bearing flags, horses gaily caparisoned with flags and bunting; followed by one man on a yellow horse, man and horse decorated with
yellow."[17]

Such tactics put Remmel and the Republicans squarely on the defensive. But Democratic leaders continued to worry that conservative Democrats would bolt. Some editors betrayed their nervousness by reassuring local businessmen that a vote for Davis was not so much a vote for a man as for a party. "If the people of Arkansas were going to elect a man for governor on his nice clothes, beautiful language, high standing . . . gentlemanly get up," one Democratic editor from South Arkansas declared, "Remmel would be the man. But it is not a fight of men, but measures. Not what they are within themselves, but that for which they represent."[18] Other papers tried to convince conservative voters that Davis had changed. "He is making his campaign on high ground," the *Arkansas Gazette* claimed. "His speeches are more conservative than those he delivered in the campaign previous to his nomination and they are winning friends for him throughout the state."[19] Davis encouraged this image. Although he consistently refused to back away from the positions that he had taken during the primary campaign, in speech after speech he apologized for the rough treatment that he had accorded fellow Democrats during the past year.[20]

Remmel, who was in a difficult position no matter what he did, proved to be his own worst enemy. It did not help his cause when he ridiculed Davis's supporters for strutting around in one-gallus outfits, or when he reminded the voters of the unpleasant fact that they had no choice but to "go east" for capital. His insistence that his election to the governorship "would be worth a great deal to Arkansas as an advertisement"—a claim he repeated over and over again—was a sincere but questionable strategy in a state where the majority of voters were struggling farmers and where sectionalism and xenophobia were strong traditions.[21] By concentrating on the businessman's vote and largely ignoring the farm vote, he insured that some conservative Democrats would join the Republican ranks; but he squandered whatever chance he had of seriously challenging Davis. Like Davis's opponents in the Democratic primary, he did not seem to understand what was happening in the canebrakes or up the forks of the creeks.

The Republican challenge, which seemed so menacing in mid-summer, did not amount to much on election day. The voters elected a completely Democratic state senate and a house of representatives made up of ninety-six Democrats, one Independent Democrat, one Populist, and two Republicans. Davis, the only statewide candidate facing Republican opposition, won a majority of the vote in all but two counties, the traditionally Republican mountain counties of Newton and Searcy. Davis's share (66.7 percent) of the total vote was actually greater than Dan Jones's share (64.3 percent) in 1896, though it was slightly smaller than Jones's vote (67.3 percent) in the off-year election of 1898.[22]

Despite the magnitude of the Democrats' victory, there were some bright spots in the election for the Republicans. Remmel received almost 5,000

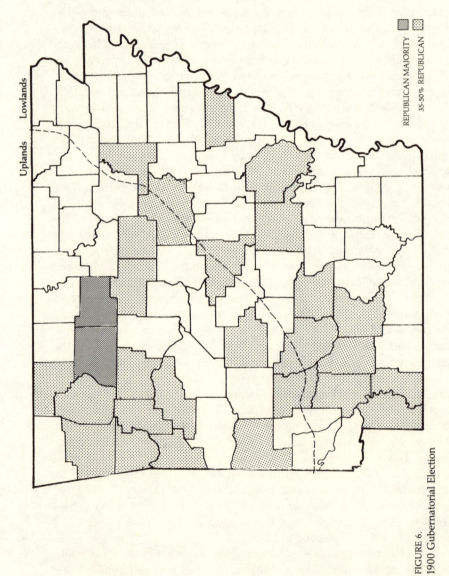

REPUBLICAN MAJORITY

35-50% REPUBLICAN

Uplands   Lowlands

Uplands

FIGURE 6.
1900 Gubernatorial Election

SOURCE: *Biennial Report of the Secretary of State of Arkansas,
1899–1900,* 419–421.

more votes than he had received in 1896, while Davis won 2,477 fewer votes than Jones had received in 1896. Thus the Democratic majority was more than 7,000 votes smaller than it had been four years earlier. Moreover, the Republican share of the gubernatorial vote (30.6 percent) was more than 5 percent higher than in 1896 (25.3 percent).[23]

These bright spots were clouded over by the fact that the improvement in the party's showing stemmed not from Democratic defections but from a combination of other factors: a relatively low Democratic turnout, an unusually large Republican turnout, and an infusion of ex-Populists into the Republican ranks. The anticipated bolt by conservative Democrats—which Remmel and the Republicans labored long and hard to bring about—did not materialize. It is impossible to estimate precisely the number of Democrats who voted for Remmel in 1900, but both county and precinct data indicate that Democratic defectors—probably between 2,000 and 4,000 voters—were few. The Republican coalition of 1900 probably contained more ex-Populists than ex-Democrats. This is not as surprising as it may seem, since a substantial minority of Arkansas Populists had voted Republican prior to the agrarian revolt, and the two parties had flirted with fusion for almost a decade.[24] After the virtual collapse of the Arkansas People's party in 1898, many Republican-Populists returned to their old party, even though Harmon Remmel had little to offer them ideologically.

Democratic leaders, too, had some cause to be concerned about their party's future. Although the number of Democratic defectors was relatively small, the number of Democrats who "went fishing" on election day was disturbingly large. It was only mildly reassuring that most Democrats who could not bring themselves to vote for Davis simply sat out the election, rather than voting for Remmel. The number of non-voting anti-Davis Democrats almost certainly exceeded 10,000. In Pulaski County alone, Davis received approximately a thousand fewer votes than Dan Jones had received in 1896. When factors such as population growth, the return of some Populists to the Democratic party, and the likelihood of increased turnout among avidly pro-Davis Democrats are taken into account, the estimated number of non-voting anti-Davis Democrats in the county swells to almost 1,500. In the city of Little Rock, where opposition to Davis was particularly intense, the Democratic vote for governor in 1900 was 32.5 percent smaller than in 1896. In nearby Argenta, the drop was a staggering 51.7 percent. In Fort Smith, the state's second largest city, where Davis had received only 35.8 percent of the vote in the primary, the decline was 38.9 percent.[25] Clearly, many conservative Democrats had not yet reconciled themselves to Davis's ascendancy.

During his first two years in state politics, Davis accomplished a great deal. He dragged his party kicking and screaming into the age of mass politics. He took the reform wing of the party from the moderate Bryanists and pushed the ideological center of the party well to the left. And he politicized a generation of Arkansas farmers whose faith in political action had been flagging, stroking their egos and giving them a renewed sense of dignity and hope. These were no mean accomplishments, especially for a thirty-seven-year-old upstart who had backed into the attorney generalship. Still, his greatest challenges lay ahead. Could he relieve the powerlessness of the Arkansas dirt farmer and halt the advance of New South colonialism? Could his movement succeed where the Brothers of Freedom, the Populists, and other agrarian protest movements had failed? Although he had effected a political rebellion, could he—and would he—provide his followers with anything more than psychological sustenance?

9

The Tribune of Haybinders

If you red-necks or hill-billies ever come to Little Rock be sure to come to see me—come to my house. Don't go to the hotels or the wagon-yards, but come to my house and make it your home while you are in the Capital City. If I am not at home tell my wife who you are; tell her you are my friend and that you belong to the sun-burned sons of toil. Tell her to give you some hog jowl and turnip greens. She may be busy making soap, but that will be all right.

—*Jeff Davis (1900)*[1]

The fall of 1900 was a busy time for Jeff Davis. Most of September and October was devoted to the national election, which once again pitted Davis's hero, William Jennings Bryan, against William McKinley. Although he had been campaigning almost continuously for more than a year, Davis tirelessly stumped the state for Bryan and various Democratic congressional candidates. He even made a couple of speeches outside the state, though there was nothing he or anyone else could do to stem the Republican tide.[2]

When he was not out campaigning for the Democracy, Governer-elect Davis was busy cementing political alliances, helping Jacobson run the attorney general's office, or attending to personal matters. Through most of his attorney generalship, he had lived at the Gleason Hotel, while his family remained in Russellville—an unsatisfactory arrangement for a man deeply attached to his wife and children. Now that his long-term political and financial prospects were more promising—as governor his salary would be $3,000 a year, twice what he was making as attorney general—he made plans to move his family to Little Rock. Although Arkansas did not provide its chief executive with a governor's mansion. Davis managed to rent a house on Scott Street spacious enough to accommodate his wife, who was expecting twins in April, his six children, and his nine hunting dogs.[3]

In December, Davis selected his official gubernatorial staff: his eldest daughter, Bessie, was hired as a stenographer; Jacobson was appointed private secretary to the governor; and a black janitor was hired to take care of the executive wing of the state house. Jacobson's appointment came as no surprise, since he had acted as Davis's right-hand man for more than two years. Despite its unimpressive-sounding title, it was an appointment that would have a profound effect on Davis's governorship. The private secretary to the governor was an important public official in Arkansas. An official member of the state government, he received an annual salary of $1,500 and was required to serve as the adjutant general of the Arkansas State Militia. In effect, he performed many of the functions performed by lieutenant governors in other states. The Arkansas lieutenant governorship was largely a ceremonial position. A member of the state senate, the lieutenant governor was elected by his colleagues at the end of each legislative session to serve in the executive office when the governor was out of the state.[4] While the position of private secretary lacked the prestige of a lieutenant governorship, it offered its holder numerous opportunities to exercise a measure of power and influence.

Davis's inauguration on January 18 was a simple, unpretentious affair, even by Arkansas standards. As one observer described the scene, "there was an entire absence of pomp and pageantry. No brass band was on hand to play "The Conquering Hero." No military companies were present in gay uniforms. Everything savored of Jeffersonian simplicity."[5] This lack of fanfare was in keeping with Davis's rustic image, though outgoing Governor Dan Jones deserved most of the credit for the ceremony's subdued tone. Still smarting from his defeat in the senatorial primary, Jones broke custom and refused to participate in his successor's inauguration. After delivering the traditional farewell address before a joint session of the legislature, he scurried from the house chamber. When Governor-elect Davis and the other new state officials arrived in the hall a few minutes later, Jones was nowhere in sight.[6]

Despite Jones's absence, or perhaps because of it, Davis was all smiles as he stepped to the podium to deliver his inaugural address. As his father, two of his daughters, and a host of friends from Pope County looked on, he deliverd one of the most restrained speeches of his career, calmly and tactfully presenting a list of necessary reforms. While he admitted that "many of the evils" that burdened and oppressed the people of Arkansas could be eliminated only by national legislation, he maintained that govermental activism at the state level was a necessary first step.[7] Though the scope of his legislative program was modest by twentieth-century standards, it was far more ambitious than any of the programs offered by his predecessors.

Most of the speech was devoted to the two issues that had catapulted him into the limelight: the Rector Antitrust Act and the proposed new state house. He implored the members of the legislature to pass an extraterritorial amendment which would put some teeth in the Rector Act, though he warned them that "a storm of opposition will be aroused and great calamities and misfortune will be prepdicted as overshadowing our common-wealth, and it will require all your wisdom, moral courage and patriotism to withstand the flood of opposition." He also reminded them that they had the power "to absolutely prohibit foreign corporations from transacting business in this State," though he admitted that at present such action was "neither expected nor desired."[8]

In his discussion of the state house issue, Davis reiterated his opposition to the Kimbell Act. "I have always thought and am still of the opinion," he declared, "that the abandonment of the present beautiful State Capitol and the destruction of the penitentiary property is a waste of public property that the State cannot afford." If the new legislature could not bring itself to repeal the Kimball Act, it could at least amend the act so that the new state house could be "built upon the proper site and under a proper and business-like management." He recommended the abolition of the present Capitol Commission, the firing of the architect hired by the commission, the creation of a new commission made up of state officials, and the use of competitive bidding and convict labor. The present plan, he contended, was a wasteful extravagance that would ultimately lead to increased taxation.[9]

Davis also called for a fellow-servant law which would give workers "the same rights of redress for injuries sustained as any other class of citizens," the establishment of a state reform school, the enlargement of the state lunatic asylum, increased appropriations for Confederate pensions, the abolition of the suicide clause in life insurance policies, and the repeal of a controversial 1897 act that provided for the construction of state-owned railroads by convict labor.[10]

Although Davis's inaugural address contained little that would please die-hard conservatives, its general tone was unmistakably conciliatory. In his closing statement he came as close as he would ever come to endorsing the spirit of New South commercialism:

> In conclusion, gentlemen, permit me to express the hope that your session will be a pleasant and harmonious one, and that you will do all in your power by wise and conservative legislation to promote the material growth and development of our State, by lending all proper and legitimate encouragement to the investment of capital in our midst, whether for the building of railroads, factories, or the development of the many natural resources of our State; and as your chief executive, I tender you my earnest cooperation in all things that will increase our prosperity and make us justly proud of the State in which we live.[11]

As Davis stepped away from the podium, the house chamber was filled with applause, not to mention a few sighs of relief from anxious conservatives. After a brief demonstration led by the well-wishers from Pope County, the new governor was sworn in by Chief Justice H. G. Bunn, the humorless judge who had scolded Davis for removing his coat while addressing the state supreme court in 1899. At long last the Davis era had begun—though no one, including Davis, was quite sure what difference it would make. Less than an hour after his inauguration, Davis confessed to Charles Jacobson that he was a bit bewildered by his new position. "Well, we have it," he declared, gazing around his new office,"—what are we going to do with it?"[12]

Davis clearly intented to do a great deal with his new position, but even he must have wondered if he had the skills or patience to handle the administrative duties of the governor's office. His restless personality, sharp wit, unrestrained sociability, and aggressive, slashing style made him unbeatable on the stump, but these traits would count for very little when he was sitting behind the governor's desk. The same personal characteristics that made Davis a great politician seemed to limit him as a public official. High-strung and impatient, he was an undisciplined administrator with no facility for bureaucratic office work. As Jacobson, who knew him as well as anyone, recalled:

> The Governor was not an office man and he was as quiet, restful and peaceful in his office as a lion in a cage during a circus parade. At times as I wended my way through the menagerie of a big circus and saw the king of the jungles . . . restlessly and carelessly pacing his six-by-ten cage, I was reminded of the man with whom I was associated, pacing the floor of his office and yearning to be out on the hustings talking to one-gallus boys.[13]

Davis's passion for sports also interfered with his administrative routine. Aside from stump speaking, his two greatest loves were hunting and fishing. On a warm, sunny day, the best place to look for Jeff Davis was out in the woods, not in the state house. In Jacobson's words "it was hard to confine Jeff to an office. He wanted to be out in the open, talking, hunting, training dogs. He was a splendid shot, passionately loved hunting quail and always kept a number of splendidly trained pointers and setters."[14] When he was not out shooting quail, he was often at the ball park rooting for the Little Rock "Arkansas Travelers." A rabid baseball fan, he threw out the first ball of the 1901 season and spent much of the summer sitting behind the Travelers' dugout. Intensely competitive, he "liked everything wherein a good scrap was to be staged whether it was a ball game, cock-fight, or what not."[15]

Finally, there was the problem of Davis's fondness for liquor. A heavy drinker, he spent much of his career either bending his elbow or nursing a hangover. By the end of his first term, Davis's drinking escapades had become legendary—so much so that he was expelled from the Baptist church in 1902 and censured by three denominational conferences. Although there is no evidence that Davis's drinking hampered his political activities—indeed, it may have helped out on the stump—there can be little doubt that it affected his performance as a public official.

Davis's first major task in office was to gain control of the legislature, which opened its biennial session on January 14. Davis's style of mass politics had revolutionized the Democratic primary system, but it remained to be seen whether he could transform the Arkansas legislature into an engine of reform. In Arkansas, as in most states, hostility between the governor and the legislature was the rule rather than the exception. Legislators were not accustomed to paying much attention to executive proposals, no matter how popular the governor happened to be.[16] Dan Jones, the most legislation-minded governor in years, had virtually no success in trying to direct the legislature's affairs. Whether Davis could succeed where the more cautious Jones had failed was an open question as the 1901 legislature began its proceedings.

It was difficult to predict how the new legislature would respond to Davis's reform program. The 1901 session was filled with new faces: in the senate there were fifteen new members (three of whom had served in the 1899 house), and in the house there were sixty-four. These figures may suggest that a political revolution had taken place; but by Arkansas standards, the number of holdovers from the previous legislature was high. In the 1899 house, only twenty-one representatives had served in the preceding legislature. In the turbulent year of 1893, there were only ten holdovers in the house.[17]

The new legislature was slightly younger and contained more businessmen—the latter statistic reflecting, among other things, the fact that Davis had goaded the business community into political action. But for the most

TABLE 10
Turnover and Persistence in the Arkansas Legislatures of 1891,1893,1899, and 1901

	Legislature			
	1891	1893	1899	1901
House Of Representatives				
N=	95	97	100	100
New Members	70	87	79	64
Holdovers	25	10	21	36
% New Members	73.7	88.5	79.0	64.0
% Holdovers	26.3	11.5	21.0	36.0
Senate				
N=	32	32	32	32
New Members	12	12	13	12
New Members Who Had Served in the Previous House	2	5	4	3
Holdovers	18	15	15	17
% New Members	43.8	53.1	53.1	46.9
% Holdovers	56.2	46.9	46.9	53.1

SOURCE: *Biennial Report of the Secretary of State of Arkansas, 1887–1888,* 284–286; *1889–1890,* 76–78; *1891–1892,* 68–71; *1897–1898,* 294–297; *1899–1900,* 434–437; *1895–1896,* 281–284.

TABLE 11
Age, Occupational, and Religious Composition of the Arkansas Legislature, 1897–1901

	House			Senate		
	1897	1899	1901	1897	1899	1901
Age:						
Average Age	41.2	40.4	40.3	45.5	40.1	39.3
# 21–35 years old	41	39	43	8	14	15
# 36–49 years old	25	36	34	16	13	10
# 50+ years old	32	23	22	8	5	7
N=	98	98	99	32	32	32
Occupation*						
Farmer	43	32	35	10	6	4
Lawyer	35	43	35	17	24	24
Teacher	15	9	11	5	3	2
Editor	8	5	5	0	0	1
Minister	4	0	2	0	0	0
Doctor	4	5	5	1	0	0
Merchant	5	5	7	3	0	2
Real Estate	0	0	3	0	0	0
Clerk	0	1	4	0	0	0
Other	3	2	4	0	0	0
N=	117	102	111	36	33	33
% in:†						
Agriculture	36.8	31.4	31.5	27.8	18.2	12.1
Professions	56.4	60.8	53.2	63.9	81.8	81.8
Business	5.1	5.9	13.5	8.3	0.0	6.1
Other	1.7	2.0	1.8	0.0	0.0	0.0
Religion:						
Baptist	27	24	22	8	7	9
Methodist	35	28	25	8	8	11
Presbyterian	7	13	16	5	5	4
Christian	10	4	8	2	3	2
Episcopal	3	4	1	2	2	0
Catholic	2	1	0	0	0	0
Other	2	4	4	0	1	1
No Membership	13	21	24	7	6	5
N=	99	99	100	32	32	32
% Baptist	27.3	24.2	22.0	25.0	21.9	28.1
% Methodist	35.4	28.3	25.0	25.0	25.0	34.4
% Presbyterian	7.1	13.1	16.0	15.6	15.6	12.5
% Christian	10.1	4.0	8.0	6.3	9.4	6.3
% Episcopal	3.0	4.0	1.0	6.3	6.3	0.0
% Catholic	2.0	1.0	0.0	0.0	0.0	0.0
% Other	2.0	4.0	4.0	0.0	3.1	3.1
% No Membership	13.1	21.2	24.0	21.9	18.8	15.6

*Some members reported more than one occupation.
†Percent of total occupations reported.
SOURCE: *Biennial Report of the Secretary of State of Arkansas, 1895–1896,* 281–284; *1897–1898,* 294–297; *1899–1900,* 434–437.

part the social composition of the 1901 legislature was strikingly similar to that of previous legislatures. Most of its members were professional men—lawyers comprised the largest single occupational group—and most belonged to either the Baptist or the Methodist church. The proportion of farmers, 31.5 percent in the house and 12.1 percent in the senate, was approximately the same as in the 1899 legislature, though somewhat smaller than in the 1897 session. A few of the farmer-legislators were modest yeomen, but most were large planters. Whatever else it was, the new legislature was no convention of "haybinders."

At the outset, it appeared that the legislature was anxious to cooperate with Davis. An ardent Davis supporter, Thomas H. Humphreys of Fayetteville, was elected speaker of the house. Born in Texas in 1865, Humphreys was a former Fort Smith city attorney serving his second term in the house. A clever parliamentarian, he proved his loyalty to Davis time and time again during the 1901 session. In 1902, Davis rewarded him with a judicial appointment.[18]

Davis's prospects in the senate, which was traditionally more conservative than the house, were less encouraging. However, he had reason to be fairly optimistic. Although his first choice for senate president, William F. Kirby, finished a distant second behind Robert J. Wilson of Fayetteville, the situation could have been much worse. Wilson was more conservative and far more independent-minded than either Kirby or Humphreys, but he had been leaning towards the Davis camp and was a potential ally.[19]

Since Robert Wilson was in no position, and had no desire, to act as Davis's unofficial floor leader in the senate, the job fell to Kirby, a second-term senator from Texarkana. Though only thirty-three years old, Kirby had already earned a wide reputation as a keen student of the law. Totally committed to the new administration, he quickly became one of Davis's most trusted advisors. From 1905 to 1907, he served as Davis's attorney general; and in 1908 Davis supported him for the governorship. Although he was defeated in the 1908 race, he later served a term in the United States Senate (1916–1921). Well-mannered and intellectual, Kirby often seemed out of place in the Davis movement.[20]

Davis also depended heavily on the talents of Senator David L. King, a thirty-eight-year-old lawyer from Hardy. Though only a first-term senator, King was an able legislator and a formidable debater. He was also a renowned trial attorney, who reportedly had never lost a felony case. One of Davis's earliest supporters, he had withdrawn from the attorney general's race in April 1900 when it became clear that Davis preferred George Murphy. Once in the senate he went down the line for the new administration; in return he was given the honor of sponsoring Davis's antitrust bill.[21]

Humphreys, Kirby, and King did their able best to infuse the legislature with the spirit of "Jeff Davisism," but they faced an uphill struggle all the

way. A powerful business lobby, ideological conservatism, institutional iner-
tia, widespread distrust of Davis's motives, a legitimate concern for legislative autonomy, and, perhaps most importantly, the fact that factionalism
was generally equated with bossism in Arkansas politics all conspired to
defeat Davis's legislative program. Although Jeff had won the hearts of the
voters and the loyalty of some politicians, he had not changed the standards
of propriety that most of Arkansas's political elite believed in. And, at the
same time that they were trying to forge a cohesive proadministration faction, Davis's legislative lieutenants had to deny that they were acting as the
governor's agents.[22] The governor's power was not supposed to interfere
with the workings of an individual legislator's conscience, even though
everyone knew the realities of political life dictated otherwise.

Davis's first jolt came on January 30, when a fellow-servant bill sponsored by Senator Robert Lawrence of Pope County was narrowly defeated
(13–14) in the senate. Lawrence was closely associated with Davis, and
everyone in the legislature was aware that passage of the bill was one of the
governor's highest priorities. Nevertheless, when a second fellow-servant
bill reached the floor of the senate in late March, it too was defeated. Then
the senate rejected Davis's antitrust legislation. An antitrust bill passed the
house by a wide margin (66–7) on March 11, but the Davis forces were never
able to get the bill out of committee in the senate. When Senator David King,
the co-sponsor of the bill, made a last-ditch effort to get the bill on the
senate floor, only eleven senators were willing to support his resolution.[23]

Davis generally fared better in the house, but not always. On April 2, the
house voted 52–30 to override his veto of a resolution calling for a constitutional amendment to alter the jury system in civil cases. On April 4, he
narrowly escaped a second major defeat when the house came within three
votes of overriding his veto of the "Sunnyside" prison farm bill, (He had
vetoed the purchase in February on the grounds that the farm was a disease-
ridden swamp.) The house did approve (52–35) the Davis-backed
Humphreys Bill, which prohibited long-term convict-lease contracts; but the
bill was killed by the senate a week later. Davis was furious, but the worst
was yet to come. When, on April 11, David King introduced a resolution
empowering the governor to investigate all existing convict-lease contracts,
the anti-Davis forces argued that the governor was trying to interfere in an
area in which he had no constitutional authority. They carried the day (16–
14) once again. Davis's efforts at prison reform suffered another setback on
April 29, when the senate rejected a bill giving the governor a greater role in
the selection of a convict farm site.)[24]

On the state house issue Davis won a partial though not a very satisfying
victory. After weeks of wrangling, the legislature ratified a compromise
which, though leaving the basic structure of the Kimbell Act intact, established a new Capitol Commission consisting of the governor and three

appointees. The compromise bill also appropriated $1,000,000 for the construction of the new state house and called for the use of competitive bidding and convict labor. Davis signed the bill on April 29, but he was clearly still opposed to building a new state house on the penitentiary grounds.[25]

Although Davis had considerable support in both houses, the 1901 legislature gave him very little of what he had asked for in his inaugural address. Ignoring what Davis claimed was a clear mandate from the people, the general assembly turned down his requests for a fellow-servant law, an antitrust law, a reform school, and an expansion of the state's charitable institutions; instead it dealt with outlawing college fraternities, establishing the apple blossom as the state flower, and other weighty matters. Davis's legislative support seemed to erode as the session progressed and was probably at its lowest point when the legislature adjourned on May 4. Davis, however—although he vetoed nine bills—was careful to avoid a full-

TABLE 12

Factionalism in the 1901 Arkansas Senate: Support for the Davis Position on Eight Important Roll Call Votes

Senator	% Pro-Davis	Pro-Davis Votes	Anti-Davis Votes	Absences	SB3: Reform School	SB20: Antitrust	SB176: Prison Farm	HB25: Anti-Scrip	HB491a: State House	HB491b: State House	SCR14: Convict-Lease	King Res..: Antitrust
Pro-Davis												
David King	100.0	8	0	0	+	+	+	+	+	+	+	+
William Kirby	100.0	6	0	2		+	+	−	+	+	+	+
Reuben Adams	87.5	7	1	0	+	+	+	−	+	+	+	+
Nelson Carlock	87.5	7	1	0	−	+	+	+	+	+	+	+
George Brown	85.7	6	1	1	−	+	+	+	+	+	+	
M. P. Huddleston	85.7	6	1	1	+	+	−	+	+	+	+	
Thomas Hardy	80.0	4	1	3			+		+	−	+	+
Paul Matlock	80.0	4	1	3		+	+	+		+	−	
R. L. Lawrence	75.0	6	2	0	−	+	−	+	+	+	+	+
W. E. Ferguson	71.4	5	2	1	−	+		+	+	+	+	−
W. T. Hammock	71.4	5	2	1	−		−	+	+	+	+	+
Neutral												
Robert Wilson	62.5	5	3	0	−	+	+	−	+	+	+	−
Robert Dowdy	62.5	5	3	0	+	+	−	+	−	+	+	−
Gibson Witt	62.5	5	3	0	+	−	+	+	+	+	−	−
Eugene Lankford	62.5	5	3	0	+	+	−	−	−	+	+	+
George Haynie	60.0	3	2	3	−	+	−				+	+
Jacob King	42.9	3	4	1	+	+	−	−	−	−	−	+
Lawrence Clark	40.0	2	3	3	+	+		−	−			−
John McNemer	40.0	2	3	3	+	+		−		−	−	−
Joseph Short	37.5	3	5	0	−	−	−	+	−	+	−	+

TABLE 12 (continued)

Senator	% Pro- Davis	Pro-Davis Votes	Anti-Davis Votes	Absences	SB3: Reform School	SB20: Antitrust	SB176: Prison Farm	HB25: Anti-Scrip	HB491a: State House	HB491b: State House	SCR14: Convict-Lease	King Res.: Antitrust
Anti-Davis												
William Cotton	33.3	2	4	2	–		–	+	–	+	–	
A. Flenniken	33.3	2	4	2	+	–	+		–	–	–	
Byron Price	28.6	2	5	1	+		+	–	–	–	–	–
John Mardis	20.0	1	4	3	+		–		–	–	–	–
George Sengel	16.7	1	5	2	+	–			–	–	–	–
Thomas Wilson	14.3	1	6	1	–	–	–		–	+	–	–
James E. Wood	14.3	1	6	1	+	–			–	–	–	–
P. T. Butler	14.3	1	6	1		–	+	–	–	–	–	–
Richard Buckner	12.5	1	7	0	+	–	–	–	–	–	–	–
Creed Caldwell	12.5	1	7	0	+	–	–	–	–	–	–	–
J. D. Shackleford	12.5	1	7	0	+	–	–	–	–	–	–	–
Hal Norwood	00.0	0	6	2	–		–	–	–	–	–	–

Key to Abbreviations:

SB3   is Senate Bill 3– – "To establish a house of correction for juvenile criminals" (introduced by John McNemer).

SB20   is Senate Bill 20—a vote to suspend the rules to consider "An act to provide for the punishment of pools, trusts, conspiracies to create prices, etc. and repeal act approved March 6, 1899" (introduced by David King.

SB176   is Senate Bill 176—"To provide for the purchase of a convict farm" (introduced by Thomas Hardy).

HB25   is House Bill 25—"An act making it unlawful for any corporation, company, firm or persons to use, to issue, sell, give or deliver to any person in payment of wages due for any scrip, token, draft, check or evidence of indebtedness, payable or redeemable otherwise than in lawful money, and for other purposes" (introduced by Rep. John Holland).

HB491a   is a motion to table Senator Eugene Lankforrd's amendments to House Bill 491—"An act to provide for the completion of the State Capitol Building."

HB491b   is a motion to table Senator Richard Buckner's amendment to House Bill 491.

SCR14   is Senate Concurrent Resolution 14—a resolution which called for the governor to investigate illegal convict lease contracts (introduced by David King).

King Res.   is the David L. King Resolution, which required a committee chaired by Senator P T. Butler to return all antitrust bills to the full senate; the King Antitrust Bill had been stalled in the Butler committee for months.

A + represents support for the Davis position; a – represents a vote against the Davis position.
SOURCE: *Journal of the Senate of Arkansas, 1901.*

scale confrontation with the legislature.[26] Like a good fighter, he knew when to retreat and when to attack. When the time was right and with the help of the electorate, he would bludgeon the legislature into submission.

Table 12. which presents the senate's voting patterns on eight important roll-calls where the pro-Davis position was clear, illustrates Davis's problems with the 1901 legislature. His legislative following was neither large enough nor cohesive enough to support an ambitious legislative program. His hold over his legislative followers was tenuous. With the exception of

David King and William Kirby, even his strongest supporters sometimes voted against him. Davis could ill afford such defections. Led by Senator George Sengel of Sebastian County, the anti-Davis forces in the legislature constituted a formidable opposition.[27] Well-organized and well-financed, they exhibited more factional cohesion than the pro-Davis forces. If Davis was to see his legislative program enacted into law, he would not only have to enlarge his following; he would also have to tighten his control over those legislators who were already sympathetic to his administration

Despite problems with the legislature, Davis's first six months in office were surprisingly peaceful. The acrimonious mudslinging that had characterized the 1900 primary campaign had all but disappeared, and the party's wounds seemed to be healing. As summer approached, some anti-Davis leaders even began to admit that the new administration had turned out to be a pleasant surprise. "Gov. Davis has made a better officer than we ever expected he would," the editor of the Arkadelphia *Southern-Standard* de-

TABLE 13

Age, Occupational, Religious, and Tenure Composition of the 1901 Arkansas Senate: Pro-Davis, Anti-Davis, and Neutral Factions*

| | | Faction | | |
		Pro- Davis	Anti- Davis	Neutral
	N=	11	12	9
Age:				
Average Age		39.0	39.1	40.0
% 21–35 years old		45.5	50.0	44.4
% 36–49 years old		36.4	25.0	33.3
% 50+ years old		18.1	25.0	22.2
Occupation[b]				
% in:				
Agriculture		27.3	00.0	11.1
Professions		72.7	83.3	88.9
Business		00.0	16.7	00.0
Religion:				
% Baptist		45.5	16.7	22.2
% Methodist		36.4	25.0	44.4
% Presbyterian		00.0	33.3	00.0
% Christian		9.1	8.3	00.0
% No Membership		9.1	16.7	33.3
Tenure:				
% New Senators		45.5	41.7	22.2
% New Senators Who Had Served in the Previous House		00.0	25.0	00.0
% Holdovers		54.5	33.3	77.8

*As defined in Table 12.

†Some members reported more than one occupation; percent of total occupations reported.

SOURCES: See Tables 11 and 12.

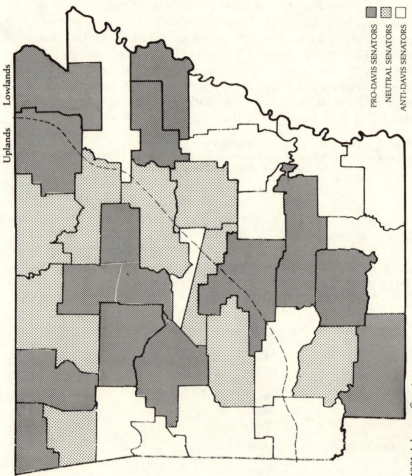

FIGURE 7.
Factionalism in the 1901 Arkansas Senate

SOURCE: *Journal of the Senate of Arkansas, 1901.*

clared in early June, "and in that capacity has shown more common sense than he demonstrated during the campaign."[28] Similarly, the editor of the *Arkansas Gazette* admitted that "so far Mr. Davis has performed his duties as governor creditably, and should he maintain his present gait he will be entitled to re-election.[29]

But as was so often the case during Davis's career, this was merely a period of calm before the storm. Many years later Jacobson recalled that during Davis's early months in office "surface indications . . . gave no evidence of the flames smouldering beneath the political horizon." As potential sources of political conflict, "the penitentiary management, State Capitol Commission, convict farm purchase, and anti-trust law were pregnant with untold possibilities," yet only when Davis decided to force these issues did they develop "into problems that were to shake the state from center to circumference."[30]

The first issue to erupt was the penitentiary controversy. When it became apparent that Davis was determined to gain control of the state's penal system, the uneasy truce between him and his critics came to an abrupt end. Although the struggle over the penitentiary eventually involved a number of explosive issues, it centered around Davis's opposition to the convict-lease system—a source of controversy for decades.

Arkansas's convict-lease system originated in 1873, when the legislature leased the penitentiary and its inmates to John M. Peck for a ten-year period. Using the penitentiary buildings at Little Rock as a base of operations, Peck issued subleases to various contractors—primarily planters, coal mine operators, building contractors, and brick manufacturers. Under this loosely administered system, the prison population was spread throughout the state, and official supervision of convict life became virtually impossible. The terms of the lease relieved the state of its responsibility for providing the prisoners with food, clothing, fuel, and medical care. Although it was illegal to force the convicts to work more than ten hours a day, the contractors essentially were allowed to treat their convict laborers as they saw fit.[31] The living conditions that developed under this system were gruesome; but public officials were reluctant to abandon an institution that poured money into the state treasury and helped to keep taxes low.

In 1881 a legislative committee investigated the convict-lease system and concluded that the institution was hopelessly corrupt and inhumane. According to the committee's report, the annual death rate for the state's prison population was a staggering 25 percent. Nevertheless, two years later the legislature approved a second ten-year lease. Despite growing public concern, treatment of convict laborers actually worsened under the administration of the new lessee, Zeb Ward. Abuses and atrocities multiplied until 1887, when an exposé of the working conditions at the Coal Hill mines in Johnson County turned into a full-blown scandal. Public pressure prompted an official investigation, which confirmed the reports that the prisoners at Coal Hill were being mistreated, tortured, and, in many cases, literally worked to death. The fallout from the Coal Hill scandal was considerable. There were several criminal convictions; the members of the State Penitentiary Board, dubbed "the blind mice" by the press, were totally discredited; and Governor Simon Hughes, who was closely identified with the Penitentiary Board, lost his bid for a third term.[32]

Although some prisoners received better treatment in the wake of the Coal Hill scandal, the convict-lease system continued to be a fount of corruption and brutality, as well as a source of considerable embarrassment for Democratic officials. In 1891, Governor James P. Eagle advised the legislature to abandon the lease system when the second ten-year lease expired in 1893. Two years later, after the leaders of the Arkansas People's party echoed Eagle's request, the legislature approved a bill that completely reorganized the state's prison system. Although it stopped short of prohibiting the leasing of convict labor, the new law placed most of the prison population in state-run convict farms; made it "lawful for convicts or ex-convicts to testify as to the treatment of prisoners, the sanitary conditions, and the food provided for them at the penitentiary or at the convict camps"; replaced the inspector of convicts with a more powerful superintendent of the penitentiary; and created a new State Penitentiary Board made up of the governor, the secretary of state, and the attorney general.[33]

The penal system that emerged after the reorganization act of 1893 was hardly benevolent; but it was clearly an improvement over the old system, which had all but precluded public scrutiny of prison life. Under the new law, prisoners were generally leased to private contractors on a short-term basis, and, in most cases, the state provided the contractor with professional wardens and guards. Most of the prisoners who were not leased out to contractors worked on state-run cotton plantations rented by the Penitentiary Board. In 1898 there were eight such plantations, but the number varied from year to year. The remainder of the prison population lived at the state penitentiary in Little Rock.[34]

The short-term convict-lease system worked reasonably well until the Kimbell State House Act called for the destruction of the state penitentiary at Little Rock. When the penitentiary buildings were torn down in the summer of 1899, the Penitentiary Board was obliged to find a new home for several hundred inmates. Since a new penitentiary could not be built without legislative approval, and since such approval could not be obtained until the legislature convened in January 1901, the board was forced to resort to a temporary solution to the penitentiary problem. Consequently, in August 1899 the board leased nearly a third of the state's prison population to the Arkansas Brick Manufacturing Company. W. W. Dickinson, the president of the brick company, knew that the Penitentiary Board was in no position to quibble over the terms of the lease and insisted on a lucrative ten-year contract.[35] The Penitentiary Board, which included Attorney General Davis, complied with Dickinson's demands, even though everyone concerned knew that the state was being fleeced.

No one paid much attention to the Dickinson contract until the 1901 legislature began to scrutinize the penitentiary situation. Since Davis had been a member of the Penitentiary Board that approved the Dickinson contract, the issue was a potential source of embarrassment for the new administration. Davis, who firmly believed that the best defense is a good offense, proceeded to solve the problem by becoming the contract's most vociferous opponent. When his critics reminded him that he had been a member of the Penitentiary Board that had signed the Dickinson contract, he claimed he had been tricked into putting his signature on it. Though nearly everyone in state government knew better, he insisted that he had never approved of the contract.[36] Concocting such a story — Davis himself could hardly keep a straight face whenever he repeated it — was obviously risky, but the stakes were high. For political as well as humanitarian reasons, Davis was determined to gain control of the penitentiary system, and the annulment of the Dickinson contract was an integral part of his plan to do so.

The legislature, of course, had other ideas. Although the governor and a majority of both houses agreed that the state should purchase a convict farm which would serve as the new penitentiary, there was widespread disagreement over how the purchase should be financed and where the farm should be located. In February Davis vetoed the "Sunnyside" farm bill, and in April the senate rejected several measures that would have enlarged the governor's role in the administration of the penal system. The Humphreys Bill, which would have nullified the Dickinson contract, passed the house, but was killed by the senate. When the legislature adjourned in May, neither branch of government had much to show for its efforts other than obstructionism.[37]

In June, Davis turned his attention to the Penitentiary Board. Except for his pardoning power, the governor had no more control over the penal system than any of the other state officials who served on the board. But Davis was hopeful that his colleagues would bow to his authority. To his dismay, several members of the board proved to be far more independent than he anticipated. When a majority of the board was reluctant to annul the Dickinson contract, Davis decided to force the issue. By exposing the brutality of the convict-lease system, he would create a scandal which would force the board to endorse his proposed reforms. In early June, he made an unannounced visit to the convict farm at England, in Lonoke County. He claimed that what he saw there was enough to make a grown man weep: food crawling with vermin, emaciated bodies, scarred backs, unsanitary living quarters, and Negro guards flogging white prisoners.[38]

At a meeting of the Penitentiary Board on July 9, Davis presented his grisly findings and demanded that the convict-lease system be reformed. At his insistence, the board voted to require wardens to serve their prisoners meat at every meal and to prohibit the flogging of convicts' bare skin. However, when he asked the board to annul the Dickinson contract, which he termed "vicious and unconscionable," only Secretary of State John Crockett supported him. The other three members of the board—Attorney General George Murphy, State Auditor T. C. Monroe, and Commissioner of Mines, Manufacturers, and Agriculture Frank Hill—voted to uphold the contract, despite Warden Hugh Nichol's testimony that the convicts leased by the Arkansas Brick Manufacturing Company were being forced to work ten to fourteen hours a day and that he had been offered a monthly bonus of $25 if he would work them even longer. Although Murphy and the others admitted that they were uncomfortable with the Dickinson contract, they argued that annulment would be a dishonorable act that would shake the business community's confidence in state government.[39] Most of the press agreed, but Davis had no intention of giving up. More than prison reform was at stake: three important officials who claimed to be his friends had defied his authority, and he was not about to let them get away with it.

In early August, Davis created a sensation when he told a reporter from the St. Louis *Globe-Democrat* that three members of the Penitentiary Board were sabotaging his efforts at prison reform. According to Davis, his opponents on the board had consigned the state's convicts to a living hell:

> It's about as bad a condition as could exist in any state. . . . I appeared before the grand jury of Lonoke County last week and produced witnesses to show to what ends the convicts are used. In that county there is a contractor who placed the convicts under guard of negroes. He feeds the convicts on greasy pork three times a day. At noon meal they receive a little cabbage of the poorest quality and some half-baked corn bread. They are fed in the fields right under the boiling sun, and permitted no recreation at all during the noon hour. It is simply outrageous and has got to stop if I have anything to say about it.
>
> I propose to go on the stump throughout the state and show up these members of the board of managers who vote to continue such a system. It should be stopped immediately. Three members of the board outvote me on every proposition, and we can do nothing. . . .
>
> We can not go on and let these men be starved and ill-treated in the manner they have been, and I do not propose to let up until the other members of the board agree to some more humane system. I think there will be some warm times in Arkansas before we are done with this question.[40]

The "warm times" that Davis predicted were not long in coming. At the Penitentiary Board meeting on August 12, an irate George Murphy introduced a resolution that implicitly accused Davis of slander and called for a full investigation of Davis's charges. When the board reconvened to consider Murphy's resolution two days later, the meeting was punctuated with several heated exchanges, and at one point Davis and Frank Hill nearly came to blows. At first, Davis tried to smooth his colleagues' ruffled feathers by insisting that he had been misquoted by the St. Louis press, but when Hill and Murphy refused to accept his explanation he became belligerent, threatening them with political extinction if they refused to knuckle under. In the end, with the help of State Auditor Monroe, who was nominally the chairman of the Penitentiary Board, Davis was able to carry the day. Although Monroe had sided with Hill and Murphy in earlier meetings, he now allowed Davis to reintroduce the motion to annul the Dickinson contract. This ruling prevented the board from voting on the Murphy resolution. Later, as Hill and Murphy looked on in horror, Monroe changed his vote on the annulment issue. By a vote of 3 to 2, the Board had reversed itself. To the surprise of everyone but Davis and Monroe, the Dickinson contract had been annulled.[41]

Though politically important, Davis's triumph proved to be more symbolic than real. Following the pattern established in the antitrust and state house controversies, the courts once again intervened and eventually nullified Davis's victory. It took the Arkansas Brick Manufacturing Company less than a week to obtain a temporary injuncton against the Penitentiary Board's annulment action; in mid-October George Murphy's former law partner, Chancery Judge Thomas B. Martin, granted the company a permanent injunction. Davis forced the board to appeal the case to the state supreme court, but no one doubted that the court would uphold the Dickinson contract. In May 1902, as expected, the court ruled against the board.[42]

The battle over the Dickinson contract poisoned Davis's relationship with Hill and Murphy, and open conflict became a routine affair at Penitentiary Board meetings. When Penitentiary Superintendent E. T. McConnell, an anti-Davis Democrat, resigned in early September after seven years in office, Davis and Crockett were jubilant. Although Hill, Murphy, and Monroe (Monroe continued to vacillate between the two factions) pushed through a resolution thanking McConnell for "his efficiency as superintendent and for his success in the financial management of the penitentiary affairs," Davis managed to have the last laugh.[43] McConnell's successor, Reese B. Hogins, was a former sheriff and county clerk of Pope County and a long-time friend of the Davis family. Although the entire Penitentiary Board endorsed Hogins's appointment, many anti-Davis Democrats feared that he would become a Davis puppet.[44]

While the penitentiary controversy simmered, Davis turned his attention to another potentially explosive issue, the proposed new state house. Under the terms of the state house act that Davis had signed in April, the original Capitol Commission had been disbanded, and a new commission appointed. The four men appointed to the new commission by the governor— Mayor Thomas Cox of Dardanelle, ex-Governor James P. Eagle, W. N. Norton of Forrest City and J. E. Martin of Conway—were all Davis stalwarts.[45]

The new commission had a mandate from the legislature to begin construction of the new state house as soon as possible. But Davis had other ideas. Throughout the summer, Davis lead the commissioners in a running feud with George Mann, the architect hired by the first commission. Davis did his best to force Mann to resign, but the architect made it clear that he would bow out only if the state made it worth his while financially. Proponents of the new state house urged Davis and the commissioners to stop squabbling with Mann and to begin construction, but as the months passed not a shovelful of dirt was turned. By late summer the state house advocates had just about run out of patience, when Davis suddenly threw them a curve. At a meeting of the Capitol Commission in early September, Davis unveiled a plan to build a new state house on the foundation of the old one. The proposal, which was tentatively endorsed by the commission, allegedly would save the taxpayers' money and thwart the plans of the special interests who had schemed to bleed the state dry. Davis's critics charged that his proposal was unrealistic—that it was simply a means of further postponing construction on the old penitentiary grounds. But Davis insisted that the proposal represented a legitimate compromise that took into account both the needs of state government and the interests of the common man. When George Mann complained that the proposal would shortchange future generations by producing a state house of inadequate size, Davis retorted: "Damn the future, it's the present I'm interested in."[46] No public statement ever revealed more about Davis's attitude toward "progressive" reform.

10

Hillbillies and Swamp Democrats

This man must be crazy. I never heard such a harangue in my life.
—*Senator James K. Jones (1901)*[1]

Davis's handling of the penitentiary and state house issues left many Democratic leaders disgruntled. But as the summer drew to a close no one seemed anxious to lock horns with him. More important, no anti-Davis Democrat had yet announced his intention to run for the governorship in 1902. Davis, never one to stand on formality and itching to get back out on the stump, decided to open his re-election campaign anyway. He kicked off in early September with a rousing speech at Searcy, in the old Populist stronghold of White County. Directing most of his fury at the legislature and the Penitentiary Board, he recounted the saga of the King Antitrust Bill and the fellow-servant bill, and pleaded with the crowd to elect a legislature that would stand up to the trusts. With the voter's help, he would finish the job that he had started—he would run "Red River" through the state house and clean out all the trust-heelers and "high-collared aristocrats."

The Searcy speech was a stem-winder that had the farmers of White County tossing their wool hats in the air before it was over. However, most Arkansas Democrats paid little attention to the fulminations of a candidate who was unopposed for re-election. Many voters were too busy preparing for the fall harvest to worry about politics; and for those who were interested in political affairs, there was a much more exciting race to watch than Davis's.[2]

All eyes were on the Senate race between ex-Governor James P. Clarke and incumbent Senator James K. Jones. Although Jones had served as chairman of the National Democratic Committee from 1896 to 1900 and was one of the most powerful figures in the Senate, most observers considered the race to be a tossup. In 1896 Jones had defeated Clarke rather handily, but nearly everyone expected the fiery lawyer from Phillips County to be a much stronger challenger in the rematch. Always aloof, Jones had grown increasingly stodgy and conservative since the Bryan debacle of 1896. The son of a prosperous Mississippi planter, he had never borne his wealth and status lightly. Habitually dressed in a "suit of black broadcloth," he had the look and manner of an Old South patrician. A successful lawyer and planter, he had recently gained a reputation as an entrepreneur by helping to orga-nize the American Round Bale Cotton Company,—a corporation holding a patent on a machine that pressed cotton into round bales. This association with the commercial elite undoubtedly improved his standing in New York and Washington, but it would not make things any easier for him out on the rural stump.[3]

Though Clarke was equally wealthy, he had more of the common touch. A clever stump speaker, he could sound like a Populist when he had to; and he was more reform-oriented than Jones, especially on the antitrust issue. But the major difference between the two candidates had little to do with ideology. Instead, the race seemed to revolve around intrastate sectionalism. Jones, a long-time resident of Hempstead County, was the candidate of South Arkansas; Clarke, who hailed from Helena, the "queen city of the Delta," was the candidate of East Arkansas. Competition between these two lowland regions was as old as the state itself, and the rivalry was never more intense than during contests between Clarke and Jones. To add to the drama, the "swamp Democrats" of East Arkansas had not elected a favorite son to the United States Senate since the 1850s.[4]

Realizing that his re-election campaign could not compete with the Jones-Clarke contest, Davis took one of the boldest steps of his career. If the Senate race was where the action was, then that's where he would go. Overlooking an unwritten party rule against mixing gubernatorial and senatorial politics, he decided to campaign for Clarke—knowing that his intervention on Clarke's behalf would shake the Arkansas Democratic party to its founda-tions. Of course, he had more to gain from an alliance with Clarke than mere excitement. As his recent problems with the legislature had demon-strated, without increased support from the voters and politicians of East Arkansas, Davis had little hope of gaining firm control of state politics. According to Jacobson, Davis's logic was simple: "He realized his weakness in eastern Arkansas. He knew that portion of the state was governed mostly by machine politics and he further knew that Senator Clarke was the strong-est man politically in that section of the state."[5] The fact that Davis admired Clarke and detested Jones made his decision that much easier. Similar in temperament and close enough in political philosophy to allow for a work-ing relationship, Davis and Clarke were natural allies.

On October 17, speaking before a huge crowd at a Labor Day celebration in Fort Smith, Davis "fired a bomb into the senatorial race." After reiterating that he had no intention of running for the Senate himself, he informed the crowd that it would be impossible for him to honor his campaign pledges if the powerful Senator Jones were re-elected. Unlike old Jim Berry, whom he described as "one of God's chosen noblemen," Jones had become a tool of the trusts, having succumbed to "personal greed and avarice." Why should an honest yeoman vote for a man who owned $850,000 worth of stock in the American Cotton Company? According to Davis, the American Cotton Company was "one of the most nefarious trusts that has ever burdened the people of the South."[6] At this point, the reporters began to run for the telephones, but Davis pressed on:

> I say to you, my fellow citizens, that all patents are in a sense a trust. . . . How much better it would be if the patent were removed and every farmer and ginner in the country were permitted to build one of these presses and have it in his back yard. If it is such a good thing why not let everbody have it? . . . He says that his stock, when last quoted on the market, was only worth ten cents on the dollar. Gentlemen, how many of you have got anything that is quoted on the market? Here we have one senator carrying around on his person stuff that is quoted in the market. Did you ever hear of old Jim Berry doing such a thing? . . . If the stock is not worth anything he ought to give it to some of these farmers to paper their houses with.[7]

By this time, most of the crowd was convinced that Jones practically lived on Wall Street, but Davis made sure that the farmers and workers of Sebastian County knew exactly what he was talking about:

> I say to you, my fellow citizens, that this American Cotton Company is a trust. . . . It was organized in the state of New Jersey, where all trusts are organized. . . . In the state of New Jersey, my fellow citizens, no private individual can look at the books, nobody can go behind the curtain and see what this thing really is, except a stockholder. . . . If he wanted to have a thing that was free from suspicion, why did he not organize it in some state where any citizen could look at the books? Why did he organize it in a state that never raised a pound of cotton on earth? Why did he not organize it in this beautiful Southland of ours right among the cotton fields? Ah, gentlemen, the pure white spotless cotton, emblematical of purity and holiness, would have blushed crimson red with shame should this nefarious creature have crept into our midst and been spawned upon us right where the greatest staple on God's green earth is grown. He knew it was a trust; therefore he got it as far away from the scene of the tragedy as possible.[8]

As the crowd buzzed with indignation, Davis delivered the clincher: Senator Jones and the trust-ridden Little Rock *Arkansas Democrat* had conspired to defeat the King Antitrust Bill. Hinting that Jones had been involved in a bribery scheme, Davis claimed that the senator had "crucified" the King Bill until it "fell dead and helpless at the very feet of the throne of Mammon." In closing, Davis insisted that he had no ulterior motives for opposing Jones's re-election. "I do not care anything about Governor Clarke especially," he declared, "but I cannot carry out my policy as your chief executive and pass you wholesome anti-trust legislation if Senator Jones is successful in this race. . . . I want to redeem my pledges; will you help me? I cannot do it with the trust-makers of all the trusts dominating the politics of Arkansas."[9]

Davis's attack on Jones sent shock waves across the state. Some observers were sure that Davis had gone mad. Others were convinced that, like most demagogues, he had become greedy and had simply overplayed his hand. Still others were a bit awed by his audacity; after all, it was not every day that a first-term governor had the nerve to declare war on one of the nation's most powerful politicians. Many anti-Davis editors claimed that the governor had proven once and for all that he was a power-hungry political boss. "Arkansas don't need any bossism in political contests," one irate editor wrote. "If Governor Davis keeps on he will, in course of time, be trying to dictate to the people whom they shall elect as city marshal, constable, and even down to who shall be night watchman."[10] Another claimed that Jones was being bullied by "Clarke, Davis and Co., a trust organized for the purpose of controlling Arkansas offices," and warned that "Davis is not satisfied with being Governor, he wants to be the whole thing."[11] As for Jones himself, he could hardly believe what had happened. After reading a transcript of the Fort Smith speech, he remarked: "This man must be crazy. I never heard such a harangue in my life.[12]

Unfortunately for Jones, the worst was yet to come. Pleased with the reaction to the charges made at Fort Smith, Davis soon dragged several other political skeletons out of the senator's closet. One Davis broadside charged that Jones had declared bankruptcy in 1868 in order to avoid paying a board bill. Another ridiculed him for serving only one month in the Confederate Army. Still another claimed that, while acting as a young woman's legal guardian, he had cheated his ward out of several thousand dollars.[13] At the same time, Davis continued to hammer away at Jones's involvement with the trusts, insisting that he had "pumped morphine" into the King Antitrust Bill. According to Davis, no man who owned stock in the American Cotton Company could legitimately claim to be an enemy of the trusts. "You couldn't find any cotton stock on Jim Berry," he exclaimed on more than one occasion, nor on "James P. Clarke, the white plumed knight of Arkansas."[14]

Many people seemed genuinely shocked by Davis's assault on Jones, but no one who knew him well could have been too surprised. Political combat was the natural order of things as far as Davis was concerned, and he was never quite himself when the political scene was peaceful. What the journalist Charles Morrow Wilson once said of Orval Faubus was equally true of Davis: he was "a fire handler, a wind feeler, a living echo of the backhill man, who would burn his bridges before he reaches them."[15] As Jacobson recalled, "It would have been a punishment to him greater than he could have withstood, to sit quietly by and watch Clarke and Jones campaign the state." Although Davis was playing with fire when he went after Jones, the Tribune of Haybinders could afford to take chances that no other politician would dare take. According to Jacobson:

> I know he deliberately brought upon himself this opposition, realizing no man in the state could defeat him, no matter what he said or did. He knew the boys in the hills and valleys would touch hands for him whenever he got out among them. He wanted to keep in personal touch with them, to meet them as often as opportunity afforded on their native heath, and weld them to him stronger politically, if that were possible. It was his constant personal contact with them that made them one and he knew no man would turn them from him, that he could not do so himself. If he urged them to vote against him they would not do so. If his record was attacked, they would not believe it. They knew he was their friend, that everything he did was for their good that he was their Governor, and so long as he served as such, their welfare and interests were being safeguarded. No man on the stump could have made any impression on them, however brilliant or oratorical he might have been.[16]

Perhaps so, but Jones was not about to throw in the towel. In early January, he issued a public letter which offered a point-by-point rebuttal of Davis's charges. The governor, he insisted, was a cheap political trickster who had no respect for the truth. Claiming that Davis had entered into an unethical factional alliance with Clarke, Jones ordered him to stop interfering with the senatorial campaign. Though he never admitted it publicly, Jones also helped to set up an anti-Davis headquarters that disseminated anti-Davis broadsides and pamphlets. At the same time, the anti-Davis press, which needed little prompting from Jones, picked up where it had left off during the 1900 campaign. One pro-Jones editor characterized Davis as "an ass in a lion's skin," while another called him "a mental, political pigmy."[17] Most important, Jones and his allies began to search for a gubernatorial candidate who could stop Davis in his tracks. Prior to Davis's attack on Jones, many anti-Davis Democrats had reconciled themselves to three more years of Jeff Davisism, but most were now convinced that Jeff had to go.

Finding a viable challenger was no easy task. Despite the consensus among anti-Davis leaders that Davis had forfeited his right to the traditional second term, no one was anxious to put his own career on the line. Some impatient conservatives, most notably James Mitchell of the *Arkansas Democrat*, seemed to believe that any respectable gentleman would suffice. Most anti-Davis leaders, however, realized that they needed someone who could beat Davis at his own game, someone who could convincingly bait the trusts and stroke the voters. In the end, it was generally agreed that the one man who had a good chance of defeating Davis was Elias Rector, the patrician-reformer who had sponsored the 1899 antitrust act. Although Rector was somewhat reluctant to join forces with the conservative wing of the party, he too had come to the conclusion that Davis had to be stopped. After several weeks of indecision, he announced for the governorship on January 2.[18] Anti-Davis Democrats were jubilant, but no one was happier than Davis. At long last, he had the race he had been hoping for.

Davis did not take Rector's challenge lightly. He knew all too well that his former ally was a formidable adversary. Not only was Rector an able campaigner, but he was also the only politician in the state whose trust-busting credentials rivaled those of Davis himself. With Rector as his opponent, Davis could not rely on the antitrust issue, which had figured so prominently in his primary victory two years earlier. Like it or not, he had to shift his attention to other matters.

Considering Rector's background, it is not surprising that Davis turned first to the issue of class. By Arkansas standards Rector was a bona fide aristocrat, and Davis was not about to let the voters forget it. Soon after Rector's entrance into the race, Davis managed to dredge up an incident that cast serious doubt on his opponent's commitment to democratic principles. In May 1900 Rector had gotten into a scuffle with Professor George B. Cook, the superintendent of the Hot Springs school system, after Cook refused to overrule a teacher's decision to flunk one of Rector's sons. Following a bitter argument—during which Rector accused Cook of being prejudiced against his child because he was the son of a gentleman—Rector drew a pistol on the unarmed professor. Although the two men were separated before any violence could take place, the fracas received a good deal of attention from the press.[19]

Rector was deeply embarrassed by the whole affair and hoped that the incident would soon be forgotten. But on January 11, with prompting from Davis, Cook released a public letter that gave a blow-by-blow account of the incident. According to Cook, at one point during the argument Rector had remarked: "Why, damn it, my children do not receive any better consideration at your hands in the public schools than do the children of common woodhaulers. . . . I will have you to understand, sir, that my son is a gentleman and the son of a gentleman, and the son of the most distinguished family in the South."[20] Davis, confident that Cook's statement would hurt Rector at the polls, flooded the state with a pamphlet edition of the letter.

On January 17, Rector angrily responded with a public letter insisting that he had been deliberately misquoted and that he was the victim of a cheap political trick. Professor Cook's embellished version of the incident had been inspired by Governor Davis, who had proven once and for all that he was a dishonorable man. According to Rector, the "woodhaulers" statement was a fabrication designed to incite the voters against him. While he could not deny that he belonged to a distinguished family, he maintained that he had always been a friend of the common laboring man. "My entire life and association," he assured the voters, "has been cast with the poorer classes. They have ever been my warmest friends and most zealous supporters. I was reared mostly on a farm and performed much of the labor incident to such a life, such as cutting and hauling wood and rails, building rail fences, driving oxen, etc, I look back on this part of my life with infinite pride and pleasure."[21] Rector insisted that his feud with Professor Cook was a private affair having nothing to do with politics. To interject such an affair into the gubernatorial campaign was an insult, not only to the Rector family, but also to the voting public.

Rector let it be known that, as a matter of personal honor, he would not tolerate any further exploitation of the Cook affair. But Davis refused to let up. In addition to reading the Cook letter at every opportunity on the stump, Davis began to ridicule Rector's high-toned lifestyle—especially his fashionable clothes. According to Davis, Colonel Rector was too proud to dress like an ordinary man. If the highfalutin Colonel were elected, a poor man would probably have to send his personal card in on a silver platter before the governor would agree to see him. "If my record don't suit you," Davis thundered, "vote for Rector, he's a gentleman.[22]

By the time the county canvass opened on January 27, at Lewisville, Rector had had enough. Clearly looking for a fight, he decided to liven things up with a personal attack of his own. He accused Davis of being a drunkard and of trying to disguise his condition by dousing himself with a sobering patent medicine called Wizard Oil. When Davis replied that "a brave and courageous man" would not try to capitalize on another man's physical afflictions, Rector jumped to his feet and, with clenched fists, warned Davis that if he continued to make such statements he would find out just how brave and courageous his opponent was. Davis backed off, but only after he had assured the crowd that Rector's challenge was a ruse concocted by a desperate man. Since he knew that he had no chance at the ballot box, Davis declared, Rector had resolved to remove his opponent from the race by physical force.[23]

At Hot Springs the next day, Rector tried to neutralize Davis's exploitation of the class issue. He charged that, while serving as attorney general, Davis had squandered the public's money on personal luxury items such as soap, combs, and worst of all, "a whirligig fan at the State's expense, to fan himself with, not being content to use a palm leaf like ordinary people."[24] Refusing to take Rector's charges seriously, Davis assured the Colonel that he could have the fan and what was left of the soap when he became governor.

When the canvass stopped at Lonoke a week later. Davis gave Rector a lesson in political theatrics and demonstrated just how vulnerable the Cook affair had left the Colonel. Styling himself as a martyr, Davis declared that his opponent was nothing more than a trigger-happy aristocrat:

I have not got any gun on me, and now, Col. Rector, I ask if you have. I will turn all my pockets inside out and let the sheriff of Lonoke County search me, and I want to know if you will let the sheriff search you? You have got a pistol on you and you dare not deny this fact. You struck an unarmed school teacher once, Prof. Cook, of your own city, with a pistol. You have got one now. Deny it, and I will prove it by letting the sheriff of this county search you. Will you submit to it? You can shoot me, murder me as Goebel was murdered, but you cannot bluff me.[25]

As Rector, who was indeed packing a pistol beneath his coat, sat in stony silence, the crowd roared for Jeff.

The class issue was not the only weapon in Davis's political arsenal. Rector's close association with Commissioner Frank Hill and former Penitentiary Superintendent E. T. McConnell—according to Davis—was part of a conspiratorial "penitentiary ring" that was trying to take over the state. Davis claimed that because he had exposed the inhumane conditions in the penitentiary system, the "ring" had vowed to destroy his political career.[26]

The "penitentiary ring" controversy had been brewing for months. During the fall, Davis had provided the Memphis *Commercial Appeal* and the St. Louis *Globe-Democrat* with photographs of a convict whom he claimed had been starved and beaten to death by prison guards. These grotesque pictures, one of which was later reproduced on a campaign broadside, showed an emaciated figure mutilated by what appeared to be whip marks. Rector produced an affidavit from a prison doctor who swore that the marks were actually bed sores, and that the governor had known from the very beginning that the convict had died of natural causes. Unflappable as ever, Davis claimed that such testimony simply confirmed the existence of a conspiracy: Rector and his friends had mistreated the state's convicts, feeding them nothing but "coarse bulk pork, cabbage leaves and corn bread," and now they were trying to cover up their crimes. Davis believed "in reforming convicts, and not in killing them," and boasted that he had promised the prisoners at one camp that he would "pardon every d——n one of them" if the penitentiary staff did not start treating them better. "We changed the penitentiary and put a new superintendent in," Davis told a crowd at Hot Springs, "and it was the greatest victory that ever took place in Arkansas when we put "Bud" McConnell out. Red River got started."[27]

The most spectacular aspect of the penitentiary controversy had little to do with penal reform. Despite a sincere desire for reform, Davis often allowed his remarks on the penitentiary issue to deteriorate into a Negrophobic harangue. He had discovered that nothing excited the voters more than the charge that Rector had sanctioned the use of "negro guards" at the state prison camp at England. In a speech at Rogers in late January, Davis described the horrors that he had discovered during an inspection of the England camp the previous July. To his utter amazement, he saw "negro guards lay a white man face down on the ground and while one stood on his neck another held his feet and a third whipped him on the bare back." "Every time the lash fell," Davis recalled, "the flesh puffed and curled like a bacon rind on a hot skillet."[28] The England story was repeated in speech after speech, in varying degrees of detail and hyperbole. "The first sight that greeted my eyes," he assured the crowd at Hot Springs "was a great, big, black negro with a pump gun guarding the white men and driving them down the row and saying: 'Hoe that cotton, damn you, or I will kill you.'"[29]

According to Davis, such outrages were primarily the work of Rector's close friend, Commissioner Frank Hill. Davis claimed that at one meeting of the Penitentiary Board, Hill, who was not a native Southerner, had openly defended the practice of hiring black guards. "Judge Hill, I told him, a nigger may be good enough up in Canada where you were reared, but he is not good enough in this sunny land of ours."[30] Both Rector and Hill issued vigorous denials and offered $100 to anyone who could substantiate the governor's charges. Davis gleefully accepted the challenge and promised to withdraw from the race if proved wrong. Then Rector produced an affidavit signed by Frank Barton, the warden at the England camp, which emphatically denied that black guards had been used at England. Davis countered with an eyewitness who swore that Barton was lying.[31] Whatever the truth, every exchange worked to Davis's advantage, since it fixed public attention on Rector's alleged breach of racial etiquette.

Frustrated and angry, Rector counterattacked as best he could. He chastised Davis for providing state convicts, 90 percent of whom were black, with a fancy turkey dinner at Christmas. Why, asked Rector, did a governor who claimed to be devoted to white supremacy pamper "negro convicts" who were already eating better than "a majority of the people in the back counties"?[32] In a similar vein, the anti-Davis press resurrected a minor racial scandal involving Davis and a well-known ex-slave, Uncle Bob Perry. While enroute to the northwestern part of the state in September 1901, Davis allegedly invited Perry and several other "rowdy negroes" into a white-only railway coach to entertain the gubernatorial party with a "drunken hoedown." According to eyewitnesses who signed sworn statements, after watching his guests "pat Juba" and dance the cakewalk, the Governor produced a bottle of whiskey from which he and the "darkeys" then drank their fill.[33]

Despite such efforts, Rector remained on the defensive where the race issue was concerned. In any event, in the latter stages of the campaign neither candidate seemed anxious to make race the central issue of the contest.

Davis, preferring to bludgeon Rector with the class issue, simply allowed the matter to drop. Nevertheless, he had introduced a new and potentially important weapon into the ever-escalating warfare of Democratic factionalism. Like most successful Southern Democrats, Davis had race-baited

Republicans and Populists throughout his political career, but never before had he done so to a member of his own party. His handling of the "negro guards" incident was a masterful performance of Negrophobic demagoguery worthy of Ben Tillman or James K. Vardaman. Looking back on the affair years later, J. N. Heiskell claimed that Davis had "anticipated *The Clansman* [by] several years."[34]

The use of the race issue against Rector represented a turning point in the history of the Davis movement. For the first time in his career, he had focused on an issue which was not directly related to the economic and cultural plight of the agrarian South. Admittedly, during the 1880s and 1890s, he had been a leading figure in a Democratic county organization that indulged in more than its share of Negrophobic politics. And the interracial and interparty violence of the Pope County Militia War of 1872 had tightly woven Democratic partisanship and white racism into the fabric of local politics. Indeed, as a candidate for district prosecuting attorney in 1890, Davis had promised to "fill the penitentiary so full of negroes that their feet would be sticking out of the windows."[35] Yet, beyond this one statement there is no evidence that Davis was an unusually militant white supremacist during his early years in politics.

Although Davis had been an active participant in the white supremacist annihilation of the Populist movement, racial demagoguery played no direct role in his rise to power in state Democratic politics. During the primary campaigns of 1898 and 1900, white supremacy was simply not an issue. Aside from emphasizing his personal identification with Jefferson Davis and the Lost Cause, Davis ignored racial themes entirely.[36] And his opponents did the same, with one minor exception: at one point during the 1900 campaign, A. F. Vandeventer criticized Davis for failing to rid the state of black strikebreakers, but the charge never developed into a full-fledged issue.[37] When it came to race-baiting Republicans and Populists, Davis could more than hold his own, as he demonstrated in the general election campaign of 1900. But the kind of white supremacist harangue that Davis used against Remmel and Files did not set him apart from other Democratic leaders. Only when he race-baited Elias Rector did he break with party tradition.

All in all, the Cook affair, the attack on the "penitentiary ring," and the black guards controversy made the Davis-Rector contest one of the most heated gubernatorial campaigns in Arkansas history. Soon after the opening of the county canvass, one editor reported that the campaign "was getting as hot as a cooking stove."[38] Another wrote that "no man who is without a thick hide has any business running for office these days."[39]

For Elias Rector, such comments were food for thought. An experienced campaigner, Rector had never encountered anything like Davis's barrage of abuse; as a man of wealth and status, he was not accustomed to being insulted to his face; a serious politician, he could not abide Davis's melo-dramatic posturing. Politics, in his view, was supposed to be the domain of gentlemen who played by the rules: Although he tried to adapt to his opponent's no-holds-barred style of campaigning, by mid-February Rector's daily confrontations with Davis had become a burden that he could no longer tolerate. Withdrawing from the official county canvass, he stumped the state alone for the final six weeks of the campaign.[40] This was an opportunity for Davis to turn his guns on Senator Jones.

This welcome change allowed Davis to return to the antitrust issue. By late February, he was concentrating almost all of his fire on the "trust-heeling" Jones, who soon realized that he was in deep trouble.[41] Sensing that he had to turn the campaign around, Jones challenged Davis to a public debate. Davis eagerly accepted, and the two men met on March 14, at Forrest City in St. Francis County. March was a slack time in the cotton belt, and thousands of East Arkansas farmers poured into the town to witness the confrontation. Davis did not disappoint them. Focusing on Jones's involve-ment with the American Cotton Company, he added a vaudevillian twist to his antitrust crusade. As one observer described the scene:

> Referring to Senator Jones' alleged sympathy with the trusts he called to know if there were any Jones buttons in the audience and several buttons were pitched to the governor. The governor took one in his hand and told the voters to look on the back and see where they were made. "Even the buttons," continued the governor, "were made in Newark, N.J., the state where Senator Jones' trust was organized." Still holding the button aloft, the governor sang the following ditty, to the tune of "She Was Bred in Old Kentucky":
>
> > They were made in old New Jersey,
> > Where the trusts were formed, you know.
> > They were made in old New Jersey,
> > Where the senator's patent grows, etc.[42]

By the time Jones got up to speak, the crowd belonged to Davis. Although the senator gave a creditable speech, his lengthy discussion of the dif-ferences between a patent and a trust could not compete with Davis's rollicking harangue. As Jones left the podium there was polite applause, but it was clear to everyone present that Davis had carried the day.[43] The senator had gambled and lost.

In the aftermath of the Forrest City debate, Davis grew increasingly confident. A week before the primary, he sent his campaign workers a wire that read: "Save Clarke, all hell can't beat me."[44] Many political observers agreed with the governor's prediction. The Rector camp however, remained optimistic. In the latter stages of the campaign, Rector pinned his hopes on one issue—Davis's drinking habits. This was the one area where Davis was vulnerable. Focusing public attention on the governor's numerous drinking escapades, Rector repeated the Wizard Oil charge at every opportunity. He produced several witnesses who swore that Davis was a shameless drunkard. In a state where voters took the prohibition issue seriously and where most of the religious establishment was "dry" to the point of obsession, this was not a bad strategy. Hoping to mobilize the Prohibitionists, anti-Davis editors added some of their own charges. The most serious charge was issued by the *Arkansas Democrat*, which claimed that Davis had compounded his sins by pardoning hundreds of convicted liquor-law violators. Depicting Davis as an immoral backslider who violated Christian principles at every turn, the *Democrat* maintained that the governor was owned lock, stock, and barrel by the liquor interests.[45]

When Davis first assumed the governorship, temperance advocates had reason to believe that the new governor would prove to be a reliable ally. Although there had been no mention of the liquor issue during the 1900 campaign, it was well known that in the early 1890s Davis had been the prosecuting attorney of the "driest" judicial district in the state. Davis's home county was an old Prohibitionist stronghold, having been one of the first (1882) counties in Arkansas to outlaw saloons. Indeed, Davis's own father had once been a well-known temperance crusader.[46] Thus, despite the disturbing rumor that the governor was a heavy drinker, Prohibitionists had high hopes that the new administration would be sympathetic to their cause.

These expectations were quickly shattered. In April 1901, less than three months after his inauguration, Davis vetoed the Holt Bill, which would have prohibited the common practice of legally transporting liquor into dry counties. The bill posed a serious threat to the local liquor industry, and was considered by many Prohibitionists to be the most important piece of temperance legislation ever passed by an Arkansas legislature. In his veto message, Davis argued that the bill was too extreme; that, if permitted to become law, it would be met "with such a revulsion of feeling that I believe at the next general election every county in the state would vote for license, and in the meantime there would be an increase in illicit distilleries in all forms from which we would have liquor with its most demoralizing and pernicious effects." Although willing to pay homage to the temperance ideal, Davis refused to align himself with the "extremists" who wanted to make the state bone dry. In his judgment, Arkansas already had "the best liquor laws of any state in the Union."[47]

Despite the veto of the Holt Bill, most Arkansas temperance leaders continued to court the governor's favor. In November, Davis was elected first vice-president of the Arkansas Baptist Association, the most temperance-conscious religious organization in the state. Although some Baptist leaders were outraged by this action, most were willing to give Davis the benefit of the doubt. Many temperance leaders were clearly troubled by Davis's alliance with James P. Clarke, who was known to be a strong supporter of the East Arkansas liquor interests. But for the most part Davis's relationship with the "morality crowd" remained relatively cordial until Rector shattered the peace with his sensational accusations.[48]

Rector's charges scandalized the Baptist hierarchy. Several leading ministers issued public statements denouncing Davis's disgraceful behavior; others called for an official investigation of his conduct. In mid-February, Frank White, an ex-chaplain of the state senate and a celebrated Baptist preacher, publicly commended the editor of the *Arkansas Democrat* for exposing "the bad conduct of Mr. Davis as a high official of church and state." "I have no hesitation in venturing," White declared, "that very few Baptists who voted for Mr. Davis as vice-president of the Paragould convention [i.e. the State Baptist Association] will support him for governor in the primar[y]. . . . With all the influence I have, I am for Rector against Davis, first, last, and all time."[49] The Reverend Charles T. Arnett, editor of *The Baptist Evangel*, claimed that it was "a notorious fact" that Davis was "a drunkard, a base slanderer, a libertine and gambler, a blasphemer and a liar."[50]

Religious leaders from other denominations soon joined in. On March 17, two weeks before the primary, the Reverend William E. Thompson, pastor of one of Little Rock's largest Methodist churches, delivered a special sermon entitled "The Church in Politics—Among the Politicians." Speaking to an overflow crowd, including the Governor and Mrs. Davis, Reverend Thompson warned that "if a man's private life is impure he hasn't got any right in a place of public trust, no matter how much he may know." Though Thompson did not attack Davis by name, there was no mistaking the anti-Davis nature of the sermon, particularly when he exhorted the crowd to "silence the voice of the demagogue and tear the mask from the face of the sycophant." Near the end of the sermon, he made a thinly-veiled plea for Davis's defeat:

> When you find one vice in a man you find a bunch. We allow men to go into public office who have debased virtue. We put men in office who are addicted to drunkenness. We have a right to demand a clean private life of a public man, as well as a clean administration. . . . The politics of our national life must be kept pure. When the church of God rises in its majesty and determines to *vote* for God and humanity it will be the most effective preaching it has ever done.[51]

Within moments of the last "amen," Davis rushed to the pulpit and pumped the preacher's hand, complimenting him on his "magnificient sermon."[52] Whether or not Jeff winked or even cracked a smile at the bewildered preacher, we will never know. Most likely he played it straight. In Arkansas, the forces of righteousness were on the march, and even Jeff Davis—a man who often flaunted social convention, a man who well deserved the sobriquet "the Wild Ass of the Ozarks"—had to step a little lightly in their wake.

The temperance crowd was a powerful social movement with a long history of political involvement. With varying degrees of intensity, Arkansas politicians had been wrangling with the liquor issue since the end of Reconstruction. In 1875, at the request of local temperance societies, the legislature passed a "three-mile law" that allowed residents living within three miles of an academy or college to petition the county court for local prohibition. Despite its limited utility, the three-mile law set the stage for the organization of the Arkansas Christian Temperance Union in January 1879. Later in the year, the temperance union pressured the legislature to pass a local option law requiring each county to hold a biennial referendum to determine the legality of local saloon licenses.[53] This institutionalized the political salience of the liquor issue and led to increased conflict between wets and drys.

As Table 14 illustrates, the early years of the local option system were lean years for Arkansas Prohibitionists. In 1882 only eleven of the state's seventy-four counties voted to outlaw local saloons. In 1884 the number of dry counties fell to seven, as nearly 70 percent of the electorate voted for license. By the mid-1880s some leading temperance advocates had become disillusioned with the license system and pressure-group tactics and had begun to talk about the need for an independent prohibitionist party. Such talk alienated many Democratic partisans and split the movement. When the Arkansas Prohibitionist party became a reality in 1892, the party's gubernatorial candidate, Judge J. W. Nelson, received less than one percent of the vote.

TABLE 14
The Growth of the Anti-License Movement in Arkansas, 1882–1910*

					Total Vote	
Year	Dry Counties	Wet Counties	% Anti-License	% Pro-License	Anti-License	Pro-License
1882	11	63	36.3	63.7	45,187	79,246
1884	7	68	31.8	68.2	44,144	94,602
1892	19	38	44.1	55.9	49,348	62,628
1894	44	31	51.1	48.9	56,978	54,490
1896	33	42	47.6	52.4	61,362	68,088
1898	26	49	44.5	55.5	45,915	57,188
1900	30	45	46.3	53.7	56,323	65,450
1902	43	32	48.4	51.6	54,935	58,545
1904	47	28	50.7	49.3	70,916	68,963
1906	54	21	55.2	44.8	82,250	66,626
1908	57	18	57.1	42.9	89,350	67,168
1910	63	12	58.1	41.9	81,699	58,947

*At each biennial state election Arkansas voters were given the opportunity to vote for or against the legalization of saloons in their respective counties. The two alternatives under this local-option system were called "pro-license" and "anti-license."
SOURCE: *Biennial Report of the Secretary of State of Arknsas, 1881–1882 . . . 1909–1910.*

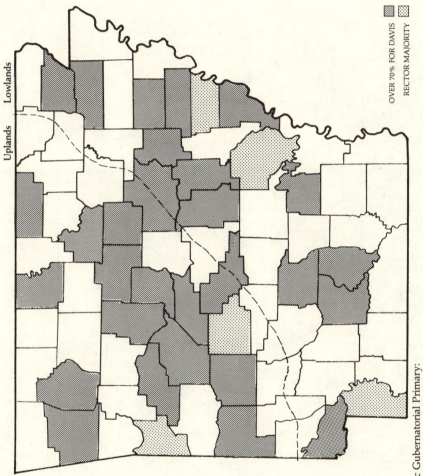

Uplands

Lowlands

OVER 70% FOR DAVIS

RECTOR MAJORITY

FIGURE 8.
1902 Democratic Gubernatorial Primary:
% for Jeff Davis

SOURCE: Little Rock *Arkansas Gazette*, April 24, 1904.

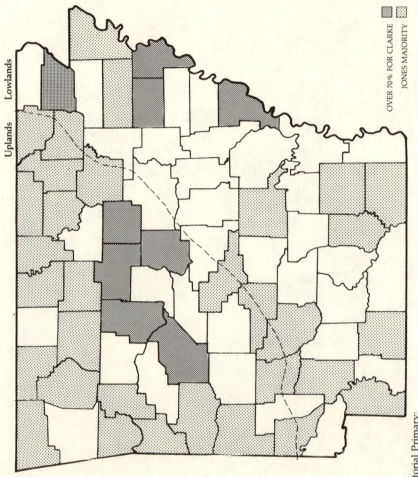

Uplands   Lowlands

OVER 70% FOR CLARKE

JONES MAJORITY

FIGURE 9.
1902 Democratic Senatorial Primary:
% for James P. Clarke

SOURCE: Arkadelphia *Southern-Standard*, April 24, 1902.

Despite the Prohibitionist party's problems, the anti-license movement began to take hold in the early 1890s. By the middle of the decade, pro- and anti-license forces were battling on almost even terms. In 1894 "No License Associations" were organized in several counties; and, for the first time, more than half of the state's counties outlawed the sale of liquor.[54] Although a dry majority would not occur again until 1902, the anti-license movement had established itself as a force to be reckoned with.

In 1899, after a relatively poor showing in the previous election, temperance advocates organized the Arkansas Anti-Saloon League. Though beset by factionalism, the league soon mobilized the anti-license vote to an unprecedented extent. The growth of the anti-license vote between 1898 and 1910 was extraordinary (see Table 14), as the number of dry counties increased from twenty-six to sixty-three. In fact, the local liquor industry found it necessary to form a State Protective Association in 1904.[55]

The temperance lobby, a rising force in Arkansas politics, was not strong enough to turn the tide in the 1902 primary. Despite the best efforts of Rector and his Prohibitionist allies, Davis won a sweeping victory on election day. Winning strong support in all areas of the state, Davis received 66.1 percent of the vote and carried seventy of Arkansas's seventy-five counties. Much to Davis's delight, James P. Clarke also emerged victorious, though his margin of victory—he won 54.3 percent of the vote—was much narrower than Davis's. Although Jones ran well in many South Arkansas and Ozark mountain counties, this did not offset Clarke's strong showing in the eastern and central portions of the state.

TABLE 15
The 1902 Davis Vote: Precinct Returns, Eleven County Sample

Type of Precinct	N	% for Davis 1902 (Group Mean)	N	% for Davis 1900 (Group Mean)	Δ 1900–1902	% for Clarke 1902 (Group Mean)
City	3	56.7	3	46.2	+10.5	52.8
Large Town–Farm	8	55.6	5	58.2	−2.6	48.5
Small Town–Farm	16	57.5	7	62.2	−4.7	35.0
Village-Farm	20	69.3	11	72.3	−3.0	59.4
Hamlet-Farm	36	73.1	19	75.2	−2.1	57.0
Farm (Suburban)	3	65.1	3	60.1	+5.0	57.0
Farm Central)	46	65.9	23	65.2	+0.7	47.1
Farm (Isolated)	49	71.7	23	74.7	−3.0	53.1
Farm (Very Isolated)	22	74.4	7	62.1	+12.3	54.5
Populist*	33	78.1	23	73.5	+4.6	60.6
Prohibitionist†	61	69.1	13	71.8	−2.7	48.3

*The 1900 Populist precincts are the same as those in Table 8. In each of the 1902 Populist precincts, the Populist candidate for governor received 40 percent or more of the vote at least once between 1892 and 1896. See Appendix B.
†The 1900 Prohibitionist precincts are the same as those in Table 9. In each of the 1902 Prohibitionist precincts, the anti-saloon license vote (i.e. the vote for a dry county) exceeded 65 percent at least once between 1906 and 1912. See Appendix B.
SOURCE: See Appendix B.

The nature of Davis's victory can be seen in Figure 8 and Table 15. The only county in which Rector polled a large vote (76.7 percent) was his home county of Garland, though he did manage to eke out narrow victories in four other counties: Sebastian (52.9 percent), the one county that Davis had failed to carry in the 1900 primary; Miller County (50.3 percent), which included the city of Texarkana; and two prosperous East Arkansas plantation counties, Lee (55.3 percent) and Arkansas (50.9 percent). Like Davis's opponents in the 1900 primary, Rector was most popular among urban voters. Conversely, Davis's support was concentrated in the rural areas, particularly in the more isolated farm precincts. With few exceptions, voting precincts that did not include incorporated towns were solidly pro-Davis. Although Davis made his strongest showing in exclusively rural precincts, he also ran extremely well in farm precincts that included villages or hamlets, just as he had done two years earlier.

As Table 15 illustrates, the 1900 and 1902 Davis coalitions were strikingly similar. The only major development was Davis's improved showing in the "very isolated" farm townships. The reasons for his increased popularity in remote areas undoubtedly varied from precinct to precinct, but in many cases it probably reflected two additional years of campaigning. By the time the 1902 primary was held, Davis had had the opportunity to spread his message farther into the backcountry (which may also help to explain why he picked up more votes in the old Populist strongholds). He also had a large campaign staff to help him, something he did not have in the 1900 campaign.

As the figures in Tables 16–18 demonstrate, this infusion of backcountry voters—many of whom were poor or illiterate—had some impact on the

TABLE 16
Illiteracy, Farm Tenancy, and the 1902 Davis Vote in Four Sample Counties:
Rank-Order Correlations

County	N (Precincts)	Rank-Order Correlation Between Davis Vote and White Illiteracy Rate, 1900*	Rank-Order Correlation Between Davis Vote and White Farm Tenancy† 1900*
Drew	12	+.853	+.015
Howard	16	−.013	−.125
Marion	20	−.045	−.078
St. Francis	11	−.214	−.046

*Among white heads of household.
†"Farm laborers" have been grouped with tenant farmers.
SOURCES: *12th Census of the United States, 1900, Population Schedules,* Manuscript Returns for Drew, Howard, Marion, and St. Francis Counties, Arkansas, located at the National Archives, Washington, D.C. The electoral data are from: *The Monticellonian* (Drew County), April 4, 1902; *Nashville News,* April 2, 1902; Yellville *Mountain Echo,* April 11, 1902; *Forrest City Times,* April 4, 1902.

TABLE 17
The Distribution of Wealth and the 1902 Davis Vote in Washington County:
Rank-Order Correlations

Township	Personal Property Per Taxpayer, 1903	Rank	% for Jeff Davis, 1902	Rank	% for James P. Clarke, 1902	Rank
Vineyard	$450	1	83.7	13	87.5	5
Springdale	357	2	77.9	17	61.5	27
Prairie	354	3	54.7	28	57.8	28
Prairie Grove	338	4	75.2	21	79.3	14
Marrs Hill	305	5	83.0	15	72.1	19.5
Illinois	284	6	88.9	8	81.9	11
Goshen	264	7	79.4	16	72.1	19.5
Wheeler	260	8	88.2	9	93.1	2
Rheas Mill	259	9	77.8	18	83.3	10
Cane Hill	258	10	52.4	29	47.4	29
Center	258	11	85.8	11	83.6	9
Price	256	12	93.3	4	85.7	6
Richland	242	13	73.2	24	65.7	25
Elm Springs	238	14	76.4	20	71.0	22
Wyman	234	15	91.7	5	75.0	16.5
Wedington	230	16	62.8	25	71.4	21
Brush Creek	228	17	74.6	22	88.5	4
Dutch Hills	220	18	73.8	23	79.7	13
Star Hill	186	19	57.5	26	91.9	3
Durham	183	20	87.0	10	63.6	26
White River	183	21	76.8	19	67.8	23
Boston	180	22	83.3	14	76.5	15
Valley	178	23	55.4	27	66.7	24
Cove Creek	164	24	95.7	3	75.0	16.5
Winslow	155	25	91.3	6	84.1	7
Reed	149	26	90.6	7	74.2	18
West Fork	147	27	100.0	1.5	81.6	12
Lees Creek	146	28	100.0	1.5	95.2	1
Crawford	145	29	84.2	12	83.8	8
			$R_s = -.533$		$R_s = -.231$	

SOURCES: Washington County Tax Book for 1903, located at the Washington County Courthouse, Fayetteville, Arkansas; *Springfield News*, April 11, 1902.

socioeconomic profile of the Davis coalition. This was certainly true in Washington County, where the rank order correlation between the Davis vote and the distribution of personal property went from +.187 in 1900 to −.533 in 1902. Nevertheless, very few of these figures support a lower-class interpretation of the Davis movement. In 1902, as in 1900, Davis's support among farmers cut across economic class lines. Although it often paralleled lines of social stratification, the factional split between Davis Democrats and anti-Davis Democrats was primarily a function of the urban-rural cleavage, not of economic class per se. This interpretation is confirmed by the relevant simple and partial correlation coefficients in Appendix A (Tables A and G).

TABLE 18
The Distribution of Wealth and the 1902 Davis Vote in Sharp County:
Rank-Order Correlations

Township	Personal Property Per Household, 1904	Rank	% for Jeff Davis, 1902	Rank	% for James P. Clarke, 1902	Rank
Lebanon	$490	1	61.0	13	48.0	10
Piney Fork	486	2	35.7	17	18.4	17
Big Rock	395	3	90.1	5	72.7	2
Hardy	387	4	46.4	15	22.6	16
Richwoods	360	5	67.0	12	58.3	8
Sullivan	349	6	38.7	16	27.5	14
Cave	338	7	74.7	10	31.8	12
Jackson	333	8	77.9	8	30.2	13
Morgan	312	9	94.9	3	65.5	5
Highland	304	10	96.3	2	69.8	2
Strawberry	299	11	80.3	7	65.8	4
Big Creek	274	12	76.3	9	50.0	9
Lave Creek	272	13	96.9	1	84.2	1
Scott	258	14	73.8	11	40.2	11
North	245	15	25.0	19	13.0	15
Washington	245	16	86.7	6	59.1	7
Davidson	226	17	93.4	4	61.0	6
Johnson	226	18	57.1	14	00.0	19
Union	211	19	32.8	18	25.0	15
			$R_s = -.081$		$R_s = +.055$	

SOURCES: The tax data appear in the *Sharp County Record,* September 30, 1904. The number of households in each township has been tabulated from the *12th Census of the United States, 1900, Population Schedules,* Manuscript returns for Sharp County, Arkansas, located at the National Archives, Washington, D.C. The electoral returns are from the *Sharp County Record,* April 11, 1902.

The coefficients in Appendix A reveal at least one other interesting pattern: the Prohibitionist forces split their vote in 1902. Despite the Wizard Oil controversy and Davis's alliance with Clarke, the temperance issue seems to have had no more impact on the distribution of the Davis vote in 1902 than it did in 1900.

The most difficult aspect of the 1902 primary to interpret is the Davis-Clarke alliance. Although Davis and Clarke did everything they could to encourage factional voting, they were dealing with an electorate unfamiliar with factional politics. Did the voters follow their advice and vote along factional lines? The precinct data in Tables 15, 17, and 18 and the +.485 correlation (see Appendix A) between the Davis vote and the Clarke vote indicate that some did and some did not. Although split-ticket voting was common in many areas of the state, particularly in the south Arkansas lowlands and in the mountain counties of northern and western Arkansas, the factional alignment between the two candidates had considerable impact on voting patterns in a number of counties. In sharp contrast to his poor showing in most upland counties. Clarke polled a large vote in Davis's home county of Pope (73.1 percent) and in the nearby Davis strongholds of Cleburne (72.0 percent), Van Buren (71.2 percent), and Yell (70.1 percent). Conversely, the Clarke forces boosted Davis's totals in several lowland counties. In addition to winning 94.7 percent of the vote in Clarke's home county (Phillips), Davis made a surprisingly strong showing throughout most of the traditionally conservative East Arkansas Delta. Significantly, not one of the five delta counties in which Davis had trouble—Arkansas, Lee, Jefferson, Desha, and Mississippi—was a Clarke stronghold.

Politically speaking the results of the 1902 primary represented a great victory for Davis. By defeating Elias Rector, he eliminated the only politician who had any hope of challenging his leadership of the local antitrust crusade. And by engineering the defeat of James K. Jones, he demoralized the conservative wing of the Arkansas Democratic party. Finally, by effecting an alliance with James P. Clarke, he transformed an embryonic political organization into a powerful statewide machine. Unfortunately, Davis paid an enormous price for his victories over Rector and Jones. The alliance with Clarke brought him added political power and security, but it also compromised the ideological integrity of the Davis movement. With few exceptions, the "swamp Democrats" who entered the Davis organization via the Clarke alliance had little sympathy for and little understanding of the one-gallus revolt that had brought Davis to power. Perhaps even more important, the racial and moralistic turmoil of the Davis-Rector campaign diverted attention from Davis's crusade against New South colonialism. To the detriment of the embattled dirt farmers of Arkansas, the 1902 campaign and its aftershocks permanently altered the course of the Davis movement.

11

Just a Pint Baptist

To be wholly respectable a man must give up many an enjoyment.
—*Opie Read*[1]

Davis's landslide victory in the 1902 primary set the leaders of the anti-Davis coalition back on their heels, but it did little to still the controversies which had dominated the campaign. Nowhere was this more evident than in the continuing controversy over Davis's moral character. Although in his hour of triumph, Davis jubilantly declared that he had been "fully and overwhelmingly exonerated" from the "vile charges" that had been levelled against him, it soon became apparent that he was whistling in the dark.[2] Curiously enough, Davis himself was instrumental in keeping the issue alive. On March 30, the day after the primary, he provoked a feud with ex-Governor James P. Eagle, the perennial president of the Arkansas Baptist Association. Although Eagle was a personal friend, Davis demanded his resignation from the Capitol Commission, ostensibly because Eagle had publicly supported James K. Jones in the recent senatorial primary.[3] When Eagle refused to step down, the donnybrook was on.

On April 7, Davis resigned as first vice-president of the State Baptist Association, complaining that "those in high authority in the denomination have taken no occasion to deny the vile slanders that have been made against me."[4] President Eagle accepted the resignation, and for the first time in months Baptist leaders breathed a sigh of relief. However, on April 18, Davis formally removed Eagle from the Capitol Commission, infuriating not only the Baptist establishment but also the state legislature, which ultimately ruled that the governor had no legal right to order Eagle's removal. The entire controversy soon became entangled in the affairs of the Second Baptist Church of Little Rock, to which both Davis and Eagle belonged. Less than a week after Eagle's ouster, a church disciplinary committee, including State Supreme Court Justice Carroll Wood, ex-Attorney General W. F. Atkinson, and former Populist gubernatorial candidate A. W. Files, drew up a list of formal charges against Davis. The charges were essentially the same as those circulated by the anti-Davis press during the 1902 primary campaign:

1. Recently he went to Hot Springs, Ark., to attend a reception to some editorial excursion, and during his stay there became thoroughly drunk and acted in a most disgraceful manner, and has brought disgrace to the cause of Christ.

2. Prior thereto he went to Hot Springs and got drunk, and went to a gambling house and bet and lost money and acted otherwise in a disorderly, unbecoming and disgraceful manner.

3. That last fall, on a trip from Camden to Little Rock, he was drunk and disorderly.

4. That recently he was drinking and treating some negroes on a train in northwestern Arkansas, in or near Benton county, Ark.

5. That he was drinking and drunk on the Choctaw train running out from Little Rock, on or about Monday after the recent primary election.

6. That sometime since he has been governor he was drunk at Texarkana, Ark.

7. That he has otherwise violated the principles of our church covenant by neglecting to perform his duties, and by grossly sinning against the purposes and principles of its organization.[5]

Davis condemned the committee's proceedings as a political witch hunt conducted by "traitors and hypocrites"; however, since he had done nothing wrong, he was "ready for trial." "My only offense," he insisted, "is that I lent humble assistance in defeating their idol, James K. Jones, who is now a political corpse, and the official decapitation of my distinguished friend Governor Eagle."[6] After more than a month of heated exchanges between Davis and his accusers, the trial finally convened on May 28. More than a hundred members of the congregation were present. Ex-Attorney General E. B. Kinsworthy acted as Davis's unofficial counsel and put up a spirited defense. But in the end only five members of the congregation voted against expulsion. On May 29, exactly two months after his primary victory, Davis—who refused to attend the trial and was away on a fishing trip in the wilds of Chicot County—was informed that he had been formally expelled from the congregation:

Now we command you brethren, in the name of our Lord Jesus Christ, that ye withdraw yourselves from every brother that walketh disorderly, and not after the tradition which he received after us.

—2 Thess. 3:6[7]

Before the ink on his expulsion notice was dry, the wayward governor managed to turn the situation to his advantage. Davis, who liked nothing better than to assume the role of the martyr, had been provided with the perfect backdrop for a political "passion play." Readmitted to the fellowship by his home church in Russellville, he implored the people of Arkansas to strike down the "high-collared" pharisees who had persecuted him for his political beliefs. "I love the Baptist church of Arkansas," he told the State

Democratic Convention in mid-June, "and a few canting hypocrites of this church cannot drive me from its blessed folds. This last thrust of the dying men of the late senatorial campaign is indeed the 'most unkindest cut of all'. . . ." Wronged and slandered by a band of conspirators, he would take his case to "the people"; he would have his trial on "the public hustings. There," he vowed, "we will settle fully, finally and forever the dirty, vile calumny that has been hurled against me."[8]

Davis proved to be a man of his word.

Throughout the 1903–1904 gubernatorial primary campaign, he used the church expulsion issue to bludgeon his opponent, Judge Carroll Wood, who suffered the misfortune of having been a member of the Second Baptist Church's disciplinary committee. Since Wood had been one of his leading accusers, Davis had no difficulty placing the opposition in a conspiratorial light. As he told a crowd at Little Rock in November 1903, it was no accident that Deacon Wood had challenged him for the Democratic gubernatorial nomination:

> My fellow-citizens, I was excluded from the Second Baptist Church in Little Rock. A lot of high-combed roosters down there, Judge Wood among the members, turned me out of the church for political purposes without a trial, without a hearing, thinking that they could ruin me in that way; but when the little church at Russellville, where I was raised, heard of this indignity, this outrage, they sent for me to come home and join the church of which I had been a member for twenty years, and more than a hundred members were present when I was restored.[9]

Wood countered Davis's claims of persecution with an abundance of evidence, including sworn testimony that only twelve members (several of whom were Davis's relatives) of the Russellville congregation had been present at the governor's alleged "restoration of fellowship."[10] Unfortunately for Wood and his friends, most Arkansas voters could not have cared less whether the actual figure was twelve or twelve hundred. Out on the backwoods stump, where Davis was the master of every situation and his word was accepted as gospel, the affidavits of a Little Rock deacon counted for very little. Even though Davis remained wedded to his whiskey and his Wizard Oil, Judge Wood never had a chance.

The church expulsion affair was an important episode in Davis's career. Coming on the heels of the controversy over his intervention in the Senate race, it severed his few remaining ties with "respectable" society and all but completed the polarization of the Arkansas Democratic party. By focusing public attention on Davis's alleged lack of respectability, it affected both the intensity and the character of Democratic factionalism. Dramatizing the cultural rift between the predominantly agrarian pro-Davis faction and the New South–oriented anti-Davis faction, the episode encouraged both sides to express their political beliefs in moral and religious terms.

Following the expulsion, Davis was openly hostile towards what he de-

risively called "the morality crowd." For the remainder of his career, he was
solidly allied with the state's liquor industry. During his second and third
terms, he vetoed several temperance bills and pardoned hundreds of liquor
law violators, including many of Arkansas's most notorious "blind tigers."[11]
As the editor of the *Arkansas Gazette* observed in 1906, through the liberal
"use of the veto pen and the pardon blank" Davis became "a valuable
friend to the liquor interests of Arkansas." In return for these favors, the
liquor interests allowed themselves to be integrated into the Davis organization. "These interests, accustomed to combination and active participation
in politics—being forced at times to engage in a struggle for their very
existence, for the right to live," the *Gazette* declared, "are a powerful
machine in themselves, but their machine has been merely a part of that far
greater and more powerful enginery that serves the political fortunes of Jeff
Davis."[12]

The extent to which the public was aware of the alliance between Davis
and the liquor interests is difficult to say. Although it was widely publicized
in the anti-Davis press, Davis himself avoided the liquor issue as much as
possible in political campaigns. Not surprisingly, the liquor interests were
similarly discreet.[13]

On those rare occasions when Davis did broach the temperance question,
he treated it with humor and a bit of gentle ridicule. "My campaign against
my opponents is going to be as easy as taking candy from a baby," he told a
crowd during the 1904 campaign, "I want all you fellows who ever took a
drink to vote for me, and all of those who haven't may vote for Judge
Wood."[14] During the general election campaign of 1906, Davis delighted a
crowd at Danville by planting a bottle of whiskey in the suitcase of John G.
Adams, the gubernatorial candidate of the Prohibitionist party:

> Davis: Old Sodapop, when did you come to town? You say you are a Prohi. I can
> take two green persimmons and squeeze on you and make you so drunk you
> wouldn't know your heels from a shotgun. Open up your old grip and let the
> crowd see that whiskey.
> Adams: I haven't got whiskey in my grip.
> Davis: Yes, you have; let's examine, and if you haven't I will donate $100 to the
> churches in Danville.

To Adams's amazement, "the bottle of whiskey was produced and the
crowd yelled for Jeff."[15]

When it came to discussing his own drinking habits, Davis was either
discreet or facetious. "I was never drunk in my life," he told the voters in
August 1902.[16] With a twinkle in his eye, he often assured his followers that
he was only a "pint Baptist," whereas his self-righteous critics were secretly
"quart Baptists." Although he never actually admitted that he was a drunkard, he came dangerously close, particularly during the closing years of his

career. For example, in the spring of 1908, he informed a crowd at Ola that John Hinemon, the gubernatorial candidate endorsed by the Anti-Saloon League, "can take as big a drink of whiskey as I can—which is saying a good deal."[17]

Davis's battles with the preachers and Prohibitionists of Arkansas have received a great deal of attention from historians, and rightly so. No other politician in the state's history compiled a comparable record of conflict. During his first term alone, Davis incurred the wrath of the local temperance movement, battled openly with several of the state's leading ministers, was expelled from the Baptist church, and formally censured by at least three denominational conferences. Unfortunately, this record of conflict has led many historians to overlook the other side of Davis's relationship with the religious and the righteous. For every anti-Davis man who regarded Jeff as a veritable Antichrist, there was a pro-Davis man who saw him as a God-fearing, Christian gentleman. Davis was the perfect embodiment of W. J. Cash's "hell-of-a-fellow" Southerner. Part hedonist and part puritan, he liked to sin on Saturday night and repent on Sunday morning. Like many of his followers, Davis played both sides of the street consistently and sincerely. Nowhere was the old aphorism that the masses will "vote dry even if they have to stagger to the polls to do it" more true than in Jeff Davis's Arkansas.[18]

The tendency to overlook religion has been a chronic problem in the biographical literature on Southern demagoguery. Most monographs have all but ignored the religio-moral aspects of agrarian politics. This is somewhat surprising, since students of Southern politics have often noted the political salience of "Bible-Belt" evangelism. Francis Butler Simkins argued that "it is impossible for the devout Southerner of the twentieth century not to vote the same way that he prays. He gets concepts of faith, righteousness, and politics so confused that they could be unraveled only in the unrealistic thinking of those who think in terms of the geometrical simplicities of the eighteenth century."[19] The Southern demagogue, in particular, has been loosely identified with the spirit and emotion of evangelical protestantism. Detecting the resonance between the rabble-rousing political barbecue and the frenetic camp meeting, many observers have concluded that political and religious primitivism went hand-in-hand in the agrarian South. Although the generic connection between rabble-rousing politics and Southern evangelism has never been explored in any depth, most political commentators seem to agree with W. J. Cash's contention that the charismatic preacher and the charismatic politician were similar in style and function. Both spoke in a rustic idiom, relied on spellbinding oratory, and, as Cash put it, "discoursed continually on the theme of the superior virtue and piety of the poor as against the stiff-necked rich, and the certainty that in heaven it would be the former who would sit at the head of the table."[20] The sociologist Howard Odum once observed that it was not uncommon for early twentieth-century Southern stump meetings to take on the appearance of a religious revival—complete with "gospel songs . . . rising fervor" and "revival symptoms" of all sorts.[21]

The concept of the Southern demagogue as a political evangelist was particularly fashionable during the 1920s and 1930s. Surrounded by the fundamentalist demonology of the Scopes trial, the ravings of the Ku Klux Klan, and the obsessive puritanism of Bible-thumping Prohibitionists, journalists and other contemporary observers often concluded that the political and religious peculiarities of the backwoods South were inextricably linked. According to H. L. Mencken, the demagoguery and "political bumpkinry" which plagued the South were directly related to "the Baptist and Methodist barbarism" that dominated the region.[22] According to the planter-poet William Alexander Percy, the men who supported demagogues like James Kimble Vardaman and Theodore Bilbo were the same kind of men "who attend revivals and fight and fornicate in the bushes afterward."[23] Evangelical fervor lay at the heart of Huey Long's political personality, insisted a young New Orleans lawyer: "Terror was what drove him," he told Jonathan Daniels in 1938, ". . . a lean, utter, muscle-jumping terror that you'll find at the protracted meetings of Methodists and Baptists and Holiness folk in the hill country and sometimes even at revivals in the little towns."[24]

The assumption that the religious dimension of agrarian politics was primarily pathological is questionable; the observation that such a dimension existed is undoubtedly correct. In the case of Jeff Davis, religion clearly played a significant, albeit a subordinate, role in his rise to power. Despite his troubles with Arkansas's temperance–dominated religious establishment, Davis had deep roots in organized religion. The son of an ordained Baptist minister, he had a devout upbringing that stressed Christian piety and reverence to the pulpit. Although Lewis Davis abandoned the ministry for a law career in 1865, he continued to be actively involved in religious affairs. During the 1870s and 1880s, the elder Davis attended several denominational, ecumenical, and temperance conventions, and served as chairman of the Pope County Sunday School Association and the Russellville Auxiliary of the American Bible Society. Jeff himself was active in both of these organizations during the late 1880s and early 1890s. In the Davis household there was a natural bond between family and religion, reinforced by Jeff's marriage to the daughter of a Methodist preacher.[25]

Like his father, Davis was a devout Baptist. Throughout most of his life, he was a member of the First Baptist Church of Russellville, which he attended faithfully whenever possible, and to which he reportedly tendered generous contributions. The Russellville church was affiliated with the powerful Southern Baptist Convention, which Davis once described as "that denomination which is dearer to me than life." "I love the Baptist cause and the Baptist church," he declared on one occasion, "better than anything except my mother and father, wife and children. . . ."[26] As noted earlier, for a brief period during his first administration, he served as first vice-president of the Arkansas Baptist Association. [27]

Davis left no record of private reflections on religious matters, but his public statements suggest that his faith was both firm and orthodox. His theology, like that of most Southern Baptists, was fundamentalist, evangelical, and centrally concerned with questions of personal piety, conversion, and salvation. "I am a sort of hard-shelled Baptist in my faith," he liked to say, "I believe in foot-washing, I believe in baptism by immersion, and I believe in using the straight edge."[28]

Though deeply committed to Baptist orthodoxy, Davis was not a sectarian zealot. Exhorting the electorate to join the Baptist fold would have offended not only his political instincts but also his sense of religious freedom. While he believed that "the Bible is plain" and "orthodox belief is explicit," he also felt that personal "conceptions of God" were best left "to each for himself."[29]

Davis's brand of evangelical Christianity was often emotional and even frenzied, but in no way was it fanatical or extremist. Within its cultural context, his religion was both respectable and moderate. It was the religion of the small town evangelical church, where revivals were spirited but never really out of control, and where sacred and secular domains remained somewhat distinct. As such, it was far removed from the unreserved zeal and hysteria of the backcountry Pentecostals.[30] Davis's religion was well within the cultural mainstream, with a potentially broad political appeal.

Although Davis did not believe in mixing sectarian proselytism with politics, he had no serious qualms about mixing religion with politics and government in a general way. To his mind, civic order and political progress were inextricably linked to religious faith and Christian righteousness. "You may . . . assure me that God no longer deals with nations," he once told his colleagues in the United States Senate, "but for myself, one thing I know . . . while Baal deals with nations for evil, God must continue to combat him and rule for good. . . . Bring, sir, to your assistance the history of Europe. What has been the doom of empires who knew not God?"[31]

Although he frequently spiced his stump speeches with religious allusions and professions of piety, Davis was not a political evangelist in the tradition of Sam Jones, Sidney Catts, or the later William Jennings Bryan.[32] He never allowed his religious views to dominate his political affairs. Like most American politicians, he employed religious themes in a supportive role, while maintaining an overwhelmingly secular political ideology.[33] Whenever Jeff Davis took to the stump, you could be sure he was after votes, not religious converts.

Considering his reputation as a demagogue, a striking aspect of Davis's public theology was his refusal to cultivate the darker side of Southern evangelism. Religious bigotry was not part of his political repertoire. Unlike

Tom Watson of Georgia, Tom Tom Heflin of Alabama, and a host of lesser-known figures, he showed no interest in playing the Pope-hating, Jew-baiting demagogue.[34]

Davis's tolerant attitude toward Catholics is particularly noteworthy. Anti-Catholicism was a common sentiment in Arkansas at the time (though not nearly as common as it would become in the 1920s), and shadowboxing with the Pope was an increasingly popular pastime. For example, in 1898 a Catholic church in Tontitown (Washington County) was burned to the ground by a band of angry Protestants, rebuilt by its parishioners, then burned again by the same culprits.[35] To his credit, Davis made no attempt to capitalize on such sentiments. In his public record there is no hint of anti-Catholic prejudice. If he did harbor anti-Catholic feelings, he kept them to himself.

Davis's behavior towards Jews was also relatively tolerant. During his fifteen years in state politics, the sum of his public anti-Semitism consisted of a few references to "the usurers, the Rothschilds" and the "little puny, hook-nosed lawyers around Little Rock."[36] Such remarks reflected a measure of anti-Semitic bigotry, but they were far removed from the hate-mongering "Christ-killer" rhetoric of the Ku Klux Klan of later years.

In any event, Davis's infrequent lapses into anti-Semitic rhetoric were completely overshadowed by his long and close relationship with Charles Jacobson, the young Jewish lawyer who served as his deputy prosecuting attorney (1893–94), campaign manager (1898), assistant attorney general (1899–1901), private secretary (1901–07), and law partner (1907). With the exception of Jeff himself, Jacobson was the most important member of the Davis organization. During the many long periods when Davis was out stumping for votes, Jacobson literally ran the state. A devout Jew, he joined the reform congregation of Temple B'nai Israel immediately after his arrival in Little Rock in 1899, and for the next two decades was probably the most active lay leader in the congregation. A close friend of Rabbi Louis Wolsey, he taught the temple's confirmation classes throughout his career in state politics. In fact, whenever Rabbi Wolsey was absent from the city on the Sabbath, it was usually Jacobson who stepped in and conducted B'nai Israel's services. He also served as secretary of the Concordia Club, Little Rock's largest and most active Jewish social organization.

The fact that Jacobson was a leader of the Little Rock Jewish community was common knowledge among Arkansas politicians and, to a lesser extent, among Arkansas voters as well. Davis made no attempt to hide the fact that his assistant was a Jew. He referred publicly to his "Jew clerk" (a phrase which, admittedly, may have had negative connotations); and in April 1904, along with Rabbi Wolsey, Davis officiated at Jacobson's wedding, which was held at the home of Charles Abeles, one of Little Rock's leading Jewish merchants.[37] Clearly, Jeff was no Tom Watson.

When Davis did try to capitalize on popular religious enthusiasms, he invariably emphasized the "soft side" of evangelical Christianity. Rather than invoking themes of sin, guilt, or damnation, or trying to terrify his listeners with images of divine wrath, he stressed the more comforting themes of divine mercy and Christian martyrdom. "Hell-fire and brimstone" was simply not his style. Although his political sermonettes often conveyed deep emotion and moralistic fervor, they communicated more sentiment than terror.

Cultivating the sentimental aspects of Christian faith was a strategy that provided Davis with numerous opportunities to reinforce his identification with the downtrodden, the unfortunate, and the forgotten. As one rather unsympathetic New York journalist described the situation, Davis had

> tears for the soldier with one leg in the crotch of a sapling; tears for the poor woman whose back was wrenched when the homicidal railroad company's train ran into the swamp with malice aforethought; tears for the horsethief; tears for the man whose horse he stole; tears for the innocent, tears for the guilty; tears for anyone with a vote in the background. He is a Baptist campaigner, and when he gets those old mothers in Israel boohooing on the hilltops, there's no power in Arkansas than can turn his course.[38]

At the center of Davis's maudlin approach to religion was the doctrine of divine mercy. "Mercy is God. God is mercy." he told a crowd at Bentonville in 1905, "without mercy we would have no God. The sunshine, the flowers, the birds, the trees, the brooks—everything in nature tells us in glad, loving tones of God and His mercy." Such rhetoric was seldom idle chatter. In this particular instance, Davis was using the image of a merciful God to justify his highly controversial pardoning record:

> Ladies, they call me the pardoning Governor of the State. I am glad to be called the pardoning Governor; I am glad that I have been able, during my administration, to lift so many shadows from the hearts and homes of the people of my state. . . . My fellow-citizens, never criticize a man because he is merciful. . . . you do not know what shadow lies across your pathway; you do not know what cloud overhangs your home. My boy today, a student at the State University, the pride of my heart, may commit an offense before nightfall that will incarcerate him in a felon's cell. . . . if it were true, I would crawl to Little Rock, if it were possible, I would crawl at the very feet of the Governor, I would wash his feet with my tears to obtain his pardon. . . . A few days ago I went into my office . . . and there sat a woman with two little girls, ragged and barefooted. . . . I asked her what she wanted, and she said the pardon of her husband. She had no lawyer, no petitions, but I listened to her pitiful story. She said her husband was accused of shooting at a man. I asked her if he had hurt that man. Her reply, my fellow-citizens, may make you laugh, but it did not make me laugh. She said, "No, Governor, he never totched the man." But, ladies and gentlemen, that pathetic story "totched" me, and I believe it touched the great White Throne of God. . . . I examined the case, with the result that I sent a pardon into the Blue Mountains of Pike County, which

"totched" that little home and the hearts of that woman and little children, and I believe that the Recording Angel of God dipped his wing in a fount of eternal gold and wrote to my credit that deed of charity, that act of kindness.[39]

Davis was roundly criticized for indulging in self-serving rhetoric; but he knew that in the agrarian South, particularly in the Ozarks, sentiment carried more weight than sophistication. When Davis appealed to the romantic side of Southern culture, he was tapping a deep well. Christian mercy, Southern womanhood, the virtues of home and hearth—this was an unbeatable combination in a society that valued family and religion above all else. Davis was happy for his opponents to wallow in detached sophistication—he would rather have the votes.

The second major theme of Davis's political theology was Christian martyrdom. For a man who liked to portray himself as both a political martyr and a defender of the dispossessed, parables of crucifixion and religious persecution had considerable political salience. Never one for false modesty, Davis often posed as a Christ-figure. At one point during the 1900 primary campaign, he compared himself to Christ in such explicit terms that one opponent charged him with sacrilege.[40] Usually the comparison was established through vague allusions to the crucifixion of Christ or the bondage of the "children of Israel." For example, during a 1908 Senate speech Davis responded to criticism from the Washington press in the following fashion:

Let scavengers of plutocracy howl! Truth, God's living truth—where are its defenders? Miserable travesty upon noble manhood, post-graduates in all arts of slander or defamation, I challenge a subsidized press! . . . Go! damnable imps of pelf and greed, I defy your taunts! Tear to fragments my political career, if it comport with your execrable will; stifle and distort my every utterance; not satisfied, if such be your brutal frenzy, lash my poor form into insensibility; then, if it be your further pleasure, gnaw from my stiffening limbs every vestige of quivering flesh; howl in wretched bestiality through my own innocent blood as it drips from your fiendish visages; drag then, if you want what remains, into the filth and vermin of your foul den and burn it upon the altar of Baal, or scatter it before the friendly winds of heaven to your betters, the carrion crows of the field . . . insignificant as I am, if my political career be marked, let them sharpen their blade, for I will be here at the appointed hour, and while here only God can stay my voice in behalf of organized, united labor and the yeomanry of America.[41]

Often the alleged victim of persecution was not Davis himself but his beleaguered followers. In the Senate speech quoted above, Davis used religious imagery to depict the victimization of the American working class:

May the God of Moses, in infinite mercy and pity, rescue liberty in America from a thralldom more abject than Egyptian bondage to the infidelity of Gold. His faithful poor in every state in the American Union may He deliver from that sweat and toil which brings no reward! Strike down the power of Pharaoh, oh, God of Israel![42]

In sum, despite his well-deserved reputation as a carouser, Davis represented himself as a God-fearing, church-going Christian gentlemen. A devout upbringing, a lifelong affiliation with the Baptist church, a penchant for the rhetoric of pietism and Christian martyrdom—these were part of Davis's public image throughout his career in state politics. Along with his romanticization of Southern womanhood, the yeoman farm family, and the Old South, this strain of religiosity gave the Davis movement a distinct religio-moral twist. To his enemies, Davis was a shameless hypocrite who violated middle-class canons of decency. But to his friends and suporters he was a sincere moralist and a man of honor. In a spirit akin to ethnic loyalty, the redneck farmers of Arkansas were willing to give their leader the benefit of the doubt. Any man who could speak so eloquently on behalf of morality and Christianity, they reasoned, could not be the devil described in the anti-Davis press. The serious charges against him merely testified to the desperation of his enemies, validating his claim that he was the victim of an unholy conspiracy concocted by the "high-collared" crowd.

The controversy over Davis's moral character was not the only issue to spill over from the 1902 primary campaign. The race issue also continued to boil. In early May, just as Rector and the prison guard issue were fading from view, Davis deliberately gave the racial cauldron another stir. At a national Woman's Club convention, a group of delegates from Massachusetts had challenged the lily-white membership policies of Southern affiliates. Davis, claiming to be infuriated by this, embarked upon the most spectacular Negrophobic escapade of his career—the Andrew Thompson affair. Thompson, a black convict serving a three-year sentence in the state penitentiary for "assault with intent to kill," became an innocent pawn in a bizarre episode involving one of the most unusual pardons ever granted by an American politician. Acting on what the *New York Times* called "an angry impulse," Davis banished Thompson to the land of Garrison and Sumner.[43] The pardon message read as follows:

> Having just returned from the North and having heard many expressions of sympathy by the citizens of Massachusetts for what they were pleased to call the poor, oppressed negro of the South, and desiring that they shall have an opportunity to reform a certain portion of the negro population of our state: Therefore, I, Jefferson Davis, Governor of the state of Arkansas, by virtue of the constitution and authority vested in me by the constitution and laws of Arkansas, do grant unto Andrew Thompson, a negro, full and free pardon on condition that he become within the next thirty days a citizen of Massachusetts.[44]

Within hours of the message's release, Davis had become a national celebrity, taking his place along with Pitchfork Ben Tillman as a symbol of the unreconstructed South. In Massachusetts, public reaction to this challenge from the canebrakes was a combination of disgust and righteous indignation. General G. W. Blackmar, commander of the Massachusetts division of the Grand Army of the Republic, judged Davis's action to be "beneath our contempt," and concluded that the governor from Arkansas had "only succeeded in showing himself worthy of his namesake." To Henry B. Blackwell, editor of the *Woman's Journal*, the pardon simply proved "that the fools are not all dead yet." Massachusetts Congressman E. B. Callender suggested that the Bay State might retaliate in kind by dispatching a few "Italian murderers to the paradise of bowie knives and revolvers." Less facetiously, Callender added that his state would "welcome the Southern culprit, remembering that God gave him a soul and that Arkansas cannot by legislation take that gift away."[45]

All of this was gleefully reported by the Arkansas press. Old Jeff had tweaked Yankeedom's tail, and even some of his worst enemies praised him for it. Congratulatory letters and telegrams poured in from all over the South, praising him for his manly act, for his "heroic missionary work," as one man put it. A group of businessmen in Texarkana actually set up an "Andrew Thompson ticket fund" to provide the convict with a one-way ticket to Boston "and 50 cents with which to buy one square meal on his arrival." In the Dallas *Times-Herald*, the pardoning governor was even lauded in verse:

> Oh Davis!
> Clever Davis!
> Governor Davis!
> of Arkansaw!
> Don't laugh, darn ye.
> For he has done
> Great things, he's won
> A victory. He's solved
> The problem that has vexed
> Us all and has perplexed
> The South in decades past.
> Oh Davis!
> Foxy Davis!
> Of Arkansas!
> He's pardoned a felonious coon
> And warned him soon
> To take his clothes and go!
> And where to?
> Why, Massachu-
> setts! Think of it!
> The Bay State proud
> Where the coon's allowed
> To sit with his feet
> On the dinner table.[46]

Flushed with victory, Davis announced that in the future no black convict could expect to receive a pardon from him without first producing a one-way ticket to Boston. Soon thereafter, Kemp Toney, a young pro-Davis legislator from Pine Bluff, received a public promise from Davis that a black client of his named Armstrong would be pardoned if he could produce such a ticket. Yet when Toney actually produced the ticket, Davis reneged. Realizing that his publicity stunt was getting out of hand, Davis refused to grant the pardon unless Toney could also provide Armstrong with a police escort to Boston. Toney, who did not have the means to comply with Davis's terms, withdrew his request, and the new pardoning policy was soon forgotten. The *New York Times* concluded that Governor Davis had proven to be just one more Southern politician "whose bark is worse than his bite." "Massachusetts," the *Times* assured its readers, "is safe."[47]

The Thompson affair was more than a malicious prank. It was also an attempt to restore party solidarity. Realizing that the recent primary campaign had placed a severe strain on the bonds of Democratic partisanship, Davis raised the banner of white supremacy. This was the time-honored means of restoring party loyalty, and most anti-Davis Democrats responded accordingly. Unfortunately for Davis, a large number of anti-Davis Democrats did not respond to his cue. At the Democratic State Convention in June, several of Senator James K. Jones's supporters made it clear that they had nothing but contempt for the upstart who had ruined their idol's career. And several prominent conservative leaders bluntly refused to campaign for the Democratic state ticket. In August, one conservative Democratic congressional candidate called Davis "the worst demagogue in the state."[48]

Despite his desire for party solidarity, Davis bore much of the responsibility for this continuing dissension. In early July, just as the general election campaign was about to begin, he needlessly antagonized the conservative wing of the party by trying to block Senator Jones's appointment to the Panama Canal Commission. Even after the opening of the county canvass, Davis continued to snipe at fellow Democrats, ignoring a long-standing tradition that forbade intraparty squabbling during the general election campaign. Although several editors warned him that he was playing with fire, Davis could not resist taunting the "high-collared roosters" who had tried to deny him a second term.[49]

Fortunately for Davis and the Democrats, the Republicans had troubles of their own. Factional conflict between Republican leaders who supported long-time party boss Powell Clayton and those who opposed him had plagued the Arkansas Republican party for years. In 1902 this factionalism turned into open warfare. After party regulars nominated a staunch Clayton supporter, Harry H. Myers, for governor at the Republican State Convention in late June, a group calling themselves "Insurgent Republicans" held a convention of their own and nominated Charles D. Greaves of Hot Springs. Representing approximately a third of the party's leaders, the Greaves faction vowed that it would remain in the gubernatorial contest until Clayton relinquished his monopolistic control over party patronage. This delighted Democratic leaders, who did everything they could to sustain the Insurgent Republican revolt. Realizing that Myers posed a far more serious threat to Davis than Greaves, the Democrats awarded all minority-party election commissionerships to the Greaves faction. Myers and Clayton immediately cried foul, but there was nothing they could to do to remedy the situation.[50]

Once the campaign actually got underway, it became clear that a biased election commission was the least of Myers's problems. Myers, a good stump speaker and an able campaigner, was not a native Southerner. Though he had lived in Arkansas since 1884, he was born in Iowa; and Davis never let the voters forget this. At Stuttgart, Davis described Myers as "a little Yankee who came down here from Keokuk, Iowa," whom "we know nothing about." On other occasions, he characterized him as "a little Yankee, wearing brogan shoes" or as a shiftless "carpetbagger" who had once backed "out of a lady's parlor . . . to keep from showing the ventilation in his trousers."[51]

Myers's Northern background made him an easy mark where the race issue was concerned. At Brinkley, Davis informed the crowd that he had sent Andrew Thompson to Massachusetts because he "wanted to give all Yankees like Myers a slap in the face." Later in the same speech, he added: "Myers accuses me of sending negroes to Massachusetts. If I were to send a few more of his constituents there he would get no votes at all." When Myers pointed out that Andrew Thompson had returned from Massachusetts and was "driving a hack in Des Arc," Davis shot back: "Yes, that's true enough. The nigger went up there and stayed sixty days, and didn't like the country and people and came back."[52] On several occasions, Davis demanded to know how many offices Myers would give to the negro delegates who had nominated him at the Republican State Convention. "You and your gang ride the negro" he thundered at one point, "and hold him between you and hell to keep from having your own skin scorched." He also did everything he could to evoke memories of "Black Reconstruction," charging that Myers represented the same party that had dispatched the negro militia to southwest Arkansas in 1868—the militia that had murdered one of his aunts and forced his family to hide in the woods. "Behind that man," he declared, shaking his fist at Myers, "I see the form of a reeking, bloody hand and a gang of lawless cutthroats who ravaged this country of ours years ago."[53]

Myers tried to counter these attacks by declaring that "white people had always ruled this country and always would"; by ridiculing Davis's claim (Davis denied that he had ever made such a claim) to be a descendant of Jefferson Davis; and by charging that during the Civil War, Davis's father had been a slacker who, even after being conscripted into the Confederate Army, "never fired a shot." Insisting that Davis had been re-elected solely because of his famous name, Myers told the story of a little boy in Newton County who had declared: "I am going to be governor." When Myers asked the little boy how he could be so certain, the boy replied: "Cause my name is Jeff Davis."[54]

Although Myers was on the defensive throughout the campaign, he put up a spirited fight. He hammered away at Davis's alleged bossism, calling him a "bombastic, imperial dictator," the "czar of Democracy," and "the great 'I am' who rules this state and the Democratic party with an iron hand."[55] An avid New South booster, Myers often directed his efforts at Democratic businessmen, who were unhappy with Davis's antibusiness stance. In addition to endorsing a tax exemption program, which he hoped would encourage northern investors to build factories in Arkansas, the scrappy Republican denounced Davis's opposition to a new state house. "He does not want it because he is not progressive," Myers declared at Brinkley. "The old owl roost, where the bats and moths run riot, is in perfect keeping with Governor Davis himself. That's the reason he likes it. Both are about thirty years behind the times."[56]

The results of the election indicate that a number of Arkansas Democrats agreed with Myers's assessment of Davis. Although Davis won the election by a huge margin—he received 77,354 votes to Myers's 29,251 and Greaves's 8,345—he ran more than 8,000 votes behind the rest of the Democratic state ticket.[57] Almost 10 percent of the active Democratic electorate refused to support him. In some counties the proportion of Democrats who could not bring themselves to vote for Davis approached 20 percent. Most of these die-hard anti-Davis Democrats were urban voters. In Fort Smith, for example, Davis received less than half as many votes as Attorney General George Murphy.[58]

Many Democratic leaders were disturbed by Davis's poor showing, but few were willing to acknowledge that a serious breach of party solidarity had taken place. "There is no doubt that a number of Democrats either voted against Governor Davis or did not vote at all," the *Arkansas Gazette* declared several days after the election. "But there is no movement in the party large enough to be called a defection. Gov. Davis's emphatic temperament has made some political enemies for him; many people do not approve of all that he has said and done; but the number of Democrats who refused to vote for the Democratic candidate for governor is so small that it need not give concern to the party."[59] There was a "whistling in the dark" quality to such reassurances. The dictates of race, tradition, and sectionalism had prevailed in 1902 just as they had in 1900. But thoughtful Democrats must have realized that the tempest surrounding Jeff Davisism was still gathering force and that the party's stiffest challenges lay ahead.

12

High Crimes and Misdemeanors

Man is conceived in sin and born in corruption and he passeth from the stink of the didie to the stench of the shroud. There is always something.

—Willie Stark[1]

The bonds of partisanship were strained by Davis's lack of respectability, by his alleged bossism, and by his disdain for New South commercialism. But the biggest threat to Democratic solidarity proved to be the continued struggle for control of the state penitentiary system. The penitentiary controversy which had erupted in 1901 showed no signs of abating during the spring and summer of 1902.

A May 16 supreme court ruling upheld the legality of the Dickinson contract, but Davis continued to press his crusade against the convict-lease system and the "penitentiary ring." Comparing Arkansas's prison system to the "mines of Siberia," he attacked the penitentiary staff at every opportunity.[2] He also became embroiled in a feud with his old friend Penitentiary Superintendent Reese Hogins. Although Hogins was a staunch Davis supporter when he took over as superintendent in December 1901, their relationship was soon poisoned by Davis's constant interference in penitentiary affairs. Davis claimed that the root of the trouble was Hogins's collusive relationship with W. W. Dickinson and the Arkansas Brick Manufacturing Company:

When he went in as superintendent of the penitentiary, the Arkansas Brick Company, a private corporation of this state, which has the most iniquitous contract that was ever made in the state, had only 130 men at their disposal. The superintendent of the penitentiary solemnly promised me before he took his oath of office that not another man should be furnished this corporation unless he was forced to do it by the courts. This is why I selected him, this is why I insisted on his appointment. He promised me most solemnly that if a convict who was working under this contract died or was pardoned, it meant one man less for the

173

corporation, that his place would never be willingly or voluntarily supplied by him. The superintendent had only been in office a short time when to my great surprise, without any order or direction from the board as such, or without consultation with any member of the board, he turned over to this corporation 170 men, making the number of men required by the contract, namely, 300, thus placing them under the protecting wing of an injunction of the Pulaski Chancery Court, there to remain for the life of this contract.[3]

According to Hogins, the feud was triggered by his refusal to hire the governor's brother-in-law. As he explained in a public letter in late August:

Soon after I entered upon my duties, the electrician resigned and I appointed in his stead, Mr. Dowell, a young man, bearing the best credentials as fully educated and possessed of practical experience in that line. . . . Shortly after I had made this appointment, the governor asked me to remove Mr. Dowell and put Mr. Sam Thach, the governor's brother-in-law, in his place as electrician. I felt that he would liable to blow things to atoms, ruining the electrical machinery, and perhaps causing death to those nearby. I told the governor so, and that I could not appoint his brother-in-law. This displeased him very much. He said that Mr. Thach . . . had sold out his business, come down here to take that position, and that he had promised it to him. He was very much out of sorts. He said that Sam could learn the business in a month and that the convicts attended to it, anyhow; in this I knew that he was in error. I did not appoint Mr. Thach, and ever since my declination to do so, the governor has been dissatisfied.[4]

The Davis-Hogins feud became public knowledge in mid-summer, when Davis's Republican opponent Harry Myers inadvertently brought it out into the open. When Myers declared that Davis's father "was conscripted and never fired a gun in the war," he cited Reese Hogins as the source of his information. Hogins insisted that Myers was lying. But Davis never forgave him for this alleged act of treachery, and publicly denounced him as a traitor who had joined forces with the "penitentiary ring."[5]

The Davis-Hogins feud captured its share of headlines but the most volatile aspect of the penitentiary controversy was the ongoing struggle over the purchase of a state convict farm. The location of the convict farm had been a major source of controversy since Davis's veto of the "Sunnyside" bill in February 1901. In October, Davis and Secretary of State Crockett urged the Penitentiary Board to purchase a six-thousand-acre farm from Louis Altheimer, a prominent Jefferson County Republican. But a majority of the board, claiming that the asking price of $87,000 was unreasonable, voted against the purchase. In January 1902 George Murphy and other members of the board endorsed a proposal to buy the Beakley Farm, located near the village of England in Lonoke County, for $175,000. Davis opposed the purchase and produced several witnesses who testified that the soil on the Beakley Farm was "poor and sterile" and that much of the property was swampy and unfit for cultivation. A number of England residents filed a petition supporting Davis's objections to the purchase, and the Murphy faction reluctantly withdrew its endorsement of the Beakley proposal.[6]

During the spring and summer, Davis continued to press for the purchase of the Altheimer property, but the Murphy faction—which now included Davis's former allies John Crockett and T. C. Monroe—remained opposed to the idea. Davis's relationship with the other members of the board steadily deteriorated. When Murphy publicly criticized Davis's liberal pardoning record in late July, Davis countered with a renewed attack on the penitentiary ring's inhumane treatment of the state's prisoners. In early August, he called for a ban on the subleasing of convict labor, but he was rebuffed by the other members of the board. Later in the month, he directed his fire at M. D. L. Cook, the penitentiary system's financial secretary. Claiming that Cook had too much power and was subject to too much temptation, he called for the abolition of the position of financial secretary. When Murphy and the other members of the board refused to take this suggestion seriously, he vowed that he would take his case to the people.[7]

The running battle between Davis and the Penitentiary Board turned into a full-scale war in late November when, over Davis's protest, the board purchased the Cummings Farm, an eleven-thousand acre tract in Lincoln County, for $140,000. Davis, who still favored the acquisition of the Altheimer property, was furious—particularly after he learned that M. D. L. Cook had secretly sold 750 bales of state-owned cotton earlier in the week in order to make the $30,000 down payment on the Cummings Farm. Calling the purchase "one of the greatest outrages ever inflicted upon Arkansas," Davis promised to do everything in his power to break the contract. The Cummings property, he insisted, was totally "unfit for a convict farm."[8] As he told the legislature in January 1903:

> It has been absolutely impossible during the entire history of this farm for any private individual to work it successfully. It is subject to overflow, more than 300 acres of the best land on the place . . . having washed and caved into the river. It is a narrow strip of land averaging from one-half to a mile wide and seven miles long, stretched up and down the Arkansas River. It is inaccessible except by boats, during stages of high water, and is covered with Johnson grass, which is the dread of all river planters. Between it and the railroad . . . is a swamp, almost inpenetrable and impassable during the high water season. Upon this tract or body of land are sloughs, lagoons and cypress breaks, from which all the valuable timber has been cut, and out of which ooze malaria, miasma, swamp fever, and other diseases absolutely dangerous and inconsistent with the health and well-being of the convicts. . . . The retention of this place absolutely thwarts and destroys every plan and purpose which I have had in the reformation of the penitentiary and the amelioration of the condition of the convicts. . . . To carry white convicts from the mountainous sections of this state to this cesspool of miasma and disease for a

long term of punishment would mean ultimately their death. None but negroes could work on such land, and humanity would dictate that they should not be forced to do so, living and confined as they are under penitentiary rules and restrictions. If this purchase stands, one of the greatest aspirations of my life is gone.[9]

Davis's desire to nullify the Cummings Farm purchase became an all-consuming passion during the winter of 1902–1903. Cook and the Penitentiary Board had outfoxed him, but he had no intention of letting them get away with it. When the new legislature convened in January, he devoted almost half of his inaugural address to the penitentiary controversy. Using language usually reserved for the stump, he issued a scorching indictment of Cook, Hogins, and the Penitentiary Board: "I say that around the city of Little Rock there is a crowd of leeches and blood-suckers that are trying to build up a penitentiary dynasty and political penitentiary ring, the object and purpose of which is to control the politics of Arkansas, and incidently loot the state treasury while doing it."[10] Davis's blunt language shocked conservatives, who thought they had seen and heard everything during his first term. Accusing fellow Democrats of mismanagement and fraud in the heat of a primary campaign was one thing, but this kind of invective in an inaugural address was something else again.

Davis's unrestrained attack on the "penitentiary ring" triggered a storm of controversy that ultimately engulfed his entire legislative program. Even some pro-Davis legislators were unwilling to follow his lead. Davis forced the issue by demanding that the legislature send an investigative team to the Cummings Farm. And, although he eventually got his way on this particular point, he lost control of the legislature in the process. Davis then began to threaten unruly legislators with political extinction. But the more high-handed he became, the more the legislature stiffened its resistance.[11]

By late February, Davis's legislative program was in shambles: the King Antitrust Bill and a Davis-backed reform school bill were bogged down in committee; the fellow-servant bill had been preempted by a conservative substitute; Davis's plan to place the management of the penitentiary under the State Board of Charities had been rejected by the house; and a senate committee had issued a scathing report condemning the removal of James P. Eagle from the Capitol Commission. On February 9, the legislature overrode three Davis vetoes in less than thirty minutes. There was no longer any doubt that the Governor and the legislature were on a collision course.[12]

Davis's lack of legislative support provided the leaders of the anti-Davis coalition with the opening they had been looking for. Accusing him of numerous offenses, anti-Davis leaders, both inside and outside of the legislature, began to call for his impeachment. The idea caught on, and by mid-February the press was filled with editorials demanding Davis's removal from office. "If the legislators will continue their good work and impeach our governor," one editor assured his readers, "they will be commended by the better element in Arkansas."[13]

The leader of the impeachment forces was Attorney General George Murphy, who organized a massive anti-Davis rally held at the Capital Theater in Little Rock on February 12. Despite an admission charge, a standing-room only crowd turned out to hear the attorney general denounce the governor. Secretary of State Crockett, State Auditor Monroe, and twenty other anti-Davis leaders sat on the stage with Murphy; scores of anti-Davis legislators were in the audience. The crowd had come to witness a roast, and Murphy did not disappoint them. As the audience roared its approval, the fiery attorney general demanded Davis's impeachment:

> Our state is in a crisis, and we have not the man for governor who can lead us out of it. Recently it has been the pleasure of this governor to deliver a message to the legislature, in which he has made against other state officers and officials libelous charges and insinuations which are unbefitting the high office which he holds. . . . If they are true they ought to be impeached. On the other hand, if the governor does not speak the truth, if his insinuations and charges are false, justice and right cry out for his own impeachment. None should be satisfied with anything else. His actions have shown him unfit to administer the laws of this state. . . . Either he or the members of the penitentiary board must be impeached.[14]

For two hours Murphy painstakingly outlined the case against Davis. Focusing on the Cummings Farm controversy and Davis's attempts to bully the Penitentiary Board, he also alluded to a host of "high crimes and misdemeanors," ranging from misuse of the governor's contingent fund to the illegal and unwarranted removal of Eagle from the Capitol Commission.[15]

The morning after Murphy's philippic, the house of representatives approved a resolution calling for a full investigation of the charges and counter-charges. The investigation was to be conducted by the House Ways and Means Committee, which has been conducting an unofficial investigation of Davis's alleged misconduct for several weeks. The committee was chaired by Edward M. Merriam, a virulently anti-Davis legislator from Pulaski County, and a majority of its members belonged to the anti-Davis faction. Most observers predicted that Davis would be raked over the coals. Davis claimed that he welcomed the investigation, but everyone concerned realized that the committee's hearings represented the first step of the impeachment process.[16]

The investigation began on February 18 and lasted for more than five weeks. Meeting nightly in the chambers of the supreme court, the eleven members of the Ways and Means Committee interviewed scores of witnesses and compiled more than eight hundred pages of testimony. Rigidly factionalized, the committee was composed of six anti-Davis legislators, three pro-Davis legislators, and two members who tried to remain neutral. To add to the drama, the nightly hearings were open to the public, with

Davis's supporters sitting on one side of the room and his critics sitting on the other. Although Davis's claim that he attended the proceedings at the risk of his life was an exaggeration, the atmosphere was extremely tense. At several points the two factions nearly came to blows.[17]

Throughout the investigation Davis was on the defensive, which was exactly where he wanted to be. For a politician who thrived on persecution and who spent much of his career trying to cultivate the image of martyrdom, the nightly melodrama in the supreme court chambers was a dream come true. In Charles Jacobson's words, through it all Davis remained "cool, collected and imperturbable . . . conscious of the fact that he was being furnished an issue about which he could talk forever. . . ."[18] Recognizing that the charges against him were too trivial to sustain an impeachment, he provided his critics with enough rope to hang themselves.

In the early going the investigation focused on Davis's alleged misuse of his contingent fund. Although the amount of money involved totalled less than $100, the committee spent several days examining Davis's expense account. His critics claimed that he had used the contingent fund to pay for telegrams and long-distance telephone calls that had nothing to do with state business.[19] They also charged that he had drawn $35 from the contingent fund to pay for a trip to the University of Arkansas's commencement exercises, even through he would be reimbursed by the university. Davis explained that he simply had forgotten to return the $35 to the contingent fund. When a hostile committee member asserted that Davis had known he would be reimbursed as soon as he arrived in Fayetteville, the unflappable governor declared: "Yes, sir, but I did not have any money. I haven't got car fare tonight, and if you will loan me five cents I will be obliged to you.'"[20]

The next charge was that Davis had accepted free coal from the company that supplied the state's charitable institutions. George Murphy and other anti-Davis leaders charged that Davis had acted in collusion with his close friend and advisor, John H. Page, who had served as secretary of the State Board of Charities since 1901. In response, Davis insisted that the coal company had charged him $100 for the coal. At present he was too poor to pay the bill, he assured the committee, but he would pay it someday. In this instance, Davis got the best of his accusers, as did Page, who was fully exonerated by the State Charities Board in early March.[21]

As February drew to a close, the committee turned to the most explosive issue at hand—Davis's running feud with the Penitentiary Board. The investigation focused on Davis's opposition to the Cummings Farm purchase and his alleged intimidation of State Auditor Monroe. Monroe testified that Davis had forced him to sign a political "compact" that required him to support Davis's position on all penitentiary matters. Monroe's allegation was corroborated by Secretary of State Crockett, a recent convert to the anti-

Davis cause, who told the committee that Davis had once shown him a copy of the compact. Murphy then spent several nights trying to convince the committee that Davis and Louis Altheimer had been involved in a kickback scheme. Altheimer testified on Davis's behalf, but most of the witnesses were vehemently anti-Davis, including Reese Hogins. Hogins defended the Dickinson convict-lease contract and insisted that his feud with the governor had been triggered by his refusal to hire the governor's brother-in-law. Davis, of course, denied everything. These "vile charges" had been trumped up by Murphy and the other members of the "penitentiary ring," who once again were trying to blacken his name and destroy his career.[22]

By mid-March everyone was growing tired of the hearings—everyone, that is, but George Murphy. On March 14, he presented seventeen new charges against Davis. The most serious of these concerned Davis's relationship with the Memphis and Choctaw Railroad and the St. Louis Southwestern Railroad. According to Murphy, on at least three occasions the railroads had bribed Davis with free transportation and other gifts. During a lengthy excursion to New York and New England in the spring of 1902, Davis had been provided with a private railway car "stocked with wines and liquors, free of charge to the governor and his party, the use of which caused such ludicrous conduct on the part of some of the party as to make the state a laughing-stock among those who saw or heard it." But subsequent testimony proved Murphy's allegations were either incorrect or greatly exaggerated, and even the anti-Davis members of the committee agreed to let the matter drop.[23] After struggling through a final week of hearings, the weary committee adjourned on March 23.

The next step was the submission of a report to the house of representatives, but this was easier said than done. At the close of the hearings, the hopelessly divided committee submitted four separate reports. Report No. 1 was known as "the majority report." Prepared by Chairman Merriman and five other anti-Davis committeemen, it defended the Penitentiary Board, endorsed the purchase of the Cummings Farm, absolved Superintendent Hogins of any wrong-doing, contradicted Davis's claim that the state's prisoners were being mistreated, and condemned Davis for misusing his contingent fund and trying to intimidate T. C. Monroe. The report concluded that Davis had accepted free transportation and other gifts, but admitted there was no evidence that he had accepted these gifts in exchange for political favors. Report No. 1 did not contain an explicit call for Davis's impeachment, but the implications of its conclusions were clear.[24]

Report No. 2, known as "the minority report," was prepared by J. Sam Rowland and J. Marion Futrell, the two "neutral" committeemen. Claiming that the Ways and Means Committee was only a fact-finding body and that the guilt or innocence of the governor was a matter for the entire house of representatives to decide, Rowland and Futrell insisted that a transcript of the hearings, along with related documents, should be presented to the house without comment. Report No. 3 was issued by the three pro-Davis members of the committee—Benjamin Wofford, George Stockard, and William Whitley. Designed to bring the impeachment controversy to a close, Report No. 3 absolved all parties of wrong-doing. Finally, even though he was willing to sign Report No. 3, William Whitley filed a fourth report, which he alone endorsed. Written by Davis's staff, the Whitley report criticized the Cummings Farm purchase, praised Davis's efforts to reform the penitentiary system, and denied that Davis had misused his contingent fund or acted improperly in any way. Whitley was dubbed "the governor's attorney" and accused of deliberately providing the Davis forces with a tailor-made campaign document, which, of course, was exactly what he was doing.[25]

The reports were put to a vote on April 9. Most of the state's editors confidently predicted that the governor would be found guilty of gross misconduct and removed from office. They were mistaken. As soon as the vote on Report No. 1 was tabulated, it became clear that the pro- and anti-Davis factions in the house were evenly matched (see Table 19 and Figure 10). In what was essentially a preliminary vote on Davis's impeachment, the house rejected Report No. 1 by the narrowest of margins, 43 to 44. This was a crushing blow to the anti-Davis forces, but they were soon consoled by the fact that the pro-Davis Report No. 3 also went down to defeat, 40 to 44. In the end, the house approved the innocuous Report No. 2 by a vote of 66 to 20.[26] Thus ended any chance of Davis's impeachment. Anti-Davis leaders tried to make the best of the situation by claiming that the adoption of Report No. 2 amounted to a formal censure, but it was clear that Davis had won a strategic victory. And, in the wake of the impeachment attempt, he was certain to be more dangerous than ever.

In the aftermath of the impeachment controversy, Davis was full of bluster. The "high-collared roosters" had tried to skin him, he repeatedly declared, but they had lost their nerve. Even so, he soon discovered that his troubles with the legislature were far from over. During the final three weeks of the legislative session, his enemies dealt him one defeat after another. On several occasions he even lost the support of legislators who had defended him during the impeachment crisis. On April 15 and 16, both houses overrode his veto of the Merriman State House Bill, which empowered the legislature to select five new capitol commissioners. In the house the vote was 71 to 10, and in the senate it was 24 to 8. When Davis, in a fit of pique, refused to acknowledge the new law and "appointed" five new capitol commissioners of his own, the legislature filed a quo warranto suit against him. On April 19, the senate unanimously overrode his veto of a reward granted by the legislature to an anti-Davis sheriff. Later, by a vote of 45 to 38, the house refused to annul the Dickinson convict lease contract. A week

TABLE 19

Age, Occupational, Religious, and Tenure Composition of the 1903 Arkansas House of
Representatives: Pro-Davis, Anti-Davis, and Neutral Factions*

			Faction		
		Total	Pro-Davis	Anti-Davis	Neutral
	N=	100	39	41	20
Age:					
Average Age		41.5	41.9	40.8	42.1
% 21–35 years old		40.8	43.6	41.0	35.0
% 36–49 years old		31.6	30.8	30.8	35.0
% 50+ years old		27.6	25.6	28.2	30.0
Occupation:					
% in:					
Agriculture		30.9	39.1	19.0	36.4
Professions		56.4	50.0	64.3	54.5
Business		12.7	10.9	16.7	9.1
Religion:					
% Baptist		18.0	17.9	22.0	10.0
% Methodist		34.0	46.2	22.0	35.0
% Presbyterian		12.0	7.7	17.1	10.0
% Christian		9.0	12.8	9.8	0.0
% Other Protestant		4.0	2.4	7.3	0.0
% No Membership		23.0	12.8	22.0	45.0
Tenure:					
% New Representatives		74.0	84.6	68.3	65.0
% Holdovers from the 1901 House		26.0	15.4	31.7	35.0

*Pro-Davis legislators voted for Report No. 3 and against Report No. 1. Anti-Davis legislators did the reverse. All legislators who did not fall into these two categories were classified as "neutral."
SOURCES: *Biennial Report of the Secretary of State of Arkansas, 1901–1902,* 439–441; *Journal of the Arkansas House of Representatives, 1903.*

later anti-Davis leaders in the senate stymied several attempts to resuscitate the King Antitrust Bill. On April 30, the last day of the session, Davis suffered a double defeat: the senate refused to confirm his appointment of James G. Wallace as a chancery judge, and both houses overrode his veto of a resolution upholding the legality of the Merriman State House Act.[27]

Davis struck back with a vengeance. On May 17, after vetoing eight bills in less than twenty-four hours, he dropped a political bombshell: despite earlier promises to retire at the end of his second term, he had decided to seek a third term. Although he was violating a time-honored custom—no Arkansas governor had ever been elected to a third term—he insisted that personal honor and political integrity required him to enter the race. In a lengthy public letter addressed "To the Democracy of the State of Arkan-

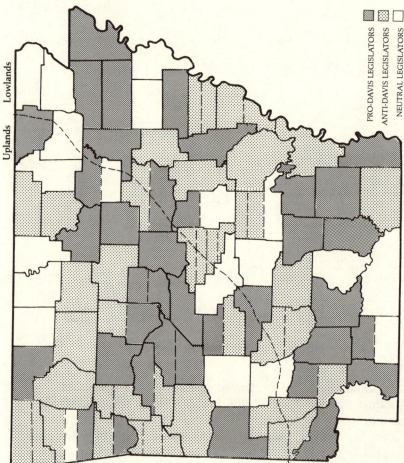

Uplands   Lowlands

Uplands

PRO-DAVIS LEGISLATORS

ANTI-DAVIS LEGISLATORS

NEUTRAL LEGISLATORS

FIGURE 10.
The 1903 Impeachment Controversy

SOURCE: *Biennial Report of the Secretary of State of Arkansas,
1901–1902, 439–441; Journal of the Arkansas House of
Representatives, 1903.*

sas," he claimed that the legislature's recent treachery left him no choice but to go before the people and try to clear his name:

> ... the vials of wrath of that body were turned loose upon me in the most unjust and merciless warfare that has ever been waged against a public officer in this or any other state. Charges involving my honor, the good name of my mother and father, my family, were preferred against me without the slightest pretext, and hurled broadcast through the press of this nation. My impeachment was sought for high crimes and misdemeanors in office, a price was placed upon my official head, and a deep-laid, well-considered, far-reaching scheme was entered into to ruin me and drag my family down to infamy and shame. Yet when the legislature came to the crucial test, they didn't have the manhood or the courage to carry out their iniquitous schemes, but adopted a report referring the whole matter to the people.
>
> Had they acquitted me before that body I should not have asked you for re-election to the office of governor, but since they have selected the people of this state as a jury to try and determine this issue, most willingly do I leave it to you and accept the challenge. ... If I can but call the old guard together again, and they will stand like Spartans as they have always done, I shall not fear the result. Twice you have borne me kindly and gently in your arms over this crowd of calumniators. To shrink from their blade now would be cowardly and unmanly; to fawn before my traducers would be unjust to myself and my family. I would want my children to forsake my memory, and my body buried in the rude rough sands of the sea, to be ever forgotten should I be guilty of such cowardice.[28]

Davis's announcement had the state buzzing, but the clincher was yet to come. On May 20, without a word of warning, he vetoed more than 300 bills. Anti-Davis leaders immediately screamed that this time he had gone too far, but in this particular instance they had no one but themselves to blame. During the final days of the leglislative session, the anti-Davis faction had concocted a scheme to nullify the governor's veto power. But as usual Davis was one step ahead of them. Charles Jacobson, who played a supporting role in this bizarre drama, described the situation:

> The faction in the Legislature of 1903 that was unfriendly to the Governor believed he intended to veto some of their bills after adjournment, so they framed up a plan not to present a number of bills until after twenty days after adjournment, being of the opinion that the Governor would then lose jurisdiction over them and could not exercise the veto power, and that the bills would, after that time, automatically become laws. It was a shrewd scheme and as the twenty-day period began to pass along the Governor was either tipped off or saw the play. ... When the twenty-day period was over the various clerks and committees began to bring in legislative bills by the armload. The Governor waited until all the bills were brought in, then prepared and published a proclamation vetoing them all, over three hundred. He had me procure a wheel-barrow, which we loaded with vetoed bills and which filled it to capacity, and then rolled the wheel-barrow loaded with legislative bills into the office of the Secretary of State and dumped

them out on the floor at the desk of Secretary John W. Crockett. It was a curious sight and as soon as the news of it leaked out people crowded in to view the destruction of many weeks of labor by the General Assembly.[29]

Attorney General Murphy challenged the legality of the mass veto, and in late June his challenge was sustained by a district judge. Undaunted, Davis appealed the decision to the state supreme court, which, to everyone's surprise, ruled in his favor on July 15.[30] Davis, the supreme political counterpuncher, had won another round.

13

The Old Guard

I want all you fellows who ever took a drink to vote for me and all
of those who haven't may vote for Judge Wood.
—*Jeff Davis (1904)*[1]

The mass veto set the stage for a tumultuous primary. "This is going
to be a bruising race," the *Arkansas Gazette* warned, "Don't enter it
unless you are prepared for a fight to a finish."[2] Despite such warnings, by mid-June, three anti-Davis candidates had announced for governorship: M. J. Manning, a forty-one year old lawyer from Monroe County, who
had served as president of the state senate in 1899; A. F. Vandeventer, the
Morrilton lumber merchant and former speaker of the house who had
opposed Davis in the 1900 primary; and Arkansas Supreme Court Justice
Carroll D. Wood. Neither Manning, who withdrew from the race less than
two weeks after the opening of the county canvass, nor Vandeventer, who
simply wanted a measure of personal vindication, posed any real threat to
Davis. But Wood's candidacy was another matter.[3] As Charles Jacobson
recalled, Wood "was selected by some of the ablest politicians in the state"
and "was one of the strongest and most formidable men who could have
been selected to oppose the Governor."[4]

The son of a prominent Baptist minister, Carroll Wood was born and
raised in Ashley County, a Black Belt plantation county in the southeastern
corner of the state. After graduating from the University of Arkansas in 1879
and reading law in his elder brother's Hot Springs law office, Wood settled in
Drew County, where he served two terms as a district prosecuting attorney
(1881–1886) and two terms as a circuit judge (1886–1893). Elected to the
Arkansas Supreme Court in 1893, he became one of the state's most eminent
jurists.[5] Considered a moderate on most political issues, he had been on
fairly good terms with Davis prior to the 1902 church expulsion controversy.
However, since that time the two men had been blood enemies.

On June 6, nearly a month before the opening of the county canvass,
Davis went after Wood by issuing a circular which implied that Wood was

involved in "a scheme . . . to change the Democratic rule of having a primary election in each county to a convention." According to Davis, Wood and his Little Rock allies planned "to take the election out of the hands of the people and put it in the hands of the politicians." An angry Judge Wood denied this, calling the scheme, "a figment of Governor Davis' imagination, hatched out for political purposes." Wood insisted that he was a strong supporter of the primary system, though he added that he had "no disposition to dictate to the various county committees" and was entirely willing to leave the matter to their judgment."[6] The Davis forces interpreted Wood's failure to make a blanket condemnation of the convention system as proof of a conspiracy. In Bonanza on June 19, Davis told the crowd that Wood and his henchmen would resort to any means to defeat him. At one point, he claimed that he had gone "to the state house every night during the sitting of the legislature at risk of his life and would have been murdered if the slightest disturbance had been raised."[7]

The first face to face confrontation between Davis and Wood took place at Corwin, in Saline County, on July 11. Davis began by ridiculing Wood's candidacy: "Judge Wood, I am glad that gang in Little Rock got you to run. I was afraid they were going to get a strong man to run against me." After charging that Wood was the hand-picked candidate of "the silk-stocking crowd in Little Rock," he claimed that during the recent session of the legislature the Judge had been "as busy as a cranberry merchant" trying to kill the antitrust bill.

Turning his attention to the Ways and Means Committee investigation, he informed the crowd that Chairman E. M. Merriam was a brigand who "had been dismissed from the 'yankee army' for immorality." According to Davis, the recent impeachment attempt was the paramount issue of the campaign: "A vote for me will be for my acquittal; a vote against me is for my conviction. The legislature has agreed to leave it to the people and I now accept and empanel you as a jury to decide my guilt or innocence. This is the fight of my life."[8]

In his rejoinder, Wood refused to respond in kind. Taking the high road of political respectability, he scolded Davis for assuming the role of a martyr, for referring to the yeomanry as "hill billies" and "red necks," and for refusing to prosecute the trusts during the final year of his attorney generalship. At one point, Wood claimed that Davis reminded him "of a mad yearling when he quit the prosecution of the trusts and went out over the state branding the supreme court of the state as five jackasses." Although Wood tried to maintain his judicial demeanor, his speech was punctuated by several angry exchanges. When he charged that the governor was the candidate of "the whiskey crowd," Davis bellowed: "I had rather be run by the whiskey crowd . . . than by the penitentiary crowd and the Dickinson Manufacturing Company."[9] After an equally heated rebuttal, the two candidates sent the farmers of Saline County back to their ploughs and headed for Perrysmith, where they started all over again. From Perrysmith the canvass travelled to several central Arkansas towns where the scene was always the same: Davis slashed away and Wood strained to keep his temper. Although this political side show attracted huge crowds, it took less than a week to convince one Little Rock editor that "Arkansas has too much politics."[10]

In late July, the campaign took an unexpected turn when a serious illness forced Wood out of the county canvass for almost a month. Davis refused to postpone the canvass until after Wood's recovery; he actually stepped up the pace of his campaign, sometimes delivering as many as four speeches a day.[11] With Manning out of the race and Wood temporarily on the sidelines, Vandeventer became Davis's chief whipping boy.

Returning to a tactic that had proved effective during the 1900 campaign, Davis constantly referred to Vandeventer, a native of Illinois, as the Gazette Yankee from Morrilton. When the two men spoke at Beebe, Davis supporters unveiled a huge flag depicting Vandeventer as a carpetbagger, with the inscription "Ain't Davis hell on carpetbaggers."[12] Vandeventer responded that "his mother was from Nashville, Tenn., and all of his folks were from Virginia, and that there were fifteen of his relatives in the Confederate army" and "that he had nothing to do with being born in Illinois and that he loved the South."[13] But Davis refused to let up.

Although Vandeventer was a game opponent, Davis invariably managed to have the last laugh. When Vandeventer criticized Davis's pardoning record in a speech at Piggott, Davis shouted back: "I wouldn't pardon you if you were in hell."[14] When he reminded Davis that such illustrious figures as George Washington and Thomas Jefferson had been opposed to third terms. Davis quipped that "they did not have the Arkansas legislature to contend with."[15] Finally, when Vandeventer ridiculed Davis's identification with the "one-gallus boys" and the backwoods "rednecks," Davis pulled up his pantlegs and showed the crowd his homemade socks. "My opponents wear silk socks," a grinning Davis declared, "but I wear the same kind you farmers wear, and if you farmers will stay with me we will whip this silk-stocking crowd one more time."[16]

Vandeventer did manage to score points against Davis with the race issue. The fireworks began when he pointed out that the governor had recently replaced B. F. Red, a white Confederate veteran who had served as the state house janitor for several years, with a "yellow negro." Davis explained that Red's permanent replacement was a white man and that the so-called "yellow negro" had only been hired for a few days, but Vandeventer refused to let the matter drop. He had struck a nerve and went on to attack Davis for other alleged racial heresies. At Beebe, the two candidates nearly got in a scuffle when Vandeventer accused Davis of pardoning a black man named Pomp Brown who had been convicted of trying to rape a young white girl.

In later speeches, Vandeventer claimed that Davis had pardoned no less than six black men convicted of raping or assaulting white women—a charge that Davis promptly labeled "an infamous lie."[17]

When Wood returned to the stump in late August he followed Vandeventer's lead. The Wood forces flooded the state with a broadside entitled "The Pomp Brown Case," which displayed a gruesome caricature of a black rapist and the inscription: "He caught me and pulled me off my horse and began trying to carry me into the woods." "How if this were your daughter Mr. Voter?" The broadside included the text of a letter from the alleged victim, Arkie Evans, condemning the Brown pardon as a "gross insult to every respectable white lady in Arkansas."[18] Wood also chastised Davis for approving pardon petitions that contained black signatures and for appointing black officeholders in Chicot and Pulaski Counties.[19]

For a time Davis tried to dodge the Pomp Brown issue, but Wood ultimately forced him to discuss the matter on the stump:

> they say that I pardoned a negro—Pomp Brown of Conway—for assaulting a white girl. Gentleman, I am a Southern man, imbibing all the traditions and sentiments of the Southern people, and you know full well that I had good reasons for so doing. In our country when we have no doubt about a negro's guilt we do not give him a trial; we mob him, and that ends it; and I want to say to you, my fellow-citizens, of Carroll County, that the mere fact that this negro got a trial is evidence that there was some doubt of his guilt. . . . The judge who tried him, Judge J. G. Wallace wrote me a letter shortly after I went in as Governor, telling me that he had doubts about this negro's guilt, and begging me to pardon him. The prosecuting attorney, at that time, Hon. C. C. Reid, of Morrilton, now Congressman of that district, wrote me a letter, saying that the negro was not guilty and insisting upon his pardon. These two letters were accompanied by a lengthy petition, signed by . . . a number of the most prominent men in Morrilton, telling me that this negro was not guilty and asking that I pardon him. What else could I do, my fellow-citizens, with such a showing?

Davis capped his defense with an affidavit from the victim's father disclaiming Brown's guilt. "More than two years have elapsed since this pardon was granted," Davis pleaded, "[yet] it was never spoken of until this campaign. The opposition is growing desperate and must find something that they think will damage me in my race."[20]

Davis dismissed the black signature charge as preposterous and insisted that the black appointments in question had been made by his private secretary without his knowledge. "I want to say to you," he told a crowd at Eureka Springs, "that I never in my life *knowingly* appointed a negro to any office . . . when I went into office as Governor . . . I announced this rule, and have never knowingly violated it: that no man could be appointed to office under my administration unless he was a white man, a Democrat and a Jeff Davis man." This declaration sent the wool hats flying in the air, but Davis's defense did not stop there. Having discovered that, as a young circuit judge in the late 1880s and early 1890s, Wood had regularly appointed black jury commissioners, Davis launched a devastating counterattack. "Did you ever hear of such a thing in Arkansas before?" he asked the crowd. "Would the circuit judge of your district do such a thing? [The judicial district in which Eureka Springs was located was more than 99 percent white.] My fellow-citizens, the statute of this state does not require that the jury commissioners be even selected from opposite political parties, and no one would presume that a white man, born and raised in the South, would select a negro . . . to pass upon the right of white people in the civil and criminal courts. . . ."[21]

Wood reluctantly admitted that he had, in fact, appointed black jury commissioners, but he insisted that such appointments had been a political necessity. The Democratic leadership of his district, like that of most Black Belt districts at the time, had entered into a fusion agreement with local Republicans, that called for a prearranged division of local offices and the black vote. He, as circuit judge, had been pledged to appoint one black jury commissioner at each term of court. The only alternative to this distasteful but necessary compromise, insisted Wood, was complete submission to negro domination and carpetbag rule.[22]

This explanation, according to Davis, was bad history; it was also confirmation that Wood's heretical racial views were still intact:

> His only excuse that he made today for his outrageous conduct was that he did it in order to secure the negro vote for circuit judge. My fellow-citizens, if he would do this to secure the negro vote for circuit judge, what would he do to be elected Governor of Arkansas? If he would give negroes this recognition to get their vote for circuit judge, what recognition would he give them if he were Governor? My fellow-citizens, he trails in the dust, the dirt and the mire, according to his own confession, the judicial ermine in order to procure votes for office, and these were the nigger votes that he sought. . . . the negro question is the biggest question now confronting the American people. Teddy Roosevelt is trying to force it upon us, is trying to force negro equality in the South. Roosevelt only wanted to eat with negroes; Judge Wood appointed them as jury commissioners and on the juries of the country. How would you, my fellow-citizen, like to sit on a jury with a negro? His campaign manager, George Pugh, has forgotten that at one term of the court in Ashley County Wood forced his father . . . to serve with a nigger as jury commissioner. . . . He says that he did it in order to get rid of the carpetbaggers in that country. I call your attention, my fellow-citizens, to the fact that there were no carpetbaggers in this State in 1887; we ousted the carpetbaggers for forcing negroes upon us, the very thing that Judge Wood is doing, and I do not imagine that a negro would smell any sweeter to a white man or be any more preferable if appointed by Judge Wood than a carpet-bagger. His action in this matter is without parallel. Neither his predecessor nor the judges that followed him ever appointed a negro.[23]

Davis went on to entertain the crowd with a grotesque parody of his opponent's crime:

Do you know what the qualifications of jury commissioners are? The statute says that they shall be men of good judgment, reasonable information and approved integrity. We do not have any negroes like that in my country; we do not have any negroes possessing these qualifications where I live. Do you in your country?

We will imagine for a moment that Judge Wood is calling up three gentlemen who are to serve as jury commissioners at a term of court. He calls up two white men and swears them, according to these qualifications; then he calls up a big, thick-lipped, kinky-headed negro, Sambo Jones, saying to him, "Come around here and be sworn as jury commissioner in this honorable court for the next term. Sambo, are you a man of good judgment?"

"Oh, yas, boss; I'se got good jedgment. My jedgment nevah is questioned. I'se got the best jedgment of any nigger in this country."

"Well, Sambo, have you reasonable information?"

"Oh, yas, Judge; I'se got good information; I knows where all the hogs is in the bottom, and I knows where all de corncribs is that has no locks on 'em. Jedge, I knows where all the hen roosts is; dat am a fac', and I is a nigger of fine inflammation."

"Well, Sambo, what about your integrity?"

"Oh, yas, Jedge; I pleads guilty dat I 'se got 'tegrity. My 'tegrity nevah is done been questioned. Now, of cose, Jedge, my hand jest fits a hog's ear, but, Jedge, I is a nigger of good 'tegrity; I doesn't shoot any craps; doesn't do nothing that a nigger oughtn't to do; I is a nigger of the most perfect "tegrity in dis country."

"Imagine a judge appointing such a character as this as a jury commissioner," Davis demanded of the crowd.[24]

Davis knew full well that Wood's justification of the black appointments was legitimate; he also knew that such appointments were part of an inglorious past that most white Democrats wanted to forget.[25] In the new age of black disfranchisement and strident Jim Crowism, Wood's actions took on an aura of sin and treachery.

Although Davis's race-baiting of Carroll Wood demonstrates that he had developed into a Negrophobic showman of the first order, he was not a single-minded racial demagogue. He had begun to turn to white supremacist politics as a sort of "trump card," as Rupert Vance put it; but racial demagoguery was no more his primary strategy in 1903 than in 1899.[26] He continued to focus on his role as an agrarian avenger. He was still, above all else, the man who kept the trusts and the "high-collared roosters" in line. Indeed, his ability to exploit antiurban, anticolonial, and class themes was never more apparent than during the 1903–1904 campaign.

It was during this campaign that Davis began to refer to his followers as the "Old Guard." Who belonged to the Old Guard? Who else but "the laboring class . . . the mechanic . . . the brickmason and the wool-hat brigade . . . . the horny-handed, sunburned sons of toil, the men that pull the bell-rope over the mule."[27] Davis, always a master of the common touch, outdid himself in the race against Wood. "Just look at Uncle Jim Bettis here," he roared at one point, "with his homespun clothes, with his home-knit socks. These are my kind of folks—fellows that chew hillside navy, smoke a cob pipe and sing in the choir."[28] Davis never missed a trick when it came to wooing the farm vote, as the following story related by L. S. Dunaway illustrates:

> One time Governor Davis addressed about three thousand people at Cabot, in Lonoke County. . . . After the speaking was over, about 1 o'clock, the reception committee took the distinguished speakers in charge and started over to the hotel for a 1 o'clock lunch. At his earnest solicitation, one Meredith Shirley, a farmer, living near the Faulkner County line, had the pleasure of entertaining the Governor instead of the reception committee. "I had rather eat turnip greens, hog jowls and cornbread with you fellows out here around the wagon than to go into the hotel and eat with the high-collared crowd," said the Governor. Before Govenor Davis had finished eating his dinner at least two hundred farmers had gathered around the wagon watching him eat and shaking hands with the guest of the day.
>
> As we returned on the train Governor Davis said: "I caught that entire crowd of farmers by staying out at that farm wagon and eating that good country grub and bragging on Mr. Shirley's children."[29]

Davis relished the role of hillbilly folk hero, but there was nothing insincere about his posturing. He practiced his folksy brand of politics with an utter lack of shame or self-consciousness, which was one of the secrets of his success. J. N. Heiskell wrote in 1906:

> Jeff Davis is genuinely and sincerely democratic. He is hail-fellow, well met, with all. His book of etiquette is his heart, and his rules of form and manners are nothing more than the promptings of his human nature. Any Governor might give an apparent welcome to the poorest and humblest man or woman that came into his office, but few besides Governor Davis could make the poor and humble feel the genuineness and sincerity of that welcome, make them feel that he was one of them and that his pleasure at seeing them was real.[30]

Rupert Vance, who witnessed the Davis-Wood campaign as a small child, made the same observation:

> There was a gusto about Davis; he played the demagogue but he liked it. It was not a distasteful business to him; it was glorious fun. Nor did he despise the people with whom he played the game. If the common people heard him gladly, let it be said he offered himself for their amusement—and his profit—gladly. None knew better how to meet the embarrassed and inarticulate haybinders from the forks of the creek, to shake hands with their bedraggled wives and kiss their grubby children. His opinion that cotton should sell for fifteen cents sounded like an edict from the state. When he asked a farmer how his crops were growing, how many melons he had, how much hill-side navy he raised, the very pleiades twinkled.[31]

Davis's re-election campaign was based on more than folksy rhetoric. He spent much of his time trumpeting the accomplishments of his administration. Boasting that he had prevented the "million-dollar state house steal" and thwarted the designs of the "penitentiary ring," Davis also claimed that he had expanded governmental services without adding to the common man's tax burden.[32] He was particularly proud of the new Deaf-Mute Institute, which, as he reminded the voters, had been financed by increased railroad taxes:

> How did I pay for this, my fellow-citizens? During my first term as Governor, I introduced a resolution before the board that assesses the railroads of the State for taxation. I got it passed, raising the assessment on the railroads of this State about $5,000,000 in excess of anything that had ever been assessed against them before. Multiply this $5,000,000 by $1.75 per thousand, which is the ordinary amount of taxes in this State for State, county, city and school purposes, and you have more than $80,000, the amount necessary to build and equip the Deaf-Mute Institute, all paid for by the railroads. . . . Do you wonder that the railroads are against me? I saw Judge Wood and Col. Ben Davidson, the general attorney for the Frisco system, with their heads together consulting the other day just like two old summer coons.[33]

Davis also defended his pardon record, which he claimed had been misrepresented by the press. "It is said . . . by my enemies," he declared at one rally, "that I pardoned too many people. That may be true, I don't know, but I do know this, that I pardoned *people* while Judge Wood pardoned the *railroads.*"[34] As Charles Jacobson once observed, Davis's political genius was never more evident than when he was justifying his pardon record:

> . . . he made it a point when he went into a county to speak, to carry with him the most voluminously signed petition granted in that county. Then he would take for his target the local editor who was opposing him and who, together with other citizens had signed the application, and point them out and refer to them in the crowd, read some of the bitterest editorials and then spring the petition and signatures on it. No process of logic or argument could offset this telling manner of answering his enemies, and without exception it carried the crowd, which lost sight of every other issue.[35]

To cite one example, when Wood tried to make an issue out of a pardon that Davis had granted to one of Jackson County's most notorious blind-tigers, the "pardoning governor" was off and running:

> Judge Wood says that I pardoned a man by the name of Simmons in Jackson County wrongfully for selling whiskey. . . . Here is the petition upon which I pardoned Simmons. It contains nearly five hundred names of the best people in Jackson County. At Fayetteville, the other day, Judge Wood said he would give me $10 if I would let him have the petition to keep over night so that he might see if there were some negroes on the petition. My dear Judge, you are very much interested in negroes. I would have given him the petition for nothing, it is a public record, and he is entitled to it, but he kept bluffing at me, and I made him

give me the ten dollars. I took it over to Goshen, a little village in Washington County, and gave it to a poor Methodist preacher, and I want to say to you now, Judge, that if you do not stop your bluffing I am going to bust you or build up every little preacher in this country.[36]

Davis occasionally admitted that he had been more successful as an obstructionist than as a legislator or an administrator. "My fellow-citizens, it is not so much what I have done as what I have kept the other fellow from doing," he asserted. "If you had a Miss Nancy, a man without a backbone, as Governor of your State, that gang down there in Little Rock would run over him in a week."[37]

One of Davis's greatest assets was his sharp wit. At every stop on the county canvass, he managed to have a laugh or two at his opponents' expense. As John Gould Fletcher put it, "rain or shine, the mad buffoonery went on."[38] For the most part, Davis's campaign humor was reasonably good-natured. After Wood—who sang in the church choir back in Little Rock—closed one speaking engagement with a song, Davis had a field day: "When Judge Wood gets up to speak I want you farmers to call on him for one of his songs. He is the singing candidate in this race. I can't sing. I ruined my voice crying for gravy when I was little. Judge Wood makes more racket singing in the choir in Little Rock than one of you farmers would calling your hogs at home."[39] On another occasion, Davis insisted that poor Judge Wood was desperate to get out of the race:

> The other day an old farmer caught Judge Wood by the nape of the coat tail and took him off to one side like he was going to ask about a horse thief and said, "Judge, who got you into this race?" The judge said, "Oh, for God's sake, don't ask me who got me into it; ask me who is going to get me out." I will tell you, ladies and gentlemen, who is going to get the Judge out of the race. It is the farmer, the mechanic, the wood-haulers, the red-necks and the patched britches brigade. They are going to put the Judge out on dry land. If the boys in the hills will only touch hands with the boys in the valleys, we will win one more victory for good government. We will whip these Yankees out on dry land and let them stink themselves to death.[40]

"I am going to put knee breeches on Judge Wood and run him for page when the Legislature meets," Davis assured the voters, "I will also try to get Vandeventer some kind of job, even if I have to have him put in as a chambermaid around the State house."[41]

No subject was too trivial for Davis's wit. At Sheridan he proved that he could even turn something as simple as a rainstorm to his advantage:

> I was sorry my friends all got mad at me yesterday at Redfield, but I couln't help it; they all got wet as drowned rats. Just before the speaking began the winds blew and the floods came. Judge Wood had his wife's parasol with him, and he got all of his friends under his wife's parasol and kept them dry. Judge Vandeventer sent

up to the store, bought a dollar and a half umbrella and kept all of his friends dry. All of my friends stayed out in the rain and got wet. Women, with babies in their arms, shuffled around for shelter, and the babies got so wet they would slip out of their mother's arms just like eels.[42]

On other occasions, Davis's humor carried a sharper sting: "A committee of you farmers can take judge Wood, Vandeventer and this Gazette Yankee out back of the smokehouse, take off their vests, shake them around like a dog would a two-year old 'possum, and you can put skates on a negro boy and have him skating around on railroad passes for ten feet."[43] Poking fun at Wood's association with the "high-collared crowd" in Little Rock, Davis told one crowd of farmers:

> The other day an old hay-binder from Skipper's Gap attended our speaking. He took Judge Wood off by the nap of the coat tail, and I supposed they were going out behind the smokehouse to get a drink of booze. The fellow asked Judge Wood who his campaign manager was, and Judge Wood replied that it was a little lawyer down at Little Rock. Yes, ladies and gentlemen, a little two-by-four of an up-start of a lawyer in Little Rock by the name of Wylie, who hasn't got sense enough to bound Pulaski County. The farmer also drug me off to one-side and I thought he was going to bum me for a chew of hill-side navy. He asked me who my campaign manager was, and I told him it was just the farmers of Arkansas.[44]

One of Davis's favorite pastimes was to ridicule Wood's judicial status: "These judges are an awfully overworked set of fellows. They come down to their office about 10 in the morning, leave at noon, come back at two and leave at 4. Judge, you must be worked to death, to stand such a constant strain. Upon what meat do you feed, Judge Wood, that you are enabled to do such heavy work?"[45] On another occasion, he killed two birds with one stone by mocking Judge Wood's identification with the Little Rock "morality crowd:"

> When I licked that gang in Little Rock during the last campaign they went around on the streets with faces as long as a saddle blanket. The barbers in Little Rock would actually charge them forty cents each shave, their faces were so long. Some of them call them Colonel, some of them call them Captain and some of them call them Judge. Judge of what ladies and gentlemen? Judge of good-looking women and good whiskey? There's where the judge shines. The high-collared crowd haven't got sense enough to beat me for Governor, but they know whether it is Schlitz, Budweiser or Pabst.[46]

This kind of biting humor infuriated Davis's stolidly conservative opposition. "The trouble at the present day with all state politics," the editor of the *Pine Bluff Commercial* complained, "is that men and not principles are engaging the crowd. . . . The desire of the people to be amused instead of to be instructed inspires the motive of every political gathering. The standards of high discussion are misplaced by those of ribaldry, fustian, and rant."[47]

An even greater cause of concern among anti-Davis leaders was Davis's talent for dispensing invective. His razor-sharp tongue could turn a proper gentleman into a street brawler, as he proved at Bismarck on August 25. During the early stages of the campaign, Wood had managed to hold his temper, but at Bismarck, Davis pushed the normally placid judge a bit too far. The fracas began when Davis accused Wood of having secret business dealings with John R. Dos Passos, a prominent New York lawyer who had recently argued a case before the Arkansas Supreme Court. Wood issued a vigorous denial, but Davis continued to taunt the judge with the charge that he was guilty of a conflict of interest. Wood proceeded to take a wild swing at the Governor's jaw. Davis managed to dodge the blow, but fell off the speaker's platform in the process. What happened next is unclear. Some observers swore that the Governor got in a couple of licks with the famous gold-headed cane—the one inscribed "Stand by your guns"—which had been presented to him by the 1899 legislature. Others insisted that neither man landed a blow. Both men escaped unharmed; however, the local sheriff, who happened to be a Davis lieutenant, promptly arrested Wood for assault and battery. Although the charges against Wood were later dropped, the "Bismarck incident" dominated local headlines for weeks.[48]

To the dismay of Arkansas boosters, the incident also attracted the attention of the national press. Blow-by-blow descriptions of the Wood-Davis "slugging match" appeared in newspapers from Maine to California. According to the *Arkansas Gazette,* the "Wood punch" and the "Davis duck" had suddenly become more famous than the "Jeffries swing" and the "Corbett shift."[49] One of the most inventive accounts of the episode appeared in the Chicago *Record-Herald,* which claimed that Arkansas had finally found something valuable to export to the rest of the nation:

What is the matter with Arkansas?

She has a glorious opportunity, and she is neglecting it. . . . Here are the facts. There is a campaign on for the governorship in the state, and two of the candidates, Governor Jefferson Davis and Supreme Court Judge Carroll D. Wood, are masters of the Arkansas argument. When they face each other on the platform they know how to conduct themselves in approved Arkansas style. They talk at each other til they choke with vehement utterance. Then up and at each other with their fists. The better man knocks the worse off the platform, while the audience howls with delight, and no doubt makes up its mind on the spot for whom to vote.

Now the spectacle of a governor fighting a public fist fight with a supreme court judge may not be of more than ordinary interest to an Arkansas crowd, but it certainly would be an unequaled attraction in other parts of the country. And herein lies Arkansas' neglected opportunity.

Let the Arkansans form a stock company and hire a good press agent. Let them codify the rules of the gubernatorial-judicial prize ring . . . and then let them send Governor Jefferson Davis and Judge Carroll D. Wood in one mammoth and colossal aggregation around the country. They will find that the . . . Jeffries-Corbett slugging match [is] not to be compared with their own native show when the gate receipts are counted.[50]

Just as the furor over the Bismarck incident began to subside, Wood and Davis went at it again. The rematch took place at Hope on December 18. Davis, clearly the aggressor, hit Wood so hard with his cane that he dented its handle. Although both men were bloodied, the Judge definitely got the worst of the exchange. The anti-Davis press later claimed that Davis's old friend Jeremiah V. Bourland "jumped in and caught hold of Wood, and while he was being held by a man twice his size Davis used his stick." Whether or not this was true, the slightly built judge was lucky to come out of the fray as well as he did, considering that Davis was a powerful man who weighed almost 250 pounds. The Judge was also fortunate in that this time the local sheriff was a Wood man. "This was the most redhanded assault I ever saw," the sheriff later claimed, "It was the most cowardly act in Governor Davis and Judge Bourland I ever saw. I think it was a put up job. . . . It is a disgrace to the human race and a blot on Christianity."[51] In the end, both Wood and Davis were arrested and fined ten dollars apiece for disturbing the peace; to the delight of the Wood camp, Davis was also fined fifty dollars for aggravated assault.[52]

In the aftermath of the Hope episode, the campaign reached "the extreme flood-water point in backwoods invective."[53] This was too much for Vandeventer, who, at the end of December, quietly dropped out of the race, leaving Wood and Davis to slug it out alone. Throughout the winter, both sides claimed that the opposition was morally unfit to run the state. Wood repeatedly declared that Davis had shown himself to be a brigand and a coward, and most of the press agreed. Davis, of course, told a different story. The "high-collared roosters" had tried to kill him at Hope, but he had shown them what he was made of. He had "licked Wood" and he would lick him again if he had to, though he would not sit on the same platform with him. During the remainder of the county canvass, Davis always spoke first and left as soon as he was finished. More often than not, a majority of the crowd left with him, which infuriated Wood. Eventually the canvass broke down altogether, and the two men went their separate ways.[54]

This was the kind of contest that Davis loved—a bruising, no-holds-barred brawl, a political war. The press often referred to Davis as the Napoleon of Arkansas politics, and with good reason.[55] The more his political struggles resembled military campaigns the more he liked them. Judge Bourland captured the spirit of Davis's combative style when he described "the white heat of his political course," and added: "Not that he loved a row for its own sake; but once in the arena, buckling abreast his bull-hide shield, he smote the enemy hip and thigh; nor did he cry at any time 'enough!' Upon the contrary, far and wide he strew the State with political carnage, working night and day, with all the precipitation of a gatling gun."[56] Davis encouraged this combative image, to the point of predicting his own death, which he was sure would come at the hands of a political assassin. "All I ask," he insisted, "is that when I am dead, you bury me in the old graveyard and write on my headstone the words: 'He died a martyr to the common people.'"[57]

This kind of campaign usually worked to Davis's advantage, but Wood had reason to be optimistic. For one thing, Davis's popularity among members of the political elite was at its lowest ebb since the early stages of the 1900 campaign. Several important politicians who had previously supported Davis, including Congressman Joe T. Robinson, broke with him during the 1904 campaign.[58] Before the campaign was over, scores of disaffected Davis Democrats were stumping the state for Wood. Secondly, Davis lacked one important advantage that he had in the 1902 campaign: he was no longer the only candidate with a powerful political organization at his disposal. Davis had out-organized the opposition in 1902, but this was not the case in 1904.

The Wood campaign was well-financed and extremely well-organized. "In my judgment the Wood campaign was one of the best managed political campaigns I ever saw in Arkansas," Charles Jacobson wrote in 1925. "It . . . was calculated to win as against any other man in the world except Jeff Davis."[59] Jacobson was not exaggerating. From one end of the state to the other, pro-Wood editors carried out a systematic campaign of political invective, swapping anti-Davis editorials and letters, publishing anything and everything that had an anti-Davis tone. Anti-Davis pamphlets and broadsides flooded the state, and local organizations known as "Wood clubs" were formed in virtually every county. Anti-Davis rallies and parades were held in many of the state's larger towns and cities, and tens of thousands of small wooden buttons, the official emblem of the Wood faction, were distributed to the voters. The Wood forces also adopted the novel tactic of polling county officials, jury members, and in some areas the entire local electorate, as to their political preference in the gubernatorial primary. The results of these straw ballots, which invariably showed a Wood majority, were then printed in the newspapers.[60]

The climax of the Wood campaign was a giant rally held in Little Rock on March 8, three weeks before the primary election. Representatives of "Wood clubs" from all across the state gathered to whip up enthusiasm for their standard-bearer. Several railroads offered the conventioneers reduced fares and "Wood followers poured into the city by train loads." The result was one of the most spectacular scenes in the state's history. Aided by several brass bands and countless orators, the conventioneers turned the rally into an anti-Davis carnival. Parading up and down the streets of Little Rock, enthusiastic Wood supporters—some of whom carried wooden buttons "as large as a dinner plate"—literally "took possession of the city."[61]

Predictably, the Davis camp scornfully characterized the Wood rally as a gathering of "trust agents" and "squirrel-headed editors." One Davis campaign worker wrote a lengthy parody of "The Grand Wood Blowout." An invaluable reflection of the Old Guard's perception of itself and its enemies, the parody, which was reproduced in pamphlet form and distributed across the state, is worth quoting at length:

ANTICIPATED PROCEEDINGS
of the Convention of the Carroll D. Wood Club, which met in the city of Little Rock, March 8, 1904.

The house was called to order at 10:00 a.m. by the president of the Wood Club of Pulaski county, who addressed the convention as follows:

Friends, Trust Representatives, Insurance Agents,
Bond-Holders, Railroad Attorneys, Ex-office Holders,
Disgruntled Politicians, Bolters and
Scratchers of
The Democratic Ticket, lend me your ears:
I come not to praise Wood but to bury Jeff,
The evil that men do live after them;
The good is oft interred with their bones;
So let it be with Jeff.
The noble Trust Agents have said that Jeff is
Ambitious;
Ah, that is a grievous fault.
And grievously shall he answer it.
For the Trust Agents are honorable men;
So are we all, all honorable men—
All working for the same cause
The cause of the Combines, the Corporations
And the Monopolies against the people.
That he is a friend, faithful and true,
To the Common people, no one can deny;
That he doth look after the Red Necks,
Hill Billeys and one-gallus crowd.
No one can deny.
Then to us that is a grievous fault;
For the Common people have no part with us.
We all know that the only use we have for
Them is to skin 'em
And all the use our man friday (Wood) has
For them is to vote them and make them sit
With negroes on juries
This same Jeff Davis as Governor treats the
Common farmer and laborer with the same consideration
He does the millionaire, and this is a
Grievous fault.[62]

As the tone of this pamphlet suggests, the factional split between Davis

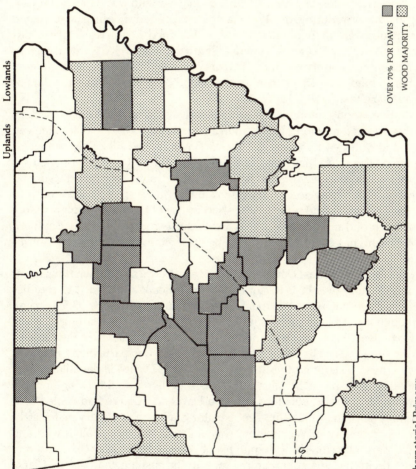

Uplands

Lowlands

Uplands   Lowlands

OVER 70% FOR DAVIS

WOOD MAJORITY

FIGURE 11.
1904 Democratic Gubernatorial Primary:
% for Jeff Davis

SOURCE: Little Rock *Arkansas Gazette*, April 24, 1904.

Democrats and anti-Davis Democrats was sharply drawn in 1904. Jacobson characterized the campaign as "a political civil war . . . which infested every channel of business and politics. No man could offer even for constable or school director, much less the higher offices, unless he in advance declared himself as between Davis and Wood. That was the only issue recognized or qualification for office required. Merits were cast to the winds, integrity, qualification, reputation were lost sight of in blazing animosity and rivalry between two contending forces."[63] L. S. Dunaway, who was with Davis every step of the way during the 1904 campaign, offered a similar assessment. "The issues were so tightly drawn and well defined . . . the respective standing of the two candidates so generally known in every city ward, as well as in the remotest county precinct," Dunaway recalled, "that it became an easy matter to name the 'Davis men' or the 'Wood men' long before the date of the primary."[64]

Despite Wood's monumental campaign, Davis won a convincing victory in the primary election. The margin of victory was more than nineteen thousand votes—71,502 to 52,216—as Davis carried 58 of the state's 75 counties. The Old Guard had done it again. When Davis telephoned his mother on election night to tell her the good news, he could hardly contain himself: "Before you close your eyes in slumber, mother, drop down on your old tired knees . . . and offer up one short prayer of thanks to Almighty God, and feel proud in your dear old heart, because you are the only Southern mother who has ever borne a son to be three times elected governor of his state."[65]

Impressive as it was, Davis's victory over Wood was somewhat narrower than his victory over Elias Rector two years earlier. Wood carried 17 counties to Rector's 5 and won 42.2 percent of the vote to Rector's 33.9 percent. Although he had little success in the uplands, Wood made a strong showing in his native South Arkansas and in the plantation lowlands of East Arkansas (see Figure 11). His strength in East Arkansas was particularly noteworthy, because it signified the deterioration of the Davis-Clarke alliance and demonstrated the artificiality of Davis's earlier popularity among the "swamp Democrats." Relations between Davis and Clarke had cooled considerably since the 1902 campaign. Senator Clarke, who was trying to establish his credibility in Washington, was embarrassed by his ally's wild and woolly second term. Thus, despite his obvious debt to Davis, he refused to take sides in the 1904 gubernatorial race. In the ensuing chaos, some Clarke lieutenants worked for Davis's re-election, but many others either remained neutral or supported Wood.[66] The result was a dramatic decline in the Davis vote in several Clarke strongholds. In Cross County, Davis's support (46.1 percent) was barely half of what it had been in 1902 (85.8 percent). In Clarke's own bailiwick, Phillips County, where Davis had made his strongest showing (94.7 percent) in 1902, the decline was a staggering 65.8 percent. Though somewhat less dramatic, Davis's losses in Woodruff (31.0

percent decline), Crittenden (22.8 percent), Greene (19.1 percent), and Monroe (10.3 percent) Counties stemmed from the same source.

Davis's popularity among urban voters also slipped in 1904. Although the urban electorate had always been the Davis movement's weakest link, in the 1902 primary Davis had managed to win at least half of the vote in most urban precincts. Of the 27 urban precincts (i.e. "city," "large town–farm,"

TABLE 20
The 1904 Davis Vote: Precinct Returns, Eleven County Sample

Type of Precinct	N	% for Davis 1904 (Group Mean)	N	% for Davis 1902 (Group Mean)	Δ 1902–1904
City	3	46.5	3	56.7	−10.2
Large Town–Farm	8	39.5	8	55.6	−16.1
Small Town–Farm	16	44.0	16	57.5	−13.5
Village-Farm	22	67.1	20	69.3	− 2.2
Hamlet-Farm	37	68.9	36	73.1	− 4.2
Farm (Suburban)	3	55.3	3	65.1	− 9.8
Farm (Central)	46	62.8	46	65.9	− 3.1
Farm (Isolated)	49	70.1	51	71.7	− 1.6
Farm (Very Isolated)	23	74.2	22	74.4	− 0.2
Populist*	35	75.2	33	78.1	− 2.9
Prohibitionist†	63	66.6	61	69.1	− 2.5

*In each of the Populist precincts, the Populist candidate for governor received 40% or more of the vote at least once between 1892 and 1896. See Appendix B.

†In each of the Prohibitionist precincts, the anti-saloon license vote (i.e. the vote for a dry county) exceeded 65% at least once between 1906 and 1912. See Appendix B.

SOURCE: See Appendix B.

TABLE 21
Illiteracy, Farm Tenancy, the Distribution of Wealth, and the 1904 Davis Vote in Six Sample Counties: Rank-Order Correlations

County	N (Precincts)	Rank-Order Correlation Between Davis Vote and:		
		White Illiteracy Rate, 1900*	White Farm Tenancy† Rate, 1900*	Personal Property Per Household,‡ 1904
Drew	12	+.580	−.133	NA
Howard	16	+.606	−.432	NA
Marion	20	−.042	+.141	NA
St. Francis	11	+.355	−.227	NA
Sharp	19	NA	NA	+.002
Washington	29	NA	NA	−.246

*Among white heads of household.

†"Farm laborers" have been grouped with tenant farmers.

‡Per taxpayer in Washington County.

SOURCES: See Tables 16–18. The electoral data are from *The Monticellonian* (Drew County), April 7, 1904; *Nashville News*, April 6, 1904; Yellville *Mountain Echo*, April 8, 1904; *Forrest City Times*, April 1, 1904; *Sharp County Record*, April 8, 1904; Fayetteville *Arkansas Sentinel*, April 6, 1904.

TABLE 22
Baptist Counties:* Democratic Primary Vote for Jeff Davis, 1898–1912

County	% Baptist,† 1906	Davis, 1898	Davis, 1902	Davis, 1904	Davis, 1906	Davis, 1912
			% for:			
Stone	85.1	28.0	80.1	79.2	55.6	48.9
Bradley	64.0	81.5	51.9	54.5	52.2	70.5
Saline	63.9	58.0	74.4	71.0	68.5	67.9
Grant	63.6	74.6	66.6	73.7	56.1	NA
Scott	63.0	39.8	57.9	69.7	62.3	65.6
Lincoln	59.8	67.4	74.1	58.1	66.0	65.1
Montgomery	57.7	68.2	84.1	75.3	82.3	78.1
Cleburne	57.4	42.9	88.6	76.6	73.0	67.4
Baxter	53.7	1.6	62.8	55.0	49.4	41.9
Ashley	53.2	40.5	68.9	47.0	55.8	68.6
Hot Spring	52.7	55.5	66.3	64.2	55.1	58.1
Columbia	52.4	17.6	65.2	58.4	60.6	59.4
Van Buren	51.4	41.8	88.9	82.8	81.1	75.1
Cleveland	50.9	88.9	65.9	71.5	74.5	71.9
Calhoun	50.1	46.4	84.6	84.1	81.4	82.6
Baptist County Mean		50.2	72.0	68.1	64.9	65.8
Statewide Mean		42.4	66.9	59.4	56.0	53.8
Difference		+7.8	+5.1	+8.7	+8.9	+12.0

*Counties where white Baptists comprised more than half of all white church members in 1906.
†The proportion of white church members who were Baptist.
SOURCES: U. S. Bureau of the Census, *Census of Religious Bodies: 1906* (Washington, D.C.: Government Printing Office, 1910), 296–298; *Arkansas Gazette*, June 17, 1898, August 19, 1900, April 24, 1904, March 29, 1912; Arkadelphia *Southern-Standard*, May 3, 1906. Because the county-level tables of the 1906 religious census did not distinguish between white and black Baptists (this was not true of other denominations, where black and white sub-denominations were identifiable), the "% Baptist 1906" has been estimated using the 1906 census figures for all Baptists and 1900 figures (printed in the *Arkansas Gazette*, August 19, 1900) for white Baptists.

and "small town–farm" precincts) listed in Appendix B, Davis carried 18 in 1902. In 1904 he carried only 9. His vote declined in 24 of the 27 precincts, and in several cases the decline exceeded twenty percent. In Little Rock, the state's largest city, his support fell from 52.0 to 37.3 percent. As the Wood camp had confidently predicted, the governor's recent antics had won him few friends on Main Street. Most of the decline in Davis's urban following can probably be attributed to disaffected middle class voters who were appalled by his lack of respectability and his militant antiurban, antibusiness rhetoric.

Fortunately for Davis, the rhetoric and behavior that alienated so many middle-class townsmen did not have the same effect on the "rednecks" and "hillbillies" of the countryside. As in earlier campaigns, a large majority of Arkansas's rural Democrats—including those who lived in or near small villages or hamlets—rallied behind the "ox-driving mountaineer lawyer" from Pope County. Once again Davis's farm support cut across class lines, though, as Table 21 demonstrates, there is some evidence that he was especially popular among illiterate voters. Following the pattern set in 1902 his support was strongest in the more isolated farm precincts and weakest in the suburban districts. Although Davis's agrarianism appealed to a broad cross section of the agricultural community, his most enthusiastic supporters were farmers who lived on the outer edge (or in some cases beyond the reach) of the new metropolitan society.

The greatest testament to Davis's popularity in the countryside was the continued support that he received from rural Baptists and Prohibitionists. As Table 22 and Appendix A (Tables A and H) demonstrate, Davis's running feud with the "morality crowd" had surprisingly little impact on voting patterns. In 1904, no less than in earlier primaries, he won his share of the temperance vote. To Deacon Wood's dismay, Davis also ran up large majorities in most of the state's banner Baptist counties. Relative to his popularity in the state at large, Davis's popularity in the Baptist strongholds was actually greater in 1904 than in 1902. The governor might be a carouser and a sinner, but to most Arkansas Democrats, Baptist or otherwise, he was still Our Jeff.

Davis's surprisingly easy victory over Carroll Wood was a bitter pill for the anti-Davis forces to swallow. The Wood camp had pulled out every stop, including the organization of a powerful political machine, and still they had come up almost twenty-thousand votes short. The fact that Wood had improved on Rector's showing was cold comfort to men who had had every expectation of winning. Once again Davis had beaten the odds, turning adversity—personal scandal, the brush with impeachment, the opposition of the state press and the religious establishment, the fact that he was seeking an unprecedented third term—into advantage. In the cold light of defeat, some anti-Davis leaders finally began to realize that Jeff Davisism was based on more than political bossism—that as long as the Democratic yeomanry considered Jeff to be their champion, nothing else would matter very much.

No one understood the implications of Wood's defeat better than Davis himself. He had emerged from a political storm, which had raged for more than two years, as the undisputed champion of the rural stump. In early May—while his political enemies were still busy trying to determine what had gone wrong—he celebrated his good fortune and his forty-second birthday. Rounding up several close friends, he rented a small steamboat and disappeared down the Red River in search of catfish.[67] No other reward could have made him happier.

14

"Multiply the White Man and Subtract the Nigger"

Naught's a naught, figger's a figger, multiply the white man and subtract the nigger.
 —*Jeff Davis, recalling a favorite childhood saying (1900)*[1]

While Davis was off in the wilds of southwestern Arkansas, the leaders of the Arkansas Republican party met in Little Rock and renominated Harry Myers for the governorship. Although Myers had had little success against Davis in the 1902 campaign, the Republicans were confident that he would fare much better in the presidential-election year of 1904. Buoyed by a popular Republican president and by the possibility that thousands of disaffected anti-Davis Democrats would "go fishing" on election day, Republican leaders were more hopeful than they had been in years.[2]

Recognizing the seriousness of the Republican challenge, Democratic leaders did everything they could to cool the fires of party factionalism. When the Democratic State Convention met at Hot Springs in mid-June, the desire for a restoration of party unity was very much in evidence. The Davis faction was in firm control of the convention: approximately sixty percent of the delegates and all fifteen members of the credentials committee were Davis men; the new party chairman O. B. Gordon was staunchly pro-Davis; and both the platform committee and the newly-elected Democratic State Central Committee were dominated by Davis supporters. But there was no attempt to humiliate the Wood forces. On the contrary, Davis made sure that both Wood and his campaign manager, George Pugh, were selected as alternate delegates to the Democratic National Convention. In return, Pugh cancelled plans to place Wood's name in nomination and urged the convention to nominate Davis by acclamation. Davis was delighted. "We are out upon the sun-crowned hill of a united democracy," he declared in his acceptance speech, ". . . ready to grapple with a common foe, ready to fight in a common cause and ready to win a glorious victory."[3]

Davis's sanguine assessment notwithstanding, the convention had its tense moments. In the early going there was a bitter credentials fight involving a contested delegation from Independence County; later, the Davis forces introduced a controversial resolution to establish a binding statewide senatorial primary. Davis planned to run against Senator James Berry in the 1906 primary, and he did not want a repeat of the 1902 convention, when the supporters of James K. Jones insisted that state convention delegates were not bound by the results of the party primary. Despite spirited opposition from the Wood camp, the resolution passed. A discordant note was also sounded by Robert L. Rogers. A fiery young lawyer from Crawford County, who had defeated Davis's close friend and advisor Jeremiah V. Bourland in the attorney general's race, Rogers pledged that he "would go into office wearing no man's yoke." The Wood delegates greeted Rogers's declaration with a resounding cheer, underscoring the fragility of the party's new-found solidarity.[4]

The rematch between Davis and Myers was a surprisingly "listless affair." Myers and the Republicans refused to take part in the traditional county canvass, and Davis was forced to stump the state alone. But without the element of direct personal combat, he had little success rousing the voters. The Prohibitionist and Socialist parties also had gubernatorial candidates in the field, but no one seemed to notice. Preoccupied with the St. Louis World's Fair and a series of violent floods in East Arkansas in July, the press gave the campaign only token coverage.[5]

Unaccustomed to being ignored, Davis tried to enliven the 1904 campaign with a barrage of racial demagoguery. He had employed Jim Crow politics in his first contest with Myers, but he outdid himself in the rematch. In 1904 there was an aggressive, Negrophobic quality to Davis's racism which had been lacking in earlier campaigns. He began to express an interest in white supremacist causes that he previously had ignored. For example, midway through the campaign he appeared to undergo an abrupt conversion to the cause of school tax segregation. A year and a half earlier, when the issue had been a subject of bitter controversy in the legislature, he had refused to take sides. Now, as he hammered away at "Rooseveltism" and "negro equality," he portrayed segregated school taxes as the last hope of the white race. By the end of the summer, his endorsement of "white taxes for white schools only" had degenerated into an all-out attack on black education itself. Brandishing the slogan "Every time you educate a 'nigger' you spoil a good field hand," he vowed to hold the line against "social equality."[6]

During the national election campaign that followed, Davis's crusade against black education became even more strident. At Malden, Missouri, his discussion of the tax issue was nothing more than a Negrophobic harangue. "We may have a lot of dead negroes in Arkansas," he assured the crowd, "but we shall never have negro equality, and I want to say that I would rather tear, screaming from her mother's arms, my little daughter and bury her alive than to see her arm in arm with the best nigger on earth."[7]

Davis's support for school tax segregation was more than a campaign gimmick. He sincerely hoped that the measure would become law, even though it would virtually destroy the state's black educational system. When he delivered his biennial legislative proposals in January 1905, school tax segregation was high on his list of priorities. The text of his statement to the legislature reveals just how Negrophobic his racial views had become:

> we have come, in my judgment, to the parting of the ways with the negro. We have tried to be his friend, we have tried to educate him, we have tried to teach him Christian morality, and we may delude ourselves for the moment into the belief that we are accomplishing some good and making some progress in this direction; but let one of the . . . "rapscallions" i.e. Republicans get a crowd of "niggers" in a back alley, or in a "nigger" church and make an inflammatory speech to them, and the good that we have tried to do for years will be wiped away in a moment; and so I have come to the conclusion, gentlemen of the Legislature, that any effort upon the part of Arkansas or the Southland to further divide her blessings with this degenerate and improvident race is futile. A negro is not susceptible of higher education, he is not susceptible of higher moral culture.
>
> A negro is a servant made so by God Almighty, bred and born as such, and no matter with what tender solicitude we attempt to raise him from his position, he is but a servant still. Attempted education proves harmful rather than beneficial, so I have come to the point where I, for one, am willing to step out and say, "From this day forward let the negroes in Arkansas educate themselves." If it is impossible, let the sympathy for them come from this carpetbag element that keeps them constantly in commotion. . . . The South for nearly half a century has done her best to try to make something out of the negro, and we have totally failed.[8]

Later in the month, Representative J. C. Burgess, a Davis crony from Pope County, introduced a segregated school tax bill similar to those introduced in previous legislative sessions. Fortunately for Arkansas's black public school system, most legislators—whether pro-Davis or anti-Davis—were unwilling to go along with the governor's hard-line approach to the "negro problem." Despite Davis's best efforts—one irate legislator claimed that the governor had threatened to ruin the political career of anyone who opposed the measure—the Burgess Bill was overwhelmingly defeated, 56 to 29. Though relatively popular among representatives from the Black Belt counties of South Arkansas, the bill received little support elsewhere. Unlike Davis, most legislators were unwilling to support a measure that promised to exacerbate an already troublesome labor shortage.[9]

Davis was something of an extremist on the segregated school tax issue, but he was not a single-minded racial fanatic. Although he was a committed white supremacist and a gifted Negrophobic propagandist, Davis never forgot that he was, above all else, a politician. He tailored his actions to political realities, not to racial theories. Whenever his racist enthusiasms threatened his political power, as in the case of the 1902 Armstrong pardon and the Burgess Bill, he withdrew to the safety of moderation. He was, in the fullest sense of the term, a racial "demagogue," an on-again–off-again bigot who knew when to use the race issue and when not to.

Davis's Jim Crow politics ensured that the Arkansas Democratic party would fend off the Republican challenge in 1904. In the September election, Davis defeated Myers by 38,093 votes, nearly matching the 39,758 vote plurality of 1902. The voters also elected a predominantly pro-Davis legislature. During both the primary and general election campaigns, Davis had pleaded with the voters to throw the rascals out of the legislature. In most cases he got his wish. Very few of the legislators who had worked for his impeachment in 1903 would sit in the 1905 legislature. Only 8 the 41 state representatives who voted for the anti-Davis Ways and Means Committee report and against the pro-Davis report, were re-elected in 1904. (Two others were elevated to the state senate.)[10]

Although Davis was approaching the peak of his power when the new legislature convened in January 1905, his frustrations with the legislative branch were not over. The anti-Davis minority proved to be cleverly obstructionist, and many pro-Davis legislators turned out to be surprisingly independent and unreliable. Waylaid by an intense corporate lobbying effort and a systematic campaign of bribery and boodling, the 1905 legislature disappointed Davis on a number of occasions. In the end, the legislators approved several of his pet projects, including an extraterritorial antitrust law, the establishment of a state reform school, and the reorganization of penitentiary management.[11] But the overall productivity of the session was not what Davis had hoped for.

Nothing symbolized the anticlimactic nature of the 1905 legislature better than the fate of the new antitrust law. The passage of such a law should have been the crowning achievement of Davis's career. But in 1905 as in 1899 Davis's victory over the trusts was more apparent than real. Immediately after the passage of the new law, several fire insurance companies withdrew from the state. But they soon discovered that they had little to worry about. Claiming that the new law was virtually unenforceable, Attorney General Robert Rogers made only a token attempt at enforcement. There was nothing Davis could do to remedy the situation. Although the constitutionality of the antitrust law was upheld by both the Arkansas Supreme Court and the United States Supreme Court, the act remained inoperative. To Davis's dismay, the 1907 legislature passed an amendment that all but exempted fire insurance companies from the law's provisions; and later legislatures added amendments that made the law a dead letter. By 1911 the antitrust law had "passed from the stage of political activity unmourned and unregretted."[12]

The mixed results of the 1905 legislative session provided Davis with a rationale for his next political venture, the race for the United States Senate. If the solutions to the problems of Arkansas's yeomanry could not be found in Little Rock, perhaps they could be found in Washington. At the 1902 Democratic State Convention, Davis had announced his intention to run against Senator James Berry in 1906; in the spring of 1905 he made it official.[13]

The year 1905 was an exciting time in American politics. The winds of political change were sweeping across the nation. In Wisconsin, the irrepressible Robert M. La Follette was elected to the United States Senate. In Chicago, Big Bill Haywood and other radical labor leaders were busy organizing the Industrial Workers of the World. In New York, a young lawyer named Charles Evans Hughes was dominating the headlines with his relentless investigation of the insurance industry. In Georgia, Hoke Smith, the beleaguered Cleveland Democrat, and Tom Watson, the old Populist firebrand, were both on the comeback trail after more than eight years of semiretirement. And most important, in Washington, President Theodore Roosevelt, backed by a huge popular mandate, was beginning to flex his political muscles. Roosevelt's landslide victory over the conservative New Yorker Alton Parker had fueled the fires of insurgency in both parties. In the wake of Parker's dismal showing, Bryanists and other "progressive" Democrats were on the rebound.[14] Moderates like James Berry, it seemed, were ripe for defeat.

Berry, the ranking Democrat on the Senate Commerce Committee, was one of the most popular men in Washington. But he was not a political heavyweight. Although he saw himself as a liberal free-silver Democrat, most contemporary observers viewed the one-legged Confederate veteran as an historical artifact, a living symbol of the Lost Cause. A proper Southern gentleman, he served as a counterpoint to rabble rousers like Senator Pitchfork Ben Tillman of South Carolina and Senator Edward Carmack of Tennessee.[15]

Davis had supported Berry in the 1900 primary, but he now claimed that the senator was too old and feeble to stand up against the trusts. According to Davis, Berry had been a fine senator in his day, but he had outlived his political usefulness. With the trusts on the rampage, Arkansas needed a fighter in Washington, not an aging gentleman.[16]

Publicly, Berry welcomed Davis's challenge; privately, he must have winced at the thought of battling Davis out on the stump. Nearing sixty-five years of age and in chronically poor health, the soft-spoken senator was hampered in his declining years by a throat condition that made public speaking extremely difficult. Thus, when the "leather-lunged" Davis insisted on a long and arduous county canvass, the senator had no choice but to beg off.[17]

With the primary election date set for March 28, 1906, Berry had hoped to avoid campaigning until early winter. Davis promised that he would not set up any speaking engagements without first consulting Senator Berry. Nevertheless, on June 9 Davis informed Berry that he had decided to open the campaign at Conway on the Fourth of July, and invited the Senator to make the occasion a joint speaking engagement. Berry angrily refused, complaining that Davis had broken his promise. In his opinion, it was absurd to begin the campaign in early July, nearly nine months before the primary election.[18]

Berry's refusal to meet Davis at Conway was understandable; but it was also bad politics. In the context of Arkansas politics, Berry had committed a cardinal sin—he had backed away from a fight. Most Arkansawyers expected their political heroes to be scrappers—ready and able to mix it up with their enemies anytime and anywhere. To be bested on the stump was one thing; to refuse to do battle was something else. Many voters must have wondered if this was the same Jim Berry who had fought the Yankees at Corinth and made such short work of Dan Jones in the 1900 campaign.

At Conway, as a boisterous crowd of more than eight thousand looked on, Davis revealed the "real" reasons for Berry's refusal to face the voters. First, as governor in the mid-1880s, Berry had signed a bill that exempted certain railroad properties from taxation. In contrast, Davis pointed out, his administration had increased railroad tax assessments by millions of dollars. A second charge concerned Berry's endorsement of an 1898 agreement ending a sixty-year-old land bond dispute between the State of Arkansas and the United States Government. According to Davis, the settlement cheated Arkansas out of millions of acres of public land. Thirdly, Davis reminded the crowd that in 1893 Berry had voted against the Hatch Bill, a measure that would have prohibited speculation in agricultural futures. All the other cotton state senators who opposed the bill had been defeated for re-election; Berry alone remained in office. Finally, Davis claimed that Berry had opposed the mandatory primary rule adopted by the 1904 Democratic State Convention.[19]

In mid-July, Berry issued a lengthy press release that rebutted Davis's charges. But he continued to refuse to meet Davis on the stump. Undaunted, Davis stumped the state alone during July and August, sometimes making as many as three speeches a day.[20]

By late summer it had become clear that, despite Davis's taunts, Berry had no intention of taking part in the county canvass. This presented Davis with a serious problem. How could he conduct a hell-for-leather, Jeff Davis-style campaign if his opponent refused to come out and fight? Jeff liked to stand toe to toe with his opponent and slug it out. For him this style of campaigning was more than a matter of preference; it was a matter of political survival. To be truly successful, he required conflict and confrontation, not only in the newspapers, but also out on the hustings where he could personally flay his opponent's hide. To rouse the Old Guard and maintain the momentum of the Davis movement, he depended upon a continuous drama of political combat. Each Davis campaign needed to be at least as spectacular as previous efforts. On more than one occasion, according to Charles Jacobson, Davis deliberately "created opposition in order to make the race interesting. He craved it, sought it, prayed for it."[21]

In late August, in an obvious attempt to create some political excitement, Davis turned his guns on Attorney General Robert Rogers, who was favored to win the Democratic nomination for governor. Most likely, Davis would have interfered in the governor's race anyway, but he probably would not have been so ferocious if his own campaign had been more engrossing. In a series of blistering speeches, Davis characterized the attorney general as a tool of the "penitentiary ring," a stalking-horse for the trusts, and a "servant of the worst gang of thieves and boodlers that ever attempted to loot the treasury of the State."[22] Rogers, who was famous for his fiery temperament, responded in kind, calling Davis everything from a hypocrite to a political dictator. He ridiculed Davis's faith in the recent antitrust act; and, he accused him of colluding with the railroads in a controversial 1904 agreement, which put a $30,000 legal fee in Senator James P. Clarke's pocket and cancelled more than $250,000 of railroad taxes. Rogers matched Davis epithet for epithet and on a couple of occasions threatened him with bodily harm if he did not let up.[23]

Unfortunately for Rogers, Davis's interference in the gubernatorial campaign went beyond a barrage of insults. He also put the entire weight of the Davis machine behind Rogers's chief opponent, John Sebastian Little, a popular six-term congressman from Sebastian County. Dubbed the Great Commoner by the *Arkansas Gazette*, Bass Little was known for his affable personality and enthusiasm for Bryanism. Although he had never been closely allied with the Davis faction, his agrarian style and reformist ideology were compatible with Jeff Davisism. Little's only serious shortcoming was poor health. At several points during the campaign, he nearly collapsed from nervous exhaustion, and for one three-week period he was forced to stop campaigning altogether. On several occasions he tried to withdraw from the race, but each time Davis persuaded him to carry on.[24]

The Davis-Rogers feud was eventually eclipsed by an even more explosive controversy. In October Davis single-handedly turned President Theodore Roosevelt's visit to Little Rock into a racial crisis. Davis's ability to dramatize and exploit the race issue in a carefully controlled and politically effective way was never more apparent than during Roosevelt's visit. Davis had race-baited Roosevelt mercilessly during the national campaign of 1904, but only at long-range. A face to face confrontation with the Lion of Sagamore Hill was heady stuff, even for Davis. But somehow he emerged from the presidential encounter with, as Rupert Vance put it, "enough ammunition to win a dozen elections."[25]

The Roosevelt affair was one of the most cleverly crafted campaign spectacles of Davis's career. Two weeks before Roosevelt's arrival, Davis threatened to boycott the official welcoming ceremonies unless the "Carpetbagger," Powell Clayton, were excluded from the presidential luncheon party. Presidential visit or not, Davis would not "break bread" with the murderous villain who had plundered the state during Reconstruction. The issue having been drawn, he announced on the following day that he would welcome the president during the ceremonies at City Park, but would excuse himself from the presidential party as soon as it arrived at the luncheon site. A masterful political stroke, this allowed Davis to share the spotlight with Roosevelt without having to socialize with his arch-enemy, Powell Clayton. In the final days before the visit, Little Rock was alive with rumors: the governor would not speak unless City Park were cleared of black spectators; he planned to insult the president; the real reason for his refusal to attend the presidential luncheon was that Roosevelt had once dined with Booker T. Washington; and so on. By the time the president's train arrived in Little Rock on October 26, the stage was set for a major political rhubarb.[26]

Informed that Roosevelt planned to speak on the subject of "Law Enforcement and Civic Righteousness," Davis tailored his welcoming speech accordingly. Ignoring the counsel of his closest political advisors, he took it upon himself to instruct the yankee President in the ways of Southern lynch-law. His speech, tempered by the nature of his audience, was a curious mixture of racial moderation and undisguised Negrophobia. Temporarily abandoning the hard-line racial exclusionism that had characterized his speeches on school tax segregation, he praised the South's many "well disposed, self-respecting, and law-abiding negroes." Only the "vicious element" of the "inferior race" was condemned. Restraint was an essential part of Davis's strategy because—while he hoped to provoke a controversy—he did not want to insult his powerful guest. This necessitated a welter of contradictory rhetoric, which was nothing new for a Southern politician discussing the lynching issue. Davis began by assuring Roosevelt that Arkansas was unsurpassed in its "love of law and order." "I make no excuses," he insisted at one point, for the man ". . . who would take the law into his own hands." Yet, seconds later, he argued that lynching was an inevitable and just reward for any black man who dared to assault a white woman:

Mr. President, when the husband or the brother, the father or the sweetheart of one of these angels of earth, comes home in the evening and finds her in the throes of death; when he sees the cruel clutch-mark on her snow white throat, and watches the pulse-beat grow fainter and fainter as the end draws near, there is not a law on the statute books of Arkansas to prevent that father or husband or brother or sweetheart from avenging that crime AT ONCE AND WITHOUT APOLOGY TO ANY TRIBUNAL ON THE FACE OF THE EARTH.[27]

Never one to shrink from a fight, Roosevelt responded by offering his intemperate host a bit of unsolicited presidential wisdom:

Governor, you spoke of the hideous crime that is often hideously avenged. . . . To avenge one hideous crime for another hideous crime is to reduce the man doing so to the bestial level of the bestial scoundrel (loud applause) and the hideous effects of lynch law are shown in the fact that three-fourths of the lynchings are not for that crime at all, but for other crimes (applause). And you as governor, and all other exponents of the law, owe it to our people, owe it to the cause of civilization, to do everything in our power, officially and unofficially, to drive the menace and reproach of lynch law out of the United States (loud applause).[28]

To Roosevelt, and to the national press reporters present, Davis's words appeared harsh and irresponsible. But to the locals his remarks were clearly standard fare—perhaps even a bit moderate, a bit apologetic—by Arkansas standards. Davis said nothing which had not been said by Arkansas politicians countless times before. In 1895 Congressman Bass Little had boldly declared on the house floor that he had "no respect for either man or community that will not invoke the authority of that higher law of the human heart and visit speedy death to the brute guilty of . . . the most heinous of crimes."[29] Four years later, Governor Dan Jones told a *New York Times* reporter that lynching was inevitable whenever the crime of rape was involved: "This crime is so heinous and revolting that all the laws in the world, no matter how severe the punishment or speedy its infliction, can not, in my judgment, prevent lynching. . . ."[30] In Arkansas, lynching was sometimes even defended from the pulpit. "While I do not justify lynching," the Right Reverend William M. Brown, bishop of the Arkansas diocese of the Episcopal Church, declared in 1903, "I can find no other remedy adequate to suppress the crime for which this has been made a punishment by the people of the South. I am a northern man, and used to look with horror on lynching, but since I have been south my eyes have been opened."[31] Even the *Arkansas Gazette*, which had editorialized against lynching for years, endorsed much of what Davis had to say. "If Theodore Roosevelt spent his life on a lonely plantation in a region where Negroes outnumber the whites, where officers of the law are seldom seen, where popular volunteers must at times supplement the efforts of officers running down malefactors," the *Gazette* argued, "he might hold sentiments much like those expressed by Gov. Davis."[32]

Of course, Davis was well aware that it was not so much what he said but to whom he said it that mattered. Standing face to face with the President of the United States, an Arkansas hillbilly had spoken his piece on the race issue. Coupled with his refusal to dine with Powell Clayton, this could only enhance Davis's image as a defender of the "Southern way of life." To no one's surprise, Davis succeeded in turning the Roosevelt incident into a major political issue. And James Berry, a one-legged Confederate veteran, found himself in the curious position of being branded a traitor to the South for having attended a luncheon with Powell Clayton. Blending the themes of racism, sectionalism, and xenophobia, Davis had little trouble placing Berry on the defensive:

> There must have been 40,000 people in our Capital City, one-half of whom were niggers. I never saw as many niggers in my life. I had to take four baths to take the smell off my person. The papers say that I did not treat the President courteously. I stayed with him all day; I showed him all the courtesy any official could show another; but when we came to the banquet table, I found that Powell Clayton was to sit at the same table, and I said, "Mr. President, I can not eat with the old one-armed villain; his hell-hounds and villains murdered my aunt in Little River County during the Reconstruction." Many a night has my mother laid out with me, a baby, in the woods, to escape the ravages of these demons. He murdered our citizens, he pillaged our homes, he depleted our treasury, and my mother would have no respect for me if I should sit down and eat with him. The food would sour on my stomach. I delivered the President to the banquet hall, where the luncheon was being served, and I said to the guard, "Cut the ropes; let me out. My God, let me away from Powell Clayton and his nigger gang!" Ah, my fellow-citizens, I did not eat with Powell Clayton, and the next time you hear from Jeff Davis he will not be sitting as Senator Berry did, at a banquet board with this despoiler of our homes.[33]

Davis's ability to turn the Roosevelt visit into a white supremacist publicity stunt, along with his subsequent manhandling of Berry on the stump, demonstrates that he was a racial demagogue of considerable skill. Like his contemporaries, Vardaman and Tillman, he had the ability to whip up a storm of Negrophobic rhetoric without being entrapped in the ensuing whirlwind. Still, campaign rhetoric does always not tell the whole story. In assessing the racial dimension of Davis's political appeal, we need to determine the extent to which his white supremacy went beyond the level of rhetoric. Did he actively promote white supremacist legislation? To what extent were his executive actions racially discriminatory? Was he really the "white man's Governor," as he claimed to be?

Davis's official behavior while governor was generally consistent with his Negrophobic campaign rhetoric. With the exception of the three "accidental" black appointments publicized by Carroll Wood, he apparently made good his promise to appoint only white Democrats to public office. In addition, several of his executive orders were openly discriminatory. In December 1902, for example, he pardoned every *white* convict in the state under the age of eighteen. Although he claimed that the mass pardon was issued to call attention to the need for a reform school, the plight of young black convicts was officially ignored. He later issued a blanket pardon to all *white* females serving time in the state penitentiary.[34]

Davis also led the successful movement for a mandatory white primary. The adoption of this rule by the State Democratic Central Committee in January 1906 was considered a major victory for the Davis faction. Although some Arkansas counties had adopted local white primary rules as early as 1898, many had held back.[35] Few Democrats openly endorsed black suffrage, but the idea of a mandatory state-wide white primary was not all that popular among Democratic leaders. Many Black Belt Democrats feared that banning blacks from the Democratic party would substantially increase the local Republican vote in general elections. As long as black disfranchisement in general elections was incomplete, an all-white Democratic primary was a risky venture, at least in the Black Belt.

The fact that Davis chose to ignore this problem is a testament to his deep personal and political commitment to black disfranchisement. More than any other racial issue, disfranchisement seemed to excite Davis's imagination. His statements on the subject tended to be uncompromising and intensely Negrophobic. "I stand for the Caucasian race in government," he told a crowd during the general election campaign of 1904, ". . . and I say that 'nigger' dominion will never prevail in this beautiful Southland of ours, as long as shotguns and rifles lie around loose, and we are able to pull the trigger."[36] He told the legislature in 1905: "The most cruel blow that was ever struck a helpless and defenseless people was the action of the general government in placing in the hands of an ignorant, illiterate and irresponsible race of people, the ballot of a free man. . . ."[37] A strong supporter of the Poll Tax Amendment of 1908 and the Grandfather Clause Amendment of 1912, Davis probably did more to complete the process of black disfranchisement in Arkansas than any other politician. "The negroes ought to be disfranchised," he declared when he announced his support for the grandfather clause, "because you can't educate a nigger, I would be glad to see the United State deport them. They look like Apes."[38]

Davis was much less active in other areas of racial legislation. Although his governorship coincided with the flowering of the Jim Crow movement in Arkansas, his responsibility for this development is questionable. Aside from contributing to a general climate of increasing racial tension, he was not directly responsible for the flood of racially restrictive legislation that swept the state during his term of office. Although he signed several pieces of Jim Crow legislation into law, there is no evidence that he played any significant role in the actual formulation or enactment of this legislation.

The one time that he did clearly initiate and promote a piece of Negrophobic legislation, the Burgess school tax segregation bill, his efforts were unsuccessful.

Davis's apparent lack of interest in racial legislation can be seen in the voting behavior of his legislative followers. As shown in Table 23, limited evidence on voting behavior in the 1903 legislature demonstrates that Davis had surprisingly little influence on his followers in matters of racial legislation. Although these data indicate that pro-Davis legislators were somewhat more inclined to support Negrophobic legislation than anti-Davis legislators, the most revealing pattern is the extent to which the Davis faction was split over these bills. Such a low level of factional cohesion was most likely a reflection of apathy at the top.

Davis's seemingly apathetic attitude toward pending white supremacist legislation is suggestive; but his failure to comment on or take credit for racial legislation after it became law is even more revealing. One looks in vain through his campaign speeches for any references to new race laws such as the Gantt Jim Crow streetcar law or the Witt Jim Crow prison law. Despite the harshness of his rhetoric, he did not seize *every* opportunity to exploit the race issue. Except for his consistent opposition to black suffrage and black officeholding, his interest in the race issue tended to be intermittent. His public attitude and behavior towards blacks varied according to political exigencies.

Despite his whitecapper rhetoric, Davis had few qualms about personally associating with blacks. His chauffeur was black; some of his favorite hunting companions were black; he hired a black man to replace a white as state house janitor; and, as we have seen, he was not averse to drinking from the same bottle as an ex-slave. Occasionally he even evidenced sentimental paternalism towards servile blacks. "If you want the best there is in barber work," he once told a crowd, "go to some old-time Southern darky—lay down in his chair and go to sleep, and he will do the rest." On another occasion he talked warmly about the special relationship between "a negro farm-hand" and "a good houn' pup."[39]

To a limited extent, the paternalistic side of Davis's racism affected his public policy. During his governorship, he pardoned hundreds of black convicts and worked long and hard to reform an inhumane prison system whose inmates were overwhelmingly black.[40] While arguing against the purchase of the "disease-ridden" Cummings Farm in 1903, he acknowledged that "negroes could work on such land," but insisted that "humanity would dictate that they should not be forced to do so."[41] Though somewhat self-serving, this public expression of sympathy for downtrodden black convicts indicates that Davis's commitment to white supremacist politics had its limits.

The race issue was by no means the only arrow in Davis's quiver during

TABLE 23
Racial Bills
Comparative Voting Behavior of Pro-Davis, Anti-Davis, and Neutral Factions in the 1903 Arkansas House of Representatives

		Pro-Davis			Anti-Davis			Neutral			Total		
		Yes	No	NV	Yes	No	NV	Yes	No	NV	Yes	No	NV
HB 2: White Taxes To Be Used For White Schools Only (1st Vote)	#:	23	11	5	15	15	11	10	4	6	48	30	22
	%:	59.0	28.2	12.8	36.6	36.6	26.8	50.0	20.0	30.0	48.0	30.0	22.0
HB 2: Reconsideration Vote	#:	12	20	7	14	25	2	6	7	7	32	52	16
	%:	30.8	51.3	17.9	34.1	61.0	04.9	30.0	40.0	40.0	32.0	52.0	16.0
HB 140: Proscription of Black Railway Porters	#:	12	13	14	11	17	13	5	5	10	28	35	37
	%:	30.8	33.3	35.9	26.8	41.5	31.7	25.0	25.0	50.0	28.0	35.0	37.0

SOURCE: *Journal of the House of Representatives of Arkansas, 1903.*

the 1905–1906 campaign. In addition to attacking the "penitentiary ring" and the "state house steal" crowd, he filled his speeches with radical, anti-business rhetoric. When he was not criticizing Berry and Rogers for being soft on the trusts, he was assailing Wall Street for "gambling in the products of the soil of the Southland."[42] At Bentonville, he told the crowd:

> You growers of the products of the soil are as helpless as an unborn babe; you do not control the prices of your hogs, your wheat, your corn, your cotton. Who does control it, then, you say, Governor? I will tell you. There is a crowd of gamblers in New York City, called the Board of Exchange, that controls these prices. Did any of you ever visit the Board of Exchange in New York? I presume not. I was there about two years ago. I visited New York with Governor Clarke to try a lawsuit, and while there we visited this gambling house. You say, Governor, you should not call it a gambling house; it is a Board of Exchange. I say to you that it is a gambling house. The poor boy in this audience that steals a pig is sent to the penitentiary for larceny. The man that steals a million dollars or a railroad of this country is called a financier and sent to Congress. That is the difference.
>
> As I say, we went to this gambling house. Let me describe it to you for a moment. . . . These men were sitting there tearing open telegrams and going yow, yow, yow. I could not understand what they said, but in less than five minutes Clarke said. "Jeff, look there!" A price had been posted; they had changed the price of cotton the world over $5 a bale. Did they ever own a bale of cotton, my fellow-citizens? Did they ever see a cotton field ripening under a Southern sun? Do they ever expect to own a bale? No. What were they doing? Gambling in the products of the South. As I came up White River the other day along that stream, more beautiful than the Hudson, out of the car window I saw little children, girls and boys, thinly clad on a cold, frosty morning, children just as dear to their parents as yours or mine are to us, picking the cotton, pulling it from the bolls, their little hands almost frozen.
>
> When I saw this sight, my fellow-citizens, my mind turned back to that other scene in New York City, where the gamblers of Wall street sat around the gambling table gambling not only in the products of the soil of the South, but gambling in the flesh and blood and bone of the children of the South, and my heart cried aloud: "My God! Is there no help in Israel? Is there no help for the children of the South?"[43]

It was no accident that Davis's words sounded like an echo of the Populist rhetoric of the 1890s. In the same speech, he made a direct appeal to the old Populists:

> I do not know whether there are any Populists here today, and I do not care. I used to hate the Populists worse than any man in the State. I used to fight them. In 1888 I was chosen by the Democracy of this State, a freckle-faced red-headed boy, as one of their presidential electors and nothing gave me more pleasure than to fight the Pops of our State. You will remember, my fellow-citizens, that in 1888 Grover Cleveland tried to turn over to the goldbugs the Government of the United

States and that 30,000 true and brave souls in this State rebelled and established the Populist Party. You will also remember that in 1896, when we nominated the grandest and truest man the world ever knew—William Jennings Bryan—for President, we stole all the Populists had; we stole their platform, we stole their candidate, we stole them out lock, stock and barrel, and today these same men have come back into the Democratic Party and are voting the Democratic ticket as bravely and loyally as any men that ever cast an honest ballot.

Populists—why, I used to hate them; but I did not know as much then as I do now; I did not have as much sense then as I have now. These old Populists twenty years ago saw what we are seeing today. Bryan today is advocating just what the Populists advocated twenty years ago; that is, the public ownership of public franchises; and I say to you, as Mr. Bryan says, that if this Government does not soon own public carriers, if it does not soon own public carriers, that the public carriers will own this Government. . . .

Ah, my fellow-citizens, this old Populist Party advocated some of the grandest doctrines that the world ever knew. Among them was this: that you could legislate prosperity into a country. I used to believe this was a fool idea, but I had not been tangled up with the Arkansas Legislature as I have since. . . . I say to you here that you can legislate prosperity into a country if you have the right kind of men to do the legislating.[44]

Some critics had a field day ridiculing Davis's belated conversion to Populism; but most were more concerned about the style than the substance of his politics. Berry complained that Davis's campaign was filling the state with needless conflict, turning "father against son, brother against brother."[45] But Davis had a different interpretation:

Senator Berry says there is too much politics. He has not seen any politics yet. I have not got started. It is like an old man that lived in Thayer, Mo., who had never seen a railroad train. . . . He said to his son, Bill, one morning: "Take me down there and let me see that thing." His son carried him down there. A freight train was running through the mountains, whizzing around the curves at about thirty miles an hour. Bill said, "Father, what do you think of it?" and the latter replied, "Stop it. Bill, stop it. It will kill somebody in the country." His son answered, "Why Father, it has been running here for two months and has not hurt anybody yet." He said, "Yes, Bill, but the durned thing is running endways now; wait till it turns sideways and it will kill everything in the country." So I say to Senator Berry that this senatorial race has hardly started yet; wait until the senatorial race turns sideways and he will see some politics.[46]

The Davis-Berry campaign generally lacked the intensity of the Davis-Wood campaign. But it had its moments. In late November, Davis and ex-Congressman Hugh Dinsmore engaged in a bloody brawl in a Fayetteville hotel lobby. In his recent speeches, Davis had been reading excerpts from a letter that Berry had written to Dinsmore—a letter Dinsmore claimed had been stolen. When Davis refused to return the letter, Dinsmore responded with several choice epithets, which led to a fight. Before the fracas was over, Davis had broken his cane over Dinsmore's shoulder, and Dinsmore had bloodied Davis's head with a pistol butt. Dinsmore was eventually fined fifty dollars for carrying a pistol and one dollar for assault and battery; but most newspapers blamed Davis for the incident. According to the *New Orleans State*, Davis's "chief aim in life" was "to earn the title of the 'Fighting Governor.'"[47]

In the final month of the campaign, with both Berry and Rogers running behind, the anti-Davis forces pulled out all stops. Several ministers attacked Davis from the pulpit, charging him with public drunkenness and general immorality. Even the prohibitionist crusader Carry Nation, who was touring the state at the time, got into the act, roasting Davis on several occasions. The Berry camp trotted out John F. Reese, a convicted bootlegger who claimed that Davis had offered him a pardon in exchange for $500. Unfortunately for Berry, an attempt to arrange a face to face confrontation between Reese and Davis was unsuccessful.[48] A more fruitful line of attack focused on an alleged surplus in the state treasury. Throughout the campaign, Davis had boasted that his frugal handling of the state budget had produced a surplus of nearly four million dollars. This was a misrepresentation, since the alleged surplus included more than three million dollars of University of Arkansas Endowment Fund bonds. Backed by State Treasurer H. C. Tipton, Berry pointed out that the university bonds represented a debit, not a credit, for the state. Thus, the actual surplus was less than six-hundred thousand dollars. Despite the evidence, Jeff refused to acknowledge the mistake, though he did admit that arithmetic had never been one of his strong points.[49]

The final week of the campaign was dominated by a tragicomic controversy. In early March, Davis's father died at the age of seventy-three. The loss was a deep personal tragedy for Davis, who had always been close to his father. Nevertheless, politics was politics, and Davis felt no shame in wringing a few votes out of his father's death:

> Only a few weeks ago I experienced the greatest sorrow that ever came into my life. My old father, after a lingering illness, passed on to his reward. I wish you could have sat with me at his bedside and listened to his whispered prayers, as he asked God to give him strength to live long enough to see his son grace a seat in the Senate of the United States. . . . But, ah, my fellow citizens, this one wish of my father was denied him. The cord of life was clipped and his spirit winged its way to Glory and to God. Today he walks the golden streets in the company of Lee and Jackson and others of the Confederacy who had gone on ahead. And speaking to you here today for possibly the last time in this campaign, I fancy I can see his dear old sainted face, leaning far over the battlements of heaven, lighted up by the splendor of the New Jerusalem, giving me the strength and the fortitude to fight the battles of the plain people of Arkansas.[50]

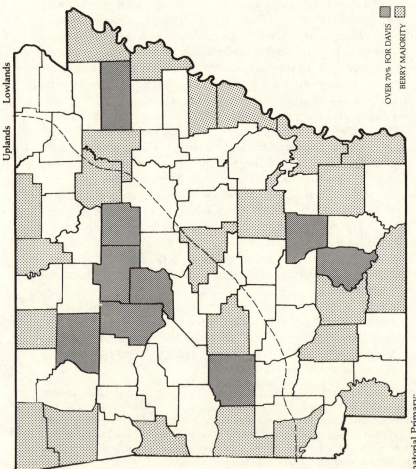

Uplands   Lowlands

OVER 70% FOR DAVIS
BERRY MAJORITY

FIGURE 12.
1906 Democratic Senatorial Primary:
% for Jeff Davis

SOURCE: Arkadelphia *Southern-Standard*, May 3, 1906.

The Old Guard undoubtedly was moved by Davis's maudlin eulogy. But the anti-Davis press pointed out that Lewis Davis had been a Confederate draftee whose military record was less than inspiring. Carping over a dead man's past was a fitting ending to a contest that the Little Rock *Arkansas Democrat* called "the vilest and meanest state campaign ever witnessed in Arkansas."[51]

On election day, heavy rains kept many voters at home, particularly in the remote precincts where the Davis vote was traditionally strong. This caused concern in the Davis camp, especially after the early returns seemed to favor Berry. In the final tally, however, Davis won the election by a margin of almost thirteen-thousand votes—67,982 to 55,074—and carried 51 counties.[52] It was his closest call to date, but considering the circumstances—he was running against a popular incumbent—he was more than satisfied with the results. Berry made a strong showing in urban areas, in the East Arkansas Delta, and in several mountain counties along the state's northern and western borders. But Davis won a solid majority of the vote everywhere else. As shown in Table 24, he ran especially well in very isolated farm precincts and in the old Populist strongholds. In the governor's race, Little won by an even larger majority than Davis, a remarkable achievement considering that he had been a heavy underdog at the beginning of the campaign.[53]

Most of Davis's critics were anything but gracious in defeat. Shocked and saddened by the loss of Berry, "the most beloved office-holder the state had ever known," they consoled themselves with cathartic expressions of outrage.[54] "The cry is going up for the Lord to help Arkansas," wrote the editor

TABLE 24
The 1906 Davis Vote: Precinct Returns, Nine County Sample*

Type of Precinct	N	% for Davis 1906 (Group Mean)	N	% for Davis 1904 (Group Mean)	Δ 1904–1906 N
City	3	44.2	3	46.5	− 2.3
Large Town–Farm	7	34.9	8	39.5	− 4.6
Small Town–Farm	11	43.2	16	44.0	− 0.8
Village-Farm	16	56.9	22	67.1	−10.2
Hamlet-Farm	33	60.9	37	68.9	− 8.0
Farm (Suburban)	3	27.0	3	55.3	−28.3
Farm (Central)	31	59.2	46	62.8	− 3.6
Farm (Isolated)	44	68.1	51	70.1	− 2.0
Farm (Very Isolated)	17	76.6	23	74.2	+ 2.4
Populist†	26	76.9	35	75.2	+ 1.7
Prohibitionist†	48	60.0	63	66.6	− 6.6

*See Appendix B. The 1906 primary returns for Crawford and Poinsett Counties are not available.
†See Table 20 for defnition.
SOURCE: See Appendix B.

of the *Fort Smith Elevator.* "Pity Arkansas with her Davis; pity Mississippi with her Vardaman; pity South Carolina with her Tillman. . . . Pity and pray. It is surely time to quit politics and call on the Lord."[55] The national press was equally pessimistic about Davis's potential for statesmanship. "The only resemblance between the Senator and a certain historic person," declared the *New York Sun,* "will be in name, not in achievements, intellect or character. . . . No one would mistake the husky, hulking, bold-faced countryman, who will figure as Jefferson Davis II, for a statesman."[56] In a similar vein, the editor of the Memphis *Commercial Appeal* warned: "There is a vast deal of difference between the stump and a seat in the United States Senate. The character capable of scooping in votes from the stump may find itself utterly incapable and useless amid the surroundings of the senator."[57] It was a prophetic warning.

15
King Jeff I

> Oh high and lordly is our chieftain Jeff,
> And in his heart the virtues congregate.
> His liquor, like his lies we swallow down
> And 'twixt the brass and brains and belly of the man
> We know not which has made him most renowned.
>
> —*From George G. Stockard's play,* King Jeff I *(1925)*[1]

Davis reached the peak of his power during the spring and summer of 1906. Although his opposition remained formidable, he clearly had the "high-collared roosters" on the run. His status as a master politician was no longer in dispute; even his most bitter enemies were in awe of his political skills. Many observers had considered Jim Berry to be unbeatable, yet Davis had made it look easy, electing John Little in the bargain. This political feat prompted a number of anti-Davis editors to take stock. In the wake of the senatorial primary, numerous editorial analyses of the Davis phenomenon were written. The most extensive and probably the most perceptive analysis appeared in the *Arkansas Gazette* on August 1. The author, *Gazette* editor J. N. Heiskell, had battled Davis for years, but he decided to give credit where credit was due. The governor, Heiskell maintained, was "a remarkable man" and an extraordinary "political prodigy." "The mere naming of his victories does not half tell the story;" he argued, "he has won his battles against odds and under circumstances that would have . . . sent down to overwhelming defeat any other man in the whole State of Arkansas." Heiskell believed nine factors were instrumental in Davis's success:

He is thoroughly democratic in speech, manner and action, and is surcharged with personal magnetism.

He makes the people think he is persecuted for their sake and stands between them and oppression.

He appeals to the human element.

He cunningly paints things to his liking and ingeniously and unscrupulously turns them to his advantage.

He continually does violence to the moral maxim that the suppression of truth is the suggestion of falsehood.

He audaciously and impudently relies on the public's lack of information about incidents in issue.

He appropriates credit for about everything creditable.

He has a powerful machine.

He has not met his match.

Heiskell closed by likening Davis to Napoleon: "Napoleon Bonaparte kept indefatigably and everlastingly at it and accomplished, at any price possible for him to pay, his set and determined purpose. So does Jeff Davis."[2]

Davis appreciated the serious attention he was receiving from political commentators; but, personally, he had little time for such high-flown analysis. Leaving the editors to ponder the implications of his political genius, he spent most of April and part of May vacationing in California with his wife. His previous travels in the West had been limited to Oklahoma and Kansas, and the trip to California fulfilled a lifelong dream. His mother, who had traveled to California with her first husband in the 1850s, had thrilled her young son with tales of a wild Pacific Arcadia. The California trip was one of the great adventures of Davis's life. As a vacation, however, it was less relaxing than it might have been.[3] To his dismay, the political pot kept boiling back home.

While Davis was out of the state, the acting governor was John P. Lee, the president pro tempore of the state senate. A conservative lawyer and banker from lowland Monroe County, Lee was solidly aligned with the anti-Davis faction. Prior to his departure, Davis had been concerned about what mischief Lee might accomplish during his absence and had instructed Charles Jacobson to remove a number of sensitive documents from his office files. Despite this precaution, Lee came very close to ruining Davis's vacation. Before the governor's return in mid-May, Lee managed to appoint several anti-Davis politicians to minor posts and to issue a pardon to a virulently anti-Davis Democrat from Washington County. At one point, he even threatened to convene a special session of the legislature. This was more than Davis could stand. "We are both well," he wired Jacobson on May 4, "but I am too mad and worried to enjoy myself."[4] In the end, the actual damage inflicted by Lee was slight; but Davis's conviction was heightened that his political enemies were an unscrupulous lot.

By the time the Democratic State Convention met in June, Davis had regained firm control of his administration. The convention enthusiastically ratified the results of the March primary, despite the protests of a few diehard Berry supporters. The delegates' endorsement was tantamount to election, though Davis's official election to the Senate would not come until the legislature polled its members in January 1907. The convention also chose Davis's political lieutenant, William F. Kirby, to be the party's nominee for attorney general. This enraged Xenophon O. Pindall, the anti-Davis candidate for attorney general. Pindall had won a plurality over Kirby in the primary, but had failed to win a majority of the total vote in a three-way race. Pindall cried foul, pointing to the hypocrisy of Davis's democratic rhetoric, but the Davis forces prevailed.[5]

During the general election campaign that followed, Davis stumped the state for the Democratic ticket and even made a few partisan speeches in Oklahoma. His sojourn among the Sooners was a great success and, like the California exposure, a fitting prelude to his impending assault on national politics. When he arrived in Washington to take his seat in the Senate, he wanted as many Americans as possible to know who he was. Nevertheless, his primary concern was the Arkansas state election. Since John Little was more acceptable to the conservative wing of the party than Davis, the threat of a bolt to the Republicans was more remote than in the previous three elections. But Davis was not taking any chances. Displaying his most respectable demeanor, he did everything he could to ensure party solidarity. As expected, Little and the Democrats won in a cakewalk over a Republican party that was beset by intense factionalism.[6]

With Little as governor and Kirby as attorney general, Davis could go off to Washington assured that his interests back home would be protected. Although he was less sure about the character of the new legislature— during the 1906 primary, factional lines were less distinct than they had been in 1904—relatively few of the new legislators had conducted explicitly anti-Davis campaigns. In any event, the upcoming legislative session could hardly be more disappointing than previous sessions.[7]

Davis's final months in office were devoted largely to pardon requests, the cementing of his relationship with Governor-elect Little, and the writing of his farewell address to the legislature. Delivered on January 18, this address was a carefully crafted effort that demonstrated what Davis could do when he applied himself. It contained his most ambitious reform proposals to date, especially in the area of economic reform where his recommendations were far more explicit and wide-ranging than they had been in the past. In addition to his standard pitch for more stringent antitrust legislation, he called for a series of innovative laws to protect farmers and workers. Directed primarily at the evils of economic colonialism, his proposals included a constitutional amendment that would place a surtax on all land owned by absentee owners, and a law that would prevent nonresidents (of the state) and nonresident corporations from owning Arkansas land except for expressly corporate purposes. Such a law, he pointed out, would have prevented the recent acquisition of Arkansas cotton lands by a large British textile company.

He went on to insist that homesteads should be exempt from all taxes other than road taxes, and that liens on farm land should be illegal except for the purpose of making improvements or securing money to purchase land. The common dirt farmer, "the man with the hoe in his hand," had to

be protected from those who would "let greed run riot." He also called for a
law prohibiting speculation in crop futures. The present cotton market, in
his view, was "nothing more or less than a simple gambling device by which
men are permitted to gamble in the products of the soil." (Unfortunately,
such unregulated speculation was consistent with the spirit of the times—an
unscrupulous form of commercialism, tied "to the merciless laws of the
survival of the fittest," was threatening to take over the nation.) After chas-
tising the railroads and other corporations for "looking upon their employees as so many chattels," he counseled the legislators "to drive the
lobbyists from your halls." "It would be more decent," he claimed, "for a
member of this general assembly to be seen talking on the streets or found
in the room of the most vile prostitute in this city than to be found in the
rooms of one of these lobbyists."[8]

Whether Davis's radical statements were uttered in a spirit of true radicalism or as a calculated attempt at demagoguery, they were disquieting to
conservatives. To their dismay, Jeff was going out with a bang. Still, he *was*
going out. Anti-Davis Democrats had been waiting for the governor's
farewell for a long time. Having Jeff in Washington might cause the state a
bit of embarrassment, but at least he would be out of Little Rock for much of
the next six years. Davis might try to run the state from Washington, using
Governor Little as a figurehead, but many were hopeful that Little would
eventually assert himself and break away from the Davis camp.[9]

Little's inaugural address, immediately following Davis's farewell, drew a
mixed response from conservatives. Although he made no attempt to match
Davis's stinging rhetoric, the new governor outlined an ambitious reform
program, not all of which pleased the business community. As Davis nod-
ded his approval, Little called for additional antitrust legislation, free school
textbooks, a fellow-servant law, the abolition of the convict-lease system, the
building of a state textile school, an improved drainage and levee system,
and better roads. Many members of the legislature—especially those who
considered themselves to be progressives—were impressed by the substance
of Little's speech and by his apparent willingness to pursue his goals with
tact and moderation. A number of observers commented that Little seemed
strangely ill at ease for a man who had been in public life for thirty years,
but no one thought much of that at the time.

Two days after his inauguration, Little suffered a complete "mental and
physical collapse." Although rumors of his death proved false, the state soon
discovered that the ailing governor had been forced to return to his home in
Greenwood and that his son Paul (who doubled as his father's secretary)
had been put in charge of the governor's office in Little Rock. For three
weeks Little did his best to run the state from his bedside. Some legislators
questioned the constitutionality of a long-distance governorship, but Attorney General Kirby quickly ruled that Little's absence from the capital

posed no major constitutional problems. In early February, the press reported that he was recovering rapidly and would soon return to Little Rock. But such reports were inaccurate. On February 11 the state was rocked by the news that the governor was being taken to the Gulf Coast of Texas for an indefinite period of convalescence. With Little out of the state, John I. Moore of Phillips County, the conservative president of the state senate, became acting governor. The Davis forces prayed that Moore's tenure would be brief, but they did not get their wish. Two weeks after his arrival in Texas, Little's condition worsened, and it became clear that he would never return to the executive office. Moore served as acting governor until the legislature adjourned on May 14. He was replaced by the newly-elected lieutenant governor (president pro tempore of the senate), Xenophon O. Pindall. Little never recovered and was eventually placed in the Arkansas State Hospital for Nervous Diseases, where he died in 1916.[10]

For Davis, Little's illness was a political as well as a personal tragedy. A carefully constructed scenario of loyal succession had disintegrated, and the Davis faction's hegemony in state politics was in dire jeopardy. John Moore, a conservative lawyer from the East Arkansas Delta, was in the governor's office, and there was nothing Davis could do about it. Although Moore was not virulently anti-Davis—the two men had been classmates at Cumberland University in 1881–82—he had little sympathy for Davis's style or ideology. To make matters worse, anti-Davis forces in the legislature wasted no time in taking advantage of the situation. With the executive branch in disarray, corporate lobbyists had a field day with the legislature. Davis's worst moment came when the legislature approved an amendment that placed fire insurance companies outside the jurisdiction of the 1905 antitrust law. In Davis's words, the antitrust law "was torn into shreds, demolished, trampled upon by the subsidized press . . . and by the hired minions of corporate wealth. . . . Rooms were fitted up at the Hotel Marion in the city of Little Rock, with champagne, whiskey and cigars; legislators forgot their people, legislators closed their eyes to their duty—they struck the fatal blow; they destroyed the law."[11]

Despite the lobbyists, the Davis faction did not come up empty-handed: the legislature approved an employers' liability act and an act prohibiting speculation in crop futures; extended the powers of the Railroad Commission; and even appropriated $3,000 to provide artificial limbs for disabled Confederate veterans. Most important, on January 30, the legislature officially elected Davis to the United States Senate. The vote was 86 to 6.[12] Since his term would not begin until March 4, and he would not leave for Washington until Congress reconvened in early December, Davis was faced with a lengthy interregnum. But the break was welcome as it gave him the opportunity to revive his private law practice. Years of almost continuous campaigning had sapped his finances, and he desperately needed to recoup his personal fortune. In mid-January, he and Jacobson opened a law office in Little Rock.

The legal partnership between Davis and Jacobson proved to be a striking financial success. Unfortunately, it had the unintended effect of poisoning the relationship between two men who were not accustomed to working together as equals. Jacobson was subsequently unwilling to go back to the status of an unquestioning subordinate. For the first time in his political career, he began to demand a degree of personal and political independence. When Davis refused to adjust, the two men came to a parting of the ways. According to Jacobson, the break was triggered by a disagreement over what his duties as Davis's legislative assistant should be. Davis, who hoped to spend much of his Senate term in Arkansas tending to his political machine and his hunting dogs, wanted Jacobson to run his Washington office. But Jacobson insisted on staying in Little Rock, arguing that with a wife and two small children to support he simply could not afford to live in Washington year-round.

The two men soon had a political falling-out that rendered the disagreement over Jacobson's new duties academic. During his years as Davis's private secretary, Jacobson had become a close personal friend of Secretary of State O. C. Ludwig. When Ludwig announced that he would run for a third term in the 1908 primary, Jacobson offered him his wholehearted support—thinking that Davis would do likewise. To nearly everyone's surprise, however, Davis threw his support to Ludwig's opponent, Julius Clary. Everyone in the Davis organization was ordered to follow suit, but many Davisites, including Jacobson, stubbornly refused. Before long the break was complete; so much so that when Davis ran for re-election to the Senate in 1912, Jacobson actually worked as a campaign aide for his opponent, Congressman Stephen S. Brundidge. At the time of Davis's death in January 1913, the two men were not even on speaking terms.[13]

Throughout the spring and summer of 1907, Davis was preoccupied with the continuing saga of John Little's replacements. When X. O. Pindall succeeded John Moore as acting governor in mid-May, things went from bad to worse, as far as Davis was concerned. According to some observers, however, he had no one but himself to blame for this development. Although Davis and Pindall had been political enemies for years—Pindall claimed that the Davis faction had cheated him out of the attorney general nomination at the 1906 state convention—the two men allegedly had struck a bargain prior to Pindall's selection as lieutenant governor. But, bargain or no, the new acting governor and the senator were soon at sword's point over matters of patronage and penitentiary management. Pindall became increasingly bold and defiant, informing Davis's emissaries that he, not the senator, was the acting governor of Arkansas. And barring Little's death, which would necessitate a special gubernatorial election, he would remain the governor until January 1909.

At one point during the summer, it appeared that Little's death was imminent. Thinking that a special election was in the offing, Davis met with his closest political advisors to choose a gubernatorial candidate. Several potential candidates were discussed, including Attorney General Kirby, Judge Jeptha Evans, and George Washington Donaghey, a prominent building contractor from Conway. But Davis did not consider any of these men to be completely satisfactory. Although he leaned towards Kirby, he refused to commit himself. In the end, Little survived, but the confusion of that summer meeting would haunt Davis later in the year.

In October, Davis found himself in a political quandary when both Kirby and Donaghey announced for the governorship. Barring a withdrawal, the March 1908 primary would pit two popular pro-Davis candidates against one another—a potentially disastrous situation that might lead to the election of John Hinemon, the anti-Davis candidate for governor. Although Kirby was more of an insider than Donaghey, both men had loyal followings within the Davis faction. To complicate matters further, the contest for secretary of state also boasted two pro-Davis candidates, Julius Clary and O. C. Ludwig. Davis faced a difficult choice: he could stay out of the state races and let the voters decide who best represented Jeff Davisism—a strategy that might work to the advantage of the anti-Davis faction; or he could throw his support behind one candidate in each race—a strategy that would almost certainly alienate two powerful allies. After several weeks of indecision, he chose the latter course. The fabric of the Davis organization had been unravelling ever since he had relinquished the governorship in January. It was time, he decided, to tighten things up. In November, Davis let it be known that he was supporting Kirby and Clary, and that he expected everyone in the Davis camp to follow suit. He hoped that his forthright stand would persuade Donaghey and Ludwig to withdraw; but he had misjudged the situation. Not only did Donaghey and Ludwig refuse to withdraw, but also several key lieutenants in the Davis organization, including Charles Jacobson and John Page, refused to follow Davis's lead.[14] Davis was nonplussed. His control over his organization had always been somewhat tenuous, but this was the first threat of a full-scale rebellion. However, the primary was still six months away, and he had plenty of time to whip the boys into line. At that moment he had other important things to worry about.

Davis spent most of October and November drafting a federal antitrust bill and an accompanying oration later known as the "cobweb speech." He labored over the speech for weeks and, for the first time in his career, committed the entire text to memory. When the Senate convened on December 2, he wanted to be ready. "If you will send me to Washington I will let that gang know I am in town," he had promised the voters during the 1906 campaign, "I will pull off a speech that will knock down the cobwebs before I am there two weeks."[15]

True to his word, on December 4, two days after the opening of the session, Davis introduced S.100—a bill for the "suppression of pools, trusts and combinations in restraint of trade." He had intented to deliver his "cobweb speech" on the spot, but Senate leaders informed him that the rules prohibited members from discussing a bill on the day that it was introduced. Bewildered, Davis initially demanded that the rules be waived; eventually, he agreed to postpone his speech until December 11. Senate veterans were flabbergasted. Even Bob La Follette, who had shocked the Senate with a two-day oration in April 1906, had waited three months before beginning his assault on Senate protocol. To Davis's delight, the flap was played up by the press. He had been in Washington less than a week, and he was already something of a celebrity.[16]

When Davis rose to deliver his speech on the eleventh, the Senate galleries were overflowing with curious onlookers. Committee meetings were adjourned to accommodate the speech, and congressmen and their staffs stood in the doorways, craning their necks to catch a glimpse of the primitive Arkansawyer. It was not every day that a wild man from the Ozarks spoke his piece on the Senate floor. The whole scene smacked of Barnum and Bailey, and everyone expected a good show.

Davis did his best not to disappoint them. Making no concessions to the setting, he delivered his speech just as he would have delivered it in the Arkansas backcountry. He began by informing his colleagues that he had no intention of abiding by the Senate tradition that discouraged new members from making speeches: "It was not my purpose when I entered this honorable body to retain my seat in silence . . . until my hair should have grown gray in service, until I had grown out of the knowledge of my constituents and lost my identity with them."[17] The trust issue, in his view, was not a subject for polite debate; it was a cause for action. The Republic was in peril, and something had to be done. After pointing out the deficiencies of the Sherman Antitrust Act of 1890, he urged the Senate to pass a law that would cripple the trusts:

> Let the great trust magnates of the land understand that they are not above the law; that the strong arm of justice can reach them. Prosecute them as you would any other felon, just as you would an ordinary horsethief. The man who steals your horse commits a very small injury to your property, but the man who steals under the trust process grinds and oppresses and destroys American manhood and shuts the door of opportunity to millions of men, does a wrong and an injury that cannot be compensated in mere fines. Put them in the penitentiary . . . the best object lesson today for the suppresssion of the trusts would be be to see John D. Rockefeller or someone just like him with stripes on.[18]

The Rockefeller statement drew gasps from the audience, but Davis plunged ahead. Rockefeller's "swollen fortune" was just the tip of the iceberg, according to Davis. Thanks to the trusts, millionaires owned "about

87.5 per cent of the nation's entire wealth," yet no one seemed to be doing anything about it. "The country has gone wild about money," he declared. "This is a day when gold is placed above God and money is placed above men, when we would sell our souls, our Government, our all for dollars." This "mad desire to get money" had brought the Republic to the brink of disaster. "I am neither an alarmist, socialist, nor anarchist," he assured the audience, "but I tell you there is something wrong. This is not the govern- ment handed to us by our fathers."[19] As his voice cracked with emotion, he pleaded for a return to "the old-time Democratic simplicity," to the days when men like Old Hickory Jackson ran the government:

When he was sworn in as chief executive of this great nation, he came to the White House on horseback. He rode his horse out here, hitched it to a rack, and, dressed in a suit of blue jeans, walked into the White House and took the oath of office. How simple was that ceremony! How plain! If a man should do that today he would be called crazy. Today there is too much glitter, there is too much gold, there is too much tinsel. If things continue for another quarter of a century as they have for the past twenty-five years the statesmen of America will be wearing knee breeches with brass buckles, and powdered wigs, and when they go to the White House they will be bowing down to semi-royalty. We are going too fast. This world is moving too fast.[20]

This tribute to the lost world of Andrew Jackson brought out a few chuckles from the Republican side of the aisle, but Davis was in no mood for levity. As the speech progressed, he became increasingly agitated. To the delight of the crowd, he began to pace back and forth, waving his arms and occasionally pounding on his desk. His voice grew louder and louder, and at several points he literally screamed at the audience. Showing no signs of tiring, he attacked everything from the tariff ("the mother of trusts") to Wall Street ("I hope the day will soon come when we can see the stock gambler of New York in felon's stripes.") to the oil industry ("I dislike Standard Oil. I hate the smell of coal oil. Petroleum makes me sick.")[21] Finally, after an hour and fifteen minutes of pyrotechnic oratory, he sat down. The immediate reaction was a hearty round of applause—and a few looks of incredulity. Whatever else could be said of the new senator from Arkansas, he was a forthright gentleman with a strong pair of lungs.

Immediately after the speech, Davis sent a wire to his friends back in Arkansas: "Spoke to the biggest crowd Senate ever had. They came to scoff; they stayed to pray."[22] He later boasted that his maiden speech in the Senate had "bearded the lion in his den," providing "the trust interests such a drubbing on the floor of that august body as they shall not soon forget."[23] But, in truth, he was bitterly disappointed by the Washington establish- ment's refusal to take him or his bill seriously. When the owner of a Phila- delphia vaudeville show offered him a $3,000 a month contract, he reportedly "did not know whether to laugh or cuss at the proposition."[24] No one seemed to appreciate the gravity of the antitrust issue. One colleague suggested that money from the Senate contingent fund should be used to replace the carpet near Davis's seat and to repair his desk, since Senator Davis "constantly paced up and down the main aisle during his discourse stamping his feet vehemently to emphasize his points against the octopus and repeatedly banged his desk with clenched fists."[25]

The national press reacted to Davis's harangue with a mixture of disdain and condescension. A few papers saw some merit in Davis's performance. "The Arkansan means well," the Philadelphia *Record* concluded. "He is explosive but not dangerous; fresh, but not uncompromising. No doubt when tamed and domesticated in his place he will prove as tolerable as Tillman."[26] But most editors were not so charitable. According to the *New York Times,* Davis's speech was "a disappointment even to his friendliest colleagues. It did consume time, but it was not even a good show."[27] A number of observers made unfavorable comparisons between Davis and South Carolina's Senator "Pitchfork Ben" Tillman. The St. Louis *Post-Dispatch* claimed that "Ben Tillman's celebrated pitch-fork" had been "melted into a mass of shapeless metal by the more torrid thought and language of the junior senator from Arkansas."[28] To Davis's dismay, most commentators focused on the style rather than the substance of the speech. The account that appeared in *The Independent* magazine was typical:

> He thundered through his maiden effort rather like a mad Nubian, only dropping occasionally and suddenly, as if to bring out the other better by contrast. He was furious, pathetic, humorous. He strode up and down the center aisle. He stamped his feet. He banged his desk. He shook his hand, his fists, his finger. . . . The first man to congratulate him was Sen. McEnery, who is deaf as a post, and by the act paid a delicately humorous compliment to the new Senator's powers of gesticulation.[29]

Davis liked being the center of attention, but he did not enjoy being viewed as a clown. As he told a number of interviewers, though he was not averse to poking fun at himself from time to time, he was not a buffoon. He was a serious reformer, and the sooner the city-slickers recognized that fact the better off everyone would be. The "subsidized press" could attack him all it liked, but no amount of ridicule would deter his crusade against the malefactors of great wealth. To prove his point, he introduced a second major reform bill—a bill to prohibit speculation in crop futures—on January 13. Based on a law enacted by the Arkansas legislature in 1907, the bill featured a clause that made it "unlawful to use the mails, or the telegraph or the telephone system for the purpose of conveying gambling propositions."[30] Davis had high hopes for the crop futures hill, but he quickly discovered that few senators shared his intense desire to "stay the ruthless hand of the gambler."[31] Like most measures that called for a radical restructuring of the

American economy, the bill was quietly referred to the judiciary committee, where it was quickly forgotten.

Davis was deeply discouraged by the rude reception accorded his reform bills. Although he had been in Washington less than two months, he had already seen enough to confirm his worst suspicions: the nation's capital was an enemy camp, a city ruled by trust-heeling Republicans. Worst of all, the Senate itself appeared to be the enemy's headquarters. He found most of his colleagues to be stuffy and decadent; he could not fathom Senate protocol; and he considered most of his committee work to be pointless. Accustomed to the forthright politics of the Arkansas backcountry, he had little respect for an institution that seemed to value politeness more than truth. With few exceptions, the debates on the Senate floor bored him; no one ever talked about the big issues, such as the growing power of the trusts; and nothing of importance ever seemed to get done. Frustrated and more than a little homesick, Davis decided to return to Arkansas in early February.[32]

Davis's disenchantment with the Senate was not the only reason for his return. The governor's race was heating up, and he wanted to do what he could to boost Will Kirby's candidacy. For a number of reasons, Davis regarded Kirby's election as essential. He needed someone whom he could trust in the governor's office, and Kirby was loyal to a fault. He also wanted a governor who shared his passion for fighting the trusts. Here too Kirby filled the bill. Unlike George Donaghey, who was both a successful businessman and a relative newcomer to the antitrust movement, he had been an inveterate trust baiter throughout his career.[33] Kirby's biggest weakness as a candidate was his lack of stump-speaking prowess, but Davis was more than willing to pick up the slack. It had been more than a year since his last campaign effort, and he longed to be back out among his beloved rednecks. Moreover, by mounting an old-fashioned, Jeff Davis–style stump campaign that tipped the balance in Kirby's favor, he could regain firm control over his organization. He not only wanted to see Kirby elected, he also wanted to demonstrate his power to sway the electorate. If he could save Kirby and destroy Donaghey, the boys at the county courthouses would think twice before they challenged his authority again.

Davis kicked off his campaign for Kirby on February 18 with a blistering speech at Ozark. Later distributed across the state in pamphlet form, the Ozark speech dwelled upon the themes of persecution and conspiracy. Those friends who counseled him to stay out of the governor's race did not know what was happening behind the scenes, he told the crowd. "I defy this whole gang of high-collared roosters that are today seeking my undoing," he declared, ". . . I will not sit quietly in my seat in Washington and allow the work that I have been endeavoring to perform in the interest of the people for the past six years to be destroyed by them." Considering what was at stake, he would have to be a fool not to champion Kirby's cause: "W. F.

Kirby is the only candidate in this race for Governor who has ever been my personal and political friend. . . . He is the only candidate . . . who is really and truly the friend of the common people." How could anyone trust a man like George Donaghey, Davis demanded of the crowd, a man who boasted that he was "worth $500,000," a man who "has never yet in any contract that he has ever had employed union labor as his workmen"? Donaghey was not an evil man, Davis admitted, but he was no less dangerous than the worst of the trust heelers. Citing Donaghey's much-publicized aversion to stump speaking, Davis portrayed him as a political novice who lacked "the manhood to meet his opponents in fair open debate." If elected, Donaghey "would be as perfectly controlled by the ringsters and politicians of Little Rock . . . as your little boy would be controlled by you."[34]

The Ozark speech was only the beginning. For six weeks Davis stormed across the state, venting his spleen at Donaghey, the trusts, the penitentiary ring, and other enemies of Jeff Davisism. Much of his wrath was directed at alleged turncoats, such as Prosecuting Attorney Lewis Rhoton and Farmers' Union secretary Ben Griffin. Although he had once praised Rhoton for having "a backbone as big as my old grip," he now claimed that the prosecuting attorney was doing the trusts' bidding by falsely accusing him of accepting free railroad passes. In response, Rhoton published facsimiles of free passes bearing Davis's signature—passes provided by T. L. Cox, a man whom Davis had frequently characterized as the head of the "Little Rock Ring." Davis eventually let the matter drop, but not before he and Rhoton had engaged in a series of mudslinging exchanges[35] The conflict between Davis and Griffin was equally intense. Griffin was a long-time Davis supporter, but early in the 1908 campaign he had cast his lot with Donaghey, who was a close personal friend. Although Griffin insisted that his support for Donaghey should not be interpreted as an attack on Jeff Davisism, Davis thought otherwise. Fearing that Griffin would pull many Farmers' Union members into the Donaghey camp, he spared no effort in trying to discredit the "red-headed, sly old fox" who was trying to hand the Farmers' Union over to "the ringsters and tricksters, trust heelers and trust magnates of Arkansas."[36]

Rhoton and Griffin were more than willing to trade insults with Davis. But Donaghey took a different tack. Instead of responding in kind, he offered himself as an alternative to the back-biting professional politicians of the Davis era. He freely admitted that he was a political amateur. He was, he assured the voters, nothing more than a "practical, plain businessman" who had been drawn into politics by a sense of responsibility. As a member of the Capitol Commission, he had helped to foil the designs of the "State House ring." Now his only wish was to preside over the completion of the new capitol, to see the building completed as quickly as possible at a minimal cost. Jeff Davis himself, he reminded the voters, had once described him as "Honest George" Donaghey . . . a man who has stood lone-handed and fought the biggest gang of grafters and thieves that ever invaded our State."[37] Why Davis was attacking him now, he was not sure, but he hinted that political bossism was the root cause of the trouble between them.

Donaghey ran a shrewd campaign, emphasizing the state house issue and portraying himself as a lone warrior fighting a powerful political machine. But he had other advantages as well. He was well-financed; he had the support of Ben Griffin and the Farmers' Union; and he espoused a program of "business progressivism" that was acceptable to many moderate anti-Davisites. He also benefited from relatively weak opposition. John Hinemon, the anti-Davis candidate for governor, was an inept campaigner, and Will Kirby was not much better.[38] In the end, this combination of factors was too much for even Jeff Davis to overcome. Despite Davis's campaign, Donaghey won a convincing victory on election day, outdistancing Kirby by more than thirteen thousand votes. Hinemon finished a distant third, but that was small consolation for Davis, who realized that he had suffered the most serious political setback of his career. Julius Clary, Davis's candidate for secretary of state, also went down to defeat. The only bright spot for the Davis camp was Hal Norwood's victory in the attorney general's race.[39]

The 1908 primary was a bitter pill for Davis to swallow. More than a third of the Old Guard had ignored his advice and voted for Donaghey and Ludwig. Although most farm voters had kept the faith, village and town voters had defected in droves.[40] Many observers interpreted these defections as a rebuke to political bossism, and to a great degree they were probably right. Nothing did more to ensure Donaghey's victory than Davis's heavy-handed tactics. By leaving his post in Washington to campaign against a former ally, Davis had violated the electorate's sense of fair play. Jeff the martyr had become Jeff the bully. For the first time in his career, he had made a serious mistake in political judgment. That one mistake cost him dearly. Even though he retained a loyal core of followers, the myth of his invincibility had been dispelled. For many voters the Davis mystique was irrevocably broken.[41]

Following the election, Davis tried to save face by insisting that Honest George Donaghey was an ally after all. In a public letter to Donaghey, he described the recent primary as "a choice between two Jeff Davis men— yourself and Kirby." "I selected one Jeff Davis man," he explained, "and the people selected the other."[42] Unfortunately for Davis, Donaghey refused to cooperate. Spurning Davis's advances, he denied that he had ever been associated with any political faction. "I wear no man's collar," he declared.[43]

Donaghey's defiance signaled a changing of the guard in the Arkansas Democratic party. Backed by a centrist "progressive" coalition that cut across existing factional lines, the governor-elect wasted no time dismantling the political arrangements of the Davis era. When the Democratic State Convention met in June, Donaghey and his allies seized control of the party machinery. In addition to drafting the platform and selecting the party's officers, the Donaghey forces successfully blocked Davis's selection as an at-large delegate to the upcoming Democratic National Convention. Even though it was customary to include the state's two senators among the four at-large delegates, Davis finished a humiliating seventh in the balloting. After nearly a decade of dominance, Davis and his cronies had been rudely shoved aside.[44]

Although Davis professed to be shocked by his sudden loss of influence, he could not have been too surprised. Even at the height of his power in 1906, his hold over local politicians had been tenuous. Unaccustomed to permanent factional loyalties, Arkansas politicians were an unruly lot. While some "Jeff Davis men" were tied to their leader by bonds of ideology and intense personal loyalty, most grudgingly bowed to his authority. As long as he provided them with a trickle of patronage, an occasional pardon to dispense, or a few extra votes on election day, local politicians tolerated Davis's disruption of local autonomy. But when he could no longer be counted on to deliver these things, the centrifugal nature of Arkansas politics reasserted itself.[45] Without a faithful lieutenant in the governor's office. Davis had no hope of maintaining the strength of his political organization. Already weakened by the ascendance of acting-Governor Pindall, the Davis machine never recovered from the Kirby-Donaghey fiasco. With its leadership in disarray and bereft of its gubernatorial patronage base, the once powerful organization went into permanent decline.

Davis's political problems were compounded by continuing frustrations in Washington. On April 28, he introduced a resolution to dislodge his antitrust bill from the judiciary committee, and three days later he delivered a lengthy philippic against the forces that had conspired to stifle the bill. The speech attracted a large crowd, which expected a repeat of the "cobweb" performance. But Davis surprised them. Tired of being portrayed as a wild-eyed, backwoods buffoon, he set out to prove that he could beat the high-falutin Yankees at their own game. Reading from a prepared text, he filled the Senate chamber with grandiose phrases and obscure historical allusions. Although the speech, which was obviously written by someone else, was designed to enhance his respectability, it had just the opposite effect. As Davis stumbled over unfamiliar words and syntax, most of the audience headed for the exits. By the time he was finished, only a handful of bemused senators remained on the floor. The resulting press reports were merciless, and Davis was deeply embarrassed by the whole affair. Hurling a few choice epithets at the "subsidized press," he retreated into stony silence. When he boarded the train for Arkansas a few weeks later, some colleagues wondered if he would ever come back.[46]

Although he was glad to be home, Davis found little solace in Arkansas during the summer of 1908. With the Donaghey forces running amuck, his only hope lay in the election of a Democratic president who would provide him with enough patronage to shore up his deteriorating organization. In the fall, he stumped several states for his hero William Jennings Bryan, who was making a third bid for the presidency. Bryan ultimately lost the election by more than a million votes to William Howard Taft, but the campaign seemed to rekindle Davis's interest in national affairs. When he returned to Washington in December, he reintroduced his crop futures bill and, a month later, delivered a long and impassioned harangue on the crop speculation issue.[47] "The money power of this Government is treading upon dangerous ground," he warned his colleagues. "I would not be an alarmist . . . but I predict here and now that unless conditions change, that unless the Congress of the United States turn a listening ear to the lamentations of an outraged public, that within ten years there may be another Shenandoah Valley, there may be another Gettysburg; the red broom of war may sweep this Government as it has never been swept before."[48] Davis's dire prediction provoked considerable comment, but it did not move the Senate to action. Like the antitrust bill, the crop futures bill was destined to die in committee.

The crop futures speech was Davis's last hurrah. Never again did he deliver a major address on the Senate floor. Although he remained a senator until his death in 1913, his subsequent participation in Senate affairs was largely inconsequential. In June 1909 he took part in the debate on the Payne-Aldrich tariff, introducing an amendment that eliminated all tariffs on imported lumber. But his efforts were quickly brushed aside by the protectionist Republican majority. Later in the summer, during the debate on a Republican-sponsored tax bill, he spoke out against an amendment that lowered taxes on corporate income. But once again no one seemed to pay much attention to him. In February 1910 he made a futile attempt to amend a postal savings bank bill—he wanted to permit deposits in all solvent banks, not just in banks examined by the federal government. And later the same month, he voiced his opposition to a bill granting Standard Oil the right to lay oil and gas pipelines across Arkansas's public lands.[49] The proposed pipeline, he declared, was an insult to the state of Arkansas. If he had his way, Standard Oil would pump its oil "straight from here to hell," and John D. Rockefeller himself would be "there to receive it."[50]

The pipeline issue raised Davis's ire, but even the specter of the Standard Oil octopus could not keep him in Washington. Tired of being ignored by his senatorial colleagues, he turned to the Old Guard for consolation. Hoping to revive the flagging spirit of Jeff Davisism, he spent most of the winter of 1910 on the Arkansas stump. George Donaghey was running for re-election, and Davis was determined to deny him a second term. Although Donaghey had proven to be a tough-minded reformer during his first year in office, Davis had developed a blind hatred for the self-styled "progressive" gover-

nor. Casting ideological considerations aside, he threw his support to Donaghey's moderate opponent, Judge William M. Kavanaugh. One of Little
Rock's most prominent bankers and business leaders, Kavanaugh was an
unlikely Davis ally. Even Jeff Davis could not convince the voters that the
president of the Little Rock Railway and Electric Company was an agrarian
insurgent. Despite Davis's efforts, Donaghey ran even stronger than in
1908, defeating Kavanaugh by more than thirty-five-thousand votes. On a
county-by-county basis, the correlation between the Kavanaugh vote and
the 1906 Davis vote was a meager +.130, and even Pope County, Davis's
own bailiwick, ended up in the Donaghey column. For the second time in
two years, a substantial portion of the Old Guard had refused to follow
Davis's lead.[51]

The growing suspicion that Jeff Davis had lost his bearings was reinforced by an unfortunate episode known as the "sunk lands" controversy.
The by-product of an 1810 earthquake, the so-called sunk lands encompassed hundreds of thousands of acres of public land in northeastern
Arkansas. In 1850 Congress ceded the entire area, most of which was
swampland, to the state of Arkansas; but some federal officials later questioned the legality of the cession. During the 1890s, the Cleveland administration ruled that the federal government had no claim to the sunk lands,
and a decade later Theodore Roosevelt's secretary of the interior, Ethan
Allen Hitchcock, made a similar judgment. Following the Hitchcock ruling,
which seemed to settle the matter, the state authorized the St. Francis Levee
Board to sell the sunk lands to private individuals for $1.50 an acre. Since
the sunk lands contained rich stands of timber, land speculators wasted no
time in buying up the entire area. Unfortunately for the speculators, the
Roosevelt administration reversed itself in 1908 and filed suit to reclaim the
sunk lands for the federal government. To complicate matters further, as the
case made its way through the courts, hundreds of poor white homesteaders, anticipating a judgment in the federal government's favor, moved
into the area.

The homesteaders' claims created a serious problem not only for the
speculators but also for Davis, who had agreed to serve as the St. Francis
Levee Board's legal counsel. Although Davis claimed that he had no personal stake in the case, a number of his friends were among the speculators
who stood to gain from a judgment upholding the Levee Board's sales.
Willing to go to great lengths to defend the speculators' interests, Davis
drafted a bill to countermand a preliminary court ruling that favored the
federal government's case. When the House Committee on Public Lands
held hearings on the sunk lands issue in February 1910, the propriety of the
bill (which was formally sponsored by Arkansas Congressman William
Oldfield) was called into serious question. Indeed, Davis's testimony before
the committee seemed to implicate him in a plot to defraud the home-

steaders of their land. When pressed by a committee member who could not understand how the self-proclaimed Tribune of Haybinders could pit himself against poor homesteaders, Davis reluctantly admitted that he had sacrificed the rights of "the little fellow" in order to promote "the great good of the public." Later, out on the stump, he boasted that his actions on behalf of the speculators had prevented the plunder of the sunk lands by predatory timber companies. In the end, the committee let the matter drop, and Davis escaped formal censure. But his apparent collusion with unscrupulous land speculators tarnished his reform image and further accelerated his political decline.[52]

During his final years in the Senate, Davis became increasingly absorbed in his family life and spent less and less time in Washington. His precarious financial situation forced him to devote much of his time to his Little Rock law practice. But his frequent visits to Arkansas were also welcome diversions from the disappointments of Senate life. At one point, he was deeply embarrassed by the disclosure that he had put several members of his family on the Senate staff payroll, even though they had never left Little Rock. The death of his wife in 1910 added to his troubles. Losing a faithful companion of twenty-eight years was a devastating blow. In October 1911, after a year of mourning and intermittent depression, he married Lelia Carter, the daughter of a prominent Franklin County physician.[53] Remarriage seemed to raise his spirits, though his new wife's social pretensions proved to be a continuing source of embarrassment for a man who had made a career out of attacking the "high-collared" crowd. When Senator and Mrs. Davis hosted a grand "cotillion" at their home in December 1911, the anti-Davis press had a field day. "Is this the same Jeff who for many years denounced the gang at Little Rock, charged them with being high-collared, bile-shirted and silk-hosed?" the *Morrilton Democrat* asked mockingly, ". . . the same Jeff who with tears in his eyes told them he could not afford to wear new pants while his wife was at home making old-fashioned soap . . . who went to Washington wearing wool socks, patched breeches, brogan shoes and a flannel shirt, a piece of corn bread tucked snugly away in his bosom and a bottle of wizard oil in his saddle bags?"[54]

In point of fact, it was the same Jeff. The "cotillion" notwithstanding, he remained alienated from polite society—especially the Washington variety. It was not easy being a Democrat in Washington during the Roosevelt-Taft era, but Davis compounded his problems by stubbornly refusing to adapt to his surroundings. He had no patience with the social conventions that ruled Washington society and made few friends outside the Arkansas delegation. Uncomfortable consorting with Republicans, he could not fathom the political truce that descended upon Washington in the evening hours. When President Taft invited him to a White House reception in 1909, he did not even bother to send his regrets. It was the last presidential invitation he ever

received. He would not attend any social function that required formal
dress; he would not wear a silk hat, regardless of the occasion; and he
refused to ride in private automobiles, which he regarded as decadent play-
things of the rich. It is not surprising that he became a social pariah, who
apparently spent most of his time in Washington either answering his constituents' letters or mailing free seeds to farmers back in Arkansas.[55] Since
few people in the capital treated him with the respect that he thought he
deserved, he preferred to keep to himself. Thus, for social as well as political
reasons, he had mixed feelings about his Senate career. As he once confided
to Congressman Russell of Missouri, "I appreciate the great honor of a seat
in the United States Senate, but I believe I would prefer to be at home with
my family and friends in Arkansas."[56]

By 1911 Davis was truly one of the forgotten men of the Senate. Dispirited
and increasingly withdrawn, he did little but brood about his lack of influence in Little Rock and Washington. He made few public appearances, and
the press paid little attention to him. Indeed, the only thing that kept him in
the public eye was speculation about his forthcoming re-election campaign.
Confident that he was ripe for defeat, anti-Davis leaders called for a challenger who could put the senator out of his misery.[57]

Despite Davis's vulnerability, the opposition had a difficult time finding a
suitable challenger. The memory of what Davis had done to Wood and
Berry was enough to discourage even the most ambitious politicians. In the
end, the only man willing to take on Davis was ex-Congressman Stephen S.
Brundidge. A close friend of former Senator Berry's, Brundidge was determined to avenge Berry's humiliating defeat in the 1906 primary. The son of a
prominent building contractor, he had practiced law in White County since
1880. During a twelve-year career (1897–1909) in Washington, he had
earned a reputation as a moderate progressive and a captivating orator.
Although he had never been known as an agrarian insurgent, anti-Davis
leaders were hopeful that he could hold his own on the backwoods stump.[58]

They were not disappointed. Displaying a sharp tongue and a caustic wit,
Brundidge was the aggressor throughout the campaign. In speech after
speech, he mercilessly recounted Davis's involvement in the "sunk lands"
fiasco and taunted him with detailed descriptions of his legislative defeats.[59] According to Brundidge, after five years in office Davis had nothing
to show but a few humorous press clippings. As a senator, Davis was not
just a failure, he was a laughingstock—an embarrassment to himself and
the state. "The senator representing Arkansas is only a joke," Brundidge told
a crowd at Camden. "He is here in Arkansas trying lawsuits most of the
time."[60] On another occasion, he quipped that he was "running to fill a
vacancy," that for all practical purposes Arkansas had been without a second senator since 1907.[61]

Brundidge maintained an exhausting speaking schedule and did everything he could to foster an exciting campaign. But Davis refused to follow suit. Abandoning "the well-beaten paths which had characterized his former campaigns," he confounded Brundidge's strategy of confrontation by refusing to engage in an extended series of joint debates.[62] At the beginning of the campaign Brundidge had proposed a lengthy county canvass, but Davis would only agree to four joint-speaking engagements. When Brundidge charged him with cowardice, Davis explained that he was simply trying to turn over a new leaf:

> Mr. Brundidge complains because I will not enter into an extended campaign with him. . . . My reason is obvious. We have had politics in this state that became so personal and abusive that it amounted to a disgrace to the participants. I am not wholly without blame for this condition of affairs and have made up my mind in this campaign to meet him at only four places and he can go his way and I will go mine. In my third race for Governor, the lines were drawn so tightly between Democrats that it put father against son, brother against brother, fist fights, knockdowns and drag-outs all over Arkansas, and I have determined never to be a party to such a scene again. . . . The press of this state belittles my efforts. They say I am not making the aggressive, fire-eating speeches I made in former days. I hope that time will so temper my disposition, will so cool my enthusiasm and so control my judgment that I may make a more manly, dignified, statesmanlike campaign during this race than I have ever made before and I intend to pitch it upon the highest ground possible and keep it there if my opponent will let me.[63]

Davis's low-key campaign insured that the senatorial primary would be overshadowed by the governor's race, which pitted George Donaghey against Congressman Joseph T. Robinson. The bitter struggle between Donaghey and Robinson captured most of the headlines, which suited Davis just fine. His determination to avoid controversy even kept him from meddling in the governor's race, at least for awhile. Although his hatred for Donaghey was hardly a secret, he did not openly campaign for Robinson until two weeks before the primary. This last-minute alliance between the Davis and Robinson camps—Robinson apparently promised to do what he could for Davis in East Arkansas—was a clear indication that Davis felt the Senate race was still up for grabs. He had good reason to be worried. The Davis machine, which had roused the Old Guard in earlier campaigns, was in shambles. And several of his former lieutenants, including Charles Jacobson, John Page, and Jesse Hart, were solidly ensconced in the enemy camp. As the campaign progressed the number of defectors increased, and during the final week of the race Brundidge took out full page ads listing former Jeff Davis men who were working for the Brundidge organization.[64]

By election day, March 27, Davis was anything but confident. In the end however, he managed to eke out a narrow victory, winning 72,005 votes to Brundidge's 62,369. Brundidge carried 30 counties and ran extremely well in the northeastern lowlands and the mountain counties along the Missouri

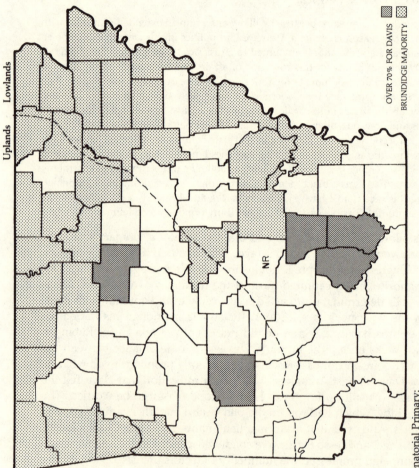

Uplands   Lowlands

OVER 70% FOR DAVIS

BRUNDIDGE MAJORITY

NR

FIGURE 13.
1912 Democratic Senatorial Primary:
% for Jeff Davis

SOURCE: Little Rock *Arkansas Gazette*, March 29, 1912.

border. But he could not overcome Davis's strong showing in central and southern Arkansas. In the governor's race, Robinson won a surprisingly easy victory over Donaghey, which gave rise to the theory that Davis owed his re-election to Robinson. Davis, of course, denied that this was the case: he attributed his victory to the steadfast loyalty of the Old Guard. And he was probably right. Although some realignment had taken place since the 1906 primary, the +.599 correlation between the 1906 and 1912 Davis votes indicates that most of the Old Guard had stuck by their hero. Despite all that had happened—the Kirby and Kavanaugh campaigns, the "sunk lands" scandal, the infamous cotillion, and five unproductive years in Washington—a large majority of the state's white farmers still considered Jeff to be their champion (see Appendix B). Conversely, he was as unpopular as ever among city and town voters. To friend and foe alike, he was, still Jeff.[65]

Davis's re-election seemed to revive his interest in public affairs. In a speech at the Democratic State Convention in June, he apologized for his prolonged absences from the Senate and vowed to do better in the future. Later in the summer, as he campaigned for Woodrow Wilson and the Democratic ticket, he talked of a new career in Washington. Although he had mixed feelings about the Wilsonian brand of progressivism, he was more optimistic than he had been in years. When the Democrats won the national election in November, he was ecstatic. With President Wilson in the White House and a Democratic majority in both houses of Congress, he would finally have a chance for a fair hearing in Washington.[66]

Unfortunately, Davis did not live to see Wilson's inauguration. On New Year's Day 1913 he left the dinner table complaining of chest pains. The family summoned a doctor, who assured the ailing senator that he had nothing to worry about. Later in the evening, however, the pains became more intense, and shortly after midnight Davis suffered a fatal heart attack.[67] He was only fifty years old. Weakened by years of heavy drinking and overeating, he had expired, as one observer put it, "at the noontime of his life."[68]

Davis's funeral was the largest in Little Rock history. At least ten thousand people witnessed the interment at Mount Holly Cemetery, and thousands more lined the streets as the funeral procession made its way from the First Baptist Church to the cemetery. Many of the onlookers were farmers who had travelled many miles to pay their respects. With their rickety wagons and bedraggled families, they gave the whole scene a rustic quality that Davis would have appreciated. At the end of the service, the sky darkened and a heavy rain began to fall. But this did not deter hundreds of weeping mourners from remaining at the graveside for hours. Jeff was gone, but the Old Guard carried on.[69]

Barely noted in Washington, Davis's death stunned his home state. For better or worse, the turbulent, brawling Davis era had finally come to a close. In some Arkansas households there was a profound sense of loss, in others an unmistakable sense of relief. Despite his setbacks in the Senate, at the time of his death Davis remained "the most beloved man, and, at the same time, the worst hated man in all Arkansas."[70] In the stirring eulogy delivered at Davis's funeral, Judge Jeptha Evans declared that "no greater tribune of the people has lived and died on the banks of the great Mississippi. Their sorrows were his sorrows and their triumphs were his triumphs."[71] Even some of the late senator's sharpest critics acknowledged that he had been a gifted politician and a sincere advocate of agrarian insurgency. Shortly after Davis's death, the editor of the Jonesboro *Tribune* wrote:

> Jeff had many faults and made many mistakes which the newspapers of the State showed up in all their glaring colors. . . . But with all his trickery and political chicanery Jeff was loyal to his friends and associates. Those who were close to him, aside from politics, claim that he had many kindly attributes and a sympathetic heart. Now that he is no more, and his great influence is dead, even those who opposed him through every trial of his life can only stand beside his bier and mingle admiration for his successful career with the tears of these who were his friends. The backbone of demagoguery may be broken throughout the State, a new era may dawn in Arkansas politics, but his influence will still live in the hearts and memory of the rural voters for all time. Arkansas never has and never will see his like again.[72]

The Davis faction outlived its founder, but not for long. George Hays was elected to the governorship (over Stephen Brundidge) in July 1913 as a "Davis candidate," and most of the Davis vote rallied behind William F. Kirby in the 1914 senatorial primary.[73] But the old pro-Davis versus anti-Davis bifactionalism rapidly faded. During the 1916 gubernatorial primary campaign, Judge L. C. "Shotgun" Smith tried to mimic Davis, declaring that if the voters would simply supply him with all the potlicker and turnip greens he could eat, he would "make Arkansas the d——dest best Governor the State ever had." Although this folksy approach seemed to excite some members of the Old Guard, Smith ultimately lost the election to Charles Hillman Brough by more than fourteen thousand votes.[74] Individual candidates continued to invoke Davis's memory well into the 1920s.[75] But by then the Davis movement had been reduced to an artifact of folk mythology. The movement was dead; but, as Rupert Vance noted in 1930, the legend lived on:

> Dead these seventeen years, Jeff Davis possesses a name that Arkansawyers, usually an outspoken race, mention before strangers with bated breath. . . . Since his day Arkansas has elevated to the governship a banker and a farmer, sundry lawyers, a professor of sociology from the state university with his Ph.D., and a travelling salesman; has sent to the Senate the redoubtable Joe T. and Thaddeus the Terrible. But the land of the Slow Train, where fact becomes folklore if it is

allowed to simmer overnight, has produced and will, God be thanked, produce no more consummate master of politics than Jeff the Little.[76]

Davis's legendary career inspired a play, a novel, and countless bits of doggerel—including a celebrated poetic lament written by Orto Finley:

> If Jeff could only come back now for one small day
> And see the petty politicians' peevish play—
> Behold the dazzling "intellects" that dare aspire
> To seats of fame that only statesmen should acquire.
> In fancy I can see the "Old Guard" fall in line,
> With guns unlimbered, waiting for the first faint sign
> To forward march—God, what a change would mark the day,
> If Jeff could only come back now to lead the way.[77]

The extraordinary affection that Finley and other members of the Old Guard felt for Davis was in keeping with the romantic character of the movement. Their faith in him was almost mystical. As J. N. Heiskell once put it, "In Arkansas Jeff Davis is more than a man; he is a sentiment, a belief, a conviction, a credo; he is a psychological fetich."[78] More than a man, perhaps, but less than a true political messiah. One thing is certain, the loyalty of the Old Guard was not based on Davis's ability to improve the material conditions of their lives. To some, Jeff was the beneficent boss who gave them a job, or the "pardoning governor" who released their son from prison. But for the vast majority of his followers there were no such payoffs. Some may have benefited from the legislation fostered by the Davis movement. But, once again, this group could not have been very large. Thanks to a series of obstructionist legislatures, a conservative state supreme court, and Davis's own ambivalence about governmental activism, his legislative accomplishments were modest at best. Even his vaunted antitrust law did little to disturb existing economic structures and basic power relationships. Arkansas farmers continued to live in a world of insecurity and economic hardship, and most were no better off in 1913 than they had been in 1900. Jeff had come and gone, leaving them with a treasure of memories, but little else had changed. The men and women between the plow handles were still scratching out a meager living from the land, and the decisions that controlled their lives were still made elsewhere.

Appendices

APPENDIX A
Arkansas County Data, 1888–1918: Simple Correlation and Multiple Regression Analysis

In an attempt to illuminate the social bases of Arkansas politics, I have compiled and analyzed a large amount of county-level (N=75) electoral and ecological data. These data were processed by a Control Data PDP-10 computer at the Brandeis University Computer Center. P-STAT, a social science software system developed at Princeton University, was used to produce descriptive statistics, simple correlation matrices, and multiple regression analyses. Table A presents the simple correlation coefficients between the Davis vote and various electoral and ecological variables (a full description of these variables and their sources appears at the end of this appendix); and Tables B–J contain the results of several multiple regression analyses. Readers desiring an explanation of the uses and limitations of correlation and regression analysis should consult John H. Mueller, Karl F. Schuessler, and Herbert L. Costner, *Statistical Reasoning in Sociology* (3rd ed.; Boston: Houghton Mifflin, 1977), Hubert M. Blalock, Jr., *Social Statistics* (2nd ed.; New York: McGraw-Hill, 1972), and Charles M. Dollar and Richard J. Jensen, *Historian's Guide to Statistics: Quantitative Analysis and Historical Research* (New York: Holt, Rinehart, and Winston, 1971).

TABLE A
Simple Correlation Coefficients (Pearson's *r*) between the Davis Vote
and Selected Electoral and Ecological Variables

Variables	Democratic Primary Vote for Jeff Davis				
	1898	1902	1904	1906	1912
% Living in incorporated towns 1910	−.072	−.406	−.406	−.416	−.321
% Living in 1000+ towns 1900	−.085	−.322	−.381	−.396	−.215
% Living in 1000+ towns 1910	−.088	−.369	−.429	−.423	−.288
% Urban 1900	−.083	−.272	−.289	−.352	−.228
% Urban 1910	−.032	−.330	−.377	−.399	−.268
% Black 1900	−.039	−.058	−.441	−.395	−.129
% Black 1910	−.039	−.043	−.439	−.387	−.130
Black population increase 1880–1900	−.224	.074	−.057	.011	−.076
White illiteracy 1900	−.007	.201	.451	.505	.163
White illiteracy 1910	−.032	.215	.464	.395	.093
Black illiteracy 1900	.042	.230	−.046	.040	.110
Black illiteracy 1910	.155	.146	.073	−.066	.161
Literacy gap 1900	.012	.129	−.220	−.149	.015
Literacy gap 1910	.146	.064	−.110	−.211	.122
Farm tenancy 1900	−.210	−.033	−.450	−.369	−.403
Farm tenancy 1910	−.218	.003	−.416	−.292	−.388
White farm tenancy 1900	−.239	−.024	−.219	−.088	−.397
White farm tenancy 1910	−.258	−.012	−.223	−.112	−.406
Increase in white farm tenancy 1900–1910	−.129	.025	−.105	−.100	−.191
Tenancy gap 1900	−.066	−.089	−.358	−.318	−.194
Tenancy gap 1910	−.036	−.027	−.352	−.164	−.092
Population per square mile 1900	−.128	−.212	−.460	−.376	−.330
Increase in PPSM 1880–1900	−.126	−.144	−.329	−.261	−.233
Settlement 1900 (farm acreage/total acreage)	−.093	.003	−.191	−.158	−.081
Settlement 1910	−.093	−.076	−.163	−.180	−.165
% of settled land (1900) settled since 1880	−.206	.192	.186	.169	−.128
% of settled land (1910) settled since 1890	−.150	.130	.282	.268	−.050
Cotton acreage 1900	.036	.004	−.136	−.254	−.035
Cotton acreage increase 1880–1900	−.038	−.095	−.107	−.008	.010
Value of farm land & bldgs. per acre 1900	−.207	−.107	−.386	−.433	−.572
Value of farm land & bldgs. per acre 1910	−.215	−.134	−.399	−.369	−.568
Inc. Val. farm & bldgs. per acre 1880–1900	−.179	−.090	−.324	−.349	−.502
Acres per farm 1900	.127	.033	.308	.213	.352
Acres per farm 1910	.120	.029	.296	.147	.220
Property per capita 1902	−.221	−.366	−.295	−.281	−.406
Property per capita 1912	−.138	−.242	−.309	−.267	−.348
Property per capita increase 1880–1902	−.150	−.338	−.103	−.170	−.323
Property per capita increase 1890–1902	.097	−.291	−.267	−.476	−.210
Property per capita increase 1890–1912	.089	−.157	−.320	−.400	−.222
Personal property per capita 1902	−.097	−.342	−.217	−.305	−.287
Personal property per capita 1912	.057	−.288	−.142	−.154	.025
Personal prop. per capita increase 1890–1902	.074	−.177	−.257	−.366	−.223
Personal prop. per capita increase 1890–1912	.099	−.196	−.157	−.132	.019
RR property per square mile 1904	−.234	−.095	−.379	−.334	−.461
Manufacturing 1900	.004	−.041	−.225	−.181	−.016
Workers 1900	.128	.013	−.149	−.074	.156
Baptist 1906	.074	.218	.388	.300	.327
Lowchurch 1906	.002	.249	.411	.302	.289
White church membership 1906	.023	−.018	−.436	−.293	.014
Ritualist 1906	.016	−.115	−.216	−.318	−.180
Union-Labor vote for governor 1888	−.008	.109	−.081	−.244	−.022

TABLE A (continued)

Variables	Democratic Primary Vote for Jeff Davis				
	1898	1902	1904	1906	1912
Union-Labor vote for governor 1890	−.042	.034	−.181	−.305	−.183
Populist vote for president 1892	.235	.098	.117	.122	.257
Populist vote for governor 1892	.097	.149	.225	.197	.246
Populist vote for governor 1894	.198	.102	.260	.210	.342
Populist vote for governor 1896	.153	.178	.213	.154	.287
Populist vote for governor 1898	.075	.043	.112	.105	.237
Populist vote for governor 1900	.057	.112	.171	.136	.234
Democratic vote for governor 1900	.022	.262	.004	−.007	.077
% for Jeff Davis 1898 (att. gen. primary)	1.000	.000	.187	.120	.466
% for Jeff Davis 1902 (gov. primary)	.000	1.000	.314	.368	.260
% for Jeff Davis 1904 (gov. primary)	.187	.314	1.000	.691	.537
% for Jeff Davis 1906 (sen. primary)	.120	.368	.691	1.000	.599
% for Jeff Davis 1912 (sen. primary)	.466	.260	.537	.599	1.000
% for James P. Clarke 1902 (sen. primary)	−.094	.485	.133	.148	.041
% for George Donaghey 1908 (gov. primary)	−.170	−.020	.018	.009	−.136
% for W. F. Kirby 1908 (gov. primary)	.026	.121	.096	.180	.246
% for John Hinemon 1908 (gov. primary)	.175	−.102	−.131	−.194	−.089
% for O. C. Ludwig 1908 (sec. of state prim.)	−.189	−.196	−.413	−.322	−.400
% for Hal Norwood 1908 (att. gen. primary)	.356	−.128	.223	.213	.379
% for George Donaghey 1910 (gov. primary)	−.147	.028	−.271	−.130	−.257
% for Jesse Hart 1908 (s. court primary)	.213	−.057	−.032	.025	.113
% for Joe Robinson 1912 (gov. primary)	.225	.044	.126	.012	.091
% for George Hays 1913 (gov. primary)	.392	.016	.028	.028	.412
% for W. F. Kirby 1914 (sen. primary)	.171	−.000	.275	.304	.496
% for C. H. Brough 1916 (gov. primary)	.106	−.023	−.232	−.250	−.144
% for Earle Hodges 1916 (gov. primary)	−.526	.007	−.067	−.060	−.366
% for L. C. Smith 1916 (gov. primary)	.457	.013	.281	.292	.519
% for C. H. Brough 1918 (gov. primary)	.060	−.021	−.258	−.293	−.265
% for Joe Robinson 1918 (sen. primary)	.130	−.192	−.238	−.178	−.046
Anti-license 1900	.020	.100	.225	.277	.230
Anti-license 1902	.129	.177	.259	.261	.260
Anti-license 1904	.091	.204	.194	.210	.279
Anti-license 1906	.093	.214	.286	.431	.275
Anit-license 1908	.084	.210	.221	.301	.228
Anti-license 1910	.108	.076	.230	.270	.097
Pro−Prohibition 1912 (Act 2)	.065	−.109	.025	.166	.140
Pro−Poll Tax 1892 (Am. 2)	−.056	−.172	−.400	−.349	−.229
Pro−Poll Tax 1908 (Am. 9)	−.221	−.087	−.367	−.361	−.241
Pro−Railroad Commission 1898 (Am. 4)	−.011	−.073	−.212	−.105	−.232
Pro−Initiative and Referendum (Am. 10)	−.031	.079	.297	.298	−.000
Pro−Turner-Jacobson Tax Bill 1912 (Act 1)	−.143	−.311	−.121	−.088	−.209
Pro−Uniform Textbook Law 1912 (Act 4)	−.103	−.216	.069	.000	−.091
Pro−Grandfather Clause 1912 (Am. 11)	−.155	−.137	−.031	−.161	−.333
Pro−Cotton Mill Tax Exemption 1912 (Am. 12)	.033	−.141	−.163	−.142	−.093
Pro−Recall Law 1912 (Am. 14)	.077	−.170	.168	.147	.096
Pro−Municipal Bonds 1912 (Am. 15)	−.117	−.250	−.335	−.320	−.304
Voter turnout, 1900 gov. election	.004	.103	.366	.423	.107
Voter turnout, 1902 gov. election	.036	.003	.324	.466	.186
Voter turnout, 1904 gov. election	.139	.163	.418	.573	.337
Voter turnout, 1906 gov. election	−.084	.025	.360	.440	.080
Decrease in voter turnout (gov.) 1890–1910	.018	−.064	−.183	−.212	−.061

TABLE B
Multiple Regression Analysis of Voter Turnout in the 1888 Gubernatorial Election

Dependent Variable:	1888 Voter Turnout	
Multiple R	.60	
Multiple R²	.36	
Mean of Dependent Variable	76.1%	
Standard Error of Estimate	72.5	
F	.000	
Independent Variables:	Partial	Simple
Acres per farm 1890	−.391	−.248
Settlement 1890 (farm acreage/total acreage)	.327	.215
Populist vote for governor 1892	.280	.301
% Living in 1000+ towns 1890	−.224	−.302
Democratic vote for president 1888	−.201	.042
Increase in PPSM 1880–1890	−.200	−.114
% of settled land (1890) settled since 1880	.150	.169
Variables Not In Final Equation:		
Upland counties (dummy)	.009	.206
Non–railroad counties 1890 (dummy)	−.064	.026
Black farm tenancy 1900	−.019	.009
% Black 1890	−.007	−.176
Black illiteracy 1900	−.020	−.077
Property per capita increase 1880–1890	.111	−.054

TABLE C
Multiple Regression Analysis of Voter Turnout in the 1888
Gubernatorial Election (White Counties)[a]

Dependent Variable:	1888 Voter Turnout	
Multiple R	.63	
Multiple R²	.40	
Mean of Dependent Variable	77.3%	
Standard Error of Estimate	68.2	
F	.032	
Independent Variables:	Partial	Simple
Personal prop. per capita increase 1880–1890	−.524	−.412
Settlement 1890 (farm acreage/total acreage)	.505	.172
White church membership 1906	−.352	−.073
Populist vote for governor 1892	.272	.233
Variables Not In Final Equation:		
Personal property per capita 1890	−.197	−.350
% Living in 1000+ towns 1890	−.234	−.173
White illiteracy 1900	.208	−.238
% of settled land (1890) settled since 1880	.162	.053
Farm tenancy 1890	.033	−.104
Republican vote for president 1888	.177	.024
Anti-license 1894	.051	−.045
Property per capita increase 1880–1890	−.075	−.203
Lowchurch 1906	−.033	−.092

[a]Counties which were less than 6% black in 1900 (n=25).

TABLE D

Multiple Regression Analysis of Decrease in Voter Turnout
1890–1910, Gubernatorial Elections

Dependent Variable:	Decrease in Voter Turnout 1890–1910	
Multiple R	.66	
Multiple R^2	.44	
Mean of Dependent Variable	34.6%	
Standard Error of Estimate	94.2	
F	.000	
Independent Variables:	Partial	Simple
% Black 1910	.421	.569
Populist vote for governor 1892	.276	−.087
Farm tenancy 1910	.225	.544
% of settled land (1910) settled since 1890	.215	.071
Variables Not In Final Equation:		
Democratic vote for governor 1908	.055	.309
% Living in 1000+ towns 1910	−.105	.054
Union-Labor county (dummy)	−.022	.207
Settlement 1910 (farm acreage/total acreage)	−.095	−.236
% for Jeff Davis 1904 (gov. primary)	.085	−.183
Personal prop. per capita increase 1880–1912	−.035	−.123
Black population increase 1880–1900	−.117	−.284
Lowchurch 1906	.020	−.268
White church membership 1906	−.073	.193
Anti-license 1910	.028	−.209
RR property per square mile 1904	−.115	.131

TABLE E

Multiple Regression Analysis of Decrease in Voter Turnout
1890–1910, Gubernatorial Elections (White Counties)[a]

Dependent Variable:	Decrease in Voter Turnout 1890–1910	
Multiple R	.87	
Multiple R^2	.76	
Mean of Dependent Variable	21.1%	
Standard Error of Estimate	55.9	
F	.000	
Independent Variables:	Partial	Simple
Property per capita increase 1880–1902	−.835	−.593
Populist vote for governor 1892	.779	.424
% for Jeff Davis 1904 (gov. primary)	−.594	.038
White farm tenancy 1900	.534	−.041
Democratic vote for governor 1900	−.388	.092
Variables Not In Final Equation:		
White church membership 1906	.037	.159
Settlement 1900 (farm acreage/total acreage)	.039	−.175
% of settled land (1900) settled since 1880	.009	−.265
White illiteracy 1900	.032	−.043
Lowchurch 1906	−.100	.063
Anti-license 1904	.085	−.061
Increase in farm tenancy 1880–1900	.044	.183
% Living in 1000+ towns 1900	−.156	−.236

[a]Counties which were less than 6% black in 1900 (n=25).

TABLE F

Multiple Regression Analysis of the 1898 Davis Vote

Dependent Variable: % for Jeff Davis in the 1898 Attorney General Primary		
Multiple R		.33
Multiple R²		.11
Mean of Dependent Variable		42.4%
Standard Error of Estimate		238.8
F		.039

Independent Variables:	Partial	Simple
White farm tenancy 1900	−.265	−.239
Settlement 1900 (farm acreage/total acreage)	−.196	−.093
Property per capita increase 1880–1902	−.190	−.150
Variables Not In Final Equation:		
% Black 1900	−.050	−.039
White illiteracy 1900	−.027	−.007
% Living in incorporated towns 1910	.065	−.072
White church membership 1906	.037	.023
Baptist 1906	−.089	.074
Ritualist 1906	.138	.016
Anti-license 1904	.055	.091
Populist vote for governor 1892	.073	.097

TABLE G

Multiple Regression Analysis of the 1902 Davis Vote

Dependent Variable: % for Jeff Davis in the 1902 Gov. Primary		
Multiple R		.41
Multiple R²		.16
Mean of Dependent Variable		66.9%
Standard Error of Estimate		108.3
F		.000

Independent Variables:	Partial	Simple
% Living in incorporated towns 1910	−.406	−.406
Variables Not In Final Equation:		
White illiteracy 1910	−.002	.215
White farm tenancy 1910	.051	−.012
% Black 1910	−.042	−.043
Anti-license 1906	.057	.214
Property per capita increase 1890–1912	.000	−.157
Settlement 1910 (farm acreage/total acreage)	−.105	−.076
White church membership 1906	.123	−.018
Baptist 1906	.041	.218
Ritualist 1906	.085	−.115

TABLE H
Multiple Regression Analysis of the 1904 Davis Vote

Dependent Variable: % for Jeff Davis in the 1904 Gov. Primary

Multiple R	.68
Multiple R^2	.47
Mean of Dependent Variable	59.4%
Standard Error of Estimate	96.42
F	.000

Independent Variables:	Partial	Simple
% Living in incorporated towns 1910	−.326	−.406
Settlement 1900 (farm acreage/total acreage)	−.316	−.191
% Black 1900	−.279	−.441
Ritualist 1906	−.250	−.216
White farm tenancy 1900	−.220	−.219
White church membership 1906	−.184	−.436
Baptist 1906	.147	.388
White illiteracy 1900	−.040	.451
Variables Not In Final Equation:		
Property per capita increase 1880–1902	−.073	−.103
Populist vote for governor 1892	.039	.225
Anti-license 1904	.080	.194

TABLE I
Multiple Regression Analysis of the 1906 Davis Vote

Dependent Variable: % For Jeff Davis in the 1906 Senatorial Primary

Multiple R	.68
Multiple R^2	.46
Mean of Dependent Variable	56.0%
Standard Error of Estimate	99.7
F	.000

Independent Variables:	Partial	Simple
Settlement 1910 (farm acreage/total acreage)	−.465	−.180
Property per capita increase 1890–1912	−.412	−.400
% Black 1910	−.400	−.387
% Living in incorporated towns 1910	−.257	−.416
Variables Not In Final Equation:		
White church membership 1906	.035	−.293
Baptist 1906	−.015	.300
Ritualist 1906	−.087	−.318
White farm tenancy 1910	−.131	−.112
Pro-Prohibition 1912 (Act 2)	.097	.166
White illiteracy 1910	−.095	.395

TABLE J
Multiple Regression Analysis of the 1912 Davis Vote

Dependent Variable: % for Jeff Davis in the 1912 Senatorial Primary

Multiple R	.64
Multiple R^2	.41
Mean of Dependent Variable	53.8%
Standard Error of Estimate	97.48
F	.000

Independent Variables:	Partial	Simple
White farm tenancy 1910	−.518	−.406
Settlement 1910 (farm acreage/total acreage)	−.449	−.166
Property per capita increase 1890–1912	−.372	−.222
% Living in incorporated towns 1910	−.185	−.321
White church membership 1906	.175	.014
Variables Not In Final Equation:		
Baptist 1906	−.048	.327
Ritualist 1906	.097	−.180
White illiteracy 1910	−.003	.093
Pro-Prohibition 1912 (Act 2)	.118	.140
% Black 1910	−.020	−.130

VARIABLE DESCRIPTION AND SOURCES

#	*Variable*	*Source*
1	% Living in incorporated towns 1910	*13th Census of the U.S., 1910, Population,* 2: 96–107.
2	% Living in towns of 1000+ population 1890	Ibid.
3	% Living in towns of 1000+ population 1900	Ibid.
4	% Living in towns of 1000+ population 1910	Ibid.
5	% Urban 1900 (% living in towns of 2500+)	Ibid., 2: 118–131.
6	% Black 1890	*12th Census of the U.S., 1900, Supplementary Analysis,* 264.
7	% Black 1900	Ibid.
8	% Black 1910	*13th Census of the U.S., 1910, Population,* 2: 118–131.
9	Increase in black % of population 1880–1900	*12th Census of the U.S., 1900, Supplementary Analysis,* 264.
10	White illiteracy 1900 (illiteracy rate among native-born white males of voting age)	*12th Census of the U.S., 1900, Population,* 1: 971.
11	White illiteracy 1910 (illiteracy rate among native-born white males of voting age)	*13th Census of the U.S., 1910, Population,* 2: 119–131.
12	Black illiteracy 1900 (illiteracy rate among black males of voting age)	*12th Census of the U.S., 1900, Supplementary Analysis,* 264.
13	Black illiteracy 1910 (illiteracy rate among black males of voting age)	See Variable 11.
14	Literacy gap 1900 (difference between black and white illiteracy rates)	See Variables 10 and 12.
15	Literacy gap 1910 (difference between black and white illiteracy rates)	See Variables 11 and 13.
16	Farm tenancy 1890 (% of all farm operators)	*11th Census of the U.S., 1890, Agriculture,* 2: 122–125.

VARIABLE DESCRIPTION AND SOURCES (continued)

#	Variable	Source
17	Farm tenancy 1900 (% of all farm operators)	*12th Census of the U.S., 1900, Agriculture,* Part 1, 60–63.
18	Farm tenancy 1910 (% of all farm operators)	*13th Census of the U.S., 1910, Agriculture,* 6: 104–119.
19	White farm tenancy 1900	See Variable 17.
20	White farm tenancy 1910	See Variable 18.
21	Black farm tenancy 1900	See Variable 17.
22	Increase in white farm tenancy rate 1900–1910	See Variables 17–18.
23	Tenancy gap 1900 (difference between the black and white farm tenancy rates)	See Variable 17.
24	Tenancy gap 1910 (difference between the black and white farm tenancy rates)	See Variable 18.
25	Population per square mile 1900	*12th Census of the U.S., 1900, Population,* 1: XXXVIII–XXXIX.
26	Increase in population per square mile 1880–1890	See Variable 25; *10th Census of the U.S., 1880, Cotton Production,* Part I, 539–540.
27	Increase in population per square mile 1880–1900	See Variables 25 and 26.
28	Settlement 1890 (ratio of farm acreage to total acreage)	*11th Census of the U.S., 1890, Agriculture,* 2: 199–200; *12th Census of the U.S., 1900, Population,* 1: XXXVIII–XXXIX.
29	Settlement 1900 (ratio of farm acreage to total acreage)	*12th Census of the U.S., 1900, Agriculture,* Part 1, 267–268; *12th Census of the U.S., 1900, Population,* 1, XXXVIII–XXXIX.
30	Settlement 1910 (ratio of farm acreage to total acreage)	*13th Census of the U.S., 1910, Agriculture,* 6: 104–119.
31	% of settled land (1890) settled since 1880	See Variable 28; *10th Census of the U.S., Agriculture,* 3: 105; *10th Census of the U.S., 1880, Cotton Production,* Part 1, 539–540.
32	% of settled land (1900) settled since 1880	See Variables 28 and 29.
33	% of settled land (1910) settled since 1890	See Variables 28 and 30.
34	Cotton acreage 1900 (ratio of cotton acreage to improved farmland)	*12th Census of the U.S., 1900, Agriculture,* Part 2, 430; Part 1, 267–268.
35	Cotton acreage increase 1880–1900	See Variables 31 and 34.
36	Value of farm land and buildings per acre 1900	Thomas J. Pressly and William H. Scofield, eds., *Farm Real Estate Values in the United States by Counties, 1850–1959.*
37	Value of farm land and buildings per acre 1910	Ibid.
38	Increase in value of farmland and buildings per acre 1880–1900	Ibid.
39	Acres per farm 1890	*11th Census of the U.S., 1890, Agriculture,* 2: 122–124.
40	Acres per farm 1900	*12th Census of the U.S., 1900, Agriculture,* Part 1, 60–62.
41	Acres per farm 1910	*13th Census of the U.S., 1910, Agriculture,* 6: 104–119.

VARIABLE DESCRIPTION AND SOURCES (continued)

#	Variable	Source
42	Property (assessed value of all property, real and personal) per capita 1902	*12th Census of the U.S., Wealth, Debt, and Taxation 1907,* 852–853.
43	Property (assessed value of all property, real and personal) per capita 1912	*13th Census of the U.S., Wealth, Debt, and Taxation 1913,* 753–754.
44	Property per capita increase 1880–1890	See Variable 42.
45	Property per capita increase 1880–1902	See Variable 42.
46	Property per capita increase 1890–1902	See Variable 42.
47	Property per capita increase 1890–1912	See Variables 42 and 43.
48	Personal property per capita 1890	*11th Census of the U.S., Wealth, Debt, and Taxation 1890,* 108–110.
49	Personal property per capita 1902	*12th Census of the U.S., Wealth, Debt, and Taxation 1907,* 893–894.
50	Personal property per capita 1912	*13th Census of the U.S., Wealth, Debt, and Taxation 1913,* 1: 799–800.
51	Personal property per capita increase 1880–1890	*Compendium of the 10th Census, 1880,* Part 2, 1535–1536; See Variable 48.
52	Personal property per capita increase 1880–1912	See Variables 50–51.
53	Personal property per capita increase 1890–1902	See Variables 48–49.
54	Personal property per capita increase 1890–1912	See Variables 48 and 50.
55	RR property per square mile 1904	*Biennial Report of the Secretary of State of Arkansas* (hereafter cited as *SSR*) *1903–1904,* 404–462; *12th Census of the U.S., 1900, Population,* 1: XXX-VIII–XXXIX.
56	Manufacturing 1900 (value of manufactured goods per capita)	*12th Census of the U.S., 1900, Manufacturers,* Vol. 8, Part 2, 26–27.
57	Workers 1900 (ratio of male wage earners over 16 to males of voting age)	Ibid.; *12th Census of the U.S., 1900, Population,* 2: 175.
58	Baptist 1906 (% of white church members) (Jewish, Mormon, and "Other Protestant" denominations have been excluded from the white church membership total.)	*Census of Religious Bodies: 1906,* 296–298; Little Rock *Arkansas Gazette,* August 19, 1900.
59	Lowchurch 1906 (% of white church members that were Baptist or Church of Christ)	Ibid.
60	White church membership 1906 (ratio of white church members to total white population)	Ibid.,; Little Rock *Arkansas Gazette,* August 19, 1900; *12th Census of the U.S., 1900, Population,* 1: 530; *13th Census of the U.S., 1910, Population,* 1: 231.
61	Ritualist 1906 (% of white church members that were Episcopalian, Lutheran, or Catholic)	See Variable 58.
62	Union-Labor vote for governor 1888 (% for C. M. Norwood)	*SSR 1889–1890,* 47–49.
63	Union-Labor vote for governor 1890 (% for N. B. Fizer)	Ibid., 53–55.
64	Populist vote for president 1892 (% for J.B. Weaver)	*SSR 1895–1896,* 71–72.
65	Populist vote for governor 1892 (% For J. P. Carnahan)	*SSR 1891–1892,* 54–56.
66	Populist vote for governor 1894 (% for D. E. Barker)	*SSR 1895–1896,* 51–53.

VARIABLE DESCRIPTION AND SOURCES (continued)

#	*Variable*	*Source*
67	Populist vote for governor 1896 (% for A. W. Files)	Ibid., 57–59.
68	Populist vote for governor 1898 (% for W. S. Morgan)	*SSR 1899–1900*, 407–409.
69	Populist vote for governor 1900 (% for A. W. Files)	Ibid., 413–415.
70	Democratic vote for governor 1900 (% for Jeff Davis)	Ibid.
71	Democratic vote for governor 1908 (% for G. W. Donaghey)	*SSR 1907–1908*, 367–370.
72	Democratic vote for president 1888 (% for Grover Cleveland)	*SSR 1919–1920*, 341–344.
73	Republican vote for president 1888 (% for Benjamin Harrison)	Ibid.
74	% for Jeff Davis 1898 (Democratic primary, attorney general)	Little Rock *Arkansas Gazette*, June 17, 1898.
75	% for Jeff Davis 1902 (Democratic primary, governor)	Ibid., April 24, 1904.
76	% for Jeff Davis 1904 (Democratic primary, governor)	Ibid.
77	% for Jeff Davis 1906 (Democratic primary, senator)	Arkadelphia *Southern-Standard*, May 3, 1906.
78	% for Jeff Davis 1912 (Democratic primary, senator)	Little Rock *Arkansas Gazette*, March 29, 1912.
79	% for James P. Clarke 1902 (Democratic primary, senator)	Arkadelphia *Southern-Standard*, April 24, 1902.
80	% for George Donaghey 1908 (Democratic primary, governor)	Ibid., April 16, 1908.
81	% for William F. Kirby 1908 (Democratic primary, governor)	Ibid.
82	% for John Hinemon 1908 (Democratic primary, governor)	Ibid.
83	% for O. C. Ludwig, 1908 (Democratic primary, secretary of state)	Ibid.
84	% for Hal Norwood 1908 (Democratic primary, state auditor)	Ibid.
85	% for Jesse C. Hart 1908 (Democratic primary, supreme court)	Ibid.
86	% for George W. Donaghey 1910 (Democratic primary, governor)	Little Rock *Arkansas Gazette*, April 3–4, 1910.
87	% for Joseph T. Robinson 1912 (Democratic primary, governor)	Little Rock *Arkansas Gazette*, March 29, 1912.
88	% for George Hays 1913 (Democratic primary, governor)	Ibid., July 1, 1913.
89	% for William F. Kirby 1914 (Democratic primary, senator)	Ibid., April 15, 1914.
90	% for Charles H. Brough 1916 (Democratic primary, governor)	Ibid., April 6, 1916.
91	% for Earle Hodges 1916 (Democratic primary, governor)	Ibid.
92	% for L. C. Smith 1916 (Democratic primary, governor)	Ibid.
93	% for Charles H. Brough 1918 (Democratic primary, governor)	Ibid., June 5, 1918.

VARIABLE DESCRIPTION AND SOURCES (continued)

#	Variable	Source
94	% for Joseph T. Robinson 1918 (Democratic primary, senator)	Ibid.
95	Anti-license 1894	*SSR 1895–1896*, 63–64.
96	Anti-license 1900	*SSR 1899–1900*, 422–423.
97	Anti-license 1902	*SSR 1901–1902*, 413–415.
98	Anti-license 1904	*SSR 1905–1906*, 441–444.
99	Anti-license 1906	Ibid.
100	Anti-license 1908	*SSR 1907–1908*, 375–378.
101	Anti-license 1910	*SSR 1909–1910*, 396–399.
102	Pro-Prohibition 1912 (% voting for Act 2, Statewide Prohibition Law)	*SSR 1911–1912*, 408–411.
103	Pro–Poll Tax 1892 (Constitutional Amendment #2)	*SSR 1891–1892*, 57–59.
104	Pro–Poll Tax 1908 (Constitutional Amendment #9)	*SSR 1907–1908*, 375–378.
105	Pro–Railroad Commission 1898 (Constitutional Amendment #4)	Arkadelphia *Southern Standard,* September 23, 1898.
106	Pro–Initiative and Referendum 1910 (Constitutional Amendment #10)	*SSR 1909–1910*, 396–399.
107	Pro–Turner-Jacobson Tax Bill 1912 (Act #1 submitted under Initiative and Referendum Law)	*SSR 1911–1912*, 408–411.
108	Pro–Uniform Textbook Law 1912 (Act #4 submitted under Initiative and Referendum Law)	Ibid.
109	Pro–Grandfather Clause 1912 (Constitutional Amendment #11)	*SSR 1911–1912*, 408–411.
110	Pro–Cotton Mill Tax Exemption 1912 (Constitutional Amendment #12) (% voting for seven-year tax exemption for new cotton mills)	Ibid., 412–415.
111	Pro–Recall Law 1912 (Constitutional Amendment #14)	Ibid.
112	Pro–Municipal Bonds 1912 (Constitutional Amendment #15)	Ibid.
113	Voter turnout, 1888 gubernatorial election (ratio of voters to males of voting age) (inter-census estimates of males of voting age have been computed.)	*SSR 1889–1890*, 47–49. *Compendium of the 10th Census, 1880,* Part 1, 562–563; *11th Census of the U.S., 1890, Population,* 8: 755.
114	Voter turnout, 1900 gubernatorial election	*SSR 1899–1900*, 413–415; *12th Census of the U.S., 1900, Population,* 2: 175.
115	Voter turnout, 1902 gubernatorial election	*SSR 1901–1902*, 404–408; See Variable 114; *13th Census of the U.S., 1910, Population,* 1: 231.
116	Voter turnout, 1904 gubernatorial election	*SSR 1905–1906*, 421–424; See Variable 115.
117	Voter turnout, 1906 gubernatorial election	*SSR 1905–1906*, 433–436; See Variable 115.

VARIABLE DESCRIPTION AND SOURCES (continued)

#	Variable	Source
118	Decrease in voter turnout in gubernatorial elections 1890–1910	See Variable 115; *SSR 1889–1890*, 53–55; *11th Census of the U.S., 1890, Population*, 8: 755.
119	Non-railroad counties 1890 (dummy) (counties without railroads in 1890)	*SSR 1889–1890*, 302–306.
120	Upland counties (dummy) (counties that include hilly or mountainous terrain)	—
121	Union-Labor counties (dummy) (counties carried by the Union-Labor gubernatorial candidate in 1888 or 1890)	*SSR 1889–1890*, 47–49, 53–55.

APPENDIX B
Arkansas Precinct Data, 1892–1912

This appendix contains electoral and ecological data for 210 Arkansas townships. These townships constitute all of the voting precincts (some small precincts have been combined so that electoral units correspond with census units) in 11 sample counties: Crawford, Drew, Hot Spring, Howard, Marion, Poinsett, Pulaski, St. Francis, Sebastian, Sharp, and Washington. The choice of counties was dictated partly by the availability of electoral data (local newspapers are the only source for Arkansas precinct returns from the period 1892–1912; unfortunately, many precinct returns were never published, while others were published in newspapers which are no longer available to historical researchers) and partly by a desire to construct a sample that accurately reflects the geographical and cultural diversity of the state. Marion, Sharp, and Washington are Ozark mountain counties. Crawford and Sebastian are semimountainous counties that straddle the Arkansas River Valley. Howard County is situated in the foothills of southwestern Arkansas. Poinsett and St. Francis Counties are located in the East Arkansas lowlands. Pulaski and Hot Spring are central Arkansas counties that straddle the division between upcountry and lowcountry. And Drew County is located in the lowlands of southeastern Arkansas.

The precincts in the table that follows have been categorized by level of "metropolitanization," defined here as a composite of urbanization and proximity to commercial shipping points. The categorization scheme includes nine categories.

City: urban areas with populations exceeding 5,000 in 1900.

Large Town–Farm: precincts which included county seat towns or towns with populations exceeding 1,000 in 1900.

Small Town–Farm: precincts which included incorporated towns with populations between 300 and 1,000 in 1900.

Village-Farm: precincts which included small (population under 300) incorporated towns or unincorporated towns on the verge of incorporation.

Hamlet-Farm: predominantly rural precincts which included one or more "hamlets" (comunities which contained a post office and at least five other business or commercial addresses in 1906, but which were too small to be incorporated).

Farm (Suburban): farm precincts which adjoined or surrounded cities or county seat towns.

Farm (Central): farm precincts located within 5 miles of a railroad stop.

Farm (Isolated): farm precincts located more than 5 miles but less than 15 miles from a railroad stop.

Farm (Very Isolated): farm precincts located 15 miles or more from the nearest railroad stop.

"Miles to the nearest railroad stop" is based on data from Polk's *Arkansas State Gazetteer and Business Directory* for the years 1892–3 and 1906–7. In each precinct the point of reference was the location of the local post office. When a precinct contained two or more post offices (an uncommon situation), the post office closest to the nearest railroad stop was used as the point of reference.

APPENDIX B (continued)

Precinct	County	% for Jeff Davis Democratic Primaries					% for J.P. Clarke 1902[b]	% Populist[c]	% Anti-License[d]	% Black[e] 1900	Miles to RR Stop	% Pop. in Incorp. Towns 1900	Pop. of Largest Town 1900
		1900	1902	1904	1906[b]	1912[b]							
CITY													
Argenta	Pulaski	46.2[a]	56.7	46.5	44.2	47.7	52.8	9.1	29.7	37.8	0	100	6,837[f]
Fort Smith	Sebastian	62.2	79.2	70.1	69.7	56.9	69.6	13.1	40.3	20.8	0	100	11,587
Little Rock	Pulaski	40.5	52.0	37.3	35.5	37.4	63.7	8.9	28.1	38.4	0	100	38,307
LARGE TOWN-FARM													
Diamond	Sebastian	58.2	55.6	39.5	34.9	38.1	48.5	16.5	51.1	13.3	0	64	1,298
Fenter	Hot Springs	59.7	52.4	23.3	21.2	—	51.8	21.0	30.8	31.2	0	52	1,582
Forrest City	St. Francis	—	68.5	46.9	35.6	45.9	54.1	4.1	58.9	53.4	0	100	1,361
Marion	Drew	53.1	61.8	47.3	48.2	37.8	68.3	6.9	28.2	57.3	0	39	1,579
Nashville	Howard	—	31.8	15.7	26.2	48.0	33.6	6.9	63.2	21.4	0	39	928
Prairie	Washington	44.4	54.5	50.2	38.8	43.0	43.1	15.8	58.4	4.4	0	51	4,061
Springdale	Washington	68.3	54.7	39.8	33.2	21.9	57.8	17.0	56.8	0.0	0	100	1,251
Van Buren	Crawford	64.6	77.9	67.6	41.4	47.7	61.5	34.4	63.0	0.0	0	41	2,573
SMALL TOWN-FARM													
Alma	Crawford	62.2	57.5	44.0	43.2	49.6	35.0	16.7	64.7	29.4	0	27	440
Bolivar	Poinsett	—	71.6	30.3	—	42.7	24.7	10.9	81.1	6.4	0	29	462
Center	Sebastian	69.7	40.9	51.2	48.8	—	40.9	1.3	19.2	7.7	0	27	491
Center Point	Howard	63.9	57.0	33.3	58.5	62.8	24.7	19.7	68.6	32.3	9	19	334
Cole	Sebastian	57.1	66.7	55.3	39.1	—	57.9	19.0	71.8	0.8	0	26	330
Dyer	Crawford	—	37.1	22.5	—	—	31.9	8.6	64.7	0.0	0	55	343
Hardy	Sharp	—	81.5	80.2	—	72.3	13.2	43.2	77.1	0.0	0	41	347
Hartford	Sebastian	58.8	46.4	38.5	31.5	46.1	22.6	—	57.1	0.0	0	31	460
Little Rock	Poinsett	—	49.3	56.3	59.3	—	24.8	12.5	61.3	27.8	0	34	352
Marion	Sebastian	75.0	79.9	90.8	—	—	74.7	2.9	92.9	2.1	0	36	906
Maxey	Crawford	—	69.9	47.6	54.3	—	35.7	14.1	12.0	3.0	0	31	361
Piney Fork	Sharp	—	55.4	36.4	—	30.5	38.1	—	77.1	6.8	0	32	312
Prairie Grove	Washington	87.7	35.7	20.0	29.3	39.5	18.4	8.4	58.5	0.7	25	43	551
Sugar Loaf	Sebastian	23.0	75.2	52.7	24.5	47.6	69.3	9.8	76.4	3.4	0	22	368
Union	Marion	—	64.5	45.4	54.8	—	40.4	—	78.2	1.6	0	30	578
Wilmar	Drew	—	65.7	35.2	38.2	55.6	20.8	50.5	67.3	43.3	0	100	844

VILLAGE-FARM												
Bartholomew	Drew	72.3	69.3	67.1	56.9	57.1	59.4	25.0	58.1	94.6	0	0	296[j]
Cave	Sharp	—	59.2	22.8	36.1	47.1	66.7	0.7	34.6	0.0	15	0	278[i]
Cedarville	Crawford	—	74.7	58.9	53.1	53.8	31.8	9.9	57.5	0.0	11	14	67[g]
Chester	Crawford	—	70.0	66.7	—	71.4	33.3	30.9	48.7	0.0	0	27	174
Collins	Drew	45.6	38.2	76.5	80.2	30.8	23.5	72.3	44.4	31.3	8	15	212
Dillard	Howard	68.4	82.6	62.2	79.3	79.5	82.5	65.5	33.3	17.9	14	6	278[h]
Elm Springs	Washington	84.2	—	86.6	48.8	90.9	—	31.9	32.0	0.0	0	0	222[i]
Fourche	Pulaski	—	76.4	66.7	52.6	39.0	71.0	13.8	66.7	18.0	0	20	173
Franklin	Drew	100.0	82.0	72.8	42.6	73.7	73.5	16.8	64.4	68.2	10	0	180[i]
Greenwood	Poinsett	44.8	41.1	38.9	—	67.8	25.4	—	73.6	—	8	0	154[i]
Griggs	St. Francis	87.8	70.2	64.6	83.3	—	62.5	22.8	81.8	66.7	27	22	245[i]
Mineral Springs	Howard	—	90.1	53.2	38.3	56.7	89.9	16.7	57.8	35.8	0	0	278[h]
Mountain	Howard	88.5	68.1	92.2	28.1	67.5	41.2	30.3	73.9	0.0	0	0	115[i]
Owen	Poinsett	65.7	36.4	88.7	—	54.9	30.1	4.5	85.1	5.8	15	0	165[i]
Prairie	St. Francis	81.8	85.9	82.3	80.4	—	65.8	69.9	58.1	77.0	0	0	196
Saratoga	Howard	—	92.5	60.5	61.9	55.8	84.3	18.6	52.1	56.7	0	0	215[i]
Starr Hill	Washington	—	71.4	70.1	58.8	28.3	82.8	26.3	45.5	2.2	0	0	292[i]
Tyronza	Poinsett	—	57.5	93.2	—	54.0	91.9	3.3	63.4	29.5	0	0	76[i]
Umpire	Howard	—	75.9	84.9	77.6	—	57.7	—	72.9	—	0	0	136[i]
West Prairie	Poinsett	—	83.3	88.8	—	79.4	59.1	6.8	71.4	0.0	0	0	232[i]
Wheatley	St. Francis	82.3	39.1	54.7	57.9	64.5	30.1	9.6	81.5	37.7	0	0	330[i]
Winslow	Washington	46.3	91.3	46.3	51.5	34.3	84.1	33.7	53.8	0.0	0	0	289[i]
HAMLET-FARM												
Badgett	Pulaski	75.2	73.1	68.9	60.9	60.8	57.0	24.7	52.8	89.7	0	0	—
Baker	Howard	58.1	66.7	57.6	90.7	58.3	81.0	1.6	10.4	0.0	16	0	—
Bass Little	Sebastian	79.2	92.9	98.8	88.6	66.2	77.8	11.8	48.6	0.0	0	0	—
Bearhouse	Drew	100.0	65.3	65.5	51.4	85.0	59.0	11.5	72.8	3.5	9	0	—
Bismarck	Hot Spring	—	76.3	61.2	70.2	82.7	84.9	50.0	46.3	0.0	15	0	—
Bloomer	Sebastian	94.9	41.5	81.3	86.7	—	88.9	28.0	71.4	1.2	.4	0	—
Blythe	Marion	25.7	67.4	50.0	64.2	65.9	21.1	19.5	54.8	0.0	0	0	—
Brown Springs	Hot Spring	—	—	50.6	48.3	71.0	65.9	—	46.3	—	0	0	—
Campbell	Pulaski	93.8	81.3	85.3	90.2	23.1	87.5	6.3	63.3	97.3	0	5	—
Cane Hill	Washington	79.4	52.4	42.4	28.5	27.3	47.4	20.2	79.2	3.2	5	0	—
Center	Washington	86.9	85.8	66.7	46.6	56.7	83.6	34.1	65.3	0.0	0	0	—

APPENDIX B (continued)

Precinct	County	% for Jeff Davis Democratic Primaries					% for J.P. Clarke 1902[b]	% Populist[c]	% Anti-Licensed[d]	% Black[e] 1900	Miles to RR Stop	% Pop. in Incorp. Towns 1900	Pop. of Largest Town 1900
		1900	1902	1904	1906[b]	1912[b]							
HAMLET-FARM (cont.)													
Clear Creek	Hot Spring	—	77.3	38.9	32.4	56.8	54.3	39.4	55.1	0.0	14	0	—
Crawford	Washington	68.8	84.2	74.4	67.9	45.0	83.8	60.4	50.8	0.0	0	0	—
Dayton	Sebastian	94.9	75.0	92.5	81.4	—	42.1	25.0	76.9	6.8	4	0	—
De Roche	Hot Spring	—	78.1	85.4	87.0	81.1	24.6	19.8	48.8	0.0	16	0	—
Dodd City	Marion	—	70.0	55.2	59.4	—	59.6	—	29.3	0.0	6	0	—
Franklin	Marion	—	83.8	75.0	76.9	—	49.3	—	27.1	0.0	17	0	—
Goshen	Washington	85.8	79.4	78.9	56.6	58.7	72.1	16.7	51.1	0.0	12	0	—
Highland	Sharp	—	96.3	89.5	46.2	40.0	69.8	—	43.8	0.0	3	0	—
Jackson	Sharp	—	77.9	69.5	20.0	45.2	30.2	—	58.5	0.0	3	0	—
Johnson	St. Francis	95.3	78.2	82.6	85.0	78.2	67.4	40.9	45.8	44.5	10	0	—
Midway	Hot Spring	—	79.5	80.8	58.6	79.5	44.0	34.3	30.5	5.1	0	0	—
Mountain	Crawford	—	15.8	80.8	—	77.3	5.3	34.5	54.2	0.0	0	0	—
Mount Sandels	Sebastian	27.9	21.4	6.8	9.0	—	8.2	4.1	60.2	6.2	0	0	—
Reed	Washington	86.7	90.6	87.9	94.4	94.7	74.2	10.0	58.5	0.0	7	0	—
Rheas Mill	Washington	70.7	77.8	77.1	63.1	50.0	83.3	24.1	68.9	0.0	5	0	—
Richmond	Washington	75.3	73.2	58.2	47.1	44.1	65.7	20.7	46.5	3.5	0	0	—
Rogers	Sebastian	69.6	66.9	37.6	35.3	—	26.4	26.8	57.6	0.0	0	0	—
Roland	Pulaski	66.7	86.5	74.0	—	78.9	86.1	38.9	—	56.4	0	0	—
Rudy	Crawford	—	70.8	64.8	—	48.2	43.1	14.9	50.5	0.0	0	0	—
Saline	Hot Spring	—	96.9	94.9	88.9	90.3	70.4	26.1	22.7	0.0	0	0	—
Sullivan	Sharp	—	38.7	37.1	32.8	30.9	27.5	—	65.2	1.0	15	0	—
Telico	St. Francis	91.3	81.7	78.4	74.3	45.2	78.0	41.0	33.3	52.1	0	0	—
Union	Crawford	—	31.7	59.7	—	18.6	1.6	16.9	70.1	0.0	14	0	—
Veasey	Drew	—	88.4	73.1	78.1	81.1	52.8	23.5	40.9	33.7	13	0	—
West Fork	Washington	73.3	100.0	88.6	54.1	76.2	81.6	15.3	70.8	0.0	0	0	—
White River	Marion	—	85.2	68.5	72.4	—	54.5	—	71.6	0.0	0	0	—
FARM (Suburban)													
Big Rock	Pulaski	60.1	65.1	55.3	27.0	49.6	57.0	22.3	36.4	70.9	0	0	—
Madison	St. Francis	70.6	54.8	53.4	40.2	47.3	50.0	34.4	46.2	95.1	0	0	—
Upper	Sebastian	36.5	40.6	28.0	25.5	—	25.1	24.1	21.6	26.9	0	0	—

FARM (Central)												
Ashley	Pulaski	65.2	65.9	62.8	59.2	63.5	47.1	24.7	50.2	93.5	0	0	—
Bates	Sebastian	20.8	35.7	20.0	—	23.8	42.9	2.2	8.8	0.0	5	0	—
Beverly	Sebastian	51.7	51.7	58.1	62.1	—	32.8	30.2	89.3	5.0	0	0	—
Big Creek	Sebastian	51.7	33.7	38.5	68.8	—	30.1	20.9	47.8	5.7	0	0	—
Brodie	Pulaski	34.4	67.0	56.8	60.6	66.7	33.3	20.2	88.7	22.3	4	0	—
Buffalo	Marion	83.3	77.7	80.3	76.3	—	80.0	8.5	46.9	0.0	3	0	—
Butterfield	Hot Spring	—	72.2	36.7	36.8	80.0	62.9	—	23.5	—	0	0	—
Cominto	Drew	—	—	88.9	88.2	87.1	—	—	39.4	5.8	5	0	—
County Line	Howard	81.0	49.2	59.3	75.0	75.5	20.7	46.5	34.8	0.0	4	0	—
Crooked Creek	Marion	—	90.0	83.3	80.7	—	72.4	—	75.8	0.0	0	0	—
Dobson	Poinsett	—	84.8	74.2	87.1	—	72.7	—	42.9	17.8	0	0	—
Dora	Crawford	—	57.1	73.5	—	82.1	57.1	5.5	56.6	0.0	0	0	—
Durham	Washington	67.6	34.3	60.0	72.7	73.0	22.2	10.5	40.3	87.9	0	0	—
Eagle	Pulaski	—	87.0	76.4	21.4	75.0	63.6	3.9	66.7	0.0	5	0	—
Eagle	Sebastian	41.9	77.1	62.7	78.8	—	—	23.5	—	91.3	0	0	—
Eastman	Pulaski	72.4	71.7	53.1	68.9	65.1	20.8	5.7	61.2	79.1	0	0	—
Franks	St. Francis	92.2	64.3	55.1	50.7	72.2	50.4	10.3	23.2	36.8	0	0	—
Gifford	Hot Spring	—	70.2	63.7	45.8	78.5	57.6	2.4	33.3	46.4	0	0	—
Goodwin	St. Francis	93.1	70.3	67.2	79.7	64.3	64.9	40.2	29.2	74.2	0	0	—
Gray	Pulaski	81.9	94.8	79.2	55.6	—	56.5	13.8	0.0	0.0	3	0	—
Greenfield	Poinsett	—	57.8	66.1	—	60.0	62.2	10.9	37.1	33.5	3	0	—
Hill	Pulaski	58.9	73.9	59.8	42.4	76.9	50.9	22.5	33.5	0.0	0	0	—
Lafayette	Crawford	—	67.3	68.8	—	65.5	65.6	50.0	47.2	0.0	5	0	—
Lancaster	Crawford	—	52.0	87.8	—	58.8	15.8	66.2	31.8	0.0	3	0	—
Lebanon	Sharp	—	61.0	60.0	62.2	35.7	31.8	—	50.0	16.3	5	0	—
Magnet	Hot Spring	—	51.0	68.4	42.0	57.6	48.0	12.7	72.1	0.0	0	0	—
Mineral	Pulaski	77.3	79.4	51.4	—	—	26.6	42.2	—	0.0	4	0	—
Mississippi	Sebastian	63.3	18.8	48.1	60.3	48.6	69.6	44.7	83.6	11.9	0	0	—
Oliver Springs	Crawford	—	78.0	50.0	—	79.2	7.1	60.2	71.3	39.5	0	0	—
Ouachita	Hot Spring	—	69.9	56.4	60.4	69.6	15.4	14.8	64.8	0.0	0	0	—
Owen	Pulaski	87.3	89.7	93.3	—	40.0	88.4	52.8	65.9	45.3	0	0	—
Porter	Crawford	—	42.9	88.2	—	85.7	14.3	19.4	67.4	0.0	0	0	—
Prairie	Drew	78.8	78.8	75.0	76.5	—	73.5	58.2	29.4		0	0	—
Prairie	Sebastian	33.8	26.3	21.4	31.5	—	12.0	7.0	73.6		0	0	—

APPENDIX B (continued)

Precinct	County	% for Jeff Davis Democratic Primaries 1900	1902	1904	1906	1912	% for J.P. Clarke 1902	% Populist	% Anti-License	% Black 1900	Miles to RR Stop	% Pop. in Incorp. Towns 1900	Pop. of Largest Town 1900
FARM (Central)—(cont.)													
Prairie Bayou	Hot Spring	—	57.9	49.2	52.6	46.6	15.9	22.5	59.4	1.4	5	0	—
Price	Washington	83.3	93.3	72.1	57.6	30.5	85.7	37.9	60.6	8.5	0	0	—
River	Crawford	—	83.3	—	—	100.0	22.9	20.8	46.2	0.0	3	0	—
Saline	Drew	—	81.1	86.9	71.8	93.1	54.8	43.9	40.3	41.5	0	0	—
Scott	Poinsett	—	64.3	61.8	—	—	55.6	1.8	33.9	25.5	0	0	—
Sullivan	Sebastian	60.6	70.6	65.2	55.9	—	26.7	20.3	31.5	8.3	5	0	—
Valley	Washington	80.2	55.4	62.1	54.2	52.6	66.7	17.5	61.1	4.1	3	0	—
Vine Prairie	Crawford	—	91.8	84.8	50.0	43.8	28.0	18.2	50.0	0.0	5	0	—
White River	Washington	55.7	76.8	69.8	—	60.3	54.5	39.5	67.9	0.6	3	0	—
Whitley	Crawford	—	86.2	100.0	—	82.9	17.2	20.0	33.6	0.0	4	0	—
Willis	Poinsett	—	59.4	59.5	—	—	56.3	—	69.6	0.0	0	0	—
Worthen	Pulaski	93.0	88.4	92.2	—	—	93.2	12.9	—	59.8	0	0	—
Young	Pulaski	33.3	00.0	7.7	18.2	00.0	50.0	27.8	—	95.0	0	0	—
FARM (Isolated)													
Antioch	Hot Spring	74.7	71.7	70.2	68.1	57.5	53.1	27.9	54.1	4.8	10	0	—
Bayou Meto	Pulaski	93.3	80.4	76.8	79.6	91.7	58.6	18.2	21.2	7.6	7	0	—
Bearden	Marion	—	95.2	92.5	90.7	86.8	94.2	39.0	57.5	0.0	7	0	—
Big Creek	Hot Spring	—	48.6	73.9	76.9	—	28.6	—	100.0	0.0	9	0	—
Blackfish	St. Francis	94.7	90.0	66.7	54.5	62.3	72.9	14.0	80.4	80.0	8	0	—
Blackland	Howard	62.3	44.8	84.3	91.3	63.3	55.6	1.5	12.1	61.5	12	0	—
Brewer	Howard	92.3	53.1	63.9	59.6	71.4	36.9	2.6	38.1	6.7	7	0	—
Brush Creek	Washington	87.8	89.7	70.1	44.7	62.8	84.5	38.2	72.6	0.0	13	0	—
Cedar Creek	Crawford	—	74.6	80.3	72.7	48.0	88.5	28.3	52.2	0.0	14	0	—
Clear Creek	Drew	—	33.3	52.6	72.8	88.9	4.8	36.4	41.5	39.1	9	0	—
Cove City	Crawford	—	68.2	72.2	—	63.7	49.2	8.1	65.0	6.4	13	0	—
Cove Creek	Washington	73.5	18.8	27.3	82.9	20.0	21.2	7.7	25.9	0.0	12	0	—
Crook	Drew	—	95.7	92.3	95.2	65.0	75.0	45.1	57.4	19.0	13	0	—
Davidson	Sharp	—	93.8	89.2	96.8	96.8	12.5	63.0	26.1	0.0	10	0	—
DeSoto	Marion	—	93.4	89.8	81.7	73.6	61.0	—	81.6	0.0	12	0	—

Place	County												
Dutch Mills	Washington	65.2	73.8	82.9	78.8	67.3	79.7	14.7	78.3	0.0	6	0	—
Ellis	Pulaski	86.6	92.9	94.4	—	80.0	100.0	48.8	—	18.8	6	0	—
Franklin	Howard	31.6	87.0	96.7	88.9	—	60.9	53.8	24.0	49.2	10	0	—
Hampton	Marion	—	80.8	65.3	60.0	—	23.6	—	66.7	0.0	11	0	—
Harrison	Hot Spring	—	31.6	62.9	47.4	57.1	26.3	11.5	50.0	1.3	8	0	—
Illinois	Washington	88.5	88.9	75.7	66.3	57.1	81.9	19.6	62.9	0.9	6	0	—
James Creek	Marion	—	84.6	39.5	45.3	—	50.8	—	46.4	0.0	8	0	—
Jasper	Crawford	—	58.3	42.9	—	20.0	4.3	43.3	78.3	5.0	7	0	—
Jefferson	Marion	—	—	63.6	63.6	—	—	—	54.5	—	10	0	—
Jim Fork	Sebastian	44.0	68.9	53.8	55.6	—	36.6	30.2	31.5	10.5	8	0	—
Johnson	Sharp	—	57.1	44.4	44.4	44.4	0.0	—	38.5	23.4	8	0	—
L'Anguille	St. Francis	89.3	77.5	85.7	93.5	40.0	73.8	54.4	15.5	55.0	6	0	—
Lees Creek	Washington	100.0	100.0	87.9	95.5	9.1	95.2	13.8	47.6	0.0	6	0	—
Liberty	Marion	—	92.9	100.0	65.4	—	65.4	—	56.7	0.0	8	0	—
Lone Hill	Hot Spring	—	83.0	38.6	40.6	60.5	25.0	10.0	64.6	16.8	7	0	—
Marrs Hill	Washington	87.0	83.0	63.8	46.5	52.6	72.1	7.7	59.1	0.0	12	0	—
North	Sharp	—	25.0	27.3	26.5	27.3	13.0	—	37.8	0.0	6	0	—
Prairie	Marion	—	71.9	55.6	73.9	—	47.8	—	52.4	0.0	7	0	—
Richmond	Crawford	—	83.1	47.1	52.4	52.4	30.2	23.1	59.7	12.7	7	0	—
Richwoods	Sharp	—	67.0	80.8	70.4	44.2	58.3	—	83.5	0.0	12	0	—
Saline	Howard	47.1	77.8	72.4	68.8	69.9	69.0	36.4	73.4	25.7	11	0	—
Sand Point	Crawford	—	54.5	71.4	28.6	—	9.1	—	27.3	—	7	0	—
Spring Hill	Drew	—	63.1	80.0	86.4	91.8	46.9	18.5	14.5	59.8	11	0	—
Strawberry	Sharp	—	80.3	75.3	70.9	74.0	65.8	—	40.4	0.0	10	0	—
Sugarloaf	Marion	85.7	81.1	75.0	85.2	—	62.7	—	29.8	0.0	8	0	—
Sulphur Springs	Howard	96.9	56.4	62.6	36.6	54.0	—	33.1	71.6	0.0	6	0	—
Union	Pulaski	—	97.9	82.3	87.7	81.1	91.8	41.1	—	20.6	10	0	—
Union	Sharp	32.8	—	34.8	28.9	39.7	25.0	—	48.8	1.9	10	0	—
Vineyard	Washington	83.3	83.7	75.8	77.9	77.1	87.5	54.1	75.0	0.0	10	0	—
Washburn	Sebastian	21.6	73.3	44.7	64.5	—	53.7	26.9	76.0	0.0	12	0	—
Water Creek	Marion	—	78.1	82.5	63.4	—	23.2	—	83.3	0.0	9	0	—
Wedington	Washington	83.9	62.8	72.0	71.7	33.3	71.4	22.4	81.6	0.0	12	0	—
Wheeler	Washington	65.7	88.2	90.0	84.2	75.0	93.1	25.9	45.7	0.0	10	0	—
White Oak	Sebastian	65.0	66.7	42.9	88.2	—	26.9	4.1	63.0	0.0	8	0	—
Winfrey	Crawford	—	—	100.0	—	00.0	—	51.9	79.2	0.0	7	0	—
Wyman	Washington	73.9	91.7	70.6	42.1	33.3	75.0	—	64.3	0.0	7	0	—

APPENDIX B (continued)

Precinct	County	% for Jeff Davis Democratic Primaries					% for J.P. Clarke 1902[b]	% Populist[c]	% Anti-License[d]	% Black[e] 1900	Miles to RR Stop	% Pop. in Incorp. Towns 1900	Pop. of Largest Town 1900
		1900	1902	1904	1906[b]	1912[b]							
FARM (Very Isolated)		62.1	74.4	74.2	76.6	71.5	54.5	46.0	48.6	1.2	16	0	—
Barker	Crawford	—	4.5	33.3	—	81.0	31.8	39.6	56.3	0.0	15	0	—
Big Creek	Marion	—	27.3	16.7	—	—	27.3	—	33.3	0.0	16	0	—
Big Creek	Sharp	76.3	76.3	61.3	65.9	51.0	50.0	—	68.6	0.0	29	0	—
Big Rock	Sharp	—	90.1	93.2	85.9	54.5	72.7	—	60.7	0.0	24	0	—
Blue Ridge	Howard	51.9	88.5	87.2	90.3	92.3	74.1	53.3	26.7	0.0	29	0	—
Boston	Washington	35.0	83.3	62.5	95.8	81.8	76.5	75.5	71.7	0.0	21	0	—
Cedar Creek	Marion	—	90.9	53.3	60.5	—	60.9	—	28.6	0.0	20	0	—
Clay	Howard	17.6	37.5	71.7	51.2	64.2	16.2	44.9	47.8	0.0	22	0	—
Crockett	Marion	—	80.0	66.7	—	—	30.0	—	17.6	0.0	20	0	—
Henderson	Hot Spring	—	95.6	93.1	97.8	96.6	54.5	26.9	71.2	0.0	18	0	—
Holly Creek	Howard	79.2	80.6	80.3	60.0	73.0	69.1	30.1	32.3	0.0	23	0	—
Keesee	Marion	—	61.5	100.0	75.0	—	53.8	—	78.6	0.0	16	0	—
Lave Creek	Sharp	—	96.9	94.7	91.2	78.8	84.2	—	38.1	0.0	16	0	—
Lees Creek	Crawford	—	19.4	24.2	—	38.5	12.5	30.0	15.3	0.0	17	0	—
Madison	Howard	93.1	100.0	100.0	93.5	79.7	88.8	64.0	24.0	0.0	17	0	—
Maumelle	Pulaski	81.4	97.2	100.0	—	—	97.2	72.0	—	0.0	16	0	—
Morgan	Sharp	—	94.9	92.2	85.7	65.8	65.5	—	28.3	0.0	16	0	—
Muddy Fork	Howard	76.5	—	68.6	70.7	63.5	—	52.6	53.7	8.0	15	0	—
North Fork	Marion	—	68.4	69.6	67.2	—	50.0	—	53.3	0.0	16	0	—
Scott	Sharp	—	73.8	78.0	71.2	74.5	40.2	—	70.0	0.0	16	0	—
Shepherd	Crawford	—	87.5	100.0	—	—	11.8	16.1	77.8	0.0	16	0	—
Valley	Hot Spring	—	96.3	88.9	78.0	90.0	73.5	46.6	88.5	0.0	16	0	—
Washington	Sharp	—	86.7	70.0	61.7	57.8	59.1	—	26.5	0.0	25	0	—

[a]All group figures are means.
[b]Senatorial primaries.
[c]The Populist vote for governor. The Howard and Crawford County figures are for 1892 (% for James P. Carnahan) and the Hot Spring County figures are for 1896 (% for A. W. Files). All others are for 1894 (% for D. E. Barker).
[d]The Crawford, Drew, Marion, and Sharp County figures are for 1912. The Poinsett County figures are for 1908. All others are for 1906.

eThe Argenta, Little Rock, and Fort Smith figures represent % of total population. The Argenta figure is from the 1910 census; the 1900 figure is unavailable because the city was incorporated in 1905. The figures for Washington County precincts represent % of those "liable to pay the poll tax" in 1903. The racial composition figures for the remaining precincts represent % of heads of household.

fThe population of Hill Township, the vast majority of which became the incorporated town of Argenta in 1905.

gThis figure is an estimate. The population of Cedarville town was 80 in 1890 and 54 in 1910. The 1900 census did not distinguish between Cedarville town and Cedarville Township.

hMost of the town of Mineral Springs was located in Mineral Springs Township; the remainder was in adjoining Dillard Township.

iThese figures represent the 1910 population of towns which existed in 1900 but which were not incorporated until sometime after 1900.

jMiles to the nearest river shipping point.

SOURCES: Little Rock *Arkansas Democrat* (Pulaski County), March 30, 1906; Little Rock *Arkansas Gazette* (Pulaski County), September 7, 1894, April 22, 1900, April 2, 1902, March 31, 1904, September 5, 1906, March 28, 1912; *Fort Smith Elevator* (Sebastian County), September 14, 1894, April 6, 1900, April 1, 1904, April 13, September 14, 1906; *Springdale News* (Washington County), September 21, 1894, April 20, 1900, April 11, 1902, April 13, September 14, 1906, April 12, 1912; *Forrest City Times* (St. Francis County), September 7, 1894, April 13, 1900, April 4, 1902, April 1, 1904, April 6, September 7, 1906, April 5, 1912; *Nashville News* (Howard County), September 24, 1892, March 21, 1900, April 2, 1902, April 6, 1904, April 11, September 12, 1906, April 3, 1912; *The Monticellonian* (Drew County), September 28, 1894, April 4, 1902, April 7, 1904, April 5, 1906, April 4, 1912; *Yellville Mountain Echo* (Marion County), April 11, 1902, April 8, 1904, April 6, 1906, September 20, 1912; *Sharp County Record* (Sharp County), April 11, 1902, April 8, 1904, April 13, 1906, April 5, September 20, 1912; *Malvern Arkansas Meteor* (Hot Spring County), April 11, 1902, April 8, 1904, April 6, 1906, April 5, 1912; *Harrisburg Modern News* (Poinsett County), September 7, 1894, April 4, 1902, April 1, 1904, September 18, 1908; *Van Buren Press* (Crawford County) April 12, 1902; *Drew County Advance* (Drew County), September 17, 1912; *Van Buren Weekly Argus* (Crawford County), September 14, 1892, April 6, 1904, April 2, September 15, 1912; *Malvern Arkansas Times* (Hot Spring County), September 16, 1896; *Malvern Times-Journal* (Hot Spring County), September 12, 1906; *Fayetteville Arkansas Sentinel* (Washington County), April 6, 1904; U.S. Bureau of the Census, *Thirteenth Census of the United States, 1910, Population* (Washington: Government Printing Office, 1913) 2:96–107, 118–131; *Arkansas State Gazeteer and Business Directory* for the years 1892–3 and 1906–7 (Chicago: R. L. Polk, 1892, 1906); *Twelfth Census of the United States, 1900, Population Schedules,* Manuscript Returns for Crawford, Drew, Hot Spring, Howard, Marion, Poinsett, Pulaski, St. Francis, Sebastian, Sharp, and Washington Counties, Arkansas, located at the National Archives, Washington, D. C.

Notes

Abbreviations
ArkHQ: The Arkansas Historical Quarterly
PAHA: Publications of the Arkansas Historical Association

Chapter 1

1. Rupert Vance, "A Karl Marx for Hill Billies," *Social Forces* 9 (December 1930): 180; John Shelton Reed and Daniel Joseph Singal, eds., *Regionalism and the South: Selected Papers of Rupert Vance* (Chapel Hill: University of North Carolina Press, 1982), 29.

2. Vance, "A Karl Marx for Hill Billies," 180–190; Charles Jacobson, *The Life Story of Jeff Davis: The Stormy Petrel of Arkansas Politics* (Little Rock: Parke-Harper, 1925), 144. The nickname "wild ass of the Ozarks" was coined by an Indianapolis newspaper man in 1911.

3. John Gould Fletcher, *Arkansas* (Chapel Hill: University of North Carolina Press, 1947), 292; Jacobson, *Life Story*, 59; Vance, "A Karl Marx for Hill Billies," 180. The description was offered by the editor of the *Helena Weekly World* in 1899.

4. Brief discussions of Davis's career appear in C. Vann Woodward, *Origins of the New South, 1877–1913* (Baton Rouge: Louisana State University Press, 1951), 376–377; Reinhard H. Luthin, "Flowering of the Southern Demagogue,"*American Scholar* 20 (April 1951): 189–190; V. O. Key, *Southern Politics in State and Nation* (New York: Knopf, 1949), 183–185; Daniel M. Robison, "From Tillman to Long: Some Striking Leaders of the Rural South,"*Journal of Southern History* 3 (August 1937): 296, 303–304; Francis Butler Simkins, *A History of the South* (New York: Knopf, 1953), 541; Monroe Lee Billington, *The American South, A Brief History* (New York: Scribner's, 1971), 321; Jack Temple Kirby, *Darkness at the Dawning: Race and Reform in the Progressive South* (Philadelphia: J. B. Lippincott, 1972), 29–30; John S. Ezell, *The South Since 1865* (New York: Macmillan, 1975), 376; Monroe Lee Billington, *The Political South in the Twentieth Century* (New York: Scribner's, 1975), 4; Harry S. Ashmore, *Arkansas: A Bicentennial History* (New York: W. W. Norton, 1978), 139–142; and David E. Rison, "Jeff Davis," in David C. Roller and Robert W. Twyman, eds., *The Encyclopedia of Southern History* (Baton Rouge: Louisiana State University Press, 1979), 332–333. The best introduction to Davis's career is Jacobson, *Life Story,* an insider's account published in 1925. L. S. Dunaway, ed., *Jeff Davis, Governor and United States Senator: His Life and Speeches* (Little Rock: Democrat Printing and Litho. Co., 1913), is a useful collection of speeches and reminiscences. Published articles on Davis include: Vance, "A Karl Marx for Hill Billies," 180–190; Paige E. Mulhollan, "The Issues of the Davis-Berry Senatorial Campaign in 1906," *ArkHQ* 20 (Summer 1961): 118–126; Cal Ledbetter Jr., "Jeff Davis and the Politics of Combat," *ArkHQ* 33 (Spring 1974): 16–37; Annette Shelby, "Jeff Davis of Arkansas: 'Profes-

sional Man of the People,'" in Cal M. Logue and Howard Dorgan, eds., *The Oratory of Southern Demagogues* (Baton Rouge: Louisiana State University Press, 1981), 12–44; Raymond Arsenault, "Governor Jeff Davis," in Timothy P. Donovan and Willard B. Gatewood, Jr., eds., *The Governors of Arkansas: Essays in Political Biography* (Fayetteville: University of Arkansas Press, 1981), 111–125; and Richard L. Niswonger,"A Study in Southern Demagoguery: Jeff Davis of Arkansas," *ArkHQ* 39 (Summer 1980): 114–124. There are several unpublished accounts of Davis's career: Bayless Walker Price, "The Life of Jeff Davis" (M.A. thesis, University of Alabama, 1929); Nevin Neal, "Jeff Davis and the Reform Movement in Arkansas, 1898–1907" (M.A. thesis, Vanderbilt University, 1939); George James Stevenson, "The Political Career of Jeff Davis: An Example of the Southern Protest" (M.A. thesis, University of Arkansas, 1949); Morton Harrison Fry, "Jeff Davis of Arkansas: A Study of Neo-Populism and Economic Democracy" (Senior thesis, Princeton University, 1968); John Richard Johnson, "The Campaign Speaking of Jeff Davis of Arkansas, 1899–1904" (M.A. thesis, Louisiana State University, 1974); Billy Travis Booth, "An Analysis of the Myths in Selected Speeches of Jeff Davis of Arkansas, 1899–1911" (Ph.D. thesis, Louisiana State University, 1977); and Raymond Arsenault, "The Wild Ass of the Ozarks: Jeff Davis and the Social Bases of Southern Demagoguery, 1888–1913" (Ph.D. thesis, Brandeis University, 1981).

5. At the University of Arkansas Library, Fayetteville, Arkansas, there are two very small collections dealing with Davis: a four-item collection entitled "Materials Relating to Jeff Davis"; and a microfilm labeled "Speeches of Jeff Davis and Other Miscellaneous Davis Material." The library also contains several other manuscript collections that have some relevance to Davis's career: Arkansas Baptists' Records (microfilm), Charles Hillman Brough Papers, Charles Hillman Brough Scrapbooks, Cumberland Presbyterian Church Papers, George Washington Donaghey Papers, William Hope Harvey Materials, George Washington Hays Papers, Thomas C. McRae Papers, John H. Page Notebook and Correspondence, Harmon L. Remmel Papers, Joseph Taylor Robinson Papers, David Y. Thomas Papers, and the George A. Thornburgh Scrapbooks. The Brough, Donaghey, Hays, Page, Remmel, and Thornburgh collections are the most useful. The Arkansas History Commission in Little Rock houses the Robert Minor Wallace Papers, the George Washington Donaghey Scrapbook, and the official gubernatorial Letterbooks of Governors Powell Clayton, James Berry, Simon Hughes, James P. Eagle, and William M. Fishback. These collections provide valuable background material on Arkansas politics, but they contain few specific references to Davis.

6. Niswonger, "A Study in Southern Demagoguery: Jeff Davis of Arkansas," 114–124; Shelby, "Jeff Davis of Arkansas: 'Professional Man of the People,'" 16, 39. On the concept of the "Southern demagogue," see Allan Louis Larson, "Southern Demagogues: A Study in Charismatic Leadership" (Ph.D. thesis, Northwestern University, 1964); Logue and Dorgan, *The Oratory of Southern Demagogues*, 1–11; Luthin, "Flowering of the Southern Demagogue," 185–195; Allan Michie and Frank Ryhlick, *Dixie Demagogues* (New York: Vanguard Press, 1939); Gerald W. Johnson, "Live Demagogue, or Dead Gentleman?" *Virginia Quarterly Review* 12 (January 1936): 1–14; Robison, "From Tillman to Long: Some Striking Leaders of the Rural South," 289–310; Rupert B. Vance, "Rebels and Agrarians All: Studies in One-Party Politics," *Southern Review* 4 (1938): 26–44; Wilma Dykeman, "The Southern Demagogue,"*Virginia Quarterly Review* 33 (Autumn 1957): 558–569; Robert Snyder, "The Concept of Demagoguery: Huey Long and His Literary Critics," *Louisiana Studies* 15 (Spring 1976): 61–84; Michael L. Kurtz, "Demagoguery," in Roller and Twyman, eds., *The Encyclopedia of Southern History*, 354; Virginius Dabney, *Liberalism in the South* (Chapel Hill: University of North Carolina Press, 1932), 265–274; Clarence Cason, *Ninety Degrees in the Shade* (Chapel Hill: University of North Carolina Press, 1935), 88–89, 107; William B. Hesseltine, *The South in American History* (New York: Prentice-Hall, 1936), 617–621; Howard W. Odum, *An American Epoch: Southern Portraiture in the National Picture* (New York: Henry Holt and Co., 1930), 132–138, 143, 147; W. J. Cash, *The Mind of the South* (New York: Knopf, 1941), 252–259, 290–294, 432–433; Harnett T. Kane, *Louisiana Hayride: The American Rehearsal for Dictatorship, 1928–1940* (New York: W. Morrow and

Co., 1941), 3–10; Ellis G. Arnall, *The Shore Dimly Seen* (Philadelphia: J. B. Lippincott, 1946), 39–50; Key, *Southern Politics*, 3–4, 232–233, 261–271, 305; Simkins, *A History of the South*, 538–546; Harry S. Ashmore, *An Epitaph for Dixie* (New York: W. W. Norton, 1958), 95–112; T. Harry Williams, *Huey Long* (New York: Knopf, 1970), 410–413; T. Harry Williams, "The Gentleman from Louisiana: Demagogue or Democrat," *Journal of Southern History* 26 (February 1960): 3–21; T. Harry Williams, *Romance and Realism in Southern Politics* (Athens: University of Georgia Press, 1961), 61–64; Allan P. Sindler, *Huey Long's Louisiana: State Politics, 1920–1952* (Baltimore: Johns Hopkins University Press, 1956), 110–113; Henry C. Dethloff, ed., *Huey P. Long—Southern Demagogue or American Democrat?* (Boston: D. C. Heath, 1967), v–viii; Hugh Davis Graham, ed., *Huey Long* (Englewood Cliffs: Prentice-Hall, 1970), 2–4; Billington, *The American South*, 320–324, 333; Kirby, *Darkness at the Dawning*, 34, 68; Francis M. Wilhoit, *The Politics of Massive Resistance* (New York: George Braziller, 1973), 85–90; J. Wayne Flynt, *Dixie's Forgotten People: The South's Poor Whites* (Bloomington: Indiana University Press, 1979), 12, 54–56, 163; David Leon Chandler, *The Natural Superiority of Southern Politicians: A Revisionist History* (Garden City: Doubleday, 1977), 118, 121–123, 148–149, 166, 238, 268, 303, 325; and Dan Carter, "Southern Political Style," in Robert Haws, ed., *The Age of Segregation: Race Relations in the South, 1890–1945* (Jackson: University Press of Mississippi, 1978), 45–66.

7. Williams, *Huey Long*, 69.

8. This definition appears in Euripides's *Orestes*. Richard H. Rovere, *Senator Joe McCarthy* (New York: Harcourt, Brace, Jovanovich, 1959), 45; *The Oxford English Dictionary* (Oxford: Clarendon Press, 1933), 3: 172; W. W. Skeat, *An Etymological Dictionary of the English Language* (Oxford: Oxford University Press, 1962) (originally published in 1879), 162; Williams, *Huey Long*, 411; Williams, "The Gentleman from Louisiana: Demagogue or Democrat," 17–18; and T. Harry Williams, "Huey Long and the Politics of Realism," in Harold M. Hollingsworth, ed., *Essays on Recent Southern Politics* (Austin: University of Texas Press, 1970), 101.

9. *The Oxford English Dictionary*, 3: 172. The term "demagogue" was first exported to Imperial Rome, where it was used for centuries. To the Romans, who had even less respect for the common man than the Greeks, the essence of demagoguery was an admixture of politics and entertainment. According to the satirist Juvenal, the mindless plebeians of Rome would support any politician who provided them with enough "bread and circuses." See Plutarch, *The Lives of the Noble Grecians and Romans* (translated by John Dryden) (New York: Random House, n.d.), 1012; Livy, Book 4, Chs. 13–15; and Polybius, Book 2, Ch. 21. "Demagogue" appeared in French literature as early as the fourteenth century, but it did not come into common usage in Western Europe until much later. Bossuet reportedly caused quite a stir when he used the word in the seventeenth century, as did John Milton who called it a "Goblin word." Hobbes (1651) and Dryden (1683) also used the term, but it did not gain currency until the Enlightenment. The French Academy put its imprimatur on the word "demagogue" in 1762, and the constitution makers and political commentators of the late eighteenth and early nineteenth centuries made liberal use of terms such as "demagogy" and "demagogical." Some people apparently regarded "demagogy" as an ancient word for democracy, while others used it as a synonym for inflammatory rhetoric. In the United States, where the politicians and intellectuals of the early national period carried on an exhaustive debate about the implications of democracy and popular sovereignty, "demagogue" became the watchword of conservative dissent. As the nineteenth century progressed and as universal manhood suffrage and mass-oriented party politics became disturbing realities for American conservatives, the term took on the status of an all-purpose epithet. See Reinhard H. Luthin, "Some Demagogues in American History," *American Historical Review* 57 (October 1951): 22–46; Reinhard H. Luthin, *American Demagogues: Twentieth Century* (Boston: Beacon Press, 1954), ix–16, 302–319; Logue and Dorgan, *The Oratory of Southern Demagogues*, 3–6; Noah Webster, *An American Dictionary of the English Language* (New York: S. Converse, 1828), 1: 57; James Fenimore Cooper, *The American Democrat* (New York: Vintage, 1956), 96–102; David Ross Locke, *The Demagogue* (Boston: Lee and Shepard, 1891); George Alfred Townsend, "Demagogues," *The Chautauquan* 17 (1893): 308–313;

Thomas Nixon Carver, "The Science of Demagogy," *The American Journal of Politics* 2 (1893): 271–277; Lord James Bryce, *Modern Democracies* (New York: Macmillan, 1921), 2: 554; Frederick E. Venn, "The Demagogue—A Text Book for Politicians," *The Independent* (April 26, 1924): 219–221, (May 10, 1924): 256–257, 268, (June 7, 1924): 303–305; Frank R. Kent, "Our Political Monstrosities," *Atlantic Monthly* (April 1933): 407–411; Samuel K. Ratcliffe, "The New American Demagogues," *Fortnightly Review* 143 (June 1935): 674–684; H. L. Mencken, *A Mencken Chrestomathy* (New York: Knopf, 1949), 150–151, 159, 200, 240; G. M. Gilbert, "Dictators and Demagogues," *Journal of Social Issues* 11 (no. 3, 1955): 51–54; Sindler, *Huey Long's Louisiana*, 110–113; Larson, "Southern Demagogues: A Study in Charismatic Leadership," 85–86; and William Safire, *Safire's Political Dictionary* (New York: Random House, 1978), 163–164. For a more detailed discussion of the problem of definition, see Arsenault, "The Wild Ass of the Ozarks," 5–19.

10. Logue and Dorgan, *The Oratory of Southern Demagogues*, 4.

11. Dykeman, "The Southern Demagogue," 559–560.

12. Mencken, *A Mencken Chrestomathy*, 191, 184–200. See also Fred C. Hobson, Jr., *Serpent in Eden: H. L. Mencken and the South* (Chapel Hill: University of North Carolina Press, 1974).

13. Mencken, *A Mencken Chrestomathy*, 200, 245. Venn, "The Demagogue—A Text Book for Politicians," 219–221, 256–257, 268, 303–305, is similar in tone.

14. Luthin, "Flowering of the Southern Demagogue," 185.

15. C. Vann Woodward, *Tom Watson: Agrarian Rebel* (New York: Macmillan, 1938), preface.

16. Hamilton Basso, *Mainstream* (New York: Reynal and Hitchcock, 1943), 188; John A. Moreau, "Huey Long and His Chroniclers," *Louisiana History* 6 (Spring 1965): 123.

17. Thomas D. Clark and Albert D. Kirwan, *The South Since Appomattox—A Century of Regional Change* (New York: Oxford University Press, 1967), 129.

18. Williams, "The Gentleman from Louisiana: Demagogue or Democrat," 18–20. See also Eric Hoffer, *The True Believer* (New York: Harper and Row, 1951).

19. On the concept of symbolic politics, see Murray Edelman, *The Symbolic Uses of Politics* (Urbana: University of Illinois Press, 1964); and Murray Edelman, *Politics as Symbolic Action, Mass Arousal and Quiescence* (Chicago: Markham, 1971).

20. On "Bourbon" politics, see Jonathan M. Wiener, "Bourbons," in Roller and Twyman, eds., *The Encyclopedia of Southern History*, 142; Woodward, *Origins of the New South*, 1–106; James Tice Moore, "Redeemers Reconsidered: Change and Continuity in the Democratic South, 1870–1900," *Journal of Southern History* 44 (August 1978): 357–378; Dewey W. Grantham, Jr., *The Democratic South* (New York: W. W. Norton, 1965), 13–14; Paul H. Buck, *The Road to Reunion, 1865–1900* (Boston: Little, Brown and Co., 1937); Paul Gaston, *The New South Creed* (New York: Knopf, 1970); Paul Lewinson, "The Negro in the White Class and Party Struggle," *Southwestern Political and Social Science Quarterly* 8 (March 1928): 358–382; William J. Cooper, *The Conservative Regime: South Carolina, 1877–1890* (Baltimore: Johns Hopkins University Press, 1968); William Ivy Hair, *Bourbonism and Agrarian Protest: Louisiana Politics, 1877–1900* (Baton Rouge: Louisiana State University Press, 1969); Allen J. Going, *Bourbon Democracy in Alabama, 1874–1890* (University, Ala.: University of Alabama Press, 1951); Allen W. Moger, *Virginia: From Bourbonism to Byrd* (Charlottesville: University of Virginia Press, 1968); Raymond H. Pulley, *Old Virginia Restored: An Interpretation of the Progressive Impulse, 1870–1930* (Charlottesville: University of Virginia Press, 1968); Roger L. Hart, *Redeemers, Bourbons, and Populists: Tennessee, 1870–1896* (Baton Rouge: Louisiana State University Press, 1975); Jonathan M. Wiener, *Social Origins of the New South: Alabama, 1860–1885* (Baton Rouge: Louisiana State University Press, 1978); and Dwight B. Billings, Jr., *Planters and the Making of a "New South": Class, Politics, and Development in North Carolina, 1865–1900* (Chapel Hill: University of North Carolina Press, 1979); and Dan T. Carter, "From the Old South to the New: Another Look at the Theme of Change and Continuity," in Walter J. Fraser, Jr., and Winfred B. Moore, Jr., eds., *From the Old South To the New: Essays on the Transitional South* (Westport, Conn.: Greenwood Press, 1981), 23–32.

21. Williams, *Romance and Realism in Southern Politics*, 63.

22. Cason, *Ninety Degrees in the Shade*, 72.

23. Sheldon Hackney, *"Origins of the New South* in Retrospect," *Journal of Southern History* 38 (May 1972): 205. For a survey of recent studies of post-Reconstruction Southern politics, see Numan V. Bartley, "In Search of the New South: Southern Politics after Reconstruction," *Reviews in American History* (Special Issue: *The Promise of American History: Progress and Prospects*) 10 (December 1982): 150–163.

24. Francis Butler Simkins, *The Tillman Movement in South Carolina* (Durham: Duke University Press, 1926); Francis Butler Simkins, *Pitchfork Ben Tillman, South Carolinian* (Baton Rouge: Louisiana State University Press, 1944). Cooper, *The Conservative Regime: South Carolina, 1877–1890*, contains a brief analysis of Tillman's supporters. See also David L. Carlton, *Mill and Town in South Carolina, 1880–1920* (Baton Rouge: Louisiana State University Press, 1982), 161–165.

25. Woodward, *Tom Watson: Agrarian Rebel*; Simkins, *Pitchfork Ben Tillman, South Carolinian*; William F. Holmes, *The White Chief, James Kimble Vardaman* (Baton Rouge: Louisiana State University Press, 1970); Wayne Flynt, *Cracker Messiah: Governor Sidney J. Catts of Florida* (Baton Rouge: Louisiana State University Press, 1977); William Anderson, *The Wild Man from Sugar Creek* (Baton Rouge: Louisiana State University Press, 1975); Williams, *Huey Long*. See also Daniel M. Robison, *Bob Taylor and the Agrarian Revolt in Tennessee* (Chapel Hill: University of North Carolina Press, 1935); Samuel Proctor, *Napoleon Bonaparte Broward: Florida's Fighting Democrat* (Gainesville: University of Florida Press, 1950); Dewey W. Grantham, Jr., *Hoke Smith and the Politics of the New South* (Baton Rouge: Louisiana State University Press, 1958); Robert C. Cotner, *James Stephen Hogg: A Biography* (Austin: University of Texas Press, 1959); A. J. Liebling, *The Earl of Louisiana* (New York: Simon and Schuster, 1961); A. Wigfall Green, *The Man Bilbo* (Baton Rouge: Louisiana State University Press, 1963); and Marshall Frady, *Wallace* (New York: New American Library, 1968). For a critical review of this literature, see Robert Dean Pope, "Of the Man at the Center: Biographies of Southern Politicians from the Age of Segregation," in J. Morgan Kousser and James M. McPherson, eds., *Region, Race, and Reconstruction: Essays in Honor of C. Vann Woodward* (New York: Oxford University Press, 1982), 89–112.

26. The most notable exceptions are Key, *Southern Politics*; J. Morgan Kousser, *The Shaping of Southern Politics: Suffrage Restriction and the Establishment of the One-Party South, 1880–1910* (New Haven: Yale University Press, 1974), 231–236; Hart, *Redeemers, Bourbons, and Populists: Tennessee, 1870–1896*, 84–154, and Appendix B; Carlton, *Mill and Town in South Carolina, 1880–1920*, 215–275; Numan V. Bartley, *From Thurmond to Wallace: Political Tendencies in Georgia, 1948–1968* (Baltimore: Johns Hopkins University Press, 1970); Numan V. Bartley and Hugh Davis Graham, *Southern Politics and the Second Reconstruction* (Baltimore: Johns Hopkins University Press, 1975); and Perry H. Howard, *Political Tendencies in Louisiana, 1812–1952* (Baton Rouge: Louisiana State University Press, 1957).

27. Samuel P. Hays, "The Social Analysis of American Political History, 1880–1920," *Political Science Quarterly* 80 (September 1965): 373–394. For some examples, see David Donald, *The Politics of Reconstruction, 1863–1867* (Baton Rouge: Louisiana State University Press, 1965); Warren A. Ellem, "Who Were the Mississippi Scalawags?" *Journal of Southern History* 38 (May 1972): 217–240; Allen W. Trelease, "Republican Reconstruction in North Carolina: A Roll-Call Analysis of the State House of Representatives, 1868–1870," *Journal of Southern History* 42 (August 1976): 319–344; Thomas Holt, *Black Over White: Negro Political Leadership in South Carolina During Reconstruction* (Urbana: University of Illinois Press, 1977); Carl V. Harris, "Right Fork or Left Fork? The Section-Party Alignment of Southern Democrats in Congress, 1873–1897," *Journal of Southern History* 42 (November 1976): 471–506; J. Mills Thornton III, "Fiscal Policy and the Failure of Radical Reconstruction in the Lower South," in Kousser and McPherson, eds., *Region, Race, and Reconstruction*, 349–394; Sheldon Hackney, *Populism to Progressivism in Alabama* (Princeton: Princeton University Press, 1969); Hart, *Redeemers, Bourbons, and Populists: Tennessee, 1870–1896*; Robert C. McMath, Jr., *Populist Vanguard: A History of the Southern Farmers' Alliance* (Chapel Hill: University of North Carolina Press, 1975); Michael

Schwartz, *Radical Protest and Social Structure: The Southern Farmers' Alliance and Cotton Tenancy, 1880–1890* (New York: Harcourt, Brace, 1976); James Turner, "Understanding the Populists," *Journal of American History* 67 (September 1980): 354–373; Kousser, *The Shaping of Southern Politics*; and the essays in Orville Vernon Burton and Robert C. McMath, Jr., eds., *Toward A New South? Studies in Post-Civil War Southern Communities* (Westport, Conn.: Greenwood Press, 1982). See also Wiener, *Social Origins of the New South: Alabama, 1860–1885*; Roger Ransom and Richard Sutch, *One Kind of Freedom: The Economic Consequences of Emancipation* (Cambridge: Cambridge University Press, 1977); Harold D. Woodman, "Sequel to Slavery: The New History Views the Postbellum South," *Journal of Southern History* 43 (November 1977): 523–554; Gavin Wright, *The Political Economy of the Cotton South* (New York: W. W. Norton, 1978); Gavin Wright, "The Strange Career of the New Southern Economic History," *Reviews in American History* (Special Issue: *The Promise of American History: Progress and Prospects*) 10 (December 1982): 164–180; Billings, *Planters and the Making of a "New South"*; and Steven Hahn, *The Roots of Southern Populism: Yeoman Farmers and the Transformation of the Georgia Upcountry, 1850–1890* (New York: Oxford University Press, 1983).

28. Richard L. McCormick, "Ethnocultural Interpretations of Nineteenth-Century American Voting Behavior," *Poitical Science Quarterly* 89 (June 1974): 351–377.

29. Samuel G. Blythe, *The Fakers* (New York: George H. Doran, 1914), 301.

30. See Grantham, *The Democratic South*; Williams, "The Gentleman from Louisiana: Demagogue or Democrat," 20–21; and Sarah McCulloh Lemmon, "The Ideology of Eugene Talmadge," *Georgia Historical Quarterly* 38 (September 1954): 226–248.

31. Cason, *Ninety Degrees in the Shade*, 89, 106–107; Michie and Ryhlick, *Dixie Demagogues*, 108–141, 221–241; Stetson Kennedy, *Southern Exposure* (New York: Doubleday, 1946), 187, 190; Arnall, *The Shore Dimly Seen*, 40–43, 107–122; Kane, *Louisiana Hayride*, 3–10; Walter Davenport, "The Fuehrer of Sugar Creek," *Collier's* 108 (December 6, 1941): 17, 71–73; Hilton Butler, "Bilbo—The Two-Edged Sword: A Mussolini for Our Most Backward State," *North American Review* 232 (December 1931): 496–503; Louis Cochran, "Mussolini of Mississippi: A Portrait of Governor Bilbo—The Builder," *The Outlook* 158 (June 17, 1931): 203–205, 222–223; James Rorty, "Callie Long's Boy Huey," *Forum* 94 (August 1935): 75; William Bradford Huie, "Talmadge: White Man's Governor," *American Mercury* 54 (February 1942): 181–190; Wallace Stegner, "Pattern for Demagogues," *The Pacific Spectator* 2 (Autumn 1948): 209–213; Victor Ferkiss, "Ezra Pound and American Fascism," *Journal of Politics* 17 (May 1955): 173–197; and Victor Ferkiss, "Populist Influences on American Fascism," *Western Political Quarterly* 10 (June 1957): 350–373. For a telling critique of the "cottonpatch fascist" approach, see Alan Brinkley, *Voices of Protest: Huey Long, Father Coughlin, and the Great Depression* (New York: Knopf, 1982), 269–283.

32. See Robert Kelley, "Ideology and Political Culture from Jefferson to Nixon," *American Historical Review* 82 (June 1977): 531–562; and Robert Kelley, *The Cultural Pattern in American Politics: The First Century* (New York: Knopf, 1979), 3–28.

33. See Lee Benson, *The Concept of Jacksonian Democracy: New York as a Test Case* (Princeton: Princeton University Press, 1961); Paul Kleppner, *The Cross of Culture: A Social Analysis of Midwestern Politics, 1850–1900* (New York: Free Press, 1970); Paul Kleppner, *The Third Electoral System, 1853–1892: Parties, Voters, and Political Cultures* (Chapel Hill: University of North Carolina Press, 1979); Richard J. Jensen, *The Winning of the Midwest: Social and Political Conflict, 1888–1896* (Chicago: University of Chicago Press, 1971); Samuel T. McSeveney, *The Politics of Depression: Political Behavior in the Northeast, 1893–1896* (New York: Oxford University Press, 1972); Ronald P. Formisano, *The Birth of Mass Political Parties: Michigan, 1827–1861* (Princeton: Princeton University Press, 1971); and Michael F. Holt, *Forging a Majority: The Formation of the Republican Party in Pittsburgh, 1848–1860* (New Haven: Yale University Press, 1969).

34. See McCormick, "Ethnocultural Interpretations of Nineteenth-Century American Voting Behavior," 351–377; Kelley, *The Cultural Pattern in American Politics*, 3–28; Richard B. Latner and Peter Levine, "Perspectives on Antebellum Pietistic Politics," *Reviews in American History* 4 (March 1976): 15–24; James E. Wright, "The Ethnocultural Model of Voting," *American*

Behavioral Scientist 16 (1973): 653–674; James R. Green, "Behavioralism and Class Analysis: A Review Essay on Mehtodology and Ideology," *Labor History* 13 (Winter 1972): 89–106; and J. Morgan Kousser, "The 'New Political History': A Methodological Critique," *Reviews in American History* 4 (March 1976): 1–14. The most important Southern contribution to date is Harry L. Watson, *Jacksonian Politics and Community Conflict: The Emergence of the Second American Party System in Cumberland County, North Carolina* (Baton Rouge: Louisiana State University Press, 1981).

35. Kelley, "Ideology and Political Culture from Jefferson to Nixon," 533; Kelley, *The Cultural Pattern in American Politics*, passim; George Brown Tindall, *The Ethnic Southerners* (Baton Rouge: Louisiana State University Press, 1976), 1–21. See also John Shelton Reed, *One South: An Ethnic Approach to Regional Culture* (Baton Rouge: Louisiana State University Press, 1982); and Forrest McDonald and Grady McWhiney, "The South from Self-Sufficiency to Peonage: An Interpretation," *American Historical Review* 85 (December 1980): 1095–1118.

36. See especially Robison, "From Tillman to Long: Some Striking Leaders of the Rural South," 289–310; Vance, "Rebels and Agrarians All: Studies in One-Party Politics," 26–44; Johnson, "Live Demagogue, or Dead Gentleman?" 1–14; and Karl Rodabaugh, "'Farmer Gene' Talmadge and the Rural Style in Georgia Politics," *Southern Studies* 21 (Spring 1982): 83–96.

37. See Robert R. Dykstra, "Town-Country Conflict: A Hidden Dimension in American Social History," *Agricultural History* 38 (October 1964): 195–204; Frank J. Huffman, Jr., "Town and Country in the South, 1850–1880: A Comparison of Urban and Rural Social Structures," *South Atlantic Quarterly* 76 (Summer 1977): 366–381; Robert C. McMath, Jr., "Community, Region, and Hegemony in the Nineteenth-Century South," in Burton and McMath, eds., *Toward A New South?*, 281–300; Barbara F. Agresti, "Town and Country in a Florida Rural County in the Late 19th Century: Some Population and Household Comparisons," *Rural Sociology* 77 (Winter 1977): 556– 568; Orville Vernon Burton, "The Rise and Fall of Afro-American Town Life: Town and Country in Reconstruction Edgefield, South Carolina," in Burton and McMath, eds., *Toward A New South?*, 152–192; Carlton, *Mill and Town in South Carolina, 1880–1920*, 13-39; and Robert P. Swierenga, "Towards the 'New Rural History': A Review Essay," *Historical Methods Newsletter* 6 (June 1973): 111–122.

38. See Ch. 7, Note 3.

39. Robert H. Wiebe, *The Search for Order, 1877–1920* (New York: Hill and Wang, 1967), xiii–75; Robert H. Wiebe, *The Segmented Society: An Introduction to the Meaning of America* (New York: Oxford University Press, 1975). See also McMath, "Community, Region, and Hegemony in the Nineteenth-Century South," 289–295, for a perceptive discussion of the changing nature of Southern communities.

40. This rough estimate is based on an impressionistic survey of business directory records and manuscript census returns for 11 Arkansas counties: Clark, Crawford, Hot Spring, Jefferson, Nevada, Phillips, Poinsett, Polk, Pulaski, Sebastian, and Sharp; and on a more systematic survey of similar records for 6 other counties: Drew, Howard, Marion, Pope, St. Francis, and Washington. A "planter" is defined here as an agriculturalist who defined himself as such. *Arkansas State Gazetteer and Business Directories for 1888-9, 1892-3, 1906-7, 1912-3* (Chicago: R. L. Polk and Co., 1888, 1892, 1906, 1912); *Twelfth Census of the United States*, Manuscript Returns, *Population Schedules* for Clark, Crawford, Drew, Hot Spring, Howard, Jefferson, Marion, Nevada, Phillips, Poinsett, Polk, Pope, Pulaski, St. Francis, Sebastian, Sharp, and Washington Counties, Arkansas, located at the National Archives, Washington, D.C.

41. On class relations in the Old South, see Eugene Genovese, "Yeomen Farmers in a Slaveholders' Democracy," *Agricultural History* 49 (April 1975): 331–342; J. Mills Thornton III, *Politics and Power in a Slave Society: Alabama, 1800–1860* (Baton Rouge: Louisiana State University Press, 1978). See also Edward Magdol, "Against the Gentry: An Inquiry into a Southern Lower Class Community and Culture, 1865–1870," *Journal of Social History* 6 (Spring 1973): 259–283; and Edward Magdol and Jon Wakelyn, eds., *The Southern Common People: Studies in Nineteenth-Century Social History* (Westport, Conn.: Greenwood Press, 1980).

42. L. S. Dunaway, *What a Preacher Saw Through a Key-Hole in Arkansas* (Little Rock: Parke-Harper, 1925), 82. On the development of the planter-merchant class, see Woodward, *Origins of the New South*, 181–184; Ransom and Sutch, *One Kind of Freedom*, 56–170; Billings, *Planters and the Making of a "New South"*; and Harold D. Woodman, *King Cotton and His Retainers: Financing and Marketing the Cotton Crop of the South, 1800–1925* (Lexington: University of Kentucky Press, 1968).

43. The impact of urbanization, industrialization, and commercial development on planter values and behavior has become a major point of debate. See Woodward, "Sequel to Slavery: The New History Views the Postbellum South," 544–554; Carter, "From the Old South to the New: Another Look at the Theme of Change and Continuity," 23–32; Billings, *Planters and the Making of a "New South"*; Wiener, *Social Origins of the New South: Alabama, 1860–1885*; Jonathan M. Wiener, "Class Structure and Economic Development in the American South, 1865–1955," *American Historical Review* 84 (October 1979): 970–992; and the "Comments" by Robert Higgs and Harold Woodman, *American Historical Review* 84 (October 1979): 993–1001. See also Wiener's "Reply" to Higgs and Woodman, *American Historical Review* 84 (October 1979): 1002–1006

44. For a strikingly different view of Southern urban culture, see David R. Goldfield, "The Urban South: A Regional Framework," *American Historical Review* 86 (December 1981): 1009–1034; and Goldfield, *Cotton Fields and Skyscrapers: Southern City and Region, 1607–1980* (Baton Rouge: Louisiana State University Press, 1982).

45. On the concept of relative deprivation, see Neil J. Smelser, *Theory of Collective Behavior* (New York: Free Press, 1963).

46. See Lawrence Goodwyn, *Democratic Promise: The Populist Moment in America* (New York: Oxford University Press, 1976); McMath, *Populist Vanguard*; Turner, "Understanding the Populists," 354–373; and Sheldon Hackney, ed., *Populism: The Critical Issues* (Boston: Little, Brown and Co, 1971), introduction.

47. See C. Vann Woodward, "Tom Watson and the Negro in Agrarian Politics," *Journal of Southern History* 4 (February 1938): 14–33; Jack Abramowitz, "The Negro in the Agrarian Revolt," *Agricultural History* 24 (January 1950): 89–95; Jack Abramowitz, "The Negro in the Populist Movement," *Journal of Negro History* 38 (July 1953): 257–289; Robert Saunders, "Southern Populists and the Negro, 1893–1895," *Journal of Negro History* 54 (July 1969): 240–261; Charles Crowe, "Tom Watson, Populists and Blacks Reconsidered," *Journal of Negro History* 55 (April 1970): 99–116; Cornel Justin Reinhart, "Populism and the Black: A Study in Ideology and Social Strains" (Ph.D. thesis, University of Oklahoma, 1972); Gerald H. Gaither, *Blacks and the Populist Revolt: Ballots and Bigotry in the "New South"* (University, Ala.: University of Alabama Press, 1977); and Lawrence Goodwyn, "Populist Dreams and Negro Rights: East Texas as a Case Study,"*American Historical Review* 76 (December 1971): 1435–1456.

48. See Bertram Wyatt-Brown, *Southern Honor: Ethics and Behavior in the Old South* (New York: Oxford University Press, 1982); John Shelton Reed, *The Enduring South: Subcultural Persistence in a Mass Society* (Chapel Hill: University of North Carolina Press, 1975), 33–43; Reed, *One South*, 53, 113, 123, 133, 136–138, 175–178; and Willie Morris, *North Toward Home* (New York: Dell, 1967), 3–145.

49. Fletcher, *Arkansas*, 314.

50. Dunaway, *What a Preacher Saw*, 82.

51. See Kousser, *The Shaping of Southern Politics*, 231–237.

52. See Vance, "Rebels and Agrarians All: Studies in One-Party Politics," 35; and Williams, *Romance and Realism in Southern Politics*, 62–64.

53. Woodward, *Origins of the New South*, 377.

54. See James R. Green, *Grass-Roots Socialism: Radical Movements in the Southwest, 1895–1943* (Baton Rouge: Louisiana State University Press, 1978); and G. Gregory Kiser, "The Socialist Party in Arkansas, 1900–1912," *ArkHQ* 40 (Summer 1981): 119–153.

55. On Southern progressivism, see Arthur S. Link, "The Progressive Movement in the

South, 1870–1914,"*North Carolina Historical Review* 23 (April 1946): 172–195; George Brown Tindall, "Business Progressivism: Southern Politics in the Twenties,"*South Atlantic Quarterly* 62 (Winter 1963): 92–106; Dewey W. Grantham, "The Contours of Southern Progressivism," *American Historical Review* 86 (December 1981): 1035–1059; Grantham, *The Democratic South,* 42–68; Woodward, *Origins of the New South,* 369–428, 456–481; Hackney, *Populism to Progressivism in Alabama,* 122–332; Kirby, *Darkness at the Dawning: Race and Reform in the Progressive South;* Williams, *Romance and Realism in Southern Politics,* 58–64; Lewis L. Gould, *Progressives and Prohibitionists: Texas Democrats in the Wilson Era* (Austin: University of Texas Press, 1973); Holmes, *The White Chief: James Kimble Vardaman,* 267–293; Albert D. Kirwan, *Revolt of the Rednecks: Mississippi Politics, 1876–1925* (Lexington: University of Kentucky Press, 1951); and Bartley, "In Search of the New South: Southern Politics After Reconstruction," 156–159. Davis has often been characterized as a progressive, but such a characterization is at best a half-truth. Despite his advocacy of certain progressive reforms—antitrust legislation, railroad legislation, penal reform, expansion of charitable institutions, and increased rights for workers and organized labor—he never described himself as a progressive and had little use for politicians who adopted the progressive label. The administrative, bureaucratic mentality that suffused much of the progressive movement had no charm for Davis.

56. Williams, *Romance and Realism in Southern Politics,* 62.

57. See Thornton, *Politics and Power in a Slave Society: Alabama, 1800–1860,* xviii–xxi, 3–58, 301–302, for a perceptive discussion of Southern Jacksonianism.

58. Goodwyn, *Democratic Promise,* 181–182, 201–211, 388–401, 582–592.

59. See Schwartz, *Radical Protest and Social Structure,* 129–198; and Billings, *Planters and the Making of a "New South",* 183–190.

Chapter 2

1. L. S. Dunaway, ed., *Jeff Davis, Governor and United States Senator: His Life and Speeches* (Little Rock: Democrat Printing and Litho. Co., 1913), 68–69.

2. Ibid., 23, 68, 228, 244, 247; David Y. Thomas, "Jeff Davis," in Allen Johnson and Dumas Malone, eds., *Dictionary of American Biography* (New York: Charles Scribner's Sons, 1958), 3: 122; Charles Jacobson, *The Life Story of Jeff Davis: The Stormy Petrel of Arkansas Politics* (Little Rock: Parke-Harper, 1925), 13; Dallas T. Herndon, ed., *Centennial History of Arkansas* (Little Rock: S. J. Clark, 1922), 3: 520; George James Stevenson, "The Political Career of Jeff Davis: An Example of the Southern Protest" (M.A. thesis, University of Arkansas, 1949), 21; Nevin Neal, "Jeff Davis and the Reform Movement in Arkansas, 1898–1907" (M.A. thesis, Vanderbilt University, 1939), 27; Bayless Walker Price, "The Life of Jeff Davis" (M.A. thesis, University of Alabama, 1929), 1; Walter Scott McNutt, Olin McKnight, and George Hubbell, *A History of Arkansas* (Little Rock: Democrat Printing and Litho. Co., 1932), 315; John Gould Fletcher, *Arkansas* (Chapel Hill: University of North Carolina Press, 1947), 288.

3. Jacobson, *Life Story,* 13, 121; Harry Lee Williams, "Jeff Davis—The Master Politician of His Period," Little Rock *Arkansas Gazette* (hereafter cited as *Arkansas Gazette*), November 21, 1965, 6e; *Arkansas Gazette,* April 6, June 22, 1898, August 26–27, 1899, July 24, August 30, 1902; Richard L. Niswonger, "Arkansas Democratic Politics, 1896–1920" (Ph.D. thesis, University of Texas, 1974), 129.

4. Dardanelle *Post-Dispatch,* April 26, 1900.

5. Rupert B. Vance, "A Karl Marx for Hill Billies," *Social Forces* 9 (December 1930): 190.

6. *Eighth Census of the United States, 1860,* Manuscript Returns, *Population Schedules,* for Jackson Township, Sevier County, Arkansas, located in the National Archives, Washington, D.C.; see also *Compendium of the Sixth Census, 1840* (Washington: Thomas Allen, 1841), 323–325, 94–95; *Seventh Census of the United States, 1850, Statistics of the United States* (Washington: Robert Armstrong, 1853), 553–562; and *Eighth Census of the United States, 1860, Population* (Washington: Government Printing Office, 1864), 18–20. See Fay Hempstead, *A Pictorial History*

of Arkansas from Earliest Times to the Year 1890 (St. Louis: N. D. Thompson, 1890), 935–937, 1121–1122; David Y. Thomas, ed., *Arkansas and Its People: A History, 1541–1930* (New York: American Historical Society, 1930), 2: 732–734, 775–777; Germaine M. Reed, "Journey Through Southwest Arkansas, 1858," *ArkHQ* 30 (Summer 1971): 161–169; and W. S. Ray, "Early Days in Sevier County," *PAHA* 4 (Conway, Ark., 1917): 170–203. Rocky Comfort served as the county seat of Little River County from 1868 to 1880. Later in the nineteenth century, after the construction of a railway through the town, the town's name was changed to Foreman, though it was sometimes called New Rocky Comfort. One of the more important railroad towns in southwest Arkansas, Foreman boasted a population of 1,408 by 1920.

7. See Harry Sinclair Drago, *Red River Valley* (New York: Charles N. Potter, 1962), 11, 33; Eugene Bowers and Evelyn Oppenheimer, *Red River Dust* (Waco: Word Books, 1969), 14–30; *Eighth Census of the United States, 1860, Population,* 18–20; *Eighth Census of the United States, 1860, Agriculture* (Washington: Government Printing Office, 1864), 6–9, 224; *Eighth Census of the United States, 1860, Manufactures* (Washington: Government Printing Office, 1865), 20; Ray, "Early Days in Sevier County," 174–178, 191; Ludwell H. Johnson, *Red River Campaign: Politics and Cotton in the Civil War* (Baltimore: Johns Hopkins University Press, 1958), 13, 47. In 1860, Sevier County ranked twelfth (out of fifty-five counties) in number of cotton bales (400 pound bales) ginned with 10,897 bales.

8. Press Woodruff, *A Backwoods Philosopher from Arkansas* (Chicago: Thompson and Thomas, 1901), 23.

9. E. E. Dale, "Arkansas: The Myth and the State," *ArkHQ* 12 (Spring 1953): 8–29; C. Fred Williams, "The Bear State Image: Arkansas in the Nineteenth Century," *ArkHQ* 39 (Summer 1980): 99–111; Lee A. Dew, "'On a Slow Train Through Arkansaw'—The Negative Image of Arkansas in the Early Twentieth Century," *ArkHQ* 39 (Summer 1980): 125–135; Foy Lisenby, "A Survey of Arkansas's Image Problem," *ArkHQ* 30 (Spring 1971): 60–71. See also Bernie Babcock, *The Man Who Lied on Arkansas and What Got Him* (Little Rock: The Sketch Book Pub. Co., 1909), 31, 41–78; Fred W. Allsopp, *Folklore of Romantic Arkansas* (New York: The Grolier Society, 1931), 2: 335; Charles Morrow Wilson, *The Bodacious Ozarks: True Tales of the Backhills* (New York: Hastings House, 1959), 28; Fletcher, *Arkansas,* 65, 94, 109, 316–319, 332; Work Projects Administration, *Arkansas: A Guide to the State* (New York: Hastings House, 1941), 4, 5, 99, which argues that "Arkansas is not like that at all, of course"; Marguerite Lyon, *Hurrah for Arkansas: From Razorbacks to Diamonds* (Indianapolis: Bobbs-Merrill, 1947), 13–14; Marion Hughes, *Three Years in Arkansaw* (Chicago: M. A. Donahue and Co., n.d.); Charles H. Hibler, *Down in Arkansas* (Kansas City: J. W. Smith, 1911); Edgar E. Bryant, *Speeches and Addresses* (Fort Smith: Chauncey A. Lick, 1893), 89–90; Bernie Babcock, *Yesterday and Today in Arkansas* (Little Rock, 1917); Charles Morrow Wilson, *Backwoods America* (Chapel Hill: University of North Carolina Press, 1934); *The Arkansas Gazette: The Book of Arkansas, 1913* (Little Rock: Arkansas Gazette, 1913), 97–146; J. Breckinridge Ellis, *Arkansaw Cousins: A Story of the Ozarks* (New York: Henry Holt, 1908); W. A. Browne, "Some Frontier Conditions in the Hilly Portion of the Ozarks," *Journal of Geography* 28 (1929): 181–188; Vance Randolph, *The Ozarks: An American Survival of Primitive Society* (New York: Vanguard Press, 1931); Wayman Hogue, *Back Yonder, An Ozark Chronicle* (New York: Minton, Balch, and Co., 1932); Fred Starr, *Of These Hills and Us* (Boston: Christopher, 1958); Milton D. Rafferty, *The Ozarks: Land and Life* (Norman: University of Oklahoma Press, 1980); James R. Masterson, *Tall Tales of Arkansaw* (Boston: Chapman and Grimes, 1943); Opie Read, *Opie Read in Arkansas and What He Saw There* (New York: J. S. Ogilvie Pub. Co., 1891); Opie Read, *Flashes of Wit Selected from the National Gloom Chaser, The Arkansas Traveler,* ed. Max Stein) Chicago: Stein, 1945): Marion Lowell, *Glimpses and Epigrams of Opie Read* (Chicago: Hill, 1902); Robert L. Morris, "Opie Read, Arkansas Journalist," *ArkHQ* 2 (September 1943): 246–254; Robert L. Morris, "The Arkansan in American Folklore," *ArkHQ* 9 (Summer 1950): 99–107; William A. Edmonds, *The Truth About Arkansas* (St. Louis: Woodward and Tierman, 1895); Avantus "Bud" Green, *Look Who's Laughing Now* (Little Rock, 1947); and "Bud" Green, *With This We Challenge . . . An Epitome of Arkansas* (Little Rock, 1945); M. E.

Dunaway, *The Philosophy of an Arkansas Farmer, and Other Poems* (Little Rock: Arkansas Writer Pub. Co., 1921), 1: 4–11; Thomas Nuttal, *A Journal of Travels into the Arkansas Territory* (Ann Arbor: University of Michigan Microfilms, 1966); Thomas W. Jackson, *On a Slow Train Through Arkansaw* (Chicago: T. W. Jackson Pub. Co., 1903); Karr Shannon, *On a Fast Train Through Arkansas* (Little Rock: Democrat Printing and Litho. Co., 1948).

10. Wilson, *Bodacious Ozarks*, 4, 236.

11. Work Projects Administration, *Arkansas: A Guide to the State*, 6–7, 13; Fletcher, *Arkansas*, 4, 8–9; Malcolm J. Rohrbough, *The Trans-Appalachian Frontier: People, Societies, and Institutions, 1775–1850* (New York: Oxford University Press, 1978), 286–287.

12. Work Projects Administration, *Arkansas: A Guide to the State*, 7; *PAHA* 1 (1906): 195; *Arkansas Gazette*, April 18, 1902, reported that 84 percent of Arkansas's land area was forest land. The second most heavily forested state was Maine (79 percent). For a discussion of the distinctiveness of South Arkansas, see George Hyman Thompson, "Leadership in Arkansas Reconstructon" (Ph.D. thesis, Columbia University, 1968), 2–20.

13. Fletcher, *Arkansas*, 4; Virgil Harold Holder, "Historical Geography of the Lower White River" (M.A. thesis, University of Arkansas, 1966), 56–97; *PAHA* 1 (1906): 203–207.

14. Work Projects Administration, *Arkansas: A Guide to the State*, 6–7, 12–13, 23; Fletcher, *Arkansas*, 5–9; Niswonger, "Arkansas Democratic Politics," 6; Rohrbough, *The Trans-Appalachian Frontier*, 282–283.

15. Wilson, *Bodacious Ozarks*, 7; Rohrbough, *The Trans-Appalachian Frontier*, 282–283; *PAHA* 1 (1906): 203; David Wiley Mullins, "History of Sharp County, Arkansas" (M.A. thesis, University of Colorado, 1934), 59, 63; S. W. Stockard, *The History of Lawrence, Jackson, Independence, and Stone Counties* (n.p., n.d.), 93; Work Projects Administration, *Arkansas: A Guide to the State,* 51–53.

16. Fletcher, *Arkansas*, 25; see Mary D. Hudgins, "Arkansas Traveler—A Multi-Parented Wayfarer," *ArkHQ* 30 (Summer 1971): 145–160.

17. Fletcher, *Arkansas*, 108–130; Rohrbough, *The Trans-Appalachian Frontier*, 272–292; Dale, "Arkansas: The Myth and the State," 14–22; Tommy R. Thompson, ed., "Searching for the American Dream in Arkansas: Letters of a Pioneer Family," *ArkHQ* 38 (Summer 1979): 167–181; Elsie M. Lewis, "Economic Conditions in Ante-Bellum Arkansas, 1850–1861," *ArkHQ* 6 (Autumn 1947): 256–274; Dallas T. Herndon, "A Little of What Arkansas Was Like a Hundred Years Ago," *ArkHQ* 3 (Summer 1944): 97–124; Thomas, *Arkansas and Its People*, 1: 55–68, 113–117; Work Projects Administration, *Arkansas: A Guide to the State*, 38–39; Robert Bradshaw Walz, "Migration into Arkansas, 1834–1880" (Ph.D. thesis, University of Texas, 1958). See also Michael B. Dougan, *Confederate Arkansas* (University, Ala.: University of Alabama Press, 1976), 1–11.

18. Stockard, *The History of Lawrence, Jackson, Independence and Stone Counties*, 93.

19. Lewis, "Economic Conditions in Ante-Bellum Arkansas, 1850–1861," 256–274; Work Projects Administration, *Arkansas: A Guide to the State*, 38–39, 50–54; Rohrbough, *The Trans-Appalachian Frontier*, 283–292; *Seventh Census of the United States, 1850, Statistics of the United States* (Washington: Robert Armstrong, 1853), 555–556; *Eighth Census of the United States, 1860, Agriculture*, 6–9; *Compendium of the Seventh Census of the United States, 1850* (Washington: A. O. P. Nicholson, 1854), 198–201; *Eighth Census of the United States, 1860, Mortality and Miscellaneous Statistics* (Washington: Government Printing Office, 1866), 339.

20. Russellville *Courier-Democrat*, March 8, 1906 (obituary); Price, "Life of Jeff Davis," 1.

21. Price, "Life of Jeff Davis," 1–2; Herndon, *Centennial History of Arkansas*, 3: 520; Russellville *Courier-Democrat*, March 8, 1906; Robert B. Walz, "Arkansas Slaveholdings and Slaveholders in 1850," *ArkHQ* 12 (Spring 1953): 67; *Seventh Census of the United States, 1850, Manuscript Returns, Population Schedules*, and *Slave Schedules*, for Jackson Township, Sevier County, Arkansas, located at the National Archives, Washington, D.C.; *Eighth Census of the United States, 1860, Manuscript Returns, Population Schedules*, for Jackson Township, Sevier County, Arkansas, Family #1026, includes: William Scott, farmer, age 40; Elizabeth Scott, age 24; William Scott, age 7; Sarah Scott, age 5; May Scott, age 3, The family's personal estate was

assessed at $1,000; its real estate holdings were assessed at $600. *Eighth Census of the United States, 1860,* Manuscript Returns, *Slave Schedules,* for Red River Township, Sevier County, Arkansas, Roll 54, p. 21, located at the National Archives, Washington, D.C.

22. *Ninth Census of the United States, 1870,* Manuscript Returns, *Population Schedules,* for Dover Township, Pope County, Arkansas, Reel 593–51, pp. 2–3, Family #9, includes: L. W. Davis, age 34; Elizabeth A. Davis, age 34; Jefferson Davis, age 8; W. M. Scott, age 17; Sallie Scott, age 14; and Mollie Scott, age 11, (located at the National Archives, Washington, D.C.; *Arkansas Gazette,* July 26, 1902, August 1, 1906; Dunaway, *Jeff Davis,* 220; Russellville *Courier-Democrat,* March 8, 1906.

23. Drago, *Red River Valley,* 103; Bright Ray, *Legends of Red River Valley* (San Antonio: Naylor Company, 1941), 147–155; McNutt, McKnight, and Hubbell, *History of Arkansas,* 167–168; Shelby Foote, *The Civil War: A Narrative,* vol. 2: *Fredericksburg to Meridian* (New York: Random House, 1963), 706–707; Leo Elmer Huff, "Confederate Arkansas: A History of Arkansas During the Civil War" (M.A. thesis, University of Arkansas, 1964); John M. Harrell, *Arkansas,* vol. 10, Part 2 of *Confederate Military History* (Atlanta: Confederate Pub. Co., 1899); Dougan, *Confederate Arkansas,* 114, 122; Powell Clayton, *The Aftermath of the Civil War in Arkansas* (New York: Neale, 1915), 17–22; Marcus J. Wright, *Arkansas in the War, 1861–1865* (Batesville, Ark.: Independence County Historical Society, 1963); Johnson, *Red River Campaign: Politics and Cotton in the Civil War:* Shelby Foote, *The Civil War: A Narrative,* vol. 3: *Red River to Appomattox* (New York: Random House, 1974), 25–77, 104.

24. Dunaway, *Jeff Davis,* 241, 248; Foote, *The Civil War,* 3: 578, 586, 723; see also Stephen B. Oates, *Confederate Cavalry West of the River* (Austin: University of Texas Press, 1961).

25. Foote, *The Civil War,* 3: 1019–1031.

26. Dunaway, *Jeff Davis,* 66–69.

27. Ibid., 44; G. W. Ogden, "Jeff Davis, Idol of the Hillbillies," *Hampton's Broadway Magazine* (n.d.), reprinted in the *Camden Beacon* (undated clipping); Russellville *Courier-Democrat,* March 8, 1906; Jacobson, *Life Story,* 13; Neal, "Jeff Davis and the Reform Movement in Arkansas," 27; Stevenson, "The Political Career of Jeff Davis," 21; Hempstead, *A Pictorial History of Arkansas,* 936, 1122.

28. Allen W. Trelease, *White Terror: The Ku Klux Klan Conspiracy and Southern Reconstruction* (New York: Harper and Row, 1971), 149–174; Clayton, *Aftermath of the Civil War in Arkansas,* 56–115; Boyd W. Johnson, "Cullen Montgomery Baker: The Arkansas-Texas Desperado," *ArkHQ* 25 (Autumn 1966): 229–239; A. W. Neville, *The Red River Valley, Then and Now* (Paris, Tx.: North Texas Pub. Co., 1948), 48–135; Drago, *Red River Valley,* 249–264; Bright Ray, *Legends of the Red River Valley,* 147–155; W. S. Ray, "Early Days in Sevier County," 180.

29. Johnson, "Cullen Montgomery Baker," 229–239; see also Ed Bartholomew, *Cullen Baker, Premier Texas Gunfighter* (Houston: The Frontier Press of Texas, 1954); Trelease, *White Terror,* 150–151, 156, 161–173; Clayton, *Aftermath of the Civil War in Akansas,* 63–70, 99–115; *Report of the Joint Select Committee to Inquire into the Condition of Affairs in the Late Insurrectionary States,* vol. 13 (Washington: Government Printing Office, 1872), *House Reports,* 42d Congress, 2d Session, #22, 329–330; Otis A. Singletary, "Military Disturbances in Arkansas during Reconstruction," *ArkHQ* 15 (Summer 1956), 140–150; Virginia Buxton, ed., "Clayton's Militia in Sevier and Howard Counties," *ArkHQ* 20 (Winter 1961): 344–350; J. H. Atkinson, ed., "Clayton and Catterson Rob Columbia County," *ArkHQ* 21 (Summer 1962): 153–157; John M. Harrell, *The Brooks and Baxter War: A History of the Reconstruction Period in Arkansas* (St. Louis: Slawson Printing, 1893), 85–89; Thomas S. Staples, *Reconstruction in Arkansas, 1862–1874* (New York: Columbia University Press, 1923), 294–302; McNutt, McKnight, and Hubbell, *History of Arkansas,* 212–217; David Y. Thomas, *Arkansas in War and Reconstruction* (Little Rock: United Daughters of the Confederacy, 1926), 421–422; Dunaway, *Jeff Davis,* 96; Vance, "A Karl Marx for Hill Billies," 186; for information on Powell Clayton, see Timothy P. Donovan and Willard B. Gatewood, Jr., eds., *The Governors of Arkansas: Essays in Political Biography* (Fayetteville: University of Arkansas Press, 1981), 43–54; Orval Truman Diggs, Jr., "The Issues of the Powell

Clayton Regime, 1868–1871," *ArkHQ* 8 (Spring 1949): 1–75; Thomas, *Arkansas and Its People*, 1: 147–155; and Clayton, *Aftermath of the Civil War in Arkansas*.

30. *Biographical and Historical Memoirs of Western Arkansas* (Chicago and Nashville: The Southern Pub. Co., 1891), 193–271; William M. Hurley, "Socializing Forces in the History of Pope County, Arkansas" (M.A. thesis, University of Arkansas, 1931), 26, 32–46, 153–155; D. Porter West, *Early History of Pope County* (Russellville, 1906); Work Projects Administration, *Arkansas: A Guide to the State*, 5, 126, 249. The population of Pope County was 8,386 in 1870, 14,322 in 1880, and 19,568 in 1890.

31. *Biographical and Historical Memoirs of Western Arkansas*, 209; Neal, "Jeff Davis and the Reform Movement in Arkansas," 27; *Ninth Census of the United States, 1870*, Manuscript Returns, *Population Schedules*, for Dover Township, Pope County, Arkansas, Reel 593–61, pp. 2–3, Family #9, lists $300 of personal property and $2,500 of real property, $1,500 of which was owned by Elizabeth Davis. Price, "Life of Jeff Davis," 3, claims that the Davis family was poor throughout Reconstruction; see also Fletcher, *Arkansas* 289.

32. See Randy Henningson, "Upland Farmers and Agrarian Protest: Northwest Arkansas and the Brothers of Freedom" (M.A. thesis, University of Arkansas, 1973), 49, 162; *Biographical and Historical Memoirs of Western Arkansas*, 195–196; see also Maude Carmichael, "The Plantation System in Arkansas, 1850–1876" (Ph.D. thesis, Radcliffe College, 1935); and Michael Schwartz, *Radical Protest and Social Structure: The Southern Farmers' Alliance and Cotton Tenancy, 1880–1890* (New York: Academic Press, 1976), 3–88.

33. Henningson, "Upland Farmers and Agrarian Protest," 9–10, 129–130; *Biographical and Historical Memoirs of Western Arkansas*, 194–196; Hurley, "Socializing Forces in the History of Pope County," 43–44, 60–61, 75–76; *Eighth Census of the United States, 1860, Agriculture*, 224; Ted R. Worley, "The Arkansas Peace Society of 1861: A Study in Mountain Unionism," *Journal of Southern History* 24 (November 1958): 445–456; see also Jack Benton Scroggs, "Arkansas in the Secession Movement" (M.A. thesis, University of Arkansas, 1948); Huff, "Confederate Arkansas," 1–33; Dougan, *Confederate Arkansas*, 23–67; Thomas J. Reynolds, "Pope County Militia War," *PAHA* 2 (Fayetteville, 1908): 174–178; and Fletcher, *Arkansas*, 230.

34. Reynolds, "Pope County Militia War," 174–198; Hurley, "Socializing Forces in the History of Pope County," 45, 172; *Russellville Democrat*, July 24, 1890; Fletcher, *Arkansas*, 221, 230; Staples, *Reconstruction in Arkansas*, 368–373.

35. See Harrell, *The Brooks and Baxter War*; James H. Atkinson, "The Brooks-Baxter Contest," *ArkHQ* 4 (Summer 1945): 125–149; Benjamin S. Johnson, "The Brooks-Baxter War," *PAHA* 2: 122–173; Thomas, *Arkansas in War and Reconstruction*, 427–435; Staples, *Reconstruction in Arkansas*, 401–441; Earl Woodward, "The Brooks and Baxter War in Arkansas, 1872–1874," *ArkHQ* 30 (Winter 1971), 315–336; and Donovan and Gatewood, *The Governors of Arkansas*, 55–60.

36. It is clear, however, that Lewis Davis was a Democrat partisan during the Militia War. *Russellville Democrat*, July 27, 1876; Dunaway, *Jeff Davis*, 96.

37. Thomas, *Arkansas and Its People*, 2: 429; *Biographical and Historical Memoirs of Western Arkansas*, 205; Hurley, "Socializing Forces in the History of Pope County, 26, 153–155, 173–175. On the lengthy struggle to remove the county seat from Dover, see Hurley, "Socializing Forces in the History of Pope County," 26–31; and the *Russellville Democrat*, March 14, September 5, 12, 1878, March 22, June 26, 1879, March 23, 1887.

38. *Russellville Democrat*, April 8, July 1, 15, 22, 29, November 18, 1875, February 15, May 31, 1877, October 16, 1879, April 26, 1883, July 27, 1887, June 28, 1888, June 26, 1890; Hurley, "Socializing Forces in the History of Pope County," 164, notes that Lewis W. Davis edited the *National Tribune* in 1873.

39. *Russellville Democrat*, March 11, June 24, July 1, 1875, July 27, September 7, 14, 1876, February 7, 1878, March 4, 1880, February 9, July 27, 1882, January 28, 1886.

40. Ibid., June 24, 1875, noted that at the closing exercises of Miss Tennie Williamson's school, "The speeches of Masters Jeff Davis and Nola Thach were especially commendable";

ibid., January 6, 1881; Price, "Life of Jeff Davis," 3–4; Jacobson, *Life Story,* 14–15; Dunaway, *Jeff Davis,* 5–6; Stevenson, "Political Career of Jeff Davis," 21; Price, "Life of Jeff Davis," 3–4; Fletcher, *Arkansas,* 288–289; McNutt, McKnight, and Hubbell, *History of Arkansas,* 315; Neal, "Jeff Davis and the Reform Movement in Arkansas," 27–28; *Arkansas Gazette,* January 4, 1913, quotes from a letter written by Davis to Vanderbilt Dean Thomas Malone in 1900: "Many years ago you refused [me] a degree. I thought I deserved it. I send you this clipping [a clipping describing Davis's election to the governship] to let you know how I am getting on."

41. Dunaway, *Jeff Davis,* 6–7; Jacobson, *Life Story,* 14; Neal, "Jeff Davis and the Reform Movement in Arkansas," 28, claims that Davis's age disability was later removed by an act of the legistature; Price, "Life of Jeff Davis," 5, claims that "the bar had to be petitioned to remove" Davis's age disability; Stevenson, "Political Career of Jeff Davis," 21–22; Fletcher, *Arkansas,* 289. One of Davis's classmates at Cumberland University was Sidney J. Catts, the anti-Catholic crusader who was elected governor of Florida in 1916. See Wayne Flynt, *Cracker Messiah: Governor Sidney J. Catts of Florida* (Baton Rouge: Louisiana State University Press, 1977), 5.

42. *Russellville Democrat,* September 14, 1876, October 27, 1882, January 17, 1885. Her natural father was Gilbert MacKenzie, a local Methodist minister. Neal, "Jeff Davis and the Reform Movement in Arkansas," 30; Jacobson, *Life Story,* 29.

43. Dunaway, *Jeff Davis,* 229; Jacobson, *Life Story,* 28–30.

44. Jacobson, *Life Story,* 30.

45. Dunaway, *Jeff Davis,* 28–29.

46. Ibid., 7, 29; Jacobson, *Life Story,* 14; Neal, "Jeff Davis and the Reform Movement in Arkansas," 28; Price, "Life of Jeff Davis," 5–6. For a general discussion of the Arkansas legal profession in the late nineteenth century, see John Hallum, *The Diary of an Old Lawyer or Scenes Behind the Curtain* (Nashville: Southwestern, 1895).

47. *Russellville Democrat,* April 26, 28, June 28, 1883.

48. Ibid., June 27, August 10, 1887.

49. Ibid., July 13, 27, 1876. In his 1876 campaign for a seat in the state legislature, Lewis Davis was forced to defend the legal profession. He argued that his status as a lawyer, in and of itself, did not make him an antifarmer candidate. For a perceptive discussion of the agrarian radical critique of speculation and commercialism, see Bruce Palmer, *"Man Over Money": The Southern Populist Critique of American Capitalism* (Chapel Hill: University of North Carolina Press, 1980).

50. See the *Russellville Democrat,* 1875–1890; *Arkansas State Gazeteer and Business Directory for 1888–9* (Chicago: R. L. Polk and Co., 1888), 589–590; *Arkansas State Gazeteer and Business Directory for 1892–3* (Chicago: R. L. Polk and Co., 1892), 439–440; *Tenth Census of the United States, 1880,* Manuscript Returns, *Population Schedules,* for Russellville Town, Illinois Township, Pope County, Arkansas, and the remaining townships of Pope County, located at the National Archives, Washington, D.C., and the University of Arkansas Library, Fayetteville, Arkansas.

51. Wilson, *Bodacious Ozarks,* 171.

52. See Sheldon Hackney, ed., *Populism: The Critical Issues* (Boston: Little, Brown and Co. 1971), ix–xiii.

53. Personal Tax Books, 1883–1903, and Real Estate Tax Books, 1880–1897, for Pope County, Arkansas, located at the Arkansas History Commission, Little Rock; *Tenth Census of the United States, 1880,* Manuscript Returns, *Population Schedules,* for Russellville Town and Atkins Town, Pope County, Arkansas; *Twelfth Census of the United States, 1900,* Manuscript Returns, *Population Schedules,* for Pope County, Arkansas, located at the National Archives, Washington, D.C.; *Arkansas State Gazeteer and Business Directories for 1888–9, 1982–3, 1906–7, 1912–13* (Chicago: R. L. Polk and Co., 1888, 1892, 1906, 1912); *Russellville Democrat,* December 21, 1882.

54. *Russellville Democrat,* March 19, 1891, October 18, 1883.

55. Henningson, "Upland Farmers and Agrarian Protest," 56; see also W. Scott Morgan, *History of the Wheel and Alliance and the Impending Revolution* (St. Louis: C. B. Woodward, 1891).

56. Henningson, "Upland Farmers and Agrarian Protest," 59–101, 117, 123; *Russellville*

Democrat, October 18, March 20, June 19, August 14, 21, September 11, 1884. The Democratic party won the offices of county clerk, sheriff, surveyor, and coroner. The Brothers of Freedom won the offices of county judge, treasurer, assessor, and state representative.

Chapter 3

1. *Russellville Democrat,* April 15, 1890.

2. Ibid., August 21, 1884, June 9, 16, August 18, 1886. Jeff Davis was selected as a delegate to the county convention by the Illinois Township Democratic Convention. At the same township convention Lewis Davis was elected (as one of three members) to the Illinois Township Democratic Central Committee. For information on Bourland, see Dallas T. Herndon, ed., *Centennial History of Arkansas* (Little Rock: S. J. Clark, 1922), 2: 273–274; Fay Hempstead, *Historical Review of Arkansas: Its Commerce, Industry, and Modern Affairs* (Chicago: Lewis Pub. Co., 1911), 2: 913; L. S. Dunaway, *What a Preacher Saw Through a Key-Hole in Arkansas* (Little Rock: Parke-Harper, 1925), 33; and L. S. Dunaway, ed., *Jeff Davis, Governor and United States Senator: His Life and Speeches* (Little Rock: Democrat Printing and Litho. Co., 1913), 5–10.

3. *Russellville Democrat,* July 28, 1886, July 12, 1888; Randy Henningson, "Upland Farmers and Agrarian Protest: Northwest Arkansas and the Brothers of Freedom" (M.A. thesis, University of Arkansas, 1973), 117–163.

4. Clifton Paisley, "The Political Wheelers and Arkansas' Election of 1880," *ArkHQ* 25 (Spring 1966): 3–21; Theodore Saloutos, "The Agricultural Wheel in Arkansas," *ArkHQ* 2 (June 1943): 127–140; Francis Clark Elkins, "The Agricultural Wheel in Arkansas, 1882–1890" (Ph.D. thesis, Syracuse University, 1953); W. Scott Morgan, *History of the Wheel and Alliance and the Impending Revolution* (St. Louis: C. B. Woodward, 1891); Granville Davis, "The Granger Movement in Arkansas" (M.A. thesis, University of Illinois, 1931); C. Vann Woodward, *Origins of the New South, 1877–1913* (Baton Rouge: Louisiana State University Press, 1951), 191–192, 203; David Y. Thomas, ed., *Arkansas and Its People: A History, 1541–1930* (New York: American Historical Society, 1930), 1: 208–214; Henningson, "Upland Farmers and Agrarian Protest," 139–163; John McDaniel Wheeler, "The People's Party in Arkansas, 1891–1896" (Ph.D. thesis, Tulane University, 1975), 116–160; Joe Tolbert Segraves, "Arkansas Politics, 1874–1918" (Ph.D. thesis, University of Kentucky, 1973), 75–88; W. Scott Morgan, *The Red Light: Southern Politics and Election Methods* (Moravian Falls, N.C.: Yellow Jacket Press, 1904); J. Morgan Kousser, *The Shaping of Southern Politics: Suffrage Restriction and the Establishment of the One-Party South, 1880–1910* (New Haven: Yale University Press, 1974), 123–126; James Harris Fain, "Political Disfranchisement of the Negro in Arkansas" (M.A. thesis, University of Arkansas, 1961) 30–39; John William Graves, "Town and Country: Race Relations and Urban Development in Arkansas, 1865–1905" (Ph. D. thesis, University of Virginia, 1978), 250–261; *Biennial Report of the Secretary of State of Arkansas, 1889–1890* (Little Rock, 1890), 47–49. The official vote was: James P. Eagle (Democrat), 99,229; Charles M. Norwood (Union-Labor), 84,223. A one-legged Confederate veteran and a medical doctor, Norwood returned to the Democratic party in 1900 and was elected mayor of the town of Stamps in 1901. Arkadelphia *Southern-Standard,* May 27, 1900, April 18, 1901, March 6, 1902. For information on Norwood, see *Biographical and Historical Memoirs of Southern Arkansas* (Chicago: Goodspeed, 1890), 574–575; and Hempstead, *Historical Review of Arkansas,* 3: 1590–1591.

5. Charles Jacobson, *The Life Story of Jeff Davis: The Stormy Petrel of Arkansas Politics* (Little Rock: Parke-Harper, 1925), 15–16; *Russellville Democrat,* May 31, 1888, July 31, 1890; Dunaway, *Jeff Davis,* 85–86.

6. Jacobson, *Life Story,* 18.

7. *Russellville Democrat,* February 13, March 20, 1890. Prior to his announcement, in February and early March, Davis served as a temporary replacement for Prosecuting Attorney H. S. Carter, who was undergoing medical treatment at the University of Pennsylvania. For information on Wallace's career, see ibid., May 31, 1877, February 14, 1878, October 16, 1879,

May 18, 1882, July 28, 1886, November 9, 1887, March 15, 1888, August 16, 1888, August 29, 1889, April 17, 1890, June 12, 1890; Jacobson, *Life Story,* 18–19, 22–23; and Jerry Wallace, *An Arkansas Judge, Being a Sketch of the Life and Public Service of Judge J. C. Wallace, 1850–1927* (privately printed, 1928) (copy in the University of Arkansas Library). For information on Charles Reid, see *Biographical Directory of the American Congress, 1774–1971* (Washington: Government Printing Office, 1971), 1596; and Fay Williams, *Arkansans of the Years* (Little Rock: C. C. Allard, 1953), 3: 165–166.

    8. *Russellville Democrat,* January 28, 1886, July 12, 1888, March 20, 1890; Dunaway, *Jeff Davis,* 7; Williams, *Arkansans of the Years,* 3: 166.

    9. Dunaway, *Jeff Davis,* 4.

    10. U. S. Bureau of the Census, *Twelfth Census of the United States, 1900, Population,* vol. 1 (Washington: Government Printing Office, 1902), 530. The individual county figures are: Pope County (8.3 percent black in 1890), Conway County (39.4 percent), Johnson County (3.8 percent), and Yell County (7.6 percent). For a description of Conway County, see *Historical Reminiscences and Biographical Memoirs of Conway County, Arkansas* (Little Rock: Arkansas Historical Pub. Co., 1890).

    11. *Russellville Democrat,* January 2, May 1, 15, 1890. The Pope County branch of the Farmers' Alliance was organized at Dover in early January 1890. For information on the Farmers' Alliance, see Robert C. McMath, Jr., *Populist Vanguard: A History of the Southern Farmers' Alliance* (Chapel Hill: University of North Carolina Press, 1975); Michael Schwartz, *Radical Protest and Social Structure: The Southern Farmers' Alliance and Cotton Tenancy, 1880–1890* (New York: Academic Press, 1976); and Lawrence Goodwyn, *Democratic Promise: The Populist Moment in America* (New York: Oxford University Press, 1976).

    12. *Russellville Democrat,* May 1, 1890. Davis's statement was accompanied by a supporting affidavit signed by James L. Tucker, the owner of the store where the argument took place. Tucker's statement was as follows: "This is to certify that I was present and heard a conversation that occurred in my store a few days ago between Mr. Jeff Davis and others and among other things that were said, after speaking of the great evils growing out of the money problem of this government and the unjustness of the tariff, Mr. Davis said that the farming element ought to unite in an agricultural way for their mutual good, benefit and protection, and spoke of the good results that he had witnessed in Monroe County in 1888, where the farmers owned two fine gins in common, fine stock, & c., and said that in one place they had a neighborhood meat market, and said that this was the kind of union needed, but said that if those leaders going over the country organizing the farmers for political purposes would stay at home and have their smoke houses and corn cribs at home and not in Kansas City or St. Louis, and stay behind the plow handles and behind a mule and work harder it would be better for them and for the country."

    13. Ibid., June 12, July 3, August 28, September 11, 1890; Jacobson, *Life Story,* 18–19.

    14. Dunaway, *Jeff Davis,* 29; see also the statements by J. V. Bourland and Senator James P. Clarke, in ibid., 7, 228–229.

    15. Jacobson, *Life Story,* 21–22.

    16. *Russellville Democrat,* October 20, 1892, notes that Davis was one of several local businessmen who planned to finance the construction of a large brick office building which would house Davis's law office and several other Russellville businesses. Charles Morrow Wilson, *The Bodacious Ozarks: True Tales of the Backhills* (New York: Hastings House, 1959), 80. For discussions of the antilegal tradition in Arkansas culture, see ibid., 77, 86; Thomas, *Arkansas and Its People,* 1: 66; and Opie Read, *Opie Read in Arkansas and What He Saw There* (New York: J. S. Ogilvie Pub. Co., 1891), 50–56.

    17. Jacobson, *Life Story,* 22, 25–26; Williams, *Arkansans of the Years, 3: 166; Russellville Democrat,* July 21, September 15, 1892. In the general election Davis was opposed by an "Independent" candidate named Fowler who received only forty-one votes. Davis received 2,325 votes.

18. Thomas, *Arkansas and Its People*, 1: 230–256; Richard L. Niswonger, "Arkansas Democratic Politics, 1896–1920," (Ph.D. thesis, University of Texas, 1974), 1–41; Segraves, "Arkansas Politics, 1874–1918," 190–250; Wheeler, "The People's Party in Arkansas," 165–394.

19. *Biennial Report of the Secretary of State of Arkansas, 1889–1890*, 53–55. The official vote was: James P. Eagle (Democrat), 106,267; Napoleon B. Fizer (Union-Labor), 85,181.

20. Wheeler, "The People's Party in Arkansas," 165, 494–516; *Biennial Report of the Secretary of State of Arkansas, 1891–1892* (Little Rock, 1892), 54–56. The official vote was: William Fishback (Democrat), 90,115; James P. Carnahan (People's party), 31,117; William Whipple (Republican), 33,644; W. J. Nelson (Prohibitionist), 1,310. Carnahan was from Washington County. *Biennial Report of the Secretary of State of Arkansas, 1895–1896* (Little Rock, 1896), 71–72. The official presidential vote was: Grover Cleveland (Democrat), 87,834; Benjamin Harrison (Republican), 46,974; James Weaver (People's party), 11,831; Bidwell (Prohibitionist), 113; scattering, 1,267. Ibid., 57–59. A. W. Files, the Populist candidate for governor, received 9.9 percent of the vote in 1896. The official vote was: Dan W. Jones (Democrat), 91,114; Harmon L. Remmel (Republican), 35,836; A. W. Files (People's party), 13,990; J. W. Miller (Prohibitionist), 851. Files was a former Democrat and a former state auditor. For a biographical sketch of Files, see *Biographical and Historical Memoirs of Pulaski, Jefferson . . . and Hot Spring Counties* (Chicago: Goodspeed, 1889), 449–450.

21. Little Rock *Arkansas Gazette* (hereafter cited as *Arkansas Gazette*), November 21, 1901.

22. Nevin Neal, "Jeff Davis and the Reform Movement in Arkansas, 1898–1907" (M.A. thesis, Vanderbilt University, 1939), 1–26; Wheeler, "The People's Party in Arkansas," 316–325; see also Hattie Farmer, "Economic Background to Southern Populism," *South Atlantic Quarterly* 29 (January 1930): 77–91; Woodward, *Origins of the New South*, 264–272; Schwartz, *Radical Protest and Social Structure*, 3–88; Senate Committee on Agriculture and Forestry, *Report on the Condition of Cotton Growers in the United States* (53rd Congress, 3d Session, 1895, S. Rept. 986); *Report of the Industrial Commission on Agriculture and Agricultural Labor*, vol. 10 (57th Congress, 1st Session, 1901, H. R. Documents 179); "Plantations in the South" *Thirteenth Census of the United States, 1910, Agriculture* (Washington: Government Printing Office,, 1913); 877–889; and Roger L. Ransom and Richard Sutch, *One Kind of Freedom: The Economic Consequences of Emancipation* (Cambridge: Cambridge University Press, 1977), esp. Appendix F.

23. *Arkansas Gazette*, June 23, July 22, 1892; see also Thomas, *Arkansas and Its People*, 1: 241; James Edgar Howard, "Populism in Arkansas" (M.A. thesis, George Peabody College for Teachers, 1931), 49; Richard B. Dixon, "Press Opinion Toward the Populist Party in Arkansas, 1890–1896" (M.A. thesis, University of Arkansas, 1953); Graves, "Town and Country," 351–382; Wheeler, "The People's Party in Arkansas," 168, 501.

24. Howard, "Populism in Arkansas," 46–109. In 1896 there was Populist-Republican fusion in ten counties; see ibid., 103. See also Wheeler, "The People's Party in Arkansas," 502 and passim.

25. Thomas, *Arkansas and Its People*, 1: 165–266, 355–373; Fletcher, *Arkansas*, 265–286; Niswonger, "Arkansas Democratic Politics," 1–123; Segraves, "Arkansas Politics, 1874–1918," 232–276; Wheeler, "The People's Party in Arkansas," 498–500. For information on Fishback's career, see Thomas, *Arkansas and Its People*, 3: 89; Timothy P. Donovan and Willard B. Gatewood, Jr., ed., *The Governors of Arkansas: Essays in Political Biography* (Fayetteville: University of Arkansas Press, 1981), 91–96; *History of Benton, Washington, Carroll, Madison, Crawford, Franklin, and Sebastian Counties, Arkansas* (Chicago: Goodspeed, 1889), 1312–1313; and John Gould Fletcher, *Arkansas* (Chapel Hill: University of North Carolina Press, 1947), 280.

26. Morgan, *The Red Light*; Paisley, "The Political Wheelers and Arkansas' Election," 3–21; Thomas, *Arkansas and Its People*, 1: 198–229; Kousser, *The Shaping of Southern Politics*, 123–130; John William Graves, "The Arkansas Negro and Segregation, 1890–1903" (M.A. thesis, University of Arkansas, 1967), 91–104; Fain, "Political Disfranchisement of the Negro in Arkansas," 19–40.

27. Graves, "The Arkansas Negro and Segregation," 33–34, 58–62.

28. Kousser, *The Shaping of Southern Politics*, 130.

29. Ibid., 123–129; Graves, "Town and Country," 292–319, 337–339; Graves, "The Arkansas Negro and Segregation," 91–104; Fain, "Political Disfranchisement of the Negro in Arkansas," 37–49; *Arkansas Gazette*, January 20–21, February 26, March 1, 1891; Arkansas General Assembly, *Acts of Arkansas, 1891* (Little Rock, 1891), 33–47; *Biennial Report of the Secretary of State of Arkansas, 1891–1892*, 57–59; Kousser, *The Shaping of Southern Politics*, 129; Arkansas General Assembly, *Acts of Arkansas, 1895* (Little Rock, 1895), 55–57, 179–180.

30. Kousser, *The Shaping of Southern Politics*, 123–130. The voter turnout levels presented here have been computed by expressing the number of total votes cast in an election as a percentage of the potential electorate, with the potential electorate being defined as the number of males of voting age reported by the federal census. Intercensus estimates have been made for elections that did not coincide with the decennial census. Unless short-term population growth fluctuated wildly during the period of analysis, which was not the case in late nineteenth and early twentieth-century Arkansas, this procedure can produce relatively accurate estimates of the size of the potential electorate at any given time, for particular counties, for selected groups of counties, or for the state as a whole.

31. *Arkansas Gazette*, June 30, September 9, 1892; Graves, "The Arkansas Negro and Segregation," 48, 95–97; Kousser, *The Shaping of Southern Politics*, 126–130; Fain, "Political Disfranchisement of the Negro in Arkansas," 40, 43; Democratic leaders seldom admitted that they looked forward to the disfranchisement of radical lower-class whites. An exception was the editor of the *Pine Bluff Commercial*, September 4, 1894: "The ignorant and uneducated whites and blacks cannot vote the ticket, which ought to be, and is a blessing to the state, for ignorance should never rule a great commonwealth like Arkansas." See also Graves, "Town and Country," 381–382; and Segraves, "Arkansas Politics, 1874–1918," 215–218.

32. *Biennial Report of the Secretary of Arkansas, 1903–1904* (Little Rock, 1905), 449–450. The official vote was: Alton B. Parker (Democrat), 64,434; Theodore Roosevelt (Republican), 46,860; Eugene V. Debs (Socialist), 1,816; Thomas E. Watson (People's party), 2,318; Swallow (Prohibitionist), 993.

33. The Democratic press worked hard to bring ex-Populists into the Democratic party, and during the late 1890s Democratic editors routinely claimed that the Democratic party had absorbed most of the old Populist coalition. *Arkansas Gazette*, September 8, 13, December 8, 1898, May 24, July 11, 29, 1900; Arkadelphia *Southern-Standard*, May 19, 1904; Thomas, *Arkansas and Its People*, 1: 258. For a description of what happened to the Populists in another Southern state, see Sheldon Hackney, *Populism to Progressivism in Alabama* (Princeton: Princeton University Press, 1969), 108–121.

34. *Morgan's Buzz-Saw* (Hardy, Ark.), March 1900.

35. Fain, "Political Disfranchisement of the Negro in Arkansas," 43; Graves, "The Arkansas Negro and Segregation," 48, 91–100; Kousser, *The Shaping of Southern Politics*, 127, 129; Woodward, *Origins of the New South*, 275; see also Jack Temple Kirby, *Darkness at the Dawning: Race and Reform in the Progressive South* (Philadelphia: J. B. Lippincott, 1972).

Chapter 4

1. L. S. Dunaway, ed., *Jeff Davis, Governor and United States Senator: His Life and Speeches* (Little Rock: Democrat Printing and Litho. Co., 1913), 85.

2. Charles Jacobson, *The Life Story of Jeff Davis: The Stormy Petrel of Arkansas Politics* (Little Rock: Parke-Harper, 1925), 19, 22–25; Jerry Wallace, *An Arkansas Judge, Being a Sketch of the Life and Public Service of Judge J. G. Wallace, 1850–1927* (privately printed, 1928) (copy in the University of Arkansas Library), 38, 49; Little Rock *Arkansas Gazette* (hereafter cited as *Arkansas Gazette*), March 16, 1889. Wallace opposed Terry for a second time in 1898, but withdrew before the campaign was completed. For information on William L. Terry, see *Biographical Directory of the American Congress, 1774–1971* (Washington: Government Printing Office, 1971), 1801.

3. Jacobson, *Life Story*, 25–26; Fay Williams, *Arkansans of the Years* (Little Rock: C. C. Allard, 1953), 3: 166.

4. Jacobson, *Life Story*, 25–27; *Russellville Democrat*, February 1896.

5. Jacobson, *Life Story*, 16; *Russellville Democrat*, July–October, 1896.

6. Jacobson, *Life Story*, 16.

7. Ibid., 16–17; Dunaway, *Jeff Davis*, 85.

8. Jacobson, *Life Story*, 17; John Gould Fletcher, *Arkansas* (Chapel Hill: University of North Carolina Press, 1947), 289–296; David Y. Thomas, ed., *Arkansas and Its People: A History, 1541–1930* (New York: American Historical Society, 1930), 1: 201, 254–266; James Edgar Howard, "Populism in Arkansas" (M.A. thesis, George Peabody College for Teachers, 1931), 123; John McDaniel Wheeler, "The People's Party in Arkansas, 1891–1896" (Ph.D. thesis, Tulane University, 1975), 471–487; *Arkansas Gazette*, September 7–8, July 29, 1900; Arkadelphia *Southern-Standard*, May 12, 1899; Fay Hempstead, *Historical Review of Arkansas: Its Commerce, Industry, and Modern Affairs* (Chicago: Lewis Pub. Co., 1911), 2: 836–838; Richard L. Niswonger, "Arkansas Democratic Politics, 1896–1920" (Ph.D. thesis, University of Texas, 1974), 54–59, 92–123; Timothy P. Donovan and Willard B. Gatewood, Jr., eds., *The Governors of Arkansas: Essays in Political Biography* (Fayetteville: University of Arkansas Press, 1981), 103–110; Joe Tolbert Segraves, "Arkansas Politics, 1874–1918" (Ph.D. thesis, University of Kentucky, 1973), 268–270, 275–277.

9. Jacobson, *Life Story*, 31; Nevin Neal, "Jeff Davis and the Reform Movement in Arkansas, 1898–1907" (M.A. thesis, Vanderbilt University, 1939), 32–33.

10. *Arkansas Gazette* editorial reprinted in the *Russellville Democrat*, November 18, 1897; *Atkins Chronicle*, January 21, 1898; Neal, "Jeff Davis and the Reform Movement in Arkansas," 33.

11. Jacobson, *Life Story*, 31–34; *Arkansas Gazette*, April 6–20, June 22, 1898; James Harris Fain, "Political Disfranchisement of the Negro in Arkansas" (M.A. thesis, University of Arkansas, 1961) 56–63.

12. *Arkansas Gazette*, March 27, April 6, 1898; Jacobson, *Life Story*, 34, 37; Fletcher, *Arkansas*, 289–290.

13. Fletcher, *Arkansas*, 289–290; *Arkansas Gazette*, April 8–9, June 22, 1898; Jacobson, *Life Story*, 31–35.

14. *Arkansas Gazette*, April 14, 1898; Jacobson, *Life Story*, 32–34. The four counties were Stone, Lincoln, Madison, and Howard. Dunaway, *Jeff Davis*, 230.

15. *Arkansas Gazette*, April 8–9, 1898; Jacobson, *Life Story*, 34–35; Dunaway, *Jeff Davis*, 230; Fletcher, *Arkansas*, 290.

16. Jacobson, *Life Story*, 37; *Arkansas Gazette*, April 8–May 31, June 17, 1898. Davis's popularity in several counties in southeast Arkansas probably stemmed from memories of his political barnstorming in the area during the state and national campaigns of 1888 and 1890. Cleveland County, for example, was the scene of Davis's most celebrated speeches of 1888. *Russellville Democrat*, July 31, 1890.

17. *Arkansas Gazette*, June 17, 22, 1898, Jacobson, *Life Story*, 35–36.

18. *Arkansas Gazette*, June 22, 1898.

19. *Biennial Report of the Secretary of State of Arkansas, 1899–1900* (Little Rock, 1900), 407–412; Arkadelphia *Southern-Standard*, September 23, 1898; Dallas T. Herndon, ed., *Centennial History of Arkansas* (Little Rock: S. J. Clark, 1922), 1: 353–354; *Arkansas Gazette*, July 4–September 4, 1898. The official vote for attorney general was: Davis, 78,103; Henley, 30, 119. Among members of the state Democratic ticket, the vote ranged from 75,363 to 80,335.

20. Lawrence Goodwyn, *Democratic Promise: The Populist Moment in America* (New York: Oxford University Press, 1976), xiv–xxi, 259–264, 388–401, 582–592; C. Vann Woodward, *Origins of the New South, 1877–1913* (Baton Rouge: Louisiana State University Press, 1951), 264–290: C. Vann Woodward, *Tom Watson: Agrarian Rebel* (New York: Macmillan, 1938), 278–331; Dewey W. Grantham, Jr., *The Democratic South* (New York: W. W. Norton, 1965), 33–47; John D. Hicks, *The Populist Revolt: A History of the Farmers' Alliance and the People's Party* (Minneapolis:

University of Minnesota Press, 1931), 238–423; Robert Durden, *The Climax of Populism: The Election of 1896* (Lexington: University of Kentucky Press, 1966); R. Hal Williams, *Years of Decision: American Politics in the 1890s* (New York: John Wiley and Sons, 1978), 97–127; see also Samuel McSeveney, *The Politics of Depression: Political Behavior in the Northeast, 1893–1896* (New York: Oxford University Press, 1973); and Richard J. Jensen, *The Winning of the Midwest: Social and Political Conflict, 1888–1896* (Chicago: University of Chicago Press, 1971); on Arkansas, see Thomas, *Arkansas and Its People,* 1: 230–262.

21. Niswonger, "Arkansas Democratic Politics," 25, 34, 46–48, 51–53, 60–61, 65–75; Thomas, *Arkansas and Its People,* 1: 249, 255, 257; *Arkansas Gazette,* June 28–29, 1894, August 8, 17, 22, September 4, 1895.

22. *Arkansas Gazette,* February 4, 1896; Niswonger, "Arkansas Democratic Politics," 46, 51, 56.

23. *Arkansas Gazette,* May 12, 16, 18, 20, 1896; *Fort Smith Elevator,* February 21, 1896; Niswonger, "Arkansas Democratic Politics," 49, 59. The vote in Pulaski County was 3,059 in favor of free-silver and 439 against. *Helena Weekly World,* March 25, 1896 The *World* poll involved 108 respondents: 87 newspapers supported free silver, while 19 supported the gold standard. Fifty-five other newspapers failed to respond. The editor of the *World* was a staunch supporter of the gold standard. Fred W. Allsop, *History of the Arkansas Press for a Hundred Years and More* (Little Rock: Parke-Harper, 1922), 626–627; and Fred W. Allsopp, *Little Adventures in Newspaperdom* (Little Rock: Parke-Harper, 1922), 133–138.

24. Niswonger, "Arkansas Democratic Politics," 10–12, 45, 114–118, 158–159; Thomas, *Arkansas and Its People,* 1: 260–262; *Arkansas Gazette,* November 18, 24, December 16, 1896; Fletcher, *Arkansas,* 287–288.

25. Niswonger, "Arkansas Democratic Politics," 10–12, 154–164; Neal, "Jeff Davis and the Reform Movement in Arkansas," 22; *Arkansas Gazette,* December 16, 1896, February 5–26, 1897.

26. *Arkansas Gazette,* December 30, 1896, February 4, July 16–18, 1897. The Bush Bill was sponsored by Representative James O. A. Bush, a Populist legislator from Nevada County. Earlier in the decade, Bush had served as a member of the National Committee of the People's Party. See *Biennial Report of the Secretary of State of Arkansas, 1897–1898* (Little Rock, 1898), 283; Howard, "Populism in Arkansas," 46, 48; *Journal of the House of Representatives of Arkansas, 1897, Including Extraordinary Session, April 26–June 16, 1897* (Little Rock, 1897), 49 (regular session), 99–100 (extraordinary session); Dallas T. Herndon, *Outline of Executive and Legislative History of Arkansas* (Fort Smith: Arkansas History Commission, 1922), 143–145. The Bush Bill passed the legislature during the 1897 extraordinary session, but it was later repealed by the 1899 legislature.

27. *Arkansas Gazette,* August 15–November 15, 1896; Niswonger, "Arkansas Democratic Politics," 25, 51, 90, 114; Jacobson, *Life Story,* 17, 43; Fletcher, *Arkansas,* 287–289.

28. These conclusions are based on an extensive impressionistic survey of local Democratic politics in nineteen Arkansas counties: Clark, Crawford, Drew, Hot Spring, Howard, Jackson, Jefferson, Marion, Mississippi, Nevada, Phillips, Poinsett, Polk, Pope, Pulaski, St. Francis, Sebastian, Sharp, and Washington. The accounts of the proceedings of Democratic county and township conventions for the period 1896–1900 are especially illuminating. See the Arkadelphia *Southern-Standard, Gurdon Times, Van Buren Weekly Argus, Drew County Advance,* Monticello *Monticellonian,* Malvern *Arkansaw Times, Nashville News, Pine Bluff Commercial, Pine Bluff Daily Graphic, Pine Bluff Weekly Press-Eagle,* Yellville *Mountain Echo, Osceola Times, Nevada County Picayune, Helena Weekly World,* Harrisburg *Modern News, Mena Weekly Star, Russellville Democrat,* Little Rock *Arkansas Democrat,* Little Rock *Arkansas Gazette, Forrest City Times,* Fort Smith *Elevator,* Hardy *Morgan's Buzz-Saw, Sharp County Record, Fayetteville Democrat,* and *Springdale News.*

29. Goodwyn, *Democratic Promise,* xiv–xxi, 181–182, 201–211, 338–401, 582–592.

30. See Arthur S. Link, "The Progressive Movement in the South, 1870–1914," *North Carolina Historical Review* 23 (April 1946): 172–195; Woodward, *Origins of the New South,* 369–396; Grantham, *Democratic South,* 51–66; George Brown Tindall, "Business Progressivism:

Southern Politics in the Twenties," *South Atlantic Quarterly* 62 (Winter 1963): 92–106; Jack Temple Kirby, *Darkness at the Dawning: Race and Reform in the Progressive South* (Philadelphia: J. B. Lippincott, 1972), passim; Sheldon Hackney, *Populism to Progressivism in Alabama* (Princeton: Princeton University Press, 1969), 122–146, 230–232; and Dewey W. Grantham, Jr., *Hoke Smith and the Politics of the New South* (Baton Rouge: Louisiana State University Press, 1958), passim. For a comprehensive survey of Southern progressivism, see Grantham, "The Contours of Southern Progressivism," *American Historical Review* 86 (December 1981): 1035–1059.

31. On the general themes of metropolitanization and conflict between localism and cosmopolitanism, see Robert H. Wiebe, *The Search for Order, 1877–1920* (New York: Hill and Wang, 1967), and Wiebe, *The Segmented Society: An Introduction to the Meaning of America* (New York: Oxford University Press, 1975).

32. Herndon, *Centennial History of Arkansas*, 2: 12, 15; Herndon, *Outline of Executive and Legislative History*, 136–137; Donovan and Gatewood, *The Governors of Arkansas*, 97–102; Jacobson, *Life Story*, 182–183; Fletcher, *Arkansas*, 292; Thomas, *Arkansas and Its People*, 1: 251–257, 261; *Arkansas Gazette*, June 12–13, 1897. The Smith Bill passed the legislature during the 1897 extraordinary session. The 1897 legislature also approved a 40,000-acre grant to the Hamburg and Texarkana Railroad. See Neal, "Jeff Davis and the Reform Movement in Arkansas," 21–22: and Niswonger, "Arkansas Democratic Politics," 66, 119, 168.

33. *Arkansas Gazette*, September 23, 1896; Niswonger, "Arkansas Democratic Politics," 45, 54–55, 123, 137–138, 166–167; William Orestes Penrose, "Political Ideas in Arkansas, 1880–1907" (M.A. thesis, University of Arkansas, 1945), 29, 62; *Morgan's Buzz-Saw* (Hardy, Ark.), September 1899; Hempstead, *Historical Review of Arkansas*, 2: 836–838; Herndon, *Outline of Executive and Legislative History*, 141–142, 144–145; Thomas, *Arkansas and Its People*, 1: 257–267; Donovan and Gatewood, *The Governors of Arkansas*, 103–110.

34. Thomas, *Arkansas and Its People*, 1: 201; Hempstead, *Historical Review of Arkansas*, 2: 836–838; Niswonger, "Arkansas Democratic Politics," 54–55, 123, 137–138, 175: Fletcher, *Arkansas*, 290; Herndon, *Outline of Executive and Legislative History*, 142, notes that Jones "was buried in a Confederate uniform, to which he had pinned an American flag a short time before his death."

35. Farrar Newberry, *James K. Jones: The Plumed Knight of Arkansas* (Little Rock: Siftings-Herald Printing Co., 1913); Niswonger, "Arkansas Democratic Politics," 37, 59–62, 68–69, 79–80; Penrose, "Political Ideas in Arkansas," 31; Woodward, *Origins of the New South*, 284–286; Goodwyn, *Democratic Promise*, 484–489, 495–496; Durden, *Climax of Populism*, 23–44; *Arkansas Gazette*, July 23–30, 1896.

36. Donovan and Gatewood, *The Governors of Arkansas*, 73–78; Paige E. Mulhollan, "The Public Career of James H. Berry" (M.A. thesis, University of Arkansas, 1962), 1–4, 12, 59, 65, 159–164; Thomas, *Arkansas and Its People*, 1: 186–194, 198–200, 253; Jacobson, *Life Story*, 120; James H. Berry, *An Autobiography of Senator James H. Berry* (Bentonville: Democrat Print, 1913), 1–24. Berry replaced Senator Augustus Garland in March 1885, after Garland accepted a position (attorney general) in President Grover Cleveland's cabinet. Arthur Wallace Dunn, quoted in Niswonger, "Arkansas Democratic Politics," 64–65.

37. *Biennial Report of the Secretary of State of Arkansas, 1889–1900*, 294–297, 407–409; Thomas, *Arkansas and Its People*, 1: 264; *Biennial Report of the Secretary of State of Arkansas, 1897–1898*, 281–284; Wheeler, "The People's Party in Arkansas," 471–485; Howard, "Populism in Arkansas," 106–123; Niswonger, "Arkansas Democratic Politics," 106–112; *Morgan's Buzz-Saw*, October 1898–October 1900; *Arkansas Gazette*, September 7, 8, 13, December 8, 1898, February 18, March 6, May 24, 27, July 25, 1900, June 10, November 21, 1901; Arkadelphia *Southern-Standard*, June 7, 28, July 8, 1900, April 18, 1901, March 6, July 17, 24, 1902, November 5, 1903, May 19, 1904.

38. *Nevada County Picayune* quoted in the *Arkansas Gazette*, September 13, 1898.

39. *Arkansas Gazette*, September 4, 1898, contains the crop report. Ibid., October 8, 12, 1898, April 16, July–December 1899; see also Woodward, *Origins of the New South*, 406–407; and U.S.

Department of Agriculture, Agricultural Marketing Service, "Cotton and Cottonseed: Acreage, Yield, Production, Disposition, Price, Value; by States, 1866–1952," *USDA Statistical Bulletin*, Number 164 (Washington: Government Printing Office, 1955).

40. *Arkansas Gazette*, October 7, 1899.

41. Ibid., January 5, March 5, August 3, 4, October 22, November 3, 30, December 5, 1899, September 12, 1902; Yellville *Mountain Echo*, 1899; *PAHA* 1 (1906): 196.

42. Thomas, *Arkansas and Its People*, 2: 413–414; and Corliss Colby Curry, "A History of the Timber Industry in Ashley, Bradley, and Drew Counties, Arkansas" (M.A. thesis, Univerity of Arkansas, 1954), 24–47; *Arkansas Gazette*, February 26, April 29–30, May 17, 25, 1899, February 18, 1900, September 7, 1902. The "Long Strike," as it was called in the Arkansas coal county, lasted for more than two years. The Arkansas coal industry did not begin to boom until the fall of 1902, when a strike shut down the Pennsylvania coal fields.

43. *Arkansas Gazette*, September 8, 16, 1900, June 26, 1901, October 28–29, November 6, 1902, January 29, May 6, June 9, 1903; Arkadelphia *Southern-Standard*, November 6, 1902; Charles Morrow Wilson, *The Bodacious Ozarks: True Tales of the Backhills* (New York: Hastings House, 1959), 177; Woodward, *Origins of the New South*, 406–408.

44. The editorial pages of newspapers such as the *Arkansas Gazette*, Arkadelphia *Southern-Standard*, *Fort Smith Elevator*, Fayetteville *Arkansas Sentinel*, and the *Pine Bluff Commercial* are good indices of this change. On the Development Association, see *Arkansas Gazette*, February–March, June 13, 1899; *Morgan's Buzz-Saw*, April 1, 1899; see also Niswonger, "Arkansas Democratic Politics," 154–174.

45. *Charleston Reporter*, quoted in the *Arkansas Gazette*, March 2, 1898; *Rison Bazoo*, quoted in the *Arkansas Gazette*, April 5, 1898; see also Niswonger, "Arkansas Democratic Politics," 159–160. In a widely publicized speech delivered at the Arkansas Commercial Convention in February 1897, Samuel Fordyce, a prominent Arkansas railroad entrepreneur, called for "more business and less politics."

46. *Arkansas Gazette*, October 10, 1899. See also ibid., May 11, 1896–December 31, 1899; Niswonger, "Arkansas Democratic Politics," 48–50; and Allsopp, *Little Adventures in Newspaperdom*, 133–138.

47. Niswonger, "Arkansas Democratic Politics," 3, 48–49; Little Rock *Arkansas Democrat*, May 1898–June 1899.

48. See Wiebe, *Search for Order*, 85–87.

49. Fletcher, *Arkansas*, 288.

Chapter 5

1. Little Rock *Arkansas Gazette* (hereafter cited as *Arkansas Gazette*), April 23, 1899.

2. Fay Williams, *Arkansans of the Years* (Little Rock: C. C. Allard, 1953), 3: 163–172; Fay Hempstead, *Historical Review of Arkansas: Its Commerce, Industry, and Modern Affairs* (Chicago: Lewis Pub. Co., 1911), 2: 702–704; *Arkansas Gazette*, July 15, 1957; Little Rock *Arkansas Democrat*, July 17, 1957; Fayetteville *Arkansas Sentinel*, January 22, 1901; see also Raymond Arsenault, "Charles Jacobson of Arkansas: A Jewish Politician in the Land of the Razorbacks, 1891–1915," in Nathan M. Kaganoff and Melvin I. Urofsky, eds., *Turn to the South: Essays on Southern Jewry* (Charlottesville: University of Virginia Press, 1979), 55–75.

3. Williams, *Arkansans of the Years*, 3: 166.

4. Ibid.; *Arkansas Gazette*, June 17, 1898; Hempstead, *Historical Review of Arkansas*, 2: 703. The primary vote in Conway County for attorney general was: Davis 1,222, Baker 198, Watson 153, and Hicks 130.

5. Charles Jacobson, *The Life Story of Jeff Davis: The Stormy Petrel of Arkansas Politics* (Little Rock: Parke-Harper, 1925), 19–20, 28, 36, 73, 120–123, 130–136, 155, 159, 163–164, 172, 179–180; Williams, *Arkansans of the Years*, 3: 167–169; L. S. Dunaway, ed., *Jeff Davis, Governor and United States Senator: His Life and Speeches* (Little Rock: Democrat Printing and Litho. Co., 1913), 76.

6. Jacobson, *Life Story* 157; Williams, *Arkansans of the Years*, 3: 166; Hempstead, *Historical Review of Arkansas*, 2: 703; *Arkansas Gazette*, Janury 13, 1900, January 10, 1901.

7. *Arkansas Gazette*, April 6, June 24, 1898, Richard L. Niswonger, "Arkansas Democratic Politics, 1896–1920" (Ph.D. thesis, University of Texas, 1974), 184.

8. *Arkansas Gazette*, June 14–17, 1897, January 6–April 18, 1899; *Journal of the House of Representatives of Arkansas Including Extraordinary Session, April 26–June 16, 1897* (Little Rock, 1897); David Y. Thomas, ed., *Arkansas and Its People: A History, 1541–1930* (New York: American Historical Society, 1930), 1: 259–265; Dallas T. Herndon, *Outline of Executive and Legislative History of Arkansas* (Fort Smith: Arkansas History Commission, 1922), 142–147; Niswonger, "Arkansas Democratic Politics," 155; Nevin Neal, "Jeff Davis and the Reform Movement in Arkansas, 1898–1907" (M.A. thesis, Vanderbilt University, 1939), 21–22.

9. Herndon, *Outline of Executive and Legislature History*, 145; *Biennial Report of the Secretary of State of Arkansas, 1897–1898* (Little Rock, 1898), 281–284; *Biennial Report of the Secretary of State of Arkansas, 1899–1900* (Little Rock, 1900), 295–297. Twenty-one of the 100 members of the 1899 House had served in the 1897 legislature. In the 1899 senate, 15 (16 if W. P. Grace, a senator who died during his term of office, is included) of 32 senators had served in the 1897 senate, and 4 others had been members of the 1897 house. *Arkansas Gazette*, January 7, 1899.

10. *Journal of the Senate of Arkansas, 1899* (Little Rock, 1899), 66–67, 165, 201; *Arkansas Gazette*, January 14, February 25, March 1, 22, 31, April 8, 1899. The first bill, sponsored by Representative John I. Alley of Polk County, never got out of committee. Arkadelphia *Southern-Standard*, April 28, 1899; Neal, "Jeff Davis and the Reform Movement in Arkansas," 36–37. The cash surrender bill, sponsored by Senator W. H. Collins of Sevier County, passed the senate but not the house. The railroad commission bill was defeated in the house by a vote of 12 to 65. The badge bill, sponsored by Senator John D. Shackleford of Pulaski County, passed the senate but not the house.

11. *Arkansas Gazette*, February 2, 17, March 12, 26, April 1–2, 11–13, 23, 1899; *Journal of the Senate of Arkansas, 1899*, 131, 150; Jacobson, *Life Story* 44–45, 143–144; Neal, "Jeff Davis and the Reform Movement in Arkansas," 25–26, 37ff; Herndon, *Outline of Executive and Legislative History*, 144; Arkansas General Assembly, *Acts of Arkansas, 1897* (Little Rock, 1897), Act XLVI, 60–62; Arkansas General Assembly, *Acts of Arkansas, 1899* (Little Rock, 1899), Act XLI, 50–51; Niswonger, "Arkansas Democratic Politics," 176.

12. Dallas T. Herndon, ed., *Centennial History of Arkansas* (Little Rock: S. J. Clark, 1922), 3: 226–231; *Biennial Report of the Secretary of State of Arkansas, 1899–1900*, 295; *Arkansas Gazette*, April 18, 1899. For a biographical sketch of Henry Massey Rector, see Fay Hempstead, *A Pictorial History of Arkansas from Earliest Times to the Year 1890* (St Louis: N. D. Thompson, 1890), 404–411; and Timothy P. Donovan and Willard B. Gatewood, Jr., eds., *The Governors of Arkansas: Essays in Political Biography* (Fayetteville: University of Arkansas Press, 1981), 30–32.

13. *Arkansas Gazette*, September 25, 1898, February 4, 17, April 2, 8, July 23, 1899; John Gould Fletcher, *Arkansas* (Chapel Hill: University of North Carolina, 1947), 290–291; Neal, "Jeff Davis and the Reform Movement in Arkansas," 37; Niswonger, "Arkansas Democratic Politics," 175; *Journal of the Senate of Arkansas, 1899*, 54–55, 152–153, 263, 297.

14. *Arkansas Gazette*, March 1, April 2, 1899.

15. Ibid., March 3, 1899.

16. Ibid., August 2, 1898, March 7, 30, July 23, 1899; *Acts of Arkansas, 1899*, Act XLI, 50–51; Fletcher, *Arkansas*, 290–291; *Journal of the House of Representatives of Arkansas, 1899*, 38; Niswonger, "Arkansas Democratic Politics," 45, 54, 123, 137–138, 155, 175; William Orestes Penrose, "Political Ideas in Arkansas, 1880–1907" (M.A. thesis, University of Arkansas, 1945), 29, 62. Jones ran unsuccessfully for the United States Senate in 1900 against the incumbent Senator James H. Berry. Paige E. Mulhollan, "The Public Career of James H. Berry" (M.A. thesis, University of Arkansas, 1962), 160–161.

17. Jacobson, *Life Story*, 44–45; *Arkansas Gazette*, March 7, 25, April 2, 11, 1899.

18. *Arkansas Gazette*, March 25, 26, April 1, 1899; Fletcher, *Arkansas*, 291.

19. *Arkansas Gazette,* March 26, April 11, 13, 1899; Neal, "Jeff Davis and the Reform Movement in Arkansas," 40.

20. *Arkansas Gazette,* March 29–April 2, 8, 11–14, 23, July 5, 23, 1899; Arkadelphia *Southern-Standard,* April 23, 1899.

21. *Arkansas Gazette,* March 26–28, 31, April 7, 1899. Bryan also visited Little Rock as a guest of the legislature in March 1897. Thomas, *Arkansas and Its People,* 1: 260; *Journal of the House of Representatives of Arkansas, 1897,* 169. The senate bill was sponsored by Senator Smith Martin of Jefferson County.

22. *Arkansas Gazette,* April 1, 1899. Two test suits were filed against each company.

23. Ibid., April 1–2, 11–13, 1899; *Pine Bluff Commercial,* April 9, 16, 1899; *Helena Weekly World,* April 9, 16, 1899.

24. The editors of the *Conway Democrat* and the *Helena Weekly World,* quoted in *Arkansas Gazette,* April 11, 1899.

25. *Arkansas Gazette,* April 2, July 16, 1899; Fletcher, *Arkansas,* 292; Jacobson, *Life Story,* 59; Rupert B. Vance, "A Karl Marx for Hill Billies," *Social Forces* 9 (December 1930): 180; Dunaway, *Jeff Davis,* 52, 54.

26. Davis filed fourteen suits, each of which called for a fine of $10,000. In the senate an amendment was tabled by a vote of 16–8; in the house the vote was 52–27. *Arkansas Gazette,* April 8, 11, 13, July 5, 16, 1899; Thomas, *Arkansas and Its People,* 1: 265; Fletcher, *Arkansas,* 292.

27. *Arkansas Gazette,* April 13, 1899.

28. Ibid., April 13, July 16, 1899; Fletcher, *Arkansas,* 292–293; Niswonger, "Arkansas Democratic Politics," 177.

29. *Arkansas Gazette,* April 13, 14, 16, 1899. The resolution to censure Wood passed the house by a vote of 43–33. However, two days later, at the request of Representative Charles J. Parker of Ouachita County, the sponsor of the resolution, the vote of censure was officially expunged from the record.

30. Ibid., April 14, 1899. Davis used the phrase "stand by your guns" in his speech at Glenwood Park. Jacobson, *Life Story,* 46–47, notes that "this cane became memorable in his subsequent campaigns by being used as an offensive and defensive weapon."

31. *Arkansas Gazette,* April 21, 1899; see also ibid., April 25, 1899; Fletcher, *Arkansas,* 291–292; and Jacobson, *Life Story,* 47.

32. *Arkansas Gazette,* March 26, April 2, 11–13, 22–23, 1899.

33. Ibid., April 28, 30, 1899. The state law in question (Sandel's and Hill's Digest #7200) was an obscure procedural law. Ibid., April 22, 30, 1899. Following a suggestion made by ex-Governor James P. Clarke on April 12, the Arkansas State Bankers' Association had petitioned Governor Jones on April 21 to grant a temporary suspension of the daily penalties. The discovery of the law noted above made such action unnecessary.

34. Ibid., April 18, May 9, 1899; Jacobson, *Life Story,* 47. The debate over the desirability of the appropriation began on April 17. Fletcher, *Arkansas,* 293, argues that $5,000 was an inadequate appropriation which indicated that the legislature was beginning to lose enthusiasm for Davis's controversial interpretation of the Rector Act. On Norwood and Hart, see *Arkansas Gazette,* February 4, 1902; Hal L. Norwood, *"Just a Book," Reminiscent of Changes in Customs, Interesting Trials and Other Events* (Mena, Ark.: Mena Star, 1938); Herndon, *Centennial History of Arkansas,* 2: 589–590; Hempstead, *Historical Review of Arkansas,* 2: 631–633; and Alexis Schwitalia, *Who's Who in Little Rock, 1921* (Little Rock: New Era Press, 1921), 71.

35. Fletcher, *Arkansas,* 293, 295; Jacobson, *Life Story,* 56; *Arkansas Gazette,* July 16, 1899.

36. *Arkansas Gazette,* May 28, July 6, 1899; Niswonger, "Arkansas Democratic Politics," 177; see *In the Supreme Court of Arkansas, The State of Arkansas v. Aetna Fire Insurance Co., and The State of Arkansas v. Lancashire Fire Insurance Co., Abstract and Argument for Appellant* in "Jeff Davis Microfilm," Film 121, at the University of Arkansas Library, Fayetteville, Arkansas; and *State v. Lancashire Fire Insurance Company,* 66, *Arkansas Reports,* 466–480 (1899); *State v. Aetna Fire Insurance Company,* 66, *Arkansas Reports,* 480–485 (1899).

37. *Arkansas Gazette,* July 6, 19, 21, August 26–27, September 19–20, 1899; Little Rock *Arkansas Democrat,* May 29–July 6, 1899; Niswonger, "Arkansas Democratic Politics," 177; Vance, "A Karl Marx for Hill Billies," 183.

38. Jacobson, *Life Story,* 43–44.

39. John Alfred Treon, "The Building of the Arkansas State Capitol, 1899–1915" (M.A. thesis, University of Arkansas, 1964); Treon, "Politics and Concrete: The Building of the Arkansas State Capitol, 1899–1917," *ArkHQ* 31 (Summer 1972): 99–149; George Washington Donaghey, *Building a State Capitol* (Little Rock: Parke-Harper, 1937); Jacobson, *Life Story,* 50–53; *Journal of the House of Representatives of Arkansas, 1901* (Little Rock, 1901), 47–49; *Journal of the Senate of Arkansas, 1903* (Little Rock, 1903), 35–38; *Arkansas Gazette,* March 21, April 15–18, 1899.

40. Treon, "The Building of the Arkansas State Capitol," 1–10, 49–52; Fletcher, *Arkansas,* 92, 109. The building was completed in 1840; Tom W. Campbell, *Arkansas Lawyer, Reminiscences of a Lifetime* (Little Rock: Pioneer Pub. Co., 1952), 71; *Arkansas Gazette,* February 3, July 5, 1899.

41. *Arkansas Gazette,* December 24, 1898, February 2, 10, July 5, 1899, November 17, 23, 27–28, 1900, May 3, 1901.

42. Ibid., November 17, 23, 1900.

43. Treon, "The Building of the Arkansas State Capitol," 1–3; Hiram U. Ford, "A History of the Arkansas Penitentiary to 1900" (M.A. thesis, University of Arkansas, 1936), 86; *Arkansas Gazette,* January 12, 1893; Thomas, *Arkansas and Its People,* 1: 243; Niswonger, "Arkansas Democratic Politics," 180.

44. *Arkansas Gazette,* March 21, April 15, 18, July 5, 1899; Jacobson, *Life Story,* 50–52; Thomas, *Arkansas and Its People,* 1: 265; Fletcher, *Arkansas,* 293; *Acts of Arkansas, 1899,* Act CXXVIII, 205–212.

45. *Arkansas Gazette,* April 16, 18, 1899; Jacobson, *Life Story,* 50; Niswonger, "Arkansas Democratic Politics," 181; Thomas, *Arkansas and Its People,* 1: 266; Donaghey, *Building a State Capitol,* 3–38.

46. *Arkansas Gazette,* May 17, 18, 21, 1899; Fletcher, *Arkansas,* 294; Jacobson, *Life Story,* 50; Thomas, *Arkansas and Its People,* 1: 266.

47. *Arkansas Gazette,* May 18, 1899.

48. Niswonger, "Arkansas Democratic Politics," 192.

49. *Arkansas Gazette,* June 6, 8, 9, 29, 1899; Jacobson, *Life Story,* 50–51, offers a summary of Davis's legal barrage, but some of the dates and details that he provides are inacccurate. See also Niswonger, "Arkansas Democratic Politics," 181.

50. *Arkansas Gazette,* July 16, 1899; Jacobson, *Life Story,* 49, 56–57; Dunaway, *Jeff Davis,* 61.

51. *Arkansas Gazette,* June 30, 1899; Jacobson, *Life Story,* 54–55.

52. Donaghey, *Building a State Capitol,* 39; Niswonger, "Arkansas Democratic Politics," 184; *Arkansas Gazette,* July 1, 1899; Little Rock *Arkansas Democrat,* July 1–6, 1899.

53. Jacobson, *Life Story,* 33–34, 54.

54. Ibid., 42.

55. *Arkansas Gazette,* July 3–5, 1899; Treon, "The Building of the Arkansas State Capitol," 24.

56. Jacobson, *Life Story,* 55; *Arkansas Gazette,* July 5–7, 1899; Fletcher, *Arkansas,* 296.

Chapter 6

1. L. S. Dunaway, ed., *Jeff Davis, Governor and United States Senator: His Life and Speeches* (Little Rock: Democrat Printing and Litho. Co., 1913), 51–52.

2. Little Rock *Arkansas Gazette* (hereafter cited as *Arkansas Gazette*), July 5, 1899; Alfred Treon, "The Building of the Arkansas State Capitol, 1899–1915" (M.A. thesis, University of Virginia, 1964), 24.

3. *Arkansas Gazette,* July 5, 1899; *Morgan's Buzz-Saw* (Hardy, Ark.), July, August, 1899. Hardy, located in Hardy Township in Sharp County, was an incoporated town with a population of 347 in 1900. See *Biographical and Historical Memoirs of Northeast Arkansas* (Chicago: Goodspeed,

1889), 729–761; Dallas T. Herndon, ed., *Centennial History of Arkansas* (Little Rock: S. J. Clark, 1922), 1: 808–809; and David Wiley Mullins, "History of Sharp County, Arkansas" (M.A. thesis, University of Colorado, 1934).

4. *Arkansas Gazette,* July 5, 7, 1899.

5. Ibid., July 5, 1899.

6. Ibid.

7. Ibid.

8. Ibid., July 6, October 15, 1899. The full written decision was not issued until October 7, 1899.

9. Ibid., July 6, 1899.

10. Little Rock *Arkansas Democrat,* July 5–7, 1899.

11. *Arkansas Gazette,* July 16, 1899; John Gould Fletcher, *Arkansas* (Chapel Hill: University of North Carolina Press, 1947), 295. Conway, an incorporated town with a population of 2,003 in 1900, was the county seat of Faulkner County. See Herndon, *Centennial History of Arkansas,* 1: 754–755; *Biographical and Historical Memoirs of Pulaski, Jefferson . . . and Hot Spring Counties* (Chicago: Godspeed, 1889); and *Arkansas State Gazeteer and Business Directory for 1906–7* (Chicago: R. L. Polk and Co., 1906), 153–155. Charles Jacobson, *The Life Story of Jeff Davis: The Stormy Petrel of Arkansas Politics* (Little Rock: Parke-Harper, 1925), 56–57, notes that: "In his Conway speech, he departed from the well-beaten paths of stump oratory and inaugurated a new peculiarly Jeff Davis type of oratory and method of campaigning. He alleged that by reason of his defense of the people he was being persecuted by the gang at Little Rock."

12. *Arkansas Gazette,* April 18, 1899, contains biographical sketches of Rector, Wood, and Vandeventer. See also ibid., July 23, August 24, September 19, 1899; Jacobson, *Life Story,* 57–58; Edgar E. Bryant, *Speeches and Addresses* (Fort Smith: Chauncey A. Lick, 1893).

13. *Arkansas Gazette,* April 13, 18, July 19, 21, August 26, 1899.

14. Ibid., August 26, 1899.

15. Ibid., August 26–27, 1899.

16. Ibid., August 27, September 1, December 17, 1899; Jacobson, *Life Story,* 57.

17. *Arkansas Gazette,* September 10, 1899. Bentonville, an incorporated town with a population of 1,843 in 1900, was the county seat of Benton County and the home of Senator James Berry. See *Arkansas State Gazeteer and Business Directory for 1906–7,* 100–101.

18. *Arkansas Gazette,* April 18, September 10, 1899.

19. Ibid., September 19, 1899; Chicago *Times-Herald,* September 15, 1899, quoted in ibid.

20. *Arkansas Gazette,* September 23, 1899, reprinted articles from the St. Louis *Post-Dispatch,* St. Louis *Globe-Democrat,* and the St. Louis *Republic.* See also *Arkansas Gazette,* September 22, 24, 1899; Arkadelphia *Southern-Standard,* October 19, 1899; and Jacobson, *Life Story,* 49.

21. *Arkansas Gazette,* September 26, 1899; Arkadelphia *Southern-Standard,* October 19, 1899; Richard L. Niswonger, "Arkansas Democratic Politics, 1896–1920" (Ph.D. thesis, University of Texas, 1974), 185.

22. For a summary of the Berry-Jones campaign, see Paige E. Mulhollan, "The Public Career of James H. Berry" (M.A. thesis, University of Arkansas, 1962), 162; and Niswonger, "Arkansas Democratic Politics," 186–188. After a dismal showing in the first eight county primaries (Berry won seven out of eight), Governor Jones withdrew from the senatorial primary campaign on March 23, 1900. *Arkansas Gazette,* March 24, 1900.

23. *Arkansas Gazette,* September 10, 1899. See especially the Little Rock *Arkansas Democrat,* November 1899–February 1900; and the Dardanelle *Post-Dispatch,* November 1899–February 1900; Fayetteville *Arkansas Sentinel,* September 19, October 17, 1899; L. S. Dunaway, *What a Preacher Saw Through a Key-Hole in Arkansas* (Little Rock: Parke-Harper, 1925), 62. Davis claimed that B. B. Battle, an associate justice of the Supreme Court and the owner of a successful Little Rock ice company, was "at the head of the most gigantic trust in Arkansas."

24. Arkadelphia *Southern-Standard,* October 19, 1899.

25. Dunaway, *Jeff Davis,* 47, 51–52.

26. Jacobson, *Life Story,* 56, 151; Fayetteville *Arkansas Sentinel,* September 19, October 17, 1899; Dardanelle *Post-Dispatch,* March 8, April 5, 19, 26, 1900; Niswonger, "Arkansas Democratic Politics," 139; Fred W. Allsopp, *Little Adventures in Newspaperdom* (Little Rock: Parke-Harper, 1922), 102–105, notes that "Jeff Davis made himself notorious among the members of the State press by being the first aspirant for an important office within the Democratic party who had the colossal nerve to try to get a public place without paying this customary tribute [a fee for publishing an announcement of candidacy] to the newspapers. He bade defiance to a time-honored custom, but broke into office whether or no." William Orestes Penrose, "Political Ideas in Arkansas, 1880–1907" (M.A. thesis, University of Arkansas, 1945), 133. At the 1900 state convention of the Arkansas Press Association, a resolution stating that Davis's victory demonstrated "the weakness of the press in Arkansas," was introduced. Neal, "Jeff Davis and the Reform Movement in Arkansas, 1898–1907" (M.A. thesis, Vanderbilt University, 1939), claimed that throughout Davis's career in state politics he had the support of no more than seven newspapers.

27. Will Holmes, the editor of the *Camden Beacon,* quoted in the Arkadelphia *Southern-Standard,* March 15, 1900.

28. Cal Ledbetter, Jr., "Jeff Davis and the Politics of Combat," *ArkHQ* 33 (Spring 1974): 16–37.

29. Jacobson, *Life Story,* 57.

30. Arkadelphia *Southern-Standard,* September 28, 1899.

31. Dardanelle *Post-Dispatch,* April 19, January 11, March 15, 1900. The editor was John Page, one of Davis's closest political advisors. See Fay Hempstead, *Historical Review of Arkansas: Its Commerce, Industry, and Modern Affairs* (Chicago: Lewis Pub. Co., 1911), 2: 855–856.

32. Jacobson, *Life Story,* 37–39; see also Ledbetter, "Jeff Davis and the Politics of Combat," 30; Dardanelle *Post-Dispatch,* December 1899–January 1900; and Russellville *Courier-Democrat,* December 1899–January 1900.

33. Dardanelle *Post-Dispatch,* January 18, 1900; Dunaway, *Jeff Davis,* 47–49; *Arkansas Gazette,* September 10, 1899. For information on Jacobson's relationship with Davis, see Raymond Arsenault, "Charles Jacobson of Arkansas: A Jewish Politician in the Land of the Razorbacks, 1891–1915," in Nathan M. Kagnoff and Melvin I. Urofsky, eds., *Turn to the South: Essays on Southern Jewry* (Charlottesville: University of Virginia Press, 1979), 55–75; Fay Williams, *Arkansans of the Years* (Little Rock: C. C. Allard, 1953), 3: 163–172; and Jacobson, *Life Story.*

34. *Arkansas Gazette,* December 17, 1899.

35. Ibid., January 5, March 5, March 26–April 14, 1899, February 8, March 6, 1900; Fletcher, *Arkansas,* 296; Hempstead, *Historical Review of Arkansas,* 2: 637–638; Jacobson, *Life Story,* 58; Dunaway, *Jeff Davis,* 47, 54, 65–66; Neal, "Jeff Davis and the Reform Movement in Arkansas," 38–39.

36. *Arkansas Gazette,* February 14, 1900; Arkadelphia *Southern-Standard,* February 15, 1900; Jacobson, *Life Story,* 59.

37. Dunaway, *Jeff Davis,* 46; Jacobson, *Life Story,* 59. For information on Howard County, see *Biographical and Historical Memoirs of Southern Arkansas* (Chicago: Goodspeed, 1890), 238–304. Center Point, an incorporated town with a population of 297 in 1890 and 334 in 1900, was located nine miles northwest of Nashville, the nearest banking and rail center. See *Arkansas State Gazeteer and Business Directory for 1906–7,*138–139.

38. Jacobson, *Life Story,* 58–59; Fletcher, *Arkansas,* 296. The entire text of the Center Point speech is reprinted in Dunaway, *Jeff Davis,* 46–70.

39. Dunaway, *Jeff Davis,* 51–52, 54, 59–61, 64–65, 67–69.

40. Ibid., 60–69. Davis stated: "I will give you his [Vandeventer's] record. He talks fluently as a free silver man, but when Wm. J. Bryan was invited to address the Legislature he was Speaker and appointed a committee to solicit funds to defray Mr. Bryan's expenses while attending to address that body. Mr. Charles Parker of Stephens, Ark., was on that committee. Each member of the Legislature assessed himself one dollar to pay these expenses. When Mr. Parker asked Mr.

Vandeventer, the Speaker, for a dollar he said: 'Damn that Bryan committee,' and refused to pay anything at that time. This kicked up such a big row that he afterwards paid the dollar." Ibid., 60–61. Fletcher accepted the 1886 Wheeler gubernatorial nomination, but changed his mind the following day. See David Y. Tomas, ed., *Arkansas and Its People: A History, 1541–1930* (New York: American Historical Society, 1930), 1: 203.

41. Jacobson, *Life Story,* 58–59; Fletcher, *Arkansas,* 296; *Arkansas Gazette,* January 12, 17, 1902; Niswonger, "Arkansas Democratic Politics," 128; Jacobson, *Life Story,* 150–151, notes: "Davis also inaugurated the system of printing his speeches for circulation throughout the length and breadth of the state, and in this campaign he distributed 125,000 copies. A portion he mailed out, some were sent by express, and a large number were delivered by him in person. He always caused to be sent to him a large package by express at every speaking place, then carried his grip filled with them, distributing a copy to every person on the train and threw out a bunch at every station passed. With such eagernness were they sought that he often remarked that he could sell them at 25 cents each."

42. *Arkansas Gazette,* February 18, March 6, 18, 1900; Arkadephia *Southern-Standard,* March 15, 1900; Fletcher, *Arkansas,* 300. William Goebel, a reform-minded Kentucky Democrat who had challenged the authority of the powerful Louisville and Nashville Railroad and who had come within 2,500 votes of winning the governorship in December 1899, was gunned down near the state capitol in Lexington on January 30, 1900. Caleb Powers, the Republican secretary of state, was convicted of murder, but he was ultimately pardoned. See C. Vann Woodward, *Origins of the New South, 1877–1913* (Baton Rouge: Louisiana State University Press, 1951), 374–375, 377–379; Caleb Powers, *My Own Story* (Indianapolis: Bobbs Merrill, 1905); and James C. Klotter, *William Goebel: The Politics of Wrath* (Lexington: University of Kentucky Press, 1968).

43. *Arkansas Gazette,* March 11, 15, 18, 1900. Ashley and Howard Counties held primaries on March 10, Desha and Lincoln Counties on March 14, and Hot Spring County on March 17. Jacobson, *Life Story,* 61–62, 150. The only possible exceptions were Ashley County, the birthplace of Davis's wife, and Howard County, which was located just north of Davis's native county, Little River.

44. Jacobson, *Life Story,* 62; Fletcher, *Arkansas,* 300–301; *Arkansas Gazette,* February 20, December 8, 1898, February 22, March 17, 21, 23, June 9, July 28, 1900. Thomas Fletcher, who died on February 21, 1900, at the age of eighty-one, was the acknowledged leader and chief financial backer of the Arkansas People's party. Originally a Whig, Fletcher vied unsuccessfully for the Democratic gubernatorial nomination in 1876 and 1878. A successful lawyer and merchant, he served several terms as sheriff of Pulaski County. In 1885 he was appointed federal marshal of the eastern district of Arkansas by President Grover Cleveland. See *Biographical and Historical Memoirs of Pulaski, Jefferson . . . and Hot Spring Counties,* 451–452; and Fay Hempstead, *A Pictorial History of Arkansas from Earliest Times to the Year 1890* (St. Louis: N. D. Thompson, 1890), 340–341.

45. The vote in Sebastian County was: Vandeventer, 1,414; Davis, 1,279. In the city of Fort Smith, Vandeventer received 681 votes, and Davis received 379. *Fort Smith Elevator,* April 6, 1900; *Arkansas Gazette,* April 1, 3, 8, 10–11, 15, 22, 29, May 9, 27, 1900. Davis carried Perry, Stone, Van Buren, Scott, and Marion Counties on March 31; Calhoun County on April 6; Drew, Jackson, Franklin, Sevier, Cleveland, St. Francis, Pike, and Clay Counties on April 7; Bradley County on April 13; Lonoke and Saline Counties on April 14; Pulaski County on April 17; Phillips, Yell, Union, Washington on April 21; Columbia, Baxter, Grant, and Mississippi Counties on April 28; Arkansas County on May 8; and White and Johnson Counties on May 26. For the Pulaski County returns, see ibid., April 18, 22, 1900. Vandeventer carried Little Rock, 1,594 to 1,083, but Davis ran up large majorities in Argenta and most of the outlying precincts. In the county as a whole, Davis received 2, 517 votes to Vandeventer's 2,039.

46. Rupert B. Vance, "A Karl Marx for Hill Billies," *Social Forces* 9 (December 1930): 180.

47. Dardanelle *Post-Dispatch,* April 26, 1900.

48. Ibid., April 5, 1900; Little Rock *Arkansas Democrat,* March 11–June 10, 1900. For a biographical sketch of Mitchell, see Herndon, *Centennial History of Arkansas,* 2: 1057–1059.

49. Dardanelle *Post-Dispatch,* May 3, 1900.

50. Arkadelphia *Southern-Standard,* April 26, 1900.

51. *Benton-Democrat,* n.d., quoted in ibid., May 10, 1900.

52. For the saga of the anti-Tillman Democrats, see Francis Butler Simkins, *Pitchfork Ben Tillman: South Carolinian* (Baton Rouge: Louisiana State University Press, 1944), 152–342. See also Simkins, *The Tillman Movement in South Carolina* (Durham: Duke University Press, 1926); and William Watts Ball, *The State That Forgot* (Indianapolis: Bobbs Merrill, 1932). Dardanelle *Post-Dispatch,* April 5, 12, 19, 26, 1900; Arkadelphia *Southern-Standard,* April 26, May 10, 1900; *Arkansas Gazette,* April 20–May 12, 1900.

53. Dardanelle *Post-Dispatch,* February 1, April 19, May 10, 17, June 14, 1900; Jacobson, *Life Story,* 62, 68.

54. Dardanelle *Post-Dispatch,* February 1, April 19, May 10, 17, 1900; *Arkansas Gazette,* June 27–29, 1900, February 19, 1902. For a full biographical sketch, see Weston Arthur Goodspeed, ed., *The Province and the States: A History of the Province of Louisiana Under France and Spain, and of the Territories and State of the United States Formed Thereafter* (Madison, Wis.: Western Historical Association, 1904), 4: 373–374. Jacobson, *Life Story,* 62, 68; Thomas, *Arkansas and Its People,* 3: 134; Dunaway, *Jeff Davis,* 61; Timothy P. Donovan and Willard B. Gatewood, Jr., eds., *The Governors of Arkansas: Essays in Political Biography* (Fayetteville: University of Arkansas Press, 1981), 109.

55. Jacobson, *Life Story,* 62; *Arkansas Gazette,* March 24, May 26, 1900.

56. *Arkansas Gazette,* May 26, 1900.

57. Ibid., May 26, June 10, 1900; Arkadelphia *Southern-Standard,* June 7, 1900; Jacobson, *Life Story,* 62.

58. Dardanelle *Post-Dispatch,* June 14, 1900; *Arkansas Gazette,* June 19, 1900; Arkadelphia *Southern-Standard,* June 7, 1900.

59. *Arkansas Gazette,* June 5, 1900.

Chapter 7

1. L. S. Dunaway, eds., *Jeff Davis, Governor and United States Senator: His Life and Speeches* (Little Rock: Democrat Printing and Litho. Co., 1913), 69.

2. Argenta, later known as North Little Rock, contained the railroad shops of several railways. See *Arkansas State Gazeteer and Business Directory for 1906–7* (Chicago: R. L. Polk, 1906), 67–73; *Twelfth Census of the United States, 1900,* Manuscript Returns, *Population Schedules,* for Argenta Township, Pulaski County, Arkansas located at the National Archives, Washington, D.C.; and David Y. Thomas, ed., *Arkansas and Its People: A History, 1541–1930* (New York: American Historical Society, 1930), 2: 810–812. Argenta was something of a Socialist stronghold later in the twentieth century. See James R. Green, *Grass-Roots Socialism: Radical Movements in the Southwest, 1895–1943* (Baton Rouge: Louisiana State University Press, 1978), 77. Dunaway, *Jeff Davis,* 20, offers a misleading analysis of Davis's urban following: "It has also been said that the country vote always elected him and that the towns and cities were against him. This is not true, as will be shown by an analysis of the vote in his three campaigns for Governor. He carried an average of 61 per cent of the county seats in the seventy-five counties in the State. In 185 of the principal incorporated towns in the State, Senator Davis carried an average of $71^1/_2$ per cent of the total vote during his three campaigns." Dunaway does not make it clear whether he is talking about Democratic primaries or general elections. His figures are plausible if he is talking about general elections, but they are grossly inaccurate if he is talking about Democratic primaries. These figures are repeated in Rupert B. Vance, "A Karl Marx for Hill Billies," *Social Forces* 9 (December 1930): 185.

3. See the *Arkansas State Gazeteer and Business Directory for 1892–3* and *1906–7;* U.S. Bureau of the Census, Special Reports, *Telephones and Telegraphs, 1902* (Washington: Government Printing Office, 1902), 24–26, 34, 80–81; U.S. Bureau of the Census, Special Reports, *Telephones, 1907* (Washington: Government Printing Office, 1910), 37–54, 116. In 1902, the federal census

enumerated 16,769 telephones in "urban" (towns of 2,500 or more) areas of Arkansas and 159 in rural areas. In 1907 the comparable figures were 37,178 and 12,403. In 1902 in the United States as a whole there were 30 telephones per 1,000 population; in Arkansas the figure was 12 per 1,000. In 1907 the U.S. and Arkansas figures were respectively 72 and 34 per 1,000.

4. The following statement was appended to the printed version of Davis's famous Center Point speech: "I have just discovered a letter which Judge Bryant has written to James E. Hogue, of Hot Springs (and I presume all over the state). In it the following statement is made. I read it in my speech in his presence at Arkadelphia the 14th day of February, and he does not deny it. The statement is this: 'Davis is the man to beat, say what you will about him. He has a large following in the back townships and is using methods that appeal to the prejudices of the masses.' This, gentlemen, shows the cloven hoof. This shows the conspiracy. This shows where the fight really is." Dunaway, *Jeff Davis,* 70.

5. These data have been gleaned from Polk's *Arkansas State Gazeteer and Business Directory for 1892-3* and *1906-7.* In each township the point of reference was the location of the local post office. When a township contained two or more post offices (an uncommon situation), the post office closest to the nearest railroad stop was used as the point of reference. See Appendix B.

6. The lone exception is Nevin Neal, "Jeff Davis and the Reform Movement in Arkansas, 1898–1907" (M.A. thesis, Vanderbilt University, 1939), 72, who argued: "Not only did the 'hillbillies,' 'the red-necks,' 'the wool hat boys,' and 'the one-gallus boys who lived up the crick' vote for him; but also, the leading business and professional men in the largest towns and cities were often his staunchest supporters."

7. Vance, "A Karl Marx for Hill Billies," 180. A native Arkansawyer (he was born in Plummerville in 1899), Vance witnessed the Davis movement as a small boy.

8. C. Vann Woodward, *Origins of the New South, 1877-1913* (Baton Rouge: Louisiana State University Press, 1951), 376. Woodward is also a native Arkansawyer. He was born in lowland Cross County in 1908. John S. Ezell, *The South Since 1865,* 2d ed. (New York: Macmillan, 1975), 376; Thomas, *Arkansas and Its People,* 1: 267–279; Richard L. Niswonger, "Arkansas Democratic Politics, 1896–1920" (Ph.D. thesis, University of Texas, 1974), 138.

9. Quoted in the Russellville *Weekly Tribune,* September 3, 1936; Neal, "Jeff Davis and the Reform Movement in Arkansas," 53.

10. Little Rock, *Arkansas Gazette* (hereafter cited as *Arkansas Gazette*), August 27, 1899.

11. Ibid., August 1, 1906; Dunaway, *Jeff Davis,* 209–210.

12. *Arkansas Gazatte,* June 11, 1902.

13. Dunaway, *Jeff Davis,* 20.

14. Ibid., 19, 40–43, 69; *Arkansas Gazette,* July 16, 1899.

15. For a sketch of Ferguson's career, see Reinhard H. Luthin, *American Demagogues, Twentieth Century* (Boston: Beacon Press, 1954), 153–181.

16. Dunaway, *Jeff Davis,* 209; *Arkansas Gazette,* August 1, 1906.

17. These estimates are based on weighted 1900 U.S. Census figures, which have been adjusted according to the results of simple correlation and multiple regression analyses of relevant electoral and ecological data. See Appendix A. Data from the *Twelfth Census of the United States, 1900,* Manuscript Returns, *Population Schedules,* for Arkansas located at the National Archives, Washington, D.C., and the *Arkansas State Gazeteer and Business Directory, 1906-7* were used to refine the estimates of occupational and urban-rural distribution. The white farm tenancy rate in Arkansas in 1900 was 35.1 percent. U.S. Bureau of the Census, *Twelfth Census of the United States, 1900, Agriculture,* Part 1 (Washington: Government Printing Office, 1902), 60–63; U.S. Bureau of the Census, *Thirteenth Census of the United States, 1910, Population* (Washington: Government Printing Office, 1914), 2: 96–107, 118–131; U.S. Bureau of the Census, *Twelfth Census of the United States, 1900, Manufacturing,* Part 2 (Washington: Government Printing Office, 1902), 26–29; U.S. Bureau of the Census, *Thirteenth Census of the United States, 1910, Population,* vol. 6, *Occupation Statistics* (Washington: Government Printing Office, 1914), 436–438.

18. Madison Township, which surrounded Forrest City, contained 13 white households and 250 black households in 1900. Eight of the 13 white heads of household were large planters, 4 were tenant farmers, and 1 was a blacksmith. *Twelfth Census of the United States, 1900,* Manuscript Returns, *Population Schedules,* for Madison Township, St. Francis County, Arkansas located at the National Archives, Washington, D.C.

19. Morton Harrison Fry, "Jeff Davis of Arkansas: A Study of Neo-Populism and Economic Democracy" (Senior thesis, Princeton University, 1968), passim; Neal, "Jeff Davis and the Reform Movement in Arkansas," 1; George James Stevenson, "The Political Career of Jeff Davis: An Example of the Southern Protest" (M.A. thesis, University of Arkansas, 1949), 5, 16–20; Clifton Paisley, "The Political Wheelers and Arkansas' Election of 1888," *ArkHQ* 25 (Spring 1966): 21; Vance, "A Karl Marx for Hill Billies," 180–181; Niswonger, "Arkansas Democratic Politics," 139; Thomas D. Clark and Albert D. Kirwan, *The South Since Appomattox: A Century of Regional Change* (New York: Oxford University Press, 1967), 111; John McDaniel Wheeler, "The People's Party in Arkansas, 1891–1896" (Ph.D. thesis, Tulane University, 1975), 478–479, 516; Joe Tolbert Segraves, "Arkansas Politics, 1874–1918" (Ph.D. thesis, University of Kentucky, 1973), 278, 320; Annette Shelby, "Jeff Davis of Arkansas: 'Professional Man of the People,'" in Cal M. Logue and Howard Dorgan, eds., *The Oratory of Southern Demagogues* (Baton Rouge: Louisiana State University Press, 1981), 14.

20. Paisley, "The Political Wheelers and Arkansas' Election of 1888," 21; Richard B. Dixon, "Press Opinion Toward the Populist Party in Arkansas, 1890–1896" (M.A. thesis, University of Arkansas, 1953), 61; Niswonger, "Arkansas Democratic Politics," 139–142. One scholar, Morton Fry, has questioned the assumption that Davis was a popular figure among the old Populist electorate. Fry conducted correlational analysis of the Davis movement's relationship with the Arkansas People's Party and found that there was no significant correlation between Davis's support and that of either James B. Weaver, the Populist presidential candidate in 1892, or D. E. Barker, the Populist gubernatorial candidate in 1894. Unfortunately, Fry used the returns from the 1904 general election, rather than the returns from the 1904 Democratic primary, as his index of Davis's support. Thus the value of his analysis is questionable. Fry, "Jeff Davis of Arkansas: A Study of Neo-Populism and Economic Democracy," 63–82. As the title of Fry's study suggests, he ultimately concluded that Davis was essentially a neo-Populist, even though his quantitative analysis uncovered little electoral continuity between Populism and Jeff Davisism. See also Raymond Arsenault, "From Populism to Progressivism in Selected Southern States: A Statistical Reinterpretation" (Senior thesis, Princeton University, 1969), 142–154; and Wheeler, "The People's Party in Arkansas," 486–513.

21. *Morgan's Buzz-Saw* (Hardy, Ark.), October 1899–July 1900; *Arkansas Gazette,* May 24, July 28, 1900; Arkadelphia *Southern-Standard,* June 28, July 8, 1900.

22. *Arkansas Gazette,* September 7, 1894. D. E. Barker, the Populist candidate for governor in 1894, received only 16.2 percent of the vote in Pulaski County; thus, the significance of the positive correlation in Table 12 is questionable.

23. Ibid., May–June 1900; Dardanelle *Post Dispatch,* May–June 1900; Arkadelphia *Southern-Standard,* May–June 1900.

Chapter 8

1. Little Rock, *Arkansas Gazette,* (hereafter cited as *Arkansas Gazette*), June 27, 1900.

2. Ibid., June 17–21, 26–28, 1900, October 23, 1902; David Y. Thomas, ed., *Arkansas and Its People: A History, 1541–1930* (New York: American Historical Society, 1930), 3: 268. See also James R. Grant, *The Life of Thomas C. McRae* (Russellville, Ark.: Russellville Printing Company, 1932). The Thomas C. McRae Papers, University of Arkansas Library, Fayetteville, Arkansas, contain very little information on McRae's relationship with Davis.

3. *Arkansas Gazette,* June 27–28, 1900. The other three at-large delegates were Senators

James Berry and James K. Jones and ex-Governor James P. Clarke. Edgar Bryant was selected as one of four alternate at-large delegates.

4. Ibid., June 28, 1900. Martin's resolution was offered as an amendment to the party's platform.

5. Ibid., June 27, 1900. See also Charles Jacobson, *The Life Story of Jeff Davis: The Stormy Petrel of Arkansas Politics* (Little Rock: Parke-Harper, 1925), 66.

6. *Arkansas Gazette,* June 27, 1900.

7. Ibid.

8. Ibid., June 24, 28, August 5, 1900; Arkadelphia *Southern-Standard,* August 2, 9, 1900; Dardanelle *Post-Dispatch,* June 21, August 9, 1900; Thomas, *Arkansas and Its People,* 1: 269. See also Series 5, Box 6, Folder 5, Item 13, in the Harmon L. Remmel Papers, University of Arkansas Library, Fayetteville, Ark. Fishback's letter was reprinted in Dardanelle *Post-Dispatch,* August 9, 1900. Davis retaliated by referring to Fishback's "sewer letter" and by charging that Fishback's record as governor had been "as base and rotten as hell."

9. Dardanelle *Post-Dispatch,* August 9, 1900; *History of Benton, Washington, Carroll, Madison, Crawford, Franklin, and Sebastian Counties, Arkansas* (Chicago: Goodspeed, 1889), 1312–1313.

10. Jacobson, *Life Story,* 67–68; *Arkansas Gazette,* July 8, 1900; Thomas, *Arkansas and Its People,* 1: 268–269; Dallas T. Herndon, ed., *Centennial History of Arkansas,* supplement (Little Rock: S. J. Clark, 1922), 5–10; *Arkansas Gazette,* December 17, 23, 1898, noted that a number of Republican leaders were pushing for Remmel's appointment as Secretary of Interior. Marcus A. Hanna to Richard A. McCurdy, June 21, 1900, and various letters in Series 1, Harmon L. Remmel Papers. See Marvin F. Russell, "The Rise of a Republican Leader: Harmon L. Remmel," *ArkHQ* 36 (Autumn 1977): 234–257.

11. *Arkansas Gazette,* July 28, 1900. Files was the only Populist candidate for statewide office in 1900. Thomas, *Arkansas and Its People,* 1: 269.

12. Thomas, *Arkansas and Its People,* 1: 269; *Arkansas Gazette,* July 19, September 7, 1900.

13. *Arkansas Gazette,* July 31, 1900. The telegram is now located in the Harmon L. Remmel Papers, Series 2, Box 3, Folder 1. Jacobson, *Life Story,* 67–68.

14. *Arkansas Gazette,* August 1, 2, 12, 14, 1900.

15. Arkadelphia *Southern-Standard,* August 30, 1900.

16. *Arkansas Gazette,* September 2, 1900.

17. Ibid., August 11, 1900.

18. Arkadelphia *Southern-Standard,* August 30, 1900.

19. *Arkansas Gazette,* August 8, 1900.

20. Ibid., August 29, 30, September 2, 1900; Arkadelphia *Southern-Standard,* August 30, 1900.

21. *Arkansas Gazette,* July 31, 1900; Dardanelle *Post-Dispatch,* August 2, 4, 1900.

22. *Biennial Report of the Secretary of State of Arkansas, 1901–1902* (Little Rock, 1903), 434–437.

23. See the New York *Evening Post's* discussion of the resurgence of the Arkansas Republican party, reprinted in the *Arkansas Gazette,* September 7, 1900.

24. W. M. Simpson to Winfield S. Holt, August 25, 1900, Harmon L. Remmel Papers; Herndon, *Centennial History of Arkansas,* 1: 346; James Edgar Howard, "Populism in Arkansas" (M.A. thesis, George Peabody College for Teachers, 1931), passim; *Arkansas Gazette,* September 9, 1898, March 6, 1900; John McDaniel Wheeler, "The People's Party in Arkansas, 1891–1896" (Ph.D. thesis, Tulane University, 1975), 490–493, acknowledges the existence of Populist-Republican voters, but he does not believe they were very common.

25. *Arkansas Gazette,* September 9, 1896, September 7, 1900; *Fort Smith Elevator,* September 11, 1896, September 14, 1900.

Chapter 9

1. L. S. Dunaway, ed., *Jeff Davis, Governor and United States Senator: His Life and Speeches* (Democrat Printing and Litho. Co., 1913), 42.

2. Little Rock *Arkansas Gazette* (hereafter cited as *Arkansas Gazette*), September 15–November

7, 1900. In Arkansas, Bryan received 81,142 votes to McKinley's 44,800. *Biennial Report of the Secretary of State of Arkansas, 1899–1900* (Little Rock, 1900), 432.

3. Fayetteville *Arkansas Sentinel*, March 19, April 16, 1901; *Arkansas Gazette*, July 16, 1900, December 14, 1902; Fay Williams, *Arkansans of the Years* (Little Rock: C. C. Allard, 1953), 3: 166, 168.

4. Williams, *Arkansans of the Years*, 3: 167–168; Fay Hempstead, *Historical Review of Arkansas: Its Commerce, Industry, and Modern Affairs* (Chicago: Lewis Pub. Co., 1911), 2: 703–704; *Arkansas Gazette*, May 4, June 6, 1901, July 8, 1903.

5. Ibid., January 19, 1901.

6. Ibid.; Charles Jacobson, *The Life Story of Jeff Davis: The Stormy Petrel of Arkansas Politics*, (Little Rock: Parke-Harper, 1925), 70.

7. *Arkansas Gazette*, January 19, 1901; *Journal of the House of Representatives of Arkansas, 1901* (Little Rock, 1901), 42.

8. *Journal of the House of Representatives of Arkansas, 1901*, 43–44.

9. Ibid., 47–49; Jacobson, *Life Story*, 70–71.

10. *Journal of the House of Representatives of Arkansas, 1901*, 44–47; Jacobson, *Life Story*, 70–71; David Y. Thomas, ed., *Arkansas and Its People: A History, 1541–1930* (New York: American Historical Society, 1930), 1: 270.

11. *Journal of the House of Representatives of Arkansas, 1901*, 49.

12. *Arkansas Gazette*, January 19, 1901; Arkadelphia *Southern-Standard*, January 24, 1901; Williams, *Arkansans of the Years*, 3: 164.

13. Jacobson, *Life Story*, 15, 40, 150. Although Davis's personality was not subjected to clinical diagnosis during his lifetime, there is some circumstantial evidence that he was a borderline manic-depressive. According to Jacobson, "For hours he would sit in his revolving chair in the Governor's office and stare into vacancy, never uttering a word. . . ."

14. Ibid., 19–20, 121; Arkadelphia *Southern-Standard*, April 24, September 11, 1902; *Arkansas Gazette*, July 14, 1900, April 13, September 9, November 7, 1902.

15. Jacobson, *Life Story*, 73; Williams, *Arkansans of the Years*, 3: 170.

16. For an institutional survey of Arkansas government, see John Gardner Lile, *The Government of Arkansas* (Arkadelphia: Chaplin Press, 1916). See also V. O. Key, *Southern Politics in State and Nation* (New York: Knopf, 1949), 183–200; Harry Lee Williams, *Forty Years Behind the Scenes in Arkansas Politics* (Little Rock: Parkin, 1949), passim; Cal Ledbetter, Jr., "Jeff Davis and the Politics of Combat," *ArkHQ* 33 (Spring 1974): 36; Ledbetter, "The Office of Governor in Arkansas History," *ArkHQ* 37 (Spring 1978): 44–73; and Richard L. Niswonger, "Arkansas Democratic Politics, 1896–1920" (Ph.D. thesis, University of Texas, 1974), 35.

17. *Biennial Report of the Secretary of State of Arkansas, 1899–1900*, 294–297; *Biennial Report of the Secretary of State of Arkansas, 1901–1902* (Little Rock, 1903), 434–437; *Biennial Report of the Secretary of State of Arkansas, 1891–1892* (Little Rock, 1892), 76–78; *Biennial Report of the Secretary of State of Arkansas, 1893–1894* (Little Rock, 1894), 68–71.

18. Fayetteville *Arkansas Sentinel*, February 26, 1901; *Arkansas Gazette*, April 5, 10, 1901, April 28, 1903; Jacobson, *Life Story*, 71; Niswonger, "Arkansas Democratic Politics," 195–196; Tom W. Campbell, *Arkansas Lawyer: Reminiscences of a Lifetime* (Little Rock: Pioneer Pub. Co., 1952), 510–511. For a full biographical sketch of Humphreys, see Dallas T. Herndon, ed., *Centennial History of Arkansas* (Little Rock: S. J. Clark, 1922), 3: 768, 771.

19. Jacobson, *Life Story*, 71; *Arkansas Gazette*, January 15–19, 1901; *Journal of the Senate of Arkansas, 1901* (Little Rock, 1901), 94. For a biographical sketch of Wilson, see Herndon, *Centennial History of Arkansas*, 3: 1143–1144.

20. Jacobson, *Life Story*, 130–136; Harry Lee Williams, *Behind the Scenes in Arkansas Politics* (Jonesboro, Ark.: privately printed, 1931), 10–15, 21–24; *Biographical Directory of the American Congress, 1774–1971* (Washington: Government Printing Office, 1971), 1239; Richard L. Niswonger, "William F. Kirby: Arkansas's Maverick Senator," *ArkHQ* 37 (Autumn 1978): 252–263.

21. *Hardy Herald*, n.d., quoted in *Arkansas Gazette*, February 15, 1900; ibid., April 27, 1900,

January 8, March 7, April 12, 1901; L. S. Dunaway, *What Preacher Saw Through a Key-Hole in Arkansas* (Little Rock: Parke-Harper, 1925), 65; Jacobson, *Life Story*, 71–72.

22. *Arkansas Gazette*, April 12, 1901.

23. The second fellow-servant bill, sponsored by Representative Thomas B. Brooks of Pope County, was defeated in the senate by a vote of 7–19. *Journal of the Senate of Arkansas, 1901*, 29, 171, 173, 177, 339; *Arkansas Gazette*, January 31, March 7, 12, 19, 27, 1901, January 12, 29, March 15, 1902; Jacobson, *Life Story*, 71–72.

24. *Arkansas Gazette*, March 20, 22, April 3, 10, 12, 30, 1901; *Journal of the House of Representatives of Arkansas, 1901*, 257; Thomas, *Arkansas and Its People*, 1: 270–271; Nevin Neal, "Jeff Davis and the Reform Movement in Arkansas, 1898–1907" (M.A. thesis, Vanderbilt University, 1939), 87; The senate voted 20–8 to postpone indefinitely the Humphreys Bill. The April 29 bill was sponsored by Senator Thomas W. Hardy of Ouachita County. The senate vote was 15–15.

25. *Journal of the State of Arkansas, 1901*, 94, 307–309; *Arkansas Gazette*, April 5, 30, May 3, 1901; John Alfred Treon, "The Building of the Arkansas State Capitol, 1889–1915" (M.A. thesis, University of Arkansas, 1964), 29–38; Jacobson, *Life Story*, 70–73.

26. Dallas T. Herndon, *Outline of Executive and Legislative History of Arkansas* (Fort Smith: Arkansas History Commission, 1922), 151; *Arkansas Gazette*, February 1, April 19, 28, May 1–2, 5, July 5, 1901; George James Stevenson, "The Political Career of Jeff Davis: An Example of the Southern Protest" (M.A. thesis, University of Arkansas, 1949), 44; Jacobson, *Life Story*, 72–73; Neal, "Jeff Davis and the Reform Movement in Arkansas," 77.

27. *Arkansas Gazette*, January 12, March 15, 1902. Sengel was a former president of the State Board of Trade. For a brief biographical sketch, see *History of Benton, Washington, Carroll, Madison, Crawford, Franklin, and Sebastian Counties, Arkansas* (Chicago: Goodspeed, 1889), 1364.

28. Arkadelphia *Southern-Standard*, June 13, 1901; Jacobson, Life Story, 72–74.

29. *Arkansas Gazette*, June 2, 1901.

30. Jacobson, *Life Story*, 73–74.

31. Hiram U. Ford, "A History of the Arkansas Penitentiary to 1900" (M.A. thesis, University of Arkansas, 1939), 78; Thomas, *Arkansas and Its People*, 2: 496.

32. *Journal of the House of Representatives of Arkansas, 1881* (Little Rock, 1881), 423 ff.; Ford, "A History of the Arkansas Penitentiary," 96–98, 103; C. Vann Woodward, *Origins of the New South, 1877–1913* (Baton Rouge: Louisiana State University Press, 1951), 214; Thomas, *Arkansas and Its People*, 1: 246–247; 2: 496; see also *Biennial Report of the Secretary of State of Arkansas, 1901–1902*, 11–14.

33. Ford, "A History of the Arkansas Penitentiary," 86–92, 100–104; Thomas, *Arkansas and Its People*, 1: 243–247, 2: 496–497. The board was later expanded to include other state officials, including the state auditor who was designated as chairman. Jacobson, *Life Story*, 69–86.

34. Ford, "A History of the Arkansas Penitentiary," 113–137; Thomas, *Arkansas and Its People*, 1: 247, 2: 497; *Arkansas Gazette*, June 16, 1898; *Journal of the Senate of Arkansas, 1895* (Little Rock, 1895), 875; *Journal of the House of Representatives of Arkansas, 1899* (Little Rock, 1899), 303. In 1899, a House of Representatives Penitentiary Committee report expressed some concern about the inhumane living conditions at some of the state's convict camps. For a look at the Arkansas penitentiary system from an inmate's point of view, see William N. Hill, *Story of the Arkansas Penitentiary* (Little Rock: Democrat Printing and Litho. Co., 1912).

35. *Arkansas Gazette*, April 4, 18, August 13, 14, 1901. The initial agreement was signed on February 3, 1899, but the contract was renegotiated after the passage of the Kimbell Act. On April 17, 1901, the house of representatives, by a vote of 60–12, endorsed a resolution which instructed the attorney general to try to annul the Dickinson contract.

36. Ibid., August 11, 1899, April 4–5, July 9, August 13–14, 1901, January 29, February 4, July 24, August 2–3, 19, 1902.

37. Ibid., March 20, September 7, October 23, 1901; Neal, "Jeff Davis and the Reform Movement in Arkansas," 87.

38. Jacobson, *Life Story,* 69, 86–87; *Arkansas Gazette,* July 28, 1901, January 29, February 4, 6, 1902; Fayetteville *Arkansas Sentinel,* February 25, 1902.

39. *Arkansas Gazette,* July 9, 1901.

40. Ibid., August 13, 1901.

41. Ibid., August 13–14, 1901, February 27, 1903.

42. Ibid., August 14, October 15, 1901, May 18, 1902. In a speech at Hot Springs, in January 1902, Davis threatened to "pardon every convict in the penitentiary if the courts sustained the 'brick contract.'" Fayetteville *Arkansas Sentinel,* February 25, 1902.

43. *Arkansas Gazette,* September 7, 1901.

44. Ibid., September 7–8, 1901, August 24, 1902. Hogins's term began December 1, 1901. Thomas, *Arkansas and Its People,* 1: 271. For a biographical sketch of Hogins, see *Biographical and Historical Memoirs of Western Arkansas* (Chicago and Nashville: Southern Pub. Co., 1891), 234.

45. *Arkansas Gazette,* May 3, 1901; Treon, "The Building of the Arkansas State Capitol," 37–42; Jacobson, *Life Story,* 73. The new State Capitol Commission convened for the first time on May 16.

46. Treon, "The Building of the Arkansas State Capitol," 29–46; Treon, "Politics and Concrete: The Building of the Arkansas State Capitol, 1889–1917," *ArkHQ* 31 (Summer 1972): 104; *Journal of the Senate of Arkansas, 1901,* 94, 238–242; *Journal of the House of Representatives of Arkansas, 1901,* 420–425; *Arkansas Gazette,* October 23, 1901. Mann claimed that the state owed him $36,267.21.

Chapter 10

1. Charles Jacobson, *The Life Story of Jeff Davis: The Stormy Petrel of Arkansas Politics* (Little Rock: Parke-Harper, 1925), 81.

2. Ibid., 75, 81–82; David Y. Thomas, ed., *Arkansas and its People: A History, 1541–1930* (New York: American Historical Society, 1930), 1: 271; Russellville *Courier-Democrat,* September 1901).

3. Jacobson, *Life Story,* 75, 79–82; Richard L. Niswonger, "Arkansas Democratic Politics, 1896–1920" (Ph.D. thesis, University of Texas, 1974), 59–87, 198–205; Little Rock *Arkansas Gazette,* (hereafter cited as *Arkansas Gazette*), October 1901. Poor health contributed to Jones's declining political fortunes: he suffered a serious heart attack in 1900. Farrar Newberry, *James K. Jones: The Plumed Knight of Arkansas* (Little Rock: Siftings-Herald Printing Co., 1913), 95–96, and passim; Willis J. Abbott, "James K. Jones," *Review of Reviews* 14 (October 1896): 427–428.

4. Jacobson, *Life Story,* 79; Niswonger, "Arkansas Democratic Politics," 4–6, 18, 66, 70–71, 197–98; *Arkansas Gazette,* December 8, 1901. See John Gould Fletcher, *Arkansas* (Chapel Hill: University of North Carolina Press, 1947), 315–353; and George Hyman Thompson, *Arkansas and Reconstruction: The Influence of Geography, Economics, and Personality* (Port Washington, N.Y.: Kennikat, 1976), 9–19, for discussions of the nature of intrastate sectionalism in Arkansas. Walter Scott McNutt, Olin McKnight, and George Hubbell, *A History of Arkansas* (Little Rock: Democrat Printing and Litho. Co., 1932), 604. Prior to James P. Clarke, the last senator from East Arkansas had been William K. Sebastian of Phillips County. First elected in 1848, Sebastian served in the United State Senate until 1861; from 1861 to 1865, he served in the Confederate Senate. See Michael B. Dougan, *Confederate Arkansas* (University, Ala.: University of Alabama Press, 1976), 13, 24; John Mula, "The Public Career of William King Sebastian" (M.A. thesis, University of Arkansas, 1969); and Thomas, *Arkansas and Its People,* 1: 108, 130–131.

5. Jacobson, *Life Story,* 75–82; Fletcher, *Arkansas,* 303; Niswonger, "Arkansas Democratic Politics," 197–198.

6. *Arkansas Gazette,* June 2, 6, 9, October 18, 20, 1901. In late May and early June, it was rumored that Davis planned to challenge Senator Jones in the Democratic primary, but on June 9 Davis formally took himself out of the running. The text of his public letter, "To the People of the State of Arkansas," was as follows:

Much discussion having arisen as to my future political course I am constantly in receipt of communications from my friends throughout the state submitting the inquiry as to whether or not I will be a candidate for the United States senate to succeed the Hon. James K. Jones; and that my friends may no longer be kept in doubt, and may be relieved of any embarrassment as to the present senatorial contest, occasioned by my silence, I feel it my duty to make known my intentions in this matter. The people of Arkansas have greatly honored me by electing me their chief executive by a majority such as is seldom given to any candidate, for which I shall always feel profoundly grateful, and with this election came duties and responsibilities of which I am not unmindful, and to the faithful performance of which I have devoted my entire energies and best endeavor, my highest and only ambition being to make the state a faithful and efficient officer. My term as governor has scarcely begun and to enter this contest for the senatorship at this time would require the sacrifice of public duty to gratify personal ambitions, and while I feel grateful to my friends for their generous offers of support should I enter the contest, still, I feel that I owe a duty to my state that is above and beyond any personal ambition I might have in this direction, and that I can best serve my people and discharge that duty in the office to which they have so kindly elected me. Therefore, feeling that I can best serve my people as governor, I will not at this time enter the senatorial contest, but will ask my friends, if my record as their chief executive meets their approval, to give me an endorsement of the same for a second term when they shall be called upon to speak at their primary election.

See also Thomas, *Arkansas and Its People*, 1: 271.

7. *Arkansas Gazette*, October 20, 1901.

8. Ibid.

9. Ibid.

10. Arkadelphia *Southern-Standard*, November 7, 1901; Jacobson, *Life Story*, 81; Little Rock *Arkansas Democrat*, October 18–28, 1901; Fayetteville *Arkansas Sentinel*, December 10, 1901.

11. Fayetteville *Arkansas Sentinel*, November 5, October 22, 1901.

12. Jacobson, *Life Story*, 81; Fletcher, *Arkansas*, 303.

13. Jacobson, *Life Story*, 77; *Arkansas Gazette*, January 12, March 15, 1902.

14. *Arkansas Gazette*, January 29, 1902.

15. Charles Morrow Wilson, *The Bodacious Ozarks: True Tales of the Backhills* (New York: Hastings House, 1959), 208.

16. Jacobson, *Life Story*, 82–83.

17. Ibid., 76–77; *Arkansas Gazette*, January 12, 1902; Little Rock *Arkansas Democrat*, January 2–12, 1902; Texarkana *Texarkanian*, n.d., quoted in Fayetteville *Arkansas Sentinel*, January 28, 1902.

18. Little Rock *Arkansas Democrat*, October 20–December 31, 1901; Jacobson, *Life Story*, 75–76; *Arkansas Gazette*, January 2, 1902.

19. Jacobson, *Life Story*, 76–78; *Arkansas Gazette*, May 17, 1900, January 17, 1902; Fletcher, *Arkansas*, 304–305.

20. *Arkansas Gazette*, January 17, 1902.

21. Ibid.

22. Ibid., January 17, 29, February 2, 6, 1902; Fletcher, *Arkansas*, 305–306; Jacobson, *Life Story*, 78.

23. Jacobson, *Life Story*, 78; *Arkansas Gazette*, February 2, 1902; Fletcher, *Arkansas*, 305.

24. *Arkansas Gazette*, January 29, 1902.

25. Ibid., February 6, 1902.

26. Ibid., January 29, February 2, 4, 6, 1902; Fayetteville *Arkansas Sentinel*, January 28, February 25, 1902.

27. *Arkansas Gazette*, January 29, February 2, 4, 1902; Fayetteville *Arkansas Sentinel*, February 25, 1902; Jacobson, *Life Story*, 87–88. William N. Hill, *Story of the Arkansas Penitentiary* (Little Rock: Democrat Printing and Litho. Co., 1912), 68, 112–118, 131–132, praises Davis's efforts to reform the Arkansas penal system.

28. Fayetteville *Arkansas Sentinel*, January 28, 1902.

29. L. S. Dunaway, ed., *Jeff Davis, Governor and United States Senator: His Life and Speeches* (Little Rock: Democrat Printing and Litho. Co., 1913), 214; *Arkansas Gazette,* January 29, 1902.

30. Fayetteville *Arkansas Sentinel,* January 28, February 25, 1902.

31. Ibid., January 28, 1902; *Arkansas Gazette,* February 6, 1902.

32. *Arkansas Gazette,* February 4, 1902; Arkadelphia *Southern-Standard,* February 6, 13, 1902; Fayetteville *Arkansas Sentinel,* February 25, 1902.

33. Arkadelphia *Southern-Standard,* January 23, 1902.

34. *Arkansas Gazette,* March 1902, August 1, 1906; Dunaway, *Jeff Davis,* 214.

35. *Russellville Democrat,* January 28, 1875–October 1893; Thomas J. Reynolds, "Pope County Militia War," *PAHA* 2 (Fayetteville, 1908): 174–189; Dunaway, *Jeff Davis,* 44.

36. Richard B. Dixon, "Press Opinion Toward the Populist Party in Arkansas, 1890–1896" (M.A. thesis, University of Arkansas, 1953), provides a good summary of the race-baiting tactics which Arkansas Democrats used to defuse the local Populist movement. *Arkansas Gazette,* March 27–June 22, 1898, June 21, 1899–June 1900.

37. *Arkansas Gazette,* March 18, 1900.

38. Ibid., February 2, 1902.

39. Ibid., February 18, 1902.

40. Jacobson, *Life Story,* 78; Fletcher, *Arkansas,* 305–306; Niswonger, "Arkansas Democratic Politics," 205; *Arkansas Gazette,* March 1902. On several occasions during the final month of the campaign, Rector debated Jeremiah V. Bourland, who served as Davis's proxy.

41. *Arkansas Gazette,* January 29, February 4, 6, 18, 26–27, 1902; Niswonger, "Arkansas Democratic Politics," 203, 205; Little Rock *Arkansas Democrat,* February 13–28, 1902; Fayetteville *Arkansas Sentinel,* February 25, 1902.

42. *Arkansas Gazette,* March 15, 1902. Earlier in the campaign, Jones had refused to meet Davis on the stump. Fletcher, *Arkansas,* 304.

43. *Arkansas Gazette,* March 15, 1902.

44. Jacobson, *Life Story,* 79.

45. Ibid., 78; Fletcher, *Arkansas,* 305; Little Rock *Arkansas Democrat,* February 2–March 28, 1902; Arkadelphia *Southern-Standard,* January 23, 1902.

46. Dunaway, *Jeff Davis,* 7; Fay Williams, *Arkansans of the Years* (Little Rock: C. C. Allard, 1953), 3: 166; George Murrell Hunt, "A History of the Prohibition Movement in Arkansas" (M.A. thesis, University of Arkansas, 1933), 50–74; *Biennial Report of the Secretary of State of Arkansas, 1881–1882* (Little Rock, 1882), 72–73. Pope County was one of only eleven Arkansas counties which outlawed saloons in 1882. *Russellville Democrat,* January 28, 1886, July 12, 1888.

47. *Journal of the House of Representatives of Arkansas, 1901* (Little Rock, 1901), 409–411; *Arkansas Gazette,* March 20, April 2, 1901; Hunt, "A History of the Prohibition Movement in Arkansas," 104.

48. The Prohibitionists' restrained response can probably be attributed to the fact that Davis did sign three minor temperance laws during the spring of 1901. *Journal of the House of Representatives of Arkansas, 1901,* 297, 381–382. Davis also signed an antigambling bill. See *Arkansas Gazette,* March 28, July 13, 1901; and Arkadelphia *Southern-Standard,* November 21, 1901.

49. Arkadelphia *Southern-Standard,* February 20, 1902.

50. Fayetteville *Arkansas Sentinel,* March 25, 1902.

51. *Arkansas Gazette,* March 18, 1902; *The Arkansas Methodist,* February 5, March 26, 1902.

52. *Arkansas Gazette,* March 18, 1902.

53. Hunt, "A History of the Prohibition Movement in Arkansas," 29–59.

54. Ibid., 59–90; *Biennial Report of the Secretary of State of Arkansas, 1891–1892* (Little Rock, 1892), 54–56. Nelson received only 1,310 of the 156,186 votes cast. George Thornburgh, "Prohibition in Arkansas," pamphlet in George A. Thornburgh Scrapbooks, University of Arkansas Library, Fayetteville, Ark.

55. Hunt, "A History of the Prohibition Movement in Arkansas," 95–117; Arkadelphia *Southern-Standard*, May 5, 1899. The George A. Thornburgh Scrapbooks, "Misc. Materials" and Folder 4, contain a wealth of information on the Arkansas temperance movement. Thornburgh was one of the founders of the Arkansas Anti-Saloon League; he was elected president of the League in 1907; and in 1917 he drafted the "bone-dry" bill which eventually became law.

Chapter 11

1. Marion Lowell, *Glimpses and Epigrams of Opie Read* (Chicago: Hill, 1902), 19.

2. Little Rock *Arkansas Gazette* (hereafter cited as *Arkansas Gazette*), March 30, April 1, 8, 1902.

3. Ibid., April 4, 8, 1902; Charles Jacobson, *The Life Story of Jeff Davis: The Stormy Petrel of Arkansas Politics* (Little Rock: Parke-Harper, 1925), 83–84. In November 1901 Eagle was elected president of the association for the twenty-first time. Arkadelphia *Southern-Standard*, November 21, 1901.

4. *Arkansas Gazette*, April 8, 1902.

5. Ibid., April 20, 22, 24, May 8, 29, 1902, February 11, 26, 1903.

6. Ibid., May 8, 1902.

7. Ibid., May 29, 1902.

8. Ibid., June 11, 1902; L. S. Dunaway, ed., *Jeff Davis, Governor and United States Senator: His Life and Speeches* (Little Rock: Democrat Printing and Litho. Co., 1913), 217–218.

9. Dunaway, *Jeff Davis*, 217–218; *Arkansas Gazette*, April 22, 1902.

10. Dunaway, *Jeff Davis*, 218.

11. Ibid., 40, 78, 215, 224; *Arkansas Gazette*, August 31, 1902, June 27, July 28, 1903; Fayetteville *Arkansas Sentinel*, March 9, 1904; Nevin Neal, "Jeff Davis and the Reform Movement in Arkansas, 1898–1907" (M.A. thesis, University of Arkansas, 1939), 92; David Y. Thomas, ed., *Arkansas and Its People: A History, 1541–1930* (New York: American Historical Society, 1930), 1: 276; Arkadelphia *Southern-Standard*, April 30, September 3, 1903, June 16, 1904; Dardanelle *Post-Dispatch*, September 26, 1907.

12. Dunaway, *Jeff Davis*, 224; *Arkansas Gazette*, August 1, 1906.

13. For some examples, see Arkadelphia *Southern-Standard*, April 30, August 27, September 3, November 5, 19, December 24, 1903, June 16, 1904; Fayetteville *Arkansas Sentinel*, November 25, 1903; Dardanelle *Post-Dispatch*, September 26, 1907.

14. Dunaway, *Jeff Davis*, 40.

15. Ibid., 21–22.

16. *Arkansas Gazette*, August 31, 1902.

17. Jacobson, *Life Story*, 99, 111; Dardanelle *Post-Dispatch*, March 19, 1908.

18. W. J. Cash, *The Mind of the South* (New York: Knopf, 1941), 46–60, 136–137; John Dollard, *Caste and Class in a Southern Town* (New Haven: Yale University Press, 1937), 13.

19. Francis Butler Simkins, *The Everlasting South* (Baton Rouge: Louisiana State University Press, 1963), 95.

20. Cash, *The Mind of the South*, 296–297.

21. Howard Odum, *An American Epoch: Southern Portraiture in the National Picture* (New York: Henry Holt and Co., 1930), 148–149.

22. H. L. Mencken, *Prejudices, Second Series* (New York: Knopf, 1920), 137–139. See also Fred C. Hobson, Jr., *Serpent in Eden: H. L. Mencken and the South* (Chapel Hill: University of North Carolina Press, 1974) passim, especially Chapter 2.

23. William Alexander Percy, *Lanterns on the Levee: Recollections of a Planter's Son* (New York: Knopf, 1941), 149.

24. Jonathan Daniels, *A Southerner Discovers the South* (New York: Macmillan, 1938), 234.

25. *Russellville Democrat*, February 9, July 27, October 26, 1882, February 21, 1884, January 28, 1886, September 28, 1887, June 20, 1889; Dunaway, *Jeff Davis*, 220; Jacobson, *Life Story*, 13;

Bayless Walker Price, "The Life of Jeff Davis" (M.A. thesis, University of Alabama, 1929), 1; *Arkansas Gazette,* May 8, 1902; Neal, "Jeff Davis and the Reform Movement in Arkansas," 30.

26. *Arkansas Gazette,* April 8, 1902; Dunaway, *Jeff Davis,* 27; Fayetteville *Arkansas Sentinel,* September 17, 1901. Davis and his wife formally joined the Second Baptist Church of Little Rock on September 8, 1901.

27. *Arkansas Gazette,* April 8, 1902; Arkadelphia *Southern-Standard,* November 21, 1901.

28. Dunaway, *Jeff Davis,* 55; see also *Arkansas Gazette,* January 29, 1902.

29. Dunaway, *Jeff Davis,* 157.

30. On the character and diversity of Southern evangelical protestantism, see Simkins, *The Everlasting South,* 79–103; Samuel S. Hill, Jr., *Southern Churches in Crisis* (Boston: Beacon Press, 1966); Kenneth K. Bailey, *Southern White Protestantism in the Twentieth Century* (New York: Harper and Row, 1964); George M. Marsden, *Fundamentalism and American Culture: The Shaping of Twentieth Century Evangelicalism: 1870–1925* (New York: Oxford University Press, 1980); Cash, *The Mind of the South,* passim; Erskine Caldwell, *Deep South: Memory and Observation* (New York: Weybricht and Talley, 1966); Hunter D. Farish, *The Circuit Rider Dismounts: A Social History of Southern Methodism, 1865–1900* (Richmond: Dietz Press, 1938); Rufus B. Spain, *At Ease in Zion: Social History of Southern Baptists, 1865–1900* (Nashville: Vanderbilt University Press, 1967); John L. Eighmy, *Churches in Cultural Captivity: A History of the Social Attitudes of Southern Baptists* (Knoxville: University of Tennessee Press, 1972); David Edwin Harrell, Jr., *All Things Are Possible: The Healing and Charismatic Revivals in Modern America* (Bloomington: Indiana University Press, 1975); Edmund de S. Brunner, *Church Life in the Rural South* (New York: George H. Doran, 1923); Liston Pope, *Millhands and Preachers: A Study of Gastonia* (New Haven: Yale University Press, 1942); and J. Wayne Flynt, "Dissent in Zion: Alabama Baptists and Social Issues, 1900–1914," *Journal of Southern History* 35 (November 1969): 523–542.

31. Dunaway, *Jeff Davis,* 157.

32. Ibid., 86; *Arkansas Gazette,* February 24, 1898, was sharply critical of Sam Jones's impending race for the Georgia governorship: "Politics and religion don't mix readily, and neither side of the mixture is particularly palatable for the people to swallow. As a general thing, their preference is to take the doses separate and apart." Thomas *Arkansas and Its People,* 1: 111, 238; Wayne Flynt, *Cracker Messiah: Governor Sidney J. Catts of Florida* (Baton Rouge: Louisiana State University Press, 1977); Ray Ginger, *Six Days or Forever? Tennessee vs. John Thomas Scopes* (New York: Oxford University Press, 1958), passim; Lawrence W. Levine, *Defender of the Faith: William Jennings Bryan, The Last Decade, 1915–1925* (New York: Oxford University Press, 1965); Laura M. Jones and Walt Holcomb, *The Life and Sayings of Sam P. Jones* (Atlanta: Franklin-Turner, 1907).

33. See Murray S. Stedman, Jr., *Religion and Politics in America* (New York: Harcourt, Brace and World, 1964); Peter H. Odegard, ed., *Religion and Politics* (New Brunswick, N.J.: Eagleton Institute of Politics, 1960); Seymour Martin Lipset, "Religion and Politics in American History," in Earl Rabb, ed., *Religious Conflict in America* (Garden City, N.Y.: Doubleday, 1964), 60–89; Cushing Strout, *The New Heavens and New Earth — Political Religion in America* (New York: Harper and Row, 1974); Russell E. Richey and Donald G. Jones, eds., *American Civil Religion* (New York: Harper and Row, 1974); Charles Reagan Wilson, "The Religion of the Lost Cause: Ritual and Organization of the Southern Civil Religion, 1865–1920," *Journal of Southern History* 46 (May 1980): 219–238; and Wilson, *Baptized in Blood: The Religion of the Lost Cause, 1865–1920* (Athens: University of Georgia Press, 1980).

34. See Leonard Dinnerstein, *The Leo Frank Case* (New York: Columbia University Press, 1968), 95–99, 119–135; C. Vann Woodward, *Tom Watson: Agrarian Rebel* (New York: Macmillan, 1938), 418–449; and Allan Michie and Frank Ryhlick, *Dixie Demagogues* (New York: Vanguard Press, 1939), 142–158.

35. See Lucille Harwood Mills, "The Presidential Campaign of 1928 in Arkansas" (M.A. thesis, University of Arkansas, 1948).

36. *Arkansas Gazette,* July 5, 1899; Dunaway, *Jeff Davis,* 40; see Raymond Arsenault, "Charles

Jacobson of Arkansas: A Jewish Politician in the Land of the Razorbacks, 1891–1915," in Nathan M. Kaganoff and Melvin I. Urofsky, eds., *Turn to the South: Essays on Southern Jewry* (Charlottesville: University of Virginia Press, 1979), 72.

37. Jacobson, *Life Story*; Fay Williams, *Arkansans of the Years* (Little Rock: C. C. Allard, 1953), 3: 163–172; Arsenault, "Charles Jacobson of Arkansas," 56–75; Fay Hempstead, *Historical Review of Arkansas: Its Commerce, Industry, and Modern Affairs* (Chicago: Lewis Publ. Co., 1911), 2: 703–704; telephone interview with Rabbi Ira Sanders, October 21, 1976; *Arkansas Gazette*, quoted in the Fayetteville *Arkansas Sentinel*, January 22, 1901; *Arkansas Gazette*, September 10, 1899.

38. G. W. Ogden, "Jeff Davis, Idol of the Hillbillies," *Hampton's Broadway Magazine* (n.d.), reprinted in the *Camden Beacon* (undated clipping).

39. Dunaway, *Jeff Davis*, 99–100.

40. Ibid., 42, 211–213; *Arkansas Gazette*, March 18, 1900, June 29, 1902.

41. Dunaway, *Jeff Davis*, 156–157.

42. Ibid., 161.

43. *Arkansas Gazette*, May 7, 9, 1902; *New York Times*, May 19, 1902.

44. *Arkansas Gazette*, May 7, 1902.

45. Ibid., May 9, 1902.

46. Ibid., Arkadelphia *Southern-Standard*, May 8, 1902.

47. *Arkansas Gazette*, May 17, 1902; *New York Times*, May 17, 19, 1902.

48. *Arkansas Gazette*, June 11, July 6, 19, August 12, 21, 1902; Thomas, *Arkansas and Its People*, 1: 272–273. The congressional candidate was Hugh Dinsmore, who engaged in a shouting match with Davis at a political rally in Fayetteville. See F. P. Rose, "Hugh Anderson Dinsmore," *ArkHQ* 11 (Spring 1952): 69–78.

49. *Arkansas Gazette*, July 6, August 12, 21, 27, 31, 1902.

50. Richard L. Niswonger, "Arkansas Democratic Politics, 1896–1920" (Ph.D. thesis, University of Texas, 1974), 239–265; Thomas, *Arkansas and Its People*, 1: 273–274; *Arkansas Gazette*, June 26–27, July 19, 1902; Tom Dillard, "To the Back of the Elephant: Racial Conflict in the Arkansas Republican Party," *ArkHQ* 33 (Spring 1974): 3–15; Willard B. Gatewood, Jr., "Theodore Roosevelt and Arkansas, 1901–1912," *ArkHQ* 32 (Spring 1973): 8–16; Marvin F. Russell, "The Rise of a Republican Leader: Harmon L. Remmel," *ArkHQ* 36 (Autumn 1977): 250–253.

51. *Arkansas Gazette*, June 27, July 24–25, August 12, 21, 27–31, 1902.

52. Ibid., July 25, 1902.

53. Ibid., July 24–25, August 29, 1902. See Powell Clayton, *The Aftermath of the Civil War in Arkansas* (New York: Neale, 1915), 366–368.

54. *Arkansas Gazette*, July 24–25, August 21, 27–31, 1902.

55. Ibid., June 27, July 25, August 27, 1902.

56. Ibid., July 24–25, August 27–31, 1902.

57. *Biennial Report of the Secretary of State of Arkansas, 1901–1902* (Little Rock, 1903), 404–408.

58. *Arkansas Gazette*, September 7, 1902; *Fort Smith Elevator*, September 5, 1902.

59. *Arkansas Gazette*, September 7, 1902.

Chapter 12

1. Robert Penn Warren, *All the King's Men* (New York: Bantam, 1968), 49.

2. *Little Rock Arkansas Gazette*, (hereafter cited at *Arkansas Gazette*), May 17–18, 1902.

3. *Journal of the Senate of Arkansas, 1903* (Little Rock, 1903), 19.

4. *Arkansas Gazette*, August 24, 1902.

5. Ibid., July 26, August 21, 24, 28, 1902.

6. Ibid., March 20, October 12, 23, 1901, March 18, 21, April 12, 15, 1903. *Journal of the House of Representatives of Arkansas, 1901* (Little Rock, 1901), 257; *Journal of the Senate of Arkansas, 1903*, 21–25. In May 1903, Davis granted a controversial pardon to Altheimer's son, Ulysses, who had

been jailed for contempt by Judge A. B. Grace of Pine Bluff. *Arkansas Gazette*, May 6–10, July 1, September 2, 1903.

7. *Arkansas Gazette*, July 29, August 2, 3, 13, 19, 28, 1902; Nevin Neal, "Jeff Davis and the Reform Movement in Arkansas, 1898–1907" (M.A. thesis, Vanderbilt University, 1939), 87.

8. *Journal of the Senate of Arkansas, 1903*, 22–25; *Arkansas Gazette*, November 22–23, 1902.

9. *Journal of the Senate of Arkansas, 1903*, 22–25.

10. Ibid., 19.

11. *Arkansas Gazette*, December 6, 1902, January 16, 29, February 1903. See *Journal of the Senate of Arkansas, 1903*, Appendix B, 435–534, for the full text of the "Convict Farm Investigation."

12. *Arkansas Gazette*, February 3–4, 10–11, 17, 19, 24–28, 1903.

13. Arkadelphia *Southern-Standard*, February 12, 1903.

14. *Arkansas Gazette*, February 13, 1903; Jacobson, *Life Story*, 88–89.

15. *Arkansas Gazette*, February 13, 1903.

16. Ibid., February 14–19, 1903.

17. *Report and Testimony of the Ways and Means Committee in Its Investigation of the Differences Between the Chief Executive and the Remaining Members of the Penitentiary Board* (Little Rock, 1903). Representatives Edward Merriman, J. F. Weaver, William Fletcher, E. M. Funk, Park Crutcher, and John H. Holland were anti-Davis. Representatives Benjamin Wofford, George Stockard, and William W. Whitley were pro-Davis. Representatives J. Sam Rowland and J. M. Futrell were nonaligned. *Arkansas Gazette*, February 19–March 24, June 20–21, July 4, 25, 1903; Charles Jacobson, *The Life Story of Jeff Davis: The Stormy Petrel of Arkansas Politics* (Little Rock: Parke-Harper, 1925), 88–93.

18. Jacobson, *Life Story*, 92.

19. *Arkansas Gazette*, February 21–25, April 26, 1903; Jacobson, *Life Story*, 90–91.

20. Jacobson, *Life Story*, 92.

21. Ibid., 90; *Arkansas Gazette*, February 24, March 4, 1903.

22. Ibid., February 19, 26–27, March 7, 18–21, April 15, 1903; Jacobson, *Life Story*, 92, 94.

23. *Arkansas Gazette*, March 14–15, 17, 1903; Jacobson, *Life Story*, 91, 94.

24. Jacobson, *Life Story*, 95; *Arkansas Gazette*, April 10–11, 1903.

25. Jacobson, *Life Story*, 89, 94–95; *Arkansas Gazette*, March 7, 20–22, April 11, 1903.

26. *Arkansas Gazette*, April 10–11, 15, 1903.

27. Ibid., April 16–17, 19, 21, 23, 28–30, 1903.

28. Ibid., May 17, 1903.

29. Jacobson, *Life Story*, 95–96; *Arkansas Gazette*, May 22–24, 1903. Davis began the veto process on May 20, but the official veto proclamation was issued on May 23.

30. *Arkansas Gazette*, May 26, June 26, July 16, 1903. Chief Justice Bunn was the lone dissenter. The test case was T. C. Monroe (State Auditor) v. Green, 71 Arkansas 527. Jacobson, *Life Story*, 97.

Chapter 13

1. L. S. Dunaway, ed., *Jeff Davis, Governor and United States Senator: His Life and Speeches* (Little Rock: Democrat Printing and Litho. Co., 1913), 40.

2. Little Rock *Arkansas Gazette* (hereafter cited as *Arkansas Gazette*), May 28, 1903.

3. On May 28 the *Gazette* compiled a long list of possible challengers: Wood, Vandeventer, Manning, Superintendent of Public Instruction John H. Hinemon, Congressmen Thomas C. McRae, John S. Little, and Stephen Brundidge, Attorney General George Murphy, State Senator George Sengel, Speaker of the House John I. Moore, Judge Jeptha Evans, and J. H. Harrod of Little Rock. Ibid., May 28, 31, June 9, 18–19, July 4, 16, 18, 1903. Manning withdrew on July 16.

4. Charles Jacobson, *The Life Story of Jeff Davis: The Stormy Petrel of Arkansas Politics* (Little Rock: Parke-Harper, 1925), 100.

5. Dallas T. Herndon, ed., *Centennial History of Arkansas* (Little Rock: S. J. Clark, 1922), 2: 457–459.

6. *Arkansas Gazette,* June 18, 1903.

7. Ibid., June 20–21, 1903.

8. Ibid., July 12, 1903. Davis, Manning, and Vandeventer spoke at Brinkley on July 3, and Davis and Vandeventer met again at Jonesboro on July 4. Wood spoke at Warren on July 4.

9. Ibid.

10. Ibid., July 12, 16, 19, 1903.

11. Ibid., July 21–30, August 5–7, 11, 18, 1903; John Gould Fletcher, *Arkansas* (Chapel Hill: University of North Carolina Press, 1947), 309–311.

12. *Arkansas Gazette,* July 24, 26, 28, August 5–7, 1903; Fletcher, *Arkansas,* 309–311.

13. *Arkansas Gazette,* August 5, 1903.

14. Ibid., August 6–7, 1903.

15. Ibid., July 28, 1903.

16. Dunaway, *Jeff Davis,* 19.

17. "Materials Relating to Jeff Davis," manuscript collection at the University of Arkansas Library, Fayetteville, Arkansas, Item 1; *Arkansas Gazette,* July 28, August 7, 1903; Arkadelphia *Southern-Standard,* August 27, 1903.

18. "Materials Relating to Jeff Davis," Items 1 and 4; Fayetteville *Arkansas Sentinel,* October 28, 1903, January 13, March 2, 1904.

19. "Materials Relating to Jeff Davis," Item 1; Fayetteville *Arkansas Sentinel,* October 28, 1903; George James Stevenson, "The Political Career of Jeff Davis: An Example of the Southern Protest" (M.A. thesis, University of Arkansas, 1949), 67–68.

20. Dunaway, *Jeff Davis,* 78–79.

21. Ibid., 74, 76.

22. Ibid., 74–76; "Materials Relating to Jeff Davis," Item 1.

23. Dunaway, *Jeff Davis,* 74–77.

24. Ibid., 75–76.

25. On the Black Belt "fusion" arrangements of the 1870s and 1880s, see John William Graves, "The Arkansas Negro and Segregation, 1890–1903" (M.A. thesis, University of Arkansas, 1967), 32–33.

26. Rupert B. Vance, "A Karl Marx for Hill Billies," *Social Forces* 9 (December 1930): 185.

27. Dunaway, *Jeff Davis,* 36, 40–41.

28. Ibid., 43.

29. Ibid., 33.

30. Ibid., 209; *Arkansas Gazette,* August 1, 1906.

31. Vance, "A Karl Marx for Hill Billies," 184.

32. See, for example, his speech at Eureka Springs, reprinted in Dunaway, *Jeff Davis,* 71–80; Jacobson, *Life Story,* 109–116.

33. Dunaway, *Jeff Davis,* 71–72.

34. Ibid., 72–73.

35. Jacobson, *Life Story,* 110.

36. Dunaway, *Jeff Davis,* 78.

37. Ibid., 71; see also *Arkansas Gazette,* July 26, 1903.

38. Fletcher, *Arkansas,* 311.

39. Dunaway, *Jeff Davis,* 39.

40. Ibid., 41; Fletcher, *Arkansas,* 312.

41. Dunaway, *Jeff Davis,* 37.

42. Ibid., 33–34.

43. Ibid., 32–33.

44. Ibid., 38.

45. Ibid., 73.

46. Ibid., 43–44.

47. Quoted in the *Arkansas Gazette*, August 20, 1903.

48. *Arkansas Gazette*, August 26, 30, September 3, 4, 1903.

49. Ibid., August 30, 1903.

50. Chicago *Record-Herald*, August 28, 1903, reprinted in the *Arkansas Gazette*, September 3, 1903.

51. Arkadelphia *Southern-Standard*, December 24, 1903, January 21, 1904; Jacobson, *Life Story*, 108–109; Fletcher, *Arkansas*, 312.

52. Arkadelphia *Southern-Standard*, January 21, 1904; *Arkansas Gazette*, December 30, 1903.

53. Fletcher, *Arkansas*, 309.

54. David Y. Thomas, ed., *Arkansas and Its People: A History, 1541–1930* (New York: American Historical Society, 1930), 1: 276; Fletcher, *Arkansas*, 312; Jacobson, *Life Story*, 114.

55. Jacobson, *Life Story*, 113; Dunaway, *Jeff Davis*, 211, 226.

56. Dunaway, *Jeff Davis*, 8.

57. Ibid., 225–226; *Arkansas Gazette*, August 1, 1906.

58. Arkadelphia *Southern-Standard*, January 28, 1904.

59. Jacobson, *Life Story*, 101.

60. Ibid., 99–109, 115–116; Fletcher, *Arkansas*, 309–310; Thomas, *Arkansas and Its People*, 1: 276; Fayetteville *Arkansas Sentinel*, January 13, 1904.

61. Jacobson, *Life Story*, 101–102; Fletcher, *Arkansas*, 310; *Arkansas Gazette*, March 9, 1904.

62. Jacobson, *Life Story*, 102–103.

63. Ibid., 115.

64. L. S. Dunaway, *What a Preacher Saw Through a Key-Hole in Arkansas* (Little Rock: Parke-Harper, 1925), 48.

65. Ibid., 49; *Arkansas Gazette*, April 24, 1904.

66. *Forrest City Times*, January–March 1904; Little Rock *Arkansas Democrat*, July 1903–March 1904; *Pine Bluff Daily Graphic*, January–March 1904; Harrisburg *Modern News*, March 1904; Fayetteville *Arkansas Sentinel*, February 3, 1904. Wood had supported Clarke in the 1902 senatorial primary.

67. Thomas, *Arkansas and Its People*, 1: 278.

Chapter 14

1. Fred W. Allsopp, *Folklore of Romantic Arkansas* (New York: The Grolier Society, 1931) 2: 332.

2. David Y. Thomas, ed., *Arkansas and Its People: A History, 1541–1930* (New York: American Historical Society, 1930), 1: 276; *Arkansas Gazette*, April 1–May 15, 1904; see also Series 1, Box 1, Folder 6, and Series 4, Box 3, Folder 1, of the Harmon L. Remmel Papers, University of Arkansas Library, Fayetteville, Arkansas.

3. *Arkansas Gazette*, June 15–18, 1904, Arkadelphia *Southern-Standard*, June 23, 1904; Richard L. Niswonger, "Arkansas Democratic Politics, 1896–1920" (Ph.D. thesis, University of Texas, 1974), 228–229; George James Stevenson, "The Political Career of Jeff Davis: An Example of the Southern Protest" (M.A. thesis, University of Arkansas, 1949), 70–71.

4. Little Rock *Arkansas Gazette*, (hereafter cited at *Arkansas Gazette*) June 16–17, 1904; Arkadelphia *Southern-Standard*, June 23, 1904; Charles Jacobson, *The Life Story of Jeff Davis: The Stormy Petrel of Arkansas Politics* (Little Rock: Parke-Harper, 1925), 117–119; Paige E. Mulhollan, "The Issues of the Davis-Berry Senatorial Campaign in 1906," *ArkHQ* 20 (Summer 1961): 118; Paige E. Mulhollan, "The Public Career of James H. Berry" (M.A. thesis, University of Arkansas, 1962), 168–169.

5. Arkadelphia *Southern-Standard*, June 23, 1904; *Arkansas Gazette*, July–August 1904; Stevenson, "The Political Career of Jeff Davis," 72. The Prohibitionist party's gubernatorial candidate was J. E. Wilmans; the Socialist party's candidate was William Penrose. Wilmans

received 2,527 votes; Penrose received 1,364. *Biennial Report of the Secretary of State of Arkansas, 1905–1906* (Little Rock, 1906), 424.

6. *Arkansas Gazette*, February 3–March 13, 1903, August 5, 7, 14, 20, 30–31, September 4, October 28, 1904; Russellville *Courier-Democrat*, July 21, 1904; Nevin Neal, "Jeff Davis and the Reform Movement in Arkansas, 1898–1907" (M.A. thesis, Vanderbilt University, 1939), 63; Stevenson "The Political Career of Jeff Davis," 73. James K. Vardaman used the same slogan as early as 1895. See William F. Holmes, *The White Chief, James Kimble Vardaman* (Baton Rouge: Louisiana State University Press, 1970), 54–56, 77–78.

7. *Arkansas Gazette*, October 30, 1904.

8. *Journal of the Senate of Arkansas, 1905* (Little Rock, 1905), 24–25.

9. Russellville *Courier-Democrat*, February 2, 1905; *Journal of the House of Representatives of Arkansas, 1905* (Little Rock, 1905), 61, 165–166.

10. *Biennial Report of the Secretary of State of Arkansas, 1905–1906*, 421–424; *New York Times*, September 6–7, 1904; Neal, "Jeff Davis and the Reform Movement in Arkansas," 77; *Biennial Report of the Secretary of State of Arkansas, 1901–1902* (Little Rock, 1903), 438–441; *Biennial Report of the Secretary of State of Arkansas, 1903–1904* (Little Rock, 1904), 504–507.

11. *Journal of the House of Representatives of Arkansas, 1905*, passim; *Journal of the Senate of Arkansas, 1905*, passim; Dallas T. Herndon, *Outline of Executive and Legislative History of Arkansas* (Fort Smith: Arkansas History Commission, 1922), 155–157; L. S. Dunaway, ed., *Jeff Davis, Governor and United States Senator: His Life and Speeches* (Little Rock: Democrat Printing and Litho. Co., 1913), 92–94; *New York Times*, June 2, 1905; *Arkansas Gazette*, June 1905. Several lobbyists and legislators who took part in the 1905 session were indicted for bribery and fraud. Thomas, *Arkansas and Its People*, 1: 278.

12. Jacobson, *Life Story*, 72; Stevenson, "The Political Career of Jeff Davis," 73–75, 85, 96; Niswonger, "Arkansas Democratic Politics," 230; Cal Ledbetter, Jr., "Jeff Davis and the Politics of Combat," *ArkHQ* 33 (Spring 1974): 27; Arkansas General Assembly, *Acts of Arkansas, 1905* (Little Rock, 1905), 2–3; Arkansas General Assembly, *Acts of Arkansas, 1907* (Little Rock, 1907), 430; Arkansas General Assembly, *Acts of Arkansas, 1913* (Little Rock, 1913), 680. For the court cases, see 76 *Arkansas Reports* 312, and 53 *United States Supreme Court Reports* 530.

13. Mulhollan, "The Issues of the Davis-Berry Senatorial Campaign in 1906," 118–119; *Arkansas Gazette*, June 11, 1902, May 1904.

14. See George E. Mowry, *The Era of Theodore Roosevelt, 1900–1912* (New York: Harper & Row, 1958), 197–225; C. Vann Woodward, *Tom Watson: Agrarian Rebel* (New York: Macmillan, 1938), 355–395.

15. Jacobson, *Life Story*, 124, 129; Mulhollan, "The Issues of the Davis-Berry Senatorial Campaign in 1906," 121–125; Mulhollan, "The Public Career of James H. Berry," 178–180; Niswonger, "Arkansas Democratic Politics," 234–235; *Arkansas Gazette*, March 4, 1906; Arkadelphia *Southern-Standard*, April 12, 1906. See also James H. Berry, *An Autobiography of Senator James H. Berry* (Bentonville: Democrat Print, 1913), passim.

16. Jacobson, *Life Story*, 119–120; Dunaway, *Jeff Davis*, 82; Mulhollan, "The Public Career of James H. Berry," 167–168; Mulhollan, "The Public Career of James H. Berry," 167–168; Mulhollan, "The Issues of the Davis-Berry Senatorial Campaign in 1906," 122.

17. Dunaway, *Jeff Davis*, 81; Jacobson, *Life Story,* 124.

18. Mulhollan, "The Issues of the Davis-Berry Senatorial Campaign in 1906," 119; Mulhollan, "The Public Career of James H. Berry," 169–170; Jacobson, *Life Story* 122–123.

19. *Arkansas Gazette*, July 5, 1905; Dunaway, *Jeff Davis*, 83–84, 88–91, 217, 221–222; Jacobson, *Life Story,* 123–124; Mulhollan, "The Issues of the Davis-Berry Senatorial Campaign in 1906," 119–120.

20. *Arkansas Gazette*, July 12–August 21, 1905; Mulhollan, "The Issues of the Davis-Berry Senatorial Campaign in 1906," 120–121.

21. Jacobson, *Life Story*, 128. See Ledbetter, "Jeff Davis and the Politics of Combat," 16–37.

22. Ibid., 124, 129; *Arkansas Gazette*, August 22–September 29, 1905; L. S. Dunaway, *What a*

Preacher Saw Through a Key-Hole in Arkansas (Little Rock: Parke-Harper, 1925), 65; Dunaway, *Jeff Davis*, 94–98; Mulhollan, "The Issues of the Davis-Berry Senatorial Campaign in 1906," 122; Niswonger, "Arkansas Democratic Politics," 230.

23. *Arkansas Gazette*, September 1–20, 1905; Jacobson, *Life Story*, 124; Niswonger, "Arkansas Democratic Politics," 231–234; Dunaway, *What a Preacher Saw*, 65; Dunaway, *Jeff Davis*, 96, 225; Stevenson, "The Political Career of Jeff Davis," 77; Ledbetter, "Jeff Davis and the Politics of Combat," 23, 25. For a biographical sketch of Rogers, see Dallas T. Herndon, ed., *Centennial History of Arkansas* (Little Rock: S. J. Clark, 1922), 3: 1123, 1129.

24. Jacobson, *Life Story*, 124, 128–129; Niswonger, "Arkansas Democratic Politics," 230–232. For a biographical sketch of Little, see Herndon, *Outline of Executive and Legislative History of Arkansas*, 158–159; and John Hallum, *Biographical and Pictorial History of Arkansas* (Albany: Parsons and Co. 1887), 440–442; and Timothy P. Donovan and Willard B. Gatewood, Jr., eds., *The Governors of Arkansas: Essays in Political Biography* (Fayetteville: University of Arkansas Press, 1981), 126–128; Dunaway, *What a Preacher Saw*, 66.

25. Rupert B. Vance, "A Karl Marx for Hill Billies," *Social Forces* 9 (December 1930): 186.

26. *Arkansas Gazette*, October 14–15, 17, 1905; *New York Mail*, quoted in ibid., October 31, 1905.

27. Dunaway, *What a Preacher Saw*, 63–64; Arkadelphia *Southern-Standard*, November 2, 1905.

28. Arkadelphia *Southern-Standard*, November 2, 1905.

29. U.S. Congres, *Congressional Record* (Washington: Government Printing Office, 1895), 53rd Congress, 3rd Session, January 15, 1895, 1002.

30. Arkadelphia *Southern-Standard*, August 3, 1899.

31. Ibid., September 24, 1903; see also William Montgomery Brown, *The Crucial Race Question or Where and How Shall the Color Line Be Drawn* (Little Rock: The Arkansas Churchman's Pub. Co., 1907).

32. *Arkansas Gazette*, October 27, 1905.

33. Dunaway, *Jeff Davis*, 96; Jacobson, *Life Story* 126; Vance, "A Karl Marx for Hill Billies," 185–186. Davis used the race issue against Berry even before the Roosevelt visit. In a speech at Rogers in September 1905, he chided Berry for referring to "colored men." "We call them niggers in our country," Davis told the crowd. *Arkansas Gazette*, September 27, 1905.

34. Dunaway, *Jeff Davis*, 76; Neal, "Jeff Davis and the Reform Movement in Arkansas," 62; *Arkansas Gazette*, December 27, 1902; William N. Hill, *Story of the Arkansas Penitentiary* (Little Rock: Democrat Printing and Litho. Co., 1912), 68, 112.

35. James Harris Fain, "Political Disfranchisement of the Negro in Arkansas" (M.A. thesis, University of Arkansas, 1961), 64; *Arkansas Gazette*, April 10, 1900, February 10, 1901, February 14, 17, 1904, February 1, 1906; Arkadelphia *Southern-Standard*, February 6, 1902.

36. *Arkansas Gazette*, August 5, 1904; Neal, "Jeff Davis and the Reform Movement in Arkansas," 24.

37. *Journal of the Senate of Arkansas, 1905*, 63.

38. *Arkansas Gazette*, September 8, 1912.

39. Dunaway, *What a Preacher Saw*, 80; "Materials Relating to Jeff Davis, "Manuscript collection at the University of Arkansas Library, Fayetteville, Arkansas, Item 1; Arkadelphia *Southern-Standard*, January 23, 1902.

40. Neal, "Jeff Davis and the Reform Movement in Arkansas, " 60–62, 87–93; *Biennial Report of the Arkansas State Penitentiary, 1901–1902* (Fort Smith: Thrash-Lick, 1902), 28–35; *Journal of the Senate of Arkansas, 1903* (Little Rock, 1903), 373–433; *Journal of the Senate of Arkansas, 1905*, 25–26; see also Hill, *Story of the Arkansas Penitentiary.*

41. *Journal of the Senate of Arkansas, 1905*, 25.

42. See Dunaway, *Jeff Davis*, 81–100.

43. Ibid., 86–88.

44. Ibid., 85–86.

45. Ibid., 91; Jacobson, *Life Story,* 126

46. Dunaway, *Jeff Davis,* 92.

47. *Arkansas Gazette,* November 28, December 1, 2, 12, 1905; Little Rock *Arkansas Democrat,* November 28, 1905; *Fayetteville Democrat,* November 30, 1905; *New Orleans States,* quoted in Stevenson, "The Political Career of Jeff Davis," 78–79; Mulhollan, "The Issues of the Davis-Berry Senatorial Campaign in 1906," 122; F. P. Rose, "Hugh Anderson Dinsmore," *ArkHQ* 11 (Spring 1952): 69–78. Haughtily respectable, Dinsmore was something of a dandy. On formal occasions he invariably wore a black cape instead of a coat—a practice which drew snickers from the Davis crowd.

48. *Arkansas Gazette,* February 16, March 1, 22, 28, 1906; Little Rock *Arkansas Democrat,* March 1906; Mulhollan, "The Issues of the Davis-Berry Senatorial Campaign in 1906," 123; Stevenson, "The Political Career of Jeff Davis," 80–82; *Nashville News,* March 17, 24, 1906.

49. *Arkansas Gazette,* March 9, 22, 1906; Dunaway, *Jeff Davis,* 85; Jacobson, *Life Story,* 125; Mulhollan, "The Issues of the Davis-Berry Senatorial Campaign in 1906," 123.

50. Dunaway, *What a Preacher Saw,* 56–57; Russellville *Courier-Democrat,* March 8, 1906. Davis appointed his father to a county judgeship (Pope County) in 1903. Arkadelphia *Southern-Standard,* March 12, 1903.

51. *Arkansas Gazette,* March 22–23, 28, 1906; Little Rock *Arkansas Democrat,* March 27, 1906; Dunaway, *Jeff Davis,* 220; Mulhollan, "The Issues of the Davis-Berry Senatorial Campaign in 1906," 119.

52. *Arkansas Gazette,* March 29–30, 1906; Mulhollan, "The Public Career of James H. Berry," 177–178; Arkadelphia *Southern-Standard,* May 3, 1906; Jacobson, *Life Story,* 127–128.

53. Jacobson, *Life Story,* 128–129; Dunaway, *What a Preacher Saw,* 65–66; *Arkansas Gazette,* March 29–April 3, 1906.

54. Jacobson, *Life Story,* 128–129.

55. *Fort Smith Elevator,* April 13, 1906; Mulhollan, "The Public Career of James H. Berry," 178.

56. Quoted in the Arkadelphia *Southern-Standard,* April 12, 1906.

57. Quoted in ibid., April 5, 1906.

Chapter 15

1. George G. Stockard, *King Jeff I* (Washington, D.C., W. F. Roberts, 1925), 12. Stockard represented Washington County in the Arkansas House of Representatives in 1903. His play was performed at the University of Arkansas in the mid-1920s.

2. Little Rock *Arkansas Gazette,* (hereafter cited as *Arkansas Gazette*), August 1, 1906; L. S. Dunaway, ed., *Jeff Davis Governor and United States Senator: His Life and Speeches* (Little Rock: Democrat Printing and Litho. Co., 1913), 208–226.

3. Charles Jacobson, *The Life Story of Jeff Davis: The Stormy Petrel of Arkansas Politics* (Little Rock: Parke-Harper, 1925), 178–179. Davis's half-sister, Sarah Scott, was born in California in 1855. *Eighth Census of the United States, 1860,* Manuscript Returns, *Population Schedules,* for Jackson Township, Sevier County, Arkansas, Family #1026, located at the National Archives, Washington, D.C.

4. Jacobson, *Life Story,* 178–180; Timothy P. Donovan and Willard B. Gatewood, Jr., eds., *The Governors of Arkansas: Essays in Political Biography* (Fayetteville: University of Arkansas Press, 1981), 258–259.

5. *Arkansas Gazette,* June 13, 1906; Donovan and Gatewood, *The Governors of Arkansas,* 259–260; Joe Tolbert Segraves, "Arkansas Politics, 1874–1918" (Ph.D. thesis, University of Kentucky, 1973), 312, notes that Attorney General Kirby later "blocked the appointment of Pindall's father-in-law to a lucrative position as state convict farm manager."

6. Fayetteville *Arkansas Sentinel,* October 31, 1906; George James Stevenson, "The Political Career of Jeff Davis: An Example of the Southern Protest" (M.A. thesis, University of Arkansas,

1949), 85; *Arkansas Gazette,* August 1–September 5, 1906. Little received 105,486 votes; his Republican opponent, John I. Worthington, received 41,689.

7. *Arkansas Gazette,* March 26–April 4, September 3–5, 1906. The roster of the 1907 legislature appears in the *Biennial Report of the Secretary of State of Arkansas, 1905–1906* (Little Rock, 1907), 465–467.

8. *Journal of the House of Representatives of Arkansas, 1907* (Little Rock, 1907), 43–64; Stevenson, "The Political Career of Jeff Davis," 85–88.

9. *Arkansas Gazette,* March 30, 1906, January 19–20, 1907.

10. Ibid., January 19–February 27, 1907; Donovan and Gatewood, *The Governors of Arkansas,* 127–128, 259–260; Jacobson, *Life Story,* 178; Dallas T. Herndon, *Outline of Executive and Legislative History of Arkansas* (Fort Smith: Arkansas History Commission, 1922), 158–159; L. S. Dunaway, *What a Preacher Saw Through a Key-Hole in Arkansas* (Little Rock: Parke-Harper, 1925), 66.

11. Dunaway, *Jeff Davis,* 122–123; Donovan and Gatewood, *The Governors of Arkansas,* 259.

12. *Arkansas Gazette,* January 31, May 14–18, 1907; *Journal of the House of Representatives of Arkansas, 1907,* 143; Herndon, *Outline of Executive and Legislative History of Arkansas,* 161–162; Segraves, "Arkansas Politics, 1874–1918," 318.

13. Jacobson, *Life Story,* 130, 132, 141–143, 169; Fay Williams, *Arkansans of the Years* (Little Rock: C. C. Allard, 1953), 3: 169. See also Raymond Arsenault, "Charles Jacobson of Arkansas: A Jewish Politician in the Land of the Razorbacks, 1891–1915," in Nathan M. Kaganoff and Melvin I. Urofsky, eds. *Turn to the South: Essays on Southern Jewry* (Charlottesville: University of Virginia Press, 1979), 65–71.

14. Dunaway, *Jeff Davis,* 129–133; Jacobson, *Life Story,* 130, 132; Donovan and Gatewood, *The Governors of Arkansas,* 259–260; *Arkansas Gazette,* May 15–June 10, December 29–31, 1907, January 4, 1908; Dunaway, *What a Preacher Saw,* 66–67; Richard L. Niswonger, "Arkansas Democratic Politics, 1896–1920" (Ph.D. thesis, University of Texas, 1974), 266–272; Segraves, "Arkansas Politics, 1874–1918," 312; Harry L. Williams, *Behind the Scenes in Arkansas Politics* (Jonesboro, Ark.: privately printed, 1931), 10–11.

15. Dunaway, *Jeff Davis,* 39; Jacobson, *Life Story,* 137, 188–189.

16. The text of the bill is reprinted in Dunaway, *Jeff Davis,* 251–255. *Arkansas Gazette,* December 5–7, 1907; *Washington Post,* December 5, 1907; *Washington Herald,* December 5, 1907; *Congressional Record,* December 4, 1907, 42: 136; David P. Thelen, *Robert M. La Follette and the Insurgent Spirit* (Boston: Little, Brown and Co., 1976), 56; *Congressional Record,* April 23–24, 1906, 40: 5688ff.

17. Dunaway, *Jeff Daavis,* 101; Jacobson, *Life Story,* 188–189. The text of the speech is printed in Dunaway, *Jeff Davis,* 101–121; and in the *Congressional Record,* December 11, 1907, 42: 272–282.

18. Dunaway, *Jeff Davis,* 106.

19. Ibid., 107–111.

20. Ibid., 111.

21. Ibid., 107, 119–120; *Arkansas Gazette,* December 13, 1907; *New York Times,* December 12, 1907; *Washington Post,* December 12, 1907; "Senator Davis," *The Independent* 64 (January 23, 1908): 185–186.

22. *Arkansas Gazette,* December 13, 1907; Jacobson, *Life Story,* 137–138.

23. Dunaway, *Jeff Davis,* 123; Jacobson, *Life Story,* 131.

24. Dardanelle *Post-Dispatch,* January 23, 1908.

25. Jacobson, *Life Story,* 188.

26. Quoted in *Arkansas Gazette,* December 16, 1907. For a sample of the press's reaction, see ibid., December 15, 1907.

27. *New York Times,* December 12, 1907.

28. Quoted in *Arkansas Gazette,* December 12, 1907.

29. "Senator Davis," *The Independent* 64 (January 23, 1908): 186.

30. *Congressional Record,* January 13, 1908, 42: 634, December 9, 1908, 43: 65, January 26, 1909, 43: 1402–1403; Dunaway, *Jeff Davis,* 179–207; Jacobson, *Life Story,* 204–205; Stevenson, "The Political Career of Jeff Davis," 100.

31. Dunaway, *Jeff Davis,* 207; Jacobson, *Life Story,* 205.

32. Dunaway, *Jeff Davis,* 234–235; Rupert Vance, "A Karl Marx for Hill Billies," *Social Forces* 9 (December 1930): 188–189; Cal Ledbetter, Jr., "Jeff Davis and the Politics of Combat," *ArkHQ* 33 (Spring 1974): 34–35; Jacobson, *Life Story,* 138–139.

33. Niswonger, "Arkansas Politics," 267–269; Dunaway, *What a Preacher Saw,* 66–68; Dunaway, *Jeff Davis,* 122–125, 134–135. Attorney General Kirby gained a great deal of notoriety for prosecuting the Hammond Packing Company for price-fixing. The case of Hammond Packing Co. v. State of Arkansas was referred to the United States Supreme Court in April 1907; Kirby and the State won the case.

34. Dunaway, *Jeff Davis,* 122–135; Jacobson, *Life Story,* 130–132.

35. Jacobson, *Life Story,* 134–135; Dunaway, *Jeff Davis,* plate opposite 144; *Arkansas Gazette,* February 19–20, 1908.

36. Jacobson, *Life Story,* 131, 133–134; Dunaway, *Jeff Davis,* 125–129, 134, and plate opposite 192; Dunaway, *What a Preacher Saw,* 67; Williams, *Behind the Scenes in Arkansas Politics,* 10–11. Both Griffin and Donaghey lived in the town of Conway.

37. Dunaway, *Jeff Davis,* 45, 127; Jacobson, *Life Story,* 135–136; *Arkansas Gazette,* February 20, 23, March 22, 25, 1908. For a biographical sketch of Donaghey, see Donovan and Gatewood, *The Governors of Arkansas,* 129–133. See also George Washington Donaghey, *Building a State Capitol* (Little Rock: Parke-Harper, 1937).

38. *Arkansas Gazette,* February–March 1908; Dunaway, *What a Preacher Saw,* 67–68; Niswonger, "Arkansas Democratic Politics," 269–270; Jacobson, *Life Story,* 133–1326.

39. Arkadelphia *Southern-Standard,* April 16, 1908. In the governor's race, the official vote was: Donaghey, 54,807; Kirby, 41,135; Hinemon, 36,185. These figures exclude Drew County, which did not report any official returns.

40. Kirby received a very low percentage of the vote in most city and town precincts, as the figures for the following sample precincts demonstrate: Little Rock (Pulaski County), 19.5 percent; Argenta (Pulaski County), 30.9 percent; Van Buren (Crawford County), 22.1 percent; Marion (Drew County), 17.9 percent; Wilmar (Drew County), 14.6 percent; Nashville (Howard County), 29.3 percent; Fayetteville (Washington County), 17.0 percent; Springdale (Washington County), 30.3 percent; Prairie Grove (Washington County), 20.1 percent; Fenter (Hot Spring County), 29.1 percent; Forrest City (St. Francis County), 25.8 percent; Illinois (Pope County), 29.2 percent. *Arkansas Gazette,* March 28, 1908; *Van Buren Weekly Argus,* April 1, 1908; *The Monticellonian* (Drew County), April 2, 1908; *Nashville News,* April 1, 1908; *Springdale News,* April 10, 1908; Malvern *Arkansas Meteor,* April 3, 1908; *Forrest City Times,* April 3, 1908; *Russellville Democrat,* April 2, 1908.

41. *Arkansas Gazette,* March 28–April 1, 1908; Little Rock *Arkansas Democrat,* March 27–29, 1908; Dunaway, *What a Preacher Saw,* 67–68; Williams, *Behind the Scenes in Arkansas Politics,* 11–12; Jacobson, *Life Story,* 135–136; Niswonger, "Arkansas Democratic Politics," 269–272; Stevenson, "The Political Career of Jeff Davis," 98–99. Shortly after the primary, Davis became involved in an ugly incident on a Little Rock street corner. At one point during the campaign, Davis had charged Deputy Prosecuting Attorney Tom Helms with accepting a $1,000 bribe in exchange for dropping a prosecution. This enraged Helms, who eventually accosted and assaulted Davis as he was walking down a Little Rock street. Davis escaped to his office, but not before Helms managed to bloody his face. A few minutes later Davis returned to the scene brandishing a revolver. Although no shots were fired and neither man was seriously injured, Davis was arrested for disturbing the peace and carrying a firearm within the city limits. Fort Smith *Southwest American,* April 1, 1908; Stevenson, "The Political Career of Jeff Davis," 97.

42. Fayetteville *Arkansas Sentinel,* April 2, 1908.

43. Conway *Arkansas Farmer,* April 2, 1908; Stevenson, "The Political Career of Jeff Davis," 99.

44. *Arkansas Gazette,* June 2–4, 1908; Niswonger, "Arkansas Democratic Politics," 272–274.

45. The strong tradition of localism in Arkansas politics is discussed in V. O. Key, *Southern Politics in State and Nation* (New York: Knopf, 1949), 183–200; and William Orestes Penrose, "Political Ideas in Arkansas, 1880–1907" (M.A. thesis, University of Arkansas, 1945), 62–63, 72–75, 165–166, 285.

46. The text of the speech is reprinted in Dunaway, *Jeff Davis,* 136–178; and in the *Congressional Record,* May 1, 1908, 42: 5521–5531. Jacobson, *Life Story,* 139–140; *Arkansas Gazette,* May 2, 1908; Little Rock *Arkansas Democrat,* May 2, 1908; Vance, "A Karl Marx for Hill Billies," 189.

47. *Arkansas Gazette,* September–October 1908. The speech was delivered on January 26. The text reprinted in Dunaway, *Jeff Davis,* 179–207; and in the *Congressional Record,* January 26, 1909, 43: 1402–1412. Jacobson, *Life Story,* 140; Stevenson, "The Political Career of Jeff Davis," 100–102.

48. Dunaway, *Jeff Davis,* 207.

49. Stevenson, "The Political Career of Jeff Davis," 102–109; *Congressional Record,* June 23, 1909, 44: 3706, June 26, 1909, 44: 3846–3852, 3869–3870, July 2, 1909, 44: 4036, February 1, 1910, 45: 1323–1325, February 17, 1910, 45: 2001–2008. Approximately 20 of Arkansas's 320 banks had been approved by federal examiners.

50. *Congressional Record,* February 17, 1910, 45: 2002. Despite Davis's objections, the pipeline bill was approved by the Senate and enacted into law.

51. *Arkansas Gazette,* January–March 1910. Unofficial returns from most Arkansas counties are printed in ibid., April 3–4, 1910. See also the Fort Smith *Southwest American,* April 1, 1910; Yellville *Mountain Echo,* April 8, 1910; *The Monticellonian* (Drew County), April 7, 1910; *Nashville News,* April 9, 1910; *Springdale News,* April 8, 1910; Malvern *Arkansas Meteor,* April 15, 1910; *Forrest City Times,* April 8, 1910; *Russellville Democrat,* April 7, 1910; *Mena Weekly Star,* April 7, 1910; and the *Nevada County Picayune,* April 23, 1910, for a sampling of precinct returns. Donovan and Gatewood, *The Governors of Arkansas,* 130–131; Niswonger, "Arkansas Democratic Politics," 273–277; Segraves, "Arkansas Politics, 1874–1918," 322–338; Dallas T. Herndon, *Centennial History of Arkansas* (Chicago and Little Rock: S. J. Clark, 11922), 1: 461–456; Thomas L. Baxley, "Prison Reforms During the Donaghey Administration," *ArkHQ* 22 (Spring 1963): 76–84; Jacobson, *Life Story,* 186–187; Dunaway, *Jeff Davis,* 240–243. For a biographical sketch of Kavanaugh, see Fay Hempstead, *Historical Review of Arkansas, Its Commerce, Industry, and Modern Affairs* (Chicago: Lewis Pub. Co., 1911), 2: 620–621.

52. Niswonger, "Arkansas Democratic Politics," 280–285; Jacobson, *Life Story,* 146; *Hearings Before the Committee on the Public Lands of the House of Representatives, February 15–March 2, 1910* (House Reports 19637) (Washington: Government Printing Office, 1910); *Arkansas Gazette,* December 5, 1911, February 1, March 3, 10, 1912; Fayetteville *Arkansas Sentinel,* May 10, 1910. Jerry Wallace, *An Arkansas Judge, Being a Sketch of the Life and Public Service of Judge J. G. Wallace, 1850–1927* (privately printed, 1928), 51, relates the following story: "The close reliance of Senator Davis upon the judgment of Judge Wallace may be illustrated by an incident from the "sunk lands" investigation in the United States Senate. Those were unhappy days for Senator Davis, and the worry and irritation incident to them were calculated to increase his natural volubility. Finally, he sent a telegram to Judge Wallace bearing the single question, "What shall I do?" and the prompt answer came back, "Keep your mouth shut." The next morning, Senator Davis is said to have entered the senate chamber in sphinxlike silence, and from that moment the squall began blowing over."

53. Vance, "A Karl Marx for Hill Billies," 189; Dunaway, *Jeff Davis,* 229, 234–235; Jacobson, *Life Story,* 140, 155–156; *Arkansas Gazette,* January 27, February 24, March 3, 9, 27, 1912; *New York Times,* October 13, 1911; Herndon, *Outline of Executive and Legislative History of Arkansas,* 149.

54. Jacobson, *Life Story,* 166–168; Dardanelle *Post-Dispatch,* January 25, 1912. See also G. W. Ogden, "Jeff Davis, Idol of the Hillbillies," *Hampton's Broadway Magazine* (n.d.), reprinted in the

Camden Beacon (undated clipping); and "Jeff Davis and the 'Red-Necks,'" *Literary Digest* 46 (January 25, 1913): 194.

55. Jacobson, *Life Story*, 140, 158, 190; Dunaway, *Jeff Davis*, 234–235; "Jeff Davis and the 'Red-Necks,'" 192; Stevenson, "The Political Career of Jeff Davis," 110; Niswonger, "Arkansas Democratic Politics," 246–247.

56. Quoted in Stevenson, "The Political Career of Jeff Davis," 110; *Jefferson Davis, Memorial Addresses* (62nd Congress, 3rd Session, Senate Document 1146) (Washington: Government Printing Office, 1913), 50.

57. *Arkansas Gazette*, June 1910–June 1911; John Gould Fletcher, *Arkansas* (Chapel Hill: University of North Carolina, 1947), 313; Wallace, *An Arkansas Judge*, 51; Dunaway, *Jeff Davis*, 234–235.

58. *Biographical and Historical Memoirs of Southern Arkansas* (Chicago: Goodspeed, 1890), 425; *Biographical Directory of the American Congress, 1774–1971* (Washington: Government Printing Office, 1971), 656; Jacobson, *Life Story*, 141–143; Paige E. Mulhollan, "The Public Career of James H. Berry" (M.A. thesis, University of Arkansas, 1962), 187–189; Dunaway, *What a Preacher Saw*, 72–73.

59. Jacobson, *Life Story*, 142–148; Stevenson, "The Political Career of Jeff Davis," 111–112; Niswonger, "Arkansas Democratic Politics," 284–286; Ledbetter, "Jeff Davis and the Politics of Combat," 35; *Arkansas Gazette*, December 5, 1911–March 27, 1912.

60. *Arkansas Gazette*, January 27, 1912.

61. Ibid., March 3, 1912.

62. Ibid., January 5–6, February 9, March 10, 1912; Jacobson, *Life Story*, 142–145, 147–148; Stevenson, "The Political Career of Jeff Davis," 111.

63. Jacobson, *Life Story*, 143–144. This statement was made in a speech at Morrilton on December 4, 1911.

64. Ibid., 142, 145, 147; *Arkansas Gazette*, March 19–27, 1912; Donovan and Gatewood, *The Governors of Arkansas*, 132. Robinson was from Lonoke County. For a biographical sketch of Robinson, see ibid., 134–137.

65. Jacobson, *Life Story*, 145–146; *Arkansas Gazette*, March 28–April 3, 1912; Dunaway, *What a Preacher Saw*, 72. Robinson received 90,520 votes; Donaghey received 46,701. Statewide the county-by-county correlation between the Davis and Robinson votes is only +.091.

66. Dunaway, *Jeff Davis*, 10, 27, 235; *Arkansas Gazette*, June 13–15, September 7–November 7, 1912; Arkadelphia *Southern-Standard*, June 13, 1912. Davis, like most Arkansas Democratic leaders, supported the candidacy of Champ Clark of Missouri prior to Wilson's emergence as the clear-cut favorite of the delegates at the Democratic National Convention. Segraves, "Arkansas Politics, 1874–1918," 246–347.

67. *Arkansas Gazette*, January 3–6, 13, 1913; Little Rock *Arkansas Democrat*, January 3, 1913; Bayless Walker Price, "The Life of Jeff Davis" (M.A. thesis, University of Alabama, 1929); Jacobson, *Life Story*, 215.

68. Dunaway, *Jeff Davis*, 249; *Arkansas Gazette*, January 3, 1913; Little Rock *Arkansas Democrat*, January 3, 1913; Price, "The Life of Jeff Davis," 61. Davis had been on a diet for several months and reportedly had lost fourteen pounds.

69. Dunaway, *Jeff Davis*, 23–30; *Arkansas Gazette*, January 6, 1913; Dardanelle *Post-Dispatch*, January 9, 11913; Fletcher, *Arkansas*, 313–314; Williams, *Behind the Scenes in Arkansas Politics*, 139; Dunaway, *What a Preacher Saw*, 70–71; Price, "The Life of Jeff Davis," 63–66.

70. Dunaway, *Jeff Davis*, 242. The speaker was William Kavanaugh. *New York Times*, January 3, 1913; *Washington Post*, January 3, 1913; Jacobson, *Life Story*, 215–217, 240. Dunaway, *Jeff Davis*, 227–250, contains several memorial addresses delivered by Davis's congressional colleagues.

71. Dunaway, *Jeff Davis*, 30.

72. Quoted in "Jeff Davis and the 'Red-Necks,'" 194; and in Williams, *Behind the Scenes in Arkansas Politics*, 139–141.

73. The special gubernatorial election in July 1913 became necessary when Governor Joseph

T. Robinson was chosen by the legislature to finish Davis's unexpired senatorial term. Hays was a pallbearer at Davis's funeral. Dunaway, *Jeff Davis,* 24–25, 30. As shown in Appendix A, the correlation between the 1912 Davis vote and the 1913 Hays vote is +.412; the correlation between the 1912 vote and the Kirby vote is +.496. Kirby was narrowly defeated by Senator James P. Clarke. Williams, *Behind the Scenes in Arkansas Politics,* 12–18; Dunaway, *What a Preacher Saw,* 71–74; Donovan and Gatewood, *The Governors of Arkansas,* 135–136, 139. For a biographical sketch of Hays, see ibid., 138–144.

74. Williams, *Behind the Scenes in Arkansas Politics,* 18–21; Dunaway, *What a Preacher Saw,* 74–75; Donovan and Gatewood, *The Governors of Arkansas,* 147; Charles W. Crawford, "From Classroom to State Capitol: Charles H. Brough and the Campaign of 1916," *ArkHQ* 21 (Autumn 1962): 213–230. The 1916 primary campaign was a three-way race between Smith, Brough, and Earle Hodges. The correlation between the 1912 Davis vote and the 1916 Smith vote is +.519 (see Appendix A).

75. Jacobson, *Life Story,* 168. Several Jeff Davis men were prominent in Arkansas politics during the 1920s, including Thomas C. McRae, who served as governor from 1921 to 1925. Donovan and Gatewood, *The Governors of Arkansas,* 152–159. Davis's memory was also kept alive by the political career of his eldest son, Wallace, who served as state attorney general from September 1915 (Governor Hays appointed him to the post after the death of Attorney General William L. Moose) to January 1917, and as a Democratic national committeeman from 1915 to 1921. *Arkansas Gazette,* October, 24, 1965.

76. Vance, "A Karl Marx for Hill Billies," 180.

77. Dunaway, *What a Preacher Saw,* 57–58; Stockard, *King Jeff I;* Charles Morrow Wilson, *Rabble Rouser* (New York: Longmans, Green, and Co., 1936).

78. Dunaway, *Jeff Davis,* 210; *Arkansas Gazette,* August 1, 1906.

Index

Abeles, Charles, 165
Adams, John G., 161
Agrarian radicalism: and Southern demagogues, 6–18; and the Bryanist shadow movement, 17, 53–60; in Pope County, 32–35; rise in Arkansas, 33–38; decline in Arkansas, 38–47, 58, 117. *See also* Agricultural Wheel; Brothers of Freedom; Davis, Jeff; Farmers' Alliance; Populism; Socialism
Agrarian subculture, 10–18, 32–33, 38, 55, 60, 98–100, 146, 154, 160, 167, 187, 190–191, 194, 202–203, 239, 243
Agricultural Wheel, 13, 33, 35, 38, 45, 88, 91
Alcorn, James Lusk, 64
All the King's Men, xiii, 173
Alley, John I., 293
Altheimer, Louis, 174–175, 179
Altheimer, Ulysses, 310–311
American Bible Society, 30, 163
American Round Bale Cotton Company, 138–140, 147
American Tobacco Company, 68–69, 81, 89
Antebellum South, 24–25; planters in, 12–13, 22
Anti-Catholicism, 165, 284
Anti-Davis faction. *See* Davis, Jeff; Factionalism
Anti-Saloon League, 153, 162, 308
Anti-Semitism, 8, 165
Antitrust movement: Davis's participation in, 3, 17, 45, 61, 64–84, 86, 89–91, 100, 111, 113–114, 120, 125–128, 135, 137–142, 147, 157, 176, 186, 190, 198, 207–208, 210, 217, 225, 227, 229–234, 236–237, 245,

279, 296; in Arkansas, 54, 56, 60, 63–91, 226, 318; conferences of, 76, 83–84
Argenta, Ark., 98, 117, 262, 298, 299, 318
Arkadelphia *Southern-Standard,* 94, 129–131
Arkansas Argicultural and Development Association, 59
Arkansas Baptist Association, 148–149, 158, 164, 308
Arkansas Brick Manufacturing Company, 132–135, 173. *See also* Convict-lease system; Dickinson, W. W.
Arkansas Christian Temperance Union, 150
Arkansas County, 95, 154, 157
Arkansas River, 53, 175
Arkansas River Valley, 23, 28, 51, 97, 260
Arkansas State Bankers Association, 294
Arkansas State Board of Charities, 176, 178
Arkansas State Board of Trade, 73, 304
Arkansas State Bureau of Immigration, 113
Arkansas State Hospital for Nervous Diseases, 227
"Arkansaw Traveller, The," 23–24
Armstrong, Carroll, 111
Armstrong pardon, 170, 207
Arnett, Charles T., 149
Ashley County, 41, 185, 189, 202, 298
Atkins, Ark., 29, 32, 49
Atkins *Chronicle,* 49
Atkinson, W. F., 158
Automobiles, 12, 240

Baker, Cullen Montgomery, 27
Baker, J. B. (Buck), 49–51, 292
Banks, 11, 32, 68, 75, 81, 88–91, 98, 113, 237–238, 294, 319

Banks, Nathaniel, 26

Baptist Evangel, The, 149

Baptists, 25, 185, 272; critical of Davis, 122, 148–149, 158–162; in legislature, 124–125, 129, 181; and Davis's religious beliefs, 163–164, 166, 168; and the Davis vote, 202–203, 248, 252–254

Barker, D. E., 108, 301

Barton, Frank, 145

Basso, Hamilton, 6

Batesville, Ark., 36

Battle, B. B., 296

Battle of Corinth (Miss.), 209

Baxter County, 202

Beakley farm, 174–175

Beauvoir, Miss., 78–80

Beebe, Ark., 187

Benton, Ark., 91

Benton County, 159, 296

Benton Democrat, 94

Bentonville, Ark., 49, 83, 166, 217, 296

Berry, James H., 111, 272, 296, 302; as a moderate Bryanist, 57–58; and 1900 senatorial primary, 84, 95, 293, 296; praised by Davis, 139–140; and 1906 senatorial primary, 205, 208–209, 213, 217–224, 240, 315

Bethel College (Ky.), 25

Bettis, Jim, 190–191

Bilbo, Theodore G., 163

Bismarck, Ark., 195–196, 263

Black Belt, 22, 185; voter turnout and disfranchisement in, 40–44; and fusion system, 40, 189, 214; legislators from, 206

Blackmar, G. W., 168–169

Blacks, 13, 18, 114, 119, 210–213, 216, 286; and slavery, 22, 24–25, 28; and Reconstruction, 27–29, 171; and disfranchisement, 40–46, 206, 214; as politicians, 94, 188–189, 215; and the penal system, 133, 144–146, 176, 192; and pardons, 168–171, 187–188, 192; as jurors, 189–190, 198; and education, 205–207, 214–215; and the Davis vote, 248, 252–254, 262–268; and voter turnout, 250–251. *See also* Black Belt; Lynching; Racism

Blackwell, Henry B., 169

Blease, Coleman Livingston, 3

Blythe, Samuel G., 10

Bonanza, Ark., 186

Board of Capitol Commissioners, Ark.: cre-

ated by Kimbell Act, 73–75; conflict with Davis, 74–75, 77, 84, 121, 131; reorganized in 1901, 126–127, 135–136, 305; Eagle's removal from, 158–159, 176–177; reorganized in 1903, 180; and Donaghey, 234. *See also* Kimbell State House Act; Merriman State House Act; State house

Borah, William, 6

Bossism: and demagoguery, 5, 172; and Davis, 173, 176, 203, 228–229, 235, 245. *See also* Davis organization

Bossuet, 273

Boston, Mass., 169–170

Boston Mountains, 19, 23

Bourbon Democrats: and romantic politics, 7; in Arkansas, 39, 55, 58

Bourland, Jeremiah V., 35, 110–111, 196, 205, 307

Bowling Green, Ky., 25

Bradley County, 202

Brinkley, Ark., 171–172, 312

Brooks, Thomas B., 304

Brooks-Baxter War, 29, 74

Brothers of Freedom, 33–35, 38, 285

Brough, Charles Hillman, 244, 249, 272, 321

Brown, Pomp, 187–188

Brown, William M., 212

Brugman, Richard, 84

Brundidge, Stephen S., 228, 240–244, 311

Bryan, William Jennings: as Davis's hero, 47–49, 72, 119, 218, 237; and 1896 election, 48–49, 91, 138, 218; and the Bryanist movement, 53–60, 117–118, 208, 210; visits Little Rock in 1899, 67, 90, 297–298; and 1900 election, 119, 303; as a political evangelist, 164; and 1908 election, 237

Bryanism, 47–60, 117–118, 208, 210; moderate versus radical, 55–60

Bryant, Edgar, 26, 82, 85, 88, 90–92, 110, 302

Buckner, Richard, 128

Bunn, H. G., 121, 311

Burgess, J. C., 206

Burgess school tax bill, 206–207, 215

Bush, James O. A., 290

Bush Bill, 54, 121, 290

Businessmen: attitudes toward corporate regulation, 54–55, 59–71, 292; and Rector Antitrust Act, 63–71, 88–89; and 1899 Little Rock convention, 68–70, 96; as gubernatorial candidates, 88, 234, 238; as Davis supporters, 101; ties to Democratic party,

113, 172; as legislators, 123–124, 129. *See also* Corporations; Merchants; New South movement
Butler, P. T., 128

Cabot, Ark., 191
Calhoun County, 202
California, 224–225
Callender, E. B., 169
Camden, Ark., 86, 159, 240
Camden Beacon, 85–86
Capital Theater (Little Rock), 177
Caraway, Thaddeus, 244
Carmack, Edward, 208
Carnahan, James P., 38–39, 108, 287
Carpetbaggers, 28, 171, 187, 189, 211
Carroll County, 57, 188
Carter, H. S., 285
Cash, Wilbur J., 162
Cason, Clarence, 7
Catholics, 124, 165, 284
Catts, Sidney J., 9, 164, 284
Center Point, Ark., 88–92, 105, 262, 297, 300
Chicago, Ill., 57, 83–84, 90, 208
Chicago *Record-Herald,* 195–196
Chicago *Times-Herald,* 84
Chicot County, 41, 159, 188
Civil War, 64, 90, 95, 112, 186, 209, 237; in southwestern Arkansas, 25–26; in Pope County, 28
Clansman, The, 146
Clark, Adam, 96
Clark, Champ, 320
Clark, Thomas D., 6
Clarke, James P., 31, 302, 321; as a moderate Bryanist, 56–57, 294; and 1902 senatorial primary campaign, 137–141, 147, 305; alliance with Davis, 138–141, 147–149, 152, 156–157, 210; analysis of 1902 Clarke vote, 152–153, 155–157, 249, 262–268; and liquor interests, 149; breaks with Davis, 200; visits New York Stock Exchange with Davis, 217
Clarke County, 96
Clary, Julius, 228–229, 235
Class conflict: and Southern demagogues, 8; and the urban-rural cleavage, 12–17; within the Davis movement, 16–17; and Davis's politics, 78, 81, 86–89, 95, 97, 100–106, 142–145, 154–155, 187, 190–191, 193, 198, 201–203, 231, 239–240

Clayton, Powell, 27–28, 39, 170–171, 211, 213, 272
Cleburne County, 157, 202
Cleveland, Grover, 36, 53, 208, 217, 238, 287, 291, 298
Cleveland County, 202, 289
Coal Hill scandal, 131–132
Coal mining, 59, 102, 131, 292
Cockrill, S. R., 80
Collins, Charles, 60
Collins, W. H., 293
Collins Insurance Bill, 65, 293
Colonial economy, 100, 103, 118, 146, 157, 190, 225, 245; and Southern demagogues, 7; and planter-merchants, 13; and Southern elite, 55, 60. *See also* Agrarian subculture; Crop lien system; Cultural politics; Metropolitan society; New South subculture; Sectionalism
Colorado, 53
Columbia County, 41, 95, 202
Communism, 34
Concordia Club (Little Rock), 165
Confederacy, 83, 94, 112; and Southern demagogues, 6–7, 28; Davis's romanticization of, 21–22, 26, 78–79, 90, 219; army veterans, 21–22, 26–27, 49, 57, 88, 95, 121, 140, 171, 174, 187, 208, 213, 221, 227, 285, 291; and Lewis Davis, 25, 171–172, 174, 219
Convention system, 47–48, 50–51, 93, 186, 224
Convict-lease system, 39, 126–128, 131–135, 173–175, 180, 186, 226, 304
Conway, Ark., 80–82, 113, 135, 188, 209, 229, 296, 318
Conway County, 36, 38, 61–62, 110–111, 286, 292
Cook, George B., 142–144, 146
Cook, M. D. L., 175–176
Corn, 24
Corporations, 54, 63–65, 81; lobbyists for, 63, 65, 126, 207, 226–227; nonresident, 225; and corporate income tax bill, 237. *See also* Antitrust movement; Insurance industry; New South movement; Railroads
Corruption: among Bourbon Democrats, 39, 139; Davis's charges of, 74, 173, 176, 195, 235; charges against Davis, 177–180, 210, 219, 234, 238–239; in 1905 legislature, 207, 227, 314. *See also* Impeachment; Penitentiary "ring"; State house

Corwin, Ark., 186

Cotton, 132, 138–140, 147, 225, 248, 280; price of, 33, 38, 58, 191, 217

County canvass, 88–89, 91, 113, 147, 185, 187, 196, 205, 209, 241

Cox, Thomas L., 135, 234

Crawford County, 205, 260–268

Crittenden County, 41, 201

Crockett, David, 95

Crockett, John W., 95, 107, 109, 134–135, 174–175, 177–178, 183–184

Crop futures: Davis's opposition to speculation in, 209, 226–227, 232–233, 237

Crop lien system, 28, 31, 33, 225

Cross County, 41, 300

Crowley's Ridge, 23, 97

Crutcher, Park, 311

Cultural politics: and Southern demagogues, 9–18, 55; and Davis movement, 9–18, 78, 99, 102, 118, 187, 190–191, 193–194, 198, 202–203, 243–245; in Pope County, 28, 33–34; and Bryanism, 55–56, 60. *See also* Agrarian subculture; Colonial economy; Metropolitan society; New South subculture

Cumberland University, 31, 227, 284

Cummings Farm, 175–180, 215

Dallas *Times-Herald,* 169

Daniels, Jonathan, 163

Danville, Ark., 161

Dardanelle, Ark., 135

Dardanelle, Dover and Harrison Railroad, 30

Dardanelle *Post-Dispatch,* 93

Davidson, Ben, 192

Davis, Bessie (daughter), 119

Davis, Elizabeth Phillips Scott (mother), 25, 28, 200, 224, 281–282, 283

Davis, Ina MacKenzie (wife), 31, 62, 80, 85, 119, 149, 163, 239, 298

Davis, James H. ("Cyclone"), 36

Davis, Jeff: summary of career, 3; and Southern demagoguery, 4–18; personality of, 14, 31–32, 48, 74, 122, 140–141, 149, 168, 196, 209–210, 223–224, 239, 303; childhood in southwestern Arkansas, 21–28, 171, 213; during the Civil War and Reconstruction, 21, 25–29, 171, 213; family background of, 25–30, 281–282; 1900 gubernatorial primary, 26, 75–109, 146, 167, 197; childhood and adolescence in

Pope County, 28–30; education of, 30–31, 51, 227, 283–284; marriage to Ina MacKenzie, 31; family of, 31, 62–63, 80, 85, 119–120, 163, 174, 219, 224, 239; law practice of, 31–32, 34, 47, 49, 51, 228, 240, 284; and Pope County politics, 32–37, 146, 148; and 1888 presidential election, 35–36, 217–218, 286, 289; and 1890 campaign for prosecuting attorney, 36–37, 148, 286; and use of political humor, 36, 83, 90–91, 143, 147, 185–187, 190–191, 193–194; as district prosecuting attorney, 37–38, 47, 49, 148, 285; financial situation of, 37, 119, 143, 227–228, 239, 286; and 1896 congressional campaign, 47–48; and Bryanism, 47–49, 55, 72, 119, 218, 237; and 1896 presidential election, 48–49; and 1898 campaign for attorney general, 49–53, 146, 289, 292; suffers stroke in 1898, 50–51; health of, 50–51, 243, 320; as attorney general, 58–120; and Rector Antitrust Act, 64–72, 74, 76, 78–84, 86, 89–91, 120; and 1899 businessmen's convention, 68–70; recreational activities of, 71, 122, 203, 224; and state house controversy, 72–80, 84, 90, 120–121, 126–128, 135–137; and 1899 antitrust conferences, 76, 83–84; and 1899 Hardy speech, 77–80; and 1899 Conway speech, 80–82; and persecution theme, 80–81, 85–86, 88, 90–91, 143–144, 158–160, 167–168, 178–180, 183, 186, 196–198, 223, 232–233, 296; confrontation with James Wood, 82–83; campaign techniques of, 86–92, 100, 114, 137–143, 146–147, 154, 180, 187, 190–198, 205, 209–211, 218–219, 233–234, 240–241, 297; and 1899 Center Point speech, 89–91; and 1900 primary returns, 91–109; and 1904 general election returns, 107; and 1900 Democratic State Convention, 110–112; and 1900 general election, 112–117, 146; and 1900 general election returns, 115–117; as governor-elect, 119–120; and 1901 inauguration, 120–122; and first term as governor, 120–175; and 1901 legislature, 120–130, 132–133; drinking problem of, 122, 143, 145, 147–149, 156, 158–162, 168, 179, 219, 223, 243; and 1902 church expulsion controversy, 122, 158–162; and penitentiary controversy, 126–128, 131–137, 173–180; and

1902 gubernatorial primary, 137, 141–159, 197; and 1902 senatorial primary, 137–141, 147, 152–153, 155–157; and 1902 primary returns, 151–157; and religion, 159–168; and 1904 gubernatorial primary, 160–161, 185–203, 311; and Thompson pardon, 168–171; and 1902 general election, 170–172; and 1902 general election returns, 172; and second term as governor, 175–206; and 1903 legislature, 175–184; and 1903 impeachment controversy, 176–180; and 1904 primary returns, 200–203; and 1904 general election, 204–207; and third term as governor, 206–226; and 1905 legislature, 206–208; and 1906 senatorial primary, 208–222; and Roosevelt visit to Little Rock, 210–213; and 1906 primary returns, 221–222; and final months as governor, 223–226; and 1907 farewell address, 225–226; and Little administration, 225–227; as Senator-elect, 227–229; and Pindall administration, 228; and 1908 gubernatorial primary, 229, 233–235; and 1907 "cobweb" speech, 229–232; and federal antitrust bill, 229–234, 236; as United States Senator, 230–244; and crop futures bill, 232–233, 237; and loss of influence after 1907, 233–244; and 1910 gubernatorial primary, 237–238; and 1910 sunk lands controversy, 238–239; and death of first wife, 239; and marriage to Lelia Carter, 239; and 1912 senatorial primary, 240–241; and 1912 primary returns, 241–243; and 1912 presidential election, 243, 320; death and funeral of, 243–244; legacy of, 244–245; and analysis of Davis vote, 247–268. *See also* Antitrust movement; Davis organization; Demagogue; Folklore; Jacobson, Charles; Mass leader; Oratory; Pardons; Personal politics; Press; Progressivism; Prohibition; Racism; Religion; Sectionalism; Violence

Davis, Jefferson (Confederate President), 3, 21–22, 78–80, 83, 94, 146, 171–172, 222

Davis, Joshua (grandfather), 25

Davis, Lelia Carter (second wife), 239

Davis, Lewis W. (father), 120; early life of, 25; as a Baptist preacher, 25, 27, 163; Confederate record of, 25–26, 171–172, 174, 219, 221; during Reconstruction, 27–29; as a leader in Pope County, 28–35, 284;

as a temperance leader, 30, 36, 148; death of, 219, 221; appointed to county judgeship by son, 316

Davis, Rebecca (grandmother), 25

Davis, Wallace (son), 321

Davis organization, 101–102, 165, 172, 195, 197, 204, 210, 224, 226, 319; and shadow movement, 17; emergence in 1899–1900, 94–95, 107–111; and governor's staff, 119–120; and legislature, 125–130, 176, 181–182, 207, 214–216; and patronage, 135, 188, 213, 236; and alliance with Clarke, 138, 140, 147, 156–157, 200; and liquor interests, 161; decline of, 228–229, 233–237, 241, 244–245; lingers after Davis's death, 244, 321

Deaf-Mute Institute of Arkansas, 192

Debs, Eugene V., 288

Debt repudiation movement, 39, 57

Demagogue, 3–18, 65, 146, 162–165; Jeff Davis as, 3–18, 72, 81, 101, 112, 140, 162–165, 170, 191, 207, 226, 244; Greek conception of, 4; problem of definition, 4–6, 273. *See also* Davis, Jeff; Southern demagogues

Democracy; and Southern politics, 10

Democratic National Committee, 57, 137, 321

Democratic National Convention: of 1896, 57; of 1900, 110, 301–302; of 1904, 204; of 1908, 236

Democratic party. *See* Bourbon Democrats; Bryan, William Jennings; Bryanism; Cleveland, Grover; Davis, Jeff; Davis organization; Democratic National Committee; Democratic National Convention; Democratic State Central Committee, Arkansas; Democratic State Convention, Arkansas; Factionalism; One-party system; Pope County

Democratic State Central Committee, Arkansas, 93, 111–112, 204, 214

Democratic State Convention, Arkansas: of 1894, 53; of 1898, 51; of 1900, 96, 110; of 1902, 170, 208; of 1904, 204; of 1906, 224, 228; of 1908, 235–236; of 1912, 243

Des Arc, Ark., 171

Desha County, 41, 157

Dickinson, W. W., 132–135, 173, 179–180, 186, 304

Dinsmore, Hugh, 218–219, 310, 316

Disciples of Christ (Christians), 124, 129, 181

Disfranchisement, 8–9, 14, 35, 39–46, 51, 249–251; of whites, 43–46, 250–251; Davis's attitude towards, 46, 214–215. *See also* Blacks; Grandfather clause; Poll tax; Voter turnout; White primary
Dixon, Richard, 106
Doaksville, Indian Territory, 26
Dogpatch, 23
Donaghey, George Washington, 229, 233–238, 241, 243, 249, 272, 318, 320
Dorgan, Howard, 5
Dos Passos, John R., Sr., 195
Dover, Ark., 28–30, 286
Drew County, 41, 154, 185, 201, 260–268, 318
Dryden, John, 273
Dunaway, L. S., 101, 191, 200, 299
Dykeman, Wilma, 5

Eagle, James P., 272; as governor, 73, 132, 285, 287; and Capitol Commission, 135, 158–159, 176–177; as Baptist leader, 158, 308
East Arkansas, 51, 68, 138, 147, 149, 205, 227; topography of, 19, 23; voter turnout in, 40–41; voting patterns in, 97, 104–105, 107, 151–152, 154, 157, 199–201, 220–221, 241–243, 260, 262–268
Economic depression of 1890s, 38, 53–54, 58–59
Education, 205–207, 214–215; and free textbooks, 226; and uniform textbook referendum, 249
Electrification, 11–12, 32, 89, 98–99
England, Ark., 133–134, 144–145, 174–175
Episcopalians, 124, 212
Ethnicity, in the South, 11, 17–18
Ethnocultural model, 10–11, 17–18
Eureka Springs, Ark., 50, 188–189
Evans, Arkie, 188
Evans, Jeptha, 31, 37, 110, 229, 244, 311
Ezell, John, 101

Factionalism: in the early twentieth-century South, 8, 11, 18; among Arkansas Democrats, 10, 39, 53–60, 94–95, 107–112, 115, 117, 127–131, 137–142, 145, 147–149, 155–160, 172, 176–183, 197–200, 203–205, 215–216, 221, 224–229, 235–236, 240–244, 321; among Arkansas Republicans, 170–172, 225. *See also* Davis organization

Farmers. *See* Agrarian radicalism; Agrarian subculture; Agricultural Wheel; Brothers of Freedom; Crop lien system; Farm laborers; Farmers' Alliance; Farmers' Union; Populism; Tenant farmers
Farmers' Alliance, 13, 33, 35–36, 286
Farmers' Union, 234–235
Farm laborers, 102, 104–105, 154, 201
Fascism and Southern demagogues, 10, 15–16, 163–165
Faubus, Orval, 140
Faulkner County, 191, 296
Fayetteville, Ark., 30, 97, 125, 178, 192, 218–219, 262, 310, 318
Fellow-servant legislation, 63, 121, 126–127, 176, 226
Ferguson, James (Farmer Jim), 102
Files, A. W., 108, 113, 146, 158, 287
Finley, Orto, 245
Fishback, William M., 39, 112, 272, 287, 302
Fizer, Napoleon B., 38, 287
Fletcher, John G., 85, 88–92
Fletcher, John Gould (poet), 14, 60, 89, 193
Fletcher, Thomas, 92, 298
Fletcher, William, 311
Florida, 9, 164, 284
Folklore: and Davis, 3, 14, 92–93, 191, 244–245; and Southern demagogues, 7
Fordyce, Samuel, 292
Foreman, Ark., 280
Forrest, Nathan Bedford, 95
Forrest City, Ark., 104–105, 135, 147, 262, 301, 318
Fort Smith, Ark., 54, 67, 82, 92, 97–98, 117, 125, 138–140, 172, 262, 298
Fort Smith Elevator, 222
Franklin County, 35, 47, 239
Free silver, 39, 47–49, 53–57, 60, 72, 90, 114, 208, 290
Free trade, 48, 55, 57, 231, 237
Frontier: legacy and persistence in Arkansas, 16, 21–24, 73; and Davis's use of "log cabin" politics, 21–22; data relating to, 248, 250–254
Fry, Morton, 301
Funk, E. M., 311
Fusion: between Populists and Democrats, 48, 58; between Populists and Republicans, 39, 117, 287
Fusion system, 40, 189, 214
Futrell, J. Marion, 179–180, 311

Gantt Streetcar Act, 215
Garland, Augustus, 291
Garland County, 111, 154
Georgia, 208, 309
German National Bank (Little Rock), 88
Gettysburg, Battle of, 237
Gleason Hotel (Little Rock), 119
Glenwood Park (Little Rock), 67–69, 72, 82, 294
Goar, Frank, 50–51
Goebel, William, 91, 144, 298
"Goldbugs," 48, 53–54, 60, 90, 217
Goodwyn, Lawrence, 16, 55
Gordon, O. B., 204
Goshen, Ark., 193
Gould, Jay, 53
Grace, A. B., 311
Grace, W. P., 293
Grand Army of the Republic, 169
Grandfather clause, 214, 249
Grand Prairie, 23
Grant, Ulysses S., 68
Grant County, 202
Grapes of Wrath, The, 17
Graves, Muley, 17
Great Britain, 225
Greaves, Charles D., 170–172
Greenback party, 35, 45
Greene County, 86, 201
Greenwood, Ark., 226, 263
Griffin, Ben, 234–235, 318

Hackney, Sheldon, 8
Hamburg and Texarkana Railroad, 291
Hammond Packing Company, 318
Hanna, Marcus, 113
Hardy, Thomas W., 127–128, 304
Hardy, Ark., 77–80, 125, 156, 262, 295
Harrison, Benjamin, 36, 287
Harrod, J. H., 311
Hart, Jesse Cleveland, 71, 241, 249
Harvey, William Hope (Coin), 53, 272
Hatch Bill, 209
Hays, George Washington, 244, 249, 272, 321
Hays, Samuel, 9
Haywood, Big Bill, 208
Heflin, Tom, 165
Heiskell, J. N., 101–102, 146, 191, 223–224, 245
Helena, Ark., 67, 138
Helena Weekly World, 53, 68, 99, 290

Helms, Tom, 318
Hempstead County, 41, 138
Henley, J. J., 51, 53, 289
Herrenvolk democracy, 46
Hicks, John T., 49–51, 292
Hill, Frank, 134–135, 144–145
Hindsville, Ark., 50
Hinemon, John, 162, 229, 235, 249, 311, 318
Hitchcock, Ethan Allen, 238
Hobbes, Thomas, 273
Hodges, Earle, 249, 321
Hoffer, Eric, 6
Hogins, Reese B., 135, 173–174, 176, 179
Hogue, James E., 300
Holland, John H., 127–128, 311
Holt Bill, 148
Hope, Ark., 196
Hotel Marion (Little Rock), 227
Hot Spring County, 92, 202, 260–268, 318
Hot Springs, Ark., 64, 68, 73, 96, 142–145, 159, 170, 185, 204, 300, 305
Howard County, 89, 92, 97, 104–105, 107–109, 154, 201, 260–268, 289
Hughes, Charles Evans, 208
Hughes, Simon, 132, 272
Humphreys, Thomas H., 125
Humphreys Bill, 126, 133, 304
Huntsville, Ark., 114

Illinois, 57, 83–84, 90, 187, 208
Illinois township, Ark., 33, 285, 318
Illiteracy: and disfranchisement, 41, 43, 214; and Davis vote, 104–105, 154, 201, 203, 248, 250–254
Impeachment controversy of 1903, 176–180, 186, 203, 207, 311
Imperialism, 110–111; Davis critical of, 114
Income tax, 57, 237
Independence County, 205
Independent, The, 232
Indian Territory, 22
Indians, American, 26
Industrial Workers of the World, 208
Initiative and referendum, 249
Insurance industry: attempts to regulate, 63–68, 70–71, 121, 208, 293; and Davis, 65–71, 90, 113–114, 121, 227; withdrawal from Arkansas, 67, 207. *See also* Rector Antitrust Act
Insurgent Republicans, 170–172
Intrastate sectionalism, 8, 23, 51, 92, 138, 153,

156–157, 193, 200, 241–243, 305

Iowa, 171

Iron Mountain Railroad, 53, 57

Isolation: as an Arkansas tradition, 22–24; and the Davis movement, 98–100, 154, 203, 221, 260–268

Izard County, 49

Jackson, Andrew, 16, 54–55, 70, 106, 111, 231

Jackson, Thomas (Stonewall), 219

Jackson County, 192

Jacksonian democracy, legacy of. *See* Jackson, Andrew

Jacobson, Charles: as Davis's biographer, 3; as deputy prosecuting attorney, 37, 61, 76; comments on Davis's Bryanism, 48–49; early life of, 61; as Davis's campaign manager in 1898 and 1900, 61–62, 86–87; as assistant attorney general, 62, 71–72; as private secretary to the governor, 119–120, 122, 131, 140–141, 178, 183, 185, 192, 197, 200, 210, 224; as Jewish leader, 165; breaks with Davis, 228–229, 241

James brothers, 27

Jefferson, Thomas, 78, 91, 106, 187

Jefferson County, 41, 157, 174, 294

Jeffries-Corbett fight, 195–196

Jesus, 70, 165, 167

Jews, 87, 165

Johnson County, 33, 37, 96, 131, 286

Jones, Daniel Webster, 74, 115, 117, 212, 287, 291; as reform leader, 49, 53, 57, 65, 123; and Rector Antitrust Act, 65–66, 71–72, 84; hostility towards Davis, 84, 90, 95–96, 120; and 1900 senatorial primary, 95, 209, 293, 296

Jones, James K., 302; as moderate Bryanist, 53, 57, 138; and 1902 senatorial primary, 137–141, 147, 152–153, 157, 159, 205, 305, 305–306, 307; and Panama Canal Commission, 170

Jones, Sam, 164, 309

Jonesboro, Ark., 312

Jonesboro *Tribune*, 244

Juvenal, 273

Kansas, 224

Kavanaugh, William M., 238, 243, 320

Kelley, Robert, 11

Kentucky, 25, 91, 144, 298

Keokuk, Ia., 171

Kimbell, John D., 73, 78

Kimbell State House Act, 73–75, 79–80, 111, 121, 126, 132, 304

King, David L., 125–129

King Antitrust Act, 125–128, 137, 139–140, 176, 181, 186, 245

King Jeff I, 223, 316

Kinsworthy, E. B., 159

Kirby, William F.: as pro-Davis legislator, 125, 127, 129; as attorney general, 224–227, 316, 318; and 1908 senatorial primary, 229, 233–236, 243, 249, 318; and 1914 senatorial primary, 244, 249, 321

Kirwan, Albert D., 6

Knights of the White Camellia, 27

Kousser, J. Morgan, 40

Ku Klux Klan, 27, 163, 165

Labor unions, 57, 167, 208, 234, 279

La Follette, Robert, Sr., 6, 208, 230

Lankford, Eugene, 127–128

Latta, George, 68

Lawrence, Robert, 126–127

Laynesport, Ark., 26

Lee, John P., 224

Lee, Robert E., 219

Lee County, 41, 68, 83, 154, 157

Lee County Courier, 82

Legislature, 214, 218, 245; 1877 session, 30; 1897 session, 49, 63, 124–125, 291, 293; 1899 session, 63–75, 90, 123–125, 195, 293, 297–298, 304; 1901 session, 115, 120–121, 123–130, 132–133, 136, 138, 148, 158; 1891 session, 123, 132; 1893 session, 123, 132; 1881 session, 131; 1883 session, 131; 1875 session, 150; 1903 session, 175–187, 207, 215; 1905 session, 206–208, 215, 224, 314; 1907 session, 207, 224–227; 1911 session, 249, 258

Levees, 39, 226

Lewisville, Ark., 143

Lincoln, Abraham, 51, 78, 112

Lincoln County, 41, 92, 175, 202, 289

Liquor interests, 61, 148–150, 153, 161, 186, 192

Little, John Sebastian (Bass), 210, 212, 221, 223, 225–229, 311, 317

Little, Paul, 226

Little River, 22

Little River County, 27, 29, 41, 50–51, 89, 213, 280

Little Rock and Fort Smith Railroad, 28–30
Little Rock, Ark., 25, 47, 51, 53–54, 59, 62,
    67–68, 75, 77–81, 88, 90, 92–93, 96–98,
    101, 110, 117, 119, 131–132, 149, 158–160,
    165, 176–177, 186–187, 193–194, 197–198,
    202, 204, 208, 210–213, 226–228, 234,
    239–240, 243, 262, 298, 318; voting pat-
    terns in, 98, 117, 202, 262, 318
Little Rock *Arkansas Democrat,* 80, 84–86, 93,
    139, 141, 148–149, 221
Little Rock *Arkansas Gazette,* 39, 53, 58–59,
    62–63, 65, 67–68, 70, 72–73, 82–83, 110,
    185, 210, 309, 311; supportive of Davis,
    49, 114–115, 131, 172; critical of Davis, 80,
    96, 161, 172, 195, 223–224; attacked by
    Davis, 84; and 1906 analysis of Davis's
    career, 101, 161, 223–224. *See also* Press
Little Rock "Arkansas Travelers," 122
Little Rock Board of Trade, 59, 66, 68
Little Rock Railway and Electric Company,
    238
Localism, 7–8, 13, 51, 55, 92, 236
Logan County, 47, 110
Logue, Cal M., 5
London, Eng., 66
Long, Huey, 4, 6–7, 9, 163
Lonoke, Ark., 143
Lonoke County, 41, 133–134, 143–144, 174,
    191
Louisiana, 92
Louisville and Nashville Railroad, 298
Ludwig, O. C., 228–229, 235, 249
Lum and Abner, 23
Luthin, Reinhard, 5
Lynching, 188, 211–212, 214

MacKenzie, Gilbert, 284
Madison County, 289
Mahoney, Emon, 101
Maine, 281
Malden, Mo., 205
Malone, Thomas, 284
Mann, George, 136, 305
Manning, M. J., 185, 187, 311, 312
Mansfield, La., 26
Manufacturing, 33, 54, 59, 63, 113, 121, 248–
    249
Marion County, 59, 154, 201, 260–268
Martin, J. E., 135
Martin, Joseph, 70, 75
Martin, Smith, 294

Martin, Thomas B., 95, 135
Martin, W. H., 111
Marx, Karl, 3, 100–102
Massachusetts, 168–171
Mass leader: term coined by Eric Hoffer, 6–7;
    and demagoguery, 9–10; Davis as, 76, 94
McConnell, E. T., 135, 144
McCormick, Richard L., 10
McCurdy, Richard A., 113–114
McEnery, Samuel D., 232
McKinley, William, 91, 119, 303
McNemer, John, 127–128
McRae, Thomas C., 110, 272, 311, 321
Melrose Cotton Mill, 33
Memphis and Choctaw Railroad, 179
Memphis *Commercial Appeal,* 144, 222
Memphis, Tenn., 48
Mencken, Henry L., 5, 163
Merchants, 60, 65, 68, 102, 124; and planta-
    tion economy, 13, 15, 28, 33. *See also*
    Businessmen; Colonial economy; Planters
Merriam, Edward M., 177, 179–181, 186, 311
Merriam State House Act, 180–181
Methodists, 124–125, 129, 149, 163, 181, 193,
    284
Metropolitan society, 10–13, 32–33, 56, 98–
    100, 202–203
Mexican War, 24
Militia, Arkansas State, 27–29, 120, 171, 213
Miller, J. W., 287
Miller County, 41, 92, 154
Milton, John, 273
Mississippi, 64, 138, 163, 222
Mississippi County, 41, 157
Mississippi River, 23
Mississippi Valley, 24
Missouri, 23, 61, 64, 205, 218, 240, 320
Mitchell, James, 80, 93, 141
Monroe, Thomas C., 95, 134–135, 175, 177–
    179, 311
Monroe County, 41, 185, 201, 224, 286
Montgomery County, 96, 202
Moore, John I., 227–228, 311
Moose, William L., 321
Morgan, W. Scott, 45, 58, 106–107
Morrilton, Ark., 61, 82–83, 185, 187–188, 320
Morrilton Democrat, 239
Mount Holly Cemetery (Little Rock), 243
Municipal bonds, 249
Murfreesboro, Tenn., 95
Murphy, George W., 172, 311; as Davis ally,

51, 95, 107, 109, 125; breaks with Davis during penitentiary fight, 134–135, 174–175; leads impeachment forces, 177–179, 184

Myers, Harry H., 170–172, 174, 204–205, 207

Napoleon, 196, 224
Nashville, Ark., 105, 297, 318
Nashville, Tenn., 30, 187
Nation, Carry, 219
Nativism, 8, 163
Nebo, Mount, 32
Nelson, J. W., 150, 287, 307
Neo-Populism, 7, 106–108, 217–218
Nevada County, 290
New Jersey, 139, 147
New Orleans State, 219
New South movement, 56, 59–60, 63, 65, 68, 88, 121; Davis's attitude towards, 78, 100, 111, 118, 121, 157, 172, 217. *See also* Businessmen; Colonial economy; Corporations; Manufacturing; New South subculture
New South subculture, 11–18, 32–34, 38, 55, 60, 98–100, 154, 160, 202. *See also* Businessmen; Colonial economy; Corporations; Cultural politics; Manufacturing; New South movement
Newton County, 115, 172
New York, 113, 208
New York, N.Y., 66, 138, 179, 195, 217
New York Board of Exchange, 139, 231
New York Mutual Life Insurance Company, 113
New York Stock Exchange, 139, 231
New York Sun, 222
New York Times, 168, 170, 212, 232
Nichols, Hugh, 134
Niswonger, Richard L., 101, 106
Norris, George, 6
Norton, W. N., 135
Norwood, Charles M., 35, 38, 285
Norwood, Hal, 71, 128, 235, 249
Nuttal, Thomas, 22

Odum, Howard, 163
Oklahoma, 50–51, 224–225
Ola, Ark., 161–162
Oldfield, William, 238
"Old Guard," 15–17, 198, 200, 210, 221, 235, 237–238, 241, 243

One-party system: and Southern demagogues, 8, 13–14, 17–18; in Arkansas, 43–47, 63, 170, 172, 225
Oratory: and Southern demagogues, 8, 15; Davis's style of, 14, 31, 35–37, 49–51, 70–71, 83–87, 89, 122, 137, 141, 164, 209, 229–232, 236, 240–241
Ouachita County, 41, 93, 294, 304
Ouachita Mountains, 19, 23, 28, 89, 97
Ouachita River, 26
Ozark, Ark., 50, 233–234
Ozark mountains, 19, 22–23, 28, 32, 51, 68, 77, 92, 97, 115, 153, 167, 230, 260

Pacific Express Company, 69
Page, John H., 93–94, 96, 178, 229, 241, 272, 297
Paisley, Clifton, 106
Panama Canal Commission, 170
Paragould, Ark., 149
Pardons, 224–225, 236, 245; criticism of Davis's record, 161, 175, 219, 310–311; Davis defends record, 166–167, 192–193, 214; of blacks, 168–171, 187–188, 207, 215
Parker, Alton B., 208, 288
Parker, Charles J., 294, 297
Payne-Aldrich tariff, 237
Peck, John M., 131
Penal system, Arkansas. *See* Convict-lease system; Pardons; Penitentiary, Arkansas State; Penitentiary Board, Arkansas State; Penitentiary "ring"
Penitentiary, Arkansas State, 131–137, 166, 168–180, 207, 214–215, 304; and new state house site, 73, 75, 79–80, 90, 121, 126–128, 136–137; and Beebe heirs, 79–80
Penitentiary Board, Arkansas State, 73, 75, 90, 132–135, 137, 144–145, 174–179, 304
Penitentiary "ring," 144–146, 173–174, 176, 179, 186, 192, 210, 217, 234
Pennsylvania, 231–232, 292
Penrose, William, 313–314
People's party. *See* Populism
Percy, William Alexander, 163
Perry, Bob, 145, 215
Perry County, 47
Perrysmith, Ark., 187
Personal politics: and Southern demagogues, 8, 10; Davis's use of, 14, 87, 143, 191, 205, 210, 223
Philadelphia, Pa., 231–232

Philadelphia *Record*, 232
Philippines, 89, 11, 114
Phillips, Bolen C. (grandfather), 25
Phillips County, 41, 138, 157, 200, 227, 305
Piggott, Ark., 187
Pike County, 166–167
Pindall, Xenophon O., 224–225, 227–228, 316
Pine Bluff, Ark., 170, 311
Pine Bluff Commercial, 194
Planters, 16, 22, 55, 58, 60, 131, 277; town-dwelling, 12–13, 33; as planter-merchants, 13, 99, 105; and the Davis movement, 17, 102–103, 105
Plummerville, Ark., 300
Poinsett County, 260–268
Poison Springs, Ark., 26
Poll tax, 43, 214, 249
Poor whites: and Southern demagogues, 5–6, 14–15; cultural identity of, 17; and Ozark stereotype, 22–24; and voter turnout, 40–46; and the Davis movement, 100–106, 154–156, 238–239. *See also* Class conflict
Pope County, 28–37, 48, 51, 62, 120–121, 126, 135, 157, 202, 206, 238, 285, 286, 304, 307, 316, 318
Pope County Agricultural and Mechanical Association, 30
Pope County Immigration Society, 30
Pope County Militia War, 29, 146
Pope County Sunday School Association, 30, 163
Populism: and the Davis movement, 13, 79, 100, 106–108, 118, 146, 153–154, 201, 217–218, 221, 249–253, 262–268, 301; and shadow movement, 16, 55–58, 138; decline in Arkansas, 38–47, 51, 53, 58, 63, 113, 115, 298; and disfranchisement, 39–46; and fusion, 39, 48, 58, 117, 287; and ex-Populists, 49, 117, 158, 208, 288; and reform measures, 54, 90, 132; analysis of electoral support, 137, 153–154, 201, 221, 249–253, 262–268, 287, 288, 301
Postal service, 11, 32, 98, 232, 237
Powers, Caleb, 298
Presbyterians, 124, 129, 181, 272
Press, 11, 82–83, 129, 131, 134–135, 144, 169–170, 288; hostility towards Davis, 3, 68, 74, 79–80, 85–87, 91, 93, 101, 106, 140–141, 148–149, 161, 180, 183, 192, 196–198, 203, 239, 244, 297; opposition to Popu-lists, 39; praises Davis in 1898, 49; and free-silver issue, 53; and New South movement, 59–60, 67–68; national press and Davis, 70, 195, 212, 219, 221–223, 230, 232, 236; endorses new state house, 73; Davis's criticism of, 79–80, 84–85, 111, 139, 227; reacts to 1900 primary results, 96; supports Davis in 1900 general election, 112, 114–115; ignores Davis, 205, 240
Price, Sterling, 26
Primary system, 47, 49–50, 76, 93, 186, 205, 209, 214, 224–225
Progressivism, 4, 6, 15, 56, 208, 225–226; and the Davis movement, 4, 14–15, 120, 136, 172, 192–193, 218, 243, 245, 279; and "business progressivism" in Arkan-sas, 15, 235, 237
Prohibition: and the Davis movement, 4, 36, 38, 61, 106–109, 122, 148–150, 153, 156, 158–163, 185, 194, 201–203, 219, 221, 249–254, 262–268, 307; movement in Arkansas, 30, 148–150, 153, 308. *See also* Prohibitionist party
Prohibitionist party, 51, 150, 153, 161, 205, 287, 288, 307, 313–314
Public Lands, United States House of Repre-sentatives Committee on, 238–239
Pugh, George, 189, 204
Pulaski County, 41, 47, 53, 88, 92, 97–98, 107–108, 117, 174, 177, 188, 194, 260–268, 290, 293, 298, 301, 318

Quantrill's Raiders, 25

Racism: and Southern demagogues, 5–8, 18; and Davis's politics, 13–14, 36, 144–146, 157, 168–172, 187–190, 192, 198, 204–207, 210–216, 315; and race-baiting of agrarian radicals in 1880s and 1890s, 34–36, 38–39; and race-baiting of Republicans, 39, 51, 94, 114, 170–172, 205–207, 210–213; and race-baiting of Davis, 145–146, 187–188, 192; and Jim Crow legislation, 205–207, 213–216. *See also* Blacks; Dis-franchisement; Lynching
Radio, 12
Railroad Commission, Arkansas, 54, 57, 59, 63, 65, 227, 248, 293
Railroads, 19, 24, 39, 56–57, 81, 89–90, 98–99, 102, 166, 197–198, 218, 226, 249–251, 260–268, 280, 291, 292, 298, 299; and

Southern urbanization, 11; and development in Pope County, 28–30, 32; resentment of, 54, 63; construction of, 59, 79, 121; and free passes, 64, 179, 194, 234; and tax assessments, 192, 209–210. *See also* Bush Bill; Railroad Commission, Arkansas

Read, Opie, 22–23, 158

Reconstruction, 9, 27–29, 35, 114, 171, 211, 213

Rector, Elias W.: as sponsor of 1899 antitrust bill, 64, 68, 72; and 1900 gubernatorial primary, 82; and 1902 gubernatorial primary, 141–149, 153–157, 168, 200, 203, 307

Rector, Henry Massey, 64

Rector Antitrust Act, 63–72, 74, 76, 78–84, 86, 88–91, 120, 141, 207–208, 294

Red, B. F., 187

Redfield, Ark., 193–194

Red River, 22, 25, 27–28, 203

Red River Valley, 21–22, 25, 71

Reese, John F., 219

Reform school, 121, 127–128, 176, 207, 214

Reid, Charles C., 36–37, 188

Relative deprivation, 13, 32, 56, 60

Religion, 124–125, 129, 185, 191, 193, 202–203, 206, 212, 219, 248, 250–254; and demagoguery, 5–6, 8, 100, 162–163; in the South, 11, 17–18; and Lewis Davis, 25, 27, 30, 163; and Jeff Davis, 122, 148–149, 158–168

Remmel, Harmon L., 96, 113–117, 146, 272, 287, 302

Republican party: and Reconstruction, 28–29, 39, 74; and national politics, 36, 189, 214, 231, 233, 237–239, 250, 287, 288, 302; during 1890s, 39, 51, 53, 287; and race issue, 39, 51, 94, 114, 170–172, 205–207, 210–213; and disfranchisement, 41, 43, 45–46, 51, 214; and fusion system, 40; and potential Democratic bolters, 93–94, 96, 113, 225; and 1900 state election, 96, 113–119; and 1902 state election, 170–172; and 1904 state election, 204–207. *See also* Clayton, Powell; Insurgent Republicans; Meyers, Harry H.; Remmel, Harmon L.; Roosevelt, Theodore

Reynolds, Abraham, 23

Rhoton, Lewis, 234

Rice, 23

Roads, 11–12, 23–24, 91, 98, 225–226

Robinson, Joseph T., 197, 241, 243–244, 249, 272, 320, 320–321

Rockefeller, John D., 230, 237

Rocky Comfort, Ark., 21–22, 25–27, 280

Rogers, Robert L., 205, 207, 210, 217, 219

Rogers, Ark., 144, 315

Romanticism: and Southern demagogues, 8, 15–16; and the Davis movement, 16, 245

Roosevelt, Theodore, 45, 189, 205, 208, 210–213, 238–239, 288, 315

Ross, J. W., 25

Rowland, J. Sam, 179–180, 311

Russell, Joseph, 240

Russellville, Ark., 29–30, 32–33, 37, 78, 110, 119, 159–160, 163, 286

Russellville, Ky., 25

Russellville *Democrat*, 33, 49

Russellville *National Tribune*, 30

St. Francis County, 41, 97, 104–105, 107–109, 147, 154, 201, 260–268, 318

St. Francis Levee Board, 238

St. Louis, Mo., 57, 76, 83–84, 134–135, 205

St. Louis *Globe-Democrat*, 134–135, 144

St. Louis *Post-Dispatch*, 84, 232

St. Louis Southwestern Railroad, 179

Saline County, 186–187, 202

Scalawags, 28, 46

Schoolcraft, Henry Rowe, 22

Scopes trial, 163

Scott, May (half-sister), 281–282

Scott, Sarah (half-sister), 281–282

Scott, William, 25, 224, 281–282

Scott, William, Jr. (half-brother), 281–282

Scott County, 202

Searcy, Ark., 137

Searcy County, 115

Sebastian, William K., 305

Sebastian County, 92, 96–97, 107–109, 129, 139, 154, 210, 226, 260–268, 298

Secret Ballot Act of 1891, 41, 43

Sectionalism: and Southern demagogues, 5, 7, 17; and Southern identity, 11; and colonial economy, 13, 56; and the Davis movement, 14, 17, 26, 72, 89–90, 103, 113–115, 145, 168–172, 187–189, 194, 211–213, 217. *See also* Agrarian subculture; Colonial economy; Cultural politics

Sengel, George, 73, 128–129, 304, 311

Sevier County, 22, 25–27, 280, 293

Shackleford, John D., 293
Sharp County, 78, 156, 201, 260–268, 295
Shattuck and Hoffman, 31
Sheridan, Ark., 193–194
Sherman Antitrust Act, 230
Sherman Silver Purchase Act, 53
Shirley, Meredith, 191
Simkins, Francis Butler, 162
Simmons pardon, 192–193
Skipper's Gap, Ark., 194
Slavery, 22, 24–25, 28
Smith, Hoke, 208
Smith, L. C. ("Shotgun"), 244, 249, 321
Smith Bill, 57, 291
Smithee, James N., 53
Socialism, 15, 34, 205, 231, 288, 299, 313–314
Social status: urban versus rural, 12–13, 17–
    18, 32–33, 155. *See also* Agrarian subcul-
    ture; Class conflict
South Arkansas, 23, 51, 92, 153, 156, 200,
    206
South Carolina, 3–4, 9, 94, 146, 168, 208,
    213, 222, 232
Southern Baptist Convention, 163
Southern demagogues, 3–18, 162–163
Springdale, Ark., 103, 155, 262, 318
Springfield, Little Rock and Gulf Railroad,
    56–57
Stamps, Ark., 285
Standard Oil, 64, 81, 89, 231, 237
Stark, Willie, 173
Starr, Belle, 27
State house controversy, 63, 72–80, 84, 90,
    111, 120–121, 126–128, 131, 135–137, 158,
    172, 176–177, 180–181, 192, 217, 234, 305.
    See also Capitol Commission, Arkansas;
    Kimbell State House Act
State Protective Association, Arkansas, estab-
    lished by liquor industry, 153
Stephens, Ark., 297
Stockard, George, 180, 223, 311, 316
Stone County, 202, 289
Streetcars, electric, 11, 98, 215
Streeter, A. J., 36
Stuttgart, Ark., 171
Sunk lands controversy, 238–240, 243, 319
Sunnyside Bill, 126, 133, 174
Supreme Court, Arkansas State, 49, 62, 71–
    72, 75–77, 79–80, 84, 121–122, 135, 158,
    173, 184–186, 195, 207, 245, 296, 311, 318
Supreme Court, United States, 207

"Swamp Democrats," 138, 157, 200
Symbolic politics: and Southern demagogues,
    7–8, 18; and Davis, 18, 118

Taft, William Howard, 237, 239
Talmadge, Eugene, 9
Taylor, Robert Love ("Fiddlin' Bob"), 4
Telegraphs, 11, 30, 89, 98, 232
Telephones, 11–12, 32, 89, 98, 232, 300
Temple B'nai Israel (Little Rock), 165
Tenant farmers, 38, 59; and the Davis vote,
    102–105, 154, 201, 248, 250–254
Tennessee, 4, 24, 30, 48, 187, 208
Terry, William L., 47–48, 288
Texarkana, Ark., 125, 154, 159, 169
Texas, 22, 25, 36, 102, 125, 227
Thach, Frank, 31
Thach, Nola, 283
Thach, Sam, 174, 179
Thayer, Mo., 218
Thomas, David Y., 101, 272
Thompson, Andrew, 168–171
Thompson, William E., 149
Thornburgh, George A., 272, 308
Tillman, Benjamin R. ("Pitchfork Ben"), 3–4,
    9, 94, 146, 168, 208, 213, 222, 232
Timber industry, 102, 238
Tindall, George Brown, 11
Tipton, H. C., 219
Todd County, Ky., 25
Toney, Kemp, 170
Tontitown, Ark., 165
Tucker, James L., 286
Turner-Jacobson Tax Bill, 249

Uniform Textbook Law Referendum, 249
Union army, 26, 28–29, 186
Union County, 41
Unionists, 28–29, 112
Union-Labor party, 35–36, 38–39, 41, 249,
    251, 287
United States Senate. *See* Berry, James H.;
    Clarke, James P.; Davis, Jeff; Jones,
    James K.
University of Arkansas (originally Arkansas
    Industrial University), 30, 50, 166, 178,
    185, 219, 244, 316
Urban-rural conflict, 55–56, 60, 78, 115, 190–
    191, 201; and Southern demagogues, 10–
    18; in Pope County, 32–34; and Davis
    movement, 98–102, 153–155, 202–203,

221, 243, 248–254, 260–268. *See also* Agrarian radicalism; Agrarian subculture; Colonial economy; Cultural politics; Metropolitan society; New South subculture; Social status

Van Buren, Ark., 262
Van Buren County, 21, 157, 202
Vance, Rupert, 3, 92, 100, 102, 190–191, 211, 244, 300
Vanderbilt University, 30, 36, 61, 284
Vandeventer, Arthur F., 82–83, 88, 90–92, 96, 110, 146, 185, 187–188, 193–194, 196, 297–298, 311, 312
Vardaman, James Kimble, 3–4, 9, 146, 163, 213, 222
Villages: and metropolitan society, 12, 16–17; and the Davis vote, 98–99, 102, 153, 201, 221, 235, 263
Violence: and Davis's childhood, 26–27, 29, 171; during 1880s and 1890s, 38, 40; and Davis era politics, 142–144, 178, 186, 195–197, 210, 214, 218–219, 241, 318
Virginia, 187
Voter turnout, 39–46, 117, 204, 221, 249–251

Wallace, James G., 35–36, 47, 181, 188, 288, 319
Wallace, Robert Minor, 272
Wall Street, 139, 217, 231
Ward, Zeb, 131
Warren, Robert Penn, xiii
Warren, Ark., 312
Washburn, Edward Payson, 28
Washington, Booker T., 211
Washington, George, 78, 187
Washington, Ark., 26
Washington, D.C., 48, 167, 200, 208, 225–233, 235–237, 239–240, 243
Washington County, 97, 103–104, 107–109, 155, 165, 192–193, 201, 218–219, 224, 260–268, 287, 316, 318
Watie, Stand, 26
Watson, E. P., 49–51, 292
Watson, Tom, 3–4, 6, 9, 165, 208, 288

Ways and Means Committee, Arkansas House of Representatives, 177–181, 186, 207, 311
Weaver, James B., 38, 287, 301
Weaver, J. F., 311
Wells Fargo, 68
West Point, 30
Whetstone, Pete, 22
Whig party, 88, 90, 298
Whipple, William, 39, 287
White, Frank, 149
White County, 49, 58, 96, 137, 240
White primary, 14, 214
White River, 217
Whitley, William, 180, 311
Wiebe, Robert H., 12
Williams, George W., 67
Williams, T. Harry, 6–7, 15
Williamson, Tennie, 283
Wilmans, J. E., 313–314
Wilson, Charles Morrow, 32, 140
Wilson, Robert J., 125, 127
Wilson, Woodrow, 243, 320
Wisconsin, 208
Witt Prison Act, 215
Wizard Oil, 143, 148, 156, 160, 239
Wofford, Benjamin, 180, 311
Wolsey, Rabbi Louis, 165
Woman's Club, 168
Woman's Journal, 169
Wood, Carroll D., 158, 160–161, 185–205, 213, 218, 240, 311, 312
Wood, James E., 68–69, 82–83, 88, 101, 128, 294
Woodruff, William E., Jr., 39
Woodruff County, 41, 200–201
Woodward, C. Vann, 6, 100–101, 300
Workers, 55, 98, 102, 121, 127–128, 138–139, 167, 198, 225, 227, 234, 248, 279, 299; as rural-to-urban migrants, 16
Worthen, W. B., 53
Worthington, John I., 317

Yell County, 37, 86, 96, 157, 286

Zinc mining, 59